Apollos Old Testament
COMMENTARY

3

LEVITICUS

TITLES IN THIS SERIES

LEVITICUS, Nobuyoshi Kiuchi
DEUTERONOMY, J. G. McConville
DANIEL, Ernest Lucas

APOLLOS OLD TESTAMENT
COMMENTARY

3

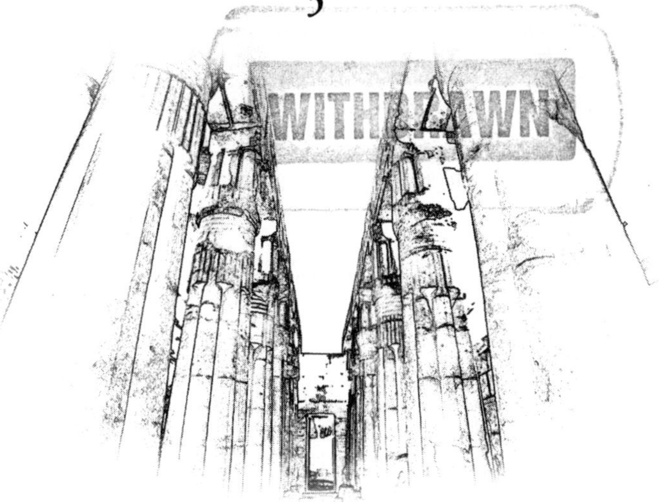

LEVITICUS

Series Editors
David W. Baker and Gordon J. Wenham

NOBUYOSHI KIUCHI

Apollos
Nottingham, England

InterVarsity Press
Downers Grove, Illinois 60515

APOLLOS
An imprint of Inter-Varsity Press
Norton Street, Nottingham NG7 3HR, England
Email: ivp@ivpbooks.com Website: www.ivpbooks.com

INTERVARSITY PRESS
PO Box 1400, Downers Grove, Illinois 60515, USA
Email: mail@ivpress.com Website: www.ivpress.com

First published 2007

British Library Cataloguing in Publication Data
A catalogue record for this book is available from the British Library.

UK ISBN 978-1-84474-177-9

Library of Congress Cataloging-in-Publication Data
These data have been requested.

US ISBN 978-0-8308-2503-5

Set in Sabon 10/12pt
Typeset in Great Britain by CRB Associates, Reepham, Norfolk
Printed and bound in Great Britain by Creative Print and Design (Wales), Ebbw Vale

CONTENTS

EDITORS' PREFACE

The Apollos Old Testament Commentary takes its name from the Alexandrian Jewish Christian who was able to impart his great learning fervently and powerfully through his teaching (Acts 18:24–25). He ably applied his understanding of past events to his contemporary society. This series seeks to do the same, keeping one foot firmly planted in the universe of the original text and the other in that of the target audience, which is preachers, teachers and students of the Bible. The series editors have selected scholars who are adept in both areas, exhibiting scholarly excellence along with practical insight for application.

Translators need to be at home with the linguistic practices and semantic nuances of both the original and target languages in order to be able to transfer the full impact of the one into the other. Commentators, however, serve as interpreters of the text rather than simply its translators. They also need to adopt a dual stance, though theirs needs to be even more solid and diversely anchored than that of translators. While they also must have the linguistic competence to produce their own excellent translations, they must moreover be fully conversant with the literary conventions, sociological and cultural practices, historical background and understanding, and theological perspectives of those who produced the text as well as those whom it concerned. On the other side, they must also understand their own times and culture, able to see where relevance for the original audience is transferable to that of current readers. For this to be accomplished, it is not only necessary to interpret the text; one must also interpret the audience.

Traditionally, commentators have been content to highlight and expound the ancient text. More recently, the need for an anchor in the present day has also become more evident, and this series self-consciously adopts this approach, combining both. Each author analyses the original text through a new translation, textual notes, a discussion of the literary form, structure and background of the passage, as well as commenting on elements of its exegesis. A study of the passage's interpretational development in Scripture and the church concludes each section, serving to bring the passage home to the modern reader. What we intend, therefore, is to provide not only tools of excellence for the academy, but also tools of function for the pulpit.

David W. Baker
Gordon J. Wenham

AUTHOR'S PREFACE

My study of Leviticus began in the early 1980s, when I was working on a PhD thesis in Cheltenham, England. Although I have found it a tremendous intellectual challenge to unpack such a puzzling book for over two decades, I now feel a great sense of release, as my long period of exploration has finally borne fruit with the appearance of this commentary.

Without the assistance of others, however, I could not have completed the task. I would therefore like to express my deep appreciation to Professor G. J. Wenham, my PhD supervisor, and Professor D. W. Baker, both of whom invited me to write a commentary on Leviticus several years ago, and gave helpful advice to improve the manuscript. Also I would especially like to record my appreciation to Dr L. Trevaskis, who read my first draft and gave me stimulating comments, while correcting my English. I am also deeply grateful for the kindness of my colleagues and the staff at Tokyo Christian University, who have created an environment where I have been able to maintain my concentration on Leviticus until the present.

Lastly, special thanks are due to Dr P. Duce and the team at IVP for their speedy and efficient work in producing this tome.

May the Lord use it for his glory!

Nobuyoshi Kiuchi

ABBREVIATIONS

TEXTUAL

11QPaleoLev, 4QLev	Fragmentary texts of Leviticus from Qumran
Arab.	Arabic
BHS	K. Elliger and W. Rudolph (eds.), *Biblia Hebraica Stuttgartensia*, 2nd ed., Stuttgart: Deutsche Bibelstiftung, 1977
Gr.	Greek
Hebr.	Hebrew
LXX	Septuagint
MS(S)	Manuscript(s)
MT	Masoretic Text
SamP	Samaritan Pentateuch
Syr	Syriac
Tg(s)	Targum(s)
TgJon	Targum Jonathan
TgO	Targum Onqelos
Vg	Vulgate

HEBREW GRAMMAR

abs.	absolute
def. art.	definite article
f.	feminine
hiph.	hiphil
hith.	hithpael
hoph.	hophal
imp.	imperative
impf.	imperfect
inf.	infinitive
m.	masculine
ni.	niphal
pf.	perfect
pi.	piel
pl.	plural
ptc.	participle
pu.	pual
sg.	singular

MISCELLANEOUS

Akk.	Akkadian
AV	Authorized (King James) Version
ch(s).	chapter(s)
ed(s).	edited by; editors(s); edition
Elberfelder	Die Elberfelder Bibel
Eng.	English
ESV	English Standard Version
FS	*Festschrift*
JPS	Jewish Publication Society translation
lit.	literally
n.	note
NASB	New American Standard Bible
NIV	New International Version
NRSV	New Revised Standard Version
NT	New Testament
OT	Old Testament
p(p).	page(s)
REB	Revised English Bible
rev.	revised (by)
RSV	Revised Standard Version
SBL	Society of Biblical Literature
s.v.	(*sub verbo*) under the word or heading
trans.	translated, translation
v(v).	verse(s)

JOURNALS, REFERENCE WORKS, SERIES

AB	Anchor Bible
ABD	D. N. Freedman (ed.), *Anchor Bible Dictionary*, 6 vols., New York: Doubleday, 1992
AJSR	*Association for Jewish Studies Review*
AnBib	Analecta biblica
AOTC	Apollos Old Testament Commentary
ASOR	American Schools of Oriental Research
ATD	Alttestament Deutsch
BBB	Bonner Biblische Beiträge
BBR	*Bulletin for Biblical Research*
Bib	*Biblica*
BJS	Brown Judaic Studies
BKAT	Biblischer Kommentar, Altes Testament
BSC	Bible Student's Commentary

BZAW	Beihefte zur Zeitschrift für die alttestamentliche Wissenschaft
CBC	Cambridge Bible Commentary
DOTP	T. Desmond Alexander and David W. Baker (eds.), *Dictionary of the Old Testament: Pentateuch*, Downers Grove and Leicester: IVP
EBC	Expositor's Bible Commentary, 1984
EM	E. L. Skenik, U. Cassuto et al. (eds.), *Encyclopaedia Miqra'it*, 9 vols., Jerusalem: Bialik Institute, 1950–88
ETL	*Ephemerides theologicarum lovaniensium*
Exeg	*Exegetica* [Japanese]
FAT	Forschungen zum Alten Testament
GKC	E. Kautzsch (ed.), *Gesenius' Hebrew Grammar*, rev. and trans. A. E. Cowley, Oxford: Clarendon, 1910
HALOT	L. Koehler and W. Baumgartner, *The Hebrew and Aramaic Lexicon of the Old Testament*, trans. M. E. J. Richardson, Leiden: Brill, 1994–2000
IBHS	B. K. Waltke and M. O'Connor, *Introduction to Biblical Hebrew Syntax*, Winona Lake: Eisenbrauns, 1990
ICC	International Critical Commentary
IEJ	*Israel Exploration Journal*
JAOS	*Journal of the American Oriental Society*
JBL	*Journal of Biblical Literature*
JNWSL	*Journal of Northwest Semitic Languages*
Joüon-Muraoka	T. Joüon-Muraoka, *A Grammar of Biblical Hebrew*, Subsidia Biblica 14/I–II, Rome: Pontifical Biblical Institute, 1991
JPSTC	Jewish Publication Society Torah Commentary
JSOT	Journal for the Study of the Old Testament
JSOTSup	Journal for the Study of the Old Testament, Supplement Series
JSS	*Journal of Semitic Studies*
Merwe	C. H. J. van der Merwe, J. A. Naudé and J. H. Kroeze, *A Biblical Hebrew Reference Grammar*, Sheffield: Sheffield Academic Press, 1999
NAC	New American Commentary
NCB	New Century Bible
NDBT	T. D. Alexander and B. S. Rosner (eds.), *New Dictionary of Biblical Theology*, Downers Grove and Leicester: IVP, 2000
NICOT	New International Commentary on the Old Testament
NIDNTT	C. Brown (ed.), *New International Dictionary of New Testament Theology*, 3 vols., Grand Rapids: Eerdmans, 1975–8

NIDOTTE	W. A. VanGemeren (ed.), *New International Dictionary of Old Testament Theology and Exegesis*, 5 vols., Grand Rapids: Zondervan; Carlisle: Paternoster, 1997
OTL	Old Testament Libray
OtSt	*Oudtestamentische Studiën*
QD	Quaestiones disputatae
RB	*Revue biblique*
SANT	Studien zum Alten und Neuen Testament
SBL	Society of Biblical Literature
SJLA	Studies in Judaism in Late Antiquity
Them	*Themelios*
ThH	Théologie historique
ThWAT	G. J. Botterweck and H. Ringgren (eds.), *Theologisches Wörterbuch zum Alten Testament*, Stuttgart: Kohlhammer, 1970–2000
TOTC	Tyndale Old Testament Commentaries
TynB	*Tyndale Bulletin*
UT	C. H. Gordon, *Ugaritic Textbook*, Analecta orientalia 38, Rome: Pontifical Biblical Institute, 1965
VT	*Vetus Testamentum*
VTSup	Supplements to Vetus Testamentum
WBC	Word Biblical Commentary
ZAH	*Zeitschrift für Althebräistik*
ZAW	*Zeitschrift für die alttestamentliche Wissenschaft*

INTRODUCTION

1. THE NAME OF THE BOOK

The name 'Leviticus' comes from the Latin term 'Leviticus', which is based on the LXX *leuitikon*. It is not certain why the LXX translators associated the book so strongly with the Levites, considering that only a single reference is made to the 'Levites' in 25:32–33. Judging from a later Jewish name for the book, namely the teaching of the priests (*tôrat hakkôhănîm*), the LXX translators may have seen its content as most relevant to the role of the priests.

The common Hebrew name is drawn from the opening phrase of the book, *wayyiqrâ*, meaning, 'and he called'. Another Aramaic name is *siphrâ*, meaning 'the book', which alludes to the special importance Leviticus had among the five books of Moses in the Jewish tradition.

2. THE SETTING OF LEVITICUS

Leviticus follows the book of Exodus, which gives an account of the historical exodus, the giving of the Sinai covenant, the building of the tabernacle, and instructions concerning basic ceremonies that would soon be conducted there by the priests. There are unmistakable signs that the two books are continuous (cf. Rendtorff 1996: 22–35). The following literary and thematic relationships between Exodus and Leviticus are noteworthy in this regard.

(1) The prescription for the priestly ordination in Exod. 28 – 29 is carried out in Lev. 8.

(2) A gradual lengthening of the time the Lord appears visibly to his people occurs across both books. On the first occasion the Lord appears only briefly to Moses within a burning thorn bush (Exod. 3). After this, there is a seven-day manifestation of his glory on Mount Sinai (Exod. 24). Then, finally, the Lord's visible presence arrives permanently after the first day service recorded in Lev. 9.

On the other hand, the beginning of Leviticus clearly presents a new stage in the development of the Lord's will. It begins with prescriptions for offerings that concern the activities of the priests and lay people in the sanctuary, which are not mentioned in Exodus except for Exod. 28 – 29. Also the connection between Exod. 40:34–35 and Lev. 1 indicates that deeper matters are revealed in Leviticus (cf. Auld 2003: 43). The material of chs. 9 – 27 is new, though some of it is, in principle, already anticipated within Exodus. The coherency and unity of Leviticus as opposed to that of Exodus will become clearer, when the structure of Leviticus is discussed below.

Thus Leviticus can be viewed as a further and deeper unfolding of the divine–human relationship that took place at Mount Sinai.

3. THE MODERN STUDY OF LEVITICUS AND ITS AUTHORSHIP

Since the nineteenth century Leviticus has been a crucial object of Pentateuchal studies. According to the hypothesis propounded by J. Wellhausen the material of Leviticus belongs to P (the priestly material), the latest of four literary sources (J, E, D, P), which reflects the social and religious condition of the post-exilic community.

Many assumptions are invoked in determining literary sources, including linguistic style, the suggestions of historical discrepancies, doublets and differences in theological stance. These observations are then interpreted with a particular evolutionary view of ancient Israel's religious history in an effort to discover the history of the Pentateuch's composition. In addition to this, the interpretative approach taken to the 'religious' rules that characterize much of Leviticus and the so-called P document has some bearing on how its material is viewed.

While Wellhausen's method has dominated Pentateuchal study since the time of its inception, namely from the end of the nineteenth century onwards, recent criticism of its fundamental presuppositions has led to challenges to many of its commonly accepted results. Among others, Israeli scholars, beginning with Kaufmann, argue on the basis of societal and linguistic evidence that the date of P was earlier than suggested by Wellhausen and others (Kaufmann 1937–56; Weinfeld 1972; Hurvitz

1982). Nevertheless, despite this trenchant and valid criticism, the assumption is still adopted by many recent scholars.

With regard to the book of Leviticus in particular, Klostermann (1983) observed in the late nineteenth century that chs. 17 – 26 constitute a different literary layer to P, concluding that it exhibited some similarities with the book of Ezekiel. He proposed calling this corpus of literature H (*Heiligkeitsgesetz* or the 'Holiness Code'), owing to its clear emphasis on holiness. Moreover he considers that H was written at a much earlier time than P. While some scholars have since distinguished further literary layers within P, the common view that P is the editor of H has remained unchallenged until the recent work by Knohl. Knohl advances his view from various considerations that lead him to posit H as the final redactor of P (Knohl 1995; cf. Joosten 1996). His thesis is basically followed in Milgrom's massive commentary on Leviticus (1991–2001), though Milgrom differs from Knohl at some points. This position holds, for example, that P concentrates on the holiness of materials such as offerings and sancta (static holiness), and not that of human beings (dynamic holiness), as is clearly the interest in H. Moreover, these scholars maintain that while H, the later redactor, has a worldview that is at times different from P's, it did not change P's rules but incorporated them, giving them new meaning. Milgrom traces P's origin to the sanctuary of Shilo, and dates H as written at the time of king Hezekiah (1991: 34).

Milgrom advances many pieces of evidence in support of his proposed relationship between P and H. Yet to me it seems that his position may derive from a failure to see, on the one hand, that the same essence of holiness is assumed in 'static holiness' and 'dynamic holiness', and on the other hand, that there is a thematic development within Leviticus. In terms of this latter oversight, a thematic development within a book could quite conceivably rely on differences in topic, terminology, style and perspective. If so, then the only question that remains is whether or not there are discrepancies in content, especially in relation to the idea of holiness, which I shall address in 7.4 below.

The recent scholarly discussion appears to revolve around the question of whether it is appropriate to view the book as divisible into two parts, as assumed by Milgrom and Knohl, while scholars, including Milgrom, are increasingly attempting to interpret the book as it stands. Warning's study on the rhetorical aspects of Leviticus may contain a serious challenge to traditional critical judgments concerning literary layers within the book (Warning 1999).

Other scholars have questioned the existence of P in addition to the traditional chronology ascribed to it. For example, in a study of Gen. 2 – 3, Wenham suggests that, assuming P exists, it could be viewed as the earliest among the four documents (Wenham 1999), an idea already espoused in the nineteenth century by scholars such as Dillmann. Yet Wenham also points out that Gen. 2 – 3, traditionally ascribed to JE, contains sanctuary symbolism (Wenham 1986), a characteristic normally used to identify P!

It must be added that alongside the so-called 'critical study' of Leviticus in the nineteenth century, conservative scholars such as Kurtz, Kellogg, Keil and others devoted considerable energy to exploring the symbolic meaning of rituals. These quests were particularly motivated by the New Testament and though their conclusions at times appear forced and speculative, their orientation remains valid, considering that Leviticus is replete with symbolic acts. It is posited in this commentary that much of the speculation concerning literary layers made in the above 'critical studies' arises from a deficient understanding of the symbolic meaning of these rites and ceremonies. Until such an understanding is gained, attempts to identify literary layers in this material are potentially misguided.

With this in mind, the present commentary will not devote discussion to proposed literary layers and sources. Rather it assumes the book as a whole makes good sense without having to resort to hypotheses about literary layers (cf. Wenham 1996).

The large majority of modern studies on Leviticus have abandoned Mosaic authorship (exceptions are Harrison [1980: 15–25] and Rooker [2000: 38–39]). To me it seems scholars have assigned the genesis of Leviticus to various stages of Israel's history (cf. Gerstenberger 1993: 9–13), partly because in dwelling on the formal aspects of its ritual and ceremonial prescriptions they have overlooked the high existential demands the Lord places on the Israelites and priests. When due account is taken of these demands, such as the need to destroy the human egocentric nature (see below), an admission that priests or any group in Israel's history could not have written Leviticus seems inevitable. The demands made of such people are just too high! Leviticus has its origin in God. Though this does not in itself reveal the book's date of authorship, in combination with what the book describes it does favour the view that it originates from the time of Moses – more so than traditional critical theories that date it somewhere in the first millennium BC (cf. Kiuchi 2003c: 523).

4. THE STRUCTURE OF LEVITICUS

Because of the preoccupation traditional critical studies of Leviticus have with identifying the life setting of the priestly material, very few scholarly attempts to understand the book as a whole have been made. Mary Douglas, one of the few who have attempted to do this, proposes what she calls 'a ring structure', where the whole book is arranged in the form of a chiasm, with ch. 19 as its centre (Douglas 1993: 3–23). Though her attempt is commendable, her characterization of each section seems somewhat arbitrary to me (see Kiuchi 1999a: 50–53). Alternatively the book is better viewed linearly.

The structure is discussed below by way of presenting the book's general content.

4.1. Chapters 1 – 7

The material of Leviticus 1 – 7 is divisible into two parts, chs. 1 – 6:7[5:26] and 6:8[6:1] – 7:38. Each section deals with five kinds of offerings, as follows:

I (1:1 – 6:7[5:26])	II (6:8[6:1] – 7:38)
the burnt offering (ch. 1)	the burnt offering (6:8[1] – 13[6])
the loyalty offering (ch. 2)	the loyalty offering (6:14[7] – 23[16]) (including the loyalty offering for the priestly ordination)
the fellowship offering (ch. 3)	the sin offering (6:24[17] – 30[23])
the sin offering (4:1 – 5:13)	the reparation offering (7:1–10)
the reparation offering (5:14 – 5:26)	the fellowship offering (7:11–21)
	injunction on food matters (7:22–27)
	the priests' portion of the fellowship offering (7:28–36)

The relationship between the two corpora is explained in various ways. The apparent repetitiveness between the two corpora is often assumed to be the result of some kind of redactional process. The simplest way of resolving this tension is to assume that corpus II was added later (e.g. Hartley 1992: 94–95; Gerstenberger 1993: 76). However, it is possible to see the two corpora from at least two different viewpoints: that of the *addressee* and that of the *contents*.

From the addressees' viewpoint, corpus I comprises four addresses (1:1–2 [to the Israelites], 4:1–2 [to the Israelites], 5:14 [to Moses], 6:1[5:20] [to Moses]. All of these are addressed first to Moses, who is subsequently to inform the Israelites, with the exception of the Lord's instructions regarding the reparation offering (5:14; 6:1[5:20]), where no such instruction to inform the Israelites or priests is given. However, apart from the reparation offering, corpus I is concerned predominantly with the Israelites.

Corpus II contains the Lord's address in 6:8[1] – 9[2] (to Aaron and his sons), 6:19[1]2 (to Moses), 6:24–25[17–18] (to Aaron and his sons), 7:22–23 (to the Israelites), 7:28–29 (to the Israelites). Corpus II is apparently addressed to the priests, but there is an exception: 7:22ff. reports instructions for the Israelites. However, section 7:22–27 is necessitated by reference to the fellowship offering, the meat of which is shared by both the priests and the offerer. Thus corpus II is predominantly concerned with the priests, with the exception of the fellowship offering.

As is clear from the above table, the position of the fellowship offering is different in I and II. In corpus I it follows the loyalty offering, whereas in II it comes last. This order is explained in different ways (cf. Wenham 1979: 116–119; Milgrom 1991: 382). Before the relationship between the two corpora can be addressed, the features of each corpus require some discussion.

The order of the offerings in Corpus I is at least due to the ritual procedure; some elements are based on those already mentioned in previous offerings (cf. 3:5; 4:8–10, 26, 31, 35; 5:7–8, 11). Yet, more importantly, the five types of offerings are clearly arranged according to their degree of pleasantness to the Lord: the *burnt offering* is the archetype for all other offerings in so far as it is completely burnt; the prescription for the *loyalty offering* stresses the soothing aroma, dealing with the offerer's existential aspect without reference to specific sin; then the *fellowship offering* follows because it is offered on occasions of thanksgiving and oath making. Its focus is not as spiritual as the loyalty offering. Last come the *sin offering* and *reparation offering*, which concern the violation of the Lord's specific commandments, a situation far more offensive to the Lord than the circumstances assumed in the bringing of the preceding offerings. Incidentally it should be noted that the literary pattern A–B–A'–B' that manifests itself from ch. 11 onwards (see below) is also discernible in Lev. 1:1 – 6:7[5:26]: A (the burnt offering), B (the loyalty offering, which begins with *nepeš* in 2:1), A' (the fellowship offering: note that 3:1 parallels 1:3), B' (the sin and reparation offerings: note that the sinner is called *nepeš* in the protases of the cases in 4:1 – 6:7[5:26]).

The arrangement of the offerings in corpus II is explained by Milgrom as grounded on their respective degrees of sanctity (1991: 382; cf. Wenham 1979: 118–119). Thus the fellowship offering comes last, since it, being shared by the offerer and the priest, is of less sanctity than those offerings called 'the most holy': the grain, sin and guilt offerings (6:25[18]; 7:6). That is, if the fellowship offering is offered in accordance with the instructions given in ch. 3, it is more pleasing to the Lord than the sin offering. Yet, since this offering is the most likely to be profaned, it is not called holy and its prescription comes last in corpus II.

When corpus I is compared with corpus II, one feature is clearly discernible. While corpus I places the emphasis on the early part of the ritual, particularly on what goes to the Lord, or what is performed before the Lord, corpus II exhibits a clear emphasis on the handling of the remaining parts of the offerings (see 6:16 – 18[9–11] [the loyalty offering], 6:26[19], 29–30[22–23] [the sin offering], 7:6–7 [the reparation offering], 7:14–21 [the fellowship offering]). Thus, corpus I stresses the Israelites' approach to the Lord with offerings, while corpus II stresses the priests' handling of, and responsibility for, the holy things.

There is yet another literary feature that transcends the two corpora. Reference to the burnt offering and the loyalty offering in 5:7–13, on the one hand, and the burnt offering and the loyalty offering in 7:8–10, literarily and theologically conclude their preceding prescriptions. So that the reparation offering in I that comes after the sin offering, and the fellowship offering in II that comes after the reparation offering, are viewed as exceptional, in that the rules concern or include the extreme cases of holiness's desecration.

Nevertheless the two corpora are not clearly delineated. For the location of the reparation offering at 5:14 – 6:7[5:26] is a fitting conclusion to corpus I, as the reparation offering deals with the sin of infringing upon holy things, and corpus II begins with the issue of safeguarding the holy things, with the purpose of securing the divine presence.

The book of Leviticus is located after the Tent of Meeting's construction. Assuming the actual ritual, it begins by prescribing how the people are to approach the Lord with offerings (chs. 1 – 5), and then details the means of preserving the holiness of the holy things; i.e. securing the divine presence (chs. 6 – 7). All of this is positioned before the beginning of actual worship in chs. 8 – 9. Given the significance of safeguarding the holy things, corpus II cannot be termed 'supplementary' to corpus I, at least from a thematic point of view.

Minor issues concerning the repetitiveness or overlap between the two corpora are dealt with in the commentary.

4.2. Chapters 8 – 16

These chapters relate the successful execution of the commands given in Exod. 28 – 29. Though they could conceivably have come at the beginning of Leviticus, there is a twofold reason for the present order of material. First, without chs. 1 – 7 much of chs. 8 – 10 remain unexplained. Second, there is a thematic shift in content between chs. 1 – 7 and chs. 8 – 10 in terms of how a human becomes holy and acceptable to the Lord: chs. 1 – 7 deal with holy offerings, while the offerer is tacitly demanded to be holy. Chs. 8 – 10 deal with the priests, who are made holy by calling. Therefore, rather than viewing chs. 1 – 7 as an insertion before chs. 8 – 10 (*pace* Milgrom 1991: 61; see Rendtorff 1996: 25–26), Lev. chs. 1 – 10 is arranged in a natural and logical order (see 'Form and structure' on ch. 12).

Ch. 10 relates the incident of Nadab and Abihu, and its aftermath. In that the chapter contains instructions concerning the role of priests within Israel (vv. 9–11), the following chapters, 11 – 16, provide a resource for their carrying out of this role. Furthermore the content of vv. 10–11, teaching the laws to the people and distinguishing between the clean and unclean, the holy and the common, adumbrate the content of all the chapters that follow until ch. 27.

The basic structure of chs. 11 – 16 is, as has been proposed (see Kiuchi 2003c: 524), as follows:

Ch. 11	Introduction
Ch. 12	A
Chs. 13 – 14	B
Ch. 15	A'
Ch. 16	B'

This literary pattern of introduction A–B–A'–B' recurs till ch. 26 (though the introduction is absent from chs. 23 – 26).

It is noteworthy that the call to holiness at the end of ch. 11 does not recur again until ch. 19 onwards. Some scholars suppose that the later H editor inserted these expressions, either interpreting the rules in Lev. 11 as moral/ethical, or as a way of transforming the 'cultic rules' into moral/ethical ones. But this conclusion is overly hasty, considering that these scholars assume that holiness is moral/ethical, without approaching the meaning of the rules in ch. 11 from their possible symbolic dimension.

As the present form of Leviticus stands, the call to holiness in 11:43–45 spans chs. 12 – 26, and it is narrow-minded simply to divide the book into chs. 1 – 16 and (17) 18 – 26 on historical-critical grounds. Rather the command for holiness in 11:43–44 is related to more than chs. 12 – 16. It is expressed by concrete conduct-oriented commandments in chs. 18 – 26. If this is so (I believe it is), it is highly dubious whether the common critical division between 'cultic' (referring to chs. 1 – 16) and 'ethical' (referring to chs. 18 – 26) was entertained by the original legislator or editor.

4.3. Chapters 17 – 22

Even though ch. 17 appears to commence a new section, it follows a clearly transitional passage at the end of ch. 16, which anticipates some terminology and ideas that recur from ch. 17 onwards, among which is the relationship between *kipper* and *nepeš* (the human soul).

The structure of chs. 17 – 23 is as follows: ch. 17 (introduction), ch. 18 (A), ch. 19 (B), ch. 20 (A'), chs. 21 – 22 (B'). It is clear that ch. 18 is closely related to ch. 20, while the concern of ch. 19, a chapter preoccupied with the holiness of the Israelites, is applied to the *holy* priests in chs. 21 – 22.

First, ch. 18, which prohibits various Canaanite customs, recurs with some variations in ch. 20, where emphasis is laid more on the punishment consequent upon their violation. Separating these chapters is ch. 19, a chapter on holiness. It forcefully commands the people to become holy.

Second, chs. 21 – 22 address the holiness of priests and offerings. Compared with ch. 19, there is a culmination in terms of the presentation of the holiness theme, for while substantial holiness is a mandate given to all Israelites in ch. 19, the same holiness is now expected of the outwardly consecrated priests, and their handling of the holy offerings.

4.4. Chapters 23 – 26 (27)

Ch. 23 introduces the theme of holy time, and this is developed in ch. 25 as the Sabbatical year and Jubilee year. The rationale for the placement of the intervening ch. 24 has previously eluded exegetes. Its rules for certain rituals within the Tent and an apparently unrelated account of an incident of blasphemy seem at odds with the surrounding chapters. However, if the two parts of ch. 24 are interpreted as dealing with eternal blessing and divine sanction, respectively (as proposed in 'Comment'), then it can be viewed as relating to the concrete historical reality of the Israelites in ch. 26, a chapter dealing with blessing and curse.

Thus, though chs. 23 – 26 lack an introduction, like chs. 11 and 17, they form the pattern A–B–A^{1}–B^{1} as found in chs. 12 – 16 and 18 – 22.

4.5. Commandments and related terms

Some terms used to refer to the Lord's commandments, such as *miṣwôt* (commandments), *tôrâ/tôrôt* (teachings), *ḥuqqôt* (statutes) and *mišpāṭîm* (rules) have implications for the structure of Leviticus (see Kiuchi 1999a: 33–64, which is revised below). Whereas the term *tôrâ/tôrôt* (teachings) occurs in the early part and *mišpāṭîm* occurs in the latter part of the book, the use of *ḥuqqâ/ḥuqqôt* extends across both. With this in mind, discussions about different literary layers, particularly those of P and H, begin to appear irrelevant to the book's correct interpretation.

First, as commented in 4:2, *miṣwôt* is a most comprehensive term encompassing the meaning of all the other related terms, *ḥuqqîm*, *mišpāṭîm* and *tôrôt*. Thus its occurrence in 27:34 is evidence that the legislator is referring not just to the commandments of ch. 27 but to all the regulations of Leviticus. Therefore the absence of *miṣwôt* at the end of ch. 26 appears deliberate; instead *ḥuqqîm*, a less comprehensive term, is used. Nevertheless that all the regulations prior to ch. 26 are considered to be *miṣwôt* is indicated by its occurrence in 26:14–15, where it reads, 'But if you will not listen to me and will not do all these commandments (*miṣwôt*), if you spurn my *statutes* (*ḥuqqôt*), and if your soul abhors my *rules* (*mišpāṭîm*), so that you will not do all my commandments (*miṣwôt*), but break my covenant (*bĕrît*) . . .'

It is likely that in v. 15, the terms for commandments are mentioned in an order that reflects their broadening semantic width, so that the 'commandments' (*miṣwôt*) covers both 'statutes' (*ḥuqqôt*) and 'rules' (*mišpāṭîm*), while 'covenant' (*bĕrît*) encapsulates the semantic realms of all of the foregoing terms. It is also noteworthy that in 22:31, the concluding part of that chapter, 'the commandments' (*miṣwôt*) refers at the very least to the rules of chs. 21 – 22.

Second, *tôrôt* refers to the rules on ritual prescriptions, such as in chs. 1 – 7 (see 7:37 and 'Comment' on 6:9[2]) and the rituals for purification in chs. 11 – 15 (see 11:46; 12:7; 13:59; 14:54, 57; 15:32). However, these parts of Leviticus are never called *mišpāṭîm*, though *tôrâ* is sometimes synonymous with *ḥuqqâ* (3:17; 7:36).

Third, *ḥuqqôt*, which means 'statutes', is synonymous with *mišpāṭîm*, which means 'judgments' (cf. 18:4–5, 26; 19:37; 20:22; 25:18; 26:15, 43), but in view of the fact that *ḥuqqôt* conjoins with the verb *hālak* (to walk), while *mišpāṭîm* occurs with verbs such as *'āśâ* (to do) and *šāmar* (to keep) and never with *hālak*, *ḥuqqôt* means 'principles of conduct'. As regards *mišpāṭîm*, since it does not occur in Lev. 1 – 17 (except in the form *kammišpaṭ* [according to the rule] in 5:10 and 9:16), it can be inferred that it has a meaning distinct from that of *tôrôt*. Yet the fact that some parts of *tôrôt* stipulate penalties (e.g. 19:5–8) means it must overlap with *mišpāṭîm* in some way.

Last, the term *ḥuqqîm* appears in 10:10 and 26:46. It is natural that its mention in 10:10 ends, at least, in 26:46. Yet since chs. 10 – 26 contain chs. 11 – 15, which are *tôrôt*, *ḥuqqîm* must also include chs. 1 – 7. Therefore the term *ḥuqqîm* is a more comprehensive term than *ḥuqqôt*, *mišpāṭîm* and *tôrôt*.

Thus the above examination of the semantic realm of each term reveals the following set of *miṣwôt* relationships.

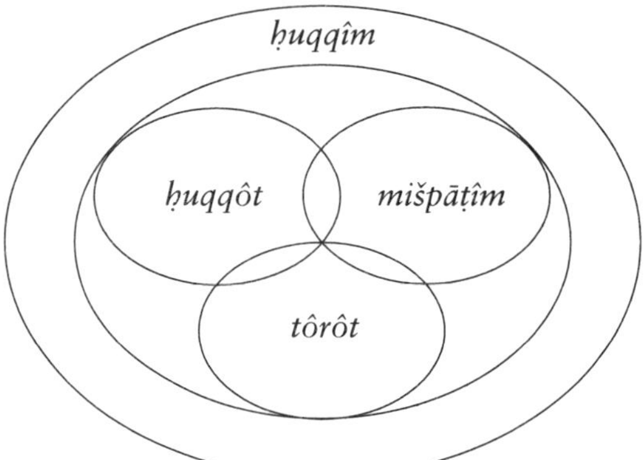

These relationships strongly imply that the summary statements in 26:46 and 27:34 are made with these interrelated semantic realms in mind.

As mentioned above, *tôrâ*/*tôrôt* covers chs. 1 – 15, and the occurrence of the term *mišpāṭîm* is limited to chs. 18 – 25, while *ḥuqqâ*/*ḥuqqôt* is used in both parts. Thus, on the whole, Leviticus first addresses itself to laws that concern divine–human relationships, expressed by rituals (*tôrôt*), and then addresses itself more specifically to human conduct before the Lord (*mišpāṭîm*), while principles for conduct (*ḥuqqâ*/*ḥuqqôt*) are found throughout.

It is noteworthy that ch. 16, which is a ritual, is characterized as a *ḥuqqâ* (vv. 29, 31, 34) and not as a *tôrâ*, and that ch. 17 contains a reference in v. 7 to *ḥuqqâ*. The book moves gradually from *tôrâ*-dominated chapters to *ḥuqqôt*/*mišpāṭîm*-dominated chapters, and chs. 16 – 17 form a transitional role from this viewpoint. Thus it is inappropriate to see ch. 17 onwards as something entirely new and distinct from the preceding chapters, as is often concluded by critics.

5. SOME DISTINCTIVE FEATURES OF LEVITICUS

5.1. Style

5.1.1. Addressees

Leviticus is dominated by laws the Lord spoke through Moses. The address formula takes the form 'The Lord spoke to X, and X spoke to Y.' In Leviticus, X is always Moses; except in 10:8, where Aaron is addressed directly. As for Y, it is ordinarily the Israelites or Aaron and his sons, but not always. Sometimes it is Aaron, and less frequently there are cases where Y is not mentioned: it is simply said, 'The Lord spoke to Moses.' As indicated by the various comments made here, these variations seem deliberate rather than accidental; in general the address used is governed by the nature of the law being given. Moses is the mediator between God and the people, and also the one who initiates the priesthood (Lev. 8 – 9). Thus, whenever the law in question concerns the very foundation of the covenant, Moses is addressed; whereas when inner priestly matters are in question, Aaron is addressed (see e.g. 1:2; 5:14; 6:19[12]). For a further implication of this, see Greenberg 1990.

5.1.2. The prescriptions as theology

Although the laws, particularly those to do with rituals, are commonly viewed as no more than an instruction manual describing how rituals should be conducted, their formulation and presentation indicates they have a different agenda. They are aimed to convey a certain message through their formulation, and not least through the symbolic meaning of the rituals found therein (see below). For example, the stipulation in 7:30 that 'His hands shall bring the LORD's food offerings' seems unnecessary if this is just a prescription. Thus we are invited to explore the underlying rationales for the various formulations.

A more widespread literary phenomenon is the use of repetitiveness or non-repetitiveness in the prescriptions. These can be classified according to various categories. The protases of the four cases in ch. 4 are suitable for the purpose of illustration.

(1) There are some variations in style that appear to be dictated purely by stylistic concerns. For instance, 'or if he is made aware of his sin' in v. 28 is not mentioned in vv. 32–33; probably because vv. 32–36 are a subcase. A little different is the forgiveness formula in v. 31, which recurs with extra details in v. 35 ('his sin that he committed'). These instances do not produce differences in meaning.

(2) However, some variations possibly reflect the nature of the case in question. For example, the content of v. 2 encompasses vv. 3, 13, 22, 27. The variation of the formulation is not just stylistic, but is conformed to the nature of the ritual; particularly to the degree of sinfulness that characterizes the person standing before God (see 'Comment'). The priest is not said to realize guilt; that being presupposed, more urgency is conveyed by the phrase 'so that the people realize guilt' (v. 3). In the second case the community realizes guilt' *and* 'comes to know the sin'. In the third and fourth cases these two conditions, a realization of guilt and 'coming to know the sin', are set out as two alternatives, being joined by *'ô* (or) in vv. 23, 28. Furthermore, while in the second case the congregation itself comes to know the sin (*nôdĕ'â*), in the third and fourth cases a sinner is informed of his sin by someone else (*hôda'*).

(3) There are cases where an explicit reference to something appears somehow related to implicit assumptions, when a comparison is possible with other cases. For example, in the prescription for the burning of fat, the appearance of the phrase 'a soothing aroma' (4:31), which characterizes the burnt offering, appears conspicuous, since it occurs for the first time in this chapter in the case of the lay individual. It should not be inferred from this that in the other three cases the burning of fat does not produce 'a soothing aroma': the omission of this phrase in relation to the other cases achieves a literary function. It stresses the serious, rather than joyful, character of those rituals.

(4) The non-mention of forgiveness as well as *kipper* in the case of the priest is possibly deliberate, having some intention behind it. This issue is related not so much to textual problems concerning vv. 10–12, but to an ideological reason; namely that the anointed priest, who mediates between God and sinner, is also a sinner.

Thus explicitness and implicitness within prescriptions do not just fulfil literary purposes: they also reflect ideological principles. Therefore the exegesis undertaken in this commentary pays special attention to such literary phenomena. Moreover if some significant key terms such as *kipper*, *nepeš*, *rēaḥ nîḥôaḥ* etc. are taken into account, Leviticus, particularly its early chapters, may exhibit a far more lively picture of the divine–human relationship than has been previously admitted.

5.2. Content

5.2.1. Its ideological relation to Exodus

How should Leviticus be read in relation to the exodus event? The question revolves around the fact that Leviticus legislation was meant to mould the Israelites into God's holy people after they were redeemed from bondage in Egypt. On the basis of the covenant/treaty background of the Pentateuchal law, Wenham (1979: 31) states:

> the law was given in a context of grace. In the treaty form the stipulations came after the historical prologue. This was analogous to the historical situation: God gave his law to Israel after they had been redeemed from Egypt, not as a means for securing their redemption. God's call to Israel to be his holy people preceded the revelation of the law at Sinai, but only obedience could make holiness a living reality. In Leviticus, whenever the exodus from Egypt is mentioned it is always as a motive for keeping the law (e.g., 11:45; 18:3; 23:43).

While this view seems to be formally right, terms such as 'grace', 'redeem' and 'holiness' should be reconsidered from an existential perspective. For, though it seems that the Decalogue was given within a context of 'grace', would not the difficulty of observing it in addition to the severe punishments associated with such violations (though this is not mentioned in the Decalogue itself, except in the case of the third commandment) militate against such a conclusion? It is true that the redemption from Egypt was an act of God's graciousness. However, before Sinai the people grumbled about their food (Exod. 16), and after the giving of the law at Sinai they made a golden calf (Exod. 32ff.). If the people had come to realize they possessed nothing in this world but the Lord, then the law would have been very easy for them to observe. Yet the people's grumbling attests to the fact that the condition of their hearts was far from the holiness expected of them (Exod. 19:6). Put simply, the Israelites left Egypt without experiencing a clinical operation on their hearts. It became necessary for their hearts to be dealt with by the law, and this is why the law is given after their physical removal from Egypt.

Moreover, while Wenham notes in the above statement that 'holiness' may be taken as a goal or ideal, my proposal that it is a term referring to a certain condition of the human heart, namely the absence of an egocentric nature (see below, especially 7.4), indicates that the Israelites standing before the Lord in Exod. 19 are as yet unredeemed (unsaved) from their sinfulness, a position roughly equivalent to having an egocentric nature. In other words, while there is a dimension where it is possible to address the exodus event not only as salvation from bondage in Egypt but also as their salvation from sin (cf. 1 Cor. 10:1–4), the spiritual reality of the people showed that they were far from being saved from their own sinfulness.

The book of Leviticus, as the further unfolding of the Sinai covenant, addresses itself to matters of the human heart through its rules on offerings, cleanness/uncleanness and holiness. The rules in the book, though mostly set forth in hypothetical forms, presume the existence of a spiritual gap between the Lord and the people. Moreover, while the people are assumed to be in a covenantal relationship with the Lord, all the rules in Leviticus constitute the covenant's very content. Thus it is inappropriate to assume the people were saved, so the rules in Leviticus were added purely to enhance or enrich the covenantal relationship between the people and the Lord. Therefore it seems necessary to conclude that unless one becomes holy, he remains unsaved from his sinfulness; i.e. his own egocentric nature (cf. Lev. 26:41; cf. Kiuchi 2003b: 1–30).

As the natural sequel of Exodus, Leviticus contains more than a few references to Exodus, which will be noted in 'Comment'.

5.2.2. *No compromise over holiness*

As in other parts of the priestly literature, Leviticus allows no compromise in matters of holiness. Though there are degrees of holiness among offerings, between the outer part of the Tent and the Holy of Holies, and between the priests and the laity, the profanation of holiness is accompanied by dire consequences. In this regard, the prescriptions and rules in this book should be viewed as given from the divine viewpoint. Inevitably the Lord does not, in principle, concern himself with the question of whether or not the Israelites can observe his commandments.

A closer look at the prescriptions shows, however, that the human propensity towards sin and uncleanness is assumed in the formulation of the prescriptions. Here are some examples. There are five kinds of offerings, the most pleasing of which from the Lord's perspective is the burnt offering, and the least pleasing are the sin and reparation offerings (see 4.1 above). The prescription concerning the remaining part of the fellowship offering reflects the covetous nature of its offerer. Lev. 17:7 reveals the book is given with an awareness that the people were involved in idolatrous practices. In particular ch. 26 clearly reflects the stiff-neckedness of the Israelites. Thus, though no comment is made concerning whether or not the Israelites can observe the Lord's commandments, the Lord appears to know the answer, and this negative answer is reflected in the way the prescriptions are formulated.

With all this in mind, the Lord remains adamant about the standard he requires of humans: he allows no compromise of his holiness.

5.2.3. *Its ideological relation to Genesis*

The high standard the Leviticus legislation demands of the Israelites becomes clearer when it is realized that it has the Genesis account of the fall as its immediate background. The literary and ideological links between Leviticus and Gen. 1 – 3, particularly Gen. 3, in the areas of sin and uncleanness were noted by nineteenth-century scholars such as Keil and Kurtz. Although the latter's way of linking these texts is unpersuasive, the connection has recently gained renewed interest among conservative scholars like Wenham (1986), Sailhamer (1992: 39–41, 334–337 *et passim*) and Parry (1994: 126–152). Particularly Wenham and Parry point out the presence of sanctuary symbolism in Gen. 2 – 3.

As explained below and in 'Comment', the cleanness/uncleanness rules are best explained by assuming Gen. 3 as their immediate background. Not a few elements in the fall, including the first man and woman's hiding of their loins and the Lord's increasing of the pain associated with childbirth, appear related to the uncleanness associated with male and female reproductive organs. The curse on the animal world caused by the serpent provides a significant clue to the rationale underlying the unclean creatures of ch. 11.

Connections between the fall and Leviticus are discernible elsewhere too. For instance the presence of the cherubim before the Holy of Holies is assumed in the ritual in 4:2–12 and 16:1–22. It probably suggests that somewhere beyond the cherubim on the ark in the Holy of Holies lies the world of the pre-fall Garden of Eden. Similarly the seven-branched lampstand in the Holy Place (24:2–4) may symbolize the Tree of Life (Meyers 1976: 5–9). Other links to Gen. 3 are noted throughout the commentary, all of which convey the message that holiness is what the first man and woman had before the fall, and that the various rules in Leviticus aim to lead the Israelites, as it were, back to this existential condition. As will be explained in 7.3.2 below, the latter requires the evisceration of so-called sin (*ḥāṭā'*), the meaning of which is to hide oneself from God, and the destruction of the egocentric nature that represents the existential condition of the human heart.

Lastly, the sacrificial idea of offerings narrated in Genesis (the burnt offerings offered by Noah [Gen. 8:20–21] and Abraham [Gen. 22:2, 9], the offerings made by Cain and Abel [Gen. 4:3–4]) may well lie behind the Levitical legislation.

6. RITUAL AS SYMBOLIC

In general it is agreed that the ritual acts have their own symbolic meanings. However, these symbolic meanings are rarely spelled out in Leviticus, except for the meaning of blood in 17:11. In an attempt to uncover the symbolic meanings Klingbeil (2004: 502) has recently proposed an appropriate approach to the ritual text. Especially he proposes to take the present form of the OT as the database upon which exegesis must be done, in so far as this area belongs to theology rather than historical study, with which I concur.

The presence of symbolic meanings in relation to the ritual acts of Leviticus is inferred from the following points.

(1) In the case of offerings, there is first the offerer's motive, such as thanksgiving or repentance. It is natural then that the offering and its ritual are related, at least in some sense, to the offerer's motive (cf. Kiuchi 1999b: 23–31). If blood symbolizes human life, then other elements of the ritual must also convey their symbolic meanings. This may be particularly supported by the symbolic meaning of the imposition of a hand before slaughtering; i.e. it probably symbolizes an offerer's identification with the animal.

(2) With regard to the uncleanness regulations in chs. 11 – 15, their symbolic dimension is betrayed by their literary and ideological links with Gen. 3 (see 'Comment' on chs. 11 – 13, 15). Since the prescriptions have the fall as their immediate background, it can be inferred that they deal with the spiritual condition of humans after the fall.

(3) Ch. 19, an important chapter on holiness, contains some rules that concern fabric and agriculture (vv. 19, 23–25). However, since holiness obviously concerns an inner quality of humans in this chapter (v. 2), it is entirely unlikely that a mixed fabric is forbidden for its own sake, or that the Lord is purely concerned with the fruit of trees. Both would seem to bear a symbolic relationship to a human heart that is holy.

(4) The Hebr. term *tôrâ*, commonly translated 'law' or 'prescription', is attached to the corpuses of rules in 6:9[2] – 7:37 and chs. 11 – 15. As proposed in this commentary, it also includes chs. 1 – 6:7, and means 'teaching'. Thus these laws are more than mere prescriptions: they are prescriptions useful for 'teaching'. If so, the quest for the symbolic meaning of rituals becomes mandatory. Therefore it is more than likely that the rituals in Leviticus have human beings as their referent, and cannot be separated from them.

The term 'symbol' is ordinarily used in relation to rituals, whereas 'metaphor' is commonly used to denote poetic description. Both are alike in that they deal with the relationship between the object and what it represents. But while a symbolic meaning is fixed, the meanings of poetic metaphors are flexible. For example, when animal blood is said to be 'life', the symbolic meaning is fixed as such. By contrast, blood could be used metaphorically of the colour red, warmth, viscosity etc.

Despite the common assumption that symbolic meanings have an inflexible nature, the symbolic meanings of the various ritual acts of Leviticus have eluded exegetes throughout the ages. Nevertheless if a ritual act or an object used within a ritual has a certain inflexible symbolic meaning, then the task for exegetes to identify it becomes mandatory (cf. Meyers 1976: 5–9). In this commentary an attempt is made to explore the symbolic dimension of Leviticus as much as possible. The reader may examine whether the various proposals fit within the context as a whole. The Leviticus text is not entirely silent regarding these meanings. Among others, terms like *'ādām* (a man), *nepeš* (a soul), *kipper* (to make propitiation) or *ḥāṭā'* (to hide oneself, see 'Comment' on 4:2) provide helpful clues for solving the problem. If no clue is found within Leviticus, we may turn our eyes to non-priestly literature. Such a procedure is justified by the assumption that the Israelites' basic view of the various symbolic meanings did not change easily over time.

One of the chief characteristics of ritual symbolism in Leviticus is the inseparableness of a symbol from what it symbolizes: the two are considered one (for the 'intrinsic' nature of the Levitical symbolism, see Wenham 1982: 118–125). For instance, in 10:16–20 Moses expostulates with Aaron regarding the latter's handling of the remaining part of the sin offering. The words of both persons (vv. 17–19) show that the flesh of the sin offering and what it symbolizes are one. The incident suggests that if the ritual is performed, its symbolic meaning is also fulfilled before the Lord. It appears that the same situation applies to all the other offerings and their respective rituals.

This assumption inevitably invites us to reflect on the relationship between the outward or literal observance of the prescription and what it symbolizes. If the ritual has a symbolic meaning, the keeping of its outward or literal observance alone is insufficient. Thus in reading the prescriptions one would need to make a provisional distinction between outward observance and what it symbolizes. For although, as mentioned above, the Leviticus prescriptions have a dimension that makes them more than prescriptions, there are many cases where their literal observance appears to meet the requirements. For instance, to follow the prescription in ch. 3 may appear to satisfy what the Lord requires. However, if the burning of fat symbolizes, as proposed in this commentary (see 'Comment' on 3:3–4), the annihilation of the offerer's egocentric nature, then simply to follow the prescription outwardly remains a long way from what is required. Likewise by following the uncleanness regulations of chs. 11 – 15 one becomes clean. However, if 'uncleanness' symbolizes the human existential condition, to attend only to the literal observance of these rules would make a person a mere hypocrite. In other words it is vitally important to recognize that the Lord commands the observance of the symbolic meaning through one's involvement in outward actions. Therefore it is ultimately meaningless to limit observance to outward acts.

Several rationales underlie the presentation of rituals replete with symbolic meanings. First of all, though the laws are meant to make the Israelites holy, it is impossible for this to occur in a direct way for an unclean or sinful individual (for the ideas of 'uncleanness', 'sin' and 'holy', see below). Moreover recourse to visible things is intelligible for human beings who often remain unaware of spiritual things. Thus spiritual matters are conveyed by tangible objects for educational purposes: in order for the people to learn what *sacrifice* is, they need to bring a costly animal, or in order that they may learn what *holiness* is, many restrictions are made, some of which will cost their physical lives.

Based on the distinction between outward observance and the spiritual truth it symbolizes, I make a distinction between *outer* cleanness/uncleanness and *inner* cleanness/uncleanness, and between *outer* holiness and *inner* holiness. And yet it is to be kept in mind that this distinction is for explanation's sake, and that outer cleanness/uncleanness or holiness enshrines within itself, and points to, inner cleanness/uncleanness and holiness.

Does the Lord accept those offerings made by people who do not truly embody the symbolic meaning of these offerings? The answer is no. For unless the offerer's heart embodies the symbolic meaning of the offering, the latter becomes a profanation of holiness. This of course raises the question of who may offer an offering in the true sense of the word.

The recognition of the spiritual gap between the offering and the offerer, for instance, brings us to another dimension of the ritual. Since it is so difficult to bridge this gap, the prescriptions on sacrifice and defilement have a universal or lifelong dimension; if one can offer a burnt offering in the true sense of the word (just like Abraham offering Isaac [Gen. 22]), he is accepted by the Lord. The same holds true for the observance of the cleanness/uncleanness regulations, given the symbolic meaning of uncleanness I propose: the state of hiding oneself (see below).

Therefore when the symbol and what is symbolized become one in reality, there is no need for sacrifices and offerings. The OT refers to such a spiritual reality or possibility in Pss. 40:6 or 51:16–19 (see 8 below).

7. SOME KEY THEMES IN LEVITICUS

In an attempt to grasp the fundamental message of Leviticus it is necessary to explain in advance some key ideas and terms; these are concerned with the *nature of human beings*, the *symbolic meanings of cleanness, uncleanness and holiness*, and the *wrath of God* (*kipper* and its related terms).

7.1. Fundamental aspects of the human being

Leviticus deals rigorously with the God–human relationship. Therefore it is vital to know how it views human beings. Humans are by no means viewed as neutral. They have to approach the Lord by making sacrifice, they have to be killed when they approach the holy realm without due qualifications, and, above all, are seen as having a strong tendency to defile themselves.

Three important terms (*'îš 'ādām* and *nepeš*) are used to refer legally to the same individual, but merit a closer look and need to be differentiated in meaning, although modern translations have treated these terms more or less synonymously. Leaving aside the exegetical details of the relevant passages for 'Comment', only my conclusions regarding the meaning of these terms in Leviticus are set out below.

7.1.1. 'îš (a person)

The term *'îš* occurs ninety-four times in Leviticus. The phrase *'îš 'îš*, in the sense of 'anyone', occurs in 15:2; 17:3, 8, 10, 13; 18:6; 20:2, 9; 22:4, 15, 18. Ordinarily *'îš* occurs in contrast with *'iššâ* (13:29, 38; 15:18; 19:20; 20:10–11, 13–14, 18, 21, 27; 21:7; 24:10). A reflexive use of *'îš* is quite common in the sense of 'each' (7:10; 10:1; 19:3, 11; 25:10, 13, 17, 46; 26:37). The remaining occurrences introduce cases that begin with 'When a person'.

Thus it is clear that the term is used to refer to an individual in interhuman relationships (between fellow Israelites or a husband and wife), and refers to individuals without reference to their inner quality (contrast *nepeš*) or the animal world (cf. *'ādām*).

7.1.2. 'ādām (a man)

The term *'ādām* appears fifteen times in Leviticus (1:2; 5:3–4, 22; 7:21; 13:2, 9; 16:17; 18:5; 22:5; 24:17, 20–21; 27:28–29; see Maass 1973: 85–94). Some general features of its usage are listed below. Since various aspects of *'ādām* are at issue, they may overlap.

'Ādām is used (1) when a human being is contrasted with animals (*bĕhēmâ*, 24:21; 27:28, 29), (2) when the corporeal side of a human being is stressed (5:3; 7:21; 13:2, 9; 18:5; 22:5; 24:17, 20–21; 27:28, 39) and (3) when an inclusive reference is made to all humanity. In this case it is

translated 'humankind' and *'ādām* is prefixed by the article (*hā'ādām*, 5:4, 22; 18:5).

Verbs conjoined with *'ādām* include *hiqrîb* (offer, 1:2), *biṭṭē'* (utter, 5:4), *'āśâ* (do, 6:3[5:22]; 18:5). However, with the exception of 5:22, *'ādām* is never the agent of *ḥāṭā'* in Leviticus.

The formula *'ādām kî* introduces two major prescriptions: that for the burnt offering (1:2), and the other concerning cases of *ṣāra'at* (13:2). Though commentators have commonly assumed females are also in view on these occasions, it probably refers exclusively to 'a man', not 'a woman' (see 'Comment' there).

7.1.3. nepeš ('a soul' or 'an egocentric nature')

The noun *nepeš* occurs sixty times in Leviticus. It has been translated 'person', 'living being' and 'life', 'soul' and 'corpse' (cf. Seebass 1986: 531–555; Schwartz 1991: 40–41). In general, Eng. translations have failed to render the distinctive meaning of *nepeš* over against those of *'îš* or *'ādām*. However, there are some occurrences of *nepeš* where a contextual reading suggests its meaning is different from *'îš* and *'ādām*.

One feature of the appearance of *nepeš* deserves special attention: it frequently occurs in connection with the *kāret* (cutting off) penalty (7:20–21, 25, 27; 17:10, 14; 18:29; 19:8; 20:6; 22:3; 23:29). The *kāret* penalty is not by itself the death penalty, but refers to the excommunication of a person from the community. At one place, 22:3, the penalty is cutting off 'from before the LORD'.

Now from the fact that *nepeš* is synonymous with *lēbāb* (a heart) in ch. 26 (vv. 36, 41; cf. *nepeš* in vv. 15–16, 43), it can be inferred that *nepeš* refers to an invisible part of a human being. This inference is further corroborated by comparing it with those cases where the verb *nikrat* (to be cut off) is conjoined with *'ādām* or *'îš*. The *kāret* penalty is mainly related to *nepeš* (Exod. 12:19; 31:14; Lev. 7:20–21, 25, 27; 17:10, 14; 18:29; 19:8; 20:6; 22:3; 23:29; Num. 9:13; 15:30–31; 19:13, 20) and sporadically to *'îš* (Exod. 30:33, 38; Lev. 17:4, 9; 20:3, 5, 17–18). It should be noted that in a few passages, such as Lev. 17:10 and Num. 9:13, *nepeš* and *'îš* appear alternately. It is remarkable that the *kāret* penalty is never associated with *'ādām*, at least, in the legal part of the Pentateuch. On the other hand, *mwt* is associated with *'îš* (Exod. 21:12, 14; 21:16, 18, 20; 21:28–29, 35; Lev. 19:20; 20:2, 4, 9–13, 15, 20, 27; 24:17; Num. 15:35; 26:10, 65; 27:8 etc.), or, less frequently, *'ādām* (Lev. 24:21; 27:29; Num. 16:29; 19:14). It is to be observed that *mwt* is never directly associated with *nepeš*. The various relationships are more easily comprehended diagrammatically:

nikrat, *nepeš*, *'îš*	(*'ādām* is not directly associated with *krt*)
mwt, *'ādām*, *'îš*	(*nepeš* is not directly associated with *mwt*)

That *'ādām* is not directly associated with *krt* is understandable, considering that the *kāret* penalty has basically no bearing on the question of whether a person is physically alive or dead. This is consonant with the inference made above that *'ādām* refers to the earthly and corporeal sides of a person. That *nepeš* is not directly associated with *mwt* may well reflect the circumstance that it is a term referring to a person's spiritual side, which does not perish or disappear with the person's physical death. The above finding also indicates that *'îš* is related to both the *kāret* penalty and dying, which suggests that *'îš* has both the spiritual and corporeal aspects of a person in view, while it has other semantic elements (interpersonal connotations) not shared by *'ādām* and *nepeš*.

The result of the above observations is as follows.

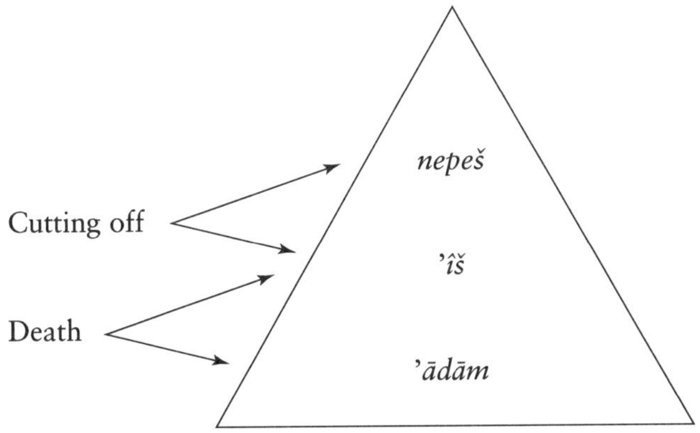

An equally important phenomenon of the *nepeš* is that in Leviticus it occurs both as a pure entity and as an entity with a strong tendency to sin and defile itself. On the one hand, 11:43–44 (see also 20:25) reads, 'You shall not make your souls (*napšôtēkem*) detestable with any swarming thing that swarms ... You shall not defile souls (*napšôtēkem*) with any swarming thing that crawls on the ground.'

In this case, *napšôtêkem* is viewed as an entity that can be inherently pure. But at the same time, as implied by all of the other regulations in Leviticus, the human *nepeš* is viewed as having a strong propensity to sin and defile itself. Although the regulations are set forth in a hypothetical form such as 'if' or 'when', where the human soul appears to be neutral, the very fact that it is conjoined with such verbs as *ḥāṭā'* (4:2), *šiqqēṣ* (11:43; 20:25), *ṭimmē'* (11:43), *'innâ* (16:29, 31; 23:27) implies that the *nepeš* is assumed to be an egocentric nature. In 21:1, 10 it is assumed that the human *nepeš* is not just something to be defiled, but is the very source of defilement. Rather than the 'living *nepeš*' of Gen. 2:7, it is now a doomed *nepeš*. I understand that it essentially refers to the egocentric nature that assumedly appeared after the fall (Gen. 3). With the 'sin' of the first man and woman their souls were dead, separated from an intimate presence of God, and came to bear the condition mentioned in Gen. 3:22. Since *nepeš* refers to the invisible side of a human being, it should be translated 'a soul', with the understanding that, despite having a pure core, it ordinarily manifests itself with egocentricity that constantly reacts, consciously or unconsciously, against God (cf. Hab. 2:4). Therefore I use 'egocentric nature' to explain the term, but in translation, 'a soul'.

It is noteworthy that no term for 'a spirit' (*rûaḥ*) occurs in Leviticus, though the human spirit, as opposed to the divine spirit, is certainly one of the human being's invisible components. In the Bible the human spirit is viewed as an entity that has become swollen with pride and arrogance, and therefore deserves destruction (Pss. 34:18; 51:17[19]; Isa. 57:15; 66:2; Matt. 5:3). Perhaps the term *nepeš* encompasses what is meant by the human spirit, and the reason why the latter is not mentioned in Leviticus is that, by concentrating on the human *nepeš*, the book intends to stress the relationships between physical life and the doomed state of the human soul, and between the doomed soul and life before God (cf. 17:11), since *nepeš* means both 'life' and 'soul'. It is notable that the Lord has his own *nepeš* (26:30).

Thus it seems that various rituals and statutes aim to convert the Israelites into people who have the same *living souls* the first man and woman had before the fall.

7.2. 'Sin'

Recent commentaries on Leviticus appear to take for granted that 'sin' means *violation* of certain of the Lord's commandments. However, this conduct-oriented understanding of sin should be challenged by the fact that the use of the Hebrew term *ḥāṭā'* (commonly rendered 'to commit a sin') and *ḥaṭṭā't* (commonly rendered 'a sin') do not match the context of chs. 4 – 5 (for the following, see Kiuchi 2003a). For example, the verb *ḥāṭā'* in Lev. 4:2 is more comprehensive than violation of a prohibition itself (see 'Comment' on 4:2). This is more explicit in the use of *ḥāṭā'* in 5:1–5. *Ḥāṭā'* in this context does not refer to violation of any specific commandment, but apparently refers to the condition of the sinner's heart. Since the verb is synonymous with the meaning of *šāgâ* and *šāgag* (to go astray), it has an existential meaning. Re-examination of other related terms such as *mā'al* (to break faith) also points to the inference that *ḥāṭā'* refers to the condition of the human heart, though in this context the latter is generated by violation of a certain prohibitive commandment.

A more specific meaning of *ḥāṭā'*, which is both comprehensive and existential, can be inferred from three points: (1) In the prescription of 4:1 – 6:7[5:26], the sinner presents himself before the Lord upon realization of his guilt that has been hidden from him (please note, I use the masculine pronoun here and elsewhere usually only for brevity's sake: the text applies equally to females). (2) In 5:6 the realization of guilt is followed by a confession (*hitwaddâ*, 'to confess', 5:6). (3) Synonyms and antonyms of *ḥāṭā'* and *ḥaṭṭā't* in the rest of the OT show it has to do with the idea of 'hiding'. From these the conclusion is drawn that *ḥāṭā'* means to 'hide oneself'.

The other contexts where *ḥāṭā'* does not appear but *ḥaṭṭā't* does, concern purification of uncleanness. In these contexts the assumed existential meaning becomes even more heightened because the contexts do not assume violation of a prohibitive commandment of God. Thus it is inferred that *ḥaṭṭā't* stands for the condition of hiding oneself.

One of the major characteristics of *ḥāṭā'* and *ḥaṭṭā't* is that, as what these terms express is existential, the agent is not conscious of his own heart's condition.

As *ḥāṭā'* and *ḥaṭṭā't* mean 'to hide oneself' and the condition of 'hiding oneself', respectively, we can assume that the function of the sin offering is to uncover the offerer's heart.

Although neither *ḥāṭā'* nor *ḥaṭṭā't* appears in Gen. 3, which relates how sin came into the world, the account assumedly relates major characteristics of *ḥāṭā'* and *ḥaṭṭā't*. Here it remains to note that as the story begins with the serpent's address to the woman, 'sin' starts from human inner thought. For the rest of the aspects of *ḥāṭā'* and *ḥaṭṭā't*, see 'Explanation' on chs. 11 – 13 and 15.

This commentary is based on these findings, and their implications for other themes such as uncleanness and holiness are far reaching.

7.3. 'Cleanness'/'Uncleanness'

Regulations concerning cleanness and uncleanness are concentrated in chs. 11 – 16, yet are assumed by some of the material that precedes this section, such as in 5:2–3 and 7:19–21. The priests are instructed to make the Israelites aware of these rules (10:10). There are essentially three sets of regulations in chs. 11 – 15, cleanness/uncleanness of animals and creatures (ch. 11), the serious skin disease called *ṣāra'at* (chs. 13 – 14), and genital discharges (chs. 12, 15). While the same terms 'clean' (*ṭāhēr*) and 'uncleanness' (*ṭāmē'*) occur in these chapters, their rationale is explored in each of the three kinds of regulation.

7.3.1. Traditional explanations of the rationale for 'uncleanness' in chapters 11 – 15

A wide range of views has been advanced for the rationale underlying the unclean creatures of Lev. 11 (for details, see Jenson 1992: 75–83; Houston 1993: 68–123). The 'hygienic' explanation that sees hygienic concerns as lying behind the selection of unclean creatures is advocated by some scholars, such as Harrison (1980) and others. However, this explanation raises at least two questions. First, why are other harmful animals and vegetables not prohibited? Second, if they reflect hygienic concerns, why do the rules of Lev. 11 not remain in force after Pentecost (see Rooker 2000: 172). The 'cultic' explanation assumes that the unclean animals prohibited in Lev. 11 were used in Canaanite religious practices (Noth 1965: 92). Yet, as pointed out by Wenham (cf. 1979: 167), this seems unlikely, considering that bulls, which are clean in Israel, were offered in Canaan. The traditional 'symbolic' explanation, championed by Philo, is one that sees the use of clean and unclean creatures as a means for teaching spiritual truths (cf. Houston 2003: 144–147). Related to this approach is that adopted by early and recent scholars, which considers that the unclean creatures represent death (Dillmann 1880: 479; Paschen 1970; Wenham 1979: 169–171; Milgrom 1991: 704–742). Though the proposed symbolic meanings of this approach are often judged as inappropriate by modern exegetes (e.g. Rooker 2000: 171), they are, in my view, close to the truth.

A recent and now dominant approach to the clean and unclean creatures is that contributed by Douglas, who suggests that the locomotion and mode of digestion are the criteria for identifying the various listed animals as either normal or abnormal: if a creature exhibits a feature that digresses from its inherent feature in the creation, it is unclean and vice versa (Douglas 1966). This view is criticized by Firmage on the basis that the criteria suggested by Douglas do not match the unclean creatures in Lev. 11, particularly the criterion of locomotion (Firmage 1990).

Lastly, some scholars hold that the rules in ch. 11 are arbitrarily commanded by God, for the purpose of making Israel a distinguished people (Rooker 2000: 171–172).

As regards genital discharges (chs. 12 and 15) and the leprous skin disease (chs. 13 – 14), two approaches, sometimes combined, deserve mention: the hygienic approach, and the symbolic approach that views the concept of 'death' as underlying the regulation (Dillmann 1880: 478–479; Wenham 1983: Milgrom 1991: 766–768, 816–820).

Thus the only rationale proposed thus far that may cover all the cases of uncleanness appears to be the 'death'-motif.

7.3.2. *The symbolic meaning of uncleanness and the meaning of sin*

Seen as a whole, the various traditional approaches, including some newer ones, have failed by and large to capture the rationale underlying the uncleanness regulations. This is, in my view, due to a failure to obtain some consistent rationale for uncleanness that covers not just part of the regulations but all of the regulations in chs. 11 – 15, all the more so since the same term 'unclean' is used, despite the apparently completely different topics.

Now, as has been noted, the biblical uncleanness regulations are restricted to topics relating to human birth, discharges from male and female reproductive organs, and *ṣāraʻat* (leprous disease), in addition to the creatures listed in ch. 11. Thus, although it is most reasonable to see 'death' as lying behind the idea of uncleanness as far as chs. 11 and 13 – 14 are concerned, that a mere cut on the human body is not said to defile suggests that physical life is not the main point of the rules, and that if 'death' is assumed, it is not physical but *spiritual* death.

From the regulations concerning the leprous disease described in ch. 13, I have recently proposed that it has nothing to do with pathological or medical concerns (partly observed by Wenham and Milgrom) but that the disease functions to describe the human propensity to hide sinfulness. The manifestations of the disease, such as its persistence and the normal human response of hiding the infected areas, are highly appropriate for describing human sinfulness (Kiuchi 2001a). From this I further propose that the description may have the fall event of Gen. 3 in view. As my comments will show, these chapters on cleanness/uncleanness exhibit links to the account of Gen. 3, not just in themes such as hiding oneself literally and spiritually (Gen. 3:7–9), childbearing (Gen. 3:14), man and woman, but also through use of the expression 'on the belly' (*hālak ʻal gāḥôn*, Gen. 3:14; Lev. 11:42). These literary and ideological links to Gen. 3 show that Leviticus forms a sequel to Gen. 3.

Then, from the meaning of *ḥāṭāʼ* and *ḥaṭṭāʼt*, commonly translated 'to commit a sin' and 'a sin', the conclusion is drawn that these terms mean 'to hide oneself' and 'the state of hiding oneself', respectively (Kiuchi 2003a). Hence the term *ṭāmēʼ*/*ṭumʻâ* (unclean/uncleanness), synonymous with *ḥāṭāʼ* and *ḥaṭṭāʼt*, refers symbolically to the state of hiding oneself when this is not occasioned by a violation of certain commandments. Furthermore I propose in this commentary that the leprous disease symbolizes the human egocentric self (see 'Comment' on ch. 13).

The reason why only specific topics such as genital discharge and leprous disease are chosen to symbolize uncleanness is that the legislator intends both to describe the human fallen condition and to encourage the Israelites to become holy (on the immediate background of the fall, see 5.2.3 above). It is vital to recognize that while certain creatures and human genital conditions are said to be unclean, this ultimately symbolizes a human spiritual condition before God. Thus uncleanness expresses the human existential condition that is essentially a matter of the human heart or soul.

Therefore, while it is not wrong to view death behind uncleanness, the latter more specifically symbolizes the state of human self-hiding before God (see 'Explanation' on chs. 11 and 13).

One of the chief problems in studying cleanness/uncleanness is the strong tendency among scholars to use the term 'cultic' in a sense opposed to 'moral/ethical' terminology, so the former connotes the amoral (e.g. Schwartz 1999: 26; cf. the recent discussion by Klawans 2000: 21–42). In a recent article Houston, while avoiding moralizing the dietary law, proposes to see it as an expression of loyalty to the covenant Lord, and as 'part of a much broader structure of moral and cosmological thinking' (2003: 160). However, in so far as uncleanness refers to the human existential condition before God, it is uncleanness that includes the moral, and not the other way round. At any rate, it is inappropriate to see the two as belonging to the same sphere and incongruous (see also on holiness below).

As far as my knowledge goes, no modern exegete has attempted to explain cleanness/uncleanness regulations in Lev. 11 – 15 in relation to the fall account in Gen. 3, which this commentary will address intensively.

As stated above, regarding the literal observation of the rules and their symbolic meaning, I call, for convenience' sake, the literal rule of cleanness/uncleanness 'outer cleanness/uncleanness' and its symbolic meaning 'inner cleanness/uncleanness'. Outer uncleanness is presented as a window through which the legislator intends to make readers aware of their inner uncleanness, and the same goes for cleanness. Thus mere outward observance of the rules ultimately fails to achieve what God requires of the readers.

One cannot offer sacrifices in an unclean state, as they do in the sanctuary. However, if all humanity is unclean, how can they offer sacrifices? The reader should not miss the high standard the Lord demands of the Israelites in Leviticus.

7.4. Holiness

In the Levitical laws, humans, objects and time are said to be holy: priests (21:7), offerings (e.g. 6:17[10]), sancta (the Tent of Meeting and all the utensils therein and altars; e.g. 16:16) and time (the sabbath, Jubilee, the festive days; e.g. 25:12). The Israelites are never *said* to be holy, though they are *commanded* to be so by observing the Lord's commandments (11:44; 20:7). While holiness at least means 'belonging to the divine sphere' (cf. Schwartz 2000), this definition still fails to clarify the relationship between holiness and uncleanness/cleanness, particularly in view of the symbolic meanings of the latter terms: the state of hiding and uncovering oneself, respectively.

The idea of holiness (*qōdeš*) is pursued throughout this commentary, yet it would be useful to sum up the major conclusions reached regarding this crucial term.

(1) The sacrificial idea intimates that the essence of holiness lies in death, especially the death of one's egocentric nature. In particular the latter is symbolized by the burning of fat (see 'Comment' on 3:3–4), which may be premised by the wholeheartedness (*tāmîm*) of the offerer.

(2) The rules in ch. 13 show that even when one is pronounced clean, this is only a temporary state, and the egocentric nature, symbolized by the leprous disease, remains latent.

(3) The Golden Rule, 'Love your neighbour as yourself,' in 19:18b can be observed only when one dies to one's egocentric nature.

From these and other exegetical observations I propose that negatively holiness refers to an inner human state where there is an absence of egocentric nature.

7.4.1. *Its relation to cleanness and uncleanness*

In 10:10 it is stated that holiness is the opposite to what is common, and cleanness is the opposite of uncleanness. How are we meant to conceive of the relationship between each pair of opposites: holy/common and clean/unclean? Milgrom notes that what is designated 'common' sometimes includes what is described as 'clean' (2000b: 29–30; cf. Péter-Contesse 1993: 241–244). However, this is correct and meaningful only when cleanness and uncleanness are not confronted with holiness. For instance, the ceremonies in chs. 8 – 9 indicate that all the participants in the ceremonies are viewed as unclean before being given a state of holiness, which means that what is clean is still viewed as unclean before holiness.

Moreover the rules, when their symbolic meanings are taken into account, show that cleanness is only a temporary state (cf. chs. 13 and 15), and behind the various rules on cleanness and uncleanness lies the assumption that human beings are essentially unclean all the time for as long as they possess an egocentric nature. This becomes most explicit in 21:1 (see 'Comment' there).

7.4.2. *Outer holiness and inner holiness*

I propose to make a distinction between outer and inner holiness, just as I have done in relation to outer and inner cleanness/uncleanness. It is convenient to use these terms in explaining the rules in Leviticus, since the latter have both practical and symbolic dimensions. As is the case for my treatment of cleanness/uncleanness the distinction is for explanation's sake, and the relationship between outer holiness and inner holiness is not formal/logical but dynamic. From this viewpoint I set out below some necessary preliminary comments regarding those things said to be holy: *offerings*, *priests*, *sancta* and *time*.

a. Sacrifices and offerings. Five types of offerings are either assumed, or explicitly mentioned, to be holy. The burnt offering is not said to be holy, while the loyalty, sin and reparation offerings are explicitly described as such. The reason why the burnt offering is not said to be holy lies in the nature of the term 'holy' or 'holiness'. The legislator chooses to use it when making the reader aware of the danger of profanation and to designate that the remaining portion belongs to the priest. In the burnt offering no such possibility of profanation exists, since it is entirely consumed; rather the absence of holiness terminology in relation to this offering implies it symbolizes the essence of holiness (see below and 'Comment' on ch. 1). On the other hand, the reason why the fellowship offering is not explicitly described as holy probably reflects that, of all the offerings, it was the most likely to be profaned. Thus there are degrees of holiness among the five types of offerings.

In view of the symbolic meaning of the imposition of a hand on the animal and of other indications in the text, the offerings symbolize the spiritual reality of an offerer. Thus, just as in connection with cleanness and uncleanness, I use the concepts of outer and inner holiness for explanation's sake: the former points to the latter, and the former is by itself ultimately meaningless. This distinction is also necessitated because a spiritual gap is assumed between the holy offering and the offerer; though the offerer is expected to be holy, the full embodiment of the symbolic meaning makes the offering unnecessary.

It must be stressed that though Leviticus is indeed concerned about the offerer's outward acts, it desires that these be the expression of their inner motives. To view the Leviticus text as just a formal prescription, as though the author is purely concerned with the ritual, is erroneous.

b. Priests. Aaron and his sons are ordained as priests. When the ordination ceremony is complete, they are assumed to be holy (ch. 8) before the Lord, not just in outer holiness but in inner holiness. However, it is unlikely that inner holiness was achieved by this ceremony. Then if they continue their activities without bearing inner holiness, they constantly profane holiness. The relationship between outer and inner holiness is dynamic. Although their holiness after the ordination ceremony is outer, it demands that they bear inner holiness. In chs. 1 – 16 the regulations frequently hint at the necessity of their being holy in the handling of offerings as mediators between the offerer and the Lord.

That the priests ought to bear not just outer but also inner holiness is particularly stressed in ch. 21 (see v. 7b). Here they are said to be holy, yet simultaneously it is said they are to be consecrated by the Lord (v. 6a).

The gap between outer and inner holiness derives from the fact that inner holiness represents the human heart devoid of an egocentric nature (see 'Comment' on ch. 21). Before holiness, however, the priests ought to be clean; i.e. in a state of uncovering themselves before the Lord. Otherwise the offerings the lay people bring to the priests will be profaned in the hands of the latter (ch. 22).

While the priests are holy (22:7), Moses, the installer of priesthood, is never said to be holy. As in the cases concerning the burnt offering and time (see below), this suggests that the absence of holiness terminology in relation to Moses suggests he already represents the essence of holiness.

c. Sancta (holy places). A major question revolves around the holiness of places. It is questionable what holiness means in connection with a holy place and, in particular, how it relates to human beings.

First of all, one cannot assume in Leviticus that the sancta are independent of human beings. The interrelatedness of the offerer–animal and blood–altar is clearly enunciated in 17:11. Moreover in the ordination ceremony the purification/consecration of the altar takes place concurrently with that of Aaron and his sons (8:24). The purification/consecration of the defiled altar is again performed on the Day of Atonement ritual concurrently with that of the priests (ch. 16). On other ordinary occasions the animal blood is daubed or sprinkled on the altar (chs. 1 – 5), which confers forgiveness of sin and cleanness to the person in question. These data imply that the altar reflects the spiritual condition of the priests or the laity.

Relevant to this is the fact that the human body symbolizes the sanctuary (see Douglas 1999: 80; though from a different perspective). In 14:10–20 the once-leprous person appears to be ascribed a high position by being treated like the altar. Yet again, this instance strongly suggests that the altar represents a person's spiritual condition (see 'Explanation' on ch. 14). Furthermore when chs. 11 – 16 are seen as a literary whole, in 11:44 the human soul (*nepeš*) is defiled, whereas in 15:31 the Lord's abode is said to be defiled (see 'Explanation' on ch. 16).

The correspondence between human beings (the Israelites) and the sanctuary/Tent emerges even more clearly when the symbolic meaning of uncleanness, cleanness and holiness are taken into account. It can also be inferred that the sanctuary, particularly the Tent of Meeting, represents the Lord's general assessment of the inner human condition: the laity can access the outer court, while the priests ordinarily work in the outer part of the Tent, but none is allowed to enter the inner part of the Tent, the Holy of Holies, except for the chief priest Aaron or his successor, once a year. The structure of the Tent and the Lord's assignment of work to the priests evince the underlying assumption that the Holy of Holies corresponds to the innermost part of the human heart. If holiness means the absence of an egocentric nature, the structure and limitation of access to the Holy of Holies attest to the rationale that the radical or thorough purification of the human soul is done unilaterally by the Lord, and that this is extremely difficult.

Thus on the basis of the correspondence between holy places and the people, the purification or consecration of sancta becomes the purification or consecration of the people. Therefore, for instance, when it is said that the priest ought to eat the remaining flesh of an animal *in a holy place*, it does not mean that this particular place is intrinsically holy or in some way separate from the person who eats it, but that the priest ought to eat it in a holy manner: without an egocentric nature (cf. Klingbeil 2004: 514).

One may well wonder why the ritual is needed, and why there ought to be sancta as intermediaries between the people and the Lord. There are two major interrelated reasons. The first is that human beings cannot approach the invisible without the visible; one cannot have a true sense of sacrifice without a concrete visible sacrifice such as one's own animals, birds, flour etc. It is desirable the people ultimately dispense with the visible sanctuary. However, since human beings remain largely unaware of their own spiritual condition, visible objects such as offerings and the sanctuary are needed for an educational purpose. The second reason is that humans are so hypocritical that if they observe the ritual, they consider they are serving God (cf. Amos 5:21–24). The ritual functions to divide human beings into two kinds of people: the hypocritical and those who seek the spiritual truth behind the ritual. In a word, humanity is so stubborn and has such a propensity to hide itself from God that it can learn the divine truth only indirectly. Or, more precisely, God adjusts himself to the spiritual condition of human beings: just as they tend to hide themselves, God conveys his message indirectly through the rituals. The situation is the same as that reflected in the parables of Jesus (e.g. Matt. 13:34; Mark 4:34).

d. Time. Chs. 23 and 25 prescribe holy times: the sabbath, various annual feasts, the Sabbatical and Jubilee years. All these times are grounded on the sabbath principle. However, that time itself is said to be holy does not mean time is considered separate from the Israelites. As for offerings and sancta, the very mention of 'holy' (*qōdeš*) shows that consecration is to be made by human beings; otherwise holy time is desecrated. To refrain from ordinary work is a minimal and outward observance of these feasts, but so long as holiness is a matter of the human heart, these festivals demand more.

Moreover it seems that all time belongs to the Lord. Thus calling a specific period of time 'holy', or demanding the consecration of a period of time, is designed for the Israelites, since it is impossible for them to consecrate all time.

Apart from time that is explicitly called 'holy', the early part of Leviticus contains many time references, particularly in the purificatory and consecration rituals. Thus a person is unclean 'until evening' (e.g. 11:24–25; 14:46; 15:5), 'for seven days' (12:2; 15:13, 19, 24, 28), and it takes 'seven days' to consecrate the priestly candidates (8:33). When considered together with the other references to Gen. 3 found in Leviticus, these time specifications clearly refer to God's creation of heaven and earth in Gen. 1. Therefore it can be inferred that purification and consecration are the Lord's re-creative work of leading people from uncleanness to cleanness, and from cleanness to holiness. The key to partaking in God's work seems to be the realization of one's own uncleanness (self-hiding), and not involving oneself in any of God's new creative work, except for awaiting the specified period.

7.4.3. The relationship between holiness in chapters 1 – 16 and holiness in chapters 18 – 26

As stated above, the common critical view is that P's concept of holiness (most of chs. 1 – 16) is different from H's concept of holiness (chs. 18 – 26). Thus Milgrom (1996: 67) states:

> H introduces three radical changes regarding P's notion of holiness. First, it breaks down the barrier between the priesthood and the laity. The attribute of holy is accessible to all Israel. Secondly, holiness is not just a matter of adhering to a regimen of prohibitive commandments, taboos; it embraces positive, performative commandments that are ethical in nature. Thirdly, Israel as a whole, priests included, enhances or diminishes its holiness in proportion to its observance of all of God's commandments.

Milgrom's third postulate is not true to the text; unless one observes *all* the commandments one is not holy. There is no question of '*enhancing* and *diminishing* holiness'. The second postulate is inexact; for instance, Lev. 1 does not belong to 'taboo'. The first is, in my view, wrong and derives from an unawareness of the relationship between outer and inner holiness, as explained in 7.3.2 above.

On the basis of 4.1 above, my position views holiness from two different viewpoints: (1) chs. 1 – 16/17 lay an emphasis on the holiness of offerings, sancta and priests in an outward sense, while (2) chs. 18 – 27, through their conduct-oriented commandments, lay an emphasis on the holiness of humans. In line with this approach the entire book can be viewed as moving gradually toward the inner holiness of the Israelites and the priests in the following way.

In chs. 1 – 7 the holiness of the offerings remains in the foreground of the prescription, yet this implicitly demands that the offerer or priests should be holy. In chs. 8 – 10 Aaron and his sons become holy in an outward sense, but the fact that it demands their inner holiness is indicated by the incident of Nadab and Abihu and its aftermath. The section 11:43–45 mentions *explicitly* for the first time that the Israelites ought to be holy, just as the Lord is.

Chs. 11 – 16, far from the matter of holiness, deal with the potentially unclean state of human beings. On the other hand, by the end of ch. 16 the legislator has established, through the rules on offerings and cleanness/uncleanness, particularly their symbolic meanings, that the essence of holiness lies in the absence of an egocentric nature, not to mention human selfishness and arrogance (see 'Comment' on chs. 1, 6, 13).

Chapter 17 stresses the urgent need for human salvation before God, and the blood as the means of this. Based on these, the rules in chs. 18 – 26 directly address themselves to human beings, the Israelites (including the priests), so they may become holy, this time by way of specific conduct-oriented commandments. These commandments are, however, designed to lead the people to such a state of heart and soul, symbolized by the holy offerings. The demand for holiness is more explicit and direct than that of chs. 1 – 16, yet the essence of holiness remains the same: the absence of an egocentric nature. Therefore the shift in emphasis need not be explained by the alleged different concepts of holiness in P and H; it is just that ch. 18 onwards stresses the demand for holiness on the basis of the holiness in chs. 1 – 16.

The seemingly strong tendency among religious people to conceive that holiness lies in observing 'moral' commandments is not mistaken by itself. But it appears that failing to realize the purpose of these commandments and the essence of holiness have inevitably made them legalistic and hypocritical. For it seems to me that the purpose of the laws is to make the Israelites aware of their egocentric nature, to destroy this nature, thereby leading them to a state of holiness characterized by a heart free of selfish motives. The above two approaches are given by the same God, but uncovering oneself (becoming clean) is the *sine qua non* for becoming holy; without uncovering oneself any efforts made toward holiness become futile and hypocritical, and place one within the vicious realm of legalism.

7.5. The wrath of God

The laconic style of Leviticus and the rare explicit references to the Lord's wrath may give the impression that the book has nothing to do with this subject, all the more so if the reader assumes that the Israelites were 'saved' (see 5.2.1 above). However, the sin and sinfulness, particularly uncleanness together with its symbolic meaning (the state of hiding oneself), assumed in the book make it clear that the Israelites remained the potential object of the Lord's wrath.

In Leviticus the expression of the Lord's wrath within the sanctuary should be distinguished from his wrath when, as hypothetically set out in ch. 26, he can no longer tolerate the spiritual condition of the Israelites and leaves the sanctuary.

The theme of God's wrath assumed within sanctuary worship is closely related to some Hebr. terms and phrases, such as *kipper* (commonly rendered 'make atonement/expiation') and *rēaḥ nîḥôaḥ* (commonly rendered 'a pleasing odour' or 'soothing aroma'). There exists an interesting literary phenomenon that 'a soothing aroma' occurs in contexts where the wrath is less expected (1:9, 13, 17; 2:2, 9, 12; 3:5, 16; 4:31), whereas it does not occur in contexts where it is most expected (cf. the first three cases in ch. 4). Thus it is inferred that the degree of the Lord's wrath is inversely related to the explicit frequency with which the soothing aroma is mentioned in a particular ritual. Moreover it is appropriate to conclude, from the relationship between *kipper* and a soothing aroma, that the latter is part of the former. Hence it is concluded that the *rēaḥ nîḥôaḥ* represents the last phase of the Lord's wrath (for more detail, see Kiuchi 2005).

As regards *kipper* itself it is a comprehensive term that includes the symbolic meaning of the burning of fat (the annihilation of the offerer's egocentric nature) as well as the symbolic meaning of the blood manipulation (the spiritual death of the offerer). The fact that *kipper* is synonymous with *nāśā' 'āwôn* (to bear guilt, Kiuchi 2005: 53) indicates that when, for instance, the priest is said to *kipper* he does not just 'purify' the sancta but also bears the guilt of the offerer. The assumed dual inverted action that occurs with regard to its agent (the priest) leads to the inference that *kipper* has a reflexive meaning. Hence it is to be rendered either 'to sacrifice oneself for propitiation' or 'to make propitiation' (see 'Comment' on 1:4, and Wright 1992: 737).

Thus not just in the so-called expiatory sacrifices like the sin and reparation offerings, but in the so-called non-expiatory offerings such as the loyalty and fellowship offerings, the offerer is viewed as the object of the Lord's wrath to varying degrees, and the offerings symbolize the offerer appeasing the Lord's wrath.

If the Lord's wrath is assumed in the offerings, what happens when one is unclean and cannot approach the sanctuary? Though the cleanness/uncleanness regulations are formulated as hypothetical cases ('when' or 'if'), their symbolic dimension of these rules imply that the Israelites are essentially unclean ('hiding themselves'; see 'Explanation' on ch. 15). Thus humans are viewed as constantly living under the Lord's wrath. Though this idea is unpopular in the modern age, I am convinced this is the message Leviticus conveys.

Indeed it is conceivable that the Lord's grace is commingled with his wrath in the very establishment of the rules that aim to make the people approach him. Yet this grace would not be appreciated without personally realizing the gap that remains between the holy God and sinful human beings.

8. LEVITICUS AND CHRISTIANS

Since the book contains rules and narratives concerning the relationship between God and humans, and more specifically the question of how humans can live in close proximity to the holy Lord, theologically it is most relevant to the atoning work of Christ. Christ became the supreme sacrifice for all humanity: his death on the cross surpassed the symbolic meanings of offerings (Heb. 9:11–14, 25–26; 10:14–18). In particular, the fact that he fulfilled all the symbolic meanings of sanctuary worship is shown by the NT's likening of him to the mercy-seat (*kappôret*, Rom. 3:25) of the Day of Atonement ritual in ch. 16, and to the high priest (Heb. 4:14 etc.; cf. Head 1995; Beckwith 1995).

While the Law is traditionally divided into moral, civil and ceremonial categories, the above treatment of the structure of the book (4.1, 7.4.3) has shown that at least the division between the moral and ceremonial is untenable. Thus the death of Christ on the cross, as the holy person, indicates the fulfilment of not just the ideas associated with the various offerings but also those attached to the rules in the latter part of the book, the goal of which is holiness. In terms of Christian interpretation of Leviticus, we ought to discern the meaning by paying attention to its original context, and only then applying the unearthed principles to the modern Christian life (cf. Wenham 1979: 34–35).

In the NT believers are saved by believing that the work of Christ was done for them. Indeed believers are expected to become priests (1 Pet. 2:5) and sacrifices (Rom. 12:1). Nevertheless, as many references as there are to sacrificial language in the NT, and accepting that the demand for holiness is even more intense in the NT than in Leviticus, the believers are still generally assumed not yet to have attained holiness, although they are sometimes called 'holy' in terms of their election (Eph. 5:27). It is vitally important to recognize that the NT writers assume the presence of the egocentric nature (equivalent to what St Paul calls 'flesh') within believers, even though faith in combination with an egocentric nature is essentially a contradiction in terms. True faith assumes an absence of the egocentric nature, which is holiness. Although one tends to envisage 'degrees of faith' prior to the disappearance of the egocentric nature, the pressing question is whether one lives according to the flesh or the spirit (Gal. 5:16–21). And as long as one lives according to his flesh, the human condition assumed by Leviticus is no different from that assumed in the NT. In this sense, while the literal observance of some parts of Leviticus is no longer necessary, the goal of such regulations (holiness) remains the same in both Leviticus and the NT.

The road to holiness is difficult in human eyes, since it involves the destruction of the egocentric nature (cf. Matt. 7:13–14).

9. A FRESH APPROACH TO LEVITICUS

Many of the main points and orientations adopted in this commentary are introduced above. On the assumption that the final form of Leviticus is theologically coherent, the present commentary aims to explain the meaning of the text as it is, and to uncover the perennial messages found therein. Particular emphasis is placed on the symbolic meanings of the rituals and offerings as well as on the results of my separate works on *ḥāṭā'* and *ḥaṭṭā't*, and ch. 13, which have made it necessary to read the book anew. This perspective demands, it seems to me, a reconsideration of modern traditional approaches to the book as a whole, which are typically reliant on the categories of 'cultic' and 'ethical' in the book's interpretation. I hope the reader will find from the interpretation offered here that a rather different book emerges from what scholars have previously conceived.

Due to the space given to the explanation of the symbolic meaning and a limitation of words, references to other works on Leviticus and the notes on the text have been kept to a minimum. However, the perceptive reader will see the differences between this commentary and others.

TEXT AND COMMENTARY

LEVITICUS 1:1–17

Translation

[1]The LORD called Moses and spoke to him from the Tent of Meeting, saying, [2]'Speak to the Israelites and say to them, If a man among you offers an offering to the LORD, you must make your offering of domestic animals from the herd or from the flock.

[3]'If his offering is a burnt offering from the herd, he must offer a male without blemish. He brings it to the entrance of the Tent of Meeting, so that he may be accepted before the LORD. [4]He lays his hand on the head of the burnt offering, so that it may be accepted on his behalf to sacrifice itself for him.

[5]'The young bull is to be slaughtered before the LORD and the sons of Aaron, the priests, offer the blood and dash it over the altar which is at the entrance of the Tent of Meeting. [6]The burnt offering is to be flayed and chopped into pieces. [7]The sons of Aaron, the priest, light a fire on the altar, lay wood on the fire, [8]and the sons of Aaron, the priests, lay the pieces of the animal, including the head and the fat, on top of the firewood on the altar. [9]Its intestines and hind legs are to be washed in water and the priest burns the whole lot as a burnt offering, an offering for annihilation with a soothing aroma for the LORD.

[10]'If his burnt offering comes from the flock, from either the sheep or the goats, he offers a male without blemish. [11]It is to be slaughtered on the north side of the altar before the LORD, and the sons of Aaron, the priests, dash its blood over the

altar. [12]Having chopped it into pieces, the priest lays them, including the head and the fat, on top of the firewood on the altar. [13]Its intestines and hind legs are to be washed with water; the priest offers the whole lot and burns it as a burnt offering. It is an offering for annihilation with a soothing aroma for the LORD.

[14]'If his burnt offering for the LORD is of birds, he is to offer either doves or pigeons as his offering. [15]The priest brings it to the altar, wrings its head off and burns it on the altar and lets its blood drain down the side of the altar. [16]He removes the crop with its contents and throws it on the east side of the altar into the ash pit. [17]He splits it open by the wings without tearing it apart, and the priest burns it on the altar on top of the firewood. It is a burnt offering, an offering for annihilation with a soothing aroma for the LORD.'

Notes on the text

1. 'The LORD called'. In MT 'the LORD' appears after 'he spoke' (*wayyĕdabber*). Syr places the Tetragrammaton after *wayyiqrā'*, but this is not the original order as evidenced by SamP, LXX, Vg and TgJon.

2. 'a man – among you': *'ādām – mikkem* The phrase *mikkem* is connected to *'ādām*. The combination of the 3rd person (*'ādām*) and the 2nd person (*mikkem*) to address the Israelites is unique in the OT. Ordinarily what comes after *'ādām kî*, *'îš kî* or *nepeš kî* is a 3rd person verb (cf. for *'ādām* Lev. 13:2; Num. 19:14; for *'îš* Lev. 13:29; 15:16; 19:20; 20:27 etc.; for *nepeš* Lev. 2:1; 4:2; 5:17; 6:2[5:21] etc.). Thus the translations 'when any of you' (JPS, NRSV), 'any one of you' (ESV) or 'anyone among you' (REB) are inexact. The correct rendering is 'a man among you' as reflected in Elberfelder (*ein Mensch vom euch*).

'your offering (sg.)': *qorbanĕkem* In SamP and LXX 'offering' is pl. but, in view of the single appearance of its pl. form in 7:38, MT is preferred.

5. 'to be slaughtered': *šāḥaṭ* The term is used in the sacrificial ritual in distinction to *zābaḥ*, which is mainly used for slaughtering the fellowship offering. LXX renders the masculine sg. verb as a 3rd person pl., as it also does in v. 11 and 3:13, probably harmonizing the number of *šāḥaṭ* with that of the following verb. The sg. verb need not imply that the agent of slaughtering was the offerer (*pace* most exegetes), for its subject is impersonal. This would apply to other verbs such as *hipšîṭ* (v. 6a), *nittaḥ* (vv. 6b, 12), *rāḥaṣ* (vv. 9, 13), *šissa'* (v. 17), where the agent of slaughtering is not necessarily one of Aaron's sons (cf. Ezek. 44:11).

'young bull': *ben habbāqār* In this construction *ben* is either interpreted as having no exegetical significance (Rendtorff 1985: 50) or as indicating a kind of bull (Péter-Contesse 1993: 43). It is more likely an indicator of age (see 'Comment').

7. 'the priest': *hakkôhēn* SamP and LXX read 'priests'. A comparison of the appellation in vv. 5b, 7a, 8a and 9b shows that these variations are

intentional. It indicates that the priest in v. 9b is Aaron, whereas all the preparations are done by his sons.

9. 'an offering for annihilation': *'iššeh* Although this term is commonly translated 'an offering by fire', it is actually distinct from fire itself. 'Food offering' is likewise inaccurate, since *'iššeh* overlaps with *leḥem* (food) in 3:11, 16. Moreover the twelve loaves of bread, called *'iššeh* in 24:7, are not burnt. 2:12 also implies that it does not always involve fire. Thus the assonance between *'ēš* and *'iššeh* suggests that the term refers to what fire brings about, since it refers to the penultimate stage to burning. Hence the proposed 'an offering for annihilation'.

10. SamP makes the beginning of this verse just like v. 14, while LXX adds 'and he lays his hand on its head'. But in view of the general tendency to omit what is mentioned in the bull's case, the LXX's additions appear secondary.

15. SamP understands *nimṣâ* as *nimṣā'*, taking the root as *mṣ'*, with the *'ālep* weakened to *hē*, while LXX (*straggiei*) and Vg (*decurrere faciet*) take the meaning as active ('squeeze out'). Probably the latter meaning is intended. Cf. 5:9.

Form and structure

The chapter's structure is simple and clear. An introductory statement (vv. 1–2) is followed by three cases of the burnt offering, introduced by 'if' (*'im*, vv. 3, 10, 14) followed by similar constructions, 'if his offering is from'. All three cases end with the same expression, 'an offering for annihilation, a soothing aroma for the LORD'.

Except for v. 2, all the rules are cast in the 3rd person. The first case is longer than the remaining two, which have almost the same length. The ritual procedure for the bull offering is as follows:

1. bringing of the *'ôlâ*
2. hand-leaning
3. slaughtering the animal
4. splashing the blood
5. flaying of the skin
6. dissecting
7. washing
8. burning

The agent of these acts is the offerer in 1 and 2, and the sons of Aaron in 4, 6 and 8. The agent's identity is unclear in 3, 5 and 7, because the verbs are 3rd person sg. and expressed indefinitely in the LXX.

In the second section, namely an offering from the flock, acts 2 and 5 are omitted. In the third, namely an offering of birds, the presentation is much different from the other two – presumably because of the bird's size.

In order to suggest the general nature of the Levitical prescription, it is necessary to comment on the second and third categories. The second section (vv. 10–13) deals with the burnt offering of a sheep or a goat. These are smaller and less expensive animals. Some of the particulars stated in vv. 5–9 are omitted from these verses. For example, the location 'at the entrance of the Tent of Meeting' (cf. v. 11 with v. 5) and prescription for flaying the animal's skin are missing (see v. 6a). Conversely the place of slaughtering, 'at the north side of the altar', is a novel feature not mentioned in v. 5. The omission of the former two makes no difference to the prescription, but the addition in v. 11 raises the possibility that the slaughtering in v. 5 also occurred at the altar's northern side. If this is correct, and there seems no reason why it is not, then the omission of this detail until v. 11 is possibly expressive (see 'Comment').

The third section introduces a sacrificial animal not mentioned in v. 2. However, since the three consecutive cases (vv. 3–9, 10–13, 14–17) deal with increasingly smaller creatures (see 'Explanation') it cannot simply be dismissed as an addition. Compared with the burnt offerings in vv. 3–13, the hand-leaning rite and specification of gender are missing.

Thus apparent additions or omissions should be interpreted not just as a matter of style but as reflecting the lawgiver's purpose.

'ôlâ

'Ôlâ is commonly rendered 'the burnt offering', or less commonly 'the whole offering' (Hartley 1992: 17; Porter 1976: 18). Strictly speaking, the idea of 'whole' is not expressed by 'the burnt offering', since the hide is not burnt (cf. 7:8). Furthermore the term *kālîl*, meaning 'totally' (6:22[15]), was available to the author if this was the intention. Thus the traditional rendering presents no serious problem.

Comment

1:1–4

1. Vv. 1–2a are not just an introduction to the *'ôlâ*, but also to the *minḥâ* (ch. 2) and the *šĕlāmîm* (ch. 3). The key term is 'to bring near' (*hiqrîb*). From this comes the general term *qorbān* (offering). Behind this term lies the assumption that a human cannot approach the Lord without meeting due qualifications. Such was unmistakably demonstrated on the occasion of the Sinai covenant (Exod. 19:10–13). The first chapter of Leviticus deals with the case where a man approaches the Lord with a burnt offering.

The beginning of Leviticus is closely associated with the end of Exodus (40:35). Moses could not enter the Tent of Meeting because it had been filled with God's glory. Thus in Lev. 1:1 God calls him from the Tent of Meeting. This parallels God's original calling of Moses from the cloud on top of Mount Sinai (Exod. 24:16; see Knierim 1992: 6).

2. 'the sons of Israel': The expression occurs fifty-three times in Leviticus, but the scope of the referent should be carefully considered in each case. Here it seems to exclude the priests, as the latter officiate in the ritual.

'If a man': It has been pointed out that on this occasion 'man' (*'ādām*) is used inclusively of men and women (e.g. Knierim 1992: 14–16). However, on the assumption that the male animal represents the offerer (see below on v. 3) it is unlikely both genders are intended. *'Ādām* occurs relatively infrequently in Leviticus, and should be distinguished from *'îš* or *nepeš*. Though the three can legally refer to the same individual, in Leviticus they refer to three different aspects of the same human being (see Introduction 7.1, 'Comment' on 2:1 and 4:2 below). *'Ādām* refers to a human's earthly existence and createdness; it does not refer to the spiritual (*nepeš*) or interhuman (*'îš*) aspects of a human. Thus the prescription for the burnt offering in this chapter concerns the dedication of a man's whole earthly existence to the Lord.

A general condition is given for sacrifice – it must be a 'domestic animal'. Wild animals were prohibited, so that the offering was the offerer's 'sacrifice' in the true sense of that word.

3. Cattle used as burnt offerings had to satisfy two qualifications. First, they had to be males. In Leviticus male animals are consistently valued higher than females. Second, they had to be 'without blemish' (*tāmîm*). This qualification deserves special attention. Although 22:17–25 suggests the animal has only to be normal, without serious defects, it was possibly extremely difficult to find such an animal (see 'Comment' on 22:17–25).

On the assumption that the offerer identifies himself with the animal (see below on v. 4), he must be without blemish in a symbolic sense: the offerer is commanded to be *tāmîm*, just like the animal. However, while *tāmîm* means 'without blemish', the term is unlikely to connote moral perfection, since this would contradict this chapter's assumption that the offerer is the object of the Lord's wrath and is assumed, in 4:3, to have sinned. Since it is more likely a matter of the offerer's heart, 'wholeheartedness' or 'perfect sincerity' (even 'innocence') is commended. Noah was such a person and the same was expected of Abraham (Gen. 6:9; 17:1; cf. Pss. 15:2; 84:11[12]; 101:2, 6; 119:1; Prov. 28:18).

Considering that all animal sacrifices were to be *tāmîm* (3:1, 6 for *šĕlāmîm*; 4:3, 23, 28, 32 for *ḥaṭṭā't*; 5:15, 18; 6:6[5:25] for *'āšām*), and that the latter are called 'holy', it is probable that being *tāmîm* constitutes part of the essence of holiness (see 'Explanation').

V. 3b specifies the location of the offering's presentation as towards the entrance of the Tent of Meeting; presumably on the altar's northern side (cf. v. 11).

'So that he may be accepted' (*lirṣōnô*) sums up the ritual's purpose for the offerer. *Rāṣôn* means 'favour', and when it constitutes a phrase (*lirṣōnô*) it describes the offerer's acceptance by divine favour (cf. 22:19; see further 19:5; 22:29; 23:11). Moreover this purpose phrase implies that the offerer was previously the object of divine displeasure.

4. The meaning of the hand-leaning rite is widely debated (see Rodriguez 1979: 193–208); the representative proposals include (1) identification of the offerer with the animal, (2) expressing the idea of substitution and (3) expressing the idea that the animal is possessed by the offerer. While it is difficult to assume that something inside the offerer, such as a specific sin or guilt, is the primary concern of the gesture (cf. with the case of the sin offering in ch. 4), it is also unlikely that the animal sacrifice is viewed as a possession (already assumed in 'from the herd'). Rather, as the term *'ādām* (a man) indicates, the gesture expresses the dedication of the whole existence of the offerer before the Lord. This idea is already expressed by the foregoing *rāṣôn* (v. 3b). Other relevant passages in Leviticus, where *rāṣôn* (acceptance) appears, also support this position (see 22:20, 29). At the very least, then, the gesture expresses the idea of identification: to say, 'This is myself'.

'on the head of the burnt offering': A hand is lain (*sāmak yad*) on the head of the animal (Lev. 1:4; 3:2, 8, 13; 4:4, 15, 24, 29, 33; 8:14; 16:21). By leaning on this vital part of the body, the offerer probably identifies with what is symbolized by the whole animal (cf. Gen. 3:15). *Hā'ōlâ* refers to the animal, but stresses the animal's purpose as a burnt offering. Since this term is mentioned again in v. 9b, the *'ādām* offerer dedicates himself to complete annihilation.

Since the gesture is followed by *nirṣâ* (v. 4b), it is probably a concrete expression of the idea of *rāṣôn* in v. 3b.

'thus sacrificing itself for him' (*lĕkapper 'ālāyw*): The term *kipper* occurs frequently in connection with the expiatory sacrifices in chs. 4 – 5 (4:20, 26, 31, 35; 5:6, 10, 13, 16, 18; 6:7[5:26] etc.). In the OT it occurs only here in connection with the burnt offering when the latter stands alone (see 'Explanation'). Moreover Lev. 1:3 is rare in that it is the animal that is the agent of *kipper*. This appears to stress that the offerer is to become the burnt offering itself, a point that supports the above interpretation of the hand-leaning rite. This, in turn, explains the unique location of *kipper* in the ritual prescription (before slaughtering); elsewhere it comes towards the end of the prescriptions. For the cases where things other than persons are the agent of *kipper*, see Exod. 30:15 (ransom money), Lev. 16:10 (the Azazel goat) and 17:11 (blood).

The concept of *kipper* is crucial for a correct understanding of the rituals in Leviticus. Nevertheless it has baffled commentators throughout the ages. As argued separately (see Kiuchi 2005: 56), it seems most reasonable to assume it derives from the noun *kôper* (ransom, ransom money; cf. Exod. 21:30; 30:12; Num. 35:31–32; see Sklar 2001). Moreover, though exegetes tend to determine *kipper*'s meaning in relation to each offering's function, namely contextually, it appears to recur with the same general meaning in each sacrificial ritual. In preference to the common assumption that *kipper* in the context of the *ḥaṭṭāt* means 'decontaminate', it is more likely related to the idea of 'ransoming' or 'making compensation'. Further a survey of the term's occurrence indicates that its interpretation ought to take the notion of God's wrath into account. From this perspective, debates over 'expiation' and 'propitiation' are unnecessary. In this commentary it is translated 'to sacrifice oneself (itself)' or 'to make propitiation' (see Introduction 7.5).

The preposition *lāmed* before *kipper* indicates purpose and should be translated 'in order to'. Still, is *kipper* related to the following ritual act or also to the presentation of the animal and hand-leaning rite that precedes? Since, in view of Lev. 17:11, *kipper* is unlikely to be achieved without the bloodshedding of v. 5, it seems appropriate to interpret the preceding (vv. 2–4a) as the prerequisite for *kipper*, and vv. 5–9 as addressing the actual process of *kipper*. Although it has been previously assumed that *kipper* in v. 4 is effected only by the shedding of blood in v. 5, it seems possible, in view of 4:31, that the reference to a 'soothing aroma' in v. 9 is also part of the concept of *kipper* (see Kiuchi 2005: 52–58, and 'Explanation').

The requirements of the offerer, that he is to offer a blameless male animal and lean his hand on that animal's head, complete his role in the ritual's performance.

1:5–13

5. It was possible that people other than the offerer, such as the Levites, slaughtered the animal (also v. 11 below). Henceforth the blood of the animal is handled by the priests.

The animal is further specified as 'a young bull'. Thus the offerer, while he is to identify with a young bull, simultaneously identifies with a filial/parental emotional struggle. This suffering is analogous to Abraham's when he prepared to offer his only son as a burnt offering.

Although nothing is stated concerning the role of the animal blood, it presumes what is said in 17:11: the shed blood gives life. The nature of this 'life', not just in the burnt offering but in all the sacrificial rituals of Leviticus, is not immediately apparent. From a broader context, the case of the ritual for a healed leper (14:13, 19–20) is illuminating. The burnt offering caters not for the sake of the leper's physical healing (he is already healed), but for the restoration of his broken relationship with the Lord. This function is not explicit in ch. 1, but this probably reflects the lawgiver's preoccupation with the need to burn the animal up in smoke and to produce a soothing aroma.

'altar': *mizbeaḥ* The sacrificial animal is slaughtered at the altar in the court (cf. Hawk 2003: 35–36). As expounded in the following chapters, the altar is the place where the worshipper encounters the Lord (Exod. 29:43). The parallel between the worshipper and the condition of the altar is found throughout the ritual prescriptions. Thus the purification of the altar parallels that of the people (16:19, 30) and the candidates for priesthood (8:15). It represents the worshipper who stands before it (see also 'Comment' on 4:7). This is an institutional development of the Sinai covenant in Exod. 24:5–8, where half of the blood was sprinkled on the people.

6–9. Before it is burnt, the priest skins and dissects the body. Reference to the parts of the body, such as the head and intestines, seem unnecessary, considering that the entire body was burnt.

The last act, burning the offering on the altar, including the head and fat, symbolizes the extinction of the offerer's worldly values (cf. Gen. 37:23; Ezek. 16:39; 23:26; Hos. 2:5; Mic. 3:3), which simultaneously functions as a soothing aroma to the Lord. It is clear the Lord abhors what is in the heart of the offerer. That is why he is pleased with its complete consumption by fire. Symbolically it is not painful for the offerer, since it takes place after his death in the spiritual sense.

'an offering for annihilation': *'iššeh* For this translation, see 'Notes on the text'.

The defining characteristic of the offering is its complete (except its skin; see 7:8) destruction by fire as 'a soothing aroma' to the Lord (cf. Gen. 8:21; Lev. 26:31). Thus, though the burnt offering includes bloodshedding, this begins only the initial stage of the ritual that culminates in the transition of the whole animal into 'a soothing aroma' by burning. The fact that *rēaḥ nîḥōaḥ* (a soothing aroma) is often related to *rāṣôn* or *rṣh* qal/ni. in other parts of the OT (Lev. 26:31, 34; Ezek. 20:40–41; Amos 5:21–22) also lends support to the interpretation that *kipper* in v. 4 refers to the symbolic meaning of all the succeeding ritual acts.

10–11. As for cattle, sheep and goats for the burnt offering should be males without defect. They are slaughtered on 'the north side of the altar'. If a symbolic meaning of this locality is intended, it possibly relates to the north side being on one's left when facing east. If so, slaughtering the smaller ruminants may symbolize their powerlessness because one's left, in the OT, sometimes represents defeat (cf. Jer. 1:14; 4:6; Ezek. 1:4; 9:2; also Porter 1976: 23).

12. The 'priest' is probably Aaron (see 'Notes on the text' on v. 12). In this case Aaron arranges the dissected pieces, which occurs at an earlier stage than it did for the young bull (cf. v. 8). Whereas Aaron's sons officiate over the sacrifice of the bull, Aaron becomes involved in the sacrifice of sheep and goats, possibly to compensate for their smaller size.

13. The first half of the verse is virtually the same as v. 9a, but the verb *hiqrîb* (bring near), not mentioned since v. 10, now appears in the second part of this verse. In other words, *hiqrîb*, which appears twice in v. 3 as the act of the offerer, occurs at the beginning (v. 10) and end (v. 13) of this section. Rather than deriving from stylistic reasons, it helps to present the offerer as dependent upon the priest, Aaron, since it is he who brings the animal closer to the Lord.

1:14–17

14. The bird should be either a dove or young pigeon. As for the young bull (see 'Comment' on v. 5), a small turtle dove or a young dove (cf. Ahitub 1982: 468–469) may symbolize the offerer's emotional involvement in separating it from its parents in addition to his identification with it.

The burnt offering of birds follows the larger animal sacrifices. The assumption that it is a man (*'ādām*, v. 2) who offers it remains the same. Thus it envisages a man offering a tiny bird as a burnt offering, symbolizing the destruction of all his earthly desires. The result of the ritual, namely a soothing aroma, is likewise the same as the previous cases (see vv. 9, 13). It is striking that the achievement of this purpose has priority over the size of the animal.

Doves are clean birds also used in purificatory contexts in Leviticus. Since no qualification is made regarding the offerer's economic condition, the choice of doves from among various kinds of clean birds requires explanation. The idea that the *'ādām* relinquishes all his worldly desires is reflected by certain traits of doves or pigeons, such as innocence or the carrying of human messages (e.g. a carrier pigeon). In other words, the dove symbolizes the *tāmîm* character. Noah released a dove three times to determine if the flood had abated (Gen. 8:8, 10). Further, the author of Genesis makes a wordplay by associating the 'resting place' (*mānôaḥ*) with the name of Noah, who is *tāmîm* (Gen. 6:9). Also in an enigmatic covenant ritual in Gen. 15, turtle doves play an important role by possibly symbolizing the Lord's protective presence. Thus these symbolic meanings make it likely that the offerer is expected to be dovelike – completely free from the world. In particular, its relatively small size concentrates attention on unseen aspects of the relationship between the offerer and the Lord, more so than the previous animal sacrifices (cf. 'a handful of the token portion' in 2:2). Seen in this way, ch. 1 is naturally followed by ch. 2, where the human soul (*nepeš*; see 'Comment' on 2:1) is prescribed as the agent of the offering of a *minḥâ*.

15. The burnt offering's practical procedure is prescribed (vv. 16–17) after the ritual's essence is related. It is probably Aaron who 'presents' the bird (see 'Comment' on v. 12 above). Even more stress is laid on Aaron's involvement with the bird to compensate for the smallness of the offering. Compared with the burnt offerings of vv. 3–13, the hand-leaning rite and specification of gender are missing (see 'Form and structure').

'To wring off' (*mālaq*) the head appears only here and 5:8. The small amount of blood and size of the bird should be kept in mind when considering this and the following verses. Nevertheless its blood is drained on to the wall of the altar before the whole bird is burnt.

16. The bird's innards are not required and the priest removes and throws them into the ash pit on the east side of the altar. Apart from the fact that the ashes of other sacrifices are thrown there, its prescription here enhances the importance of the bird case. For 'east' is a primary direction in relation to the sanctuary (cf. Num. 2:3; Ashley 1993: 71; Drinkard 1992), and in this regard the mention of 'east' possibly suggests that the sanctuary as a whole is viewed as a counterpart to the Garden of Eden (see Gen. 3:24, and also 'Comment' on 16:14).

17. Tearing the bird open without dismembering it preserves its shape – in contrast to other animal sacrifices, which are chopped into pieces (cf. vv. 6, 12; see also Gen. 15:10). Especially the emphasis on the bird's *wing* here concerning the act of dismembering (*yabdîl*), as opposed to its *head* in 5:8, also renders support to the presence of the idea that the bird leaves the ground (symbolic of this world), which is cursed (see 'Explanation' on ch. 11). In view of the fact that the burning symbolizes annihilation of the offerer's worldly desires, the gesture may signify that its offerer has less to be annihilated.

The total effect of the bird burnt offering is the same as that of ruminants – it produces 'a soothing aroma to the LORD'.

Explanation

After the completion of the construction of the Tent and its utensils, the Lord calls Moses to deliver his words concerning five major offerings to the Israelites, the first of which is the burnt offering. This offering forms the pattern upon which the following offerings are built, both ideologically and procedurally.

The function of the offering can be inferred from key terms or phrases such as *'ādām*, *rṣh*, *kipper* and *rēaḥ nîḥôaḥ*. The central message of the offering is that a man cannot be accepted by the Lord without complete surrender and a laying bare of his egocentric nature before the Lord.

The ritual's meaning

The present prescription assumes that in offering a burnt offering the offerer requires acceptance by the Lord, and this further implies that he is the object of the Lord's wrath. This is clearly indicated by the clauses 'so that he may be accepted' (v. 3b), 'to sacrifice itself for him' (v. 4b) and 'a soothing aroma' (v. 9b). As argued separately (Kiuchi 2005: 53–55; see also Introduction 7:5), the meaning of *kipper* is the same throughout Leviticus, and it means to 'sacrifice himself (itself) for appeasement (propitiation)'. The recurrent phrase 'a soothing aroma' marks the last phase of appeasement, while the more serious side of the Lord's wrath is dealt with by the expiatory sacrifices in chs. 4 – 5.

That the offering is not just a gift in a narrow sense but also represents the offerer is indicated by the following points: (1) The hand-leaning rite probably symbolizes the idea of identification and/or substitution. (2) The term *tāmîm*, one of the important prerequisites for the offering, has the symbolic meaning of wholeheartedness (see below). (3) The agent offering the burnt offering is specified as *'ādām*, which, in distinction from *nepeš* (see 'Comment' on 2:1), refers to the sinful earthly existence of humans *since the fall*. Thus the prescription implies that whatever the motive of an offerer (see below), he requires acceptance by the Lord.

At any rate, the offerer's motive must be interpreted in view of the ritual's purpose as a whole. The burnt offering takes the place of the offerer in order to appease the Lord's wrath against his general sinfulness. Thus, while the purpose of the burnt offering is often associated with the idea of self-dedication, its essence lies in the death of one's sinful and worldly desires (a forsaking of this world).

Occasions

As for the other offerings, the offerer must have a subjective motive (an occasion) for his offering. From other occurrences of the burnt offering in the OT it is clear that it not only expressed thanksgiving, but also served to assuage the Lord's wrath. The diversity of occasions presented by these data pose an apparent difficulty in harmonizing the presence of divine wrath with the offerer's joy. But this distinction is fallacious.

Within the context of Leviticus it is offered on various occasions for purification (12:6; 14:13; 15:15), ordination of candidates for the priesthood (8:18–21), the eighth-day service (9:2–3), and the Day of Atonement (16:5–6). From Lev. 7 and 22 we learn that it was offered on occasions of making vows or expressing thanksgiving. Furthermore the description of its smoke as a soothing aroma is also included in the ritual of the sin offering (see 4:31).

It is evident that while the occasions for the offerings or the offerer's motives vary, what is required remains the same. Moreover, as stated above, the burnt offering deals with the last phase in the appeasement of the Lord's wrath. Apparently the Lord's demand of the offerer, reflected in the burnt offering's symbolic meaning, has eluded exegetes. It is not that the Israelites are accepted by the Lord at a time when they have no reason to offer it. Rather the fact that all the offerer's earthly desires must be destroyed before he is accepted suggests he is under the Lord's wrath even more so at these other times. This tension is ameliorated by the priests' offering of a daily burnt offering (Exod. 29:38–39). But again, if this burnt offering was not embodied in the hearts of the people, it was ineffective. Further substantiation of this is demonstrated from the cleanness/uncleanness regulations of ch. 11 onwards.

Thus it is implied that human beings as they are remain the objects of the Lord's wrath, if not on those particular occasions when the Israelites make a vow, or give thanksgiving (cf. 22:18). How far the Israelites recognized this fact, particularly when they offered a burnt offering, is a matter that goes beyond the exegesis of Lev. 1. But to recognize this basic premise is fundamental for understanding the sacrificial ritual as well as all the prescriptions in this book (see Introduction 7.5).

Options for what animal is offered

Although the offerer determines whether he presents an animal from the cattle or a bird, the text says nothing about the economic status of the offerer, as it does in 5:7–13. The burnt offering remains valid regardless of whether it is a bird or one of the other options. From the Lord's perspective, it was sufficient for the bird to symbolize the offerer.

For instance, though a wealthy man was expected to offer a bull, he might not have done so. In fact, a poor man might have offered a bull. The absence of specification highlights all the more the condition of the offerer's heart (cf. Mark 12:42//Luke 21:2).

However, the identification of the offerer with the animal invites the reader to explore the possibility that the animal for the burnt offering reflected the offerer's heart. Thus an ox or bull was a costly sacrificial animal and generally represented a person's wealth. If the offerer felt his earthly desires lay with his material possessions, he was expected to offer such an animal. While animals such as sheep and goats were smaller than a bull, they by no means represented an inferior sacrifice. For although they represent helpless, weak animals that require a shepherd's care, spiritually the weakness they represent is comparatively better than the weakness of worldly wealth represented by the bull. Thus when an offerer offered himself as a sheep or a goat, he was presenting himself before the Lord as a helpless creature. This is, in a sense, more spiritual and, as it stands, comes closer to the purpose of the burnt offering that symbolizes the destruction of sinful human power. Pigeons and turtle doves are the smallest of the three options, but they are, in a sense, most desirable in symbolizing both a transparency in transmitting a human message and a dislocation from worldliness. Those who offered a pigeon or a turtle dove as a burnt offering were less concerned with the destruction of the material side of their desires.

The burnt offering – the essence of holiness

Nowhere in Leviticus is the burnt offering called 'a most holy thing' (*qōdeš qodāšîm*; cf. 2:3, 6:17[10], the loyalty offering; 6:25[18], the sin offering; 7:1, the reparation offering). Nor is it called 'holy' (*qōdeš*), as is the case with the fellowship offering (22:2–4, 6–7 etc.). Why is the burnt offering not referred to as such? Apparently scholars have not addressed this question. Three fundamental facts should be kept in mind. First, *qōdeš qodāšîm* always appears in reference to edible, thus visible, parts of the offerings. Second, in the burnt offering there is nothing left for the offerer and the priest. Third, other kinds of offerings are also wholly offered to the Lord. These observations imply it is the burnt offering that represents the essence of 'the most holy thing': it is entirely burnt to ashes. But why is only the burnt offering not described as most holy? Because as an offering destroyed completely by fire, there was no reason to warn the Israelites against touching remaining parts. Since part of the *minḥâ*, *ḥaṭṭā't* and *'āšām* remained, it was essential to alert the offerer to its holy nature because it represents what was to be wholly offered to the Lord: it must disappear. This remaining part was consumed by the priest or lay individual. Thus it seems that the mention of 'the most holy' in reference to the *minḥâ*, *ḥaṭṭā't* and *'āšām* functions simply to warn the Israelites that the remaining parts of the offerings ought to be handled with utmost care. It by no means indicates that those offerings were *holier* than the burnt offering. Thus the essence of holiness is expressed by the burnt offering, which is never explicitly called 'holy'.

The essence of holiness, then, lies in relinquishing one's desires about the things of this world. In other words, *holiness is essentially a matter of the human heart*. Furthermore, in so far as those things completely dedicated to the Lord, such as the sanctuary and all its utensils, are called 'holy', the designation itself stands in contrast to the human nature entangled with this world: the egocentric nature (see Introduction 7.4).

Now, the holiness of the burnt offering tacitly demands that the offerer ought to be holy as well. In other words, the symbolic dimension of the burnt offering undermines the common assumption that the offering was qualified by simply meeting outward requirements. Just as the animal ought to be holy, so should the offerer. And the holy nature of the offerer consists of, among other things, wholeheartedness and a willingness to forego all earthly desires. This means that when the offerer is unholy (not meeting these requirements), he is unacceptable to the Lord – not to mention that he is not entitled to offer a burnt offering. Yet it is doubtful if one can be wholehearted or perfectly sincere, particularly considering that such a condition of the heart is meant to be long lasting rather than temporary. That holiness is not essentially an ethical concept is discussed in ch. 19.

The essence of the burnt offering is illuminatingly portrayed by Noah and Abraham. Noah was wholehearted (Gen. 6:9) and offered a burnt offering after the flood (Gen. 8:20). He could offer it because he was wholehearted before the Lord. Abraham was told to be 'wholehearted' in Gen. 17:1, but this was not a command to initiate such action from that moment onwards. The fact that he already believed in the Lord (Gen. 15:6) suggests he was wholehearted. So wholeheartedness is an important prerequisite for Abraham's preparedness to offer his son Isaac. Thus a sacrificial character was evident in the persons of Noah and Abraham; indeed their whole lives embodied the essence of the burnt offering.

Many exegetes tacitly assume that Noah's motive in offering a burnt offering after the flood was to be accepted so he could start a new beginning with the other creatures. However, Noah's burnt offering symbolized that he hoped for nothing in this earth. Similarly Abraham, after receiving a blessing on his posterity from the Lord, was told to offer his only son as a burnt offering. The Lord's command to offer Isaac as a burnt offering required both father and son to forgo their hopes for this world. Thus the wholeheartedness of these two men was expressed in their preparedness to lose all hope in the present world.

In other words, a person's acceptance by the Lord necessitates that he or she comes to despair of and forsake any hope in this life. When a person's heart is in such a condition, he or she becomes uninterested in the cost of sacrifice.

However, some psalms reflect that there are degrees of sophistication of the idea of self-dedication (cf. Greenberg 1976), which culminates in Ps. 51:17–19. Only after the psalmist's heart and spirit were broken, was his burnt offering accepted (v. 19).

New Testament implications

In the NT, Jesus' work on the cross bears the character of the burnt offering, the essence of which lies in a soothing aroma (Eph. 5:2). With the appearance of this ultimate sacrifice, the believer is also encouraged to be an offering to the Lord (Rom. 12:1). In Rom. 12:1 the believers are exhorted to present their bodies as a 'sacrifice, living, acceptable, and holy'. The burnt offering eminently represents these three requirements. Yet the difference between the OT burnt offering and the Christian sacrifice in Rom. 12:1 lies in that while in Lev. 1 there is still a formal gap between the animal and sacrifice, the Christian believer is encouraged to be the sacrifice itself. Thus the expectation to become a burnt offering is even more urgent for believers in Christ. As stated above, this presupposes the annihilation of the believer's hope for this world. St Paul also employs sacrificial metaphors in describing the believers' lifestyle. Among other things, they are to be *amōmos* (without blemish). While, again, this term has previously been taken as referring to moral perfection, it should be taken as suggested above. It refers to the condition of the believers' hearts. It lies not in trying to observe the Lord's commandments *as much as possible*, but in laying bare the heart and becoming completely honest before the Lord, without which any apparently pious endeavour is hypocritical. Lastly, it should be added that *amōmos* occurs in conjunction with *hagios* (holy) in Eph. 5:27 and Col. 1:22.

Moreover, while Lev. 1 suggests the offerer ought to be wholehearted, it often happens that without reckoning the human egocentric nature, one cannot say he forgoes everything in this world. This is made evident by the disciples of Jesus: before the crucifixion they were conscious they had abandoned everything (cf. Matt. 26:31–46, 69–75), but the master's road to the cross laid bare the fact that their decision was made only in their egocentric nature. For, once people are self-conscious of the sacrifice they make to the Lord, they inevitably credit the work to themselves, which falls short of offering the whole of their person. In order for people to offer themselves as burnt offerings to the Lord, their wholeheartedness must become unconscious.

LEVITICUS 2:1–16

Translation

[1]When a soul presents a loyalty offering to the LORD, his offering shall be of choice
flour; he pours oil upon it, lays frankincense on it, [2]and brings it to Aaron's sons, the
priests. After taking from it a handful of choice flour and oil, with all its frankincense,
the priest turns this token portion into smoke on the altar, an offering for annihilation for a soothing aroma to the LORD. [3]The rest of the loyalty offering shall be for
Aaron and his sons; it is a most holy thing of the LORD's offering for annihilation.

[4]When you bring a loyalty offering baked in the oven, it is to be unleavened
loaves of fine flour mixed with oil or unleavened wafers smeared with oil. [5]If your
offering is a loyalty offering prepared on a griddle, it is to be of choice flour mixed
with oil, unleavened. [6]Break it in pieces, and pour oil on it; it is a loyalty offering.
[7]If your offering is a loyalty offering cooked in a pan, it is to be made of fine flour
with oil. [8]When you bring the loyalty offering that is made of these things to the
LORD, that is, when he presents it to the priest, then he shall bring it to the altar.
[9]The priest takes from the loyalty offering its token portion and burns this on the
altar, an offering for annihilation for a soothing aroma offering to the LORD. [10]But
the rest of the loyalty offering shall be for Aaron and his sons; it is a most holy part
of the LORD's offering for annihilation.

[11]No loyalty offering that you bring to the LORD shall be made with leaven, for
you shall burn no leaven nor any honey as an offering for annihilation to the LORD.
[12]As an offering of first fruits you may bring them to the LORD, but they shall not be
offered on the altar for a soothing aroma.

[13]You shall season all of your loyalty offerings with salt. You shall not let the salt

of the covenant with your God be missing from your loyalty offering; with every offering you shall offer salt.

[14]If you offer a loyalty offering of first fruits to the LORD, you shall offer for the loyalty offering of your first fruits fresh ears, roasted with fire, crushed new grain. [15]And you put oil on it and lay frankincense on it; it is a loyalty offering. [16]And the priest burns as its token portion some of the crushed grain and some of the oil with all of its frankincense; it is an offering for annihilation to the LORD.

Notes on the text

1. 'when a soul': *wěnepeš kî* In Leviticus this introductory phrase appears in 2:1; 4:2; 5:1, 4, 15, 17, 21; 7:21.

'a soul': *nepeš* LXX follows MT in rendering it *psychē*. *Nepeš* should be translated 'soul' rather than 'person', which is adopted by almost all the modern English translations (see 'Comment' on v. 1). A loss of distinction between *'ādām* and *nepeš* is apparent in some ancient translations such as TgO (*'nš*) and TgJon (*br nš*).

'choice flour': *sōlet* The word order seems to stress that the *minḥâ* from now on should be *sōlet* as opposed to the *minḥâ* described heretofore in the Pentateuch (Gen. 4:3–4; 32:14, 21; 43:11).

2. 'with all its frankincense': *'al kol lěbōnātāh* It also appears in v. 16. In line with its occurrence in 3:4, 4:11 etc. *'al* means 'with' and not 'upon'.

'token portion': *'azkārâ* LXX *mnēmosynon, mnēmosynē*. Vg *memoriale*. It appears seven times in the OT and is variously translated 'a memorial portion' (Wenham 1979, NIV, ESV), 'token portion' (NRSV, JPS), *Gedenkopfer* (Luther). See Rendtorff 1990: 100 and 'Comment'.

'an offering for soothing aroma': *rēaḥ nîḥôaḥ* See 'Comment' on 1:9.

3. 'the rest': *hannôteret* The feminine form is possibly an abbreviated form of *hamminḥâ hannôteret*.

4. 'oven': *tannûr* See Lev. 7:9; 26:26.

'When you bring': *wěkî taqrîb* It is unclear if this is 2 m. sg. or 3 f. sg.; v. 5 is in the 2 m. sg. From a structural viewpoint, Rendtorff (1990: 103) takes *taqrîb* as parallel to 2:1, where *taqrîb* is 3 f. sg. But the remoteness of v. 1 makes the link tenuous. It is more naturally taken as 2 m. sg. This means that from v. 4 to v. 8a the Lord addresses the offerer in the 2nd person.

'loaves': *ḥallâ* *HALOT* explains it as 'ring-shaped bread'. Cf. 1 Chr. 16:3, where *kikkar leḥem* is synonymous with *ḥallat leḥem* (2 Sam. 6:19).

'or' In *wěrěqîqē*, *wě* means 'or' and not 'and', as these are two similar things.

5. 'a griddle': *maḥabat* *HALOT* explains it as '(metal) plate'. See Lev. 6:14; 7:9; Ezek. 4:3; 1 Chr. 23:29.

6. 'break in pieces': *pātôt* LXX reads *kai diathrypseis*, which corresponds to *wěpattōtâ*. Inf. abs. can function as an imperative (see *GKC* 113bb). See Hartley 1992: 26 (Notes 6a).

7. 'a pan': *marḥešet HALOT* gives 'baking pan'. See Lev. 7:9.

8. 'you bring': *hēbētā* LXX and 4QLev[b] read it as 3 m. sg. Although this reading may well be a paleographically caused error due to the following *'t*, MT is preferable on contextual grounds (see Wevers 1997: 17 and 'Form and structure').

'he brings it': *hiqrîbāh BHS* margin suggests reading the verb in the imperative. The change from 2nd person address to 3rd person address should be understood in terms of the content (see 'Comment').

11. 'burn': *taqṭîrû* LXX, SamP and TgJon reads *taqrîbû*. In view of the fact that v. 12b provides a further explanation of v. 11b, MT is preferred.

13. 'your (sg.) loyalty offerings': *minḥātěkā* LXX translates this word here and in v. 13b as pl.: it takes the whole verse as addressed to the 2 pl.

'your God': *'elōhêkā* LXX reads *kyriou*. But the choice of 'God' instead of 'the LORD' is significant (see 'Comment').

Form and structure

The prescription of the *minḥâ* (the loyalty offering; see below) follows that of the burnt offering. On this occasion the *minḥâ* consists of cereal, and the chapter prescribes how the offering should be prepared and presented to the priest. The rules are introduced by *nepeš kî*, followed by subcases introduced by *'im*. The content is as follows:

1–2	Simple *minḥâ* [*nepeš kî*]
3	Direction regarding the remaining part
4–10	Cooked *minḥâ*
4	The *minḥâ* made with an oven [*wě'im*]
5–6	The *minḥâ* made with a griddle [*wě'im*]
7	The *minḥâ* made with a pan [*wě'im*]
8–9	A summary of the priest's ritual act
10	Directions regarding the remaining part
11–13	Ban on leaven and honey, directions regarding the first fruits and salt
14–16	Cooked *minḥâ* in the case of first fruits [*wě'im*]

There are some remarkable stylistic variations; particularly the change of person between cases:

1–3:	3rd person sg.
4–8a:	2nd person (on v. 4 see Notes)
8b–10:	3rd person (in relation to the priest's duty)
11–12:	2nd person pl.
13–15:	2nd person sg.
16:	3rd person sg. (in relation to the priest's duty)

The fact that the previous chapter is in the 3rd person except for 1:2 ('from among you') and the following chapters (Lev. 3 – 5) are in the 3rd person, with the exception of 3:17, suggests that more than stylistic reasons are responsible for the variation in Lev. 2. In this chapter the priest's duty is consistently cast in the 3rd person (see vv. 2a–3, 9–10, 16), while the offerer is addressed in the 3rd person when offering a simple *minḥâ* (vv. 1–3), but in the 2nd person when he offers the more elaborate *minḥâ*. Together with other stylistic features (see 'Comment' on vv. 8–9), this reflects differing degrees of eagerness to seek the Lord on the offerer's part: the 2nd person address is made when it is more intense.

It should also be noted that the two elements of 'an offering for annihilation, a soothing aroma' (vv. 2, 9) are separated in vv. 11b–12 and that 'a soothing aroma' is omitted in vv. 13–16.

minḥâ

Minḥâ is variously translated; mostly as 'grain offering' (NIV, NRSV, NEB, ESV) but also as 'an offering of meal' (JPS), 'a meal offering' (Noth 1965), 'a cereal offering' (Wenham 1979) and *Speisopfer* (Rendtorff 1985). The main ingredient of the *minḥâ* in the priestly literature is stipulated as cereal. This distinguishes it from other occurrences of the offering in the OT where the ingredients are either non-cereal or unspecified (Gen. 4:3–5). Though translating *minḥâ* to take into account its main ingredient is not unreasonable, the fact that cereal was sometimes the main ingredient of the *ḥaṭṭā't* makes such a rendering somewhat inexact (5:11). 'Meal offering' is no better, since every kind of offering was to some extent a meal except for the burnt offering. It seems more appropriate to translate in terms of the offering's function rather than its ingredients. A translation such as 'gift offering' is possible though somewhat tautological. A number of factors must be taken into account in translating *minḥâ*. These include the text's specification that a *nepeš* is the agent of this offering, the idea of *'azkārâ* (to remind), the plain nature of the ingredients and the stress placed on the offering's small size. Together these factors suggest that the purpose of the *minḥâ'* was to confirm and renew the covenantal relationship. I would like to propose 'the loyalty offering' as a translation for *minḥâ*, since its purpose was to express one's allegiance to the Lord.

Comment

2:1–3

1. The introductory *wĕnepeš kî* parallels 1:2ab. Thus it is an offering distinct from the burnt offering, and can be offered independently. As stated in Introduction (7.1.3), most of the occurrences of *nepeš* in Leviticus mean a person with an 'egocentric nature'. That this is also the case here is suggested by the appeasement of the Lord's wrath not only by the act of burning but also by the addition of frankincense (see below).

'pour oil': *yaṣaq šemen* The phrase appears elsewhere in Gen. 28:18; 35:14; in the former it has a parallel term *māšaḥ* (anointed) in 31:13. The phrase appears in oath contexts (cf. Sarna 1989: 200), and the rite may symbolize covenantal commitment. However, it is evident that oil itself has a symbolic value, since along with frankincense, it is prohibited from the *minḥâ* substituted for the sin offering in 5:11 and from the suspected adulterer in Num. 5:15. They are prohibited because they represent something pleasing to the Lord. Nevertheless it is necessary to consider the symbolic meaning of each separately.

Although oil was a primary foodstuff in ancient Israel, it also served a plethora of other purposes, many of them symbolic. Since the ingredients of the offerings in a ritual context must have a fixed meaning, an investigation into oil's symbolic meaning is called for. Its use in the softening of objects and its fragrance when burnt make it a powerful symbol of gladness and gentleness. Nevertheless a prohibition against adding it to the *minḥâ* of v. 11 makes this general symbolic meaning unlikely. Its meaning within a ritual context is more likely related to what it symbolized in the anointing and ordination of kings and priests: qualifying them to serve in God's presence. Thus oil is related to *the presence of the Lord*, which the worshipper craves. Oil is also commanded for the priestly ritual inside the Tent (the Holy Place, 24:1–4). Yet the modus operandi of achieving the symbolic meaning is different: here in the *minḥâ* of the court, oil is burnt along with flour and frankincense to produce a soothing aroma to the Lord. Its complete destruction by fire indicates that this is of primary importance to the means by which the Lord's presence is experienced. By contrast, oil in the Holy Place, while it is also burnt, is intended to produce light (see 24:1–4; cf. 9:4).

'frankincense': *lĕbōnâ* Assigning a symbolic meaning to frankincense is difficult, since it is nearly always combined with 'oil' in the Pentateuch. However, the finest quality of frankincense was used for ritual activities in the Holy Place (24:7; Exod. 30:34), and it is probable that frankincense was used when Aaron entered the Holy of Holies with burning incense taken from the incense altar (16:12; cf. Exod. 30:34–38). Thus frankincense, by its rare fragrance, most likely functioned to appease the Lord's wrath. Moreover, while in the forecourt it appeased the Lord's wrath against the offerer, inside the Tent it appeased his wrath towards the people.

'the loyalty offering': *minḥâ* See 'Form and structure'.

2. Lev. 24:7 and 5:12 indicate that the term *'azkārâ* (token portion), made of 'pure frankincense', refers not to the material side of the loyalty offering, but to the offering's symbolic meaning. The Hebr. form is causative; therefore it may mean 'to remind'; the question remains – whom does it remind? For a discussion of the term, see Nielsen 1986: 75–76. See 'Explanation'.

3. In chs. 1 – 5 no mention is made of the priestly due except 2:3, 10 (noted by Rendtorff 1990: 101). There are two possible reasons for this. First, the prescription in ch. 2 is addressed to the Israelites in general (1:2aa). In other words, ch. 2 views what remains after burning from the perspective of the offerer. It is interested in what happens to it rather than to whom it belongs: the priests. This conclusion is supported by the omission of *ḥôq* (due, Lev. 6:18[11], 22[15]; 7:34), as well as 'eating', in ch. 2. The second reason relates to the significance of the very mention of 'a most holy thing'. See below.

'a most holy thing': *qōdeš qodāšîm* The phrase occurs here for the first time in Leviticus. The loyalty offering along with the sin and reparation offerings are called 'a most holy thing' (6:17[10]; 7:1), in distinction to the fellowship offering, which is simply called *qōdeš* (21:22). As Rendtorff (1990: 102) notes, the phrase refers to those parts of the offerings that are not burnt: the priestly dues. It is important to observe that such parts are visible. By contrast, the burnt offering, which is completely burnt (thus becoming invisible), is never qualified by this phrase. As stated in ch. 1, the essence of holiness lies in being wholly burnt up. In line with this, nothing of the loyalty offering, symbolizing the total forfeiture of a soul (for 'soul' see Introduction 7.1.3), should be left on earth. By describing it as 'a *most* holy thing' the lawgiver stresses that the remaining portion comes from the Lord and must be consumed by the priest, just as the burnt offering must be completely consumed by fire in the ritual of Lev. 1. Nevertheless the remaining part of an offering is not always called 'a most holy thing' in Lev. 1 – 5, as evidenced in the prescription for the fellowship offering. Therefore, although the very mention of 'a most holy thing' indicates that the loyalty offering is a lesser quality offering than the burnt offering, it remains higher in quality than the fellowship, sin and reparation offerings (see 'Explanation' on ch. 4). In view of this, the loyalty offering comes next to the burnt offering in sanctity. In a word, this phrase is mentioned here because of its relatively higher sanctity than the offerings of chs. 3, 4 and 5.

2:4–7

Three kinds of loyalty offering, grouped according to how the fine flour is cooked (in an oven [v. 4], a griddle [v. 5] or a pan [7]) are prescribed (vv. 4–7) and followed by a prescription of what is common to all three (vv. 8–10). The first two kinds are baked unleavened. Though no reference is made to leaven in the third, v. 11 prevents the conclusion that leaven was permitted.

The unleavened bread symbolizes what it symbolized in the Passover festival. The Israelites had to eat it because they were in a hurry (cf. Exod. 12:11). But this does not exhaust its symbolic meaning. For the Israelites, leaven (yeast) symbolized fermentation, which could potentially lead to corruption (cf. Wenham 1979: 71; Sarna 1986: 89–91). In other words, in line with the symbolic significance of honey (see below on v. 11), it symbolized various materialistic concerns that hinder the offerer from maintaining his or her allegiance to God.

2:8–10

These verses refer back to vv. 4–7 and prescribe the offering's preparation and handling. A transition is made from the 2nd person in v. 8a to the 3rd person in vv. 8bff. The former reflects a more intense relationship between the offerer and the Lord (see 'Form and structure'), whereas the latter merely describes the practical side of this relationship. Contrary to appearance, the offerer's bringing (*hiqrîb*) of the offering *to the priest* is unique; elsewhere it is said that either 'the offerer brings the offering near to the LORD' (cf. 1: 3; 27:11) or 'the priest brings the offering near *to a place*' (cf. 1:15). This possibly reflects the offerer's viewpoint that the priest's status is higher than his own. V. 10 is the same as v. 3.

2:11–13

11. A general ban on yeast and honey is given. Both ingredients are related to the Passover event. For the prohibition against using yeast, see Comment on vv. 4–7 above. Honey was used as a symbol of the Promised Land's fertility (Exod. 3:17; 13:5; 33:3 etc.). It is possibly prohibited on this occasion because it symbolizes the opposite of what is symbolized by '*bitter* herbs' (Exod. 12:8). The prohibition against adding honey indicates that the offering for annihilation (*'iššeh YHWH*) is incongruous with yeast and honey, probably because their fermentation connotes corruption. Given the implied link to the exodus this symbolic meaning is probably intended here rather than the more general meaning it has, such as 'strength' and 'luxurious food' (Deut. 32:13; 1 Sam. 14:27; Ezek. 16:13, 19). Moreover the prohibition at once brings to mind the Passover meal (yeast) and the as yet inexperienced Promised Land (honey), and appears to signify that the offerer ought to revert to the initial covenant allegiance exhibited by Israel in the exodus.

12. If the offering is of first fruits, yeast and honey may be offered to the Lord, but must not be offered as a soothing aroma (see Lev. 23:17; and further Lev. 23:10; Exod. 23:19; 34:26; Num. 15:20; 18:12). This suggests that the Lord's property includes things other than what is called *'iššeh* (an annihilation offering) or *rēaḥ nîḥôaḥ* (a soothing aroma; cf. Lev. 27).

The relationship between this *rēšît* and *bikkûr* in v. 14 has been discussed. Milgrom convincingly posits that *bikkûr* refers to 'the first-ripe' of agricultural produce, while *rēšît* refers to 'the first-processed' of things such as grain, wine, oil, fruit syrup, leaven and dough (1991: 190–191; cf. Num. 18:12–13, 27).

13. The commandment for the application of salt to the offering constitutes the final prescription for the various loyalty offerings. The personal nature of the offering is stressed by the 2nd person sg. address, particularly by the use of 'your God' instead of 'the LORD' (cf. LXX). While 'the LORD' (Tetragrammaton and not the common reading *'ădonāy*) connotes intimacy to the people at large, the personal intimacy is expressed by the pronominal suffix '*your* God' (see 4:22).

As 'the salt of the covenant', the salt symbolizes the covenantal relationship, a bond. Furthermore the presence of the phrase 'the eternal covenant of salt' in Num. 18:19 suggests, first, that the salt itself represents a covenant relationship, and, second, that salt is associated with the idea of duration, being itself a preservative (cf. Latham 1982: 64–65). However, the very command to add salt betrays that one's allegiance to God is easily abandoned.

2:14–16

14–16. In terms of its ingredients, the *minḥâ* of first fruits is the vegetable offering par excellence. The offering of first fruits symbolizes that all agricultural produce is a gift from the Lord. As the fruit of the Israelites' labour (Exod. 23:16; Lev. 23:17) the offering may have functioned to sanctify their labour. Nevertheless the purpose of the *minḥâ* remains the same: to remind, or be reminded, of the covenantal relationship between the Lord and the offerer, this time through the offering of produce on the particular occasion of the first fruits.

As the last of offerings in Lev. 2, the loyalty offering of first fruits was apparently inferior to the other kinds despite its choice ingredients. The omission of 'a soothing aroma' in v. 16, which is unlikely to be accidental, also supports this conclusion. A 'soothing aroma' and 'an offering for annihilation' have already been separated in vv. 11b–12. Thus the omission of the phrase 'a soothing aroma' in v. 16 indicates that the offering of first fruits has relatively less significance than the offerings of vv. 1–2 and 4–9.

Explanation

The purpose of the loyalty offering in ch. 2 is clearly indicated by the mention of *'azkārâ*: to remind the Lord of his covenantal relationship with the offerer. The idea of 'reminding the LORD' appears strange, since the Lord is always faithful to his promises. But it results from the offerers' recognition that they are the object of the Lord's wrath, symbolized by the need to produce a soothing aroma, and that they are protected only by the Lord, who remembers his covenant. That the offering appeases the Lord's wrath is amply suggested not only in the priestly literature (Lev. 5:12; Num. 5:15) but also in Genesis (see 32:21; 33:10; 43:11, 15, 25–26). This purpose is further qualified by the symbolic meanings of other elements in the prescription.

The addition of oil and frankincense symbolizes, respectively, the offerer's desire for the Lord's presence and the appeasement of his wrath. That salt was added on every loyalty offering indicates that the covenantal relationship was permanent. Honey and leaven symbolize material blessing; hence the potential for corruption. In line with the prohibition against leaven at the Passover and honey's symbolic representation of a life of blessing in the Promised Land, the prohibition against using these ingredients in the loyalty offering was meant to transfer the offerer's mindset back to Israel's original Passover experience. More specifically, this offering facilitated their embodiment of the covenantal relationship God forged with Israel at that time. That is, the omission of leaven and honey from the offering symbolically removed the offerers from their life of blessing in the Promised Land to become again the recipients of God's unilateral salvation of them from Egypt. In so far as honey and leaven symbolize human corruption, their prohibition excludes any human elements or humanism in Israel's relationship with God.

The offering focuses on restoring the broken relationship in terms of the offerer's soul by means different from the burnt offering. First, unlike the burnt offering, where 'a man' (*'ādām*) offers a sacrifice, it is a 'soul' (*nepeš*) with an egocentric nature that offers the loyalty offering. Thus the condition of the offerer's heart is at issue in the loyalty offering. Since the covenantal relationship between the Lord and the Israelites essentially lies in the heart and mind of the latter, their forsaking this relationship is fatal. Second, the ingredients are vegetables, salt, oil and frankincense, which are meant to nourish the offerer's physical life. Considering that the grains are to be burnt, albeit only partly, they represent the egocentric nature of the offerer's soul (*nepeš*, v. 1); the doomed 'life' of the offerer should be replaced by true life brought about by visibly burning the grain. In other words, the ritual expresses that true bread must come from the Lord. Third, grain is not as expensive as animal sacrifices. This is also in keeping with the offering's function. Since it concerns a person's inner being, not only can the material afford to be simple and modest, but this must be so. In addition to this, only a handful of it goes to the Lord. Despite the inexpensiveness, smallness and plainness of the ritual, it inversely suggests the difficulty in embodying its symbolic meaning, because it aims to destroy the worshipper's egocentricity (cf. 1 Kgs 19:12

with 18:29, 36). As with the burnt offering, the soothing aroma appeases the Lord's wrath.

On the other hand, vv. 12–16 deal with a loyalty offering offered on specific occasions such as the first fruits. This occasion marks the joy and thanksgiving of the people in the Promised Land, where the potential for corruption may become a reality.

In a sense, this offering is a sequel to the burnt offering ritual in ch. 1, particularly the bird burnt offering (see 'Explanation' on ch. 1). However, since it is not completely reduced to smoke, but some is removed for the priests, it is of relatively less sanctity than the burnt offering. The next chapter deals with the *šĕlāmîm* offering, much of which is left and shared by the offerer and the priests, thus making it even more remote from the idea of complete offering, and therefore of less sanctity than the loyalty offering. The loyalty offering made on occasions of remembering the Lord's blessing (vv. 12–16) has elements of joy, and this leads to the next offering, the *šĕlāmîm* offering in ch. 3.

My evaluation of these offerings sheds light on the Cain and Abel narrative, where Abel's *animal* sacrifice was accepted and Cain's *vegetable* offering rejected (Gen. 4:1–5). The arrangement of Lev. 2 and Lev. 3, which, while following the order of Cain's and Abel's, reverses the offerings in terms of their sanctity stated above, indicates that the ingredients of the Gen. 4 offerings were immaterial to the Lord's response. It was what the Lord saw in their hearts that was important (for the meaning of *šā'â*, 'gaze at', in Gen. 4:4–5, see Kiuchi 2001b: 1–29). This is already alluded to in Lev. 1 (see the bird burnt offering), but is also confirmed in various other occurrences of *minḥâ* (e.g. 5:13; Num. 5).

New Testament implications

NT believers do not need to offer the loyalty offering to the Lord, because his wrath was appeased by Christ's death on the cross. This is on the assumption that men and woman become believers in Christ only by dying to their egocentric souls and by being renewed by the Holy Spirit. However, the difficulty in dying to the egocentric soul makes it necessary for would-be believers to confirm their bond with Christ repeatedly throughout their lives, until he returns. Practically this involves the destruction of all their selfish concerns. As Israel would continue within the covenant by embodying the relationship initiated at the Passover, so the way forward in the Christian life is to maintain strenuously the initial spiritual condition one had upon first believing in Christ.

In the OT it was the priest who burned the token portion to the Lord. In NT times it is the risen Jesus Christ and the Holy Spirit who take care of this vital aspect of the human soul. The connection with Christ is faith in him only: other things or persons are unnecessary. Indeed things and persons other than Christ may become hindrances to faith. Rather, as stated above, it is because humans tend to trust in objects and people, which amounts to idolatry, that they lose the Lord's presence. The loyalty offering is one that deals with this kind of spiritual longing for the Lord's presence, or for the confirmation of the never-failing relationship between ourselves and the Lord.

LEVITICUS 3:1–17

Translation

1If his offering is a fellowship offering – if he presents an animal from the herd, whether it is male or female, he is to present before the LORD an animal without blemish. 2He lays his hand on the head of his offering and slaughters it at the entrance to the Tent of Meeting, and Aaron's sons, the priests, dash the blood against the altar on all sides. 3From the fellowship offering he presents the offering to the LORD: fat that covers the entrails and all the fat that is on the entrails, 4the two kidneys and the fat that is around them on the sinews and the long lobe of the liver he is to remove with the kidneys. 5Aaron's sons burn it on the altar on top of the burnt offering, which is on the wood on the fire. It is an offering for annihilation for a soothing aroma to the LORD.

6If his offering is from the flock for a fellowship offering to the LORD, he is to present a male or female without blemish. 7If he presents a lamb as his offering, he presents it before the LORD. 8He lays his hand on the head of his offering and slaughters it before the Tent of Meeting. Then Aaron's sons dash its blood against the altar on all sides. 9From the fellowship offering he presents as an offering for annihilation to the LORD its fat: the entire fat tail is to be cut off close to the backbone, also the fat that covers the entrails and all the fat that is on the entrails, 10the two kidneys and the fat that is around them on the sinews and the long lobe of the liver are to be removed with the kidneys. 11The priest burns it at the altar as food, an offering for annihilation to the LORD.

12If his offering is a goat, he presents it before the LORD. 13He lays his hand on the head of his offering and slaughters it before the Tent of Meeting. Aaron's sons dash its blood against the altar on all sides. 14He presents a part of his offering as an offering for annihilation to the LORD; the fat that covers the entrails and all the thick fat that is on the entrails, 15the two kidneys and the fat that is around them on the sinews and the long lobe of the liver, which he is to remove with the kidneys. 16The priest burns them on the altar as food, an offering for annihilation for a soothing aroma. All the fat belongs to the LORD.

17This is a perpetual decree for your generations in all your settlements: never eat any fat or any blood.

Notes on the text

1. 'from the herd' LXX adds *tō kyriō* (to the Lord).

2. 'and slaughters' LXX adds *enantion kyriou* (before the Lord).

'the altar' LXX adds *holokautōmata*; i.e. *mizbaḥ hā'ōlâ* (the altar of burnt offering).

3. 'he presents' LXX and Vg read the verb in pl., according to which Aaron's sons present the *'iššeh*. Cf. vv. 9, 14. The sg. is preferred as original; it refers to the offerer (Rendtorff 1990: 115–116).

5. 'Aaron's sons' Vg omits this, whereas LXX adds *hoi hiereus* (the priests), also in vv. 8, 13.

'on the fire' SamP and LXX add *'šr 'l hmzbḥ*, as in 1:8, 12. The shorter form of MT is already found in 1:17.

8. 'before' LXX adds *tas thyras* (the entrance) before 'the Tent', while Syr inserts 'the LORD at the entrance of' before 'the Tent'.

9. 'to the LORD' LXX renders *tō theō* (to God), which is unusual in view of vv. 3, 5, 11, 14, 16.

'its fat, (namely) the entire fat tail' etc.: *ḥelbô hā'alyâ* LXX renders *to stear kai tēn osphyn*; thus rather than viewing the 'fat tail' as a subcategory of the 'fat', it assumes they are different 'fat' offerings. But as 7:3 and 9:19 suggest, 'fat tail' (*'alyâ*) appears to be considered as part of 'fat' (*ḥēleb*).

11. 'burns it': *wěhiqṭîrô* 4QLev[b] reads *wěhiqṭîr*. LXX also reflects the form without 3 m. sg. suffix.

13. 'and (he) slaughters': *wěšāḥaṭ* LXX renders it in pl. as in 1:5, 11, whereas in 3:2, 8 they render it in the sg. However, in the fellowship offering the agent of slaughtering is consistently presented as the offerer (see 'Comment' on v. 2).

16. 'a soothing aroma' LXX and SamP add *tō kyriō* and *lYHWH* (to the LORD) respectively. Although Rendtorff takes v. 16b as forming a sentence, it seems preferable to take v. 16bb as an independent sentence (see 'Comment' on v. 16).

Form and structure

After the burnt offering (ch. 1) and the loyalty offering (ch. 2) comes the prescription for the fellowship offering (*šělāmîm*; see below). While the fellowship offering was offered along with other kinds of offerings, this chapter concentrates on how it was offered. Unlike the burnt offering, animals for the fellowship offering could be either male or female. Even though the ritual culminated with the offerer and priest consuming the remaining flesh (cf. 7:15–21), this part of the ritual is not prescribed in ch. 3.

The prescription is sequential to 1:2, but read simply, 3:1 also follows 2:1. In view of the designation of the offerer ('a man' in 1:2 and 'a soul' in 2:1), it appears that this offering relates to both (see 'Comment' on v. 1).

The structure of this chapter is divisible into two sections, the case of a bull (*bāqār*) and the case of small ruminants (*ṣō'n*). The latter is subdivided into two: sheep (*keśeb*) and goats (*'ēz*). Each of the three cases begins with *'im* ('if', vv. 1, 6, 12). The addressee is consistently referred to in the 3rd person sg.

šĕlāmîm-case (1a)
cattle (1b–5)
flock (6)
  1. sheep (7–11)
  2. goats (12–16)
A prohibition against eating fat and blood (17)

The three cases share the same ritual procedure. After an animal is brought to the Lord and slaughtered, the priest pours the blood around the altar and burns the fat portions, along with the kidneys, on the altar. This uniform procedural repetition is possibly significant considering the variations between cases for the burnt offering in Lev. 1. While the presence of three cases is partly explained by the need to deal with the sheep's fat tail, this hardly explains the relatively small variations between the repeated prescriptions (cf. vv. 5, 11, 16). As in ch. 1, the biblical writer's ideology is latent in this literary phenomenon (see 'Explanation').

The prescription for the goat ends with the burning of fat, which occasions the Lord to make an injunction against consuming fat and blood (v. 16–17).

šĕlāmîm

The phrase *zebaḥ šĕlāmîm* occurs predominantly in the legal parts of Leviticus and Numbers. The relationship between the three terms *zebaḥ*, *zebaḥ šĕlāmîm* and *šĕlāmîm* is debated. Some take these terms as referring to the same sacrifice, while others rigorously argue that they reflect different sacrifices (see Rentdorff 1985: 120–126). It seems reasonable to posit that while *zebaḥ* is a general term for sacrifice, and sometimes refers to the *šĕlāmîm*, the term *šĕlāmîm* came into use with official worship in the sanctuary. In fact, the term *šĕlāmîm* first appears in Exod. 24:5 when the Sinai covenant was made between the Lord and the people.

English translations for the Hebr. *zebaḥ šĕlāmîm* include 'peace offering', 'offering of well-being' and 'fellowship offering'. *Šĕlāmîm* derives from *šlm*, meaning 'peace' or 'well-being'. Several proposals have been made for the root meaning of *šlm* (cf. Milgrom 1991: 220–221). The question is, while the basic sense of the root means a state of peace, does the *šĕlāmîm* also express such a state? This would seem to conflict with the prescription itself, where the offerer is still in need of the Lord's acceptance, indicated by the production of a soothing aroma to the Lord. While the peace or fellowship between the offerer and the Lord is the purpose of the ritual, the ritual itself expresses the process leading to that state. Therefore it may be inferred that the sacrifice, representing the offerer, brings the offerer's spiritual state from one of not-yet-accepted to one of peace or fellowship with the Lord. Thus in view of the communal eating it is reasonable to call the offering a fellowship offering in the sense that the ritual achieves fellowship between the worshipper and God.

Comment

3:1–5

1. 'If' (*'im*) indicates that this is a subdivision of the general case where a 'man' (*'ādām*) brings an offering (cf. Lev. 1:2). However, although the burnt offering in Lev. 1:3ff. is offered by a 'man', and a 'soul' (*nepeš*) offers the loyalty offering of 2:1ff., it is remarkable that the offerer in Lev. 3 is identified as neither an *'ādām* nor a *nepeš*. He is simply identified as 'the one who offers' (*maqrîb*). That the term *nepeš* predominates in passages dealing with the handling of the fellowship offering's blood and remaining meat elsewhere in Leviticus (7:18, 20, 25, 27; 17:10–11) suggests a link between 3:1 and 2:1. Further it is noteworthy that these rules in chs. 7 and 17 discuss the potential desecration of the meat of the fellowship offering. Thus perhaps the offerer in this instance should be viewed in terms of both an *'ādām* and a *nepeš*. The lack of a specific designation in Lev. 3 may derive partly from the fact that it is already mentioned, but more importantly from the circumstance that the prescription aims to draw attention to the ritual's symbolic meaning, the burning of fat, rather than the agent who offers it.

The worshipper can offer male or female animals as a fellowship offering. In this regard, the *šĕlāmîm* offering is less stringent than the burnt offering, and in fact the offering is made after the burnt offering (see v. 5). However, the animal must still be without blemish (see 'Comment' on 1:3).

2. The hand-leaning rite is the same as for the burnt offering (see 1:4). However, unlike the burnt offering (see 'Notes on the text' on 1:5), it is the offerer who slaughters the animal (see vv. 8, 13). This requirement is necessary because the animal was not completely burnt, reflecting the offerer's need to become a sacrifice, as it was for the burnt offering. Thus by slaughtering his animal for a fellowship offering the offerer identifies with the requirement that he sacrifice himself. The priest handles the blood. The term *kipper* is not mentioned, because neither the priest (as in ch. 4) nor the offering (as in 1:4) deals with *all* the components in this offering (see Introduction 7.5 and Kiuchi 2005).

3–4. Only some parts of the animal are offered to the Lord on the altar: the fat portions of the intestines (v. 3b), the kidneys, and fat associated with the hind legs (v. 4). The repetitive directions concerning the fat portions are unique to the fellowship offering (vv. 9–10, 14–15). On the assumption that the animal represents the offerer, through the hand-leaning rite, the fat and kidneys symbolize something of the offerer.

The symbolism of the burning of fat and the prohibition against eating fat (vv. 16–17) has remained elusive to exegetes (cf. Milgrom 1991: 205–207; Eberhart 2002: 88–96). *ḥēleb* can refer metaphorically to 'the best' or 'the choicest' part (Gen. 4:4; 45:18; Num. 18:12; Deut. 32:14; Pss. 81:16[17]; 147:14, cf. Ps. 63:5[6]), but it does not necessarily follow that fat was a delicacy (e.g. Wenham 1979: 80). Moreover the proposal that fat represented the source of 'strength' (Heller 1970: 106–108) also appears to be a possibility.

Of particular exegetical importance for the fat's ritual symbolic meaning is that the *ḥēleb* is accepted by the Lord as a soothing aroma *when burnt* (cf. 'Comment' on 1:6–9); the *ḥēleb* itself is not something pleasing to the Lord. Indeed Israelites apparently considered fat inedible. Elsewhere the imagery of human fat refers negatively to human arrogance (Pss. 73:7; 119:70; Job 15:27). It can be inferred from these observations that fat symbolizes something the Lord detests. Therefore the offerer must completely destroy it by fire and, of course, its destruction is inevitably pleasing to the Lord. The burning of fat symbolizes the destruction of detestable things within a human's inner being. Since the above-cited passages indicate a connection with *lēb* or *lēbāb* (heart; see also Ps. 17:10), these detestable things probably reside in the human heart: a person's egocentricity.

The above interpretation finds support when the symbolic meaning of the kidneys is considered. Not only does the term 'kidneys' (*kĕlāyôt*) refer literally to the two organs located within the body cavity but, along with *lēb* (heart), it often refers to a human's inner being (Jer. 17:10; 20:12; Pss. 7:9[10]; 16:7; 26:2; 73:21; Job 19:27; Prov. 23:16).

It is the offerer's hand that presents the fat portions, symbolizing his egocentricity, to the Lord. The Lord is pleased with, and accepts the offerer, when the latter eviscerates his heart of selfishness and uncovers his innermost heart.

5. All the enumerated things, fat, kidneys and the long lobe of the liver, were burnt by the priest. The smoke, particularly its fragrance, became a soothing aroma for the Lord. These animal organs were not the Lord's literal food: they are presented as such only when they become smoke. This verse explicitly states that the sacrifice follows the burnt offering ('upon the burnt offering'). However, it does not say the same person ought to have offered both.

3:6–11

7. As hinted at in 'Form and structure', variations in phraseology and the omission of certain terms may serve to indicate authorial purpose. In this regard there is one significant difference among the three prescriptions: the characteristics of the animals themselves (see 'Explanation'). For the moment, I restrict myself to some minor variations. V. 7 contains three terms that share the root *qrb*: *maqrîb* (presents), *qorbān* (offering) and *hiqrîb* (he presents). In the corresponding v. 1, *maqrîb* and *hiqrîb* appear, but not *qorbān*. The use of these three terms in v. 7 appears to stress the identification between the offerer and the sheep even more so than in the case for the bull. In particular, the participial form *maqrîb* stresses the agent of the action without reference to the tense.

9. The case for a lamb includes the unique prescription for the complete (*tĕmîmâ*) removal of its tail. Since the idea of 'all' could easily have been expressed by the common term *kol* (cf. 4:35), it appears that the legislator deliberately chose the term *tāmîm* to stress the lamb's *tāmîm* character (see v. 6). Since the head and tail signify a totality (cf. Kiuchi 1997), reference to the tail being *tāmîm* may symbolize the complete wholeheartedness of the offerer. That is, the offerer ought to be a person without selfishness and arrogance.

11. In contrast to v. 5, where Aaron's sons burn the fat, a single priest burns the equivalent parts of the lamb. This presumably relates to the lamb's relatively smaller size. Considering its occurrence in vv. 5 and 16, the omission of 'a soothing aroma' in v. 11 is conspicuous. That this is not accidental is indicated by the same omission in the case of a lamb in Lev. 4, even though it is included for the offering of a goat (see 4:31, 35). While the three types of ritual assume the production of a soothing aroma, the phrase's omission in the sheep offering suggests it is inferior to that of the bull. Nevertheless the *'iššeh* still belongs to the Lord (cf. v. 16).

The mention of 'food, an offering for annihilation' reflects the offerer's spiritual acceptance that the destruction of his egocentricity is food for the Lord. Thus the whole phrase 'food, an offering for annihilation, *for* a soothing aroma' describes the process by which his egocentric nature disappears.

3:12–17

12. The introduction to the goat's case is briefer than that for the lamb in v. 7.

13. Compared with vv. 2 and 8, the head of the goat is simply stated 'his head': among the three cases *qorbānô* (his offering) is omitted only in this case.

14. Compared with vv. 3 and 9, *mizzebaḥ šĕlāmîm* (from the fellowship offering) is changed to *mimmennû qorbānô* (from it his offering). The phrase *zebaḥ šĕlāmîm* does not occur in the case of the goat.

16. The latter half of this verse is not the result of connecting vv. 5b and 11b (*pace* Rendtorff 1990: 133). Rather it is deliberately formulated to complete the goat case, where the relationship between the offerer and the Lord is presented implicitly (see above on v. 11). Note that unlike 1:9, 13, 17, the phrase 'an offering for annihilation' is connected with 'a soothing aroma' in v. 16b. Moreover rather than explicitly stating that the soothing aroma is offered 'to the LORD', the normal word sequence is interrupted by the statement that 'All the fat belongs to the LORD'. Thus v. 16 effectively equates the destruction of fat, and what the fat symbolizes, with what pleases the Lord. Moreover this must have obliged the offerer not to withhold the fat from the Lord, for to do so symbolized one's reluctance to destroy one's egocentric nature. Although the statement 'All the fat belongs to the LORD' serves to make a transition into v. 17, its omission from the goat case would have meant that the offerer was not explicitly commanded to offer smoke to the Lord.

The intention of the offerer is also reflected by the priest's burning of 'them' (*hiqṭîrām*). They are both conscious in that every piece of fat must be burnt (cf. vv. 5, 11).

17. This is the first instance in the Pentateuch where 'blood' appears in connection with 'fat' (cf. Lev. 7:33; 17:6). It chiastically refers back to the ritual procedure; namely blood and then fat. While a prohibition against eating blood comes in chs. 7 and 17, that for fat is uniquely connected with the prescription of the fellowship offering in Lev. 3. Indeed apart from the blood-handling the ritual mainly consists of burning the fat portions to the Lord. The prohibition indicates that the fellowship offering is liable to desecration (7:23, 25; see also Ezek. 39:19; 44:7).

'Eating of fat' has an ironic connotation, for obviously the people will not eat it as it is – all the more so when its symbolic meaning is taken into account.

The mention of *ḥuqqat 'ôlām* does not mean that other rules are not eternally binding. The term *ḥuqqâ* refers to a principle, since it appears as the summary statement of particular laws (cf. Exod. 12:14, 17; 27:21; 28:43; Lev. 7:36; 10:9; 16:29 etc.; cf. Tomes 1988: 20–33). In this chapter, the principle is summarized by the prohibition against consuming blood and fat. The symbolic dimension of this principle implies that in distinction to *lĕdôrôtēkem* (for your generations) *'ôlām* is a term related to the divine holy realm as well as to time humanly experienced (cf. 'Explanation' on ch. 23).

Explanation

Contrary to expectations, this chapter does not give the whole ritual procedure for the fellowship offering. Rather it deals with the early part of the ritual, focusing on how a worshipper should draw near to the Lord with a fellowship offering. This stands in agreement with the general concern of Lev. 1 – 5: access to the Lord. Thus, while the ritual ends with a meal symbolizing fellowship between the Lord and worshipper, ch. 3 reveals the essence of this fellowship rather than the mundane meal it anticipates.

Since most of the animal is left after the burning of fat portions, there is a danger of profaning it and making the eating of its meat an end in itself (7:15–21), even though the latter is legitimate (see further 17:1–7). It is partly with this background in mind that this chapter lays special emphasis on bringing the sacrifice 'to the LORD' (vv. 1, 7, 12; *lipnê 'ōhel mô'ēd* in vv. 8, 13). These observations make this chapter's location after the loyalty offering logical. In fact, 1:1 – 6:7 can be seen as arranged according to the evaluation of the offering by the Lord; the later the chapter, the more the offering is related to the *potential* for human sinfulness.

The meaning of the ritual

By the hand-leaning rite, the offerer symbolically identifies himself with the animal. As for the burnt offering, the animal's blood symbolically takes the place of the offerer's. This statement needs qualification. By its shed blood taking the place of the offerer's condemned soul, the animal gives its life for him (see 'Comment' on 1:5). Thus though the animal's meat is ultimately consumed by the offerer, the animal ought to be offered wholly to the Lord. This is conveyed by the offerer's slaughtering of the animal and presentation of the fat portions to the Lord.

A striking characteristic of the fellowship offering is the burning of the fat and kidneys. Fat symbolizes the unnecessary parts of the human heart, the egocentric nature, while the kidneys symbolize the innermost part of the human heart (see 'Comment' on vv. 3–4). The two elements are sinful and abhorrent to the Lord. Therefore their fiery destruction produces a soothing aroma for the Lord. This soothing aroma is described as the 'food' by which the offerer can have communion with the Lord (v. 11). For the offerers, the food shared with the Lord was the destruction of their own selfishness, not the remaining meat of the sacrifice. The actual eating of the meat following the enactment of this ritual merely symbolizes this spiritual truth. In so far as the burning of fat produces a soothing aroma, the ritual assumes that the offerer has been under the Lord's wrath, though this is different from the situation when he commits a particular 'sin', as in Lev. 4 – 5.

The overlapping of symbolic meanings is natural in rituals: the death of the offerer is expressed not just by the animal's slaughtering but also by the burning of the fat portions and kidneys.

The fellowship offering is thus offered when the offerers seek fellowship with the Lord as a man or a woman needing to relinquish all earthly desires. Thus they cannot approach and offer a sacrifice with egocentricity or complacency, since this conflicts with the very idea of this sacrifice. Unless they die spiritually, which means giving up their investiture of hope in earthly matters, they are not entitled to offer the fellowship offering. One naturally wonders if such a requirement could have been met, even temporarily, by the Israelites.

Occasions

As for the burnt offering, the variety of motives underlying this sacrifice's offering has made its function elusive to scholars (cf. Wenham 1979: 77–80). The fellowship offering is offered on occasions of thanksgiving, making a vow and dedicating oneself voluntarily (cf. 7:15–16; 22:18, 21) as well as covenant-making (Exod. 20:24; 24:5). However, whatever the offerer's emotion, it is important to discern that the Israelites may not always have embodied the *symbolic* meaning of the ritual set out in Lev. 3. Since this text claims that a person ought to destroy his own egocentric nature in order to have fellowship with the Lord, clearly it is inappropriate to restrict the significance of the fellowship offering to particular occasions. In so far as one's whole existence before the Lord is symbolized by the offering, it is not just salvation from a particular predicament but salvation of one's soul that is at stake. As for the burnt offering, one wonders what the human reality is before the Lord when a person does not offer this sacrifice (cf. Ps. 50:13–14). Thus, while the Israelites offered fellowship offerings on particular occasions, seeking fellowship with the Lord, the existential transformation symbolized by the burning of fat is unlikely to have taken place on each occasion. It is doubtful, for instance, if they really had fellowship when they offered the offering at Sinai (Exod. 24:5), as is evidenced by the golden-calf incident soon afterwards (Exod. 32).

Salvation at stake

Additionally, but not least important, is the observation made in 'Comment' that differences in formulation between the three cases betray authorial intention. This is related to the imagery of the animals themselves in relation to the role of the fellowship offering, which should be interpreted on a different level to the basic symbolic meaning of the ritual. As the offering represents the offerer, the animals can symbolize three types of personalities. However, this is not to say that the offerer of a bull shares its particular characteristics, but that the animal in a more general sense symbolizes a certain type of personality.

The ritual of the bull is the most comprehensive: it is the most costly of the three animals. While lay individuals offered it (chs. 1 and 3), elsewhere the bull is offered for the expiation of the sins and uncleanness of the anointed priest (4:2–12; 16:3) and the whole community (4:13, 21; cf. 16:6), the consecration of Aaron and his sons (8:2), and the purification of the Tent on the Day of Atonement (16:2). On each occasion, the bull's blood was handled within the Tent, which suggests the bull is related to the divine sphere, the Tent. This in turn suggests that the young bull of the burnt and fellowship offerings, if offered by lay individuals, was closely associated with the divinity, though not in an idolatrous sense (cf. the association of imagery between *'abbîr* [the mighty] and bulls or cows in Gen. 49:24; Isa. 1:24; 34:7; 49:26; Pss. 22:12[13]; 50:13).

The case of the lamb, despite its smallness, stresses identification between the offerer and the animal to the same degree as the bull offering: by the repeated use of the root *qrb* in v. 7 and the term *tĕmîmâ* in v. 9. The sheep is pictured in the Bible as a symbol of helplessness of individuals and the people who cannot survive without a shepherd.

The low estimation of the goat, despite its being costlier than a lamb, is conveyed by its not being referred to as 'the fellowship offering', and through the indirect way in which the soothing aroma is related to the Lord in v. 16. By contrast with the lamb offering, the goat is merely presented as a means of approaching the Lord, as is hinted at in the formulation of the 'soothing aroma' (vv. 11, 16). The goat is also related to idolatry; in particular it is described as an object of idolatrous worship to the Israelites (17:7). In ch. 4, while a bull is required when the anointed priest or the whole congregation sins, the sin of the tribal leader is expiated by a male goat (4:23). In other words, when human sin is at issue, a goat is preferred to a sheep. This seems to indicate that the goat, because of its relatively greater strength than a sheep, is intrinsically associated with human sinfulness. Ironically its strength is reflected by the offerer not dedicating himself in the offering of the goat as he does for the sheep. Thus it may be that two types of human beings (sheep and goats) are seen before God the judge (bull): helpless and dependent sheep, and relatively strong and stubborn goats.

Such an evaluation of the animals themselves persisted even into NT times, when Jesus described the final judgment scene in Matt. 25:31–46 where the saved are classed as sheep and those destined to eternal punishment as goats.

Thus the imagery of the goat at the end of ch. 3 paves the way both literarily and ideologically for the prescription in ch. 4. This view may be corroborated by the above-mentioned fact that the further one reads in chs. 1 – 6:7, the more the text deals with the potential sinfulness of the offerer. It goes without saying that such a symbolic meaning of the goat was, in all likelihood, not in the mind of the Israelites when they offered it to the Lord, nor that a person who offered a goat was such a person.

New Testament implications

The NT assumes that true believers are those who have died to themselves. If one does not die spiritually in the above sense, he is still in the same position the offering of Lev. 3 attempted to overcome. In fact St Paul also assumed 'believers' still had egocentric selves when he said, 'So you also must *consider yourselves dead* to sin and alive to God in Christ Jesus' (Rom. 6:11 ESV; my emphasis). In this sense NT believers are essentially no different from the OT believer Lev. 3 envisages, though, at least, the former knew all about Jesus Christ in theory. As long as the worshipper is in such a condition, the meaning of the fellowship offering is also relevant for NT believers. In particular this chapter requires that the worshipper, being wholehearted, should willingly destroy his own selfishness and hidden parts of heart. It seems, however, that this is hard even for NT believers.

LEVITICUS 4:1 – 5:13

Translation

1The LORD spoke to Moses, saying, 2'Speak to the Israelites: When a soul hides himself inadvertently from all the commandments of the LORD which may not be broken, and does any one of them:

3'If an anointed priest hides himself, so that the people realize guilt, he is to bring a young bull without blemish for the self-hiding that he has committed as a sin offering to the LORD. 4He brings the bull to the entrance of the Tent of Meeting before the LORD, lays his hand on the bull's head and then slaughters the bull before the LORD. 5The anointed priest takes some of the bull's blood and brings it into the Tent of Meeting. 6The priest dips his finger in the blood and sprinkles some of the blood seven times before the LORD, towards the veil of the sanctuary. 7The priest puts some of the blood on the horns of the altar of fragrant incense before the LORD that is in the Tent of Meeting. The rest of the bull's blood he pours out at the base of the altar of the burnt offering that is at the entrance to the Tent of Meeting. 8He removes all the fat from the bull of the sin offering, the fat that covers the entrails and all the fat that is on the entrails, 9the two kidneys and the fat that is on them, at the loins, and the long lobe of the liver he removes with the kidneys, 10just as it is removed from a member of the herd for the offering of the fellowship offering. The priest burns them on the altar of the burnt offering. 11But the bull's hide and all its meat together with its head and its legs, and its entrails and its offal – 12all the rest of the bull he brings outside the camp to a clean place where the fat ashes are poured out and burns it on a wood fire; it is to be burned on the place of the fat ashes.

13'If the whole community of Israel go astray inadvertently and a matter be hidden from the assembly's eyes, and they break any one of the LORD's commandments that are not to be broken, and they realize guilt, 14when the self-hiding that they have committed becomes known, the assembly is to present a young bull for a

sin offering and bring it before the Tent of Meeting. [15]The elders of the
congregation lay their hands on the bull's head before the LORD, and the bull is to
be slaughtered before the LORD. [16]The anointed priest brings some of the bull's
blood into the Tent of Meeting. [17]The priest dips his finger into the blood and
sprinkles some of the blood seven times before the LORD, towards the veil. [18]Some
of the blood he puts on the horns of the altar that is before the LORD, which is in the
Tent of Meeting. The rest of the blood he pours out at the base of the altar of the
burnt offering that is at the entrance to the Tent of Meeting. [19]He removes all its fat
and burns it on the altar, [20]and does with this bull just as he did with the bull for the
sin offering. And the priest sacrifices himself for them, and they will be forgiven.
[21]Then he brings the bull outside the camp and burns it just as he burned the first
bull. It is a sin offering for the community.

[22]'If a tribal leader hides himself by breaking inadvertently any one of the
commandments of the LORD his God which may not be broken, and he realizes his
guilt, [23]or if he is made aware of the self-hiding that he has committed, he is to bring
as his offering a male goat without blemish. [24]He lays his hand on the goat's head
and slaughters it in the place where the burnt offering is slaughtered before the
LORD. It is a sin offering. [25]The priest takes some of the blood of the sin offering
with his finger and puts it on the horns of the altar of the burnt offering, and he
pours out the rest of the blood at the base of the altar of the burnt offering. [26]He
burns all its fat on the altar, like the fat of the fellowship offering. The priest
sacrifices himself for him because of his sin, and he will be forgiven.

[27]'If any soul of the common people hides himself inadvertently in breaking any of
the LORD's commandments, which are not to be broken, and he realizes guilt, [28]or if
he is made aware of the self-hiding that he has committed, he is to bring as his
offering a female goat without blemish for the self-hiding that he has committed.
[29]He lays his hand on the head of the sin offering and slaughters the sin offering in
the place of the burnt offering. [30]The priest takes some of its blood with his finger
and puts it on the horns of the altar of the burnt offering, and he pours out the rest of
the blood at the base of the altar. [31]He removes all its fat, just as the fat of the
fellowship offering is removed, and the priest burns it on the altar for a soothing
aroma to the LORD. The priest sacrifices himself for him, and he will be forgiven.

[32]'If he brings a lamb as his offering for a sin offering, he is to bring a female
without blemish. [33]He lays his hand on the head of the sin offering and slaughters it
in the place where one slaughters the burnt offering. [34]The priest takes some of the
blood of the sin offering with his finger and puts it on the horns of the altar of
the burnt offering and pours out the rest of the blood at the base of the altar. [35]He
removes all its fat, just as the fat of the lamb from a fellowship offering is removed,
and the priest burns it on the altar on top of the offering for annihilation to the
LORD. The priest sacrifices himself for him for the self-hiding that he has
committed, and he will be forgiven.

[5:1]'If a soul hides himself in that he hears a public oath, namely he has been a
witness, either that he has seen or that he has come to know the matter, yet he does
not make it known, he bears his guilt.

[2]'Or if a soul touches anything unclean, such as the corpse of an unclean animal, wild or domestic, or the corpse of an unclean creature that moves on the ground, and it is hidden from him, while he is unclean, and he realizes guilt.

[3]'Or if he touches any human uncleanness, any uncleanness by which one becomes unclean, and it is hidden from him, while he is conscious about it, and he realizes guilt.

[4]'Or if a soul swears rashly for a bad or good purpose, any sort of rash oath that a human swears, and it is hidden from him, while he is conscious about it, and he realizes guilt for any of these oaths.

[5]'Whenever one realizes guilt in any of these cases, he must confess that he has hidden himself, [6]and he is to bring as his reparation to the LORD for the self-hiding that he committed a female lamb from the flock or a goat for a sin offering, and the priest sacrifices himself for him because of his self-hiding.

[7]'If one cannot afford livestock, he is to bring to the LORD as his reparation for the self-hiding that he has committed two doves or two young pigeons, one for a sin offering and one for a burnt offering. [8]He is to bring them to the priest, and the priest is to offer first the one for the sin offering. He wrings its head from its neck without severing it. [9]He sprinkles some of the blood of the sin offering on the side of the altar, and the rest of the blood is drained out at the base of the altar. It is a sin offering. [10]He then makes a burnt offering of the second according to the regulation, and the priest sacrifices himself for him because of the self-hiding that he has committed, and he will be forgiven.

[11]'If one cannot afford two turtle doves or two young pigeons, he is to bring as his offering for his self-hiding one-tenth of an ephah of fine flour. He may not put oil on it, he may not put frankincense on it, because it is a sin offering. [12]He is to bring it to the priest, and the priest takes a handful as its token portion. He burns it on the altar upon offerings for annihilation to the LORD. It is a sin offering. [13]The priest sacrifices himself for him for the self-hiding that he has committed in any of these things, and he will be forgiven. It shall belong to the priest like the loyalty offering.'

Notes on the text

2. For the interpretation that *ḥāṭā'* means 'to hide oneself', see Kiuchi 2003a: 5–27. There is a problem with the translation of the preposition *min* that appears three times in this verse. Although the first *min* has been taken by almost all the Eng. translations as partitive, this is unlikely, as the phrase '*one* of all the commandments' etc. in v. 2a makes 'one of them' in v. 2b redundant. Nor can the first *min* be translated 'against' as *min* has no such meaning (see Milgrom 1991: 229). It is more natural to take the first and second *min* to mean 'from', and the meaning of *'āśâ* in v. 2b as intransitive (cf. Rendtorff 1990: 149; Kiuchi 2003a: 16–18). This means that the verb *ḥāṭā'* is conjoined with the preposition *min*, 'from'. Thus the meaning of v. 2a would be as proposed above, given that *ḥāṭā'* means to

'hide oneself' (see Introduction 7.2 and 'Comment' on 4:2 below). LXX adds *enanti kyriou* after *ḥāṭā'*.

'from all': *mikkōl* As in vv. 13, 22 and 5:17 *kōl* should be taken literally.

3. 'an anointed priest' See 'Comment'.

'so that the people realize guilt': *lĕ'ašmat hā'ām 'ašmâ* is a verbal noun of *'āšēm* and means 'realizing guilt', rather than 'being guilty', as has traditionally been understood. Equally important is the point that 'the people' are the agent of realizing guilt; i.e. subjective genitive.

LXX uses *peri tēs hamartias* both for the name of the offering and for the sin.

4. LXX adds *enanti kyriou* after *pār*.

5. SamP adds *'ăšer millē' 'et yādô* (who is ordained; cf. Exod. 29:29). So does LXX.

6. 'sprinkles' SamP adds '*b'ṣb'w*' (in his finger). Likewise LXX adds *tō daktylō*.

'towards': *'et pĕnê* Normally *hizzâ* (to sprinkle) is followed by *'al* (e.g. Exod. 29:21; Lev. 5:9; 6:27[20]; 16:15). Here, similar to Num. 19:4 (*'el nōkaḥ pĕnê*), the phrase appears to indicate the direction of sprinkling.

'the sanctuary': *haqqodeš* This term refers to the Tent (cf. 6:30[23]; 10:4, 18; 16:2–3, 16, 20, 23, 27).

8. 'which covers the entrails': *hamĕkasseh 'al haqqereb* SamP, TgJon and Syr read *'et* instead of *'al*, in line with 3:3, 9 and 14.

12. 'brings' – 'burns' Both verbs are sg. in MT, but pl. in SamP and LXX.

13. 'community': *'ēdâ 'ēdâ* and *qāhāl* are near synonyms (Carpenter 1997: 327), yet in this context, *'ēdâ* appears to mean 'community', while *qāhāl* signifies 'an assembly' (cf. vv. 14–15, 21; 8:3–4; 16:5, 17, 33).

'realize guilt' See 'Comment'.

14. 'becomes known': *nôdĕ'â* For the meaning of this term, see 'Comment'.

'a young bull': *par ben bāqār* SamP adds *tmym*; so does LXX, *amōmon*. This is the only case where *tāmîm* (without blemish) is missing in the MT of ch. 4.

15. 'is to be slaughtered': *šāḥaṭ* LXX reads this verb in the pl.

17. 'towards the veil' SamP and LXX read *haqqodeš* ([of] the sanctuary) after 'the veil', as in v. 6.

20. 'sacrifices himself for them' For the meaning of *kipper*, see 'Comment' on 1:4.

22. 'If' The Hebr. is *'ăšer*, yet structurally parallel to *'im* in vv. 3, 13, 27, and has a conditional sense (cf. *HALOT*).

23. 'or if' MT is simply *'ô*. For the possibility that *'ô* has the meaning of 'or if', see Exod. 21:36, and 'Comment' on 26:41. The same introduction of an alternative case is found in v. 28 below. Thus this is unlikely to present a textual problem. See 'Comment'.

24. 'slaughters' LXX reads it in the pl. But MT indicates that the offerer is the slaughterer. So in vv. 29 and 33 below.

27. 'any of the LORD's commandments'; lit. 'one of the commandments of the LORD'. SamP and LXX read 'one of *all* (*kol*)' etc., conforming it to vv. 2, 13, 22. However, if v. 2 is the summarizing statement, *kol* is not necessarily required.

35. 'its fat': *ḥelbāh* As *BHS* margin suggests, the lack of *mappiq* ought to be supplemented.

5:1a. 'either ... or ...': *'ô – 'ô* See 'Comment'.

2. The first *'ô* (or) gives an alternative to v. 1. The following three *'ô* give three examples for the general 'touching every unclean thing'.

'while – unclean': *wĕhû' ṭāmē'* Tg reads *wĕhû' yāda'*, harmonizing the clause with those in vv. 3–4.

For the syntactic structure of vv. 2–4, see 'Comment'.

4. 'any of these oaths' As *'aḥat mē'ēlleh* is repeated in v. 5a, most exegetes take this case as a dittography (e.g. Milgrom 1991: 300; Rendtorff 1992: 193–194). However, it is possible that 'these' (*'ēlleh*) refers to all the occasions on which one may swear rashly (cf. 6:7[5:26]).

5. 'Whenever – these cases' This part is missing in LXX and Tg perhaps because it is taken as *homoioteleuton*. However, *'aḥat mē'ēlleh* refers to the preceding four cases, and the phrase in v. 4 has a different referent from that in v. 5a.

SamP reads *yĕḥṭā'* instead of *yĕ'šam*. As Rendtorff (1990: 143) notes, it is not certain if it represents a deliberate change or if the two terms should be taken as conveying the same idea.

'confess that': *hitwaddâ 'ăšer* LXX and TgJon adds 'a sin' after 'confess'. Yet the substantival use of the relative pronoun makes such an addition unnecessary (cf. 5:16).

6. 'because of his self-hiding': SamP adds '*wkpr 'lyw hkhn 'l ḥṭ'tw 'šr ḥṭ' wnslḥ lw*', in conformity with 4:35b, 5:10b. This shorter formulation compared with vv. 10 and 13 may derive from the fact that the same formula has already appeared in 4:35.

7. 'livestock': *śeh* A collective noun for small livestock.

'his penalty': *'ăšāmô* LXX reads 'for his sin' (see on 4:3 above).

'et 'ăšāmô 'ăšer ḥāṭā' This phrase appears to be an abridged form of *'et 'ăšāmô laYHWH 'al ḥaṭṭātô 'ăšer ḥāṭā'* in v. 6.

11. 'as his offering for his sin': *'et qorbānô 'ăšer ḥāṭā'* For this construction, cf. 'as his reparation for the sin that he has committed' in v. 7 above.

'an ephah' This is a dry measure, but its exact mordern equivalent is uncertain. According to Powell (1992: 903), it varies between ten and twenty litres.

'put oil': *yāśîm šemen* SamP, LXX and Syr read *yiṣṣôq* (pour) as in 2:1.

12. 'its token portion': *'azkārātāh* Mappiq is missing in MT but should be added.

13. 'It shall – the offering' LXX apparently paraphrases MT and translates 'and the rest belongs to the priest like the loyalty offering'.

Form and structure

Lev. 4:1 – 5:13 deals with an offering called the *ḥaṭṭā't*, commonly translated 'a sin offering'. In ch. 4, four or five different rituals are presented according to the offerer's spiritual status before the Lord: the anointed priest (vv. 3–12), the whole community (vv. 13–21), a tribal leader (vv. 22–26) and an individual (vv. 27–35). On the whole, the main protasis is introduced by 'If a soul' (*nepeš kî*, v. 2ab) and is followed by subcases introduced by 'if' (*'im, wĕ'im, 'ăšer*, vv. 3, 13, 22, 27). 'If' in v. 32 is a subcase of vv. 27–31. The content is as follows:

1–2aa	The Lord's address to Moses
2ab	Main case
3–12	The sin of an anointed priest
13–21	The sin of the whole community
22–26	The sin of a tribal leader
27–35	The sin of an individual

The structure of ch. 4 is clear. The conditions anterior to bringing the sacrifice are part of an introductory statement in v. 2ab, which is repeated with variations in vv. 3, 13–14, 22–23, 27–28. As regards the ritual, the first two (those of an anointed priest and the whole community) are the same, while the latter two (those of a tribal leader and an individual) are *almost* the same, containing some stylistic variations. In the former two the blood is brought into the Tent and the remaining flesh is burnt outside the camp, whereas no mention is made of the remaining flesh in the latter two.

5:1–13 also belongs to the sin offering. Yet the structure is rather different from ch. 4. While the section begins with 'If a soul' (*nepeš kî*, v. 1), three cases follow, comprising the same prescription, yet introduced by *'ô nepeš* (v. 2), *'ô kî* (v. 3) and *'ô nepeš* (v. 4). These cases are followed by the direction to make confession (v. 5). The ritual is prescribed with the economical condition of the offerer in mind: a female sheep or a female goat (v. 6), two turtle doves or pigeons (vv. 7–10) and one-tenth of flour (vv. 11–13). In v. 6 the ritual in 4:27–35 is assumed, while reference is made to the ritual of the burnt offering (v. 10) and the loyalty offering (v. 11–12).

ḥaṭṭā't

The term *ḥaṭṭā't* is traditionally translated 'a sin offering'. However, this translation causes difficulties in integrating the sacrifice's twofold function in dealing with both 'ethical' sin and situations where no such sin is envisaged: the 'cultic' uncleanness regulations (e.g. 12:7–8; Num. 6).

Milgrom understands uncleanness as a quasi-material entity that threatens the holy sanctuary; it is the function of *ḥaṭṭā't* to cleanse it from such defilement. Hence his proposal 'the purification offering' (Milgrom 1991: 253–292). This view is commonly accepted in the study of this offering, though sometimes with much dissension regarding his other theories relating to the sacrifice (most recently Dennis 2002: 108–129). However, a survey of *ḥāṭā'* and *ḥaṭṭā't* has shown that the verb means to 'hide oneself' and that the noun means the state of hiding oneself (see Kiuchi 2003a). Despite the fact that the idea of purification is basic to the text, and that *ḥāṭā'* means to 'hide oneself', it is proposed that *ḥaṭṭā't* be translated as 'a sin offering', owing to the familiarity of the term 'sin', with an understanding that 'sin' means to hide oneself, unlike the traditional assumption that it is a heavily conduct-oriented term. However, 'self-hiding' and 'to hide oneself' are used in this commentary as explanatory terms.

Comment

4:1–2

1. This address marks a new beginning. Cf. 1:1. But the similar address does not necessarily delineate literary units of the same level. Cf. 6:1[5:20]; 6:19[12], 24[17].

2. *Nepeš* should be translated 'soul' as in 2:1, where it is the object of the last phase of the Lord's wrath. The presence of the egocentric nature was indicated by the fat's symbolic meaning in the previous chapter, and it is also to be destroyed at the end of the sin offering (vv. 8–10, 19, 26, 31, 35). Clearly self-hiding is an inevitable manifestation of the egocentric nature.

'hides himself': *ḥāṭā'* Péter-Contesse perceives that the Hebr. term here does not match the moral sense of sin. He says that it is rather a relational notion (1993: 75). That the term expresses something more than violation of certain of the Lord's prohibitions and thus has a comprehensive meaning is clear by the fact that it is conjoined with *min* (from), and the violation itself is mentioned in v. 2b (see 'Notes on the text'). While the verb may still appear to include violation of one prohibitive commandment, the case in 5:1–4 tells against it, as *ḥāṭā'* does not lie in violating any particular commandment (see 'Comment' there). As argued separately for *ḥāṭā'* and *ḥaṭṭā't* (Kiuchi 2003a) and mentioned in Introduction 7.2, *ḥāṭā'* means to 'hide oneself' and is not the conducted-oriented laden term 'sin'. In Lev. 4 – 5 this is particularly highlighted by its synonyms *šāgâ*, *šāgag* and the noun *šĕgāgâ*, the basic sense of these being to 'go astray inadvertently'. Like the root *šgh/šgg*, *ḥāṭā'* expresses an existential situation, and does not refer to the infringement of certain rules as such. Self-hiding in this chapter is inadvertent, which means he 'hides himself from the LORD without knowing'. His ignorance in this regard allows him to feel justified in his behaviour even though he is violating a particular prohibitive commandment. For convenience' sake the term 'sin' and 'sinner' are sometimes used in this commentary, although not in a conventional conduct-oriented sense, but in the sense stated above.

'inadvertently': *bišĕgāgâ* This phrase suggests there are other cases of *ḥāṭā'*. E.g. 5:1–4; 6:1–3[5:20–22]; 16:16. The case in Num. 15:30–31 is often called 'high-handed sin'. But note that *ḥāṭā'* is not used there.

'the commandments of the LORD': *miṣwôt YHWH Miṣwôt* includes both positive and negative commandments (cf. Lev. 26:15; 27:34; Num. 15:40). The negative ones are intended here. Though Knohl restricts the meaning of the phrase to cultic prohibitions (Knohl 1995: 138 n. 55; cf. Milgrom 1991: 21–26), it is a comprehensive phrase encompassing what is referred to by *ḥuqqîm* and *mišpāṭîm* (see Lev. 26:14 and Kiuchi 2003b: 7–10). Thus this verse reveals that the violation of *one* prohibitive commandment is deemed the same as violating *all* of the prohibitive commandments. Though this may strike one as NT-like (cf. James 2:10), this truth is expressed in the following corresponding verses in various ways (see vv. 13, 22, 27).

4:3–12

3–4. 'an anointed priest': *hakkôhēn hammāšîaḥ* Opinions are divided as to whether the phrase refers to the high priest or to the priests in general. It is questionable whether all the priests were anointed. Though some texts appear to refer only to the anointing of Aaron (Exod. 29:7; Lev. 8:12), most assume the anointing of all priests (Exod. 28:41; 29:29; 40:15; Lev. 7:36; 10:7; Num. 3:3). However, Exod. 29:7 and Lev. 8:12 must be considered in relation to Exod. 29:29 and Lev. 8:30 respectively. Thus probably all the priests were anointed (cf. Rendtorff 1990: 150–151; I hereby retract my former view in Kiuchi 1987: 166 n. 3). As regards the article *hē* in *hakkôhēn hammāšîaḥ*, it should not be taken as expressing definiteness but as 'denoting a single person or thing as being present in the mind under given circumstances' (*GKC* 126 q–r).

Inadvertent self-hiding committed by a priest involves the whole community. Until now in the history of interpretation *ḥāṭā'* has been taken as referring to specific conduct, which raised the question of whether this 'sin' was public or private in nature. But since *ḥāṭā* refers to his whole existence, this question becomes irrelevant. In the phrase 'so that the people realize guilt' (*lĕ'ašmat hā'ām*; see 'Notes on the text' and 'Comment' on v. 13 below) there is a correlation between the priest's self-hiding and the people's realizing the priest's guilt. The Lord providentially designed the spiritual matter so that the priest's 'sin' is parallel to the people's bearing the consequence of it. Thus the fact that no explicit mention is made of the priest's realizing guilt highlights the priest's heavy responsibility. The spiritual correlation is similar to that between a king and his people (cf. 2 Sam. 24). At any rate, it is assumed that the priest also realizes his own guilt, since it is he who offers the sacrifice.

Conformable to his great responsibility, his sacrificial animal must be most costly (cf. 8:2; 16:3, 6, 11): a young bull 'without blemish' (*tāmîm*). After bringing the young bull, the priest who has sinned lays his hand upon the head of the animal and slaughters it.

5–6. He brings the animal's blood to the Tent of Meeting, dips his finger in it and sprinkles it towards the *pārôket*, 'veil', seven times (cf. 14:16, 27, 51; 16:14, 19). Elsewhere blood is sprinkled towards the Tent (4:17; 16:14–15, 19; Num. 19:4), Aaron and his garments (Exod. 29:21; Lev. 8:30), the altar of burnt offering (5:9), and the house afflicted with a leprous disease (14:51). Oil is also sprinkled towards Aaron and his sons (8:30) and 'before the LORD' in conjunction with the healed leper (14:16, 27). In addition to the sprinkled blood symbolizing the cleansing of the objects upon which it is sprinkled (16:19), the act of sprinkling apparently attributed holiness to these objects. This is suggested by two considerations: (1) *Hizzâ* here is synonymous with *zāraq* in chs. 1 and 3, yet a practical difference between them is evident from the different prepositions they take; while *zāraq* is conjoined with *'al*, *hizzâ* is conjoined with *'el*, *'al pĕnē* and *lipnē*, in addition to *'al*. (2) The *zāraq* rite is always associated with the altar of burnt offering. By contrast, the *hizzâ* rite is predominantly related to the purification of the Tent (for 5:9, 14:16, 27, 51, see 'Comment' there). If not the Tent, it is associated with the *consecration* of its objects. Thus, although the *zāraq* and *hizzâ* rites both purify objects, the *hizzâ* rite's cleansing of the altar of the burnt offering is more potent than that of the *zāraq* rite. Thus the idea of 'purification' is not limited to the *ḥaṭṭā't* offering but is found in other animal sacrifices that contain such rites. This also lends support to our understanding of the *ḥaṭṭā't* offering as the sin offering. Consequently purification, though biblical, deals externally with the more significant deeper issue: existential self-hiding. The offering deals with this deeper issue through the giving of the animal's life, which takes the place of the offerer's life, symbolized by the blood sprinkling (*zāraq* and *hizzâ*).

The Pentateuch accounts for thirteen of the eighteen times the priest's finger is mentioned in the OT, all in connection with blood. The symbolic meaning of the finger is uncertain, but since it is one of the most sensitive parts of the body, and the priest represents the Lord, it may symbolize the Lord's creative or salvific power (cf. Exod. 8:19[15]; 31:18; Ps. 8:3[4]).

Since the cherubim are woven into the veil (Exod. 26:31; 36:35), the direction of the sprinkling is obviously towards the Holy of Holies. Sprinkling seven times and the allusion to the cherubim adumbrate the ritual on the Day of Atonement (Kiuchi 1987: 129; Rendtorff 1990: 160).

Thus this ritual is provisional in nature due to the fact that this is not the Day of Atonement.

7. 'Horn' occurs for the first time in relation to the sacrificial ritual. And it is noteworthy that the daubing of blood on to the altar's horns appears only in the ritual of the sin offering. It is generally assumed that the altar's four horns (Exod. 27:2) symbolize divine power or divine presence (cf. Ratschow 1978: 306; Kedar-Kopstein 1993: 186). However, the altar's dual role, representing both the divinity and the offerer, should be kept in mind. As mentioned (see 'Comment' on 1:5), the altar represents the offerer who stands before it. Thus, while the altar is holy and inaccessible to the offerer, it is more likely that the four horns represent human, not divine, power. The human power in view is that of the egocentric nature that must be destroyed to allow the person to live before the Lord. Since the worshipper cannot approach the altar as he is, the priest appeases the Lord's wrath by daubing the animal's blood on the altar.

As regards the daubing of blood, it probably symbolizes protection, just as the Israelites daubed blood on to the door at the time of the exodus to protect them from the destroyers (Exod. 12:23). Since 'four' in the 'four horns' may well symbolize all directions, the rite symbolizes the Lord's complete protection from evil powers.

The daubing of blood on the incense altar also symbolizes protection. The higher the responsibility towards God, the more serious the punishment for his sin becomes. However, it is incorrect to infer from this rite that defilement reached the Holy Place but not the Holy of Holies (see v. 6 above). The expedient nature of this ritual act is highlighted when compared with the ritual on the Day of Atonement in ch. 16 (see vv. 12–16), on which Aaron enters the Holy of Holies.

The term 'pour' (*šāpak*) is distinct from the term used in the prescriptions for the burnt offering and fellowship offering (*zāraq*; see 1:5; 3:2 etc.). The phrase *šāpak dām* (spill the blood, Gen. 9:6; 37:22) is used for murder. The association between the phrase and murder is found in Lev. 17:4, 13. The sinner's need of spiritual death seems to be conveyed by this particular way of formulation.

8–10. The fat, kidneys and lobe of the liver are treated as they were in the case of the fellowship offering (see 'Comment' on 3:3–4 and 4:2 above). This indicates why Lev. 4 follows Lev. 3; the former ritual is built upon the latter. The rite symbolizes that the worshipper's egocentric nature must be annihilated.

11–12. In this case for the priest's sin, however, all the remaining animal is burnt: its skin, flesh, head, legs, entrails and dung. In the burnt offering, no mention is made of the animal's skin: it is given to the priests (7:8). But here even the skin is burnt. As will be explained, this is because the priest who sinned is not entitled to the priestly dues; he cannot, and should not, benefit from his own sin (cf. 8:17; 9:11; 16:27).

All the remaining flesh is burnt (*śārap*) in a clean place outside the camp.

V. 12 indicates that the ash heap is a 'clean' place. Presumably an area was assigned for this purpose. Although 'clean' is probably used in a ritual sense, a symbolic meaning of 'clean' in the phrase 'in a clean place' possibly indicates that the agents of burning were to be inwardly clean (cf. 6:4; 10:14; Num. 19:9; see Introduction 7.4.2.c).

However, the burning of all the remaining flesh raises the question as to who or what the agent of purification was in the case of the priest. No-one is mentioned. That no reference to *kipper* (cf. vv. 20, 26, 31, 35) or forgiveness is made in vv. 12–13 suggests the priest is not forgiven. Although the anointed priest bears his own guilt, he is not forgiven, due to the fact that he broke one of the Lord's prohibitive commandments. The insufficiency of the ritual for the priest is suggested by his inability to enter the Holy of Holies to expiate his sin (see on vv. 5–6). Thus as a whole the ritual saved Israel only in a temporary sense.

4:13–21

13. The second case deals with a situation where the whole community goes astray inadvertently by breaking one of the Lord's prohibitive commandments.

The content of 'go astray inadvertently' (*šāgâ*) is explicated by two factors: (1) a certain matter (*dābār*) is hidden from the assembly, and (2) they transgressed one of the Lord's commandments. The concept of *ḥāṭā'* as well as *ḥaṭṭā't* is expressed by using the common term *šāgâ*. The latter expresses the community's going astray in an existential way, so they were unaware of this (cf. 1 Sam. 26:2; Isa. 28:7; Job 6:24). The subject of *ne'lam* (be hidden) is 'a matter'. Thus, although both *ne'lam* and *šāgâ* express what occurs in the community's unconsciousness, *šāgâ* is more comprehensive than *ne'lam*. This subtle difference is crucial in interpreting 5:2–4 below.

'realize guilt': *'āšēmû* The meaning of *'āšēm* has been debated in recent years. The traditional rendering is to 'be guilty'. However, this translation expresses an objective aspect of guilt, and cannot answer the question of when a person should offer an offering (see 4:22–23, 27–28; 5:2–5, 17; 6:4[5:23]; Num. 5:6). While Milgrom, duly noting the consequential meaning of the root *'šm*, proposed 'to feel guilt' (Milgrom 1976: 3–12), more recently, after re-examining previous renderings, Sklar proposed the rendering 'to suffer guilt's consequences' (2001: 22–38), partly drawing upon the use of the term in non-Levitical texts (Ps. 34:21[22]; Hos. 13:16[14:1] etc.). Indeed *'āšēm* must have accompanied either, or both, spiritual or physical suffering. In particular, the offender would become conscience-stricken upon realization of guilt. Yet in this context, the term does not appear to denote the accompanying suffering as the recognition of guilt, as the alternative cases in vv. 22–23 and vv. 27–28 suggest (for 4:3 see above). Moreover the text does not state how the offender comes to realize his guilt. The proposed rendering 'to realize guilt' seems suitable for this context in that it expresses both the objective and subjective sides of guilt.

14. 'and the sin becomes known' Since *'āšēm* presumes a knowledge of sin, *wāw* at the beginning must mean 'when' rather than 'or' or 'and'. 'Or' is expressed by *'ô* in vv. 23, 28. The realization of guilt is further explicated by 'becoming aware of sin'. *yd'* ni. suggests that the way of becoming aware is passive, which is natural because all the community has been going astray. But more importantly, since the meaning of *yāda'* is essentially experiential, *yd'* ni. means not just to 'become known', but the sin becomes a reality to the community.

The ritual for the entire community is the same as that for the priest, which indicates that thc priest's responsibility is equivalent to that of the whole community. It may also be surmised that since the priest plays the role of a mediator between the community and the Lord, he is deemed guilt-free. In this case the cause of the community's sin does not come from the priesthood, though it is the responsibility of the priests to teach the law to the people (10:10–11).

15–19. The elders of the community, as the latter's representatives, lay their hands on the head of the young bull, as in the first case (v. 4), and it is slaughtered. In the OT the elders (*zĕqēnîm*) are to be invested with wisdom, and are therefore responsible for spiritual matters (Exod. 3:16; 24:1, 9, 14; Lev. 19:32; Num. 11:16, 30 etc.). This time it is the officiating priest who mediates between the Lord and the community.

The prescription for the burning of fat (v. 19) is shorter here, since it is already detailed in vv. 9–10.

20. Unlike the case of the priest, mention is made of *kipper* and forgiveness (*nislaḥ*).

'sacrifices himself': *kipper* This is the second occurrence of *kipper* in Leviticus (see 'Comment' on 1:4). Here it means the priest's substitutional bearing of guilt in the context of the divine wrath. That the agent of *kipper* is the priest indicates he is free from the guilt of the sin in question.

'will be forgiven': *wĕnislaḥ* The reason for the passive form is questionable. As Sklar points out, the root is not always passive in the Priestly literature (see Num. 30:6, 9, 13) and, if qal were used, that might have implied that the priest was the one who had granted forgiveness (2001: 81–82). This question can be approached by observing that the 3rd person address is basic to Lev. 1 – 5, and that all these prescriptions presume the wrath of the Lord in varying decrees. Since sins have been committed in this chapter and the highest degree of the Lord's wrath is assumed, it is natural that the Lord is not presented as facing the offender directly; hence forgiveness is formulated indirectly. Evidently it is the Lord who grants forgiveness.

On the traditional understanding of 'sin', that it is almost the same as a violation of any of the Lord's commandments or, at most, a disruption of the divine–human relationship, many tend to see this forgiveness as that of such violations. But the meaning of *ḥāṭā'* suggests it concerns only the disruption of the divine–human relationship; to be granted forgiveness is not viewed as an alternative to whatever kind of penalty one may have to endure in this world.

21. The fact that the mention of *kipper* and forgiveness precedes directions concerning the burning of the sacrifice suggests the latter does not constitute part of the act of *kipper*.

4:22–26

22–23. The third case concerns the sin of a *nāśî'* (tribal leader, clan chief). A community consists of many tribal leaders (Exod. 34:31; Num. 1:16, 44; 2:3; 4:34 etc.).

Although the protasis is similar to those of vv. 2, 13, they all differ from each other in some respect. Here it is remarkable that his offence is against one of the negative commandments of the Lord *his* God; indeed the offence against one commandment is envisaged as a sin against *his* God.

Two ways of becoming aware of guilt are presented: either the leader 'realizes his guilt', or 'someone else informs him of guilt'. The use of the active form *hôda'* is deliberate in view of *nôdě'â* in v. 14. As in v. 13, *yāda'* is experiential, so the protasis means someone informs the leader of his guilt in such a way as to remind him of this particular reality concerning his lifestyle. Alternatively a person may become aware of his own self-hiding through some other means.

Although carrying relatively less responsibility than the elders or priests, the leader's sin remains more serious than that of a lay individual. This is reflected by the requirement that he offer a male goat without blemish. The value of the sacrificial animal is scaled according to the degree of a sinner's responsibility before the Lord.

24–25. After the offerer lays his hand on the head of the animal, the animal is slaughtered. The blood rite is far simpler than that for the priest and tribal leader. Unlike the two earlier rituals, the blood is daubed on the horns of the outer altar and the rest is poured on to the altar's base. For the rite's symbolic meaning, see 'Comment' on v. 7 above.

26. The formulation for the burning of the fat is much shorter than that for the case of the priest: whereas the verbs *rûm* (hiph.), *sûr* (hiph.) and *qṭr* (hiph.) are used in vv. 8, 10, 19, only the last is used in this case.

4:27–35

27. The fourth case deals with sin committed by ordinary Israelites. 'Any [lit. 'one'] soul' (*nepeš 'aḥat*) forms a phrase with 'from the people of the land' (*'am hā'āreṣ*). This use of 'one soul' is remarkable in that it forges a connection between v. 2 and the 'one (*'aḥat*) commandment' that follows, thereby emphasizing that through the violation of 'one commandment' 'one soul' hides itself from the Lord. In the OT the phrase *'am hā'āreṣ* (lit. 'the people of the land') can refer to different kinds of people, depending on the context ('the landed aristocracy' in Jer. 1:18, 'the populace, the mass' in Hag. 2:4, and 'the uneducated' in Acts 4:13; see Hartley 1992: 66). The question is whether 'the land' refers to a real land within the present context. Its usage in 20:2, 4 suggests the phrase refers to the common people, populace.

28. When the lay individual commits a sin inadvertently and only later realizes his guilt, or is made aware of it by someone else (see 'Comment' on vv. 14, 23 above), he is to bring a female goat to the priest. The ritual differs from the case of the tribal leader only in the sacrificial animal's gender: a female is less costly than a male. However, this first reference to a female animal in this chapter coincides with the assumption that women are included in the reference to 'one soul' (v. 27).

29–31. The remaining part of the ritual is the same as the ritual for the tribal leader.

'the head of the sin offering' The term *ḥaṭṭā't* refers not only to the 'hiding of oneself' but also to the animal that deals with this existential condition (cf. 'the head of the burnt offering' in 1: 4). The tangible animal and the (theological) meaning are united as one. As for the burning of fat, *sûr* (hiph., hoph.) and *qṭr* (hiph.) are used. It appears that the practical act of *sûr* (hiph., hoph.), and not the dedicatory overtones of *rûm*, are employed to stress the less solemn nature of the ritual. At the same time, the phrase 'a soothing aroma' occurs for the first time in this offering. It is self-evident that the soothing aroma is also present in the preceding rituals, but its explicit mention in this ritual indicates that, as with *'iššeh* in v. 35 below, the ritual for the lay individual is of a less serious nature than the preceding ones.

32–35. This section presents an alternative case for when a lay individual offers a sheep. The sheep must be a female without blemish. The ritual is the same as that for the female goat. Reference to 'the Lord's offering for annihilation' in v. 35 naturally evokes the 'soothing aroma' in v. 31, as these are often paired in chs. 1 – 3.

The phrase 'on top of the LORD's offering for annihilation' (*'al 'iššeh YHWH*, v. 35) is relatively rare (cf. 5:12). This phrase assumes that when this sacrifice is burnt, some other offerings have already been made, such as the burnt and/or fellowship offerings. This is unusual in that the sin offering is ordinarily offered first among a combination of offerings (e.g. ch. 9). The inexpensiveness of this animal, relative to the goat, seems to be compensated for by the smoke from other offerings such as the burnt and/or fellowship offerings.

5:1–6

Nepeš kî in v. 1, which parallels *nepeš kî* in 4:2, suggests a new set of prescriptions before the sin offering commences. One major exegetical issue in this section concerns which offering vv. 1–13 deal with, since *'āšām* (reparation offering) appears in vv. 6–7 along with *ḥaṭṭā't* (sin offering). Two points are noted. First, in 4:1 – 6:7[5:26] the frequency of the root *ḥṭ'* (*ḥāṭā'/ḥaṭṭā't*) diminishes, while that of the root *'šm* (*'āšēm/'āšām*) increases. Moreover this section (5:1–13) lies halfway between Lev. 4 and Lev. 5:13 – 6:7[5:26]. The latter of these clearly deals with the reparation offering, since it stresses the idea of reparation. Second, just as *ḥaṭṭā't* means both 'to hide oneself' and the name of the offering, so *'āšām* refers both to the act of 'reparation' and the reparation 'offering'. Thus, though the idea of reparation begins to surface in 5:6–7, this section (5:1–13) is a continuation of the prescriptions for the sin offering.

The four cases are variegated in content, yet are unified by their common purpose in dealing with the negative attitude of a sinner towards divine ordinances, expressed through either negligence or ignorance. They progress from the taking of such ordinances lightly or superficially to a person's direct violation of divine holiness. Nevertheless the nature of these offences is not as blatant as those made against the Lord in 5:14 – 6:7[5:26] below. More importantly, the offences in these cases lie not in the failure to perform a prescribed ritual or to fulfil an oath, but in the hiding of oneself.

1. 'a soul': *nepeš* See on v. 4 below. The kind of situation envisaged is debated. *'ālâ* is said to mean 'a public imprecation' (JPS), 'adjuration' (Levine 1989: 26), 'a public imprecation' (Milgrom 1991: 294). In so far as testifying to the truth is the general theme of this verse, *'ālâ* appears public in character. In this sense, a judicial court is a fitting scene for the situation. However, it should not be limited to that in view of Deut. 29:18 and Prov. 29:24.

'Ēd means 'witness': either one who has seen wrong done or heard about it from someone else. Therefore the following *'ô – 'ô* details what the witness has seen or come to know (see *HALOT* under *'ô*). However, since in this instance *yāda'* is a subcategory of *'ēd*, which is experiential, the former means not knowing by the mind, but by the senses – it is an experiential knowledge.

If an oath or curse is proclaimed in defence of the truth, and the witness keeps silent, he is held guilty. Thus the first case deals with a particular case of the willful breaking of the Ninth Commandment through silence (cf. the case in 6:1–5[5:20–24]). Special attention should be paid to the fact that *'ālâ*, often synonymous with *bĕrît*, implies that the judicial setting assumes the involvement of the deity (cf. Gen. 26:28; Num. 5:21; Deut. 29:13).

It is easily assumed that if this takes place, the curse contained in the proclamation must befall the witness. However, *nāśā' 'ăwônô*, which is translated 'bear the responsibility of guilt/bear guilt', refers to the guilt consequent upon not testifying to the truth, which is different from the guilt related to *'ālâ*. Thus the offender faces a double penalty, and it is his guilt consequent upon withholding testimony that the priest deals with via this sacrifice.

While this offence apparently comes close to being a criminal case (cf. Porter 1976: 41; Péter-Contesse 1993: 86), contra the common view, the same must be true of the cases in ch. 4, since the latter are classified under the phrase 'all the prohibitive commandments' (4:2). It is one thing to be judged in a human court but quite another to be judged in the divine court, and it is self-hiding on which the present text focuses.

The reference to 'bearing guilt' in this particular case does not mean that in the rest of the cases, in vv. 2–4 and in Lev. 4, the sinners need not bear their guilt. Rather it is explicitly mentioned here possibly to indicate the objective aspect of the offenders' bearing of guilt.

2. The second case concerns a person who touches something that makes him unclean, but the crux lies in how the following two clauses, 'it is hidden from him' (*ne'lam mimmennû*) and 'while he is unclean' (*wĕhû' ṭāmē'*), stand in relation to the phrase 'touching the unclean'. It is assumed that the person is somehow aware of it, since he later realizes his guilt. It is often assumed that the clause *ne'lam mimmennû* refers to a subsequent situation in the person's consciousness. However, the next two verses exhibit the same syntactic structure, and in view of Num. 5:13 the clause should be taken as referring to a situation concurrent with touching the unclean thing. In this case the other clause *wĕhû' ṭāmē'* is also concurrent with the touching, since the unclean state begins from the moment of contact. The situation is different from 4:13, where a certain matter is hidden from the assembly. In the latter the cause of going astray is not known, whereas in 5:2–4 it is known subconsciously (v. 2) or consciously (vv. 3–4).

This passage presupposes various cleanness and uncleanness regulations in Lev. 11 – 15. While it is commonly assumed that the sin lies in the person's failure to perform a proper purificatory ritual (e.g. 'the prolonged period of uncleanness because of one's forgetfulness or negligence' [Milgrom 1991: 298]), this is not mentioned in the text. Rather the sin lies in the fact that he hides himself from the Lord by not being clearly aware of what is unclean. Note the contrast drawn between 'unclean' and *ne'lam mimmennû*, which is repeated four times.

In so far as the person realizes his guilt, he can remember his act: his touching the unclean thing is stored in his memory (see 'Comment' on 4:14).

3. The third case exhibits the same syntactic structure as v. 2, and deals with defilement caused by human uncleanness. In line with the syntactical structure of v. 2, the clause 'while he knows (it)' (*wĕhû' yāda'*) refers to the incident of touching. Thus a conscious act is in view. Nevertheless the verb *yāda'* in Lev. 4 – 5 means to 'be conscious about', and it does not follow that since he *knew* about his act, he deliberately touched the unclean thing (see 'Comment' on 5:17). For the question of what constitutes a sin, the same answer given in v. 2 may apply here.

4. The fourth case concerns a rash oath.

'utter light-mindedly': *biṭṭē' biśĕpātayim* This act itself implies that the person does not take what he swore by invoking the name of the Lord seriously (*šb'* ni.). Thus this violation is of a flippant, rather than a deliberate or unwitting, nature.

Lĕhāra' 'ô lĕhēṭēb should be rendered 'for a bad or a good purpose' as in NRSV, and not 'to do good or to do evil'. A study of *hēṭîb* (Kiuchi 2001b: 16–17) shows that in such a case as this, where no object is indicated, it is likely to be an internal hiph. (to do good / to be good-hearted to oneself). The phrase has no ethical overtones. It concerns the nature of an oath's consequence (cf. Ps. 15:4), particularly 'evil' in connection with swearing as a means of calamity; e.g. if such and such will not take place, such and such a calamity may befall me! Moses' offence at Meribah is also described by the phrase *biṭṭē' biśĕpātayim* (Ps. 106:33), but it had the nature of *mā'al* (Deut. 32:51). Since the present case is not described as *mā'al*, something deeper in one's heart than a simple light-minded oath is integral to the nature of the offence.

wĕhû' yāda' As in v. 3 this is concurrent with the swearing of the oath. Swearing by using the divine name is evidently a conscious act.

Is there a reason for why both *nepeš* and *hā'ādām* are used in this protasis? *Nepeš* is used in vv. 1–2 as well. In Leviticus, *'ādām* prefixed by the article appears in 5:4, 6:3[5:22], 18:5 and 27:29. These passages show that *hā'ādām* means humanity, a man with corporeal aspects, more general than *'ādām* alone. *Nišba'* is always related to *nepeš*, not to *'ādām* (cf. Lev. 5:4; 6:2–3[5:21–22]; Jer. 51:14). In Lev. 4 – 5, *nepeš* is always related to *ḥāṭā'*. Thus it appears that while *nepeš* means 'soul', referring to the spiritual aspect of the human, *'ādām* means 'a man', referring to the corporeal aspect of the human. One may argue that in v. 2 the spiritual aspect of *nepeš* is in error, since a *nepeš* understood in this sense cannot touch the unclean thing. However, this argument rests on the mistaken assumption that the touching of the unclean thing is only a physical act. Unclean things symbolize spiritual matters, and the lawgiver says it is one's *nepeš* (soul) that touches the spiritual matter which is alien to the Lord (see Introduction 7.1.3 and 7.2). Further cf. the oath formula *ḥēy napšĕkā* (1 Sam. 1:26; 20:3; 25:26; 2 Sam. 4:9).

The fourth case concerns any kind of rash oath that, while hidden from a person, remains in a person's subconscious and only later comes to his awareness. All oaths involved the divinity in ancient Israel, even when the divine name was not explicitly stated. Thus the case specifically refers to an infringement of the Third Commandment. The sin consists in taking lightly what God is directly involved in.

5. On 'one of these' (*'aḥat mē'elleh*), see 'Note on the text' on vv. 4 and 5.

It is unlikely that the confession of sin (*hitwaddâ*) is restricted to the cases enumerated above. Rather it presumably occurred, in practice, for the four cases in Lev. 4 as well (cf. 16:21; 26:40; Num. 5:7). The verbal nature of the confession befits the fact that the four offences involve the blurring of the divine and common/unclean realms. At any rate, any outward act of redressing the offence is not mentioned in the apodosis.

6. As in 4:27–35 he is to bring either a female lamb or goat.

'his reparation': *'ăšāmô*. *'Āšām*, in the sense of 'reparation', appears here for the first time in Lev. 4 – 6:7[5:26]. It is not the name for the offering. Thus the female lamb or goat is deemed as reparation for the person's hiding of himself. The ritual is the same as in 4:33–35 and 4:28b–31a. The lamb and goat are referred to in the reverse order of that given in 4:28b and 4:32 and this takes the reader's attention back to that prescription.

5:7–13

The special feature of this offering is its adjustability to the sinner's economic status. This allowance implies that the Lord regarded the offences of vv. 1–4 as less serious than those of ch. 4. The first option is to bring either two turtle doves or pigeons, one for a sin offering and the other for a burnt offering. The bringing of a burnt offering is not so strange, considering that the phrase 'a soothing aroma', an essential element of the burnt offering, has already appeared in 4:31. The present ritual can accommodate the burnt and loyalty offerings, not only because the material of those offerings (birds and flour) is allowed for economic reasons, but also because the Lord regards these offences as less serious than those of ch. 4. In chs. 1 and 2 these offerings symbolized appeasement and self-rededication respectively. However, in the present context their symbolic meanings become a requirement for gaining the Lord's forgiveness. The reference to the burnt and loyalty offerings literarily rounds out the section 1:1 – 5:12 (see Introduction 4.1).

7–9. The wringing off of its head is the same as in the bird burnt offering (1:15), but the sprinkling (*hizzâ*) of the blood on the altar's wall is unique to the sin offering. The small volume of blood is not the reason for the rite, since the priest, *with his finger*, daubs a small amount of blood on the horns of the altar in 4:30, 34. The clue lies in sprinkling blood on the side of the altar, and not on the horns, as occurred in the rituals of ch. 4. In view of the symbolic meaning of the horns (see 'Comment' on 4:7 above), the penalty for self-hiding is deemed less serious. Yet equally importantly, the sprinkling (*hizzâ*) suggests a potent means of purification (see 'Comment' on 4:5–6). Thus the less expensive offering of the poorer offerer is made up for by the symbolic significance of the *hizzâ* rite.

While in the bird burnt offering *lō' yabdîl* (it shall not be severed) is mentioned in connection with the bird's wing (1:17), here it is mentioned in connection with its head. The prohibition against completely severing the wings (1:17) and head (5:8) from the whole bird appears to stress their symbolic meanings in the respective rituals. Perhaps this directive derives not from the smallness of size, but from the fact that the head represents the offerer as *pars pro toto*.

10. 'according to the regulation': *kammišpaṭ* It refers to the prescription in 1:15–17. Since one of the emphases of the bird burnt offering lies in its unsevered wings that symbolize the foresaking of this world (see 'Comment' on 1:17), the ritual of the two birds, despite their smallness, achieves what is required in ruminants.

11–13. A second allowance is made for those who cannot even afford birds. In this case a sinner could bring 'one-tenth of an ephah of choice flour' for a sin offering. The ritual is similar to that of the loyalty offering, except for the significant rule that oil and frankincense are not to be included, since they are otherwise used to express God's presence positively. The serious nature of the present case precludes oil and frankincense (cf. Num. 5:15). The core aspect of the loyalty offering (allegiance to the Lord) is used yet again, as in 4:35 with the help of the smoke of the other offerings.

The phrase in v. 13 'one of these' (*'aḥat mē'elléh*) refers back to vv. 1–4, and hints at the unity of vv. 1–13. While this offering is a sin offering, it can be handled as a loyalty offering, in which case the remaining part belongs to the priest.

Explanation

Lev. 4:1 – 5:13 deals with various cases where a person commits a *ḥaṭṭā't*, commonly translated 'sin', and offers a *ḥaṭṭā't* offering. As noted in 'Comment', and argued separately (Kiuchi 2003a), these terms lexically mean 'to hide oneself' and 'hiding oneself', and have existential, rather than 'cultic' or 'ethical', conduct in view. Put simply, sin is a matter of the human heart. Furthermore this finding is not limited to this short literary unit, but is applicable to nearly all the occurrences of these terms in the OT. In Lev. 4 – 5 in particular, the idea of hiding oneself provides a key to understanding the two different offerings, *ḥaṭṭā't* and *'āšām*, and the principles enunciated in these offerings can apply to NT believers. Some of the primary aspects of the offering and the ritual are summarized below.

Occasions and the nature of self-hiding

In Lev. 4 – 5 the agent of *ḥāṭā'* is a *nepeš*. However, this *nepeš* is not a *living nepeš* but a soul that has a propensity for violating divine prohibitions. The *nepeš* that hides itself is a doomed *nepeš*, the object of the Lord's wrath (see 'Comment' on 1:2 and 2:1). This alone attests to the fact that the prescription in this chapter deals with one's *spiritual* and *eternal* relationship with the Lord. This self-hiding occurs when one breaks one of the Lord's prohibitive commandments. The sinner is not aware of his self-hiding in this chapter, because, as narrated in Gen. 3, the divine prohibition in question is ignored once the sinner is overwhelmed by covetous desire. In such a situation the sinner can even assume his conduct was justified. Thus 'inadvertently' is not an extenuatory term. Therefore the sinner unconsciously exerts his will in hiding himself against the Lord, remaining unaware of both his hiding and the violation itself.

The root of self-hiding is the presence of an egocentric nature that the loyalty and fellowship offerings deal with. The latter alone indicate self-hiding, though 4:1 – 5:13 deals with self-hiding occasioned by violation of one divine commandment.

In Lev. 5:1–4 self-hiding is not inadvertent, since the person is, however vaguely, aware of his initial act. In this sense, it is less hypocritical. It must not be overlooked that even in this vague situation he has exerted his will to hide himself from the Lord.

Apparently the sins of 5:1–4 are more serious than those in ch. 4 in that the former deal with a more direct infringement of the Lord's holiness. However, as will become clear from a comparison of these cases with the cases of the reparation offering, it is the self-hiding the Lord abhors, and the higher the degree of hiding, the more abhorrent it becomes. This is correlated with intensification of the associated punishment (see 'Explanation' on 5:13–26). Consequently the appearance of 'reparation' (*'āšām*) in 5:6–7 is natural; this reflects his greater awareness of his initial act than the case in Lev. 4.

Consequence of self-hiding and recognition of guilt

Self-hiding inevitably has its consequence. However, in the traditional understanding of sin its punishment consists of suffering in various senses due to a particular violation itself. This is not incorrect on the whole: there are natural and legal consequences associated with such violations. But in that sin means existential self-hiding, its punishment is more severe than previously assumed. For when *ḥāṭā'* means to 'hide oneself' and *nepeš* means 'soul', the punishment becomes eternal, though the latter concept is unclearly expressed in the present text. Moreover it should be stressed that the guilt (*'āwōn*) accompanying self-hiding is not associated with the violation of a particular prohibition itself. Thus the consequence of self-hiding must be assumed as having two sides: that administered by both human and divine courts. Certainly, although a person may realize his guilt by suffering, this particular section focuses on the self-hiding itself, rather than on the suffering that may accompany it.

As 4:2 shows, the prohibitive commandments of the Lord include all kinds of prohibitions ranging from sabbath observance (Exod. 16:28) to the Ten Commandments (Exod. 20) to the covenant as a whole (Exod. 24:12; Lev. 26:15). It is one thing to be punished by a human court for particular offences, but quite another to be forgiven by the Lord for self-hiding (cf. 2 Sam. 12:13; Luke 23:39–43). This situation becomes acute when the commandments in ch. 18 onwards come into play.

Indeed one should realize how difficult it is for a person to realize his own guilt when his whole existence is hidden from the Lord. Since his whole way of thinking is darkened, he has no way of realizing his own guilt, a situation compounded when it is maintained that his own conduct is justified. A possible human means of realizing one's own guilt is through the comments made by other people. But even this means of realizing guilt may be thwarted by one's self-justification of what one has done. Indeed if a man is informed of his self-hiding, as in the cases of the tribal leader and the individual, what is the normal reaction? Does he admit it? Human experience shows that such a person is rare – all the more so when the self-hiding in question is that of the human lifestyle. Thus these prescriptions assume a human who honestly admits his own faults, and follows the Lord's prescription. The qualification of the sacrificial animal as being 'without blemish' indicates that he has such a heart, a heart that unreservedly admits fault. In my view, such a man rarely appears in the OT, although Noah, Abraham, David, Job and Daniel are exceptions. In other words, the prescription simply presents the Lord's standard, but it is feasible only when a man has such a heart.

This does not appear to correspond to what has been commonly called 'repentance'. Until now repentance from sin has been taken as repentance from the wrong act or conduct. By itself this is venerable, but the lawgiver questions his total way of life that has surfaced in a particular kind of misconduct, albeit so-called cultic or ethical.

Ritual types

Typologically there are two kinds of ritual in this chapter, some details of which must be supplemented from elsewhere. First, there is a ritual for the priest and the whole congregation, where the blood is to be taken into the Holy Place and the remaining flesh is burnt outside the camp. Second, there is the ritual where the blood is daubed on the altar of burnt offering and the flesh is consumed by the priest (6:26[19]). For the relationship with another type in chs. 8 – 9, see 'Comment' on 8:14–17.

There is an imbalance between the first two rituals and the latter two regarding the handling of the remaining flesh: while in the former it is burnt outside the camp, in the latter it goes to the officiating priest and his family. But the latter is not mentioned at all. This is probably not because it will be addressed in ch. 6, but because the sin offering is, along with the fellowship and reparation offerings, regarded as of less sanctity than the burnt and loyalty offerings (see 'Comment' on 2:3).

Specific symbolism of the ritual

The four types of ritual are common in their depiction of the priest's blood manipulation and burning of fat. The blood (read 'life') sacrifices itself for the *nepeš* of a sinner (Lev. 17:11). It has been assumed that the blood expiates his sin. But this postulate should be radically reformulated; for in this the term 'sin' is commonly understood as a violation, while it actually means to 'hide oneself' in an existential sense. Also, by expiation exegetes have understood that the animal blood as life takes the place of the sinner's condemned life. Yet the life dealt with by the ritual is life before God, and not physical life. It seems that by offering the animal *nepeš*, which symbolizes '(spiritual) life', the condemned human *nepeš* (soul) is made alive (see 'Comment' on 17:11).

The function of the sin offering has been taken as decontaminating the defiled sancta like a detergent (Milgrom 1991: 253–292). The Hebr. verb *ḥiṭṭē'* (e.g. Exod. 29:36; Lev. 6:26[19]; 8:15; 9:15; 14:49, 52) appears to describe the role of the blood of the sin offering. However, an examination of this term shows that in keeping with the meaning of *ḥāṭā'* (to hide oneself) it means to 'uncover', or 'make something uncovered' rather than 'purge' or 'decontaminate' (Kiuchi 2003a: 107–118). By laying a hand on the animal the sinner identifies himself with the animal. Then the animal blood as life, representing the sinner's life, functions to *uncover* the sinner's condemned soul before the Lord. This is the very meaning of *ḥiṭṭē'*, which leads to the process expressed by *kipper*. Next comes the burning of fat. Its symbolic meaning is stated in relation to the fellowship offering: annihilation of the egocentric nature, by which a person forfeits his relationship with the Lord. Then comes the mention of the *kipper* act by the priest, which summarizes the total effect of his work. The priest sacrifices himself (*kipper*) by bearing the guilt of the worshipper in order to appease the wrath of the Lord against him.

However, there is a fundamental flaw in this system of atonement. First, the priest himself may hide himself from the Lord. Second, he cannot enter the Holy of Holies even though this need is expressed in the ritual. Third, in the first ritual for the sin of the priest, he cannot bear his own guilt. No mention is made of *kipper* or forgiveness. Clearly these factors point to the ritual of the Day of Atonement. This is not to say that the rituals in Lev. 4 are inefficacious; these are efficacious to some extent but the same sins must be dealt with on another dimension (see further

'Comment' in ch. 16 and Kiuchi 1987: 125–126). Thus in line with this, it is likely that the burning of flesh outside the camp adumbrates the Azazel goat ritual in ch. 16. Furthermore the fact that the Day of Atonement ritual deals with 'the uncleanness of the Israelites and their rebellions, all their sins' (16:16) shows that the sins committed in ch. 4 are to be viewed from another perspective again. At any rate, in so far as the priest is invariably deficient in inner holiness, the ritual itself points to a fuller system. Thus it could be concluded that the rituals in Lev. 4 are meant to be performed on ordinary situations and are temporary in nature, while the one in Lev. 16 is definitive.

Forgiveness

After the priest's appeasement of the Lord's wrath, the sinner is granted the Lord's forgiveness (for the priest's case, see 'Comment' on vv. 11–12). Forgiveness relates to his hiding himself from the Lord, and not his violation of specific conduct-oriented commandments, though the self-hiding began through them. It is important to note that this text mentions no remedy for his wrong. That the Lord forgives means that he forgets everything about the act of self-hiding.

Forgiveness is given when the priest completes the atoning work for a sinner. This means that a man's realization of his guilt and repentance is a prerequisite for bringing a sacrifice to the Lord, but cannot replace the ritual itself. The atonement ritual is absolutely necessary for the forgiveness of sin. In other words, while sin has its consequences, among which physical and spiritual suffering are included, human suffering cannot by itself atone for sin. This is self-evident once sin is defined as sin against God. However, the point is significant in that sin often lies in offending other people and one tends to think that compensation or reconciliation between humans is sufficient. However, the text reads otherwise. Priests, sacrifices and the sanctuary are all divinely instituted and termed 'holy'. Only through divine means can one be granted forgiveness.

Four kinds of sinners

The four kinds of sinners in 4:1 – 5:13 are classified from the viewpoint of the spiritual responsibility they bear before the Lord. The overall message is clear: the more responsibility one's status carries before the Lord, the greater the punishment. The closer to God a man is, the more costly an animal he must prepare and the further into the Tent the blood must be taken. And yet this reason is not exhaustive. When this is compared with the three cases of the reparation offering (5:14 – 6:7[5:26]), where no such differentiation is made, an important additional reason seems to exist;

since self-hiding is the theme of 4:1 – 5:13, it is the lawgiver's concern to expose the real situation of the soul before the Lord – he ought to reveal even his status, such as being a priest or a tribal leader.

In the ritual of 5:6–13, allowance is made in regard to the sinner's economic situation. A most plausible reason, therefore for the economic differentiation would be that he ought to expose even his economic situation, since he has hidden himself. For humanity, which always tends to hide itself, the provision of these options is both gracious and scrutinizing. This can be further qualified as follows. In the case of the self-hiding of a lay individual in Lev. 4:27–35, two options are provided for the animal he ought to prepare, whereas in 5:6–13 three options according to one's economic status are given. The former is more stringent in that the prescription does not consider the economic situation of a sinner. Thus the more lenient rule in 5:5–13 suggests that these cases are lenient in that the sinner does not hide himself as brazenly as the sinner does in Lev. 4. Clearly the principle at work is that the more he exposes himself, the lesser the penalty he bears before God. The degrees of self-hiding are the criterion for classifying the cases for the sin offering, and the ritual, particularly the kinds of animal. This reflects the Lord's mind, which is unlike human standards, where consciousness or deliberateness makes the offence heavier. Indeed the cases in 5:1–4 appear more 'sinful' than the inadvertent cases in Lev. 4, but the Lord is more offended by the sinner in Lev. 4 than in 5:1–4, and these are reflected in the prescriptions for the offering in vv. 6–13.

Last, but not least, the very order of the cases, namely an anointed priest, the whole assembly, a leader and then a lay individual, indicates that the heavy representative responsibility of the priests is already underscored in this early part of Leviticus (L. Trevaskis, personal communication). This is natural, since all the expiatory work hinges on the guiltlessness of the priests. Yet this last requirement certainly deepens the scepticism surrounding whether expiation was really made by the priests in a true sense.

New Testament implications

Lev. 4:1–13 has some significant implications, but only the idea of 'self-hiding' needs to be addressed in relation to the traditional understanding of sin.

While the application of the Law to the gaining of righteousness ended with the resurrection of Christ (Rom. 10:4), self-hiding remained inherent in people after this time. Yet while sin is intricately bound up with the Law in the OT, it appears to be taken up in the NT more in reference to a human's inner self. Thus Pharisaic hypocrisy is a manifestation of what is meant by self-hiding, even though the term 'sin' is rarely mentioned (cf. e.g Luke 7:47; John 15:22). Though there are degrees of self-hiding, it refers, for example, to the inner condition of those who crucified Jesus (Luke 23:34), or of St Paul when he persecuted the Lord's church (1 Tim. 1:13; note the 'ignorantly') etc., where a 'firm belief' is nothing but stubbornness without knowing one's own real state before God, just as in Lev. 4:1 – 5:13 (for a survey of the OT occurrence of *ḥāṭā'* and *ḥaṭṭā't*, see Kiuchi 2003a: 51–84).

It is for this human self-hiding that Jesus Christ died on the cross, becoming *hamartia* (2 Cor. 5:21, 'self-hiding' or 'a sin offering'; Rom. 6:10; Heb. 7:27). Yet it is equally true that Christ died on the cross because of the human egocentric nature. This presumes that all humans hide themselves before God and are doomed to experience eternal damnation, so that the only hope for all humanity is to believe in him. But faith is not as easy as one might have thought, once it is recognized that it is not the same as understanding and accepting a set of doctrines. Rather faith is the condition of a human heart whose egocentricity is annihilated (cf. Cranfield 1975: 371ff.). Since this rarely takes place, humanity constantly tends to modify the Law into a humanly made set of rules, pretending that a person can be accepted by God through showing his or her attitude or eagerness to observe 'the Law' as much as possible (cf. Rom. 9:31–32). However, to have faith in Christ in the true sense means to experience the destruction of one's egocentric nature, just as St Paul did (Gal. 2:20; Rom. 7:7–24). Consequently the idea of purity or purification lies not in the observance of the commandments as much as possible, but in the uncovering of oneself and exposing one's shameful inner self before the Lord. This certainly requires courage. Yet this is the meaning of bearing one's cross (see 'Explanation' on chs. 13, 15). This principle does not change throughout the life of a believer. When undergoing sanctification, a person becomes increasingly able to uncover his innermost self to the Lord, or other people, if necessary (1 John 1:6–7).

LEVITICUS 5:14 – 6:7[5:26]

Translation

14The LORD spoke to Moses, saying, 15'When a soul commits a trespass in hiding itself inadvertently from the holy things of the LORD, he is to bring, as his reparation to the LORD, a ram without blemish from the flock, valued in silver by the sanctuary shekel; it is a reparation offering. 16And he is to make restitution for what he hid himself from the holy thing, and add one-fifth to it and give it to the priest. The priest sacrifices himself on his behalf with the ram of the reparation offering, and he will be forgiven.

17'If a soul hides himself by breaking any of the LORD's commandments, which are not to be broken, while he does not know it, and realizes guilt, he shall bear his guilt. 18He is to bring to the priest a ram without blemish from the flock as valued, as a reparation offering; and the priest sacrifices himself on his behalf for the error that he committed inadvertently and did not know, and he will be forgiven. 19It is a reparation offering: he has indeed incurred guilt to the LORD.'

6:1[5:20]The LORD spoke to Moses, saying, 2[21]'When a soul hides himself in committing a breach of faith against the LORD by deceiving a fellow in a matter of a deposit or a pledge, or by robbery, or if he has defrauded a fellow, 3[22]or has found something lost and lied about it – if he swears falsely in any of all the things that a man does, and hides himself thereby – 4[23]when he has hidden himself and realizes his guilt, and restores what he took by robbery or by fraud or the deposit that was committed to him, or the lost thing that he found, 5[24]or anything else about which he has sworn falsely, he shall repay the principal amount and shall add one-fifth to it. He shall pay it to its owner when he realizes his guilt. 6[25]And he shall bring to the priest, as his reparation offering to the LORD, a ram without blemish from the flock as valued, for a reparation offering. 7[26]The priest sacrifices himself on his behalf before the LORD, and he will be forgiven for any of the things that one may do and realize guilt thereby.'

Notes on the text

15. 'valued': *'erkĕkā* This expression is archaic in that the pronominal suffix has lost its force, and came to mean simply 'valuation' or 'valued'. (See Speiser 1960: 29–45.) See further 'Comment'.

17. 'If a soul': *wĕ'im nepeš kî* LXX reads *kai hē psychē hē an*. Yet this rendering is found also for *'ô nepeš kî* in 5:4 (cf. LXX in 7:21). This beginning has duly been felt to be anomalous, as it is found nowhere else. So proposals have been made either to delete *'im* or to take the beginning as a whole as a conflation. However, the beginnings of the four cases in 5:1–4 suggest that *nepeš kî* is not necessarily a stereotyped phrase introducing a main case (see further 'Comment').

19. In LXX 'It is a reparation offering' is missing.

6:5[5:24]. In LXX 'or' is missing.

'anything else': *mikkol* SamP, LXX, Syr and TgJon add *'dābār'* (thing).

'one-fifth of it': *ḥamiššîtāyw'* Many Hebr. MSS, as well as SamP and TgJon, read *ḥamiššîtô*, as in v. 16.

6[5:25]. 'to the priest' SamP and LXX lack it.

Form and structure

This section deals with three cases: first, the inadvertent misappropriation of the holy offering (14–16), second, the serious case during a person's inadvertent breaking of one of the divine prohibitive commandments and not knowing about it (17–19), and third, a breach of faith in the form of false witness regarding a past transgression (20–26). Thus this offering is considered different to the one in 4:1 – 5:13, and is commonly referred to as 'the guilt offering' or 'the reparation offering' (see below). The three cases begin with *nepeš kî* (when a soul, v. 15), *wĕim nepeš kî* (and if a soul, v. 17) and *nepeš kî* (when a soul, 6:2[5:21]).

This section is closely related to the section of the sin offering in that it too deals with *ḥāṭā'* (to hide oneself). Yet the offering remains distinguishable from that of 4:1 – 5:13 by its description as an *'āšām* (5:15, 18; 6:6[5:25]). As opposed to *'āšēm* (realize guilt), *'āšām* occurs five times from 5:6 (see 'Comment' there). In addition to this, the form *'āšam* appears in 5:19.

When considered as a unit, 4:1 – 6:7[5:26] displays a clear intention on the part of the legislator to associate the root *ḥṭ'* more with the sin offering, and the root *'šm* with the reparation offering. Thus while the verb *ḥāṭā'* appears in all the cases covered in this section, the noun *ḥaṭṭā't*, meaning 'the state of hiding oneself', does not appear after 5:13. In particular, in Lev. 5:17–19, though *ḥāṭā'* appears, the nature of the offence is described by the roots *šgg* and *'šm*. By contrast, even though the verb *'āšēm* occurs in all the cases of 4:1 – 6:7[5:26] (except for 5:1, 15), the incidence of the noun *'āšām* (reparation) becomes increasingly frequent from the cases of the graduated sin offering onwards.

'āšām

While *ma'al* characterizes the first and third cases, it is not found in the second case; in fact, the second case is similar to the four cases in ch. 4, particularly to 4:27. Thus the idea of *mā'al* is not the common denominator of the three cases, but *'šm* is. Hence either 'guilt offering' or 'reparation offering' is suitable for the translation of *'āšām*. However, when the functional differences between the sin offering and the *'āšām* are considered, 'the reparation offering' appears more commendable, since it is portrayed as a reparation to the Lord (see Milgrom 1991: 339–345).

Clearly the offering deals with a situation where a direct affront against the Lord has occurred. How the offences differ from the ones in 4:1 – 5:13 is addressed in 'Explanation'.

Comment

5:14–16

5:14. Though such an address to Moses by the Lord does not necessarily mark a new beginning for the rule on a different offering (see 6:1[5:20] below), this is certainly the case, since the following three subsections relate to the reparation offering rather than the sin offering. However, it is unusual that the sole recipient of the Lord's address is Moses and not the Israelites (cf. 4:2). The same formulaic address is found in 6:1[5:20]. This is possibly related to the sacrifice's nature, dealing with an individual's direct affront against the divinity. Such an incident is capable of putting the offender outside the covenant. Thus only Moses is addressed here, because as a mediator between the Lord and the people he presides over the covenantal relationship (see Introduction 5.1.1).

15–16. The first case for the reparation offering concerns trespass regarding the Lord's holy things (*qōdšê YHWH*); i.e. sacrifices and offerings to the Lord (cf. 19:8).

'soul': *nepeš* The agent of self-hiding is a soul, as is the case in the sin offering (4:1 – 5:13) and in the following two cases. But the distinctive feature of this protasis is that *ḥāṭā'* follows *mā'al*, while in the rest of the cases of Lev. 4 – 5 *ḥāṭā'* is positioned first as the summarizing term (cf. 4:2, 22, 27; 5:1). The emphatic positioning of *mā'al* in this verse probably stresses the offence's *mā'al* character (cf. 6:2[5:21] below).

'commit a breach of faith': *mā'al* The term *ma'al* characterizes the *'āšām* offering, with the exception of the case in 5:17–19 (see 6:2[5:21]; Num. 5:6). It occurs in the context of breaking covenantal relationships, such as the relationship between the Lord and the Israelites (Lev. 26:40; Josh. 22:16; 22:31; Ezek. 14:13; 17:20; 20:27; 39:23 etc.), and husband and wife (Num. 5:12; see Hugenberger 1994), and it means to 'behave treacherously'. In view of Num. 20:12 and Deut. 32:51, the term conveys a psychological factor of 'disbelief' (Kiuchi 2003a: 18–21). Therefore I translate it 'commit a breach of faith'. The term has nothing to do with intentionality. In fact here the term 'inadvertently' qualifies *ḥāṭā'* and not *mā'al*.

'hiding itself from': *ḥāṭā' min* The preposition *min* is not partitive; it means 'from' as in Lev. 4:2 (see 'Comment' there). Note that the person hides himself from *one* holy thing, as occurs in the next verse. The verse seems to imply, as for 4:2, that self-hiding from one holy object is equivalent to hiding from them all. The offence's nature is inferred from Lev. 22:14, where it is stipulated that a person who inadvertently eats a holy offering must add to it one-fifth of its value in making reparation. However, this may be just one case of the trespass on the holy things. There is no mention of 'realizing guilt' (*'āšēm*), probably because it was obvious to the person that he had made the offence.

Certainly this kind of offence is included in the 'prohibitive commandments' in Lev. 4:2, but since it is a direct affront against the divine property, it is viewed as particularly serious (for its relation to 4:2, see 'Explanation'). Accordingly a ram is required for the expiation, which is costlier than a female lamb (cf. 4:27–35; 5:6).

The expression *'erkĕkā* appears twenty-four times in Leviticus, and most frequently in chs. 5 (vv. 15, 18; 6:6[5:25]) and 27 (vv. 2–3, 16, 23, 25, 27 etc.; see also Num. 18:16). As the ram is indispensable for expiation, it seems unlikely it is 'convertible' to money (so JPS, NRSV, Noth 1965: 36; cf. Rendtorff 1992: 202–203). Hence *bĕ'erkĕkā* should be rendered 'valued'. The offender first pays what he has damaged to the priest, adding one-fifth of it as a penalty (120% of its original value). The priest sacrifices himself for him by offering a ram, and then the offerer is forgiven.

As for the following two cases (v. 18 and 6:6[5:25]) the ram ought to be the one evaluated by the priest according to the sanctuary currency. An indication of what the required ram's value should be is not given (cf. Péter-Contesse 1993: 93–94). While the animals for the sin in 4:1 – 5:13 could also be valued, this explicit reference to valuation in the case of the reparation offering is remarkable. While the idea of uncovering the offerer (his status before the Lord, economic situations and how far the offender is conscious about his act) is emphasized in the rituals of 4:1 – 5:13, the idea of debt to the Lord, irrespective of the offerer's condition, may have necessitated the mention of monetary evaluation.

5:17–19

17. The second case for the reparation offering is formulated almost the same as that for the sin offering (cf. 4:22, 27). This has raised a crux for exegetes regarding the difference between the sin offering and the reparation offering. Here in 5:17 the crux lies particularly in the phrase *wĕlō' yāda'*. A similar phrase also appears in the next verse in the form *wĕhû' lō' yāda'*. Those who take the verb *yāda'* as meaning to 'know' assume that here the passage is concerned with a particular unknown sin. The possibility has also been advanced that since rules for the transgression of sancta precede vv. 17–18, v. 17 concerns the same trespass (see 'Notes on the text'). Recently Schenker (1992: 53–55) has argued that while the expiation for a suspected sin, as the rabbis interpreted it, is unlikely in the biblical literature, there are cases for the expiation of sins that have not come into the conscience of the sinner *for a long period*. However, such a time lapse is not mentioned in the text.

As for its occurrence in 5:2, *yāda'* means to 'be conscious about' and this case is more extreme than those found in Lev. 4. In view of the fact that the root *šgg* presupposes the knowledge of a concrete act (Lev. 4), the sinner is unconscious of the act itself. In so far as he realizes his guilt, the verse assumes he somehow remembers his former situation, which indicates that though he is unaware of his own action, the latter has perhaps been stored in his subconscious memory.

The person's offence in 5:17–19 is indeed self-hiding. However, from the Lord's perspective the offence goes beyond self-hiding in that the person remains ignorant of the significance of this conduct with regard to the Lord's prohibitive commandments. That is why this case is regarded as a direct affront against the Lord, which requires a reparation offering (see Kiuchi 2003a: 85–90).

'he bears his guilt': *nāśā' 'ăwônô* This is the second appearance of the phrase in Lev. 4 – 6:7[5:26] (see 5:1). There is a stark contrast between 5:1 and 5:17; while in the former the sinner is clearly aware of his act, in the latter he is completely unaware of it. Further, in 5:17 the same phrase occurs after the person realizes his guilt, the purpose of which is perhaps to stress that though he has been ignorant of the violation, he still ought to bear the guilt (there is no mercy).

This is a case for a reparation offering for the breaking of one of the divine prohibitive commandments. It is unnecessary to limit these commandments to 'cultic regulations', as the text explicitly mentions '*kol miṣwôt YHWH* (all the commandments of the Lord). See 'Comment' on 4:2 and 5:1.

18–19. The seriousness of the offence is emphasized by 'he has indeed incurred guilt to the Lord'. The emphasis is expressed by the use of the infinitive absolute followed by a finite verb, a pointer that it concerns not just a legal matter, but the personal relationship between the Lord and the offender. The idea of *self-hiding* is minimal (it appears only at the beginning of v. 17); instead the idea of *reparation* has come to the fore. Note the frequent occurrence of the root *'šm* in vv. 17–19.

6:1–7[5:20–26]

6:1[5:20]. See 'Comment' on 5:14 above.

6:2–3[5:21–22]. The third case for the reparation offering appears to deal with a particular wrong done to one's neighbour where the divinity is invoked in an oath. Nevertheless the emphasis is placed on his direct affront against the Lord in committing a breach of faith. This is indicated by the beginning of 6:2[5:21] 'When a soul hides himself in committing a breach of faith against the Lord'. The perfidy (*ma'al*) is exemplified by the following three practical examples: (1) deceiving his neighbour in a matter of deposit, security or robbery, (2) oppressing his neighbour, and (3) lying about finding lost property. As v. 3b[5:22b], 'in any of all the things that people do and sin thereby', indicates, these are examples, and the main thrust of the case lies in swearing falsely using the Lord's name.

2[5:21]. 'deceiving': *kiḥēš* This term appears to be synonymous with the root *šqr* (lying), but on closer scrutiny it is not just lying but deception with malicious intent. The nature of the offence is first defined as *ḥāṭā'* followed by *mā'al*, which is further explicated by giving some examples: deception (*kiḥēš*) and fraud (*'āšaq*); 'deception' is further subdivided into 'in the case of deposit, pledge and robbery'. As a further example, the case is mentioned in 6:3a[5:22a], where a person denies with a sworn oath his finding of lost property. Thus the cases envisaged in 6:2–3[5:21–22] are offences of a double nature: they deal not only with wrongs committed against one's neighbour but also with false oaths made in connection with these. Moreover these offences are, unlike the cases in Lev. 4, deliberate in nature.

3[5:22]. 'in any of all the things that a man (*hā'ādām*) does and hides himself (*ḥāṭā'*) thereby'. First, *hā'ādām* should be differentiated from *nepeš* at the beginning of 6:2[5:21]. It means 'a man' with all his earthly nature and manifestations, particularly in this case, the propensity towards hiding himself. It does not follow that because the oppression of one's neighbour is an outward act the meaning here of *ḥāṭā'* means 'to commit a sin' in the traditional sense. As the *lāmed* before the infinitive construct of *ḥāṭā'* shows, doing wrong should not be compared on the same level with *ḥāṭā'*.

4–5[5:23–24]. When the person hides himself and realizes guilt, he ought to make compensation for his wrong in two steps: first, to the person he offended (vv. 4–5), and second, to the Lord (v. 6). The listed order of the misappropriated property does not correspond to the order in which they were mentioned in vv. 2–3. Second, additional compensation is to be given for the guilt related to the deception of a neighbour: he must repay the monetary equivalent of the property about which he deceived, *plus* one-fifth (120% of the original value).

'when he realizes the guilt': *bĕyôm 'ašmātô 'ašmātô* means 'his realizing guilt' just as *'ašmat hā'ām* in Lev. 4:3. That the person does not realize his guilt for all his malicious doing indicates that he is unaware of his whole situation even in the midst of carrying out his intention. This may be startling, but it is one of the important aspects of self-hiding (cf. David in 2 Sam. 12:7, 13).

6[5:25]. As the envisaged offences are deliberate in nature, the penalty is presumably heavier than the previous cases. Nevertheless the same ram and the compensation of six-fifths of the original are required, as in the previous two cases.

7[5:26]. 'for any of the things that one may do (*'āśâ*) and thereby realize guilt (*'ašmâ*)' Compare this syntactic construction with that in 6:3[5:22]. Both express the distance between 'doing' and 'realizing guilt' with the preposition *lāmed*; this expresses the whole process from 'doing', 'self-hiding' and to 'realizing guilt'.

The mention of *'ašmâ* forms an inclusio with *'ašmâ* in 4:3 that encapsulates the whole section 4:1 – 6:7[5:26].

Explanation

The distinction between the sin offering and the reparation offering has vexed exegetes. While the first two cases are inadvertent, the third is no doubt deliberate. Based on the interpretation of vv. 17–19 (see 'Comment' there) the three cases in Lev. 5:14 – 6:7[5:26] all concern the making of a direct offence against the Lord.

On this assumption all the cases of the two kinds of offering may be seen from the viewpoint of the degrees of self-hiding (see Kiuchi 2003a: 85–96): (1) The four cases in Lev. 4 (the sin offering) correspond to the case in Lev. 5:17–19 (the reparation offering); the latter is an extreme case in the sense stated above. (2) The four cases in Lev. 5:1–4 correspond to the cases in Lev. 5:14–16; all concern trespasses made against the divinity, but the latter are more direct than the former. (3) The case in Lev. 6:2–7[5:21–26] exceeds all the preceding cases in degree of seriousness: it is extreme both in relation to the inadvertent self-hiding in ch. 4, and the cases of Lev. 5:1–4 and 5:14–16, for it involves the denial of an offence.

Therefore the difference between the two offerings lies in the degree of self-hiding. When a person is conscious about his act but does not realize he has hidden himself from the Lord, his offence is classified under the sin offering (4:1–35). Moreover when a person remains vague about his initial act, being ignorant of or simply neglecting the Lord's ordinances, even though he is conscious of this, it is a case regarding a sin offering (5:1–4). In both cases the person hides himself from the Lord by his own will, though the person may claim it was done out of fear, anxiety, forgetfulness etc. On the other hand, if the degree of self-hiding is low (if a violation is committed against the divine property or the Lord himself), this requires a reparation offering. In these cases, something more than self-hiding comes into play: tangibleness, total unawareness and deliberateness. They all concern not only the infringement of the divine prohibitive commandments but an affront against the Lord himself. Indeed both offerings expiate self-hiding, but these cases are more directed to the divinity than the ones for the sin offering; the former are a sort of robbery (the first, and the third), or a complete ignorance of all the Lord's prohibitive commandments as well as the act itself (the second). Therefore it is remarkable that a way to forgiveness and reconciliation is provided for the third case, which deals with the denial of an offence. Apparently it is hopeless if one denies his own fault. On principle any forgiveness is possible if one admits his own fault. The law graciously provides a way of expiating that kind of sin if the sinner realizes his guilt.

The way for a reconciliation with God and neighbour is more demanding than the case of the sin offering. The sinner has to pay six-fifths of the value of the damaged holy things plus a ram, which is costlier than the sin offering.

While the ritual itself is presented in 7:1–6, it is missing here. The rationale for the omission is not self-evident, for the rituals for the sin offering are minutely set out in Lev. 4:1 – 5:13. Since the sinner has not hidden himself from the Lord as much as in the cases for the sin offering, he need not uncover himself through the ritual to the extent of the case of the sin offering. The blood manipulation and the burning of fat of the reparation offering are performed just like the burnt and fellowship offerings.

Thus, humanly speaking, marked paradoxes exist between the two offerings. On the one hand, the offences requiring the reparation offering are certainly grave. They represent the making of a direct affront against the divinity and this is reflected by the costlier nature of the prescribed sacrificial animal – a ram. Nevertheless they are not considered to defile the Tent. When reparation is made, everything is over. On the other hand, as stated in 'Explanation' on 4:1 – 5:13, nothing is mentioned in the sin offering regarding the remedy of the supposed damage done to one's neighbour because of its primary concern with the divine–human relationship. Furthermore full expiation is not achieved by these rituals. In view of the fact that the offences of the sin offering defile the sancta, and even the Holy of Holies, and the offences of the reparation offering do not, it is evident that the Lord abhors self-hiding more than anything else, particularly in the form of unconscious hypocrisy (see 'Explanation' on ch. 4). These observations contradict the normal human evaluation of these offences: that those committed against the Lord's holy things are of a more serious nature.

In that all the cases in 4:1 – 6:7 concern the human conscious or subconscious memory, the offender determines what kind of animal and ritual procedure he will take and perform respectively. But these fine distinctions of the human consciousness in regard to self-hiding indicate that the Lord looks at, and fully knows, the condition of the human heart.

New Testament implications

These three cases are applicable to NT believers in the following ways.

The first case, profaning the holy things, corresponds to profaning the name of Christ, who became all the OT offerings for us. One such example would be to use his name to achieve one's materialistic desires, most notably in business. One may assume he uses the name of Jesus out of reverence to him (e.g. Matt. 7:21–23). However, the use of his name may actually be motivated by an unconscious desire for material prosperity. In such a case Christ's name is desecrated, despite a person's religious fervour. Since Christ died to remove all sin, such an offence is pardonable upon that person's realization of guilt, but such a person will still suffer in this world for profaning Jesus' name (Matt. 12:31–32; Acts 9:16).

The second case of the reparation offering concerns a person's inadvertent violation of all the divine prohibitive commandments, thus of the Lord himself. Analogous to this in NT times is a person's complete ignorance of the Lord's word. This similarly represents a complete ignorance/violation of the Lord. Such a violation is not necessarily of a malicious nature. It is possibly well meaning. Nevertheless he remains unaware of his violation until he offends Christ directly without knowing it.

The third case of the reparation offering concerns breaking faith with the Lord by damaging a neighbour's property. The order of the steps taken towards forgiveness is significant. It is only after he has made compensation to the neighbour that he offers a ram to the Lord through the officiating priest. While restitution of the stolen goods to the initial owner constitutes an indispensable step towards reconciliation with God, it cannot by itself substitute for the ritual. Nor does repentance itself constitute expiation. A series of acts on the part of the offender (his realizing guilt, his restoration of the stolen object to its original owner and his bringing of sacrifices to the priest) are necessary for the forgiveness of sin. Without interhuman compensation no divine pardon is given. Yet it is appropriate to see the ritual as the preparation for, or training towards, the forgiveness granted by God. Forgiveness by others does not simultaneously imply one's forgiveness by God. As clearly prescribed by the text, the offender ought also to pay separate compensation to the Lord. It is notable that though interhuman forgiveness often feels so difficult, the Lord has provided a way to forgive an offence so heinous as the profanation of his name (cf. 1 John 4:20).

As for the previous two cases, this one shows the turning of a sinner's soul, where he, despite the robbery and fraud followed by a false oath in using the divine name, comes to his senses and realizes his guilt. The law assumes a certain kind of human (who, like this one, having committed severe wrongs both to his neighbour and God) later comes to his senses and recognizes his guilt. Such a person is commonly looked down upon in society even after he repents, but the challenge of this third case is for the church to receive such a person as a brother. In fact, the law challenges those who look down on the culprit through their own moral-ethical criteria. Moreover the reader should observe that the offender, having perpetrated the wrong, can still come to his senses (cf. Zacchaeus, Luke 19:1–10). In NT terms, this results from the Holy Spirit's guidance. The biblical God transcends any humanly fabricated moral-ethical criteria, and unless one experiences the abounding grace expressed in the divine forgiveness, he cannot forgive others.

Humans tend to see themselves more as the offended than the offender. But the text prescribes the ritual for the potential offender. Thus the law summons the reader to reflect on his own situation before the Lord.

Indeed, while the offering in the OT period could have led the Israelites to experience the Lord's forgiveness, it is in NT times by faith in Christ that a person is pardoned. The pitfall with this change lies in that the NT believer tends to assume his guilt is all borne by Christ, so he need not pay compensation for the damage he causes to his neighbour or the Lord. This is entirely erroneous. It is true that Christ bore the guilt of the believer, but what Christ bore is the guilt of self-hiding before the Lord. Therefore if the believer commits offences, he has to pay for them in this world. St Paul, after his conversion, devoted the rest of his life to proclaiming the gospel. But this is just the positive side of the coin: it was perhaps the due payment for all his sacrilegious acts both in words and deeds against the Lord's disciples (Acts 9:16).

LEVITICUS 6:8[1] – 7:10

Translation

8[1]The LORD spoke to Moses, saying, 9[2]'Command Aaron and his sons, saying, This is the teaching concerning the burnt offering. It is the one that shall remain on the hearth upon the altar all night until the morning, while the fire on the altar shall be kept burning in it. 10[3]The priest puts on his linen vestments after putting on his linen undergarments next to his body; and he takes up the ashes to which the fire has consumed the burnt offering on the altar, and places them beside the altar. 11[4]Then he takes off his vestments and puts on other garments, and carries the ashes out to a clean place outside the camp. 12[5]The fire on the altar shall be kept burning: it shall not go out. Every morning the priest shall add wood to it, lay out the burnt offering on it, and turn the fat of the fellowship offerings into smoke on it. 13[6]A perpetual fire shall be kept burning on the altar; it shall not go out.

14[7]'This is the teaching concerning the loyalty offering: The sons of Aaron shall offer it before the LORD, in front of the altar. 15[8]They take from it a handful of the choice flour and oil of the loyalty offering, with all the frankincense that is on the offering, and turn its token portion into smoke on the altar as a soothing aroma to the LORD. 16[9]Aaron and his sons shall eat what is left of it; it shall be eaten as unleavened cakes in a holy place; in the court of the Tent of Meeting they shall eat it. 17[10]It must not be baked with leaven. I have given it as their portion of my offerings for annihilation; it is most holy, like the sin offering and the reparation offering. 18[11]Every male among the descendants of Aaron shall eat of it, as their perpetual due throughout your generations, from the LORD's offerings for annihilation; anything that touches them will become holy.'

19[12]The LORD spoke to Moses, saying, 20[13]'This is the offering that Aaron and his sons shall offer to the LORD on the day when he is anointed: one-tenth of an ephah of choice flour as a regular offering, half of it in the morning and half in the evening. 21[14]It shall be made with oil on a griddle; you shall bring it well soaked, as a loyalty offering of baked pieces, and you shall present it as a soothing aroma to the LORD. 22[15]The priest from among Aaron's sons, who is anointed to succeed him, shall prepare it; it is the LORD's perpetual due to be turned entirely into smoke. 23[16]Every loyalty offering of a priest shall be wholly burned; it shall not be eaten.'

24[17]The LORD spoke to Moses, saying, 25[18]'Speak to Aaron and his sons, saying, This is the teaching concerning the sin offering. The sin offering shall be slaughtered before the LORD at the spot where the burnt offering is slaughtered; it is most holy. 26[19]The priest who makes it uncovered shall eat of it; it shall be eaten in a holy place, in the court of the Tent of Meeting. 27[20]Whatever touches its flesh shall become holy; and when any of its blood is splashed on a garment, you shall wash that on which it was splashed in a holy place. 28[21]An earthen vessel in which it was boiled shall be broken; but if it is boiled in a bronze vessel, that shall be scoured and rinsed in water. 29[22]Every male among the priests shall eat of it; it is most holy. 30[23]But no sin offering shall be eaten from which any blood is brought into the Tent of Meeting for propitiation in the Holy Place; it shall be burned with fire.

7:1'This is the teaching concerning the reparation offering. It is most holy; 2at the spot where the burnt offering is slaughtered, they shall slaughter the reparation offering, and its blood shall be dashed against all sides of the altar. 3All its fat shall be offered: the fat tail, the fat that covers the entrails, 4the two kidneys with the fat that is on them at the loins, and the long lobe of the liver, which shall be removed with the kidneys. 5The priest shall turn them into smoke on the altar as an offering for annihilation to the LORD; it is a reparation offering. 6Every male among the priests shall eat of it; it shall be eaten in a holy place; it is most holy. 7The reparation offering is like the sin offering, there is the same instruction for them; the priest who makes propitiation with it shall have it. 8So, too, the priest who offers anyone's burnt offering shall have the skin of the burnt offering he has offered. 9And every loyalty offering baked in the oven, and all that is prepared in a pan or on a griddle, shall belong to the priest who offers it. 10But every other loyalty offering, mixed with oil or dry, shall belong to all the sons of Aaron equally.'

Notes on the text

6:9[2]. 'the hearth': *môqĕdâ* It is questionable whether or not a *mappîq* is supposed to be in the last *hē*. If it is, the word means 'its hearth'; if not, it is a feminine noun. LXX translates 'on its burning', which reflects the presence of *mappîq*, whereas SamP reads *hmqdh*, thus apparently assuming a feminine noun. On the other hand, many Hebr. MSS read without the first *mēm*. For other proposals, see Rendtorff 1992: 234. Perhaps it is the masculine noun *môqēd* with a 3rd person sg. pronominal suffix.

LXX adds 'it shall not go out' after 'while the fire ... in it', as in vv. 5 and 6. But this is probably unnecessary (see 'Comment' on vv. 12–13[5–6]).

'in it': *bô* 'It' probably refers to the 'hearth' (*môqēd*), as the pronominal suffix is masculine, and not to 'the burnt offering', in which case the feminine would be expected.

10[3]. 'his linen vestments': *middô bad* SamP, Syr, TgJon read the first Hebr. word as pl. However, there is no problem in taking *bad* as indicating the material.

14[7]. 'shall offer': *haqrēb* While SamP reads *hqrybw* as 2 pl. imp., LXX, TgJon, Vg reflect the understanding that it qualifies the preceding 'the loyalty offering', *'šr yqrybw*. The reason for the use of inf. abs. here is uncertain. However, the inf. abs. often adds solemnity to the verbal meaning. The lack of concord in number is unimportant (see 25:14).

17[10]. 'my offerings for annihilation': *'iššāy* SamP and LXX add 'of the LORD'. In view of the 1st person address ('I have given'), MT is preferred.

18[11]. *Kol zākār* is sometimes translated 'only male' (JPS, Levine 1989; see Ibn Ezra), but the rendering 'every male', found in most translations is preferable (NRSV; see Num. 18:10). The same applies to *kol* in 6:22; 7:6.

'perpetual dues': *ḥoq 'ôlām Ḥōq* has the sense of 'share, portion, due' in similar contexts (Exod. 29:28; Lev. 7:34; 10:15; 24:9; Num. 18:8, 11, 19; see also Gen. 47:22 and cf. with v. 26).

'anything' See 'Comment'.

21[14]. 'well soaked': *tupînê* The Hebr. term is a hapax legomenon and its exact meaning is uncertain. Syr reads *tĕfuttennāh* (Syr), 'you will crumble', and reflects the root *ptt*. Recently Van Leeuwen (1988: 268–269) suggested 'the folded parts of the meal offering of pieces', based on LXX (*helikta*).

22[15]. 'a perpetual due to the LORD': *ḥoq 'ôlām laYHWH* LXX omits 'to the LORD'. Despite Hartley's conclusion that the idea is strange, the connection between 'being totally burnt up' (*kālîl toqṭār*) with *lYHWH* is common in Leviticus (1:9, 13, 17; 2:9 etc.).

27[20]. 'you shall wash': *tĕkabbes* SamP reads *ykbs*, perhaps understanding it as passive.

7:3 After 'entrails' LXX and SamP add 'and the fat which is on the intestines', as in 3:3, 9, 14 and 4:8.

8. LXX omits *lakkôhēn* 'to the priest', but MT should be retained, considering the legislator's emphasis (see 'Comment').

Form and structure

This section, together with 7:11–38, deals with various regulations relating to the later stages of the rituals given in Lev. 1 – 6:7, with a view to safeguarding holy things (see 'Form and structure' in ch. 1). It is addressed to the priests (6:9[2]).

The content of the section 6:8[1] – 7:10 deals with the burnt offering of fire (6:8[1]–13[6]), the loyalty offering (14[7]–23[16]), the sin offering (25[18]–30[23) and the reparation offering (7:1–10). Each is introduced with *zō't tôrat* (This is the teaching of). Most rules are first mentioned in this section, although those of the loyalty offering overlap with the earlier rules given in ch. 2. Also notable is that the section for the reparation offering gives its ritual procedure. These elements may support the assumption that the section 6:8[1] – 7:10 is supplementary to 1:1 – 6:7[5:26], but it is important to note that these rules are addressed to the priest.

Of particular interest are the apparently digressive rules of 7:8–10. Although these verses are sometimes viewed as 'out of context' (Hartley 1992: 95), it would appear, just as in the reference to the burnt and loyalty offerings in 5:7–13, that the legislator has deliberately rounded out the early part of 6:8 – 7:38 as a section on 'most holy things' (see 'Comment').

Comment

6:8–13[6:1–6] (perpetual fire)

9[2]. From 6:8 the priestly *tôrâ* (teaching) begins solemnly with the use of 'Command' (*ṣaw*). The term *tôrâ* is understood to mean 'standard, rule, instruction'. The use of *tôrâ* in this sense is most frequently found in passages addressed to priests (6:9[2], 14[7], 25[18]; 7:1, 7, 11), but not always (11:46; 12:7). Further attestations such as Lev. 11:46, 12:7, 13:59, 14:54–57 (cf. also Num. 5:29–30; 6:13, 21; 15:16, 29; 19:2, 14; 31:21) indicate that the use of this term is not confined to cases where the priest is an addressee. Why is one of the possible synonyms of *tôrâ*, such as *ḥuqqâ* (cf. 7:36), not used instead? Furthermore the significance of this term's appearance in a ritual context should be considered in view of the symbolic dimension of the preceding rituals. Thus it is likely that though the term *tôrâ* in such a context refers to specific practical instructions, it refers to teaching concerning the relationship between the Lord and humans. It happens that the human on view in 6:8 – 7:21 is predominantly a priest. Thus contrary to the common view that only the specific meaning of *tôrâ* is in view in 6:8 – 7:38 (e.g. Milgrom 1991: 382–383; Rendtorff 1992: 233; Hartley 1992: 94), the meaning of *tôrâ* in this context is no different from its occurrence in other contexts. Hence I propose it means 'a teaching'.

The fact that the term does not appear in chs. 1 – 6:7[5:26] calls for an explanation. But the appearance of the term from 6:8[6:1] onwards, vis-à-vis 1:1 – 6:7[5:26], appears to stress the presence of a symbolic dimension behind the outward ritual acts of 6:8[1] – 7:38. In other words, the reason for the term's appearance is literary. As such, whether or not the preceding chapters are *tôrâ* is an unrelated question. Thus the section 1:1 – 6:7[5:26] is possibly *tôrôt* also. Compared to synonyms such as *ḥōq* and *mišpāṭ*, which refer to particular and explicit principles or rules, *tôrâ* appears to relate to the overall relationship between God and humans. In this regard, every ritual prescription in 1:1 – 6:7 is pre-eminently *tôrâ* (see 'Explanation').

This section is not about how to offer the burnt offering (ch. 1), but is a teaching about the burnt offering. It reveals that its essence lies in the perpetual fire, known as *tāmîd* (perpetuity), which is the foundation of the burnt offering in ch. 1. *hā'ōlâ* in v. 9b[2b] refers to the evening burnt offering stipulated in Exod. 29:38–42. Yet as the flow of the rules indicates, the fire and its symbolic meaning are revealed as the core of the regulations.

First of all, 'fire' in this context symbolizes the Lord's presence as a consuming power. What does it consume? Since this burnt offering is analogous to the burnt offering in ch. 1, which symbolizes the annihilation of all the offerer's worldly desires, the same meaning for 'fire' can be assumed here (the priests' desires for worldly matters are consumed; however, see below).

Another symbolic meaning can be inferred from the fire's continual burning at night: that the presence of the Lord is light. And this, in turn, indicates that where there is no presence of the Lord, there is darkness. A similar symbolic meaning of fire occurs in 24:1–4; note that in both places the imperative of *ṣiwwâ* appears in connection with the perpetuity of the fire.

From the priests, as representatives of the whole people, is demanded a higher self-dedication than from the laity, which is reflected in the direction in which the former ought to offer burnt offerings every day (Exod. 29:42). It appears that in line with this, the 'burnt offering' is here futher specified as 'a fire' (cf. *'ôlat tāmîd* in Exod. 29:42 and *'ēš tāmîd* in 6:13[6]; see also v. 21[14] below). In view of these considerations, the direction given to the priests to keep the fire burning indicates tacitly that they ought to be like the consuming fire themselves, which is far more demanding than the offering of a burnt offering.

10–11[3–4]. This is not a separate rule from v. 9, but a continuation of it. The rule concerning priestly clothing is mentioned in connection with the handling of the ashes of the burnt offering. The linen clothes of the priests are holy and worn only when they officiate at the altar and Holy Place (see also 16:4, 23, 32). When they take the ashes away from the altar outside the camp, they must change their clothes to prevent the defilement of their holy garments. Ashes are placed in a ritually clean place, as in 4:12. The designation 'in a clean place' does not mean that certain places were inherently 'clean'. Rather, while some definite place for the disposal of the ashes may have existed, the designation indicates that a person ought to be clean before the Lord – as 'clean' refers to the state of heart (cf. Introduction 7.4.2.c). The changing of the priestly clothing in this procedure reflects the distinction made between the holy and secular realms. More practically the cool linen clothes would have made the priest's job of approaching fire more bearable (cf. 16:4, 23, 24).

12–13[5–6]. While in vv. 9b–11 the topic changes from the burnt offering to its ashes, and to the priests who remove them, the sequence is now reversed: from the fire to the priest's burning and placing the burnt offering on the altar. *Tāmîd* in *'ēš tāmîd* (13[6]) is not an adverb but forms a noun phrase, meaning 'perpetual fire' (Rendtorff 1992: 239). Thus an emphasis on the perpetuity of the altar fire gradually increases from v. 9[2], until in v. 13[6] the fire is called 'perpetual fire'.

The priestly work of disposing of the ashes of the offerings, particularly the way this is described, symbolically depicts not only how the priests ought to destroy their egocentric selves, but that they ought to become consuming fires themselves (see 'Explanation' on ch. 11).

6:14–18[6:7–11] (loyalty offering)

14–18[7–11]. The section 6:14–23 regulates the loyalty offering from a priestly perspective. V. 14[7] onwards appears to overlap with some passages in Lev. 2. However, the two differ in viewpoint: in 6:14[7]ff. the ritual is prescribed for the priests who officiate in the ritual, whereas in ch. 2 details about the offering and ritual are prescribed for the laity. Thus, though 6:15[8] is similar to 2:2, it is written from the perspective of the priests and in this regard is a mixture of 2:2 and 2:9. Cf. also the beginning of v. 16[9] with 2:3. The limitation to males for partaking in the remaining part of the sacrifice is also mentioned in 6:29[22] (the sin offering) and 7:6 (the reparation offering).

V. 17[10] is couched in the divine 1st person. This is not surprising, considering the priestly due of the loyalty offering was already mentioned in ch. 2, which reflects the Lord's special command to his priestly representatives (cf. also 'command' in v. 9[2]), as well as the fact that many rules in ch. 2 were addressed in the 2nd person even to the laity.

The designation 'the most holy thing' indicates the remaining portion of the loyalty offering is just as holy as the burnt portion. From here arises the need for extreme care in handling the remaining portion (its eating).

As leaven symbolizes corruption (see 'Comment' on 2:4–7), priests should see to it that even in partaking in their dues, they should not bring corruption into their souls. That is, since the individual Israelite's offering is the loyalty offering, the priests who partake of it ought to share the same spiritual concern of the offerer in their eating. It is further explained that the remaining portion of the loyalty offering is most holy, like the remaining flesh of the sin and reparation offerings: it is the Lord's.

18[11]. 'Anything that touches them will become holy': *kol 'ăšer yigga' bāhem yiqdāš'* A similar formula appears three times elsewhere (Exod. 29:37; 30:29; Lev. 6:27[20]). The meaning of *kol 'ăšer* as well as *yiqdaš* is variously interpreted. A traditional understanding is that whoever touches the offering must be clean (LXX, Vg, Luther). On the other hand, Elliger sees this as a warning that whoever touches the most holy things provokes

God's wrath (1966: 97). Wenham, though he also sees the same motive of involuntary consecration here, notes that if a man becomes holy, it is not clearly prescribed how he can be desecrated (1979: 121). Levine, followed by Hartley, suggests that *yiqdaš* should be understood as saying that the priest must be holy before handling the sacred (1989: 37–38), since holiness is not contagious. Recently Milgrom has taken up this formula and rejected Levine's solution. Milgrom (1991: 443–451) concludes: (1) *Kōl* should be translated 'whatever' and not 'whoever'. Thus holiness is contagious only to inanimate objects. (2) *Yiqdaš* should be rendered 'he shall become holy', just as *yiṭmā'* in the antonymic expression *kōl-hannōge' b- yiṭmā'* means 'shall become impure'. (3) *Bāhem* (them) refers to nothing but *'iššēh YHWH*, thus comprehending all the food offerings.

It seems that Milgrom is basically right in his interpretation of this passage. Thus here in 6:18[11] the offerings are said to convey holiness to things only, probably only to foodstuffs or garments. However, considering the symbolic dimension of the offerings prescribed in Lev. 1 – 6:7, there is likely to be more to this rule than purely physical concerns.

Holiness contagion in v. 18[11] takes place in a rather limited space (the Holy Place), unlike the uncleanness contagion where every thing and human being becomes defiled by coming into contact with the unclean (Hag. 2:12–13). What does the 'most holy thing' mean? First, it belongs to the Lord. But more specifically it is the outcome of the offerer's egocentric nature's death, and since this is the case of the loyalty offering it is regarded as part of the offerer's faith (loyalty) in the Lord that is renewed by this offering. Thus, though the holiness contagion can be envisioned as working materially, the symbolic meaning of the offering makes it unlikely that the contagion is material matter only (see Introduction 7.4.2). The rule essentially intends to convey a spiritual matter.

6:19–23[12–16] (loyalty offering)

19[12]. The prescription in vv. 20–23[13–16] also concerns the loyalty offering, the so-called priestly *minḥâ*. Here the Lord addresses Moses, but Moses is not told to relate the teaching to Aaron and his sons, as in vv. 8–9[1–2]. This may be an abbreviation. However, the offering prescribed here concerns the priest's ordination performed by Moses and this makes it likely that the Lord limits his address to Moses because only Moses is responsible for presiding over this occasion.

20[13]. It is questionable how the *b* in *bĕyôm* should be translated. To translate the phrase 'on the day of' clashes with the stipulation that this offering ought to be presented perpetually (*tāmîd*). It has been duly suggested that it be translated 'from the day of' (e.g. Ibn Ezra; Milgrom 1991: 397; for *b* meaning 'from', see *UT*).

21[14]. Unlike the ordinary loyalty offering, this priestly *minḥâ* has no 'token portion' (*'azkārâ*), since it is completely burnt, like the burnt offering. See 2:5.

22–23[15–16]. As commented in 4:3–4, Aaron and his sons were anointed, yet here it is one of his sons who is commanded to offer a loyalty offering. However, these verses do not imply that he is and must be 'the high priest'. The reference to the chief priest in Leviticus reflects a formulation less than 'the high priest' (cf. 6:22[15]; 16:32; 21:10; and see Num. 35:25, 28).

Kālîl (wholly burnt up) suggests that the priestly *minḥâ* resembles the burnt offering in that both cannot be eaten. However, the theological meaning of each offering remains the same; by this common factor the idea is emphasized that the person who offers a sacrifice cannot benefit from it.

Indeed if the priest is a mediator between the Lord and the people, and labours to maintain the divine presence for the people, how much more should the spiritual truth surrounding his duty apply to himself? In particular, the priest's loyalty to the Lord is essential, since everything else hinges on it (cf. 4:3–12). The priest is the spiritual leader who has the role of bringing the Israelites near to the Lord; therefore a higher degree of loyalty to the Lord is required of him. His loyalty offering ought to be completely burnt. Moreover it ought to be offered every morning and evening. Thus a continuous renewal of loyalty to the Lord is demanded of the priests, which involves a denial of their egocentric thinking about all kinds of matters. They mediate between God and the people by the smoke of the burning, which soothes the wrath of the former. But it is unlikely that the priests ever embodied this symbolic meaning in their everyday lives. Rather the very presence of the prescription implies that their egocentric selves constantly returned to them. Thus these rules reflect both the limitations of the priestly work and the ideal the priests should struggle for.

6:24–30[17–23] (sin offering)

24–26[17–19]. Here again the Lord's address is in a form similar to 6:1–2[5:20–21]; i.e. Moses is given further instructions on what he is to say to Aaron and his sons. This time they concern the sin offering, although the same address extends to the fellowship offering (7:11–21). Vv. 24–30[17–23] complement the prescription in Lev. 4 from a priestly perspective. They address matters such as the sin offering's holy nature, the place where the priests should eat, holiness contagion and the prohibition against eating the flesh of those offerings that had their blood taken into the Holy Place.

If this offering functions to uncover a soul, the priests should exhibit the same characteristic of holiness when they eat of it; i.e. they should not only uncover themselves before the Lord, but also make themselves free of self-centredness. This is reflected in the directions on the place of slaughtering in v. 25 [18] and the place of eating in v. 26[19]. The designation of the place for slaughtering indicates the animal ought to be slaughtered in the same spirit as the burnt offering. On the other hand, while the place must have been assigned somewhere in the court, the intent of the rule is that they ought to eat the flesh in a holy manner; i.e. in a state of being inwardly holy.

27[20]. The meat and blood of the sacrifice are to be handled cautiously. This verse contains two rules. First, anything that touches the sacrificial meat becomes holy. Since priests and their garments become holy by anointing, things like cooking vessels in the next verse are intended here. Second, v. 27b[20b] concerns the handling of splashed blood; both the area of clothing and the sacrificial meat on which the blood was splashed should be washed in a holy place.

Ritually, holiness is contagious only to things. Furthermore it is significant that something like clothing is not said to become completely holy, but just the part that was splashed with blood. So the effect of contagion is restricted. These rules reflect the principle that blood ought not to be used for any purpose other than expiation. All this applies to outer holiness; yet on a symbolic dimension the rule is applicable to humans (see 'Explanation').

28[21]. Here is a rule about vessels used for cooking the meat of the sin offering. If the vessel is earthen, it must be broken, while a bronze one must be scoured and rinsed in water.

Three verses, vv. 27–29, are devoted to holiness contagion. For the general principle on holiness contagion, see 'Comment' on v. 25b[18b] above. The linguistic resemblance of holiness contagion to uncleanness contagion (11:33) should not be seen in such a way that the sacrificial animal absorbs the uncleanness. Rather the resemblance is probably intended to stress the different nature of the two kinds of contagion; while the effects of the uncleanness contagion are rampant and pervasive, those of the holiness contagion are modest and minimal. The sacrificial animal is holy and has nothing to do with uncleanness: the blood and flesh of the animal substitute for the death of the offerer, and remain holy throughout.

Differences in the teachings on this matter exist between the loyalty and reparation offerings, on the one hand, and the sin offering on the other. These possibly derive from the different degrees of sanctity of the respective offerings: that of the loyalty offering is higher than the sin offering, while the reparation offering deals with a lesser degree of self-hiding that does not defile the sanctuary (see 'Explanation' on 5:14 – 6:7[5:26]). Thus the fact that even the objects that obtain holiness must be broken or cleaned points to the offerer's lack of power, relative to other offerings, to communicate holiness to others (see 'Explanation').

29[22]. This verse may appear to be at odds with the rule in v. 26[19], which says that the officiating priest eats the meat of the sacrifice.

However, v. 29[22] is a supplement to v. 26[19] rather than a later expansion of the rule; i.e. in addition to the officiating priest any male who is a priest may partake of the meat.

30[23]. On the other hand, the offering, which had its blood taken into the Tent of Meeting to make propitiation in the sanctuary, should not be eaten by the priests: it must be burnt. This is already stipulated for the sacrificial meat of the sin offering offered by the anointed priest or the whole congregation in Lev. 4:2–12. The underlying assumption is that since the propitiation of the holy objects in the sanctuary is caused by the sins of the priests themselves, priests cannot partake of the remaining meat.

Qōdeš refers to the area in the Tent (cf. Exod. 28:29, 35, 43; 29:30; Lev. 16:2–3). Yet the term also includes the courtyard (10:4).

For the two kinds of sin offering, see 'Explanation' on ch. 4.

7:1–7 (reparation offering)

This section prescribes the ritual for the reparation offering, which was not given in 5:14 – 6:7. The most holy nature of the offering is stressed by the positioning of the phrase 'the most holy thing' in the introduction (v. 1) and ending (v. 6b), thus forming an inclusio. It may well be that by stressing the offering's holy nature, the Lord draws attention to the offering's purpose of dealing with the desecration of holy things or the divinity. At the same time this section stresses the priestly dues in vv. 6–7.

2b–5. Since no clear demarcation is made between the ritual procedure and the priestly due in this section, one may wonder whether it really bears a supplementary nature to 5:14 – 6:7. For a possible meaning of the specification of the place of slaughtering in v. 2, see 'Comment' on 6:24–26[17–19] above. As Hoffmann comments (1905: 241), dashing blood (*zrq*) is the same as for the *šělāmîm* and the '*ôlâ*, burning fat is the same as for the *šělāmîm* and the *ḥaṭṭā't*, and eating the meat is the same as for the *ḥaṭṭā't*. Thus it is the combination of these elements in these verses that is unique to the '*āšām* rather than the elements themselves.

6–7. The remaining flesh is allocated to the priest as his due, and all the male members of his family may eat it. This verse is similar to 6:29[22]. However, while in 6:26[19] it is the officiating priest who eats it in the Holy Place, here every male member of the priestly family is entitled to it. Since 6:29[22] states that every male can eat the sin offering, it may follow that 7:6 brings together these two elements, the place for eating and masculinity, as what qualifies one for eating.

As regards the handling of the remaining meat, the same rule applies to both the sin and the reparation offerings: the meat belongs to the priest who makes propitiation with it. Although the officiating priest's right to eat is in the background in v. 6, it is made explicit in this generalizing statement about the same standard regarding the remaining flesh of the two sacrifices. For the meaning of 'a holy place', see 'Comment' on vv. 24–26 [17–19].

However, in view of the priests' propensity to become unclean and sin, the requirement that they ought to be inwardly holy when they consumed the flesh was unlikely to be met, so that they always tended to profane holiness by eating the flesh. Thus by repeatedly stressing in v. 7 that the remaining flesh belongs to the officiating priest, the legislator implicitly stresses that he ought to be holy. Such a rigorous requirement produces an irony over the potential gap between the holiness of the reparation offering and that of the priest, for the priest ought to be holy before he eats it; yet holiness is a matter of the human heart.

7:8–10

8. The mention of 'the officiating priest' (v. 7) prompts the Lord to add rules about priestly dues relating to the burnt and loyalty offerings. Yet at the same time, by their reference to the first two offerings (the burnt and loyalty offerings in vv. 6:8–18[1–11]), these verses form a concluding part to 6:8 – 7:10, in that the whole section deals with the offerings called 'the most holy things'.

'anyone's burnt offering': *'ôlat 'îš* is unique in the OT. *'îš* appears here for the first time in Leviticus. Since *'îš* is used with an awareness of interpersonal relations, and an *'ādām* (1:2), which connotes frail and sinful created existence before God, denotes the offerer of the burnt offering in Lev. 1, renderings such as 'any man's burnt offering' (RSV, NASB) or 'a man's burnt offering' (JPS) are inappropriate. Nor is it the burnt offering for others that the priest offers (NIV). It actually refers to the burnt offering in ch. 1.

Though no mention was made in ch. 1 about the hide of the burnt offering, it belongs for practical use to the officiating priest. The collocation of the skin (*'ôr*) of the animal and 'anyone' (*'îš*) merits special attention. 'Skin' occurs fifty-three times in Leviticus out of ninety-nine occurrences in the whole OT. It is concentrated in Lev. 13 (forty-six times) with prescriptions for the so-called leper. Human skin is the most external part of the body, and is used there as the symbolic location of the inner being's manifestation (see 'Comment' on ch. 13). Since the sacrificial animal represents the offerer, the skin of the burnt offering probably symbolizes the interpersonal aspects of the offerer. Certainly in view of the essence of holiness (see 'Explanation' on chs. 1 and 11) it would be better for the interpersonal aspects of the offerer to be burnt up. Yet the Lord sanctioned that the skin not be burnt: the skin is, in the case of the burnt offering, evidence in the hand of the officiating priest that the man (*'ādām*) really sacrificed his innermost self. That the officiating priest is the beneficiary is thrice emphasized: first, the topic (the *priest* who offers a person's burnt offering) is introduced, then the burnt offering is further qualified as 'the burnt offering that *he presented*', and lastly *lākôhen* is further stressed by *lô*. Ironically the more the priestly due of the skin is stressed, the more the inner holiness of his interpersonal matters is stressed.

9–10. While the *minḥâ* cooked in an oven, a pan or a griddle belongs to the officiating priest, the *minḥâ* mixed with oil and dried belongs to all of Aaron's sons. Interestingly in ch. 2 the remaining part of the *minḥâ* was said to belong to Aaron and his sons (2:3, 10; 6:9–11[2–4]), and this creates some tension between this passage and vv. 9–10, which prescribes two different kinds of handling for the *minḥâ*. However, this tension is ameliorated when it is remembered that the prescription of ch. 2 is addressed specifically to lay individuals. It is enough for them to know who receives the remaining part of the *minḥâ*. In addition to this, as in the case of the skin of the burnt offering in v. 8, which was not mentioned in ch. 1, it is natural that more detailed rules are set out here.

It is common sense that a distinction is made between the officiating priest and his sons who do nothing. The criterion depends on the kind of loyalty offering the worshipper brings: as the cooked meal is costlier than the raw grain, the more expensive cooked meal goes to the officiating priest, though it may be permissible for him to distribute it to other members of his family. While the dues are a privilege enjoyed by the officiating priest and his family, they are quite demanding when the offering's holy nature is taken into account. By eating the cakes, an act symbolic of their allegiance to the Lord, the priest and his family are to confess they have nothing to desire in this world.

Explanation

The section 6:8[1] – 7:38 includes various teachings (*tôrôt*). Over against the traditional understanding that these regulations merely concern the outward handling of the ritual materials, this term should be translated 'teachings' (see 'Comment' on v. 6:9[2]). As *tôrâ* deals with the relationship between the Lord and humans on an existential dimension, this understanding of the term invites the reader to explore the symbolic meaning of every prescription in 6:8[1] – 7:10. On the whole, the teaching concerns priestly responsibility and privilege.

Perpetual burnt offering (6:8–13[1–6])

The priest's duty of tending the fire symbolizes not only that his egocentricity should be removed, but that he ought to *become* the consuming fire itself. It is the duty of the priest to experience this truth himself daily and teach the people. Moreover it is simplistic to assume that such an age has passed because of Christ's coming. It is true that all the barriers between God and humans were removed by Christ (Eph. 2:14–16), but the situation of NT believers remains the same so long as their egocentric selves are not destroyed. Indeed, more than the removal of egocentric selves, here Christians in general, and leaders in particular, are exhorted to become the consuming fire itself. Can such a command be embodied by humans?

Loyalty offering (6:14–23[7–16])

The priest deserves to receive the prebends due for his work, but in so far as they are a gift *from the Lord*, he must make them holy, which means he has to treat them in keeping with what the original offerer intended. Therefore, since Aaron's sons also partake of the prebends, the same loyalty is demanded of them. However, in that holiness is a matter of the human heart it would be extremely difficult for the priest to maintain such a condition.

As the later history of the Israelites bears witness, this ultimately proved to be impossible (e.g. Ezek. 44:9–14): if the human ego is not completely destroyed, the call for a renewal of heart or rededication remains an agenda, or is reduced to a formal observance of humanly invented customs. Thus this passage challenges Christian leaders as to whether they became leaders after their egos were completely destroyed. Just as the priest was expected to have the capability of identifying himself with the spiritual concerns of the individuals, present Christian ministers must also have this same personal quality. One may argue that sanctification is a matter of degrees, but Leviticus shows there is a sharp distinction between what belongs to God and what does not. Can God use a leader who is not perfectly equipped with faith in, and loyalty to, the Lord?

The loyalty offering and what it symbolically achieves is communicable, in a very limited way, to other people who are within the holy realm. A NT example of this principle may be found in the Canaanite woman who, likening herself to a dog, even requested that Jesus give her the crumbs that had fallen from the master's table (Matt. 15:21–28; see also Mark 5:25–34).

Sin offering (6:24–30[17–23])

Negative and limited holiness contagion warn Christian believers that they ought not to mix what is the Lord's with human things. Jesus said, 'Do not give dogs what is holy, and do not throw your pearls before pigs' (Matt. 7:6 ESV).

In terms of sanctity, the sin offering is, alongside the reparation offering, graded as the least among the five major offerings. The negative contagion of holiness symbolically indicates that if a person becomes holy away from self-hiding, he or she will not have the power to communicate holiness (e.g. spiritual life), to the extent of the loyalty offering or the reparation offering. Hence the NT warnings to those who come to believe in Christ: unless such believers are careful, they are easily swept away by evil (e.g. Matt. 12:43–45; 13:3–23).

Reparation offering (7:1–7)

The work of our Saviour is also described in terms of a reparation offering (Isa. 53:10; cf. NIV and JPS). He became a ransom for the many who believe in him. The supremacy of Christ's offering is obvious in that his offering of himself on the cross (reparation) bears the character of the burnt offering. Therefore, on a dimension different from the sacrificial ritual, the Lord proclaims in Isa. 53:12a that he will receive a portion for his bearing the punishment, which here corresponds to the priestly dues.

7:8–10

The skin of the burnt offering is reserved for common use. In view of the consideration that the skin symbolizes interhuman relationships, the above-mentioned Messiah's work seems to derive from his heart, which he did not entrust to humans (John 2:24): he even spiritually cut himself off from any human relationship (Matt. 12:48–50; for this aspect of holiness, see 'Explanation' on chs. 10 – 11, 21). In this respect his offering is superior to the OT burnt offering.

Christ, by dying on the cross, became the true loyalty offering, and in an analogical but perfect way, distributed himself to many others who belong to him (cf. Ps. 68:18[19]; Eph. 4:7–8). He achieved and even surpassed all the ideals of OT offerings in that he presented his own body, leaving nothing of himself on earth.

In this section, which deals mainly with the priestly dues, the teaching of these *tôrôt* focuses on the priests' privilege and responsibility. 'Privilege', because they receive the remaining flesh, having laboured to offer offerings presented by the people. This means they have the right to be in greater proximity to the Lord than ordinary people. However, such a privilege would become a burden if their hearts still had room for selfishness or earthly desires: in such cases the holy offerings are profaned. Hence their responsibility for not profaning the offerings.

Although not explicitly stated in this text, it would be extremely difficult for the priests to become free of their selfishness or earthly desires. Therefore the holy things were constantly profaned so that the wrath of the Lord accumulated. The need for thoroughness in this matter is indicated by the perpetual fire. More than the annihilation of the egocentric nature, the mediatorial work cannot be accomplished unless the priests become a fire that consumes others' burnt offerings. This is even more so, as their function is to 'sacrifice themselves' (*kipper*). But since this would be impossible, one would naturally wonder how an offering can be truly offered to the Lord through the hands of the priests. It is thus only natural for one to expect that it would be said of the true priest, who has come to this world to cast fire (Luke 12:49), 'the one who falls on this stone will be broken to pieces; and when it falls on anyone, it will crush him' (Matt. 21:44 ESV).

Lastly, some comments are in order regarding what later came to be called the observance of the Law, as the proposal is made that *tôrâ* should be translated 'teaching'. The term *tôrâ* came to have a variety of meanings, ranging from its narrow use in referring to ritual prescriptions in Leviticus, to its widest possible use in referring to the whole Pentateuch or OT. However, it appears that when the observance of the Torah is mentioned by modern believers, these ritual prescriptions have been left in the periphery of the scope of the Law, particularly because the Temple no longer exists and sacrificial worship has ceased. Rather they tend to have in mind the observance of the so-called ethical commandments as set out in chs. 18 – 20. Yet the principles lying behind the ritual prescriptions are still valid today and are applicable, not in a superficial way of jumping to the Christ event, to God–human relationships as a whole.

LEVITICUS 7:11–38

Translation

[11]This is the teaching of the sacrifice of fellowship offering that one may offer to the LORD. [12]If he offers it for thanksgiving, then he shall offer with the thanksgiving sacrifice unleavened loaves mixed with oil, unleavened wafers smeared with oil, and loaves of fine flour well mixed with oil. [13]With the sacrifice of his fellowship offerings for thanksgiving he shall bring his offering with loaves of leavened bread. [14]And from it he shall offer one of each kind as an offering of contribution to the LORD. It shall belong to the priest who dashes the blood of the fellowship offerings.

[15]The flesh of the sacrifice of his fellowship offering for thanksgiving shall be eaten on the day of his offering. He shall not leave any of it until the morning. [16]But if the sacrifice of his offering is a vow offering or a freewill offering, it shall be eaten on the day that he offers his sacrifice, and on the next day what remains of it shall be eaten. [17]But what remains of the flesh of the sacrifice on the third day shall be burned up with fire. [18]If any of the flesh of the sacrifice of his fellowship offering is eaten on the third day, he who offers it shall not be accepted, neither shall it be

credited to him. It is a desecrated offering, and he who eats of it shall bear his iniquity.

19Flesh that touches any unclean thing shall not be eaten. It shall be burned up with fire. And as for the flesh he who is clean may eat flesh, 20but the person who eats the flesh of the sacrifice of the LORD's fellowship offerings while uncleanness is on him, that person shall be cut off from his people. 21And if anyone touches an unclean thing, whether human uncleanness or an unclean beast or any unclean detestable creature, and then eats some flesh from the sacrifice of the LORD's fellowship offering, that person shall be cut off from his people.

22The LORD spoke to Moses, saying, 23'Speak to the Israelites, saying, You shall eat no fat, of ox or sheep or goat. 24The fat of an animal that died and the fat of one that was torn by beasts may be put to any other use, but you shall not eat it. 25For anyone who eats the fat of an animal of which an offering for annihilation may be made to the LORD shall be cut off from his people. 26And you shall eat no blood whatever, whether of fowl or of animal, in any of your dwelling places. 27Any person who eats any blood, that person shall be cut off from his people.'

28The LORD spoke to Moses, saying, 29'Speak to the Israelites, saying, Anyone who offers the sacrifice of his fellowship offering to the LORD shall bring his offering to the LORD from the sacrifice of his fellowship offering. 30His own hands shall bring the LORD's offerings for annihilation. He shall bring the fat with the breast, that the breast may be waved as a wave offering before the LORD. 31The priest shall burn the fat on the altar, but the breast shall belong to Aaron and his sons. 32And the right thigh you shall give to the priest as a contribution from the sacrifice of your fellowship offerings. 33Whoever among the sons of Aaron offers the blood of the fellowship offering and the fat shall have the right thigh for a portion. 34Surely the breast that is waved and the thigh that is contributed I have taken from the Israelites, out of the sacrifices of their fellowship offerings, and have given them to Aaron the priest and to his sons, as a perpetual due from the Israelites. 35This is the anointing of Aaron and the anointing of his sons from the LORD's offerings for annihilation, from the day they were presented to serve the LORD as priests, 36which the LORD commanded to be given them by the Israelites, from the day that he anointed them. It is a perpetual due throughout their generations.'

37This is the teaching of the burnt offering, of the loyalty offering, of the sin offering, of the reparation offering, of the ordination offering and of the fellowship offering, 38which the LORD commanded Moses on Mount Sinai, on the day that he commanded the Israelites to bring their offerings to the LORD, in the wilderness of Sinai.

Notes on the text

11. 'offer': *yaqrîb* SamP and LXX read it in pl.

12. 'loaves well mixed': *ḥallôt bĕlûlôt* in v. 12b is not translated in LXX.

13. *zebaḥ tôdat šĕlāmāyw* This phrase appears twice in the OT, here and v. 15. It has been translated 'thanksgiving sacrifice of his well-being'

(JPS), 'fellowship offering of thanksgiving' (NIV), 'the sacrifice of peace offering' (NASB). It is unnecessary to see the idiom as a conflation of two kinds of sacrifices (cf. Milgrom 1991: 415). A development of appellations can be observed within this small pericope: *zebaḥ šělāmîm* (11), *zebaḥ tôdâ* (12), *zebaḥ tôdat šělāmāyw* (13), *běsar zebaḥ tôdat šělāmāyw* (15). Also, later in this chapter (7:29) comes the phrase *zebaḥ šělāmāyw*. Thus, as the suffix of *šělāmāyw* refers to the worshipper, *zebaḥ tôdat šělāmāyw* should be translated 'the sacrifice of his fellowship offering for thanksgiving'.

14. 'a contribution': *tĕrûmâ* Normal word for 'contribution'. It does not carry the more technical connotation it does in v. 34.

'one of each kind': *'eḥād mikkol qorbān* LXX reflects 'from all his gifts'. However, *'eḥād* means 'each' and refers to each of the three kinds of *minḥâ* mentioned in v. 13.

15. 'the flesh of the sacrifice of his fellowship offerings for thanksgiving' LXX adds 'will be his' and divides the first half of the verse into two parts. However, MT makes sense if the phrase is understood as introducing a new topic.

16. 'and on the next day': *umimmoḥorat* LXX translates 'and on the next day' but connects this part with the main verb 'shall be eaten', while omitting 'what remains of it shall be eaten' – presumably because the same expression *wĕhannôtar* occurs in v. 16 and at the beginning of v. 17.

18. 'a desecrated offering': *piggûl* This term refers not just to the physical state of the meat (putrid), but also to the state of the meat in connection with eating. See Wright 1987: 140–143.

19. 'as for the flesh': *wĕhabbāśār* LXX, Syr and Vg omit the phrase, probably because *bāśār* at the end of the verse makes it redundant. Some Eng. translations paraphrase it as 'as for other flesh' (JPS, NIV, NRSV, Wevers 1997: 90), but the whole can be taken as syntactically introducing a topic, while talking about a certain principle.

20. 'from his people': *mē'ammêhâ* The Hebr. for 'people' is pl. The pl. form of *'am* (people) refers to the multitude of individuals who make up a group of people (*IBHS* 7.4.1b). The same form or similar grammatical feature appears in vv. 21, 25, 27 and 17:9; 19:8, 16; 21:1, 4, 14–15.

21. 'any unclean detestable creature': *šeqeṣ ṭāmē'* The Hebr. phrase is unique in the OT. Some Hebr. MSS, as well as SamP, Syr and Tg, read 'unclean swarmers' (*šereṣ*) as in 5:2. It may be that the two terms *šereṣ* (5:2) and *šeqeṣ* (7:21) are mentioned in anticipation of ch. 11 (see vv. 10, 20, 23, 41–43).

25. *Kî* at the beginning of the verse is not translated in LXX and some Eng. translations. However, this *kî* should be taken as having a speaker-oriented function (see Claassen 1983): it introduces the reason for *stating* the prohibition.

30. 'a wave offering': *tĕnûpâ Tĕnûpâ* is traditionally rendered 'wave offering' (NIV, NASB). However, Milgrom argues that *nwp* hiph. means 'elevate' and not 'wave' (1972: 33–38), and that it is synonymous with *rwm* hiph. Hence he proposes to translate it 'elevation offering'. This understanding is followed by JPS, NRSV and other exegetes (e.g. Hartley 1992: 101; Rooker 2000: 137). However, passages such as Isa. 10:15, where it is used in relation to a wood saw, suggest that *nwp* hiph. still has the meaning of 'wave' (see Ringgren 1986: 318–319). On the whole, the term appears to refer to a swinging motion without specifying direction (up–down or front–back motion). Since it also takes persons as its object (Levites; cf. Num. 8:11, 13, 15, 21), *tĕnûpâ* can be translated figuratively as 'dedication', and *tĕrûmâ*, which appears in v. 32, may be translated 'contribution' (see 'Comment').

34. *Kî* probably carries the sense of 'surely, certainly' rather than an introduction to the reason for the previous statement, for much of the content of this verse is already mentioned in the previous verses. This verse stresses the agent who legislated the previous rules; i.e. the Lord.

35. 'anointing': *mišḥâ* Only here is this term used without reference to 'oil'. As *mišḥâ* refers to the breast and thigh in v. 34, it must mean something like 'share'. Hence the root *mšḥ* II, the Akk. cognate being *mašāḥu* (to measure, Seybold 1986: 47), is suggested, and accordingly translated 'share' (cf. *HALOT*) in almost all Eng. translations. Wenham renders it 'the anointed right' (1979: 115). However, there are two other possibilities: (1) It means 'anointing-due' (as in Elberfelder, *Salbungsteil*) in the sense that the breast and thigh are the share received after one is anointed. (2) It means 'anointing' in a metaphorical sense, since the breast and thigh are not oil. It seems that 2 is preferable, because 'due' is elsewhere expressed in Leviticus by *ḥôq* (see v. 34). LXX also renders it simply 'anointing', although the translators may have understood the intent of the verse differently.

'from the day': *bĕyôm* See 6:20[13] and 7:36 for the *bêt*, meaning 'from'.

38. *'Ăšer* at the beginning of the verse, which is similar in style to *'ăšer* in v. 36, refers back to *hattôrâ* in v. 37.

Form and structure

The section 7:11–38 deals with the fellowship offering from the perspective of priestly dues and responsibility. Though the laity's right to eat the remaining part of the sacrifice is presupposed, other aspects of the ritual such as an injunction not to profane the offering are emphasized. This accords with the general character of chs. 6 – 7: safeguarding the holy from uncleanness and profanation. The content is as follows:

A.	11–21	The fellowship offering
	12–14	The thanksgiving sacrifice
	15–21	Regulations concerning consumption of meat
		a. Time limit for consumption (15–18)
		b. Contact with uncleanness (19–21)
B.	22–27	Injunction on fat and blood
C.	28–36	The breast and right thigh as priestly dues
D.	37–38	Concluding remarks

On the whole, though these sections are clearly marked off from each other either by content or address formulae, they are unified by a common train of thought (see 'Comment').

In terms of the thematic structure of 1:1 – 7:38, the section 7:11–38 corresponds to 5:14 – 6:7[5:26] in that the latter (the reparation offering) deals with extreme offences that profane the holy, while the former (the fellowship offering) deals with the dangerous aspects of the fellowship offering by regulating how its flesh is eaten (see 'Form and structure' on 6:8[1] – 7:10). Within section 6:8[1] – 7:36, it may be observed that just as the priestly *minḥâ* section (6:19–23[12–16]) follows the ordinary *minḥâ* section (6:14[7]–18[11]), so the section on the priestly portion from the fellowship offering on the day of ordination (7:35–36) follows that for the ordinary priestly due from the fellowship offering (7:29–34).

Section A above still belongs to the matter of priests (see 6:25[18]). That is, since the fellowship offering is also handled by the laity, the priests must guard its sanctity by following these rules. This section prescribes how the flesh of the fellowship offering for thanksgiving should be consumed, and it warns of the dangers associated with its coming into contact with human uncleanness or unclean flesh. Topically, the section falls into three parts (12–14, 15–18, 19–21), yet they remain connected by common ideas.

Sections B and C are addressed to the Israelites. Section B deals with the essential elements of the offering (fat and blood), which is an expansion of the rule given in 3:17b. Thus C is based on B. Indeed C also deals with the offerer's potential concern, temptation to partake of the choicest parts of an animal: the breast and right thigh. The rules in C gradually shift to the theme of priestly dues. The section ends by linking the dues with the ordination of Aaron and his sons in the next chapter.

Section D not only concludes section 6:8[1] – 7:38 but also 1:1 – 7:38 (see 'Comment').

Comment

7:11–14

11. The section beginning from this verse (vv. 11–21) is still addressed to the priests (see 6:24–25 [17–18]). So it is the prescription for them, first and foremost.

This clause 'that one may offer to the LORD' (*'ăšer yaqrîb lYHWH*) sounds self-evident. Moreover such a clause does not follow after 'This is the law of' in 6:25[18a] and 7:1. Milgrom (1991: 413) sees in this clause 'an admission that it is permitted to eat the meat of pure, non-sacrificial animals, for example, blemished animals (22:21–25) and game (17:13–14), as well as sacrificial animals slaughtered profanely for their meat'. This is indeed true, but he further infers from this that the purpose of the offering is 'to provide meat for the table'. It is questionable if this is what is in the mind of the lawgiver. In my view this is just the point the lawgiver endeavours to remedy in an attempt to put all aspects of the sacrifice into a balanced perspective: the intention is to stress that the *zebaḥ šĕlāmîm*, though the worshipper ultimately can partake of its meat, ought to be brought before the Lord in the first place. Therefore it was the possibility that the *zebaḥ šĕlāmîm* might not be completely relinquished to the Lord that motivated the lawgiver to give the following prescription.

12–13. The term *tôdâ* means 'confession' or 'acknowledgment', not 'thanks'. It denotes the act of acknowledging that particular salvation has been granted by the Lord. The following details of the sacrifice assume the immensity of the thanksgiving on the part of the offerer. First, he adds to the thanksgiving sacrifice three items: unleavened loaves mixed with oil, unleavened wafers smeared with oil, and loaves of fine flour well mixed with oil. V. 13 stipulates that leavened bread must also be added. The latter, normally excluded from the Lord's altar (see Lev. 2:12), suggests rich communion between God and the worshipper. Since he offers both unleavened bread and leavened bread, he thereby expresses that the Lord brought the offerer a great salvation ('leavened bread'; see 'Comment' on 2:11–12) because of his faith in him (unleavened bread). Thus the offering expresses fellowship between the Lord and the worshipper.

14. The offerer presents to the Lord as a contribution each of the three kinds of fellowship offering mentioned in v. 13. 'Contribution' (*tĕrûmâ*) here bears no sacrificial significance. It is something given over to the other party whether willingly or dutifully (see 'Comment' on vv. 30–33 below). It then becomes the possession of the officiating priest. By the expression 'who dashes the blood', the officiating priest appears to be viewed as one who prepared for the offerer to pave the way for a fellowship with the Lord. It is important to observe that first the offerer presents his offering to the Lord, after which the Lord's property is given to the priest.

7:15–18

15–17. The phrase 'the flesh of the sacrifice of his fellowship offerings for thanksgiving' (*bĕśar zebaḥ tôdat šĕlāmāyw*, 15) comes last in the development of the similar appellations (see vv. 12–13 and 'Notes on the text' on v. 13) and simultaneously functions to introduce a new topic: the *flesh* of the thanksgiving sacrifice.

'Eating the flesh' probably symbolizes communion with the Lord, which is the purpose of the fellowship offering. Though the eating of blood or fat was prohibited in 3:17, the rules for eating the remaining flesh are not introduced until now. The Lord is willing to have fellowship with the worshipper with the best of the latter's sacrifice that symbolizes destruction of egocentric nature. Yet the very injunction not to leave any of the flesh until the next day or the third day suggests the egocentric nature's ongoing existence. It reflects the Lord's apprehension that the offerer's resolve is only momentary. Thus the Lord sets out different time spans for eating the flesh, depending on the offerer's indebtedness to the Lord (see below). Just as the Lord would not like to be hosted with meat of a lesser quality, he would not like to have communion with people who still bear their egocentric nature.

The difference between *nēder* and *nĕdābâ*, on the one hand, and the *tôdâ*, on the other, is that the votive sacrifice (*neder)* is offered when the prayer is answered (Pss. 22:25[26]; 50:14 etc.), while the freewill offering is offered when there is no specific obligation to do so (Ps. 54:6[8]; cf. Kurtz 1980: 258–263). Moreover the thanksgiving sacrifice is offered in response to the Lord's gracious unilateral salvific act. Thus the more a worshipper owes to the Lord, the stricter the rules of eating the meat become. In other words, the Lord naturally expects more hospitality in the offering of *tôdâ* than of the *nĕdābâ* and *nēder*. The common element of the three kinds of offering is the Lord's desire that the offerer's self-centredness be removed by the time the communion meal is held.

The phrase 'burn in fire' (*śrp bā'ēš*, 17) in Leviticus designates disposal of the disqualified meat or what is abhorrent to the Lord (4:12, 21; 8:17; 9:11; 10:6, 16; 16:28 etc.).

18. If a person violates the injunction on eating the flesh on the third day, both the offerer and the offering are not accepted, and the former must bear his own guilt: he has committed an offence against the Lord. It is inappropriate to ask about the details of bearing guilt: it is punishment on his soul (*nepeš*). As the terms *rāṣâ* and *ḥāšab* imply, the sacrifice and the offerer are, though distinct, regarded as one (see 'Comment' on 1:4 and 17:4, and 'Explanation' on chs. 1 and 3).

From this verse onwards, the term *nepeš* appears frequently as the agent who eats the flesh (v. 18), touches uncleanness (v. 21) or is cut off from the people (v. 21). All modern translations render the term as either 'the person' or 'he who'. However, as in previous chapters, the term is obviously and deliberately used in distinction to *'îš* (person, vv. 8, 10) or *'ādām* (man, v. 21). As stated in 'Comment' on 2:1 and 4:2, *nepeš* stresses an invisible aspect of a human ('soul') that is characterized by egocentricity. It may be observed that since *nepeš* constitutes an invisible entity of a person, there is a gap between *nepeš* and the tangible act of eating. This is evidence that the act of eating flesh is not simply physical. Since the agent of eating is a soul, the act of eating also takes place on a spiritual dimension. Indeed eating disqualified meat expresses a manifestation of the offerer's egocentric nature in the presence of the Lord, which is nothing less than profaning his name.

7:19–21

Here the Lord addresses the nature of the meat and the worshipper in terms of uncleanness. The fundamental principle that the unclean ought not to have any contact with the clean is set out with a gradually increasing emphasis on the qualification of the agent of consumption, the worshipper.

19–20. Meat coming into contact with the unclean is disqualified as food: it must be burnt. Meat qualifying as food is eaten by clean people only. V. 20 is an elaboration of v. 19b, dealing with a situation where the meat is eaten by an unclean person. It is explicitly stated that the flesh belongs to the Lord, as it has been offered to him. The rule does not reveal the intentionality of the act; it simply states its consequence: he will be cut off (*krt* ni.) from the people. This is the first occurrence of the *kāret* penalty in Leviticus. It is the penalty associated with a breach of the covenant (Gen. 17:14), yet how it was practically executed is not mentioned. While it is sometimes related to the death penalty, the presence of the *kāret* penalty without mention of death leaves room for the supposition that it is something other than the death penalty (cf. Sklar 2001: 14–18).

Also of significance is that from this verse onwards the term *krt* is always followed by *mēʿammāyw* (from one's people), where *ʿām* is pl. (except 22:3). As mentioned in 'Notes on the text', it refers to the multitude of individuals making up a group of people. Though the pl. *ʿammîm* is not limited to the *kāret* penalty in Leviticus (17:4, 10), when the penalty is stated, the term *ʿām* often takes its pl. form. Thus the reference to individuals or individual groups may suggest that as a penalty he is to be cut off from every member of the people to whom he belongs, not to mention from the covenantal community as a whole. He becomes absolutely isolated, cut off from any humans he may have recourse to in time of need. Thus this penalty is virtually no different for the offender from the death penalty. For the antonymous relation of the *kāret* penalty to the idea of *kipper*, see 'Comment' on ch. 17.

In Leviticus there is no absolute guarantee that the Lord always dwells among his people, which is consonant with the observation that 'his people' in the *kāret* penalty is never explicitly stated as the Lord's or God's, people. The reason may be related to the Lord's implicit wrath against the spiritual reality of the people. At any rate, the Lord's distancing himself even from the people makes the *kāret* penalty an extreme misery for the offender.

The addition of 'of the Lord's offering' (*'ăšer lYHWH*, also in the next verse) shows that the Lord hosts as well as being hosted. Therefore the breach is all the more serious, since it constitutes an assault against a holy thing.

21. The same principle is expressed, this time, through the reversal of the sequence of eating and uncleanness in v. 20a. The causes of uncleanness are detailed in language similar to Lev. 5:2–3, and they assume the regulations in Lev. 11 – 15 (see 'Notes on the text').

As in the previous case in v. 20, it is not certain whether the person in question was conscious of his act. After all, he cannot be perfectly certain he is in a clean state, for he may be unaware of his inadvertent contraction of uncleanness. The conclusion is inevitable that the offences in vv. 20–21 have nothing to do with the intention of the offender. It is extremely difficult, then, for any Israelites to offer a fellowship offering to the Lord in the true sense, as they cannot do so unless it is objectively certain they are clean.

However, once the symbolic meaning of uncleanness is taken into account, it becomes even more impossible to offer a fellowship offering to the Lord with a clean state of heart. For uncleanness symbolizes the state of hiding oneself in varying degrees, and in most cases it is unconscious. But, why are such complicated rules necessary when offerers have symbolically died to their selfishness by the shedding of animal blood and burning of fat? The reason is that the law assumes the problems of the human heart are not fully dealt with by the sacrificial ritual: the ritual tends to be formal, while the heart remains the same.

7:22–27

The prohibition in 3:17b against eating fat and blood is expanded in vv. 23b–27. The rationale underlying the blood prohibition is gradually developed through Leviticus, and on each occasion its mention relates to the fellowship offering: first, in 3:17, next in more detail in 7:23b–27, and lastly in 17:10–11, where the rationale for the injunction is explicitly stated.

22–24. These rules are addressed first to Moses. For the first time in 6:8[1] – 7:38, Moses is instructed to address the Israelites and not just the priests, as has been the case up till now (see 6:24–25[17–18]). A possible reason for the placement of the rules on fat and blood at this point would be to draw attention to their significance for the meaning of the ritual. For if the symbolic meaning of shedding blood and burning fat are actualized in the soul of the offerer, there would have been no problem in the eating of the flesh, which symbolizes communion with the Lord. But as the rules in vv. 18–21 have shown, the root of the potential trouble in eating the remaining flesh is traced back to the blood and fat of the animal. The

Lord's address in v. 22 suggests that these verses constitute a new beginning, but in content they are closely related to the handling of the fellowship offering; i.e. its fat and blood (cf. 3:16–17). In fact, the topics address the constituent elements of the ritual before eating.

The injunction in 3:17b is slightly expanded by adding 'of ox, or sheep or goat'. The main reason for the injunction is that these belong to the Lord (3:16b). More specifically, they belong to the Lord in the sense that they should be set apart to make a soothing aroma to the Lord by burning. While they remain in the form of fat, it is inedible or unfavourable to the Lord. To eat the fat, which symbolizes the offerer's egocentric nature, would demonstrate contentment with his selfish heart.

The allowance for using the fat of an animal that died or was torn by beasts, for purposes other than eating, may reflect the people's desire to use it. Such animals are unclean (17:15; 22:8) because they are dead. Thus the law allows a certain amount of defilement in taking the fat parts from dead animals (cf. Exod. 22:31[30]).

25. The case of the violation of the above injunction and its consequent punishment follows: if a soul ingests this fat, he is inevitably cut off from the people, since he has profaned the Lord's holiness. In fact, prior to divine punishment the offerer brings about punishment on himself by his own act.

26. Following the prohibition against eating fat comes the prohibition against eating blood. The sequence of fat and then blood in vv. 22–27 may reflect the order from the outer to the inner: fat covers flesh and flesh contains blood.

'your dwelling places': *môšĕbōtêkem* This remark says that the injunction applies not just to the sanctuary area, but also to the Israelites' homes. Animal blood is a means for making propitiation (Lev. 17:11), and it is at their homes that reverence for the sanctity of blood should be nurtured, which adumbrates the prohibition of profane slaughter in Lev. 17. The mention of 'fowl' and its placement (before the 'animal') may be unexpected. Why is the bird mentioned in a context where the fellowship offering is at issue? The answer is to be found in the general nature of vv. 22–27. It has both the fellowship offering and the burnt offering in view (cf. 1:14–17). Even the potential for profaning the blood of the burnt offering may be contemplated!

27. The punishment of the *kāret* penalty is laid down against anyone who consumes blood. As stated above, eating blood symbolizes destroying the very means of making propitiation, thereby losing the very means that enables the offerer to live before the Lord. However, shedding animal blood symbolizes the offerer's spiritual death. This is the foundation of the whole ritual of the fellowship offering. The Lord regarded it necessary to add the injunction on fat and blood in order to suggest that unless people die to their egocentric nature, the whole ritual symbolizing joy and fellowship becomes meaningless. For the idea of 'a soul' eating 'blood', see 'Comment' on v. 18 above.

7:28–36

28–29. The Lord again directs Moses to address the Israelites, this time regarding the breast and right thigh of the fellowship offering, both of which are mentioned for the first time in Leviticus. The former is called the wave offering of breast, and the latter the contribution of the right thigh.

The rule is expressed in a peculiar way if this is simply a prescription. Two elements are apparently stressed: (1) The offerer brings his fellowship offering from *his own* fellowship offering (*mizzebaḥ šĕlāmāyw*). (2) He brings it to the Lord ('to the LORD' is mentioned twice). First, from a factual point of view, the rule as a whole appears to be common sense. For self-evidently the offerer brings his fellowship offering from his fellowship offering. Since it is unlikely the legislator has the possibility in mind that the offerer is different from the owner of the animal, the emphasis on '*his* fellowship offering' is aimed at something else. It seems, from the context, that the present verse stresses the offering ought truly to be a sacrifice by the same person (but see below). Second, it appears also to be common sense that the offerer brings his offering *to the Lord*. The emphasis appears to stress it is the Lord who accepts it. But this is strange, since the offerer has offered the sacrifice to the Lord. Why is this emphasized here? The possibility looms large that the legislator assumes an offerer who would not willingly offer the sacrifice, despite the fact that he officially and publicly offered it to the Lord. This unwillingness possibly results from the offerer's tendency to dwell on the material outcome of the offering (the eating of meat) rather than its spiritual significance.

30–33. The offerer's actions are described gradually and in a concentrated way: first, *his hands* bring 'the offering for annihilation to the Lord', then 'the fat together with the breast', and lastly 'the breast'.

'his own hands shall bring' This is a unique expression and should be taken as reflecting the legislator's continuing concern that the offerer may be unwilling to offer to the Lord. This concern is highlighted by the emphasis on the giving of the breast, which is one of the choicest parts of the animal. 'The breast' part can be shared among the priests' family (31). But the command that it ought to be brought together with the fat suggests the offerer expresses his willingness to give the breast portion, the best part, over to the Lord, as the burning of fat symbolizes the death of selfishness. But the way in which the rule is presented appears to assume the opposite spiritual reality.

This is, then, a continuation of the legislator's concern, reflected in the placement of the prohibitions on eating fat and blood in vv. 22–27, that the offerer has the constant propensity to defeat his initial motive, which was expressed by the shedding of blood and burning of fat.

'wave offering': *tĕnûpâ* See 'Notes on the text'.

'the right thigh': *šôq hāyyāmîn* The right thigh perhaps refers to the 'hindquarter', which is one of the choicest parts alongside the breast (cf. 1 Sam. 9:24). From Exod. 29:26 and Lev. 8:29 both the breast and the right thigh are termed *mānâ* (portion). The offerer then gives the right thigh to the priest as a contribution. Only the officiating priests can partake of the right thigh. On 'Contribution' (*tĕrûmâ*), see on 7:14.

It seems possible to suppose, particularly from the present context, that both 'waving' and 'dedicating' symbolize the transference of property from one party to another. The distinction between the two may lie in the difference of the two roots *nwp* and *rwm*. The *nwp* hiph. (to wave) is more elaborate than *rwm* hiph. (to dedicate). And it appears that these express two different kinds of transference. One describes an offering given indirectly to the priest via the Lord; the other, an offering given directly to the priest. A further distinction between these rites can be surmised from the immediate context. These verses are located after the prohibition against eating fat and blood, which, in turn, reflects unwillingness on the part of the offerer. However, the context of these acts concerns instructions on what to do with the choicest parts of the animal flesh. It must be recalled that the offerer had offered the whole animal to the Lord. Moreover the telltale expressions of 'from *his* fellowship offering' and '*his own hands* bring' suggest strongly that these rituals are meant to cope with the inner life of the offerer. In other words, the genuineness of the offerer's motive is verified by his adding the best part of the animal (its breast) on to the fat parts. This appears symbolically to mean, as mentioned above, that the offerer is unselfish, and that, in addition, he is willing to offer one of the choicest parts of the animal to the Lord. Before burning fat, the priest waves the breast before the Lord.

On the other hand, the offerer is commanded to dedicate the contribution of the right thigh directly to the officiating priest (33). It is observable that while the gesture of the wave offering ritual is elaborate, that of the contribution of the right thigh is simple: it goes directly to the officiating priest. In view of the potential unwillingness of the offerer to abandon the possession, the contribution represents a simple abandonment of the best part. Thus it may be inferred that the two rites express transference of possession to the Lord or the priest, and that those are meant to cope with the potential unwillingness of the offerer. While the wave offering describes the process from unwillingness to willingness, the right thigh contribution describes the resolution (note the 2nd person address in v. 32).

34. In the section of 6:8[1] – 7:34 'I have given' (*nātattî*) appears in 6:17[10] in connection with the priestly loyalty offering, while here in 7:34 'I have taken' (*lāqaḥtî*) and 'I have given' (*wā'ettēn*) appears in connection with the breast and the right thigh. The offerer's motive and willingness to dedicate the choicest parts of the animal are expressed here in such a way that it is the Lord himself who takes them and gives them to Aaron and his sons as their priestly dues.

35–36. These verses relate the breast and right thigh to the ordination of Aaron and his sons (Exod. 29:24, 26–27; Lev. 8:27, 29). The metaphorical reference to anointing of the breast and the right thigh in v. 35 (see 'Notes on the text') aims to remind the priests of their divine calling every time they receive them.

'from the day that he anointed them' Anointing the priest has been mentioned in 6:20[13] and here. Both anticipate the ordination ceremony that will follow in the next chapter.

7:37–38

37. This and the next verses constitute a summary statement of all the rules in 6:8[1] – 7:36. While the burnt offering, the loyalty offering, the sin offering and the reparation offering are in the same order as they have been presented, the order of the ordination offerings (*millû'îm*) and the fellowship offering needs some comment. The ordination offerings (*millû'îm*) refer to the priestly loyalty offering in 6:19–23[12–16] and the breast and the right thigh (7:28–36), and each follows the ordinary loyalty offering and the ordinary fellowship offering respectively. Yet here *millû'îm* comes before the ordinary fellowship offering. It may be surmised that here is at work the logic that the priestly matters come first, a logic that pervades the whole section of 6:8[1] – 7:36: the ordinary offering presented by the laity is mentioned last.

38. The sentence structure of vv. 37–38 is very similar to that of vv. 35–36: both begin '*This* (*zō't*) is', followed by 'which (*'ăšer*)'. All the teachings in 6:8[1] – 7:36 are given at Mount Sinai about offerings to be offered to the Lord, in the Sinai desert. It may be that 'he commanded' (*ṣiwwâ*) in 6:9[2] forms an inclusio with 'he commanded' (*ṣiwwâ*) in 7:36, 38. The second half of the verse, especially the mention of 'the sons of Israel', makes it clear that 6:8[1] – 7:36 is given by the Lord on the same day as 1:1 – 6:7[5:26].

Explanation

Why are the three occasions for offering the fellowship offering mentioned in this chapter and not in ch. 3? The prescriptions of ch. 3 are not dictated by the various occasions of offering, because it is assumed a person offers his sacrifice *wholeheartedly*. By contrast, the instructions regarding the handling of the remaining flesh in ch. 7 indicate that this ideal is not reflected in practice (see 'Comment' on vv. 11, 28–29, 30–33). Indeed the very presence of prescriptions for different kinds of fellowship offerings along with the accompanying prohibitions suggest that vv. 11–38 assume the continuing presence of the offerer's egocentric nature.

It is somewhat surprising to see so many cautions made in relation to the fellowship offering. That the holy flesh may potentially become defiled by the offerer himself is something unexpected and disheartening in view of the supposed joy and thanksgiving that should be the basic tenor of the offering (see ch. 3). The repeated mention of these matters after the directions on the eating of flesh indicates that the egocentric nature may persistently remain. Furthermore the rules on the wave offering and the contribution appear very odd when it is remembered that the offerer gave the whole of his fellowship offering to the Lord out of sheer joy or thanksgiving, and all the more so if his selfishness was actually removed. Fellowship with the Lord assumes purity, but these prescriptions assume that the offerers are far from fellowship with the Lord, even when they decide to offer themselves.

Thus the text functions not just to provide additional rules to ch. 3 but expresses the Lord's concern about the spiritual reality of the offerer. In other words, the prescription for the fellowship offering is provided on the premise that 'the spirit indeed is willing, but the flesh is weak' (Matt. 26:41 ESV; Mark 14:38).

These considerations possibly shed light on the question of why the fellowship offering is not called 'holy' (*qādôš* or *qōdeš*) in chs. 3 or 7, although it is assumed to be so in ch. 21 (v. 22) and ch. 22 (vv. 2–3 etc.). That chs. 21 – 22 concern the priests and not the laity appears to suggest that the mention of 'holy' in Leviticus is reserved for the priests and their dues. It has been pointed out that the mention of *qōdeš qodāšîm* is only to illumine the essence of the burnt offering, for which no mention is made of 'holy' (see 'Explanation' on ch. 1). Thus a different rationale to that in the burnt offering appears to be operating for the fellowship offering. Apparently 'holy' or 'holiness' is not mentioned because the offerer's and priest's supposed spiritual conditions are far from the holy status of the fellowship offering itself.

This is reflected in the prescriptions for the wave offering and the contribution of the right thigh. An offerer is to bring the choicest part to the Lord *with his own hands*. This reflects his awareness that it is the choicest part. Such a consciousness of its value is at odds with the fact that he offered the whole animal to the Lord in the first place. In this kind of situation, it is easily imaginable that true fellowship with the Lord is incomplete regardless of how meticulously the offerer and the officiating priest follow the procedure. To put it another way, since the egocentric nature is not easily destroyed, the Lord provided rules to prevent fellowship from being marred.

Such a situation may well derive from the fact that, as in the burnt offering, the offerer may offer his fellowship offering as a response to his salvation from suffering or death, but not from his own egocentric nature, even though the offering essentially deals with the latter. The offerer ought to bear in mind that the purpose of the fellowship offering is, first and foremost, the destruction of his egocentric nature. Though the ritual of the fellowship offering must have been conducted in a single day, it seems clear the required qualification of the offerer cannot be met within the framework of the ritual: the ritual must also be seen as representing the divine–human relationship in a person's whole life. At any rate, a fellowship offering is not easily offered according to the prescription in ch. 7.

New Testament implications

In the NT Christ became a fellowship offering, making the sacrificial ritual obsolete. But needless to say, this does not make the Leviticus message on the fellowship offering irrelevant to NT believers. It would only have lost relevance if the human egocentric nature were completely dead. But, partly because our egocentric nature does not disappear, we are given the Lord's Supper as a means to remember and give thanks for the Lord's death. In both the Law and the NT there is a danger of profaning the holy thing: in the Law it is the blood, fat and flesh of the animal, and in the NT it is the Lord's body. This may give rise to a situation where one is convinced one is worshipping God, but is in fact just using his name merely to serve one's own desires. Yet one needs reminding that in profaning the Holy Communion one's eternal fate is at stake (see below).

Indeed we may believe fellowship with Christ is free and always given. Yet such fellowship can be enjoyed only by those whose hearts are humble. Strictly it cannot exist if one has an egocentric nature. Therefore fellowship with God is extremely difficult. St Paul also states a similar warning concerning Holy Communion in 1 Cor. 11:27–30. It is not certain what NT punishment corresponds to the *kāret* penalty of the OT Law. From Matt. 12:31–32 (cf. Heb. 6:4–8; 10:26–31) it can be inferred that it is related to blaspheming against the Lord or the Holy Spirit. For further argument, see 'Explanation' on ch. 24. In principle, the punishment of the *kāret* penalty applies to NT times too, where rejecting the means of salvation (Christ or the Holy Spirit) deserves eternal punishment.

This chapter also indicates the dangers associated with being a Christian leader. As stressed by this prescription, the offerer presents his offering to the Lord, and then it is granted to the priest(s) as a prebend. Obviously the priests need to be fed. But according to the prescription in Lev. 7:11–34, the Lord gives them their portion only *after* they have fulfilled their duty to ascertain the death of the offerer's selfish ego (even though the latter may be temporary). If this is done improperly, the priest's work at the altar becomes nothing more than formal business. Thus the spiritual condition of the lay individual depends a lot on the priest's duty: the offerer is responsible for his own spiritual condition, but the priest is also responsible for the offerer in so far as he is the guardian of the holy things. Eating is essential for human life, but if the priest becomes content with this only, simply expecting to receive the choicest parts of the animal flesh, there is no divine presence in the ritual.

In the Law it is strongly emphasized that the offerer should treat the Lord with the best part of his sacrifice to express appreciation for the salvation reveived. Yet in heaven it is *Christ* who serves true believers at the table (Luke 12:36–37). He is the one who became a servant, and remains so forever. Who will ultimately be entitled to enter this fellowship? Not everyone who utters 'Lord, Lord', but only those who do the will of the Father in heaven (Matt. 7:21). In terms of the OT fellowship offering, the death of the selfish ego must become permanent, so that such a person does not calculate the worth of his contribution, or seek the choicest parts of the animal, since he has offered it to the Lord (cf. Matt. 25:31–46).

LEVITICUS 8:1–36

Translation

[1]The LORD spoke to Moses, saying, [2]'Take Aaron and his sons with him, and the garments and the anointing oil and the bull of the sin offering and the two rams and the basket of unleavened bread. [3]And assemble the whole community at the entrance of the Tent of Meeting.' [4]And Moses did as the LORD commanded him, and the community was assembled at the entrance of the Tent of Meeting.

[5]Moses said to the community, 'This is the thing that the LORD has commanded to be done.' [6]Then Moses brought Aaron and his sons and washed them with water. [7]He put the tunic on him and tied the sash around his waist and clothed him with the robe and put the ephod on him and tied the skillfully woven band of the ephod around him, binding it to him with the band. [8]And he placed the breastpiece on him, and in the breastpiece he put the Urim and the Thummim. [9]He set the turban on his head, and on the turban, in front, he set the golden plate, the holy crown, as the LORD commanded Moses.

[10]Then Moses took the anointing oil and anointed the tabernacle and all that was in it, and consecrated them. [11]He sprinkled some of it on the altar seven times, and anointed the altar and all its utensils and the basin and its stand, to consecrate them. [12]He poured some of the anointing oil on Aaron's head and anointed him to consecrate him. [13]Moses then brought Aaron's sons and clothed them with tunics and tied sashes around their waists and bound caps on them, as the LORD commanded Moses.

[14]He brought the bull of the sin offering, and Aaron and his sons laid their hands on the head of the bull of the sin offering. [15]And it was slaughtered. Moses took the blood, and with his finger put it on the horns of the altar around it and made the altar uncovered and poured out the blood at the base of the altar and consecrated it by making propitiation for it. [16]He took all the fat that was on the entrails and the long lobe of the liver and the two kidneys with their fat, and Moses

burned them on the altar. [17]But the bull and its skin and its flesh and its dung he
burned up with fire outside the camp, as the LORD commanded Moses.
[18]Then he presented the ram of the burnt offering, and Aaron and his sons laid
their hands on the head of the ram. [19]And it was slaughtered. Moses dashed the
blood against the sides of the altar. [20]He cut the ram into pieces, and Moses burned
the head and the pieces and the fat. [21]He washed the entrails and the legs with water,
and Moses burned the whole ram on the altar. It was a burnt offering with a soothing
aroma, an offering for annihilation for the LORD, as the LORD commanded Moses.
[22]Then he presented the other ram, the ram of ordination, and Aaron and his
sons laid their hands on the head of the ram. [23]And it was slaughtered. Moses took
some of its blood and put it on the lobe of Aaron's right ear and on the thumb of his
right hand and on the big toe of his right foot. [24]Then he presented Aaron's sons,
and Moses put some of the blood on the lobes of their right ears and on the thumbs
of their right hands and on the big toes of their right feet. And Moses dashed the
blood against the sides of the altar. [25]Then he took the fat, namely the fat tail and
all the fat that was on the entrails and the long lobe of the liver and the two kidneys
with their fat and the right thigh, [26]and out of the basket of unleavened bread that
was before the LORD he took one unleavened loaf and one loaf of bread with oil and
one wafer and placed them on the pieces of fat and on the right thigh. [27]He put all
these in the hands of Aaron and in the hands of his sons and waved them as a wave
offering before the LORD. [28]Then Moses took them from their hands and burned
them on the altar with the burnt offering. This was an ordination offering with a
soothing aroma, an offering for annihilation to the LORD. [29]And Moses took the
breast and waved it for a wave offering before the LORD. It was Moses' portion of
the ram of ordination, as the LORD commanded Moses.
[30]Then Moses took some of the anointing oil and blood that was on the altar and
sprinkled it on Aaron and his garments, and also on his sons and his sons' garments.
So he consecrated Aaron and his garments, and his sons and his sons' garments with
him. [31]Moses said to Aaron and his sons, 'Boil the flesh at the entrance of the Tent of
Meeting, and there eat it and the bread that is in the basket of ordination offerings,
as I commanded, saying, Aaron and his sons shall eat it. [32]And what remains of
the flesh and the bread you shall burn with fire. [33]And you shall not go outside the
entrance of the Tent of Meeting for seven days, until the days of your ordination are
completed, for it will take seven days to ordain you. [34]As has been done today, the
LORD has commanded to be done to make propitiation for you. [35]At the entrance
of the Tent of Meeting you shall remain day and night for seven days, performing
what the LORD has charged, so that you do not die, for so I have been commanded.'
[36]And Aaron and his sons did all the things that the LORD commanded by Moses.

Notes on the text

4. 'was assembled': *watiqqāhēl* LXX reads 'and he assembled' (corresponding to Heb. *wayyaqhēl*), taking the subject as Moses. However, a change from *tāw* to *yôd* is difficult to assume. So the MT should be retained.

10. 'the anointing oil': *'et šemen hammišḥâ* LXX translates 'from the oil'. 'and anointed ... consecrated them' LXX has placed this after v. 11.

11. 'and anointed the altar' LXX adds 'and consecrated them'. Yet the idea of consecration is expressed at the end of the verse.

14. From v. 14 onwards the construction *wāw* + *yiqṭōl* or *wāw* + *qāṭal* followed by *wāw* + *yiqṭōl* + subject appears frequently (see vv. 15–16, 18–24). LXX supplies 'Moses' as the subject of the first verbs in vv. 16, 18–19, 22, 24, 28. This understanding is probably correct.

15. See 'Comment'.

19. 'and it was slaughtered': *wayyišḥaṭ* Although *BHS* margin recommends placing *sôp pāsûq* after *wayyišḥaṭ*, linking it with the preceding verse, this seems difficult in view of the frequent Hebr. construction mentioned in v. 14 above. So v. 23 below.

25. See 'Comment' on 3:9.

26. 'the basket of the unleavened bread': *sal hammaṣṣôt* LXX reads 'the basket of the ordination' (reflecting *sal hammillû'îm*), probably in conformity with v. 31.

34. 'As has been done today' There is a possibility that this clause is a continuation of v. 33b, though this position ignores the Masoretic accent, because *kēn* does not follow *kāk*. However, as it stands, it is impossible to say *kāk*, as v. 34b starts with *ṣiwwâ*, and not *'āśâ*. See Péter-Contesse 1993: 146.

Form and structure

From chs. 8 to 10 the book of Leviticus concerns itself with the actual events that occurred to Aaron and his sons, and the whole people. Lev. 8 reports the ordination of Aaron and his sons, already commanded by the Lord in Exod. 29. Lev. 9 describes how the first Tent service was conducted, while Lev. 10 narrates a sad incident involving the Aaronic family, which happened that same day. For the reason why Lev. 8 – 10 is preceded by Lev. 1 – 7, see Introduction 4.1.

The chapter as a whole can be viewed as follows:

Preparation (1–4)	The Lord's command to Moses to take Aaron and his sons, and the necessary materials for offerings and its execution
A. (5–9)	Moses' clothing of Aaron with the priestly garments
B. (10–13)	Moses' anointing of sancta, Aaron and clothing of his sons with the priestly garments
C. (14–17)	The sin offering
D. (18–21)	The burnt offering

E. (22–29)	The ordination offering
F. (30)	The sprinkling of blood and oil on Aaron and his sons and their garments
G. (31–35)	Instructions for the eating of leftovers by Aaron and his sons, and for remaining in the holy realm for seven days

Concluding note (36)

As this chart shows, the ritual proper can be divided into seven stages. Its purpose is to make Aaron and his sons and sancta holy, and this process takes seven days. The stress on the number seven may point to the legislators' intention to instil a creation motif within the ceremony: just as God created heaven and earth in six days and pronounced the seventh day on which he rested 'holy', here the Lord created his own holy servants/ priests out of their sinful state (see 'Explanation').

Some differences between Exod. 29 and Lev. 8 have led scholars to speculate about each text's historical growth and interrelationship. It is not possible to engage in the detailed discussion concerning this issue here (cf. Hartley 1992: 109; Fleming 1998: 411–412). However, on the whole, while both Exod. 29 (1–30) and Lev. 8 deal with the consecration of sancta and the priestly candidates, Exod. 29 focuses on the holy items (including the priestly candidates) and their use, while Lev. 8 stresses the organic relationship between the two.

There are similarities and divergences between the rituals of Lev. 8 and those prescribed in Lev. 1 – 7. The divergences need not reflect different authorial hands, but simply highlight the special occasion of the priestly ordination and the eighth-day service.

Although Lev. 8 – 10 is generally perceived as narrative rather than law, Lev. 8's content is simply the outcome of the commandments given in Exod. 28 – 29 for the Aaronic ordination. Thus, rather than a straightforward narrative genre, it is narrative-like. The modern clear distinction between narrative and law does not do justice to Lev. 8 or Lev. 8 – 10. Nor should the isolated instances of law in sections that look like narrative, as in Lev. 10, be viewed as foreign (see 'Comment' on 10:9).

Comment

8:1–4

8:1–2. 7:38 signals the end of the previous section. Thus 8:1 represents a new beginning. The introductory address directs Moses to 'take Aaron' etc. in a way reminiscent of 6:8–9[1–2]. Preparation for the priestly ordination requires not only Aaron and his sons, but also their garments, the anointing oil, the bull for a sin offering, two rams and the basket of unleavened bread.

3. Since all the people cannot meet at the entrance to the Tent of Meeting, the *'ēdâ* refers to the representatives of the whole community.

4. 'Moses did as the Lord commanded him' recurs frequently in this chapter (vv. 4, 9, 13, 17, 21, 29). Eleven of the thirty-five occurrences of 'commanded' (*ṣiwwâ*) in Leviticus are found in this chapter, and its subject is almost always the Lord or Moses. The whole congregation are to witness what Moses will do to Aaron and his sons. This is the ordination ceremony on the first day that is to continue for six more days (see vv. 33–34).

8:5–9

Since Moses presides over the installation of the priesthood, he is greater than the priests. Moreover his role in this chapter is more central than that of Aaron and his sons, because he makes propitiation for them. Though the text does not state so much, and though he is never the object of anointing in Exodus, Moses is presumed holy (see 'Explanation'). But if the anointing symbolizes the ordination of a person for a specific mission, it is possible that Moses was ordained through his encounter with the burning bush (cf. Exod. 1 – 3).

Splendid garments worn by the priests do more than cover nakedness (cf. Exod. 20:26): they represent the Lord's majesty. In the fall the first man and woman made a covering to hide their nakedness (shame). Later the Lord made them more durable clothing (Gen. 3:21), which implies the death of an animal. While the first clothing of humans at the fall meant a covering for nakedness/shame (Gen. 3:7), this clothing bears a different significance. As a divine provision, it represents a glorious task of mediating between sinful humans and a holy God, 'for dignity and adornment' (Exod. 28:40). Moreover the fact that Aaron and his sons are dressed by Moses indicates that the calling to priesthood comes entirely from outside the human realm: all the rights and honour that belong to the priesthood are considered a divine provision (although in ancient Israel priestly candidates were conditioned by human factors such as lineage).

Aaron's role is particularly remarkable because he bears the guilt related to all the offerings made by the Israelites (Exod. 28:38). When on the Day of Atonement his own self-hiding is dealt with, he is also to wear similar attire (Lev. 16:4).

5. *Zeh haddābār 'ăšer ṣiwwâ* (This is the thing that he has commanded) is a formula with strong enforcing overtones in Exod.–Lev.–Num. (Exod. 16:16, 32; 35:4; Lev. 8:5; 9:6; 17:2; Num. 30:2; 36:6). In all cases, the formula is used for actual actions, mostly followed by sg. or pl. imperatives. Here also in Lev. 8:5 the formula is followed not by speech, but by Moses' actions reported in v. 6 onwards. The Hebr. *dābār* has the meaning of both 'word' and 'matter', and there is no distinction in this formula. In this context this also suggests Moses' integrity in word and deed: there is no incongruence between his word and action.

6. From this verse onwards Moses demonstrates by his actions to the congregation what the Lord told him. In this verse Moses washes the bodies of Aaron and his sons. He clothes Aaron's sons only after Aaron's anointing in v. 13. The procedure reflects the priority of Aaron, as head of the priestly family, over his sons.

Moses brings Aaron and his sons and washes them with water. The rite is similar to that for the burnt offering (see Lev. 1:9). That they become naked in order to wear the splendid garments, which symbolize God's majesty (see below), suggests that their cleansing by water is symbolic of their inner spiritual cleansing (cf. Wenham 1979: 139). More specifically it can mean 'uncovering oneself' in a spiritual sense (Kiuchi 2003a: 107–118). The tension between the outer and inner cleansing continues to the end of the ordination ritual.

7–8. A *kĕtônet* is a 'tunic' made of fine linen (Exod. 39:27; 28:39). An *'abneṭ* is a 'sash' in the form of an embroidered belt (Exod. 28:39). *Mĕʿîl* means 'a robe' with a long undergarment over which an ephod was put. Nothing certain can be said about *'epôd*, yet Jenson (1997: 477) describes it as 'a sleeveless overgarment with shoulder pieces (Exod. 28:25) and bound by rings to the breastplate (28:28)'.

Ḥošen is a 'breast piece' that contains the Urim and Thummim. The latter phrase appears in Exod. 28:30, Deut. 33:8, Ezra 2:63 and Neh. 7:65. *'Ûrîm* alone occurs in Num. 27:21 and 1 Sam. 28:6, but its exact role is unclear. Probably the Urim and Thummim are used for inquiring of the Lord's will (cf. 16:7–8; cf. Van Dam 1997: 329–331). Even where no mention is made of the Urim and Thummim the practice of casting a lot may be presupposed (see Josh. 7:15–17; 1 Sam. 10:20–21). Since by this Aaron bears (*nāśā'*) judgments (*mišpāṭ*) for the people of Israel (Exod. 28:29), Aaron is the final human authority on the judgment of the Israelites. Actual practice in ancient Israel is attested in 1 Sam. 14:41 (cf. LXX).

9. Then Aaron puts on the 'turban' (*miṣnepet*) fitted with a gold plate (*ṣîṣ zāhāb*), on which is inscribed 'holiness to the Lord' (Exod. 28:36). This 'to the Lord' means he is in the divine sphere. By wearing the turban with the gold plate, Aaron 'bears the guilt of the Israelites concerning the holy things' (Exod. 28:38). The bearing of guilt in Exod. 28:38 has been interpreted as referring to 'cultic' offences committed in relation to the handling of offerings. But this interpretation is too restrictive. Instead it means that whatever Aaron does in the ritual is accepted by the Lord because of his standing before the Lord, which is symbolized by the gold plate. Thus outer holiness is linked with inner holiness, in the sense that without the latter Aaron cannot bear the guilt of the Israelites.

8:10–13

10. The anointing of the tabernacle and all the utensils within it is performed in accordance with the directions given in Exod. 40:9–11. Since the oil itself symbolizes the presence of the Lord (see 'Comment' on 2:1), anointing with oil could symbolize the conferring of divine authority and power. Moreover being anointed, Aaron and his sons are considered as heightened forms of the offerings: in the loyalty offering oil was added to the grain, but here oil is applied to humans. Yet *anointing* with oil may well symbolize not just God's presence but the conferring of authority to carry out God's mission, as is clear from other occurrences (1 Sam. 16:13; Isa. 61:1). Therefore from now on the tabernacle and all its utensils become active in carrying out God's work.

11–12. The sprinkling of oil symbolizes consecration. Elsewhere it occurs only in Lev. 14:16, 27 in connection with the cleansing ritual for a so-called leprous disease. As for Lev. 14, the *initial* consecration of the sancta and Aaron is in view here. Both Aaron and the sancta receive the same sprinkling with oil.

There is an apparent inconsistency in that these verses present only Aaron as anointed, while Exod. 28:41, 30:30, 40:15, Lev. 7:36 and 10:7 present his sons as anointed. However, these passages speak about anointing generally, and since Aaron's sons were anointed (Exod. 29:21; Lev. 8:30), there is no essential discrepancy. Moreover this method of anointing (pouring oil on his head) appears as though it was reserved for the chief priest (cf. Exod. 29:7; Lev. 21:10).

13. Aaron's sons are dressed as prescribed in Exod. 29:8–9. Though the turban is an adornment conveying dignity (Exod. 28:40), the ordinary priest's garment is, on the whole, much simpler than the chief priest's. Presumably the holiness of his son's garments hinges on the holiness of his own garment, as this verse comes after mention of Aaron's clothing (v. 7). When all the necessary rites are over, in v. 30 both Aaron and his sons are sprinkled with blood and oil by Moses.

8:14–17

See Exod. 29:10–14. From this rite to the end of the ceremony Moses behaves as a priest, while Aaron and his sons on ordinary occasions play the part of lay persons.

The laying on of hands by the priestly candidates signifies they are the beneficiaries of what the sin offering achieves: the purification of the altar. This factor significantly suggests an important aspect: the sancta and priests are essentially one, so that the priests share the same destiny as the sancta. In fact, the consecration of both the sancta and Aaron and his sons is described in a way that suggests their inseparableness.

The ritual typology deviates from that of Lev. 4 because this is an inaugural ritual for both the priestly candidates and the altar (see 'Explanation' on Lev. 4). Contra the case in 4:1 – 5:13, no particular offence is assumed.

14. The bull is the typical animal for the self-hiding of the priest (see 4:3; 16:3, 6, 11, 14). The sin offering is required because it is assumed that when the common confronts the holy, the former is conceived of as unclean and in need of purification. Common things may be either clean or unclean. But even if they are clean, they are regarded as unclean before a holy God. As *ḥaṭṭā't* means 'hiding oneself', Aaron and his sons are assumed as hiding themselves from the Lord. It is the function of the sin offering to *uncover* them before him.

15. Only here and on the Day of Atonement ritual (16:18) is it said that blood is applied around (*sābîb*) each of the horns of the altar.

'made (the altar) uncovered': *ḥiṭṭē'* As has been argued, it is unlikely to mean 'de-sin', or 'purge' as traditionally interpreted. Rather it means to 'uncover' (see Kiuchi 2003a: 107–118). This implies that the altar is assumed to be in a state of hiding before the Lord. Daubing the blood on the horns and pouring the rest of the blood around the altar's base makes simultaneous propitiation for the altar and the priestly candidates standing before it.

'poured': *yāṣaq* Another peculiarity is that only here and in 9:9 is *yāṣaq* used in connection with blood. The verb is firmly associated with oil in biblical usage (Gen. 28:18; 35:14; Exod. 29:7; Lev. 2:1, 6, etc.), while the blood of the sin offering is otherwise collocated with *šāpak* (see Exod. 29:12; Lev. 4:7, 18, 25, 30). Therefore the present usage is not coincidental, but deliberate. Apparently the legislator is attempting to relate Aaron's anointing with oil (v. 12) to the altar's consecration (v. 15; see 'Explanation'). Second, the term's use may be prompted by the negative connotation that *šāpak dām* has, namely the shedding of blood (see 'Comment' on 4:7), as this is an inaugural ceremony.

'by making propitiation for it': *lĕkapper 'ālāyw* The holiness of the altar (*qiddēš*) is the result of making propitiation (*kipper*) rather than the means thereto. However, while the altar is made holy, the holiness of the priestly candidates is another matter; more is to come in the following rites.

16–17. While in 4:19, 26, 31, 35 the burning of fat appears to have a partial role in making propitiation, here reference to propitiation (v. 15) precedes the burning of the fat. This is probably caused by the circumstance that in v. 15 the purification of the altar and priestly candidates was presented as simultaneous. These rites symbolize the destruction of any selfishness within the priestly candidates (see 'Comment' on ch. 3). V. 17 is the same as the rite in Lev. 4:11–12. But the burning of the remaining flesh was performed outside the camp. Since the priests are the recipients of propitiation, they naturally cannot eat the flesh. The rule in 6:25–30[18–23] does not apply here. As evident there, here too a complete destruction of selfishness and any propensity towards humanism is expressed by burning the skin of the animal as well as the flesh.

8:18–21

See Exod. 29:15–18 and Lev. 1. By offering the burnt offering, Aaron and his sons dedicate themselves to the Lord. Their burnt offering symbolizes they have abandoned all earthly desires. Why is a ram (*'ayil*) required for the sin offering? It is entirely optional for ordinary Israelites to offer a ram (Lev. 1). The ram is required for the reparation offering, and is assumed to be costlier than a female goat (Lev. 4 – 5). Thus this specification possibly conveys an upgraded dedication.

8:22–29

See Exod. 29:19ff. Moses is to offer the second ram in the ordination of Aaron and his sons. Though the ritual is basically that of the fellowship offering, some aspects are unique to this occasion. The need to offer another ram suggests that the first ram was insufficient for ordination. In contrast to the first ram that purified the altar and priests, the blood of the second ram is directly applied to Aaron and his sons, a symbolic ritual that relates more to their work and specific roles (see below). Here Aaron and his sons are even more explicitly conceived as one with the altar than in the preceding offerings.

22. While Moses takes the role of the priest, Aaron and his sons take that of the laity. By identifying with the ram, Aaron and his sons commit themselves to the priestly work, which is simultaneously the Lord's work.

23–24. 'lobe' (*tĕnûk*) appears eight times in the OT and only in connection with the ordination (Exod. 29:20; Lev. 8:23–24) and reparation offerings (Lev. 14:14, 17, 25–26). Moreover the occurrence of *bôhen* is concentrated within the same contexts. The rite of daubing the blood on the lobe of Aaron's right ear, on the thumb of his right hand and on the big toe of his right foot may appear to be obscure in meaning. However, Kurtz (1980: 334), observing that the three bodily members are meant *pars pro toto* and that the right side (which signifies power) is preferred to the left, offers a plausible solution when he says, 'The *ear* was to be consecrated to listen to the command and will of God, as the rule of their priestly walk and conduct; the *hand* and the *foot*, to observe the walk and conduct prescribed.' However, as it is suggested in v. 15 that Aaron and his sons are to be purified just as the altar, the former can be compared to the latter, both requiring consecration: just as blood is daubed on the specific parts of the altar, so blood is daubed on specific parts of the bodies of Aaron and his sons.

Moreover those acts precede the dashing of blood around the altar (v. 24b), which is the last act of blood handling. Daubing (*nātan*) blood has a specific connotation (see 'Comment' on 4:7), and except for the contexts of ordination and the cleansing of the so-called leper, it is always performed on the altar's horns (4:7, 18, 25, 30, 34; 8:15; 9:9; 16:18). Thus it is likely the three body parts are likened to the horns of the altar, in that both symbolize human power. Furthermore it can be speculated that *three* parts are chosen in combination with the altar's *four* horns to make the total number *seven*. Since the daubing of blood at the very least symbolizes death, the same act performed in connection with these three prominent parts of the body signifies the dying of each of these bodily members from serving human desires, so they can be made alive to serve in God's work (for the purification of the so-called leper, see 'Comment' on 14:14–18).

25–28. From this passage it is clear that the ordination offering has the character of the thanksgiving sacrifice, as similar kinds of loyalty offerings are included in 7:12 (see also Exod. 29:34). What is novel on this occasion is that these additional loyalty offerings are put on top of the fat and right thigh, and handed over to Aaron and his sons to wave with their own hands. Fat portions symbolize the egocentric selves of Aaron and his sons, while the right thigh represents one of the best parts of the animal, which was given to the officiating priest on ordinary occasions for his work. Thus Moses' waving and burning of them as a soothing aroma to the Lord signifies that Aaron and his sons indicate their willingness to dedicate the fruit of their priestly work to the Lord, not to mention their egocentric selves.

29. On the other hand, Moses receives the waved breast on the assumption that he is like the priest who receives both the breast and right thigh from the offerer on ordinary occasions (see 'Comment' on 7:30–33).

8:30–36

30. The sprinkling of oil and blood constitutes the second and concluding rite of consecration, for Aaron in v. 12 was consecrated by the sprinkling of oil. However, the sprinkling of *blood* is performed here for the first time. The rite symbolizes a potent means of purification, the deeper meaning of which is to give life to the object (see 'Comment' on 4:5–6). Ordinarily blood is sprinkled on the inner sancta such as the incense altar and ark. Here it is sprinkled on humans, which further suggests that Aaron and his sons, as well as their garments, are equivalent to the sancta, in so far as consecration is concerned. The symbolism of blood and oil indicates that this rite signifies a death to selfishness on the part of Aaron and his sons and guarantees the Lord's presence.

This concluding rite has particular significance for Aaron's sons, for only after they offer the sin offering, the burnt offering and the ordination offering do they receive the sprinkling of blood and oil on their garments (cf. v. 13). The holiness of Aaron's sons is subsumed under that of Aaron's.

31–32. For the first time in this chapter Moses speaks directly to Aaron and his sons, and the speech continues to v. 35; until now Moses presumably performs in silence what the Lord commanded him to do. The content of the speech consists of two parts. The first relates to the eating of the remaining flesh from the ordination offering in the Holy Place and the burning of the leftovers on the same day (vv. 31–32; cf. Exod. 29:31–34). The other concerns Aaron's and his sons' obligation to stay in the holy space for seven days (vv. 33–35). Nevertheless the ceremony proper is concluded by Moses instructing Aaron and his sons in v. 32 about the burning of leftovers.

33–35. Aaron and his sons ought not to go out of the Holy Place for seven days, for they become ordained on the seventh day. If they violate this command, they must die. Opinion is divided as to whether the ceremony on day one was repeated on each of the following six days. The literal translation supports the conclusion that the same was done each day. At least, Exod. 29:36–37 commands that expiation ought to be made by the sin offering for seven days.

The number 7 is a significant number, and in the context of Leviticus 'seven days' occurs in connection with the purification of the altar (4:6, 17; 16:14, 19), the *ṣāra'at*-afflicted house (14:51), the unclean period for a new mother (12:2), the quarantine period of the suspected case of the skin disease (13:4–5, 21 etc.), the healed leper before entering his tent (14:8), the man healed from a dysfunctional reproductive organ (15:13), and the unclean woman (15:19). In particular 'seven days' are required for the feasts of unleavened bread (23:6) – obviously related to the sabbath principle, in turn derived from God's creation of heaven and earth. The 'seven days' are mostly related to the unclean period or to the stage leading towards purity. Thus, though there is no explicit association of the 'seven day' principle with God's creation in Leviticus, it remains implicit. Theologically, then, it is not just time, but time in which the divine creative power is at work (see Introduction 7.4.2.d).

'to make propitiation for you': *lĕkapper 'alêkem* (v. 34) This use of *kipper* is inclusive of all the offerings used for the ordination of Aaron and his sons: not just the so-called expiatory sacrifices such as the sin offering and the burnt offering, but also the fellowship offering and the loyalty offering.

36. Aaron and his sons implemented what the Lord commanded through Moses. This note indicates that the seven days conclude at the end of ch. 8, and that Aaron and his sons became holy together with sancta (for the idea of 'holiness', see 'Explanation'). Both the priests and sancta can operate in the service of the Lord. Their major role is to mediate between the Lord and the people, and to bring the latter into closer proximity to the former.

Explanation

Ch. 8 reports the ordination of Aaron and his sons as priests. Yet considering what sacrificial rites were performed, the sinful human state assumed by the occasion may surprise the modern reader. As Wenham (1979: 144) comments, 'In this section one doctrine emerges very clearly: the universality and pervasiveness of sin.'

The consecration of Aaron and his sons is essentially achieved by Moses' anointing of them with oil, his sprinkling of them with blood, and the presentation of offerings and sacrifices (see below).

While all the rituals are performed outwardly by Moses or the priestly candidates, the consecration process loses its significance when the symbolic meanings of these rites are ignored. Indeed, as noted in 'Comment', every rite or component of the ritual appears to have a symbolic meaning. Recognition of this is vital to an understanding of the idea of holiness.

In particular this chapter sheds new light on the idea of holiness by tacitly contrasting Moses' holiness with that of Aaron: while Aaron must go through various rites, no mention of expiation is made in relation to Moses who installs the priesthood. And in this regard, it sets out a new perspective on holiness over against the one espoused in chs. 1 – 7. In ch. 1 the essence of holiness was expressed by a sacrificial animal, whereas nowhere is the holiness of the sacrifice explicitly mentioned. Concurrently the ritual suggests the need for a human (offerer) to become holy. The ordination ceremony in ch. 8 aims at making actual humans (Aaron and his sons) holy, whereas Moses is tacitly presented as a model who bears inner holiness, requiring no sacrificial ritual (see below). In this sense, there is a deepening of the essence of the idea of holiness even within chs. 1 – 10.

Significance of the ritual order

Viewed as a whole, this ordination ceremony proceeds from Moses' anointing of Aaron and his sons, their being uncovered by the sin offering, their dedication to the Lord by the burnt offering, their fellowship with the Lord via the fellowship offering, and lastly by Moses' anointing them with oil.

Why is purification of Aaron and his sons performed after they are anointed to be consecrated to the Lord? This, at least, suggests that priestly consecration is achieved by two means: (1) consecration by anointing, and (2) consecration by purifying from self-hiding/uncleanness. Both are required for him to be ordained by the Lord and to be fully equipped for the work. Thus, though anointing is basic to ordination, an anointing without purification from self-hiding/uncleanness does not qualify a man as a fully fledged priest. There is a significant gap, even on the symbolic dimension, between holiness achieved by anointing and holiness acquired through the cleansing with animal blood. The former is given irrespective of the beneficiaries' condition, whereas the latter assumes the presence of self-hiding and guilt. That is why the sin, burnt and fellowship offerings combined with the thanksgiving sacrifice follow. In these latter rituals the voluntary aspect of Aaron and his sons is expected to come to the fore: their willingness to uncover themselves, dedicate themselves and have fellowship with the Lord in response to their calling. The priests become holy again when their self-hidings and guilt are purified on the Day of Atonement. The divine sanction ought to match the inner quality of the priests. Significantly these rituals deal with their symbolic dimension, so that negatively Aaron and his sons are not assumed really to have died from their egocentric selves, even though the latter is the purpose of the whole ritual. Nevertheless within the symbolic dimension the ritual as a whole portrays inner holiness: the process of how one becomes holy in reality.

Repeated elements in the offerings, such as blood handling and the burning of fat, are not redundant: they stress the importance of the killing of Aaron's and his son's egocentric selves. Indeed the blood manipulation is repeated in the sin, burnt and ordination offerings. So is the burning of fat. The order of the three kinds of offerings reveals the logical process by which sinful humans become holy. The process must begin with an uncovering of oneself before the Lord. Only after this can the priest offer the burnt offering, which symbolizes complete self-dedication. These offerings are followed by the ordination offering, which symbolizes intimate fellowship with the Lord. Thus, though the individual elements of the ordination offerings (blood and fat) overlap with the preceding two types of offerings, the overall emphasis of the ordination offering is on something other than that of the preceding offerings: the fellowship aspect is expressed by this offering with special emphasis on the priestly activities. This suggests that only when the priests die spiritually and completely in their egocentric selves can they perform mediatory work.

Inseparable relationship between priests and altar

The inseparableness of sancta, Aaron and his sons is highlighted at some points in the ordination ceremony. In vv. 10–12 the anointing oil is sprinkled on to the sancta *and* Aaron. In vv. 14–15, as mentioned above, the purification of the altar is concurrent with that of Aaron and his sons. In vv. 23–24, Moses' daubing of the blood on to prominent body parts of Aaron and his sons strongly suggests that Aaron and his sons are regarded as though they are sancta.

More specifically, as mentioned ('Comment' on v. 15), the term 'to pour' (*yāṣaq*) is used for pouring oil and blood (vv. 12, 15). Furthermore the term *qiddēš*, which appears in v. 12, may betray the legislator's attempt to round out the consecration of the sancta.

The inseparableness of sancta and priests is only elsewhere evident in the ritual for the Day of Atonement (ch. 16), where both sancta and priests are purified on the same occasion too. Also it should be stressed that both the sprinkling of blood in v. 30 and the word *sābîb* in v. 15 have counterparts only in ch. 16, though a similar ritual is found in ch. 14.

Thus the ritual for the purification of sancta and Aaron and his sons probably represents an archetype of what happens on the altar on regular occasions: the priest puts some of the blood on the altar because the altar reflects the spiritual situation of the one who offers the animal (see 'Explanation' on ch. 1, 'Comment' on 4:7). As the priest sanctifies the altar by placing blood on it, he simultaneously sanctifies the worshipper.

Idea of holiness

In this ordination ceremony Aaron and his sons undergo many rites to become holy. However, the holiness referred to by 'consecrate' (*qiddēš*) is outward, and inner holiness is not necessarily implied. However, on this assumption some aspects of holiness deserve special attention.

First, holiness concerns the whole being of Aaron and his sons, rather than the observance of particular commandments. This is first expressed by the sin offering, which deals with their self-hiding. By offering this sacrifice Aaron and his sons express their will to uncover themselves before the Lord, which means, first and foremost, to reveal all their inner human motives, feelings and intentions – their egocentric selves – to the Lord. This certainly involves a painful process of heart, since they had to abandon any human pride and fear of man. Then they offer the burnt offering, and this expresses their willingness to abandon all earthly desires. At any rate, holiness is a matter of the human heart.

Consequently these offerings all require the death of the egocentric nature, and in this regard holiness lies beyond the spiritual death of the offerers. The series of offerings, though they may symbolically involve spiritual pain and shame, ultimately introduce the offerers into a sphere of freedom, and this is what is denoted by the term *qdš* (holiness). In a word, a holy heart is free of selfishness, earthly desires and, most significantly, the pain associated with these two things.

Second, there are two approaches to holiness. One is by the Lord's calling, expressed by the anointing with blood and oil (vv. 10–12, 15, 30). The other is represented by the priestly candidates dedicating themselves to the Lord, which is symbolized by the rituals for the various offerings. The latter is contingent upon the former. Since both take place in the form of rituals, the question arises as to how far they can obtain inner holiness by these two approaches. It appears the consecration of both sancta and priests is done on the same dimension, and it belongs to outer holiness in the sense that the consecrated persons and things belong to the divine realm. If all the symbolic meanings of the ordination ceremony are embodied in Aaron and his sons, it would be easier for them to perform their work. But a gap remains between their hearts' condition and their symbolic status. Thus holiness confronts the priests as a threatening force, because their egocentric nature remains. Until their egocentric nature dies, their job requires special vigilance and imposes a heavy spiritual load upon them.

Inner holiness is exemplified by Moses. A comparison between Moses and Aaron suggests that the need for the latter's consecration betrays an absence of inner holiness. Offering sacrifices is demanded, because the offerer ought to die in himself spiritually. While both are called to the Lord's work, Moses is superior to Aaron because he installed the priesthood. Though the process of consecration symbolically involves a number of inner sacrifices on the part of Aaron and his sons, holiness is what characterizes Moses. Thus holiness is essentially a matter of the human heart that finds its expression in personality. An aspect of holiness, then, can be found in the conduct of Moses recorded in this chapter and the Pentateuch as a whole. Repeatedly it is said, 'Moses did as he was commanded.' At the very least this suggests a holy person must be a vessel who obeys the Lord without questioning. Moreover that the essence of holiness lies in self-sacrifice is clearly apparent from the golden-calf incident, where Moses even offered his life to take the place of the Israelites if the Lord would destroy them (Exod. 32:32). He does not quarrel with the people when the latter complain. He is said to be 'very meek, more than all people who were on the face of the earth' (Num. 12:3 ESV). Thus meekness, fear of no man and a habit of giving priority to the Lord's will characterize Moses' personality (for further examples, see 'Comment' on 10:16–20).

New Testament implications

It seems this understanding of holiness applies, by and large, to NT believers. They are encouraged to become holy both in calling and in substance. On the one hand, the NT assumes believers are *given* faith in Jesus Christ from above (John 3; Heb. 3:1), but on the other, they are exhorted to *be* holy (e.g. Rom. 12:1; 1 Pet. 1:15).

Christian leadership should imitate Christ. Leaders need to be called by God and, like Aaron and his sons, must go through the process of sanctification – unless all selfish motives (egocentricity) are removed, such people are unlikely to be used as God's instruments.

LEVITICUS 9:1–24

Translation

[1]On the eighth day Moses called Aaron and his sons and the elders of Israel, [2]and he said to Aaron, 'Take for yourself a bull calf for a sin offering and a ram for a burnt offering, both without blemish, and offer them before the LORD.

[3]'And say to the Israelites, Take a male goat for a sin offering, and a calf and a lamb, both a year old without blemish, for a burnt offering, [4]and an ox and a ram for fellowship offering, to sacrifice before the LORD, and a loyalty offering mixed with oil, for today the LORD appears to you.'

[5]They brought what Moses commanded in front of the Tent of Meeting, and the whole community drew near and stood before the LORD. [6]Then Moses said, 'This is the thing that the LORD commanded you to do, that the glory of the LORD may appear to you.'

[7]Then Moses said to Aaron, 'Draw near to the altar and offer your sin offering and your burnt offering and make propitiation on behalf of yourself and the people, and bring the offering of the people and make propitiation for them, as the LORD has commanded.' [8]So Aaron drew near to the altar and slaughtered the calf of the sin offering, which was for himself. [9]And the sons of Aaron presented the blood to him, and he dipped his finger in the blood and put it on the horns of the altar and poured out the blood at the base of the altar. [10]But the fat and the kidneys and the long lobe of the liver from the sin offering he burned on the altar, as the LORD commanded Moses. [11]The flesh and the skin he burned up with fire outside the camp. [12]Then he slaughtered the burnt offering, and Aaron's sons handed him the blood, and he dashed it against all sides of the altar. [13]And they handed the burnt offering to him, piece by piece, and the head, and he burned them on the altar. [14]And he washed the entrails and the legs and burned them with the burnt offering on the altar.

[15]Then he presented the people's offering and took the goat of the sin offering that was for the people and slaughtered it and made it uncovered, like the first one. [16]He presented the burnt offering and sacrificed it according to regulation. [17]He presented the loyalty offering, took a handful of it, and burned it on the altar, besides the burnt offering of the morning. [18]He slaughtered the ox and the ram, the sacrifice of fellowship offering for the people. Aaron's sons handed him the blood, and he dashed it against all sides of the altar. [19]But the fat pieces of the ox and of the ram – the fat tail and what covers the entrails and the kidneys and the long lobe of the liver – [20]they put those fat pieces on the breasts, and he burned the fat pieces on the altar, [21]but the breasts and the right thigh Aaron waved for a wave offering before the LORD, as Moses commanded.

[22]Aaron lifted up his hands towards the people and blessed them, and he came down from offering the sin offering and the burnt offering and the fellowship offering. [23]And Moses and Aaron went into the Tent of Meeting, and when they came out they blessed the people, and the glory of the LORD appeared to all the people. [24]Fire came out from before the LORD and consumed the burnt offering and

the pieces of fat on the altar, and when all the people saw it, they shouted and fell on their faces.

Notes on the text

1. 'the elders of Israel' *BHS* margin proposes its deletion in view of 'the sons of Israel' in v. 3. However, this is unnecessary if it is understood that the elders represent the sons of Israel. The body of elders are rephrased as *hā'ēdâ* (the congregation) in v. 5 or *hā'ām* (the people) in v. 7.

3. 'the Israelites' Lit. 'the sons of Israel': *bĕnê yiśrā'ēl* SamP and LXX read 'the elders of Israel' in conformity with v. 1b. But see above on v. 1.

4. 'appears': *nir'â* The expected form is either *yĕrā'eh* (ni. impf.) or *nir'eh* (ni. ptc.), 'is to appear', as LXX and other ancient versions translate. However, if the consonants are retained, the future meaning is unlikely. Thus the participial form becomes the only possibility, and should be vocalized *nir'eh*. Milgrom interprets the MT's perfect form as an attempt to avoid anthropomorphism (1991: 574).

7. 'on behalf of the people': *bĕ'ad hā'ām* LXX reads 'for your house' in conformity with 16:6, 11, which is followed by more than a few commentators (e.g. Hartley 1992: 118; Milgrom 1991: 578). See 'Comment'.

17. 'took a handful of': *ml'* pi. + *kap* here means 'take a handful of' (JPS). A unique idiom in the OT. LXX and SamP translate *kap* in pl.

19. After 'what covers the entrails and the kidneys' LXX inserts something similar to 4:9. However, this may well be judged as a paraphrase.

20. 'they put': *wayyāśîmû* LXX and SamP read it in sg., while LXX reads the following *wayyaqṭēr* in pl. However, it is possible that in this ceremony the preparatory stage of the rites is done by Aaron's sons, whereas the last act towards the Lord or sancta is done by Aaron (see 'Comment' on v. 12). So MT is justified.

21. 'as Moses commanded' This part of the verse is considered strange, and many Hebr. MSS as well as LXX and SamP read 'as the LORD commanded Moses'. However, as far as the content is concerned, there is nothing strange in Moses commanding Aaron and his sons (cf. 9:5).

22. 'towards': *'el* LXX and SamP read 'upon'.

23. 'blessed the people' LXX adds 'all' before 'the people', probably in view of v. 24b.

24. 'saw (it)': *wayyar'* SamP and TgJon read the verb in pl.

Form and structure

On the day following the seven-day ordination, Moses summons both the newly ordained priests and the elders as representative of the whole people.

The purpose of the gathering is to witness the Lord's manifestation. To that end, they must prepare by making various sacrifices and offerings.

The prescriptions for the offerings and their execution in this chapter are not mentioned before Lev. 9. But, when stipulating the daily burnt offerings for the altar of burnt offering, the Lord said in Exod. 29:43–46:

> There I will meet with the people of Israel, and it shall be sanctified by my glory. I will consecrate the tent of meeting and the altar. Aaron also and his sons I will consecrate to serve me as priests. I will dwell among the people of Israel and will be their God. And they shall know that I am the LORD their God, who brought them out of the land of Egypt that I might dwell among them. I am the LORD their God. (ESV)

This expresses the idea that the consecration and sanctification of the priests, the altar and the Tent of Meeting guarantee the Lord's dwelling among the people. In the ordination ceremony Aaron and his sons are consecrated. But they, along with the sancta, are not yet instrumental in making the Lord's dwelling possible: it is merely the necessary preparation for this event. Now, since Aaron and his sons and the outer sancta became holy in the seven-day ordination, the preparation is over. So it stands to reason that the ceremony in Lev. 9 served to make possible the Lord's dwelling among the people. In this sense, the people's participation in the ceremony has an important role in actualizing the Lord's words in Exod. 29:43–46.

This chapter is narrative-like (cf. ch. 8). Both in content and style ch. 9 is similar to ch. 8. With regard to content, the priests approach the altar of burnt offering in the court, and not the Tent of Meeting; the ram is used for the burnt offering; and the 'congregation', consisting of elders, is summoned in front of the Tent (8:3; 9:1, 5). Stylistically, 'pouring blood' (*yāṣaq dām*) is unique to these chapters (8:15; 9:9). Other features common to chs. 4 and 16 are noted in 'Comment'. The content is as follows:

Preparations (1–4)
- For the priests (2): animals for the sin offering, the burnt offering
- For the people (3–4): animals for the sin offering, the burnt offering and the fellowship offering

Stationing of the priests and the people before the Lord, and the purpose of the ceremony (5–6)

Aaron's offering of sacrifices for priests (7–14)
- The sin offering (7–11)
- The burnt offering (12–14)

Aaron's offering of sacrifices and offerings for the people (15–21)
The sin offering (15)
The burnt offering (16)
The loyalty offering (17)
The fellowship offering (18–21)
The response from Moses and Aaron, and the Lord (22–24)
The blessing of Moses and Aaron (22–23a)
The manifestation of the Lord's glory (23b–24)

Comment

9:1–4

1. This chapter records Israel's first act of worship after the Tent of Meeting's construction. The service is of an inaugural nature and this is reflected in the sacrifices offered on this day.

'on the eighth day' 'Eighth' is counted from the first day of the ordination ceremony recounted in ch. 8. 'Eight' in the sacrificial context signifies a new beginning (Lev. 12:3; 14:10, 23; 15:29; 22:27; 23:36). Equally important is that the sequence 7–8 occurs relatively frequently in ritual contexts. These contexts can be divided into (1) circumcision and firstborn (Exod. 22:29–30; Lev. 12:3; 22:27), and (2) the purification ritual (Lev. 9; 14:10, 23; 15:14, 29; Num. 6:10), and (3) festivals (Lev. 23:10–14, 15–22, 36, 39; Num. 29:35). All of these occasions share a common seven-day period as a prerequisite for sanctification or purification, and a common eighth day to signal a new beginning. Thus on the eighth day a person emerges with a higher status than on the previous seven days.

The 'elders', who apparently represent the whole people, were also present at the time of the Sinai covenant (Exod. 24:1, 9). And in fact, the event reported in ch. 9 is a sequel to the Sinai event. Just as the Lord descended on Mount Sinai, so here he manifests himself at the altar, though now more intimately, since he begins to dwell permanently among the people.

Although the ordination period is over, Moses still takes the initiative in the first worship service. Nevertheless he recedes more into the background than in the ordination ceremony.

2–4. Moses instructs Aaron to prepare offerings for himself and the whole people. The offerings for Aaron are a calf for the sin offering and a ram for the burnt offering (2). The offerings for the whole people comprise a goat for the sin offering, and a one-year old male calf and sheep for the burnt offering (3). In addition to this, the Israelites are required to bring a bull (or cow) and a ram for a fellowship offering and a loyalty offering mixed with oil (4). These offerings will make the Lord's appearance possible (4b).

The qualification of 'one year old' is often found for animals offered on occasions suggestive of new beginnings (Exod. 12:5; Lev. 12:6; 23:12, 18–19; Num. 6:12, 14 etc.). This seems in harmony with the inaugural nature of this occasion as well. The value of the sacrificial animals used for the sin offering for both the priests and the whole people is less than that for those prescribed for when the anointed priest or whole congregation commits self-hiding (Lev. 4:3–21) or when Aaron and his sons are consecrated (Lev. 8). This is explained by the fact that in Lev. 9 the priests did not commit self-hiding in the way envisaged in Lev. 4: the sin offering for the priests in ch. 9 deals with general sinfulness, the condition of self-hiding before the Lord, which is assumed to exist when they confront the holy God.

On the other hand, the prescribed animals for the fellowship offering, a ram and bull, are the most costly options for that offering. Thus, when the animals for the fellowship offering are compared with the animals for the sin offering, it becomes clear the ceremony lays greater stress on the fellowship between the Lord and the people. In a sense, the sin and burnt offerings are a preparation towards fellowship.

2. Aaron must offer a calf as a sin offering to make propitiation for himself and his house. Why a calf? Since the sin offering for the self-hiding of the anointed priest is a bull (Lev. 4:3–21), a calf identifies this as a lesser sacrifice on the part of Aaron and his sons. A Jewish midrash links this with the incident of the golden calf (cf. Wenham 1979: 148; Rooker 2000: 150). However, that Aaron makes propitiation for the offence relating to the golden-calf incident is unlikely on two grounds. First, no specific offence is mentioned in this chapter. Second, Aaron was ordained and became holy in the ordination ceremony. It is entirely unlikely that he became holy without expiation of his self-hiding. Therefore a calf is required for the general sinfulness of Aaron and his sons when they confront the divinity. Since this ritual is not occasioned by their will, as in the case of Lev. 4, a lesser sacrifice is demanded.

'a ram for the burnt offering' Lev. 1 required only that a burnt offering from the flock be a male without blemish. It is left to the offerer to decide whether he will offer a ram or a male goat. Thus the specification of a ram in this ceremony is significant. A ram is required for the burnt offering in the previous ordination ceremony (Lev. 8:2) and on the Day of Atonement (Lev. 16:3). Since a bull is not required, this sacrifice is less significant than that offered when a priest commits self-hiding. Nevertheless the ram is the costliest of animals taken from the flock, and therefore should be regarded as next to the bull in importance.

3. 'a goat for the sin offering' A male goat was used in Lev. 4 to make propitiation for a tribal leader's self-hiding. Since on this occasion it is offered for the whole people rather than an individual, it appears a costlier animal than a female goat (4:27–28), but less expensive than a bull (4:13–14), is reasonable. This is because the whole congregation has not hidden themselves from the Lord by violating a certain prohibitive commandment.

'a calf and a lamb, both a year old, for a burnt offering' Compared with the ram for the burnt offering of the priests, this specification indicates that while individually these animals are less costly than a ram, taken together they equal it in value.

4. The Israelites are to bring a bull and a ram for the fellowship offering accompanied by grain mixed with oil as the loyalty offering (cf. Lev. 2 – 3).

'ox': *šôr* This term can refer either to a male or a female ox: either a bull or a cow. Thus flock animals are excluded on this occasion. No stipulation is given concerning gender, which indicates this ceremony is more lax than those where gender is specified (see Lev. 1). Yet the gender of the other animal *is* specified: it must be a ram, the costliest of animals taken from the flock.

At this stage it is not specified how the Lord will appear. The Lord appeared to the patriarchs, Moses and various other people. It is not known how these appearances were manifested. Quite possibly they varied on each occasion (cf. Gen. 12:7; Exod. 3:2; 16:10; 24:15–18; Num. 14:10).

9:5–6

5. Aaron and his sons obey Moses' command, bringing what he commanded. *'Ēdâ* refers to the representatives of the people (cf. 8:3). All the congregation drew near and stood before the Lord. On two previous momentous occasions the sequence of the verbs 'draw near' and 'stand' occurs: at the burning bush (Exod. 3:5) and the Sinai event (Deut. 4:11). Permission to draw near and stand before the Lord is specifically granted to the Israelites. As the burning bush and Sinai event demonstrate, it is a matter of life and death to approach the divinity.

6. Moses commands all the congregation, including the priests, in a manner reminiscent of 8:5. The Lord's appearance (v. 4b) is specifically described as the appearance of his *glory*. See v. 23b. The following offerings facilitate the people's acceptance before the Lord. It is a biblical principle that the Lord's glory manifests itself only when the human egocentric nature, with its diverse manifestations of pride, arrogance and hope in this world, dies. Thus their sinfulness must first be removed.

9:7–14

7. Moses commands Aaron to offer the prescribed offerings for himself and the people, and to make propitiation for himself and the people. In Leviticus the phrase *kipper bĕ'ad* (make propitiation on behalf of) appears only in this verse and 16:6, 11, 17, 24. In this context *bĕ'ad*, unlike *'al*, always takes *people*, not inanimate objects, as the object, thereby indicating the final beneficiary of the *kipper* act. By making propitiation for himself, Aaron makes propitiation for the people as well, on the principle that Aaron represents the whole people in his capacity as the chief priest. Therefore the latter half of the verse is not redundant, as possibly suggested by LXX's correction. It refers to the ritual mentioned in v. 15 onwards.

In terms of *kipper*'s meaning, note that v. 7a indicates the term is related to the sin offering and the burnt offering, while 'the offering [*qorbān*] of the people', in v. 7b, suggests it is related not only to those kinds of offerings, but also to the fellowship and loyalty offerings (cf. 'Comment' on 8:34).

In 4:2–13 it was observed that the anointed priest was not forgiven. The situation there does not apply here for two reasons. First, this ritual deals with general sinfulness, and not the forgiveness of a particular offence. Second, the ritual has a dedicatory nature aimed at making the Lord's appearance possible.

8. From this verse to v. 21 Aaron performs what Moses commanded. First of all, Aaron's sinfulness is dealt with. He slaughters the calf for the sin offering. This assumes Aaron is regarded as hiding himself. Although he became holy, his holiness is not inner holiness (see 'Explanation'). Though not mentioned, the hand-leaning rite must have been done before slaughtering. In fact the gesture is never mentioned in this chapter (see vv. 12, 15, 18); but it is assumed, since it was prescribed in chs. 1 – 4.

9. Aaron's sons assist Aaron in his handling of the blood. His sons bring the blood to Aaron, who dips his finger into it, and smears it on the four horns of the altar. Symbolically this act represents the death of Aaron's egocentric nature. Then he pours (*yāṣaq*) the rest of the blood at the base of the altar. For *yāṣaq*, see 'Comment' on 8:15.

10. Then Aaron burns the fat portion on the altar, symbolizing the annihilation of his egocentric nature.

'As the Lord commanded Moses' Where is this commanded? Considering the nature of the purification ritual here (propitiation for the chief priest), this seems to refer to the burning of the fat and parts of the liver from the sin offering mentioned in Lev. 4:8–10.

11. The flesh is burned outside the camp. In this the ritual deviates from what is prescribed in 4:3–12 and 6:30[23]: though the blood is not brought into the Tent, the flesh is burned outside the camp. Since this is not the case of self-hiding as it was in Lev. 4:3–12, the blood is not brought into the Tent. On the other hand, the priests cannot eat the remaining flesh, because they cannot or should not benefit from sacrifices offered for their own sinfulness.

12. After offering the sin offering, Aaron offers a ram burnt offering for himself. This ritual follows the prescription of ch. 1.

'handed' *mṣ'* hiph. appears in Leviticus only in this chapter (vv. 12–13, 18), and it means 'pass, present, make something available'. As *hiqrîb* is used in v. 9 in the same situation, *mṣ'* hiph. may be used for more than stylistic variation. Probably *himṣî'* is used when the sons of Aaron hand blood to Aaron, while *hiqrîb* is used when they present the blood to the sancta or the Lord. The practical meaning of *himṣî'* highlights Aaron's responsibility for the entire ritual on this occasion.

14. See 1:9.

9:15–21

15. After offering the burnt offering for himself, Aaron offers the offerings for the people. As in the case of Aaron's own sacrifices, the order begins with the sin offering, followed by the burnt offering. First, he offers a male goat for the sin offering. See v. 7b. V. 15a is a general statement, followed by details (Hoffmann 1905: 287–288).

wayĕḥaṭṭĕ'ēhû: 'and he uncovered it' *Ḥṭ'* pi. in such a case has been interpreted as meaning 'present as the sin offering', but as argued elsewhere (Kiuchi 2003a: 107–118), it more likely means to 'uncover, make something uncovered'. See Exod. 29:36; Lev. 6:26[19]. The verb refers to the handling of blood and its symbolic meaning. Therefore the meaning does not include the handling of the remaining flesh (cf. 10:16ff.).

16. The burnt offering here refers to the two animals mentioned in v. 3: a yearling calf and lamb.

'according to regulation': *kammišpāṭ* As in 5:10 it refers to the regulations in ch. 1. As for *kārîšôn* (like the first one) in v. 15, it is evident the legislator has abbreviated the description of the ritual process.

17. After offering the burnt offering for the people, Aaron offers the loyalty offering, followed by the fellowship offering (vv. 18–21). This order is not that commanded in v. 4. Why does the loyalty offering come before the fellowship offering? It is because this is the normal order (the burnt offering, loyalty offering and fellowship offering) given in Lev. 1 – 3. There is a symbolic rationale for offering the loyalty offering after the burnt offering. That is, only after all earthly desires are annihilated by fire (burnt offering) and the worshippers concentrate on the unique bond between them and the Lord (loyalty offering) can they enjoy fellowship with the Lord (fellowship offering).

Aaron takes a handful of grain from the loyalty offering. It is virtually the same as taking a handful of the token portion in 2:2. The nature of this type of *minḥâ* is basically the same as the normal loyalty offering without the three kinds of oil and incense accompaniments (cf. 10:12–13).

'besides the burnt offering of the morning' See Exod. 29:38–42. As Hartley comments (1992: 123), the text assumes the daily burnt offering was already being offered.

18–21. Lastly, Aaron offers the fellowship offering for the people. The ritual is the same as in Lev. 3. The blood is thrown on to the sides of the altar, and the fat portions are burnt up. The right thigh and breast belong to the priests. The dedication thigh is also waved (cf. 10:15). Symbolically this last ritual signifies the person's fellowship with the Lord by the former giving over all unnecessary selfish thoughts to destruction (see 'Comment' on 7:30–33). The Lord smells the odour of the burnt fat and is pleased.

9:22–24

22–23. When Aaron finishes offering all the prescribed offerings, he blesses the people, and then together with Moses blesses them again. A miracle follows.

'and (he) blessed'. *Brk* pi. appears twice in Lev. (9:22–23). So the people are doubly blessed. Aaron first blesses the people, presumably in the forecourt; and then, after entering the Holy Place and coming out with Moses, Aaron blesses the people again. It is debated why there is a twofold blessing. Resolution comes when the significance of blessing in this context is taken into account. Blessing in general accompanies both its gesture and words. It is an act performed at the end of a certain ceremony. Thus blessing that involves a superior performing action towards inferiors or subjects is found in such contexts as (1) priestly blessing (Num. 6:22–27; Deut. 21:5; 1 Chr. 23:13), and (2) royal blessings (2 Sam. 6:18; 1 Kgs 8:55–61). Blessings in such contexts assume that the person who blesses bears divine authority, undertaking a mediatory role between God and people. Thus it is probable that by blessing the people on this occasion, Aaron presents himself as the divinely ordained priest entitled to convey the Lord's blessing to them. Since Aaron will bear all the guilt dealt with by the offerings of the Israelites (Exod. 28:38), the blessing in this context assumes that those sacrifices and offerings are borne by him, and therefore accepted by the Lord. What kinds of words accompanied Aaron's benediction is not known. In this context, more stress is laid on the agency of the blessing: first, Aaron, and then Moses and Aaron together.

Now this first blessing by Aaron concerns the priestly work in the forecourt. It was in the Tent of Meeting that the priests ordinarily worked. Therefore Aaron must be accompanied by Moses, the one who installed the priesthood, in entering the Tent. Thus the second blessing by Aaron and Moses over the people indicated that the priests' work on behalf of the people in the Tent was effective.

This is the first time Moses enters the Holy Place (*pace* Hartley 1992: 124), though Moses used to have free communication with the Lord outside the sanctuary. Until now he is addressed by the Lord from the Tent (see Exod. 40:34–35; Lev. 1:1). Therefore this occasion marks a change in the way the Lord deals with his people and the priests.

The glory of the Lord must have been perceived in a cloud (Exod. 16:10; 19:9; Lev. 16:2), yet with the coming of fire before the Lord (see below) the self-manifestation of the Lord is unmistakable, since both cloud and fire have led the Israelites thus far.

24. That fire came from before the Lord is a miracle. It is unnecessary to see this as contradictory to the fact that those offerings were already burnt (vv. 10, 13–14, 17). Possibly the burnt offering and all the fat pieces smouldering on the altar were consumed instantly, an event that indicated to all present that the fire on the altar was of divine origin. At the sight the people cried and fell on their faces, presumably out of joy and fear.

Ordinarily the officiating priest would complete his work in offering sacrifices by blessing the offerer. However, on this occasion, the manifestation of divine fire following the blessing revealed that the priest's work was sanctioned by the Lord.

Explanation

The eighth-day service is the inaugural service that makes the divine manifestation possible (vv. 4, 23), so the priests may work at the altar and within the Tent. This occasion is the last of a series of divine manifestations that started with the episode of the burning bush (Exod. 3). After the burning bush came the Sinai event, where the Lord descended on top of the mountain. Once the instructions for the Tent and its utensils are complete, Lev. 8 describes the ordination ceremony, and in Lev. 9 the Lord reveals himself to all the people in an even more intimate way than experienced at Sinai. There are ascending degrees in the length of period the divine manifestation continues: in the burning bush it was temporary, at Sinai it was for forty days and nights and on the eighth-day service its continuance is permanent – so long as the priests and people obey the Lord. In this chapter, however, though Moses is presented as superior to Aaron, the fact that the people are accepted by the Lord, so they may approach the outer altar, indicates a closer relationship between the Lord and the people than what was experienced at Sinai.

Since the ceremony as a whole is inaugural, it is not surprising that it differs from the regular rituals reflected in 1 – 6:7[5:26]. The differences are found in the sacrifices offered on this occasion, and their nature (see 'Comment' on vv. 2–4). The rituals assume that Aaron and his sons, along with the people, have not committed any offence, although they are assumed as sinful (in a state of self-hiding).

In this ceremony Aaron makes propitiation for himself, his house and the whole people (cf. ch. 16). Typically the eighth-day service exhibits the permanent relationship between the priests and the people. Aaron is responsible not only for himself and his house, but also for the people. The following figure shows the relationship of the responsibilities:

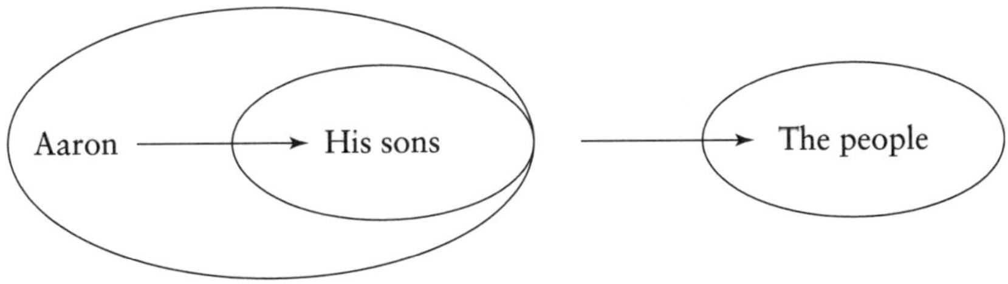

This relationship reveals that though the people bear their own responsibility, it is Aaron and his sons who make propitiation for the people's sinfulness. This assignment of responsibility is reflected in Lev. 4. With regard to Aaron's responsibility, see Exod. 28:38. The propitiation for Aaron and his family's sinfulness must come before propitiation for the sinfulness of the people. Also notable is that the animals for the propitiation of the priests are costlier than those for the propitiation of the people. This stands to reason, for if the agent making propitiation is not free from sinfulness, how can he make propitiation for others? Thus the same order of offering sacrifices is found in other contexts, such as in Lev. 16. However, this spiritual principle implies that the OT sacrificial system has in it some serious defects, because the agent making propitiation always has the potential to continue self-hiding.

One may wonder, however, why Aaron and his sons must offer the sin offering *after* they were consecrated. The fact that Aaron and his sons must again offer various sacrifices and offerings to approach the Lord stands on the assumption that inner holiness was not gained by the ordination ceremony in ch. 8. If, for instance, Aaron and his sons really and literally died from their egocentric selves, which the offerings symbolized from different perspectives, they would not have had to offer sacrifices on the eighth day. Since that was not the case, they must repeatedly offer sacrifices and offerings. This means that their becoming holy in the ordination ceremony refers, at most, to outer holiness (cf. Zechariah, in Luke 1:6–20, who is said to be blameless in observing the Lord's commandment but does not *believe* the angel's message). The gap between their holiness received by divine calling and their actual inner condition is the major hurdle priests were to overcome. This becomes the main theme in chs. 21 – 22.

Also one may wonder why Aaron and his sons do not enter the Tent on this occasion. Since the rituals inside the Tent concern expiation of self-hiding or purification of uncleanness, it is best if Aaron and his sons can dispense with such rituals, though this is impossible. Such a dichotomous tendency with regard to the outer altar and inner sancta can already be found in the arrangement of the materials in Exod. 25 – 30. At the end of Exod. 29 the Lord's dwelling is guaranteed. But the items inside the Tent, such as the incense altar and the incense, which are related to a higher degree of the Lord's wrath, come in ch. 30. In Leviticus as well, the weekly duties of the priest, which consist of changing the bread of the presence, keeping the lamp burning etc. are mentioned not in Lev. 8 – 10 but in Lev. 24, after the dangers of losing the presence of the Lord are discussed.

The inaugural ceremony in Lev. 9 reveals something of the essence of divine service. Not just the sin offering, the primary function of which is the uncovering of the egocentric nature, but also the following offerings can be viewed under the rubric of self-uncovering (see 'Comment' on 4:5–6). The burnt offering is the uncovering of the worshippers par excellence, for by offering it they dedicate themselves to the Lord through their relinquishment of all earthly desires. The loyalty offering also makes the offerer aware of the disloyalty of his soul and lays bare his egocentric soul before God. And the fellowship offering focuses on the uncovering and annihilation of the worshipper's egocentricity in so far as it focuses on the burning of fat. It is because, at least symbolically, the priests and the people uncovered themselves that the Lord revealed himself at the end of the ritual. It is the Lord's custom that when a human hides himself (commonly termed as 'sin') from him, the Lord also hides himself from that person; the latter case involves the wrath of God. All these offerings, except the loyalty offering, are common in that each includes the shedding of blood, which symbolizes the death of the worshipper's ego. As mentioned concerning the ordination ceremony (see 'Explanation' on ch. 8), the more the worshipper's spiritual death is actualized, the less pain he has in subsequent offerings. That is why joyous elements increase in the offerings after the sin offering. Therefore simply stressing joy in the religious life is deceitful and hypocritical unless that joy springs from one's spiritual death (cf. Matt 5:4; Jas 4:9).

Sanctuary and the human heart

It is noteworthy that the Lord reveals himself at the outer altar. The Lord does not desire more than this as far as the people are concerned. The priests may have something to do inside the Tent, but the people, who were barred from approaching it, need not concern themselves with the inside of the Tent; to do this would be for the people to hide themselves and defile it. Thus the scene in Lev. 9 is the fulfilment of the promise in Exod. 29:45–46, and to maintain this stance is the responsibility of the priests. Thus the OT sacrificial system shows that the Israelites cannot approach the place where the Lord resides, the Holy of Holies, nor are they expected to do so: that is strictly forbidden.

Yet, on the other hand, the Lord dwells in the Holy of Holies. As has been noted by some exegetes, the Sinai event shows some parallels to the structure of the establishment of the priesthood (see Milgrom 1970: 44–46). At Mount Sinai, Moses alone could ascend to the top, the Levites and elders could approach the mountain, but the general Israelite populace could not even touch the mountain. This tripartite division of the theocratic community is typically reflected in the relationship between Moses and Aaron, on the one hand, and Aaron and the people, on the other. The tripartite division of the realm of the sanctuary suggests the limitation of the priests and the people alike in approaching the Lord freely. Already the rituals in Lev. 4, though temporal in nature, suggest that the realm where the priests work is limited to the Holy Place and the outer court where the altar of burnt offering is located. By contrast, the lay people can only approach the outer altar.

The veil separating the Holy Place from the Holy of Holies indicates the general limitation of the priests, in that even they cannot approach the place where the Lord dwells. Only on the Day of Atonement can Aaron enter there, yet still under the threat of death (Lev. 16:2).

Now, with regard to the ordination ceremony it was noted that the purification of the priests takes place concurrently with the purification of the altar of burnt offering, and this assumes that the sancta invariably represent the people (see 'Explanation' on ch. 1, 'Comment' on 4:7; 8:14–15). This principle is also at work in the ceremonies of Lev. 4. Because of this representation, purification of the sancta is the same as the purification of the people. In Lev. 9 the Lord accepts the priests and the people alike at the outer altar, and this implies that the general welfare of the people is, if possible, guaranteed by the priestly work at the outer altar. Thus it can be envisaged that the Tent represents the further inner part of the worshippers or people. In other words, the *sanctuary as a whole represents the human heart and soul*. As is indicated in Lev. 4 and 16 it is the self-hiding of the people that defiles not only the Holy Place but also the Holy of Holies. By self-hiding, the people in general defile the Holy of Holies. But self-hiding before the Lord is a matter of the human heart, for the agent of self-hiding is the human *nepeš* (4:2). Thus the innermost part of the human soul is represented by the Holy of Holies. But this will become clearer as we move into the following chapters.

On this assumption it follows that the rationale for the people being unable to enter the Tent while the priest is able to enter lies in the Lord's general evaluation of the human heart. The fact that the Holy of Holies is off-limits to the priests implies that the purification of their hearts is extremely difficult (cf. 4:3–12).

New Testament implications

From the viewpoint of divine service this eighth-day service is not easily compared with Christian worship, where expiation need not take place. Yet in reference to some elements in the Christian church, the following point could be made. What is required of worshippers in divine service is their courage to uncover themselves. But the subsequent Christian church should be accused if they have considered that the ugly parts of the human heart and soul should be hidden before God, in favour of 'proper' outward conduct. Where people's hearts and souls are uncovered, where no self-deception or hypocrisy is found, the divine presence is guaranteed.

What is the main factor that urges humans to turn from this principle? Essentially it is their egocentricity, which always encourages them to hide themselves. Similarly when people encounter Christ and enjoy resting with him, they soon forget the initial love the Lord showed them, and begin their own journey. In NT terms this is called 'falling from grace' (cf. Gal. 3:1–4). To be within the grace of the Lord, to become content with gifts such as talents, work and family, and not to move spiritually from where one is placed is God's will (cf. Rom. 12:3–8). In fact, just as trespassing the boundaries set by God in Leviticus risked Israel's spiritual life permanently, so NT believers risk their eternal lives by moving away from God-given conditions. The latter includes, for instance, desiring to be a different person or to be famous and to earn more, which are dangerous when Christians justify their ways in the name of the Lord, both privately and publicly. God's glory manifests itself when people are deprived of all these motives and thoughts, or, at least, the latter are uncovered. Does this inaugural service not remind them of the love they first had (Rev. 2:4)?

LEVITICUS 10:1–20

Translation

1Now Nadab and Abihu, the sons of Aaron, each took his censer and put fire in it and laid incense on it and offered unauthorized fire before the LORD, which he had not commanded them. 2And fire came out from before the LORD and consumed them, and they died before the LORD. 3Then Moses said to Aaron, 'This is what the LORD had said, By those who are near me I will be sanctified, and before all the people I will be glorified.' Aaron was silent.

4Moses called Mishael and Elzaphan, the sons of Uzziel the uncle of Aaron, and said to them, 'Come near; carry your brothers away from the front of the sanctuary and out of the camp.' 5So they came near and carried them in their coats out of the camp, as Moses had said. 6Moses said to Aaron and to Eleazar and Ithamar his sons, 'Do not let the hair of your heads hang loose, and do not tear your clothes, lest you die, and wrath come upon all the congregation; but let your brothers, the whole house of Israel, bewail the burning that the LORD has kindled. 7And do not go outside the entrance of the Tent of Meeting, lest you die, for the anointing oil of the LORD is upon you.' And they did according to the word of Moses.

8The LORD spoke to Aaron, saying, 9'Drink no wine or strong drink, you or your sons with you, when you go into the Tent of Meeting, lest you die. It shall be a statute forever throughout your generations. 10You are to distinguish between the holy and the common, and between the unclean and the clean, 11and you are to teach the Israelites all the statutes that the LORD has spoken to them by Moses.'

[12]Moses spoke to Aaron and to Eleazar and Ithamar, his surviving sons, 'Take the loyalty offering that is left of the LORD's offerings for annihilation, and eat it unleavened beside the altar, for it is most holy. [13]You shall eat it in a holy place, because it is your due and your sons' due, from the LORD's offerings for annihilation, for so I am commanded. [14]But the breast that is waved and the thigh that is contributed you shall eat in a clean place, you and your sons and your daughters with you, for they are given as your due and your sons' due from the sacrifices of the fellowship offerings of the Israelites. [15]The thigh that is contributed and the breast that is waved they shall bring with the offerings for annihilation of the fat pieces to wave for a wave offering before the LORD, and it shall be yours and your sons' with you as a due forever, as the LORD has commanded.'

[16]Now Moses diligently inquired about the goat of the sin offering, and behold, it was burned up! He was angry with Eleazar and Ithamar, the surviving sons of Aaron, saying, [17]'Why have you not eaten the sin offering in a holy place, since it is a thing most holy and had been given to you that you may bear the guilt of the community, to sacrifice yourselves for them before the LORD? [18]Behold, its blood was not brought into the Holy Place. You certainly ought to have eaten it in holiness, as I commanded.' [19]And Aaron said to Moses, 'Behold, today they have offered their sin offering and their burnt offering before the LORD, and yet such things as these have happened to me! If I had eaten the sin offering today, would the LORD have approved?' [20]When Moses heard that, he approved.

Notes on the text

1. 'Aaron's sons': *bĕnê 'ahărōn* LXX adds 'two' before 'sons'.

3. 'was silent': *wayyiddōm* ESV renders 'held his peace', while LXX renders it 'he was stunned' (*katanyssō*). The latter may indeed reflect Aaron's emotion. As the chief priest the Lord's words pierced his heart (see 'Comment').

6. 'his sons': *bānāyw* LXX adds 'remaining', probably in conformity with v. 12. However, as there is a literary reason for mentioning 'remaining' in v. 12 (see 'Comment'), this is unnecessary.

'bewail': *bākâ* On this occasion the Hebr. term is broader than just 'to weep'. It probably includes fasting (cf. Brongers 1977: 4).

9. 'when you go into the Tent of Meeting' LXX adds 'or when you approach the altar' (cf. Exod. 30:20), probably for legal considerations.

10. LXX and Syr omit the *wāw* at the beginning of this verse, linking it as a purpose clause with v. 9. However, the general character of the content in vv. 10–11 indicates that the *lāmed* at the beginnings of these verses designates neither purpose (Elberfelder) nor reason (JPS), but it is an injunction (NIV, NRSV, ESV, Luther). For this use of *lāmed* see *GKC* 114 h–k.

'the unclean': *haṭṭāmē'* Tg omits it. But since in that case there is no corresponding word for *ṭāhôr*, the MT should be retained.

14. 'in a clean place': *bĕmāqôm ṭāhôr* LXX reads 'in a holy place', probably in harmony with vv. 13, 17 (see 'Comment').

17. See 'Comment'.

18. See 'Comment'.

Form and structure

Lev. 10 relates an incident that happened on the same day as the eighth-day service: two sons of Aaron, Nadab and Abihu, offered strange fire before the Lord. Fire came from before the Lord and consumed them, and they died instantly. Thus the joy of both the priests and the whole people was swept aside by sorrow.

The chapter is divisible into three sections:

A. The incident of Nadab and Abihu (1–7)
B. Instructions on the role of priests (8–11)
C. Instructions on the remaining flesh, and the priests' failure to eat from the sin offering (12–20)

The second (B) and third (C) sections naturally echo the Nadab and Abihu incident. The third section poses the dilemma Aaron has in regarding the eating of the remaining sacrificial flesh. In particular C becomes related to A when Aaron justifies his conduct by having recourse to the very principle Moses enunciates in v. 3. Significantly the narrative as a whole ends with a question about the propitiation for the priestly family left pending.

If v. 10 anticipates the regulations from ch. 11 to ch. 15, it may well be that v. 11, considering its literary relationship with 26:46, refers to all the regulations from ch. 11 to ch. 26.

After this shocking incident takes place, the Lord solemnly gives instructions, in vv. 8–11, regarding the responsibility of the priests: first in connection with the incident (v. 9), and second in connection with their permanent duties (vv. 10–11). This suggests that the Lord still assumes that the normal priestly duties began from this day onwards despite the incident of vv. 1–2.

Vv. 17–20. It is crucially important to consider why Aaron allowed his remaining sons to burn the flesh of the sin offering outside the camp (v. 16). V. 19 implies that without expiation of the sins/sinfulness of the priests they are not entitled to engage in expiatory work, a principle reflected in the ritual in 4:2–12 (see 'Comment' there), 6:23[16] and 6:30[23].

Critics tend to find the presence of rules amid the narrative somewhat awkward (cf. Hartley 1992: 131). However, it was pointed out in ch. 8 that the drawing of a clear distinction between narrative and law is artificial. More importantly, given that the priestly work inside the Tent is anticipated by 9:23, directions concerning the priests' entrance of the Tent is hardly surprising.

Comment

10:1–7

1. Nadab and Abihu are Aaron's eldest sons. It is not stated here why they took incense and brought strange fire before the Lord. The phrase 'unauthorized (lit. 'strange') fire' (*'ēš zārâ*) is qualified by 'that the Lord did not command' (*'ăšer lō' ṣiwwâ YHWH*). 'Strange' connotes both that it is unauthorized, and that the fire was taken from a place other than that authorized. The offence lies in their offering incense to the Lord in their own way. Further circumstances surrounding the offence are hinted at in v. 9: that they were drunk (see below), and that they even entered the Holy of Holies (cf. 16:1–2). In that case, the phrase 'before the Lord' in this verse and the next means the Holy of Holies. At any rate, it is emphasized that the fire was not what was commanded by the Lord. The narrator's method of emphasizing this point is significant: each of the factors leading to the incident are treated in relation to appropriate laws. In this way the background to the incident emerges only gradually for the reader.

2. Nadab and Abihu were killed instantly by the fire that came from before the Lord. The literary concord between this verse and 9:24 emphasizes that the occasion for joy is now overturned by sorrow. In 9:24 'the fire came out from before the Lord' and 'devoured the burnt offering'. Lev. 10:2 reads, 'And fire came from the Lord and devoured them.'

Is the nature of the fire here the same as that of the fire at 9:24? Though the reason for burning is different, there is no reason to assume that the fire itself is different: the fire in 9:24 consumed the offerings and the fire in 10:2 consumed Nadab and Abihu. Both are consuming fires that symbolize destruction or annihilation. In retrospect, in 9:24 the people rejoiced, or could rejoice, because the offerings took the place of the offerers, whereas in 10:2 there was no substitution for Nadab and Abihu.

And yet the conduct of Nadab and Abihu is not described by using the terms *ḥāṭā'* or *ḥaṭṭā't*. Traditionally their offence has often been called 'a sin'. But their offence requires a more exact description. It lies outside the cases anticipated by ch. 4 that deal with inadvertent self-hiding through the violation of one of God's prohibitive commandments. Instead it resembles the case for the reparation offering that deals with infringements against holy things. Nevertheless their actions constitute a much more serious, inexpiable offence than those referred to in 5:14–26. As inexpiable, it claimed their lives. Just as the cases for the reparation offering deal with *ḥāṭā'*, this case can also be explained as *ḥāṭā'*, though its nature is different from those of the reparation offering. This is a case of *ḥāṭā'*, where the reparation offering is ineffective (cf. the case of Uzzah in 2 Sam. 6:6–7; 1 Chr. 13:9–10).

3. Moses conveys the Lord's words. Perhaps Moses is expostulating with Aaron by citing the words the Lord *had told* Moses. It is formulated in a parallelism:

> By those who are near me I will be sanctified,
> and before all the people I will be glorified.

The intent is clear: the glory of the Lord manifests itself by 'those who are near me' (through the priestly work). Hence priests carry a heavy responsibility. The parallel pairing of *qdš* ni. with *kbd* ni. is unique in the OT, but a near counterpart is found in Exod. 29:43. This latter verse is the culminating summary of the preceding account of what Moses is instructed to do. If Moses' 'cited words' in 10:2 are not a literal citation, they are possibly a summary of Exod. 29:44–45, 40:34–35 or of what took place in ch. 9.

4. Moses orders the sons of Uzziel, Mishael and Elzaphan, to carry the two dead bodies out of the sanctuary and the camp.

The reason why Mishael and Elzaphan, and not Aaron and his sons, are chosen to carry the dead bodies is explained by what Moses says next: Aaron and his sons ought not to come into contact with death, which would profane their holiness.

'your brothers': *'ăḥêkem* This does not mean brothers of first degree. In v. 6 the same term is extended to the whole house of Israel.

'out of the camp' This phrase suggests that the dead bodies are treated like the remaining flesh of the sin offering that is to be burned outside the camp. However, while the latter is part of a propitiation ritual (see 8:17; 9:11), the former, having been burned inside the sanctuary, only needs to be carried out.

5. Mishael and Elzaphan comply with Moses.

'Carrying them by their coats' At first sight 'their' is ambiguous and appears to refer to Mishael and Elzaphan, but since they are not priests, it refers to Nadab and Abihu (see Péter-Contesse 1993: 163). Reference to their coats created rabbinic speculation about the way they were killed: burning of breath and the body exists (Siphra). It is, anyway, a miraculous burning that left the holy coats intact. The fact that they grabbed them by the coats gives a miserable impression in view of the holiness they were given.

6. Moses instructs Aaron and his remaining sons not to dishevel their hair nor to tear their clothes, and says that it is the house of Israel that ought to mourn Nadab and Abihu.

'Do not let the hair of your heads hang loose': *lō' tiprōmû Pāram* occurs just three times in the OT and only in Leviticus (10:6; 13:45; 21:10). The dishevelment of hair is a symbolic gesture of mourning. Certainly the gesture is related to death and uncleanness (Num. 5:18). In 21:10 the chief priest is prohibited from dishevelling his hair or tearing his garments, the latter another symbolic act of mourning. In other words, the chief priest is prohibited even from bewailing the loss of his parents. It is important to bear in mind, at this point, that the gesture is not considered separate from its symbolic meaning; i.e. he still breaks this rule if he mourns without dishevelling his hair.

However, this is the case where the brothers of the priests die, and 21:2 appears to allow the priest to mourn for his brother. Here Aaron's sons are treated by Moses as equal to Aaron in terms of holiness, and this appears inconsistent with the rule in 21:2. However, first, in ch. 10 an abnormal death caused by the profaning of holiness is at issue, whereas in 21:2 natural death is at issue if a funeral is assumed (see 'Comment' there). Second, a higher standard is applied here because of the occasion's inaugural nature.

Whether one obeys the Lord or not can be tested when one faces one of the saddest events within the family. The Lord demands their allegiance to him, as they are holy (see 'Explanation').

'wrath come upon all the congregation' The potential for divine wrath to rush out against all the community in the event of the priests' mourning reflects the same principle reflected in 4:3.

'The house of Israel' are called 'your brothers'. Already 'brothers' has appeared in v. 4. Thus the same word is used in an extended sense here, probably to stress the priests' spiritual identification with the people (cf. 'brother' in 19:17).

The anointed priests who are holy to the Lord ought never to mourn for their family's dead. This may seem unnatural, but it stands to reason because, once committed to the Lord, they are responsible to align themselves with him even when members of their family die. Furthermore, since the death of Nadab and Abihu resulted from their disobedience to the Lord's will, mourning them would imply allegiance to Nadab and Abihu.

7. The Lord prohibits Aaron and his remaining sons from exiting the Tent of Meeting. The verse is similar to 8:35. Were it not for the incident, they could have left. But since God's holiness has been profaned by Nadab and Abihu who were members of the Aaronic family, they can no longer leave. If the rest of Aaron's family go out of the sanctuary, this means further profanation of their holy anointing as well as coming into contact with death.

10:8–11

In this section the Lord addresses Aaron and gives general rules for the priests. From vv. 9–10 it is known that the priests were to work inside the Tent from this day onwards. The instruction in v. 9 is given with an awareness of the current situation Aaron and his remaining sons are in, and its formulation is affected by the Nadab and Abihu incident.

8. This is the only place in Leviticus where the Lord directly addresses Aaron, without Moses' mediation. Considering the fundamental and general role of the priests mentioned in the following verses 9–11, Aaron is clearly addressed in his capacity as the head of the priests; i.e. as the one responsible for the priesthood.

9. That the Lord's words begin with the prohibition against wine and strong drink when entering the Tent strongly implies that Nadab and Abihu may have entered the Tent of Meeting drunk. At any rate, sobriety is required of the priests during their activities in the Tent, for their mistakes can claim their lives.

10. The fundamental priestly duties are set out here and in the next verse. The very mention of these roles indicates that Aaron has not been disqualified as head of the family, though he is partially responsible for the death of Nadab and Abihu. More importantly, this reflects the Lord's forward-looking attitude, which is also found in Moses' attitude in vv. 16ff. (cf. Gen. 19:26).

It is only here that a contrast between the holy (*qōdeš*) and the common (*ḥôl*) is explicitly mentioned (cf. 1 Sam. 21:5–6; Ezek. 22:26; 42:20: 44:23). When 'uncleanness' (*ṭāmē'*) and 'cleanness' (*ṭāhôr*) are in apposition, they appear in this order (11:47; 14:57). These two pairs of concepts have profound significance for the literary structure of Leviticus. These pairs, holy–common and unclean–clean, have their legal counterparts in chs. 18 – 27 and 11 – 16, where there is a chiastic structure. In other words, 10:10–11 adumbrate the contents of the following chapters (see Kiuchi 2003c: 524).

11. Another major role of the priests is to teach the sons of Israel all the Lord's statutes. 'Statutes' (*ḥuqqîm*) appears in Lev. only twice, here and in 26:46, and this unites the entire legislation of Leviticus, with the exception of ch. 27 (see Kiuchi 1999a: 62).

10:12–20

This section reports the priests' eating of their dues from the loyalty, fellowship (vv. 12–15) and sin offerings (vv. 16–20; cf. 9:17–21). In evaluating this section, the reader, as well as Aaron himself, is challenged with what is more important: eating the remaining flesh that relates to the state of priests and people before the Lord, or the death of Aaron's sons. Moses is consistent in obeying the Lord's commandments even after this sad incident.

12–13. The wordplay created by the narrator between the remaining (*nôtarîm*) sons, and the remaining (*nôteret*) loyalty offering (cf. v. 6) clearly expresses a message. Eating the remaining loyalty offering indicates that the priests continued in their loyalty to the Lord. Therefore by twice repeating 'remaining', Moses is demanding that the priests *complete* their loyalty, which, humanly speaking is extremely hard, following the sad incident of Nadab and Abihu. Here, at least, Moses is demanding that the priests show more loyalty to the Lord than to their family. All this suggests that the offerings made in ch. 9 had real spiritual reference to the inner attitude of the priests. Offering a sacrifice is more than a formality: it is a matter of life and death (see 'Explanation').

Because the offering is most holy, it must be eaten 'beside the altar'. The altar of burnt offering is holy, so that the surrounding area may be called a holy place. But the phrase 'it is a most holy thing' is made with an awareness of the inner attitude of the offering's partakers: the priests ought to be dead to this world, including towards their family (for the holiness of the place see 'Explanation').

14. 'in a clean place' refers to somewhere in the Tent or within the sanctuary. But the intention of 'clean' is that the partaker of the meat should eat with inner cleanness, not simply that the place itself be clean. That no terms such as 'holy' or 'holiness' are ascribed to the fellowship offering coincides with the regulation in 7:11–38, where these terms are also absent.

15. See 9:21.

16. Moses found that the 'goat' for the sin offering had been burned. The goat is the one for the propitiation for the people, as is clear from the following verses. It is not proper to have recourse to passages like 6:24–30[17–23] to explain the reason why the goat was burned, for in the eighth-day service the blood of the two kinds of sin offering, one for the priests and the other for the people, was not brought into the Tent of Meeting. That the priests should have eaten the meat is deduced from the principle that the agent of the propitiation ought to eat the meat.

'He was angry': *yiqṣôp* In v. 6 the same term was used to describe the Lord's wrath. Here the narrator ascribes the same feeling to Moses.

17. The reason for Moses' anger is that Aaron, moved by his own consideration, did not obey the Lord's commandment. So he accuses Aaron and his sons for their not having eaten the flesh in a holy place, with an explanation of the function of the sin offering.

'in a holy place': *bimqôm haqqōdeš* The phrase means the same as in v. 3 (*bĕmāqôm qādôš*). The word *haqqōdeš* is an adjectival use of a noun. In this verse the use of the noun form creates an emphasis, since the phrase is followed by 'because it is a most holy thing' (*qōdeš qodāšîm*). See on vv. 12–13 above.

The flesh of the sin offering ought to be consumed just as the flesh of other offerings (see 6:26[19]). This prebend for the officiating priest must be consumed simultaneously since it belongs to the Lord. Here the privilege and responsibility are one (see 'Explanation' on 6:8[1] – 7:10).

The latter half of the verse requires rigorous attention. *'āwōn* means 'guilt', not simply 'rcsponsibility'. The relationship of the two infinitive constructs, *lāśēt* (to bear) and *lěkapper* (to make propitiation), is such that the first is explicated by the second: conceptually they are synonymous. From the purpose clause 'to bear the guilt' one tends to assume that by eating the meat the priests bear the guilt of the community (Milgrom 1991: 624–625). However, there are some counter-arguments. First, nowhere in Leviticus is eating the flesh conceived as part of the *kipper*-concept (see 4:20, 26, 31). Second, it is vital to observe that the 'it' in 'and it was given to you' refers to the flesh of the *ḥaṭṭā't*, and not to the *eating* of the flesh. In other words, v. 17b, following the statement 'for it is the most holy thing', discusses the relationship between the flesh and the priestly role of bearing guilt / making propitiation. In fact, Moses' argument in v. 17 proceeds in three stages from the last part of the ritual (eating the flesh) to the statement 'it is the most holy thing' (v. 17a) to the early part of the ritual by blood handling (bearing guilt / propitiation, v. 17b). Moses' reversal of the ritual in giving explanation makes unwarranted the assumption that eating the flesh leads to the bearing of guilt. Therefore the interpretation that eating the flesh removes the guilt of the congregation does not commend itself. The flesh of the sin offering for the people is a priestly due received after propitiation is made, and eating it symbolizes they have borne the guilt of the people, and thus made propitiation for them. Moses' words in this verse show an inseparable relationship between the priests' eating of the flesh and the *kipper act*. The flesh is not something the priests are free to handle because it is a due, but something that ought to be consumed.

18. A reference is made to the rule mentioned in 6:30[23]. Since the blood was not brought to the Tent of Meeting, the flesh of the sin offering ought to have been eaten.

The term *haqqōdeš* appears twice in this verse. Does the first *haqqōdeš* mean 'the sanctuary' or the Holy Place (the Tent of Meeting)? Because the second appears to refer to 'in a holy place', which is parallel to 'a holy place' in v. 13, some exegetes take the twice-repeated *haqqōdeš* in this verse to mean 'the sanctuary' in a wider sense, including the outer court. Péter-Contesse finds confirmation in the term 'inner' (*pěnîmâ*), as this word is required because *haqqōdeš* means the 'sanctuary' (Péter-Contesse 1993: 167–168). But 'inner' (*pěnîmâ*) probably qualifies 'was brought' (*hubbâ*). Therefore 'the inner part of the sanctuary' (NRSV, ESV) is inappropriate.

baqqōdeš Though this second *qōdeš* is often taken as meaning the same as the first (referring to a location ['the sanctuary', 'the sanctuary area']), this *qōdeš* may well be different in meaning from the first, if the first *qōdeš* means 'the Holy Place'. First, it is unlikely the term for 'place' is abbreviated. Second, it is also unlikely Moses is saying the priests ought to have eaten the flesh of the sin offering inside the Tent, as they have still not officially entered it. Rather than the location of eating, the priests' inner attitude is stressed here. Thus the translation 'in holiness' fits here. Interestingly the expressions concerning the location of eating gradually change in this chapter, as follows:

12Beside the altar (*'ēṣel hammizbēaḥ*)
13In a holy place (*bĕmāqôm qādôš*)
17In a place of holiness (*bimqôm haqqōdeš*)
18To the Holy Place (*'el haqqōdeš*)
In holiness (*baqqōdeš*)

Particularly in v. 17 the mention of 'in a place of holiness' is stressed by the following 'the most holy thing', while in v. 18 the mention of 'the Holy Place' (*haqqōdeš*) together with eating 'in holiness' highlights the holy way of eating; in the latter an awareness of *the place* disappears.

Obviously there was a specific place in the sanctuary, which was deemed holy. But holiness cannot be separated from a person. Thus the above development in phraseology relating to the location of eating emphasizes that the priests should eat the flesh in holiness because the offering is the most holy thing. Eating the flesh *in holiness* refers to more than an outer holiness: it refers to the eater's inner attitude, particularly, in this context, towards the sin offering. It was a priestly due and simultaneously eating it symbolizes that the priest has borne the guilt of the community, thus sacrificing himself for them. In other words, holiness in v. 18b means the priest's becoming a substitutionary sacrifice.

19–20. Aaron, as head of the priestly family, excuses the conduct of his two sons, Eleazar and Ithamar. The verse consists of three parts. For the following, see Kiuchi 1987: 72–77:

A. Today they have offered their sin offering and their burnt offering before the Lord.
B. and yet such things as these have happened to me!
C. If I had eaten the sin offering today, would the Lord have approved?

A. 'Today' refers to the same day (the eighth day). 'They' should be taken as impersonal rather than as referring to Aaron's four sons, while 'their' refers to the four sons. Thus this part of v. 19 refers to the fact that the priests made propitiation for themselves. The two offerings refer to the ones mentioned in 9:2, which concern the propitiation *for the priests*.

B. 'such things as these' refers to the violation made by Nadab and Abihu: their sudden death, and its aftermath. It is questionable, however, if Aaron is expressing his sorrow here as head of the priestly family.

C. Note the change of the subject from 3rd person pl. to 1st person sg.

Aaron recognizes it as his responsibility that the two remaining sons burn the flesh under his supervision. Aaron, in addressing the sin offering *for the people*, excuses himself by explaining that he cannot eat its flesh as a due.

It is often assumed that the reason Aaron and his sons did not eat the flesh was because they were mourning (Hartley 1992: 137). Is Aaron having recourse to the emotional shock at the death of his two sons here? An affirmative answer flatly contradicts the injunction in v. 6 (note the verb *bākâ* [to bewail]). Moreover there is no apparent distinction made between mourning in public and in private (*pace* Averbeck 1997: 703). Despite these criticisms, there are still exponents who stress the emotional aspect of the priests. This position, however, cannot sufficiently explain why Aaron appealed to propitiation for the priests in A, as S. D. Luzzatto noted long ago (Luzzatto 1965: 406). Offerings are not just formal. The form of the symbol cannot be separated from its meaning.

Two points are to be made. First, the outward gesture of mourning cannot be separated from its symbolic meaning: dishevelling one's hair and tearing one's clothes cannot be separated from mourning (cf. Hartley 1992: 137). There is no such distinction between formal mourning and internal mourning. It is crucially important to observe that in v. 6 inner holiness is demanded of Aaron and his sons in not mourning the death of his sons. Since it may be assumed that Aaron followed Moses' direction, it is improbable that in v. 19 Aaron is appealing to his own emotion or feelings about the incident in order to justify his conduct.

More essentially, here Aaron is first pointing to the propitiation of priests, in contrast to Moses, who is worried about the propitiation of the people (vv. 17–18). This shows that the reason for the two sons' not eating the flesh revolves around the propitiation for the priests. Here the principle enunciated in 10:3, the responsibility of the priests, must be recalled. Propitiation for the people is possible only when propitiation is made for the priests. Therefore Aaron is saying that though propitiation was made for him and his sons, a situation contrary to the joyful acceptance of the Lord has occurred. Therefore it is inappropriate for the priests to partake in the priestly dues. Since Aaron bases his argument on the same principle Moses gave in v. 3, Moses concedes Aaron was right. This implies Moses recognizes Aaron's taking responsibility to some extent as the head of his family.

Though this is Aaron's intention, he exhibits inconsistency in burning only the flesh of the sin offering, and not the remaining parts of the other offerings such as the loyalty and fellowship offerings. These were also concerned with propitiation for the priests. Thus his judgment remains humanistic anyway.

A question relating to what happens when the priesthood is left unatoned for hangs over the end of this chapter. In my view, part of the solution is presented in ch. 16.

Explanation

Humanly speaking, the Nadab and Abihu incident turned a joyful occasion into a sorrowful one. Yet the aftermath of the incident narrates the heavy responsibility the priests carry before the Lord. It is only when the priests carry out their duty in accordance with the Lord's commandment that the Lord is glorified before the people (v. 3). Moses' directions to Aaron (vv. 3–8) and the latter's response to Moses (vv. 16–19) underscore the nature of the holiness conferred.

There are two preliminary considerations. First, because they are anointed and holy, the priests should avoid any contact with death. Because of this special occasion, the holiness of Aaron's sons is deemed equivalent to Aaron's. The prohibition to mourn came to Aaron and his two remaining sons as something that compels them to abandon natural feelings about their family members. Thus the Lord leaves the mourning to the house of Israel who are said to be the 'brothers' of the priests (v. 6). Moses' directions to Aaron and his sons clearly demonstrate an important aspect of holiness: that the priests ought not to mourn even for their own family members. This aspect is developed in ch. 21.

The prohibition against mourning shows that holiness is diametrically opposed to contact with death. More essentially mourning means not only to come into contact with death, but to take side with, and sympathize with, the rebellious Nadab and Abihu. This would be to take an indirect stance against the Lord. In this light, then, the essential meaning of uncleanness that is the major theme in Lev. 11 – 15 is already suggested in this part of the incident: contact with death has the symbolic meaning of approving the violations of the Lord's commandments or his will. Thus, though harsh for Aaron and his remaining sons, the way of holiness sometimes involves a separation of the family bond, which is deep in the emotions and consciousness of familial members. In this latter sense, the way of holiness is definitely different from the *common* way.

Second, whatever happened, it is in Moses' mind that what the Lord has commanded must be carried out punctiliously. The section vv. 12–20 concerns the handling of the remaining parts of the offerings: the loyalty, fellowship and sin offerings. It is at this point that the modern readers of Leviticus are challenged to examine their own assumptions regarding the sacrifices and offerings in this book. For without an appreciation that the offerings have definite symbolic meanings one cannot realize Moses' anger, nor what had happened to the offering at the end of ch. 9. Basically one must realize that the offerings have dealt *in a real sense* with the lives of the Israelites before the Lord, so the mishandling of the offerings endanger their very lives before the Lord. This assumption explains some of Moses' anger about the sin offering (see also 'Comment' on vv. 12–13). The modern perception of a loose relationship between the symbol and the symbolized is responsible for confusion regarding the fate of the offerings here. The same can be said regarding the mourning gesture: it cannot be separated from the participants' inner attitude to the dead, at least, in Leviticus. In this instance, that meant giving allegiance to Nadab and Abihu who rebelled against the Lord.

Thus Moses' anger in v. 16 derives from the fact that Aaron does not obey the Lord's commandment regarding the remaining flesh of the sin offering. In response to Aaron's excuse, Moses concedes, but this episode along with the rest of the chapter relates some important aspects of holiness, which are of perennial value.

(1) Moses clearly demonstrates that the way of holiness is characterized by punctilious obedience to the Lord's commandments. Not only was the death of Nadab and Abihu caused by ignoring the Lord's command (v. 1); Moses himself uses the term 'to command' (*ṣiwwâ*) in vv. 13, 15, 18. This obedience must be simple and perfect.

(2) The way of holiness is, in essence, different from the common way. It places priority on the Lord's commandment or concern, so it separates itself from humanism of a kind that puts the priority and ultimate value on human biological life. But herein lies the great principle 'Leave the dead to bury their own dead' (Luke 9:60 ESV). For, as this incident concerning Nadab and Abihu shows, their death is the result of disobedience. Moreover Leviticus views so-called 'natural' death not as natural but as the consequence of disobedience to God's commandments (see 'Comment' on 18:5; cf. 2 Sam. 12:15b–23). In a word, holiness places priority on one's obedience to the Lord – even amid the death of a close relative (for participation in the funeral see further 'Explanation' on ch. 21).

(3) Thus Moses' insistence on the consumption of the remaining flesh reflects the assumption that one's state before the Lord is more important than whether one dies physically or not. It points to a further assumption that holiness lies in a different dimension to one's physical life.

(4) Holiness is individualistic in the sense that it even divides the family bond. Note that only Nadab and Abihu died, while Aaron, the head of the family, is spared. This is because each individual belongs in the first instance to God: interhuman, even familial, relationships are secondary.

(5) Holiness lies in an inner attitude that never dwells on the past. The Lord concerns himself with the priestly roles (vv. 10–11), and Moses just concerns himself with fulfilling the Lord's commandment. In common terms, it is nobility, the courage to forget the sorrowful past (Luke 9:62), that is required.

All these aspects of holiness are prone to be misunderstood and misapplied by those who think that holiness lies somewhere in the extension, or an elevated form, of humanism in the sense mentioned above. But the essence of holiness lies beyond the death of the human egocentric nature, as indicated by the symbolism of the *holy* sacrifices. To fail to understand this affects one's reading of this chapter. Some exegetes appear to sympathize with Aaron's excuse in v. 19, thus failing to see the presence of a contrast between Moses' holiness and Aaron's (e.g. Hartley 1992: 137–138; Rooker 2000: 163). But Aaron did not obey the Lord's commandment. Moreover he is ultimately responsible for the offence of Nadab and Abihu and their subsequent death. His excuse in v. 19 stands on his own fault, and yet he justifies his own conduct, appealing to the very words of Moses in v. 3. Though Moses approves Aaron's conduct, Aaron remains a man who cannot place priority on the Lord's cause, overwhelmed by his family tragedy; he cannot accept the fact that the Lord treats each priest individually. It is the same Aaron who consented to the people's desire to make a golden calf, and then later excused himself to Moses (Exod. 32:1–5, 21–24). As an ordained priest, Aaron's holiness appears to remain outward at best. And if this is Aaron's limitation, then it is no wonder that the priests are prevented from entering the Holy of Holies. In other words, the spiritual condition of not only Nadab and Abihu but of the rest of the priest's family corresponds to the area in the Tent where they are to work, which, however, cannot deal with their own self-hiding in the true sense.

Similarly the same limitation of priestly holiness is seen from the discrepancy between the most holy offerings, which aim at inner holiness corresponding to the holiness of the Holy of Holies, and the outward holiness of the priests. As the episode in vv. 16–19 has shown, it is the egocentric nature that represents the priests' limitation. Therefore it is conceivable that the veil separating the Holy Place from the Holy of Holies symbolizes the presence of the human egocentric nature. Certainly even the ego of a lay individual can be broken, so he becomes spiritually alive to God, and in this sense holier than the priests. But the structure of the Tent, particularly the presence of the veil, implies that the death of human selfishness is not yet a possibility for the people.

As a whole, this chapter presents to the reader the limitation of outer holiness with regard to Aaron and his sons, and their need to bear inner holiness in order to sacrifice themselves for the people.

New Testament implications

The OT sacrificial worship ended with the sacrifice of Christ on the cross, and with his death the curtain in the temple was torn from top to bottom (Matt. 27:51). This has cosmic significance for the salvation of all humanity. It is insufficient just to say that by his death on the cross sacrificial worship came to an end. His death brought about such a situation that even the lay individual in the OT times can enter the Holy of Holies without any qualms.

However, it is one thing to believe what Christ did for all humanity, but another to believe that so-called believers themselves experienced the spiritual process the splitting of the curtain symbolized. This can be tested, above all, by whether such people can follow what Jesus taught. Believers can follow Jesus only when they are prepared for self-sacrifice, and do not turn back (Luke 9:57–62). This becomes a reality when they experience the death of self (the destruction of their egocentric nature).

As with the previous chapters, this chapter also suggests the heavy responsibility of those people who take upon themselves spiritual leadership in the church. What emerges from this chapter is the question of how far church leaders are vigilant against their own spiritual conditions. They should imitate the holiness of Moses featured above; in particular they should undertake spiritual work only if the Lord commands them to do so (cf. 1 Thess. 2:4).

LEVITICUS 11:1–47

Translation

1And the LORD spoke to Moses and Aaron, saying to them, 2‘Speak to the Israelites,
saying, These are the creatures that you may eat among all the animals that are
on the earth. 3Whatever parts the hoof and is cloven footed and chews the cud,
among the animals, you may eat. 4Nevertheless among those that chew the cud or
part the hoof, you shall not eat these: the camel, because it chews the cud but does
not part the hoof, is unclean to you. 5And the rock badger, because it chews the cud
but does not part the hoof, is unclean to you. 6And the hare, because it chews the
cud but does not part the hoof, is unclean to you. 7And the pig, because it parts
the hoof and is cloven footed but does not chew the cud, is unclean to you. 8You
shall not eat any of their flesh, and you shall not touch their carcasses: they are
unclean to you.

9‘These you may eat, of all that are in the waters. Everything in the waters that
has fins and scales, whether in the seas or in the rivers, you may eat. 10But anything
in the seas or the rivers that has not fins and scales, of the swarming creatures in the
waters and of the living creatures that are in the waters, is detestable to you. 11You
shall regard them as detestable: you shall not eat any of their flesh, and you shall
detest their carcasses. 12Everything in the waters that has not fins and scales is
detestable to you.

13‘These you shall detest among the birds; they shall not be eaten; they are
detestable: the eagle, the bearded vulture, the black vulture, 14the kite, the falcon of
any kind, 15every raven of any kind, 16the ostrich, the nighthawk, the sea gull, the
hawk of any kind, 17the little owl, the cormorant, the short-eared owl, 18the barn
owl, the tawny owl, the carrion vulture, 19the stork, the heron of any kind, the
hoopoe and the bat.

20‘All winged insects that go on all fours are detestable to you. 21Yet among
the winged insects that go on all fours you may eat those that have jointed legs

above their feet, with which to hop on the ground. [22]Of them you may eat the locust of any kind, the bald locust of any kind, the cricket of any kind and the grasshopper of any kind. [23]But all other winged insects that have four feet are detestable to you.

[24]'And by these you shall become unclean. Whoever touches their carcass shall be unclean until the evening, [25]and whoever carries any part of their carcass shall wash his clothes and be unclean until the evening. [26]Concerning every animal that parts the hoof but is not cloven footed or does not chew the cud: they are unclean to you. Everyone who touches them shall be unclean. [27]And all that walk on their paws, among the animals that go on all fours, are unclean to you. Whoever touches their carcass shall be unclean until the evening, [28]and he who carries their carcass shall wash his clothes and be unclean until the evening; they are unclean to you.

[29]'These are unclean to you among the swarming things that swarm on the ground: the mole rat, the mouse, the great lizard of any kind, [30]the gecko, the monitor lizard, the lizard, the sand lizard and the chameleon. [31]These are unclean to you among all that swarm. Whoever touches them when they are dead shall be unclean until the evening. [32]Anything on which any of them falls when they are dead shall be unclean, whether it is an article of wood or a garment or a skin or a sack, any article that is used for any purpose. It must be put into water, and it shall be unclean until the evening; then it shall be clean. [33]If any of them falls into any earthenware vessel, all that is in it shall be unclean, and you shall break it. [34]Any food that could be eaten, on which water comes (from such a vessel), shall be unclean. And all drink that could be drunk from every such vessel shall be unclean. [35]Everything on which any part of their carcass falls shall be unclean. Whether oven or stove, it shall be broken in pieces. They are unclean and shall remain unclean for you. [36]Nevertheless a spring or a cistern holding water shall be clean, but whoever touches a carcass in them shall be unclean. [37]And if any part of their carcass falls upon any seed grain that is to be sown, it is clean, [38]but if water is put on the seed and any part of their carcass falls on it, it is unclean to you.

[39]'If any animal that you may eat dies, whoever touches its carcass shall be unclean until the evening, [40]and whoever eats of its carcass shall wash his clothes and be unclean until the evening. And whoever carries the carcass shall wash his clothes and be unclean until the evening. [41]Every swarming thing that swarms on the ground is detestable: it shall not be eaten. [42]Whatever goes on its belly, and whatever goes on all fours, or whatever has many feet, any swarming thing that swarms on the ground, you shall not eat, for they are detestable.

[43]'You shall not make your souls detestable with any swarming thing that swarms, and you shall not defile yourselves with them, and become unclean through them. [44]For I am the LORD your God. Consecrate yourselves therefore and be holy, for I am holy. You shall not defile your souls with any swarming thing that crawls on the ground. [45]For I am the LORD who brought you up out of the land of Egypt to be your God. You shall therefore be holy, for I am holy.'

[46]This is the teaching about beast and bird and every living creature that moves through the waters and every creature that swarms on the ground, [47]to make a

distinction between the unclean and the clean and between the living creature that may be eaten and the living creature that may not be eaten.

Notes on the text

1. 'to them': *'alêhem* Tg reads *lhm*, while it is omitted by LXX and Vg.

3. 'cloven footed': *šōsa'at šesa' pĕrāsōt* Lit. 'dividing the division of hoofs'. Some Hebr. MSS as well as SamP, LXX and Syr add 'two' before 'hoofs', conforming to Deut. 14:6.

19. LXX begins the verse with 'owls', corresponding to *hattaḥmās*, already mentioned in v. 16.

21. *'Ak* is necessary (cf. *BHS* apparatus), because what follows lists exceptional flying insects that have four legs.

25. 'wash his clothes' SamP adds after this *wrḥṣ bmym* (and bathes in water), which is reflected in the LXX of v. 40 below. However, 'bathing in water' is mentioned nowhere else in this chapter.

26. 'concerning every': *lĕkol* LXX and Syr reflect *ulĕkol*, 'And in every'. LXX thus takes v. 26 as independent, but by translating *bāhem* as 'with the carcass', v. 26 is connected to v. 25 in content. However, the referent of 'these' at the beginning of v. 25 is not specified until v. 26. Therefore it would be better to see the first word of v. 26 asyndetically (cf. Elberfelder and Luther). In other words, this verse deals with a case of touching the carcass of an animal.

27. 'on their paws': *'al kappāyw* Tg and 11QPaleoLev read *'al gāḥôn* (see v. 42). But this would seem secondary, since SamP and LXX coincide with MT.

29. 'unclean': *haṭṭāmē'* In contrast with *ṭāmē'* without an article in vv. 4–8, 26–28, in this verse and vv. 31, 47 *ṭāmē'* is prefixed by the article. From the content of these verses, the presence of the article expresses generalization.

34. 'water': *mayim* Though this Hebr. term is anarthrous, it refers to water coming from such a vessel as mentioned in v. 33, as NIV and NRSV paraphrase.

35. 'shall be broken in pieces': *yuttaṣ* Most ancient versions, SamP, LXX, TgJon, Vg read the verb in pl. However, its subject can be 'everything', as translated above.

40. LXX adds 'and bathes himself in water' before 'and be unclean until evening'. See Notes on v. 25.

43. 'make your souls detestable': *tĕšaqqĕṣû napšōtêkem* Some versions take *napšōtêkem* as a substitute for a reflexive pronoun, and translate 'detest *yourselves*'. But such a translation would underestimate both the importance of the term as well as the context. The verb *šiqqēṣ* has appeared in vv. 11 and 13 with *nĕbēlâ* (a corpse) and *'ēlleh* (these) as its object, and appears here with 'your souls' as its object.

Form and structure

From this chapter begin the regulations on cleanness and uncleanness, which is one of the major roles the priests are to teach the Israelites (Lev. 10:10).

While the chapter as a whole has often been seen as giving dietary laws, it is questionable if this is the chapter's major concern. In the first part of the chapter the edible and inedible creatures are listed, but from v. 24 onwards the rules begin to concern uncleanness. Moreover the latter half of the chapter unevenly concentrates on the swarming animals called *šeqeṣ*. As v. 47 states, the ultimate goal of this regulation is that the Israelites become holy like the LORD their God, who brought them out of Egypt. One may question the originality of vv. 24–28 and vv. 29–38. It is pointed out that vv. 29–38 deal solely with defilement by contact as opposed to eating, and that the section vv. 24–40 is an insert, because it deals with diet and 'interrupts the sequence of prohibited animal food' (vv. 2–23, 41–42; Milgrom 1991: 692). However, when the intention of the lawgiver is explored, there is no need to separate the two concerns, diet and defilement, in terms of sources.

The overall content of the chapter can be analysed as follows:

I *Clean/edible and unclean/inedible creatures*
1. Edible and inedible quadrupeds (vv. 2–8)
2. Water creatures (vv. 9–12)
3. Birds (vv. 13–19)
4. Flying insects: borderline cases (vv. 20–23)

II *Defilement caused by the death of the quadrupeds and swarming creatures (vv. 24–42)*
- A Carcasses of *unclean* quadrupeds, and their defilement (vv. 24–28)
- B Swarming creatures and defilement by coming into contact with their carcasses (vv. 29–38)
- A^{I} Carcasses of *clean* quadrupeds (vv. 39–40)
- B^{I} Swarming creatures with special emphasis on multifooted ones (vv. 41–42)

III *Summary and purpose of observing the laws (vv. 43–45)*

IV *Concluding remarks (vv. 46–47)*

Some comments are in order regarding II. While B is lengthy, with the rules connected by associations of ideas, the whole section can be viewed as set out as above: that carcasses of the unclean quadrupeds and their defilement, and swarming creatures and their defilement in A and B, are thematically repeated in A^{I} and B^{I} respectively.

A mere glance of the rules indicates that the rules in this chapter are arranged with a view to highlighting the defiling force of the swarmers. It is true that vv. 2–23 appear to deal with diet, and the theme recurs in vv. 39–42, while the middle section, vv. 24–38, deals with defilement. But the question whether the law concerns itself with diet or defilement cannot be the most important criterion in reading this chapter, for various reasons.

First, it can be observed that by presenting the unclean creatures in vv. 2–23 the legislator paves the way towards what he really wants to stress, particularly by mentioning the carcasses (*nĕbēlâ*) of the creatures (death) (vv. 8, 11), and the swarming nature (*šereṣ*) of the creatures (vv. 10, 20, 23). It is in vv. 29ff. that the swarming creatures which have not been mentioned are introduced as a new theme just after the *carcasses* of the unclean quadrupeds (vv. 24–28).

Second, it can be observed that in vv. 20–21, 23, 27 the legislator paves the way for some of the reptiles (vv. 29–30) by regulating that the *four-legged* winged insects are unclean. In fact, the four-legged creatures are arranged with an awareness of a polarity of clean cloven-footed and cud-chewing animals, on the one hand, and of unclean creatures walking on or nearly on their belly, as follows:

2–8	Quadrupeds with divided *hoof* (no full contact with the ground)
20, 23	Four-legged insects
26–27	Quadrupeds that walk on paws (full contact with the ground)
29–30	Swarming creatures walking on or nearly on their belly

Thus there is an unmistakable emphasis on the four legs in the flow of the rules, which shows that uncleanness of the four-legged creatures lies in touching the ground closely; hoofs may be regarded as preventing full contact with the ground (see 'Explanation').

Third, equally obvious is the legislator's intention to present the materials *focusing gradually* on the swarming creatures and their devastating defiling power. Incidentally II is the longest section in this chapter. This is seen in the use of some key terminologies in relation to each of the sections and the way in which new elements such as carcasses and touching are introduced. Even a superficial survey shows that elements of the swarming creatures are introduced bit by bit: *ṭāmē'* – *šeqeṣ*, *šeqeṣ* – *šereṣ*, *šeqeṣ* – *šereṣ* – *ṭāmē'*.

The term *šeqeṣ* is stronger in nuance than *ṭāmē'*, so if a creature is not said *ṭāmē'*, but is still described as *šeqeṣ*, all the rules regarding eating, touching and carrying apply. See I.2 and I.3 above. When it is said that some creatures are detestable, it is self-evident that they ought not to be eaten or touched. Thus when in IIB' the touching is not mentioned with regard to the swarming creatures, it is self-evident that eating presumes touching.

Fourth, in terms of eating and touching, vv. 2–23 mention only eating and touching, and the latter is restricted to *touching the carcasses*. On the other hand, vv. 24–38 mention not only touching the carcasses but *carrying* them. The apparent indifference of vv. 24–38 to the diet of the Israelites and the non-mention of eating any swarming creature can be explained partly by the fact that the section concentrates on the defiling force of the swarming creatures, and partly by the fact that it is part of the message of the section that eating of any swarming creature is out of the question: This is clear from v. 34, which addresses itself to the swarming creature defiling even *food*.

On the whole, it is clear that this chapter is concerned with uncleanness rather than cleanness, as the terms for 'cleanness' (*ṭhr*) occur just four times (vv. 32, 36–37, 47) in contrast to forty-five occurrences of 'uncleanness', expressed by the roots *ṭm'* and *šqṣ*. Thus, without entering the details of the flow of the rules (see 'Explanation'), it is clear the legislator aims his material at the most detestable creatures: the swarming ones.

The last few verses are replete with words and phrases that appear in chs. 18 – 26. Though this literary feature has been taken by some exegetes as secondary, it should be taken positively as pointing to structuring of the whole book of Leviticus. It was mentioned in Lev. 10:9–11 that these verses present the priestly roles in a chiastic order with regard to Lev. 11 – 16 and 17 – 26, the former dealing with cleanness/uncleanness, while the latter with holiness and the common. Lev. 11 is the first of the sections dealing with cleanness and uncleanness, but in concluding the chapter the legislator points to the goal of the observance of the rules set out in the chapter. And in this respect Lev. 11 is similar to Lev. 17: both chapters have a theme of *eating* and *non-eating*.

Comment

11:1–8 (edible and inedible quadrupeds)

1. Aaron is included in the Lord's address. As exegetes have noted (Ibn Ezra, Abrabanel and recently Milgrom), it is because the priests have the role of teaching the difference between pure and impure (cf. 10:10).

2. *Ḥayyâ* means 'creature', under which is subsumed quadrupeds (*bĕhēmâ*), fish (vv. 9–12), birds (vv. 13–20) and flying insects (vv. 21–23).

3. Only the animal that has a cloven hoof *and* chews the cud can be eaten (for the rationale for this criterion, see 'Explanation'). Concerning the question of why cattle, sheep and goats, listed in Deut. 14:4–5, are not mentioned here, Milgrom points out that the animals listed in this chapter are all ineligible for the altar, and that the legislator's concern is with non-sacrificial animals, which are mainly wild (1991: 647). But it is more likely that the two criteria are thorough, excluding the following four exceptional animals, and that sacrificial animals are assumed as edible. Though diet is certainly one of the legislator's concerns, the question of whether an animal is sacrificial or wild is not primary to his purpose.

The rationale for the uncleanness of the quadrupeds has challenged exegetes as a seemingly insoluble mystery, but a solution appears when the two criteria are viewed along with other features of this chapter (see 'Explanation').

4–7. Four animals are cited to illustrate this principle: camels, rock badgers, hares and pigs. As Douglas observes, the principle implicitly exhausts all land animals (1999: 139; cf. Milgrom 1991: 733–735).

In what sense are these unclean? Certainly they are said to be unclean as food, but the Israelites are not prohibited from touching the animals while they are alive. In fact the camel is a major vehicle for transportation in desert areas (e.g. Gen. 24:10; 31:17; 1 Sam. 30:17; Kiuchi 1997: 873–874).

8. Both ingestion of the flesh and contact with the carcasses of these four are prohibited. 'Carcass' (*nĕbēlâ*) occurs thirteen times in this chapter (forty-eight times in OT). By saying that both the flesh and carcasses of the unclean animals are unclean, the legislator suggests that 'uncleanness' has something to do with death, since touching the unclean animals while they are alive poses no problem.

11:9–12 (water creatures)

Only water creatures that have fins and scales can be eaten. All kinds of fish without scales and fins, and all kinds of flying insects listed in vv. 13–20 (see also v. 23) are called *šeqeṣ*. The term *šeqeṣ* conveys contempt in other contexts (Isa. 66:17; Ezek. 8:10) and thus appears to encourage stronger avoidance than what is achieved by the term *ṭāmē'*. Another feature of the fish and flying insects in vv. 13–20 is that there is no prohibition against 'touching'. However, it is likely that by saying *šeqeṣ* the prohibition against touching is assumed (*contra* Milgrom 1991: 656–685; see Grisanti 1997: 244). Though the two terms are synonymous (see v. 43), they are used discreetly in the rest of this chapter. The use of *šeqeṣ* instead of *ṭāmē'* is partly explained by its assonance with *šereṣ*. In fact both *šeqeṣ* and *šereṣ* occur several times in the same verse (vv. 10, 20, 23, 41–42).

Theoretically, then, one became unclean by touching carcasses or eating the unclean creatures, not by touching live unclean beasts (cf. camels). But it is common sense that what is called *šeqeṣ* ought not to be touched or eaten. It should be noted that water creatures without fins and scales, such as eels and lobsters, resemble in shape the snake (see 'Explanation'). This rationale is also discernible in the following cases.

11:13–23 (birds)

13–19. 'These' (*'elleh*) refers to the twenty birds listed in vv. 13b–19. Most cannot be accurately identified. All except for the last ('bats') are carrion-eaters, and owls of the kind mentioned are probably nocturnal. At least these are called *šeqeṣ hā'ôp*, meaning flying insects that have four legs (v. 20). They are unclean for food because they are either carrion-eaters or nocturnal (see 'Explanation').

20–23. This section, a subsection of the birds, deals with *swarming* winged four-legged insects. These rules come at this place to provide borderline cases. On principle, the four-legged flying insects are unclean (v. 20), whereas those with additional lower legs to hop with, such as the locust, the bald locust, the cricket and the grasshopper, are clean and edible (vv. 21–22). The principle is repeated in v. 23. As Douglas says, 'If it crawls it is unclean. If it hops it is clean' (1966: 56). The rationale for this seems to lie in that as long as they can leave the ground they are clean, because they are unlike the swarming creatures that crawl on the ground.

Some ambiguity revolves around the identification of the creature in v. 20. It has been taken as referring to creatures such as flies and hornets (Tgs, TgJon). But, as has been noted, insects normally have six legs, not four. Thus it is unlikely that v. 20 addresses itself only to insects. Péter-Contesse (1993: 185), recognizing this difficulty, suggests that a horizontal posture is envisaged here, and that creatures with two legs in the vertical posture are said to be unclean. However, v. 20 speaks about winged swarming creatures that *walk on all fours*. It would seem very difficult to find such a creature on earth, unless one considers it Sphinxlike.

Focusing on the four-legged winged creatures appears strange. In fact, four clusters of rules address four-legged animals/creatures: vv. 2–8, 20–23, 26–27 and 42. It is suggested in 'Explanation' that part of the reason lies in the legislator's intention to focus gradually on the swarming animals mentioned from v. 29 onwards: four-legged winged creatures (vv. 20, 23), quadrupeds walking on paws (vv. 26–27) and swarming creatures (vv. 29–38).

The section vv. 21–23 deals with the swarming winged creatures that *walk on all fours*, and in this respect, they are associated with the quadrupeds at the beginning of the chapter. This section forms a thematic inclusio to the whole section of vv. 2–23, thus marking it off from the following.

11:24–42 (defilement by the death of the quadrupeds and swarming creatures)

For the structure of this section, see 'Form and structure'.

11:24–28 (defilement by the death of quadrupeds)

This section introduces a new theme: defilement caused by coming into contact with carcasses. Headed by 'By these you shall become unclean', the section is structured chiastically in view of 'defilement' and the kinds of unclean animals, as follows:

24b–25:	Touching and carrying carcasses
26:	Regarding various kinds of quadrupeds that die
27a:	Various kinds of animals that walk on four legs that die
27b–28:	Touching and carrying carcasses

24. 'These' (*'elleh*) refers not just to the various kinds of animals that follow but also to what is stated in v. 24b and the following as a whole.

'shall be unclean until the evening' This time specification occurs frequently as the means to purification from light defilement (see vv. 25, 27, 28, 31 etc.), and is probably related to God's creation in Gen. 1 (L. Trevaskis – a personal communication; see also Introduction 7.4.2.d).

25. Here the touching of carcasses (as opposed to live unclean animals) and the uncleanness that results is at issue. With regard to carcasses the text appears to make a distinction between touching and carrying in terms of the degree of defilement that results: the former requires waiting until evening, while the latter requires the washing of clothes in addition to waiting until evening. Milgrom comments that ablutions were also required when the text simply says 'wait until evening' (1991: 667). But this would blur the presence of the clearly differing degrees of uncleanness.

26. The principle in vv. 4–8 is to be recalled, and here it is added that touching the carcasses of unclean quadrupeds makes one unclean.

27. In vv. 2–8 the quadrupeds that go on paws (cf. vv. 2–8) are implicitly unclean for eating. This is made explicit here. Animals 'walking on paws' refers to dogs, cats, bears etc. They are unclean, and the person who touches their carcass is defiled until evening. The rationale for this defilement appears to be associated with their direct contact with the ground.

28. The same defilement applied to unclean quadrupeds in v. 25 is applied to quadrupeds walking on paws.

11:29–38 (swarming creatures and their defiling power)

The last unclean creatures mentioned are swarming creatures, and the rules continue from v. 29 to v. 38, the longest section in this chapter. Through setting out the rules on defilement, the lawgiver simultaneously introduces the theme of death and also of life (vv. 36–37). Uncleanness is transmitted to everything immediate to human life, such as utensils, clothes, vessels, food, ovens and stoves (vv. 32–35), but not to things outside the immediate surroundings, such as springs and cisterns (v. 36). Is this not a subtle hint that uncleanness is found close to humanity, and further that humans are unclean?

29–30. Small swarming animals such as mole rats, mice and lizards (v. 29). The lizards are further exemplified in v. 30: the gecko, monitor lizard, lizard, sand lizard and chameleon. They not only swarm, but move on their belly or hide in dark places.

31. 'These': *'elleh* This term refers not to the animals listed above but to all the rules up to v. 38 (see 'these' in vv. 13, 22, 24). From the latter half of this verse to v. 38 the rules concern defilement that results from touching these creatures when they are dead.

32–33. Anything that the carcasses of the unclean animals contact becomes unclean: an article of wood, cloth, skin and sacking. When they fall into an earthen vessel, its contents become unclean and the vessel must be broken. The rationale for the difference between vv. 32 and 33 lies not 'because of the difficulty in removing all the impurity from a vessel made with earthenware' (Rooker 2000: 179), but in the materials: since the ground is assumed as unclean (see 'Explanation'), any vessel made of mud or dust is much more vulnerable to uncleanness than those made of wood, skin or cloth.

The uncleanness the carcasses of these creatures cause is of a higher degree than that associated with unclean quadrupeds and other animals. With regard to the latter, no rules are given for when they defile inanimate objects (see vv. 26–27).

34–35. Permissible food is defiled by water that comes from such a vessel described in v. 33. Water conveys uncleanness. If the vessel is an oven or stove, presumably made of earth, it must be broken into pieces. The rationale for this is the same for the earthenware mentioned in v. 33.

Thus the carcasses of swarming animals defile not only humans, inanimate objects like vessels and ovens, and the water they contain, but also food through polluted water and drink.

36. The previous verses deal with defilement caused by death. Now the theme shifts to life by using an association of ideas. While contact with carcasses makes one unclean, water in a cistern or a spring remains clean. Water in any small earthenware vessel is contrasted with water in a cistern or a spring. The view that this role is governed by a hygenic concern (that a defiled cistern or spring will greatly affect the daily lives of the Israelites) is unlikely. This is because the rules in vv. 24–34 show no concern for the practical side of daily life. This is, first of all, probably because the spring and cistern are considered as a source of water that symbolizes 'life-giving sources'. This also applies to the 'seas' in vv. 9–10. As for the life-giving forces such as blood and running water, spring and cistern are not called 'clean', 'unclean' or 'holy' (see the next two verses and 'Explanation'). Another reason why this is equally important is that springs and cisterns are typically situated in locations remote from the immediate sphere of human life.

Thus various functions of water appear in vv. 34–38. It is a means of purification in v. 32, a transmitter of uncleanness in vv. 34, 38 (see below), and a source of life in v. 36.

37–38. When a carcass comes into contact with any seed that is to be sown, the latter remains clean, but when the carcass makes contact with water-dampened seed, it becomes unclean. Here seed is envisaged as a potential life source, while the water, unlike that in a cistern or a spring, is envisaged as a medium conveying uncleanness. In the case of seed that is to be sown, which belongs to the immediate realm of human activity, its life is not vulnerable to the uncleanness of the carcass, since its life has not started. However, after the seed is watered, it begins to have life, and can potentially become unclean. The underlying principle is life: if life has started, the seed becomes vulnerable to uncleanness. Conversely if life has not started, it is not vulnerable. In sum, the life-giving force is invulnerable to uncleanness, whereas life can be defiled by uncleanness. The rules in vv. 36–38 suggest that behind uncleanness lies the idea of death. Thus it is probable that cleanness is related to life, whereas uncleanness relates to death.

The theme of life and death in terms of a 'seed' reappears in the next chapter.

11:39–42 (carcasses of clean quadrupeds and swarmers)

This section thematically repeats what was presented in vv. 24b–28 and vv. 29–38 (see 'Form and structure'). As for the fact that the eating of the carcasses of clean quadrupeds and swarming creatures both come in this section, two points can be made. First, as evident from the order of material in this chapter, clean and edible quadrupeds (vv. 1– 8) are diametrically opposed to swarmers. The thematic pairing of these animals with the swarmers in vv. 39–42 underscores the message that death cancels the distinction between cleanness and uncleanness, bringing them closer. Second, since the swarmers are self-evidently inedible, the deliberate restatement of the fact is ironical. Thus it is inappropriate to say that what is not mentioned in vv. 29ff. is mentioned in vv. 41ff. as a sort of afterthought.

39–40. In addition to the same purificatory measures concerning the carcasses of unclean quadrupeds (vv. 24–25), here a case where defilement is caused by 'eating' the carcasses of clean quadrupeds is mentioned. 'Eating' and 'carrying' are mentioned as representing higher degrees of defilement. On the whole, these verses constitute an expansion of the rule in v. 8.

41. Any swarming creature on the ground is detestable and must not be eaten. This idea is stressed by a wordplay between *šereṣ/šōreṣ*, *'ereṣ* and *šeqeṣ*. Since those creatures are self-evidently inedible in the light of vv. 29ff., the prohibition against 'eating' them is mentioned as an ironic statement of the unthinkable.

42. The creatures that swarm on the earth are recapitulated from the viewpoints of locomotion or feet. They crawl and have four feet or more, and they keep close to the ground. Indeed the term 'swarms on the ground' identifies those creatures that walk close to the ground. It is proposed that these are related to the salient features of the snake.

It should be stressed that not only does the term *gāḥôn* (belly) appear only in Lev. 11:42 and Gen. 3:14 in the whole OT, but that in both it also appears in the form of *'al gāḥôn hālak* (to walk on the belly), a pointer to the literary and theological link between the creation/fall account and the law in Lev. 11. The connection is not just lexical, but is in content also. The 'snake' (*nāḥaš*) is tantalizingly absent in this chapter. But the mention of the multifooted swarming creatures suggests this chapter clearly reflects the fallen world, resulting from human self-hiding (see 'Explanation').

'any swarming thing that swarms on the ground': *lĕkol haššereṣ haššōreṣ 'al hā'āreṣ* The phrase *lĕkol* comprehends all the creatures that swarm on the ground. Thus a great emphasis is laid on creatures that swarm on the ground.

'detestable': *šeqeṣ* There is a wordplay between *šereṣ* (swarming creatures) and *šeqeṣ* (detestable). The same wordplay was noticed in vv. 10, 20, 23, but occurs in every verse of vv. 41–43 (in v. 43 as a verbal form), though there are other markers that make a creature unclean.

11:43–47 (purpose of the rules and the conclusion)

43. That the swarming creatures are the most detestable is stressed by the negation of the pi. verb *šiqqēṣ* (to make something detestable).

'your souls': *napšōtêkem* It is possible to take this Hebr. term as reflexive, but the sequence of the verbs in this verse, *šiqqēṣ* (make detestable), *hiṭṭammā'* (defile oneself) and *nitmā'* (become unclean) shifts from transitive to reflexive, so the object of the first verb appears to be stressed. Moreover the presence of the pi. verb *ṭimmē'* (defile) in the next verse suggests that the shift of the verbal form in this verse is deliberate, and that *napšōtêkem* in the next verse must not be taken as expressing a reflexive sense, because the reflexive form already appears in this verse. Thus the term *nepeš*, which occurs in this verse and the next, in all likelihood means 'a soul'. Yet, since in the next verse the *nepeš* is vulnerable to uncleanness, it is unholy. Thus defilement is not just an outward matter, but an inward one. The distance between outer and inner cleanness requires explanation (see 'Explanation').

44. The ground for observing these rules is stated. Because these rules appear ritualistic and unrelated to ethical concerns, some awkwardness has been sensed by exegetes, all the more so when this passage resembles closely the one in 20:7, which is located in a context that addresses itself to 'ethical' issues. But such a judgment derives from a particular view of biblical holiness (see Introduction 7.4.2). As for this chapter, the understanding of *nepeš* to mean 'a soul' indicates that the rules in this chapter are not just 'cultic'. See 'Explanation'.

'For I am the LORD' This self-identification by the Lord appears in Leviticus for the first time in this verse and the next, and frequently occurs from ch. 18 onwards (18:2, 4–6, 21, 30 etc.).

The three clauses 'I am the LORD your God', 'Consecrate yourselves' (*hitqaddištem*) 'and be holy' are found in Lev. 20:7 in a chiastic order.

'For I am holy' The same expression is found in Lev. 11:45; 19:2; 20:26; 21:8.

It is noticeable that the term 'unclean' (*ṭāmē'*) occurs frequently in this chapter, whereas the term 'clean' (*ṭāhēr/ṭāhôr*) is limited to vv. 32, 36–37, in the latter of which the life-giving source is also at issue. Clearly the idea of cleanness is marginal to the legislator's concern in this chapter: the predominant concern is given to the cases of uncleanness and defilement. Thus the idea of holiness is mainly contrasted with the idea of uncleanness.

Furthermore two significant inferences come out of the fact that *nepeš* means 'a soul' (see 'Comment' on v. 43 above): (1) Vv. 43–44 indicate that *qādôš* and *ṭāmē'* relate to the condition of the human soul (*nepeš*). (2) Holiness lies in not defiling oneself by coming into contact with death or swarming creatures. Since people can become clean after defiling themselves, the holy state must lie outside the realm of clean/unclean.

'any swarming thing that crawls (*hārōmeś*) on the ground' This expression 'crawling on the ground' evokes an association with Gen. 1:21, 24–26, 28, 30. If the link with Gen. 1 is intended, it follows that the swarming creatures, originally seen as good in the Creator's eyes, have become detestable through the fall (see v. 42 above).

45. A similar reason for the necessity of observing the laws is given, but this time with reference to the recent exodus. If, in the previous verse, a reference is made to God's creation, it follows that the legislator is saying that the Israelites must observe the laws because the Lord is holy and is the one who created heaven and earth, and who, despite the fall, brought them up out of Egypt. Both creation and fall are implied, while the exodus is explicit. All this means that the observance of these rules is designed to bring a new status to the Israelites, not just as those who were redeemed from bondage in Egypt but also as those created by the holy God.

'who brought you up': *hammă'alēh* Hiph. of *'ālâ* also occurs at vv. 3–6, 26 in the phrase *ma'aleh gērâ* (chewing the cud). Since 'bringing out' from Egypt is expressed by *hôṣî'* in other parts of Leviticus (19:36; 22:33; 23:43; 25:38, 42, 55; 26:13, 45), it is likely that the use of the hiph. of *'ālâ* in

11:45 is intended to evoke imagery of the cud-chewing mentioned at the beginning of the chapter, thereby forming an inclusio (Rendsburg 1993: 418–421). Also 'the cud' (*gērâ*) may be a play on the word *gēr* (the resident alien), so the Lord is pictured as one who brought the resident aliens (the Israelites) out of Egypt. Thus the edible quadrupeds that chew the cud and have divided hoofs may symbolize something godly (see 'Explanation').

46. This verse and the next form a concluding remark about the content of these rules.

'every living creature that moves through the waters': *kol nepeš haḥayyâ hārōmeśet bammayim* The formulation closely resembles the one in Gen. 1:21.

'every creature that swarms on the ground': *kol nepeš haššōreṣet 'al hā'āreṣ* In Gen. 1 references to the swarming animals are never formulated in this way: they are rather expressed by *rāmaś* (Gen. 1:24–26, 28, 30). Only in Gen. 7:21 does a similar expression occur; until then the root *šrṣ* is reserved for water creatures.

The order of the creatures listed in this verse (beasts, birds, water creatures, swarming creatures) is different from the order of the presentation of the rules in this chapter: beasts (vv. 2–7), water creatures (vv. 8–12), birds (vv. 13–19), winged insects (vv. 20–23), swarming creatures (vv. 29–38, 41–44). The order of birds and water creatures is reversed. If the order remained the same, the reader would not have noticed that the order of the presentation was deliberate. By this change it seems that the beasts are viewed as the furthest removed from the habitat of the swarming creatures, despite the fact that both were created on the sixth day and move on the ground. What caused the change is undoubtedly the fall (see 'Explanation').

47. This verse continues the previous verse, indicating the purpose of the rules in this chapter. The expression 'to make a distinction between the unclean and the clean' recalls the reader's attention to one of the major priestly roles the Lord informed Aaron about in 10:10.

'the living creature that may be eaten': *haḥayyâ hanne'ĕkelet* The Hebr. term *ḥayyâ* comprehends all the various kinds of living creatures listed in this chapter, and corresponds with the one in v. 2, thus summarizing all the rules.

Explanation

Although this chapter has been commonly viewed as a dietary law (see Introduction 7.3.1), it is a surprise to find that the animals, birds and small creatures listed as examples do not appear to be part of the potential Israelite food source. For example, the frequent mention of 'detestable' seems to suggest that these animals were repulsive to the Israelites and not the kinds of animals they would consider eating. Not only the reptiles in

vv. 29–30, but the birds in vv. 13–19 and fishes without fins and scales in v. 10 are hard to catch. In a word, except for the quadrupeds in vv. 2–8 the habitat of the unclean fishes, birds and reptiles is the periphery of, or outside, the Israelite environment. Subsequently the rules on these creatures appear almost unnecessary. Why was it necessary to provide such rules? And why does the observance of these rules lead the Israelites to holiness?

The view that Lev. 11 is a dietary law is only partially correct. It does not explain many other factors in the rules: among others, the one mentioned above. Indeed some modern exegetes have attempted to grasp the total message of Lev. 11 mainly in relation to the rules' symbolic meaning, such as *life* and *death*, or *holiness*. Yet as the rationale for uncleanness is not established, any reading that has been proposed remains uncertain. As regards the rationale for uncleanness, it is remarkable that modern exegetes have had recourse to the creation account, but not to the fall account, when uncleanness is unlikely to be present in the good creation of God (cf. Houston 2003: 155). In this regard, older exegetes were closer to the truth when they saw a connection between uncleanness and sin (e.g. Kurtz 1980: 415–422), but again their vague reference to Gen. 3 failed to ground their interpretation of Lev. 11 soundly on the text.

Under the limitation that a complete certainty about the identities of the listed creatures is unavailable, any new hypothesis about the rules is inevitably tentative. However, presented below is an attempt to interpret the rules with special attention to their symbolic meaning.

Genesis 3 as the background of Leviticus 11

Although a modern tendency of not viewing 'uncleanness' as a pejorative term, as well as modern source-critical labelling of Gen. 2 – 3 as JE, may have hampered exegetes from linking Lev. 11 with the fall account, evidence suggesting both literary and ideological links to this material is too persuasive to be ignored. For a general treatment of this issue, see Wenham 1986 and Parry 1994. Below are some significant pointers to the connection between the list of unclean creatures and Gen. 3.

After the first man and woman violated the Lord's commandment, the Lord passed sentence on each of the perpetrators: the serpent, the woman and the man. The man and woman were not directly cursed (Gen. 3:16–19); it was the serpent, the animal world and the ground that were cursed (Gen. 3:14, 17). The crucial passage is Gen. 3:14, which states, 'Because you have done this, cursed are you above all livestock and above all beasts of the field; on your belly [*gāḥôn*] you shall go, and dust you shall eat all the days of your life' (ESV).

Three points should be noted: (1) The serpent is cursed directly. (2) The curse on the serpent affects other livestock and beasts; it is implied the latter are also cursed. (3) The serpent is to eat dust and go on its belly.

(1) It is only by the Lord's mercy that humans were not directly cursed. But this should not overshadow the fact that man violated God's commandment. All the responsibility is his and his wife's.

(2) Because of the serpent's deed, God also cursed the other animals and creatures, but (3), not as severely as the serpent.

Gen. 3:17–18 reads:

> And to Adam he said,
>
> 'Because you have listened to the voice of your wife
>   and have eaten of the tree
> of which I commanded you,
>   "You shall not eat of it",
> cursed is the ground because of you;
>   in pain you shall eat of it all the days of your life;
> thorns and thistles it shall bring forth for you;
>   and you shall eat the plants of the field.' (ESV)

On the one hand, it is stated here that the ground is cursed because of Adam's obedience to his wife's voice, which led to his disobedience of the Lord's voice. That the ground is cursed provides an additional explanation for the curse on the serpent, which now eats of the dust of the ground; the ground, the source of this dust, is cursed. No wonder the ground in Lev. 11 symbolizes the world of death.

All of these observations are reflected in the prescriptions of Lev. 11. First, the very theme of 'eating and not eating' is found both in Gen. 2 – 3 and Lev. 11. It is evident that the theme of 'eating' from the forbidden tree in Gen. 3 is developed in Lev. 11, where this time the number of prohibited items grows due to the fall. Thus more than a matter of diet appears to be intended. Indeed if Lev. 11 has Gen. 3 as its background, it may be that keeping the rules in Lev. 11 functions to remind the Israelites of the fall. Since the chapter lists what creatures ought or ought not to be eaten, the rules have the character of commandments similar to the one given in Gen. 2:16–17.

Second, as explained in 'Comment', the literary and ideological links to Gen. 3 are strong. Two conspicuous omissions stand out in this chapter. One is the fact that the serpent is not mentioned. This is not coincidental, but deliberate. The other omission is the non-mention of human death, for which the first man and woman are responsible. Given Gen. 3 as the immediate background of Lev. 11, there is only a small step from the omission of the serpent to the omission of human death. Thus the text appears to give a subtle hint that human beings are at the heart of the lawgiver's concern. Moreover by these omissions the legislator tacitly conveys the message that all the unclean beasts and creatures listed are victims of the offence and disobedience of the serpent and humans.

Basically creatures that resemble the serpent in appearance are 'unclean' and 'detestable'. The features of the serpent include swarming, creeping on the ground, having no legs and, certainly, having no cloven hoofs. That this is the case appears to be emphasized more and more towards the end of the chapter, where *šereṣ* on the earth is emphasized in vv. 41–44 as though they are the only detestable creatures. The root *rms* (creep), which appears twice in vv. 44, 46 and is synonymous with the root *šrṣ* (Gen. 1:21; 8:17), also seems to contribute to the allusion to the serpent's mode of locomotion.

Setting aside for a moment the land animals in vv. 2–8, we may survey the rest of the creatures in this chapter from the viewpoint of serpent-like features. It is important to keep in mind that since the rationale for the uncleanness is grounded in the narrative of the fall, its essence is conveyed pictorially in terms of the fall narrative rather than science.

First, water creatures without fins and scales (vv. 10, 12) resemble serpents. Second, though the serpent can be included in the swarming creatures (see v. 42), it is not mentioned in vv. 29–30. The swarmers listed in these verses are either those connected with the ground (*'āpār*) or amphibians that move on their belly using four legs. On this assumption it is possible to infer that unclean water creatures receive such a status not because they are abnormal, having no fins and scales, but because they have a serpent-like appearance.

With regard to birds, they are mostly carrion-eaters and therefore are directly connected with death. While birds that have no contact with death are clean, the carrion-eating birds come into contact with the cursed ground; therefore they are unclean.

In view of the serpent-like feature of creeping on the belly, it seems that paws (v. 27) are considered similar to the serpent's belly: in both cases the skin touches the ground. Such creatures resemble the serpent not only in swarming, but also in 'licking the dust'; though these points of resemblance are more explicitly mentioned in vv. 42–43.

Now with regard to the land animals in vv. 2–8, the two criteria mentioned, namely having divided hoofs and the chewing of the cud, can be construed as also something to do with the features of the serpent. First, the fact that the clean land animals and their features constitute a polar opposite to the serpent and its features can be gathered from the chapter's structure (see 'Form and structure'): The passages that refer to them when they are alive are positioned as far from each other as possible. By contrast, when their death is in view, these animals are juxtaposed. Second, the serpent certainly does not chew the cud, but swallows. Thus in view of this, its split tongue appears similar to the divided hoofs of the quadrupeds, but they may be different symbolically. Third, while the serpent creeps on the ground, the clean quadrupeds do not touch the ground with their skin. The symbolic meanings of these features will be given below. Fourth, the two pairs of verbs at the beginning and end of the chapter are conspicuous: they are *'lh* hiph. and *prs* qal / *šs'* pi. versus *'lh* hiph. and *bdl* hiph. They are related to the ideas of 'bringing up' and 'dividing'. The association of the two ideas 'bringing up' and 'making a distinction' makes it plausible that the two criteria at the beginning of the chapter suggest that those edible quadrupeds symbolize the potentially holy Israelites. Just as those animals are fit for food and some have the potential for becoming sacrifices and are thus holy, so the Israelites are expected to become holy, as they were delivered from the bondage of Egypt.

These considerations lead to the inference that animals and creatures in this chapter are presented as pointing to human nature.

Uncleanness

Thus the various creatures in this chapter are presented in terms of those features that characterized the cursed serpent at the fall: those creatures that share similar features are unclean, whereas those that have features dissimilar to them are clean. Indeed the fall is not just a background to these rules, but the prescription serves to remind Israel of its ongoing effect.

In Introduction (7.3.1, 7.3.2) it was pointed out that the oft-expressed view that uncleanness is symbolic of death appears to have a textual basis. However, if by death is meant physical death, uncleanness may well mean spiritual death. Nonetheless, if this view is not wrong, it is, at least, inaccurate, being too general. The exact meaning of uncleanness is not so obvious in Lev. 11, but in view of the following chapters, two considerations that tell against the death symbolism may be presented here.

First, in ch. 12 not only a mother who gives birth to a baby, but also the baby is assumedly unclean (see 'Comment' on 12:1–2). One may wonder why on such a life-giving occasion as birth both mother and baby are deemed unclean. At any rate, if the child is regarded as unclean, this indicates that cleanness and uncleanness are a matter that goes beyond biological life and death.

Second, while death may be assumed behind 'unclean(ness)' in the leprous disease in chs. 13 – 14, it is hard to explain why this particular skin disease was chosen to symbolize death. For there are deadly diseases other than this skin disease. As the features of leprosy, such as persistence and the afflicted person's wanting to hide the disease, show, it probably symbolizes something other than death.

Independently from the rules on cleanness/uncleanness, it has been argued that *ḥāṭā'* (commonly translated 'to sin') means to 'hide oneself'. Although the term *ḥāṭā'* does not appear in Gen. 3, the proposed sense can refer to the existential *state* of the first man and woman before and after their violation of God's commandment rather than the *violation* of the commandment as such. The manifestations of self-hiding are Adam's and Eve's covering (lit. covering their loins), hiding behind trees, fearing the

Lord's voice, not admitting to their own guilt, and imputing their responsibilities to one another. It is proposed that the state of hiding oneself before the Lord is symbolically called uncleanness in Lev. 11. As regards the difference between *ḥāṭā'* and uncleanness, *ḥāṭā'* involves human will, while uncleanness is the state of hiding oneself (see Kiuchi 2003a: 104). It is a spiritual matter, and is portrayed by various creatures and animals. Further aspects of uncleanness are given in ch. 13.

Now as the fall was that of the first man and woman, human beings introduced uncleanness into the animal world, but, other than the serpent, the animals would bear no responsibility for this. Various manifestations of uncleanness in this chapter can be, or should be, seen as reflecting various manifestations of what the serpent is and what it did, to which the first man and woman succumbed. Thus various animals and creatures in ch. 11 are intended to portray various spiritual features of human beings: those of fallen men represent uncleanness, whereas those close to holiness represent cleanness. Moreover it is not too much to say that those animals and creatures represent various types of human beings (see below and 'Explanation' of ch. 3). Also in this portrayal, we need to ascertain what is symbolized by water, sky and earth. First, water in vv. 8–11 appears unaffected by the unclean fishes. This is in accord with the spring water mentioned in v. 36. Second, the sky is also unaffected by unclean birds. Moreover, as indicated by the hopping four-legged winged insects, they are clean so as long as they have the capacity to leave the ground. These aspects are natural in view of the fact that it is the earth that is cursed in Gen. 3. Third, the creatures moving or crawling on the ground are unclean. This is explained partly by the fact that they are similar to the serpent, and partly by the fact that the earth was cursed. Further the uncleanness of moles and owls may indicate that the ground symbolizes darkeness. It is, however, the earth on which humans live and die. Therefore it is not too much to say that the earth represents the human sphere: this world as opposed to God's world. Since the Israelites are summoned to be holy like their God, it is obvious they should shun all of the serpent's spiritual characteristics: swarming, closeness to the ground, swallowing and death; i.e. the propensity towards forming groups, loving this world, indiscriminately ingesting both the words of God and humans – in a word, to love death.

With the above symbolic meaning of the earth in mind, I propose below what the legislator possibly intends by arranging the different types of creatures in the reverse order to their appearance in the biblical account: from swarming creatures to animals walking on paws to winged insects to carnivorous birds to fishes and land animals.

The swarmers refer to the spiritual aspects of those humans who are most unclean: they love the ground and dust; i.e. things belonging to death. Just as the serpent is the symbol of hiding oneself, those people hide themselves in various ways. In Gen. 3 they have the propensity to hide themselves before both God and man, pretending to be just and pious (see below). Flying insects with four legs are unclean, because they cannot completely leave the ground despite their wings. But those with hopping legs are clean. The latter may refer to those people who have hearts not attached to this world, thus being able to see themselves objectively and free from the world of death. Carnivorous birds are unclean. These creatures are likened to those people who, while free from death environmentally, still make a living through this world (i.e. they love death). Fishes without fins and scales are unclean because their appearance is that of the serpent. Although they move in the water and have nothing to do with the world of death, they still behave like the serpent. There are humans who rest on a spiritually clean environment, and yet behave selfishly.

Lastly, as for the rationale for the two criteria for the clean and unclean quadrupeds, this cannot be gained without recourse to its symbolic dimension that relates to humans. First, cud-chewing facilitates digestion. Since the serpent in Gen. 3 made no distinction between what belongs to the Lord and what does not, it obliterated the distinction between what God's word is and what it is not; the clean and edible animals symbolize the human spiritual feature of having the capacity to distinguish God's word from what it is not. So this trait symbolizes those people who thoroughly digest words, divine and human; namely they listen, understand and test them in their experience. The other criterion is that of the divided hoofs. This trait also points to a similar symbolic meaning. It refers to a human capacity to differentiate between the clean and unclean, what belongs to the Lord and what does not. While the serpent, being unclean, has no sense of perspective about cleanness (cf. Pss. 12:2; 17:1; Prov. 19:1), those people symbolized by the animals with divided hoofs have a sense of perspective about uncleanness as well as cleanness. This is because the concepts of cleanness and uncleanness are existential: they refer not to human emotions, will and mind as such, but to the total condition of human existence before God. Thus, while a 'clean' person has the ability to differentiate between the clean and unclean, 'unclean' people do not have that ability in the true sense, although they may have their own idea of 'cleanness'.

However, in view of the fact that the legislator arranges his list of animals and creatures with an increasing degree of emphasis on the swarming creatures, his message may well be that all human beings are swarming creatures, detested by God if they remain as they are. They have a strong tendency to 'swarm', forming various groups and institutions, even apart from societies where they make a living. Thus a surprising message comes out of the list of unclean animals and creatures and their defiling force: that the readers must see themselves as detestable before the Lord, and that they are commanded not only to separate themselves spiritually from other human beings but also to abhor themselves, as they observe the prescriptions in this chapter.

Nature of the regulation

Some features other than what was shown above may be mentioned. While observance of the rules is mandatory, literal observation alone makes the Lord's intention meaningless. The symbolic meaning of the rules as well as their goal, namely holiness, is what is commanded. However, not only the literal observation but the observation of the symbolic meaning appears impossible for the Israelites. For ultimately they are commanded to abhor themselves.

Yet such a negative aspect is not all there is to the rules: they also have a positive side. One indication is that the rules in Lev. 11 are arranged in such a way that except for the quadrupeds (vv. 2–8), fishes and birds come first, the creatures and animals walking on the ground, second, and the swarmers last. This is the order of creation in Gen. 1. This means that the rules have the creation as their background, but based on that good creation this chapter assumes the defiled state of the animal world in that not all of them are said to be clean. Moreover despite the emphasis on human fallenness in this chapter, the rules with their symbolic meanings are given to be observed. It is conspicuous that while the message of the chapter is that the Israelites must abhor themselves, they are commanded at the end not to defile their souls (*nepeš*). One has the impression the Lord encourages the Israelies to extract themselves from their present condition of spiritual death.

However, in addition to the hard aspects regarding the human spiritual condition reflected in the list of unclean animals and creatures, there is an additional factor that makes these even harder – so hard that it becomes doubtful if it is possible to observe the commandments in this chapter in the true sense, even more so when their symbolic meaning is taken into account. First, although a purification procedure is provided when one becomes defiled, it is not restricted to cases where one is conscious of a defiling act. This leaves room for the possibility that one unknowingly defiles many other people and things. Second, uncleanness means the state of hiding oneself before God. Yet the latter is usually unconscious (see 'Explanation' on ch. 13).

Furthermore was it possible for the Israelites to abhor themselves and separate themselves from other people? And if humans are likened to unclean swarming creatures, they cannot change their ways, just as the swarming creatures cannot change their ecology to that of fishes or birds: humans by nature are incorrigible. There is no clue in this chapter as to how they may extract themselves from their degenerate nature – only a picture of what humanity looks like from God's perspective, and the goal he desires us to reach. At least, this prescription on unclean animals and creatures has an educational function in reminding the Israelites, and hence every reader, of the spiritual condition of humans.

New Testament implications

'Nothing outside a man can make him "unclean" by going into him. Rather, it is what comes out of a man that makes him "unclean"' (Mark 7:15 NIV). By this saying Jesus pronounced that uncleanness comes from inside human beings. St Paul also says that nothing is unclean in itself (Rom. 14:14, 20; Titus 1:15). As the Jews had committed themselves to literal observance of the food law, it was clear to see how difficult it was for them to accept this new interpretation (Acts 10:14–16; 11:9). However, from my understanding of Lev. 11, what Jesus said is already taught in Lev. 11, though implicitly (cf. Hübner 1992). What is commanded in Lev. 11 is the symbolic meaning of the rules, and not the creatures themselves. Thus the principle reflected in the symbolic meaning of these rules is still at work in NT times.

Both Jesus and John the Baptist labelled human beings a brood of vipers; this evaluation is directed not just at the Pharisees but at all humans, including those who believe they are followers of Jesus. Which is why Jesus encouraged his disciples, saying, 'If anyone would come after me, let him deny himself and take up his cross and follow me' (Matt. 16:24 ESV).

Swarming, one of the chief characteristics of uncleanness, can be found in every sector of human society: humans tend to flock together. By this they show they cannot stand alone before God, which also means they cannot realize their existential situation. By sticking to this world and flocking together, humans have a strong tendency to remain as they are. It also appears that by doing so they are never happy, for hatred, envy, strife and war never cease. But unless one denies himself and hates this world, the oft-encouraged *koinōnia* turns out to be a swarm of reptiles (1 Tim. 5:22; 1 Pet. 4:15).

Although humans must establish themselves in a certain group and society for their living, holy living means they have perspectives on faith that concern what is beyond these frameworks. This is the symbolic meaning of abhorring the swarming creatures. Man is alone before God. Any desire to have fellowship with others is not problematical in itself, so long as humans have no egocentric nature, or, at least, uncover themselves.

Another important lesson derives from the clean animals and creatures that can be eaten. Clean animals and creatures are eaten by humans. Symbolically humans who do not hide themselves are closer to, and are loved by, God, and always tend to receive unworthy suffering and persecution without cause in this world. Jesus Christ as well as all the true prophets in the Old Testament were persecuted, and some, notably Christ, were killed. This world is not a place for them (Heb. 11:38). While suffering and persecution tend to be seen in dark colours, the self-sacrificial Christ who said 'Truly, truly, I say to you, unless you eat the flesh of the Son of Man and drink his blood, you have no life in you' (ESV) is the greatest wonder and hope for all human beings. A person who suffers but does not think he is suffering or that he is a victim is holy.

Cleanness, uncleanness and holiness

As argued above, uncleanness and cleanness are symbolic concepts and symbolize the states of hiding oneself and uncovering oneself respectively. Moreover, although 'death' and 'life' lie behind cleanness and uncleanness, the former concepts are distinct from, and wider than, the latter. Further it has been proposed that uncleanness, cleanness and holiness all essentially concern the human heart. Though various aspects of holiness are mentioned throughout this commentary, here it is in order to comment on the relationship between these three concepts in relation to 'death' and 'life'.

As is clear from Lev. 10:10, cleanness is the opposite of uncleanness. It is also certain that uncleanness is related to death, which in turn suggests that cleanness is related to life. However, what is the difference between cleanness and holiness? Cleanness is a relative state in that when it confronts the holy it is deemed as unclean (see chs. 8 – 9). Another insight from ch. 11 is that, as v. 36 shows, potential life is unaffected by the defiling force. Only once life begins is it vulnerable to uncleanness. This suggests that potential life is related to holiness.

But the principle that potential life is unaffected by uncleanness produces an irony, because humans become defiled by coming into contact with the unclean; the inference is inevitable that humans (in this case, the Israelites) have no life. In other words, because the Israelites are viewed as having no life, they become defiled. Contrary to all the commentators, it is wrong to assume that a clean person has life, whereas the unclean does not. *No-one* has it, and because of that a clean person becomes defiled by coming into contact with unclean creatures or things.

The principle that *life* (true life) is unaffected by the defiling force should be applied to the ritual of the sin offering that concerns the inner sancta, in such a way that uncleanness cannot affect the holiness of the inner sancta. Thus if it is said to defile the Tent or Holy of Holies, the latter should not be envisaged as becoming unclean in the sense that the people become unclean by touching the carcasses. The fact that the holy Tent can be defiled by the Israelites shows that holiness can be affected by uncleanness. But, on the other hand, the fact that the Holy Place or utensils in it remain holy despite defilement shows that holiness is unlike cleanness. Then where is *life*?

Here comes a consideration about the relationship between Gen. 3 and Lev. 11. Cherubim prevented humans from approaching the tree of *life*. Since Levitical legislation can be seen as the renewal of the original human condition in the Garden of Eden, as shown by the motifs common to both, it is highly likely that similarly the way to *life* is shown by the presence of cherubim on the ark. This means that *life* is not found even in the Holy of Holies (see 'Comment' on Lev. 16).

Thus the relationship can be shown in the following way:

In this relationship, cleanness is opposite to uncleanness, but the fact that cleanness becomes unclean in the face of holiness indicates that cleanness is just a temporary state, though it is closer to holiness. In terms of the rules on clean/unclean animals and creatures, to make a distinction between cleanness and uncleanness is the way towards holiness.

Interestingly this representation apparently conforms to the structure of the sanctuary: the realm of holiness is represented by the Tent, while the realms of cleanness and uncleanness are represented by the outer court and outside the sanctuary respectively.

In the chart above, the Israelites are excluded from the realm of holiness most closely related to *life*.

Such a truth that *life* is unaffected by the presence of uncleanness can be found in the person of Jesus Christ. He touched ritually unclean people such as a leper and a woman suffering from haemorrhaging and healed them. But in fact this is already seen in the works of Elijah (1 Kgs 17:20–23; see Kiuchi 1994) and Elisha. Christ's purifying power is incomparable to any purificatory ritual in Leviticus (Heb. 9:11–14).

LEVITICUS 12:1–8

Translation

1The LORD spoke to Moses, saying, 2'Speak to the Israelites, saying, If a woman conceives and bears a male child, then she shall be unclean seven days; as at the time of her menstruation, she shall be unclean. 3On the eighth day the flesh of his foreskin shall be circumcised. 4She shall remain for thirty-three days in a state of blood purification. She shall not touch anything holy, nor come into the sanctuary, until the days of her purification are completed.

5'If she bears a female child, then she shall be unclean two weeks, as in her menstruation, and she shall remain in a state of blood purification for sixty-six days.

6'When the days of her purification are completed, whether for a son or for a daughter, she shall bring to the priest at the entrance of the Tent of Meeting a lamb a year old for a burnt offering, and a pigeon or turtle dove for a sin offering, 7and he shall offer it before the LORD and make propitiation for her. Then she shall be clean from the flow of her blood. This is the teaching for her who bears a child, either male or female.

8'If she cannot afford a lamb, then she shall take two turtle doves or two pigeons, one for a burnt offering and the other for a sin offering. The priest shall make propitiation for her, and she shall be clean.'

Notes on the text

2. 'conceives': *tazrîʿ* hiph. of *zrʿ* A rare term that occurs elsewhere only in Gen. 1:11–12 in relation to plants. Usually *hārâ* is used for human conception. So hiph. of *zrʿ* may be inherently associated with the seed of a plant. While in Gen. 1:11–12 the term has the object *zeraʿ* (seed), here it does not. The hiph. form may be explained either as an internal hiph. or as a brachylogy that omits *zeraʿ*. So there is no particular reason to assume the ni. form reflected in the SamP or LXX (*spermatisthē*).

'as at the time of her menstruation': *kîmê niddat dĕwōtāh* The particle *kĕ* (just as) does not refer to 'seven days' but to the mode of her becoming defiled (cf. v. 5a). Both *niddâ* and *dĕwōt* (inf.) refer to menstruation or a menstrual flow.

3. 'flesh': *bĕśar* It euphemistically refers to the male organ.

7. 'she shall be clean': *ṭāharâ* LXX reads the consonant as 'he shall purify her'. But no necessity exists in view of the fact that what comes after *kipper* is the result of *kipper* and not other separate action (with Péter-Contesse 1993: 194).

Form and structure

Following the prescription for clean and unclean creatures is a short prescription on defilement caused by birth.

In content and terminology this chapter is related to ch. 15, particularly vv. 19ff., but it is unnecessary to suppose that this chapter was originally part of ch. 15 only to be later inserted in its present location due to the special nature of human birth (Dillman 1880: 550; Elliger 1966: 157).

First, it could be pointed out that this chapter is related to 11:37–38 in terms of the theme of 'seed' producing life. Moreover it is likely that the legislator's intention was to arrange his material starting from the environment of the human world (ch. 11), to birth (ch. 12), and then to various human conditions within life (chs. 13 – 15). Therefore it is natural that after dealing with the human environment the legislator moves on to the theme of childbirth, the beginning of life. The content is as follows:

1–2aa	The Lord's address to Moses
2ab–5	Uncleanness following birth
6–7a	The purificatory ritual in the sanctuary
7b	Summary
8	Alternative offerings for the poor

The main case is introduced by *kî* (v. 2) and the subsidiary case by *'im* (v. 5). For a Judaeo-Christian history of this regulation's interpretation, see Schearing 2003.

Comment

12:1–8

1–2. Unlike 11:1, the Lord addresses Moses and not Aaron. This is probably because the following regulation concerning human birth is the most fundamental occasion that belongs to Moses' responsibility (cf. 22:26). Aaron bears responsibility for inner priestly matters.

When a mother gives birth to a male child, she remains unclean for seven days. This is the same as the period of defilement associated with menstruation, the rule of which is given in 15:19ff.

With regard to the cause of the mother's uncleanness, some modern scholars consider it is caused by the discharge of blood from her reproductive organ, as v. 7 explicitly mentions 'the source of her blood'. Thus they consider that it is not the child but the blood discharge that defiles (Wenham 1979: 188; Wright and Jones 1992: 205).

This approach is based on some other assumptions commonly applied to other cleanness/uncleanness regulations. First, blood is life. Therefore the loss of blood symbolizes a loss of life, uncleanness. This conclusion is often supported by Douglas's assumption that a bleeding body is incomplete and that what is incomplete is unclean. Second, childbirth is a blessing and cannot be a matter of uncleanness.

While it is true that the blood discharge is the cause of her uncleanness, the assumption that blood is life is questionable. True, the blood of a sacrificial animal symbolized life (17:11), but it is doubtful whether human blood symbolizes life in the same sense that sacrificial blood does. As mentioned in 'Explanation' of the previous chapter, *life* is unlikely to be found in human beings if it refers to life before God. Moreover the above assumption presumes that this life is biological, but the very terms 'clean', 'unclean' and 'holiness' refer to a person's state before the Lord and thus must be distinguished from biological life.

The second assumption that childbirth is a divine blessing is indeed true (cf. 'childless' in Lev. 20:20–21). But this matter may belong to a dimension different from that of ritual uncleanness. It is entirely possible to see these two things as harmonious in so far as childbirth is a blessing, while retaining a negative aspect. Further details concerning this matter are given below. At any rate, methodologically, the blessing of childbirth should not dictate the exegetical discussion of this prescription.

Older or precritical commentators considered that the mother's uncleanness was due to original sin (e.g. Kellogg 1988: 330–336). As discussed below, this viewpoint is ultimately correct, but since they failed to demonstrate the close literary and ideological links between Lev. 12 and Gen. 3, their position has not been heeded by modern exegetes. Moreover the older exegetes of Leviticus characteristically made no distinction between sin and uncleanness (cf. Kurtz 1980: 419).

Part of the clue in determining the rationale underlying the mother's uncleanness lies in the term 'conceives' (*tazrîa'*). Besides here, *zr'* hiph. (to conceive) occurs only twice in the OT, in Gen. 1:11–12, which refers to seeds yielding plants. In general, there is a correlation between the world of animals and the world of vegetables, as there is in the terms *'ārēl* (see below on v. 3) and *zera'*. Yet the choice of *hizrîa'* is probably motivated by the legislator's intention to associate it with the root *zr'* and the principle reflected in 11:37–38. The theme of childbirth is, in a sense, similar to the growth of a seed. The principle there was that a potential life symbolized by a seed is unaffected by uncleanness, while new life is contaminated by uncleanness. Since human life begins in the mother's womb, the newborn child is prenatally unclean (*pace* Wenham 1979: 188; Ross 2002: 270).

In line with the above, it is proposed that the rules in vv. 2aa–5 bear a symbolic meaning in view of the symbolic meaning of uncleanness and the rules' relation to the fall, and that the symbolic meaning rather than literal observation is ultimately what is commanded (see further 'Comment' on v. 5 below).

3. Circumcision on the eighth day marks the initiation of the newborn baby into the God–Israel covenantal community. The practice was already established in Gen. 17:11, 14. That the eighth day marks a new stage permeates various ceremonies in Leviticus (see 9:1; 14:10, 23; 15:14; 23:36). The point of the circumcision ceremony relates to the fact that the newborn baby becomes a member of the covenantal community, before which he is assumed to be unclean.

This rite should also be seen from a symbolic point of view, along with the purifying period that precedes it. Several explanations have been offered for the symbolic meaning of circumcision, including the suggestion that it wards off evil spirits (cf. Hall 1992: 1026). A more likely explanation can be gained from this context, since we have already ascertained that uncleanness stands for the state of hiding oneself. The baby comes from the womb of his mother in an unclean state. The seven-day period until the circumcision on the eighth day is a purifying period for both baby and mother. The possibility that circumcision symbolically breaks the state of self-hiding is enhanced by the fact that in other contexts of circumcision or uncircumcision (e.g. Lev. 26:41; Deut. 10:16) it refers to the negation of stiff-neckedness. Moreover in Gen. 17 circumcision apparently takes place in order to symbolize 'wholeheartedness' (Gen. 17:1). Since the male genital is the most hidden part of the body, could not the rite symbolize the uncovering of the most hidden part of the human heart? Seen this way, the later tendency for the Israelites to boast of their identity by referring to their outward circumcision constitutes a plain denial of the rite's original symbolic meaning (cf. Jer. 9:24–25). For, its symbolic meaning indicates that there is no difference between the Israelites and the aliens with regard to the condition of their heart. Without such a symbolic meaning of circumcision, it is possible to maintain outer purity, but the male baby is doomed unless he embodies in his own lifetime what is symbolized by the rite.

4. The mother has to wait another thirty-three days for the purification of her discharge.

Though the discharge may last a month or so, the term 'blood' in 'in a state of blood purification' (*biděmê ṭohorâ*) is unlikely to refer to the literal discharge alone. This is confirmed by the case of the female baby, which stipulates an eighty-day waiting period (v. 5). Though the first seven and then thirty-three days may correspond roughly to her physical condition, the thirty-three days are probably just as ritualistic as the previous seven days. Thus, while the phrase is grounded on the literal blood discharge, it can have a symbolic meaning (see 'Comment' on ch. 15).

Porter comments that the reason for 'thirty-three' is probably to make the total purifying period forty, and surmises that the number is one of the chief sacred numbers (Porter 1976: 94). But this must be qualified. The number forty appears in the Pentateuch in relation to the deluge (Gen. 7:4), the Israelites' wandering in the desert (Exod. 16:35; Num. 14:34) and Moses' stay on Mount Sinai (Exod. 24:18). Most probably the number has something to do with purifying the sinful and defiled (cf. 'the conception of trial and testing' [Kellogg 1988: 332]).

Not only must the mother not touch holy things during this period, but she must refrain from approaching the sanctuary. For the mother this period functions as a purifying period: she remains unclean. The degree of her uncleanness is such that it is higher than ordinary menstrual uncleanness (ch. 15) but not as high as the leprous person who had to stay outside the camp indefinitely for as long as the diseased area remained (13:46).

5. If the mother gives birth to a female child, she is unclean for two weeks, twice as long as the period stipulated for a male child (see v. 2). Moreover she remains unclean for sixty-six days, again twice as long as for a male child. Thus she remains unclean for a total of eighty days. The longer period of defilement is caused by giving birth to a female child. Modern exegetes have provided various speculative answers, which can be divided into two types: (1) scientific reasons and (2) anthropological or social reasons.

(1) It is said that the mother remains unclean for her female child either because more toxins are released, or because a longer time is needed to form a female embryo. That this kind of explanation is a modern imposition on the Leviticus text (Jenson 1992: 75–76; cf. also Magonet 1996) is indeed true. Moreover exegetically this position does not take the nature of the 'unclean' and 'clean' language seriously.

(2) Some scholars give an anthropological explanation. For instance, Levine mentions that a female child has 'a greater potential role in human reproduction, and that childbirth should be distanced from the cult' (Levine 1992: 314–315). However, the 'cult' in ancient Israel refers to various rituals and ceremonies conducted *before the Lord*. Since childbirth is God's blessing, it would seem unintelligible as to why childbirth is distanced from the 'cult'.

Thus some more satisfactory solution remains to be looked for, but the orientation adopted by older exegetes (see above on vv. 1–2) could be elaborated here: it is the literary and ideological link with the fall in Gen. 3. That Lev. 12 assumes Gen. 2 – 3 is clear from the order of those things dealt with in Lev. 11 – 15. After Lev. 11 deals with the human environment, this chapter deals with the uncleanness of a woman's childbirth, and the next chapter (ch. 13), with the uncleanness of an *'ādām* (a man, v. 2). This was the order of God's sentence on the serpent, woman and man in Gen. 3:14–16. Thus it seems appropriate to interpret the rationale for the woman's uncleanness in childbirth in terms of the fall. Gen. 3:16 reads as follows:

> To the woman he said,
>
> 'I will surely multiply your pain in childbirth;
> in pain you shall bring forth children.
> Your desire shall be for your husband,
> but he shall rule over you.' (my trans.)

Here the Lord pronounces that he will intensify the pain of childbirth. However, while eating from the forbidden tree constitutes the core of the violation, one spiritual aspect of the violation deserves attention. It is that immediately after Adam and Eve ate of the tree of knowledge, they hid their *loins* with fig leaves (Gen. 3:7). This indicates that they not only felt ashamed of their genitals, but that in an existential sense they had to hide themselves from God. The Lord's verdict also indicates that the supposed original harmonious relationship in Gen. 2 had become a harsh one, where the woman had to experience the relationship with pain.

It is proposed here that the prescription in Lev. 12 should be interpreted in view of the above interpretation of the woman's destiny in the wake of her disobedience. Bleeding from her womb is said to be unclean, but the meaning of 'unclean' is a spiritual state before the Lord. The deeper dimension of the rationale for this uncleanness is discussed in ch. 15 (see 'Comment' there), but by referring to the literal discharge from her reproductive organ, the law aims to remind the mother of her spiritual condition (hiding herself). When the significance of this command is ignored, the rite's observance loses its meaning. The very stipulation of defilement by childbirth serves as a strong reminder to the Israelites that the divine sentence on the woman remains the same, and it also reflects the same ongoing situation.

It is not only the mother but also the child who is alienated from the Lord's presence. As stated above, the newborn child also becomes unclean.

6. After the purification period, the woman brings a year-old lamb for a burnt offering and a young pigeon or dove for a sin offering (cf. Luke 2:22–24). She is still in the process of purification, as she becomes clean only after the priest makes propitiation for her. It is assumed that after forty or eighty days she is allowed to access the holy sanctuary.

'for a son or for a daughter': *lĕbēn 'ô lĕbat* V. 2 has stated that 'if a woman conceives (*tazrîʿ*)'. In v. 2 the son was expressed by 'a male' (*zākār*), and in v. 5 the daughter was expressed by 'a female' (*nĕqēbâ*), and here 'son' and 'daughter', and in the next verse 'for male or for female'. Thus the legislator uses the language of plants, then of animals in general, and lastly of humans. What could this possibly mean? Since she appears to be treated as a human only when she concludes the long period of purification, the literary trait seems to suggest a serious degree of the woman's uncleanness before the Lord.

The specification that the lamb must be a year old probably stresses 'newness' (see 'Comment' on 9:2–4). A bird sacrifice for the sin offering is mentioned in 5:7–8, but here it is not poverty that is contemplated, but the seriousness of the uncleanness. Still, though, this is not a sin (*ḥāṭā'*) involving the exertion of one's will. This latter circumstance may explain the relatively cheap sacrifices used for propitiation.

In spite of the order in which the two kinds of offering are mentioned, the actual order of offering was the sin offering followed by the burnt offering.

7. The need for making propitiation for her uncleanness must be explained. Does this suggest she had polluted the altar of burnt offering throughout her period of uncleanness? I have noted in ch. 8 that the altar represents the people, so the altar's purification reflected the purification of the unclean. Therefore the statement that the mother had polluted the altar can be accepted, provided the altar is assumed as representing her. More essentially, since uncleanness symbolizes the hiding of oneself, her appearance at the sanctuary signifies that she now uncovers herself before the Lord.

The reference to 'making propitiation' (*kipper*) presupposes that she has been under the Lord's wrath. Wrath is directed against her for hiding herself. Indeed she did not do this by her will, but the law, by prescribing the rule, affirms that the primordial degenerate nature still persists and that the woman must know her own nature by observing it. Yet her uncleanness should not be confused with 'hiding oneself' in ch. 4, which is brought about by inadvertently violating divine prohibitions.

Lastly, and not of least importance, the location of *kipper* after the last of a series of rites indicates that uncleanness is not a matter of physical cure or healing alone; it is clear that when she appears before the priest she has physically recovered. Likewise the statement 'she shall be clean from the source of her blood' is ritual language, and does not refer to her literal discharge of blood alone. Propitiation is made for the state of hiding herself.

8. Economical consideration is given for the poor: either two turtle doves or two pigeons or doves can be offered: one for the burnt offering, the other for the sin offering. And the provision of these options to match the financial situation of the person to be cleansed implies the Lord's lenient handling of uncleanness. A possible reason is that this kind of uncleanness is deemed less severe than the cases of a man with gonorrhoea and a woman discharging blood in ch. 15. See also 'Comment' on 14:21–32.

Explanation

Although this regulation is often taken as reflecting childbirth's problematical nature, the occasion is actually appointed by the Lord as one to remind the mother of her spiritual condition, through birth pain and her period of alienation from the sanctuary. Thus the prescription reaffirms the reality of the fall and its ongoing nature, which tends rarely to be considered by humanity.

The idea of original sin has been neglected or ignored by modern exegetes, but is tacitly assumed in various rules that have been discussed thus far. Ch. 11, which immediately precedes this chapter, tacitly but strongly assumes it. Further, people who offer sacrifices are deemed as being under God's wrath in some way or other, not necessarily because of some specific wrong, but because of their existence (Lev. 1 – 3). As clearly assumed in the rationale for the purification of Aaron and his sons in chs. 8 – 9, humans are deemed as unclean when they confront the holy. More will be said on this topic in the exposition of the following chapters, chs. 13 – 15.

In view of the fact that individuals rarely realize their own self-hiding (see 'Explanation' on 4:1 – 5:13), it is understandable that the OT presents very few passages where an individual experienced this reality. One such passage is Ps. 51:5[7], where David says:

> Behold, I was brought forth in guilt,
> and in punishment did my mother conceive me. (my trans.)

Despite the Judaeo-Christian controversy over the 'doctrine' of original sin (cf. Weiss 1987: 115–122; Scharbert 1968), here David manifestly experiences that spiritual reality which was produced at the fall, tracing it even to his prenatal condition.

LEVITICUS 13:1–59

Translation

1The LORD spoke to Moses and Aaron, saying, 2'When a man has on the skin of his body a swelling or an eruption or a spot, and it turns into a case of leprous disease on the skin of his body, then he shall be brought to Aaron the priest or to one of his sons the priests.

3'The priest shall examine the diseased area on the skin of his body. And if the hair in the diseased area has turned white and the disease appears to be deeper than the skin of his body, it is a case of leprous disease. When the priest has examined him, he shall pronounce him unclean.

4'But if the spot is white in the skin of his body and appears no deeper than the skin, and the hair in it has not turned white, the priest shall isolate the diseased spot for seven days. 5The priest shall examine him on the seventh day, and if the disease remains unchanged in his eyes and the disease has not spread in the skin, then the priest shall isolate the diseased spot for another seven days. 6The priest shall examine him again on the seventh day, and if the diseased area has faded and the disease has not spread in the skin, then the priest shall pronounce him clean: it is only an eruption. He shall wash his clothes and be clean. 7But if by any chance the eruption spreads in the skin, after he has shown himself to the priest for his cleansing, he shall appear again before the priest. 8The priest shall look, and if the eruption has spread in the skin, then the priest shall pronounce him unclean: it is a leprous disease.

9'When a man is afflicted with a leprous disease, he shall be brought to the priest. 10The priest shall look, and if there is a white swelling in the skin that has turned the hair white, and there is raw flesh in the swelling, 11it is a chronic leprous disease in the skin of his body, and the priest shall pronounce him unclean. He shall not isolate him, for he is unclean. 12If by any chance the leprous disease breaks out in the skin, so the leprous disease covers all the skin of the diseased person from head to foot, so far as the priest can see, 13then the priest shall look, and if the leprous disease has covered all his body, he shall pronounce him clean of the disease: it has all turned white, and he is clean. 14But when raw flesh appears on him, he shall be unclean. 15The priest shall examine the raw flesh and pronounce him unclean. Raw flesh is unclean, for it is a leprous disease. 16But if the raw flesh recovers and turns white again, then he shall come to the priest, 17and the priest shall examine him, and if the disease has turned white, then the priest shall pronounce the diseased person clean: he is clean.

18'If there is in the skin of one's body a boil and it heals, 19and in the place of the boil there comes a white swelling or a reddish-white spot, then it shall be shown to

the priest. [20]The priest shall look, and if it appears deeper than the skin and its hair
has turned white, then the priest shall pronounce him unclean. It is a case of leprous
disease that has broken out in the boil. [21]But if the priest examines it and there is no
white hair in it and it is not deeper than the skin, but has faded, then the priest shall
isolate him for seven days. [22]If by any chance it spreads in the skin, then the priest
shall pronounce him unclean: it is a disease. [23]But if the spot remains in one place and
does not spread, it is the scar of the boil, and the priest shall pronounce him clean.

[24]'Or, when the body has a burn on its skin and the raw flesh of the burn becomes
a spot, reddish-white or white, [25]the priest shall examine it, and if the hair in the
spot has turned white and it appears deeper than the skin, then it is a leprous
disease. It has broken out in the burn, and the priest shall pronounce him unclean: it
is a case of leprous disease. [26]But if the priest examines it and there is no white hair
in the spot and it is no deeper than the skin, but has faded, the priest shall isolate
him for seven days, [27]and the priest shall examine him on the seventh day. If by any
chance it is spreading in the skin, then the priest shall pronounce him unclean: it is a
case of leprous disease. [28]But if the spot remains in one place and does not spread in
the skin, but has faded, it is a swelling from the burn, and the priest shall pronounce
him clean, for it is the scar of the burn.

[29]'When a man or woman has a disease on the head or the beard, [30]the priest shall
examine the disease. If it appears deeper than the skin, and the hair in it is yellow and
thin, then the priest shall pronounce him unclean. It is an itch, a leprous disease of the
head or the beard. [31]If the priest examines the itching disease and it appears no
deeper than the skin and there is no black hair in it, then the priest shall isolate the
person with the itching disease for seven days, [32]and on the seventh day the priest
shall examine the disease. If the itch has not spread, and there is in it no yellow hair,
and the itch appears to be no deeper than the skin, [33]then he shall shave himself, but
the itch he shall not shave; and the priest shall isolate the person with the itching
disease for another seven days. [34]On the seventh day the priest shall examine the itch,
and if the itch has not spread in the skin and it appears to be no deeper than the skin,
then the priest shall pronounce him clean. He shall wash his clothes and be clean.
[35]But if the itch spreads in the skin after his cleansing, [36]then the priest shall examine
him, and if the itch has spread in the skin, the priest need not look for the yellow hair:
he is unclean. [37]But if in his eyes the itch is unchanged and black hair has grown in it,
the itch is healed and he is clean, and the priest shall pronounce him clean.

[38]'When a man or a woman has spots on the skin of the body, white spots, [39]the
priest shall look, and if the spots on the skin of the body are a dull white, it is
leucoderma that has broken out in the skin: he is clean.

[40]'If a man's hair falls out from his head, he is bald: he is clean. [41]If a man's hair
falls out from his forehead, he has baldness of the forehead: he is clean. [42]But if
there is on the bald head or the bald forehead a reddish-white diseased area, it is a
leprous disease breaking out on his bald head or his bald forehead. [43]The priest
shall examine him, and if the diseased swelling is reddish-white on his bald head or
on his bald forehead, like the appearance of leprous disease in the skin of the body,
[44]he is a leprous man, he is unclean. The priest must pronounce him unclean: his
disease is on his head.

45 'The leprous person who has the disease shall wear torn clothes and let the hair of his head hang loose, and he shall cover his upper lip and cry out, Unclean, unclean! 46 He shall remain unclean as long as he has the disease. He is unclean. He shall live alone. His dwelling shall be outside the camp.

47 'When there is a case of leprous disease in a garment, whether a woollen or a linen garment, 48 in warp or woof of linen or wool, or in a skin or in anything made of skin, 49 if the disease is greenish or reddish in the garment, or in the skin or in the warp or the woof or in any article made of skin, it is a case of leprous disease, and it shall be shown to the priest. 50 The priest shall examine the disease and isolate what has the disease for seven days. 51 Then he shall examine the disease on the seventh day. If the disease has spread in the garment, in the warp or the woof, or in the skin, whatever be the use of the skin, the disease is a persistent leprous disease: it is unclean. 52 He shall burn the garment, or the warp or the woof, the wool or the linen, or any article made of skin that is diseased, for it is a persistent leprous disease. It shall be burned in the fire. 53 If the priest examines, and if the disease has not spread in the garment, in the warp or the woof or in any article made of skin, 54 then the priest shall command that they wash the thing in which is the disease, and he shall isolate it for another seven days. 55 The priest shall examine the diseased thing after it has been washed. If the diseased area has not changed its colour, though the disease has not spread: it is unclean. You shall burn it in the fire, whether the rot is on the back or on the front. 56 But if the priest examines, and if the diseased area has faded after it has been washed, he shall tear it out of the garment or the skin or the warp or the woof. 57 Then if it appears again in the garment, in the warp or the woof, or in any article made of skin, it is spreading. You shall burn with fire whatever has the disease. 58 But the garment, or the warp or the woof, or any article made of skin from which the disease departs when you have washed it, shall then be washed a second time, and be clean.'

59 This is the teaching for a case of leprous disease in a garment of wool or linen, either in the warp or the woof, or in any article made of skin, for pronouncing it clean or unclean.

Notes on the text

2. 'a man': *'ādām 'ādām* is deliberately distinguished from *'îš* or *nepeš*. See 'Comment'.

'an eruption': *sappaḥat* This term occurs only here and in 14:56. *HALOT* renders it 'scabs, flaking skin'. Since *spḥ* qal means to 'associate with', this rendering seems reasonable.

'a case of leprous disease': *lĕnega' ṣāra'at* The explicit mention of *ṣāra'at* at this stage may have led the JPS translators ('a scaly infection'; cf. vv. 3, 8) to think that it is either an early stage or an uncertain case of *ṣāra'at*. But v. 2a can be taken as either a summary statement for the case, or as an indication that the man knows that his infection is leprous to some extent.

'he shall be brought': *hubbā'* JPS renders it 'it shall be reported' (similarly

Ehrlich 1908: ad loc.; Milgrom 1991: 776). However, the subject appears to be the man; hence the proposed translation (cf. v. 9; 14:2).

3. 'examined him': *rā'āhû* The pronominal suffix is missing in SamP and LXX. This phenomenon appears also in vv. 5, 17, 27, 36. Conversely ancient versions appear to supply pronominal suffixes or subjects where they are absent in the MT. As Péter-Contesse concludes (1993: 201), such a phenomenon is stylistic, and does not point to a different *Vorlage* behind the MT.

5. 'remains unchanged in his eyes': *'āmad bĕ'ênāyw* See v. 37. JPS renders it 'has remained unchanged in color', NRSV and ESV 'sees that (the disease) is checked' and NIV 'is unchanged'. LXX's 'remains before him' is closest to the literal meaning. The phrase *b'nyw* should be distinguished from *b'ynw* in v. 55.

7. 'by any chance ... spread': *pāśō tipśeh* The construction *'im* followed by inf. abs. and then a finite verb appears frequently in this chapter (vv. 12, 22, 27, 35, 44). As the context shows, it probably conveys the notion of least possibility (cf. Joüon-Muraoka 123g; Merwe 159).

11. 'chronic': *nôšenet* The basic idea of the Hebr. term is 'repeating intermittently'. Cf. *ṣāra'at mam'eret* (v. 52; 14:44; malignant).

20. 'it appears': *mar'ehā*; lit. 'its appearance' The f. pronominal suffix ('it') refers either to the 'swelling' or the 'spot' in v. 19. One Gr. MS (LXX) and SamP take it as referring to 'the boil' in v. 19.

22. 'it is a disease': *nega' hî'* LXX enlarges by adding 'it is a plague of leprosy; it spread in the open sore', thus conforming it to v. 20.

27. 'it is a case of leprous disease': *nega' ṣāra'at hî'* LXX enlarges just as in v. 22 (see above).

30. 'an itch': *neteq HALOT* surmises it refers to 'herpes of the head and beard, richophytia', following Elliger (1966: 184). JPS and Milgrom (1991: 791–793) render it 'scales'. The occurrence of this rare word is concentrated in this section of the chapter (vv. 30–37; 14:54).

41. *mippĕ'at pānāyw yimmāret rō'šô* 'Hair' is implied in the verb *mrṭ* pi. In this case *pē'â* does not mean 'temples' (*pace* RSV and NRSV). The phrase *mippĕ'at* means 'from the front part'. So the meaning is either as proposed above or 'from the front of his scalp' as in NIV.

'baldness of the forehead': *gibbeaḥ* This Hebr. term is unique in the OT (cf. *gabbaḥat* in vv. 42, 55). *HALOT* referring to Ar. *'ajbah* notes 'with receding hairline'. Perhaps this distinguishes this particular form of baldness from that occurring on other areas of the head.

44. 'a leprous person': *'îš ṣārûa'* The Hebr. qal passive ptc. *ṣārûa'* always refers to a person afflicted with *ṣāra'at*, while the pu. ptc. *mĕṣôra'* can refer both to a person afflicted with *ṣāra'at* and the afflicted condition (for *ṣārûa'*, see 13:44–45; 14:3; 22:4; Num. 5:2; for *mĕṣôra'*, see Exod. 4:6; Lev. 14:2; Num. 12:10; 2 Sam. 3:29; 2 Kgs 5:1, 11, 27; 7:3, 8; 15:5; 2 Chr. 26:20–21, 23).

51. 'persistent': *mam'eret* The phrase 'a persistent *ṣāra'at*' appears for the first time in this verse; outside Lev. 13 – 14 (13:51–52; 14:44) it occurs only in Ezek. 28:24, where it is synonymous with *mak'îb*. LXX translates it *emmonos* (chronic). Yet from Ezek. 28:24 *mam'eret* possibly has a harsher nuance than *nošenet* (chronic) in 13:11.

55. 'its colour': *'ēnô* The verb *hāpak* (change) is transitive; therefore *'ayin* is not 'before him' as in SamP. The question is the meaning of sg. *'ayin*. Its meaning can only be 'colour', as instances such as Exod. 10:5, Num. 11:7, Prov. 23:31 indicate (see Milgrom 1991: 813).

'a rot': *pĕḥetet* Although the exact nuance of this hapax legomenon is uncertain, another term coming from the same root, *paḥat* (a pit, 2 Sam. 17:9; 18:17), makes it likely that *pĕḥetet* here means a perforation caused by rot.

Form and structure

Lev. 13 deals with *ṣāra'at* and its handling by the priest. Ch. 14 deals with a purificatory ritual performed when a diseased person is healed. While much discussion of this chapter focuses on the modern identification of *ṣāra'at*, it is highly dubious if its identification will unveil the prescription's message. The interpretive assumption is germane not just to an analysis of the prescription's content but also to the question of whether the legislator would like the reader to read the prescription pathologically.

Lev. 11 – 15 has the fall of Gen. 3 as its immediate literary and ideological background (see Kiuchi 2003c). Moreover, as commented below, the location of ch. 13 after chs. 11 and 12 is in keeping with the order of the divine verdict given after the fall in Gen. 3:14–19: first to the serpent, then the woman and then the man. Ch. 11 has the divine curse on the serpent as its background, while ch. 12 expands, in legal fashion, on the divine verdict on the woman. Ch. 13 reveals man's responsibility in self-hiding against God, since v. 2 mentions, 'When a man (*'ādām*)' etc. (see 'Comment'). It is thus most appropriate to interpret the prescription in relation to the fall.

The chapter is long, and refers to many cases of *ṣāra'at*. It is divisible into the following units, taking the main subjects as division markers:

'ādām

I vv. 2–8	Typical cases of *ṣāra'at*: outward symptoms and two criteria
II vv. 9–17	Obvious cases of *ṣāra'at*

bāśār

Cases that develop in areas that had some previous complications

III 1. vv. 18–23	The prior complication – a boil
IV 2. vv. 24–28	The prior complication – a burn

'îš or *'iššâ*	
V vv. 29–37	The potential case of *ṣāra'at* on one's head or beard
'îš or *'iššâ*	
VI vv. 38–39	A white bright spot in the skin that is not *ṣāra'at*
'îš	
VII vv. 40–44	Various symptoms on a man's head
VIII vv. 45–46	The handling of persons pronounced unclean
IX vv. 47–58	*Ṣāra'at* on clothes and articles made of skin

Insufficient attention has been paid to the significance of the terms *'ādām*, *bāśār* and *'îš* or *'iššâ* in this chapter's interpretation. Apparently they are neglected due to a preoccupation with each case and its specific handling. *'ādām* together with *bāśār* are used to bring to mind the various manifestations of man's earthly existence; in this case his corporeal aspects. Alternatively *'îš* and *'iššâ* are used with interpersonal connotations. This means that the early part of the chapter focuses on *ṣāra'at* on man's skin, while the later part of the chapter focuses on the interpersonal aspects of *ṣāra'at*. This difference affects how the treatment's message is interpreted. Thus there are seven treatments for *ṣāra'at*, followed by a direction (VIII) applicable to each case of *ṣāra'at*. The last prescription (IX) follows, both in style and actual procedures, the treatment for *ṣāra'at* in human beings.

However, while the nine sections seem distinct in terms of content, they remain unified by an association of words and ideas, apart from the two criteria set out in I that are found in I, IV, V (with slight differences regarding the hair). For instance, sections I and II are distinct, but in I, of the three symptoms, namely a swelling, eruption or spot, only the latter two are dealt with, while the remaining 'an eruption' becomes the theme of II; thus I and II form a literary unit in a secondary sense. Section VI looks strange when studied in isolation from its context, because it deals not with a case of *ṣāra'at* but with a skin complication not called *ṣāra'at*. It would remind men and women of the criteria given in section I. Moreover section VIII is distinct in content from the foregoing treatments, but some of the language is the same as that found in section VII (note *ṣārû'*).

Problems with the term ṣāra'at

Ṣāra'at is etymologically uncertain. Modern exegetes commonly follow the opinions of medical doctors, who are, however, not unanimous regarding the identification of *ṣāra'at*. Most modern scholars suggest it is impossible to identify it with any modern skin disease, or that *ṣāra'at* cannot be identified with Hansen's disease (e.g. Milgrom 1991: 816–817), while others identify it with 'clinical leprosy' (e.g. Harrison 1997).

As an amateur in the realm of medical science, it is impossible for me to make a final judgment on this matter. But two comments are in order regarding the exegetical method that underlies this discussion. First, if the text is mainly concerned with hygiene or pathology, it is very strange that it does not provide a comprehensive list of the symptoms of *ṣāra'at*. The prescription only arms the priests with two criteria and a colour test (white hair) as diagnostic tools. By contrast, pathological or clinical conditions are found in other contexts such as Num. 12:12. It seems likely that diagnostic criteria given in Lev. 13 are all that both the laity and the priest were able to use. More importantly, if the two criteria and colour test symbolize something theological and if this was what was of primary importance to the legislator, then it is conceivable that he focused on them, considering it unnecessary to provide detailed symptoms of the *ṣāra'at*.

Second, in attempting to identify *ṣāra'at* with a modern disease scholars have noticed that biblical *ṣāra'at* is found not only in human skin, but also in clothes and houses. When it grows in clothes and houses, it is commonly envisaged that *ṣāra'at* is something like mildew. But it is significant that the text does not say 'fungus' or 'mildew', but simply *ṣāra'at*. Crucially important to the interpretation of this evidence is whether one assumes that *ṣāra'at* must have had a wider meaning than leprosy or Hansen's disease, since it can infect things other than human skin in the OT. Almost all the commentators take this position. Yet, though not previously voiced, it is possible that since human *ṣāra'at* infected things such as clothes and houses, these latter complications derived from human beings. Obviously this kind of *ṣāra'at* is extremely rare. In fact, no OT text mentions an actual case of *ṣāra'at* like this. This implies that *ṣāra'at* on clothes and houses is extremely rare, even though the prescription assumes it is possible. It is beyond me to corroborate this with scientific arguments. But it seems that this is the most appropriate interpretation of the evidence available in the OT text.

In what follows, the Hebr. term is translated either *ṣāra'at* or 'a leprous disease' on the understanding that the medical identification of biblical *ṣāra'at* is not yet available. Rather I argue that the Levitical prescription stresses that there is something more important than the disease or even physical death in view (see below).

Comment

This chapter exhibits the essence of uncleanness and cleanness more markedly than chs. 11 – 12 and 15 by portraying the nature of uncleanness through a particular skin disease called *ṣāra'at* (see Kiuchi 2001a). 'Uncleanness' and 'cleanness' symbolize the states of 'hiding oneself' and 'uncovering oneself' respectively (see 'Explanation' on chs. 11 – 12 and Kiuchi: 2003a). It is added here that just as the swarming creatures (typically not part of the human diet) in Lev. 11 tacitly represent the spiritual reality of humanity, so does the rare disease *ṣāra'at* in Lev. 13.

Furthermore it seems possible to identify the symbolic meaning of *ṣāra'at* from viewing it within the wider Leviticus context. My proposal is that it symbolizes the human egocentric nature, and this is surmised by (1) the meaning of uncleanness being the state of hiding oneself (Kiuchi 2003a: 101–106), (2) reference to the *nepeš*, which constantly tends to hide and defile itself (see 'Comment' on 4:2; 7:20–21; 11:43–44), (3) the symbolic meaning of the veil in the Tent (see 'Explanation' on ch. 10), and (4) the fall background to the cleanness/uncleanness regulations (for the last, see 'Explanation'). Thus it is probably the egocentric nature that is symbolized by *ṣāra'at*. As we shall see below, the prescription makes good sense on this assumption.

The legislator's concern is thus consistently spiritual. Although *ṣāra'at* is viewed as a serious skin disease, the prescription uses a number of its symptoms to portray various manifestations of the human egocentric nature (it is a skin disease that can portray the human propensity to hide oneself). Therefore, although some exegetes have assumed that 'death' or an 'aura of death' underlies the concept of uncleanness (e.g. Dillmann 1880: 479; Wenham 1983: 432–434; Milgrom 1991: 816–820), it is more appropriate to postulate that the prescription describes spiritual manifestations of the egocentric nature in terms of physical skin complications and their treatments. However, as 'cleanness' is ultimately concerned with spiritual things, it should be distinguished from physical healing: healing of *ṣāra'at* presumes cleanness, but cleanness does not always presume healing.

The following comments are based on the above postulates, so the comment will often be accompanied by reference to the symbolic significance of the prescription in question.

1. The prescriptions from v. 2 onwards are addressed not only to Moses but also to Aaron, as in 11:1 (see 'Comment' on 11:1). However, the reason why they are not in turn addressed to the Israelites, as in 12:1–2, is not at all clear. Milgrom, comparing ch. 13 with ch. 15, suggests it reflects the legislator's 'apprehension lest the Israelites themselves, armed with this information, would make their own diagnosis – and misdiagnoses – instead of calling in the experts, the priests'. He adds that skin diseases anyhow soon become public knowledge in contrast to genital discharges in ch. 15 (Milgrom 1991: 772). However, the prescriptions of this chapter do not seem to require expertise. The address formulae in chs. 13 – 14 (13:1; 14:1, 33) differ from those in chs. 11 – 12 and 15 in that they lack any reference to 'the sons of Israel'. Considering that the themes of chs. 11 – 12, 15 (food and genital discharges) concern all the Israelites, whereas *ṣāra'at*, despite its detailed and lengthy prescription, really concerns only a minority of people, suggests that the comparatively low degree of relevance to the people may have prompted the legislator to omit any reference to 'the sons of Israel'. This, in turn, creates an irony, because the symbolic meaning of the prescription has universal significance (see below).

13:2–8

The first section presents some typical symptoms of *ṣāra'at*, which are also mentioned in other manifestations of this disease. There are basically two criteria: (1) the hair in the diseased spot becomes white, and (2) the diseased spot appears to penetrate below the skin.

First, by appearing deeper than the skin, *ṣāra'at* fittingly expresses how the human egocentric nature is ordinarily hidden within a person (under the skin) but in due course manifests itself outwardly.

The other criterion, white hair, also has symbolic value. Some modern exegetes interpret the whiteness of the hair, and also that of the human body that becomes completely white (vv. 12–13), as a sign of flakiness. But the emphasis on whiteness in these two different connections cannot be accidental. And in view of vv. 12–13, where a person whose entire body becomes covered with *ṣāra'at* is pronounced clean, whiteness appears to symbolize cleanness or purity (see Kiuchi 2001a). The rationale for this is that patchy whiteness on a person is pronounced unclean, but a body completely covered with *ṣāra'at* is pronounced clean. Thus, since a person completely covered with *ṣāra'at* is clean, the whiteness symbolizes cleanness. Therefore in terms of cleanness and uncleanness, to be stricken by *ṣāra'at* is not as evil as it is to be unclean before the Lord, though the former condition is indeed a difficult experience for humans.

Even though the man knows of his own condition to some extent, he must have the priest examine his complication. This case is the first of a series of prescriptions on the *ṣāra'at*, and presents criteria for diagnosing it on the basis of outward manifestations on the skin: a swelling, an eruption or a spot. For the priest to identify the complication as a case of *ṣāra'at*, all symptoms must be present. If not, a seven-day period of quarantine follows. If the disease has not spread, another seven days are required before the priest examines the person again. But it still remains possible for a spot to turn out as *ṣāra'at* even after it was declared clean. Though the first prescription ends at this point, the person's cleanness was just a temporary state in this case.

The temporary nature of the clean state corresponds to the temporary spiritual state of humans: while people may manage to hide their egocentric nature from manifesting itself before God, sooner or later it will appear outwardly. But a man, rather than uncovering the condition, desires to hide it, because of the fear involved in knowing his true condition.

Superficial purity and the persistence of the egocentric nature are typically presented in this prescription. To purify outward conduct is honourable, but if this is all that is purified, then the problem associated with the human ego, which is deep-seated in the human heart, remains.

2. The term *'ādām* (man) is relatively rare in Leviticus; thus far it occurs only in 1:2; 5:3–4, 22; 7:21. In distinction to *'îš* or *nepeš*, *'ādām* expresses the earthly manifestations of a human, such as the body, the making of mistakes, and the propensity to hide oneself from God and other humans. As mentioned in 'Form and structure', this heading is significant from the viewpoint of the arrangement of chs. 11 – 15 which are arranged roughly according to the order of the divine verdict in Gen. 3:14–19. The relevance of the fall is discussed in 'Explanation'. While one may assume that a woman is included in this occurrence of *'ādām*, that women are introduced by *'iššâ* in vv. 29 and 38 suggests that only men are intended here.

The priest is to distinguish between the symptoms, 'a swelling', 'an eruption' and 'a spot', and the *ṣāra'at*.

'into a case of leprous disease': *lĕnega' ṣāra'at* The very mention of *ṣāra'at* at the stage where no clear pronouncement is made by the priest suggests the man in question is already aware his infection is possibly leprous.

'he shall be brought': *hubbā'* Note the passive form. This is partly because *ṣāra'at* is a dreadful disease, and partly because he is unwilling to be exposed before the priest and the public (see vv. 45–46). See 13:9 and 14:2 as well.

3–5. Two symptoms of the *ṣāra'at* are listed: the hair in the diseased area has become white and the diseased area appears deeper than the skin. Prescriptive instructions are given for the dubious case of a white spot. If a white spot appears that is not deeper than the skin, and the hair within this diseased area is not white, then it is not a leprous disease. Since it remains a dubious case, the person is isolated for seven days. Moreover, because a diagnosed case of *ṣāra'at* necessitates a person's exclusion from the camp, the isolation for this case appears to take place inside the camp.

'pronounce him unclean' (v. 3) This does not mean that until the priest pronounces the person unclean the latter is not yet unclean. The hiding nature of the leprous disease is evident. So it is wrong to take the pronouncement as signifying that the case *becomes* one of a leprous disease only when the priest pronounces so. The priest's pronouncement has the function of officially uncovering the case before God.

'isolate the diseased spot' (v. 4) Certainly the 'diseased spot' refers to the person, but the spot also represents the person (cf. v. 5 and many more similar cases in this chapter; see Kiuchi 2001a: 510).

6. The significance of the washing of clothes is uncertain. Since the rite interrupts the priest's pronouncement of his cleanness and the person's state as clean (cf. vv. 34, 37), it is probably a preventive measure, since *ṣāra'at* has a degree of infection. This latter point is assumed in the later prescription on the *ṣāra'at* of clothing in vv. 47–58.

7–8. The course of events from 'a bright white spot' to 'an eruption', and further to 'a *ṣāra'at*' implies that before the person was declared clean, the *ṣāra'at* had been hiding. It is not correct to say that only when the diseased spot meets the conditions of the *ṣāra'at* does a person become leprous; hence the insidious nature of *ṣāra'at*.

13:9–17

The second section deals with more obvious cases of *ṣāra'at*. Concurrently this section provides some important clues to the ritual's meaning as a whole. It starts with a clear case of *ṣāra'at*, and introduces the new element of 'raw flesh'; i.e. instead of *ṣāra'at* appearing deeper than the skin, raw flesh appears in the swelling. This is called 'a persistent *ṣāra'at*'. Since it is an obvious case, the priest need not segregate him. Again, as the passive verb 'shall be brought out' indicates, the man does not want to present himself before the priest.

The *ṣāra'at* symptoms correspond to a man's spiritual attitude: that of hiding himself. However, unlike the first case, his egocentric nature is obvious to other people, even though he remains unaware of his own propensity to hide himself – it is very common for us to see the spiritual reality in others far better than in ourselves.

The only way in which a person is purified in the first and second prescriptions is through the affliction of *ṣāra'at* all over his body (vv. 12–13). Spiritually this means that his self-hiding is totally uncovered, so he cannot hide himself from others or even from himself: he realizes he has been hiding himself. The Lord views this condition of uncovering himself before him as clean.

Thus, since a person completely covered with *ṣāra'at* is clean, the whiteness symbolizes cleanness. In other words, cleanness is experienced when the entire body manifests the symptoms of *ṣāra'at*. As mentioned above, though the term 'clean' refers to outer cleanness, the prescriptions suggest the presence of inner purity or a deeper dimension of cleanness. However, the clean state is only temporary. Therefore the legislator anticipates that the person pronounced clean may relapse into his old condition and develop symptoms of exposed raw flesh again. Such a prescription, then, appears to assume it is impossible for a man to become completely clean, at least by human endeavour. If he appears totally uncovered and thus becomes clean, this may not remain his final condition. However, the second prescription clearly conveys the principle that the only solution to purity before the Lord is to be found in uncovering oneself before him.

Since self-hiding is existential and not particularly concerned with any specific wrong action, or even the violation of God's commandments, it is the uncovering of all the soul and heart before God that is required. But that is, as these first two prescriptions suggest, concerned with the hidden or unconscious part of the heart.

9. Note the chiastic word order of 'a man' (*'ādām*) and *ṣāra'at* in vv. 2a and 9a. Further, both of the protases are followed by 'he shall be brought to the priest'. The very beginning of this verse implies that what follows concerns cases of *ṣāra'at* obvious even to the person in question, though, as explained below (see 'Explanation'), the symbolic dimension remains veiled to them.

10–11. A swelling (*śĕ'ēt*) was the first of three symptoms in v. 2. As mentioned in v. 3, the white hair in the diseased spot is characteristic of *ṣāra'at*. However, instead of identifying it on the basis of whether or not the spot appears deeper than the skin, the priest diagnoses it as *ṣāra'at* if there is 'raw flesh in the swelling'. Since this is a clear case of *ṣāra'at*, there is no need for the priest to examine it. Further, nor must the person be isolated within the camp. According to vv. 45–46, he is to dwell outside the camp because he is unclean.

12–13. A subcase of the preceding one. Some exegetes maintain that in this case the person is healed from *ṣāra'at*, which is why the person is clean. But as argued elsewhere (Kiuchi 2001a: 507), cleanness is not necessarily equated with healing. And if cleanness guarantees one's approach to the divinity, it may well be that to be clean is more important than healing.

'Whiteness' is one of the diagnostic factors of *ṣāra'at* in vv. 3–4, 10. But here it functions to support the priest's declaration that the person is clean. For the symbolic meaning of whiteness, see 'Comment' on vv. 2–8 above. It symbolizes cleanness when whiteness covers the entire body.

In retrospect, it is apparent that since the diseased area is patchy, the person in question is unclean. If the area covers all the body, and there is no possibility of hiding it, then the person is pronounced clean. For this paradoxical aspect of *ṣāra'at*, see Kiuchi 2001 and 'Explanation'.

14–15. But when raw flesh appears again in the skin, the person is pronounced unclean. This implies that in the previous case, where *ṣāra'at* covers the entire body, the raw flesh disappeared. Thus the raw flesh is the *ṣāra'at* and the cause of uncleanness in this section of vv. 9–17.

16–17. This is a subcase of vv. 14–15. Upon the recurrence of the characteristic raw flesh, if its colour becomes white, the priest upon examination declares the spot clean. The transformation of the spot's colour to white is evidence of the flesh's death. It is only a small step towards concluding that its symbolic meaning is that the death of flesh brings purity (see 'Explanation'). In contrast to the transition from the clean to the unclean state in vv. 6–8, here the change is from the unclean to the clean state; just as the clean state is temporary, so is the unclean state.

13:18–23

This new section presents further ways *ṣāra'at* may manifest itself: it is *ṣāra'at* that develops in the spot of a healed boil. Thus it stresses the problem of distinguishing *ṣāra'at* from other common skin complications. The criteria mentioned in the first section (v. 3) help the priest to distinguish if the disease is really *ṣāra'at*.

The area of skin affected by ordinary skin complications becomes weakened so that *ṣāra'at* may develop. Thus these cases symbolize that the selfish ego manifests itself in weak areas of a person, and that it is indistinguishable from this weakness. What are spiritual weaknesses other than the most comprehensive self-hiding? There are various human weaknesses that may prompt one to hide oneself from man and God, but they are not evil or inadequate in themselves. But because they are weak they turn into areas where pride and arrogance tend to be nurtured, so it is difficult to distinguish them from the inherent weaknesses. For instance, human anger is justifiable in many cases, but being slow to anger is what characterizes God. In the midst of anger humans easily go beyond the justified bounds of their anger. On such occasions it becomes difficult to differentiate between the weakness and the eruption of the selfish ego.

Or, since the prescription assumes a boil or a burn as the prior complication, it is also possible to envisage a condition arising from particular spiritual damage so that a person becomes weak in this particular spiritual area, and his or her egocentric nature finds its expression there. Various kinds of human suffering provide sufficient examples. Suffering that leads to humility can be used as an opportunity to turn weakness into strength. But more often than not, humans tend to take pride in overcoming hardship, forgetting that God may have disciplined them for their arrogance. In this way, man shows himself to be unteachable, and his egocentric nature may continue to persist until his death. True strength lies in the kind of humility where the Lord can dwell (Isa. 57:15).

18. This verse and the next section begin with *bāśār kî* (when a flesh). It is clear from the flow of rules that the corporeal aspects of *'ādām* are stressed in this chapter. While the skin of a person is at issue in all of these cases, more and more focus appears to be on the indistinguishable nature of *ṣāra'at* from other ordinary skin complications. This case deals with the potential situation where *ṣāra'at* might grow on the very spot where the boil was previously found. Boils are sometimes a manifestation of the divine curse (Exod. 9:9; Deut. 28:27, 35). Here, however, *ṣāra'at* is presented as a more dreadful disease. It is apparent that the boil has weakened the area of skin so that other complications may grow in the same spot.

19–23. When a white swelling or a reddish-white spot appears in the area of the healed boil, the priest examines it according to the two criteria mentioned in v. 3.

13:24–28

This section deals with a case of *ṣāraʿat* that had potentially developed in a burn. The same opening clause (*bāśār kî*) indicates that this section thematically continues the preceding one (see v. 18). Once again, the priest's examination is based on the two criteria given in v. 3.

Symbolically this case is analogous to a situation where one's egocentric nature manifests itself in relation to the spiritual damage inflicted by others. Instead of being humbled, one tends to become self-assertive or revengeful.

13:29–37

This rather long prescription deals with a skin complication developing on the head or in the beard of a man or woman. Although these are areas that may well be ordinarily covered by a turban or veil, they can be seen by others more frequently than the other parts of the human body. While one of the two criteria for *ṣāraʿat* is the growth of white hair in the diseased spot, the colour of the hair in this case is yellow.

Contrary to the previous case, the potential problem is to be known not just by the afflicted person but also by others. In that there is no way his disease can be hidden from the public, the case is more threatening to him. As in the preceding cases, this case is apparently indistinguishable from other common complications. Moreover the head/beard symbolizes human dignity (cf. van Rooy 1997: 1016), so it is most shameful and threatening for a person to realize that he or she may have contracted *ṣāraʿat*.

Symbolically it appears that the egocentric nature may manifest itself in such a way that it destroys a person's public dignity. However, is it not ultimately good to be deprived of such a thing?

29. 'a man or a woman': *'îš 'ô 'iššâ* This is the first verse in this chapter where not *'ādām* but *'îš* (*'iššâ*) appears. After this verse, *'îš* occurs in this chapter in vv. 38, 40, 44. Apparently, since *'ādām* does not have the feminine form, the words *'îš* and *'iššâ* are used. But this does not exhaust the possible reasons for the choice of these words. Though these terms have a general connotation of 'a man' and 'a woman', they may refer to married persons. And since these terms connote the interhuman aspects of an individual, skin complications that cannot be hidden from human eyes, particularly in a family situation, are dealt with: those on one's head and beard (vv. 29–37, 40–44), and his or her skin (vv. 38–39).

30. 'an itch': *neteq* The itches can be *ṣāraʿat*. Fine yellow hair is an indication of *ṣāraʿat*.

31–34. The rules from v. 31 to v. 34a are expressed in such a way that the priest, not the person, deals with the itch. The concentration on the itch is based on the assumption that the itch represents the person (see 'Comment' on v. 5).

For washing the clothes in v. 34, see 'Comment' on v. 6.

35–36. If the itch spreads after it is declared clean, the priest does not have to check if the hair is yellow. The expansion of the infected area identifies it as *ṣāra'at*. Since this should take place within two weeks, the *ṣāra'at* must have been hidden.

37. If, on the other hand, the itch appears to remain the same and black hair begins growing in it, then it is a sign that the itch is healed, and that it is clean. This is the second time in this chapter where the verb 'heal' (*nirpâ*) occurs (the first time in v. 18). In this case, the healing guarantees cleanness, though the reverse may not always be the case. This is the only occurrence in this chapter where it is related to the healing of *ṣāra'at* (see 14:3, 48).

13:38–39

This short section deals with white spots on the skin. Apparently this case is similar to the case in v. 4, though unlike v. 4 no reference is made to hair: a simple bright white spot is at issue. In this case the person can examine his own condition.

The finding of a bright white spot on one's skin would be a frightening prospect because whiteness is a potential symptom of *ṣāra'at* (cf. v. 4 above). But the prescription simply says that such a case is not *ṣāra'at* but leucoderma. As 'man or woman' indicates, the matter is interpersonal (see 'Comment' on v. 29). A possible human reaction against this prescription would naturally be that the person would look intently, but fearfully, for white hair and something that appeared deeper than the skin *all over the body*. Understandably the situation would lead both a man and woman to separate from each other, and hide themselves from each other for fear of shame. Though this is not what the Lord expects, it is inevitable, and its outcome is that men and women begin to examine themselves. Thus more than the preceding cases, this prescription demands self-examination.

From the Lord's standpoint there is no difference if the disease is found by the afflicted person or someone else. But since at the fall the man and woman become godlike in a spiritual sense, even though they are not God, they inevitably try to hide their true condition, albeit unconsciously. The prescription inculcates that self-examination is the beginning of the God–human relationship. It is not about some offence within oneself, but whether a person hides by pretending to be clean. Now, as this is an existential matter, it is very difficult to locate where he or she hides. Ordinarily it may appear possible to see what kind of man or woman one is by one's close human relationships, particularly within marriage or sibling relationships. But is it not possible that even within these intimate human relationships one still does not dare to see oneself and admit to self-hiding?

13:40–44

The last human skin complication concerns the hair of a man's head, which is of course most visible to others and difficult to hide. The complications include common ones such as baldness, in which case he is clean, but also a case where a reddish-white spot appears in the bald area, in which case it is a symptom of *ṣāra'at* and the person is deemed unclean. Thus one of man's common conditions – baldness – is foundational to the latter case. The person is not only examined by others but also by himself. In this way, a most common skin complication becomes the object of other people's attention before he presents himself before the priest.

By laying down this prescription the legislator undoubtedly aims to urge men to uncover themselves, especially their egocentric selves before the Lord. It is clear that this prescription emphasizes the man's responsibility, as the text explicitly states *'îš* (a man) at the beginning, and this forms a thematic inclusio with the first prescription (vv. 2–8), which also deals with a man (*'ādām*). However, this is not to say that the woman has less propensity to self-hide. But as Gen. 3 implicitly indicates, the chief responsibility for the violation of God's commandment lay with the man: he must have supervised his wife and rejected her suggestion. After the fall, however, the man is required to check his own egocentric nature and his propensity to self-hide (see 'Form and structure', and 'Explanation' on ch. 12).

40. 'a man's hair' In Hebr. the beginning of the verse runs *wě'îš kî* (and when a person) in contrast with the foregoing cases, which are introduced by *'îš 'ô 'iššâ* (a man or a woman). This probably reflects the fact that baldness occurs most frequently in men.

41. See 'Notes on the text'.

43. 'like the appearance of leprous disease in the skin of the body' This indicates that though 'reddish' was not mentioned for the case in v. 3, the latter included such a case. At the same time, this additional explanation incidentally, but perhaps deliberately, refers back to the first case in this chapter.

44. See 'Notes on the text'.

13:45–46

What is stipulated in these verses applies to all the preceding cases. In this sense the section forms a literary unit distinct from the preceding one. However, a seamless flow of the regulation is achieved by the mention of *ṣārûaʿ* in v. 44, giving the impression that vv. 45–46 form a natural sequence to the preceding baldness cases.

When a person is pronounced unclean, that person is to dwell alone outside the camp. Dwelling outside the camp means being cut off from the people. It should be recalled that the person is declared unclean because his *ṣāraʿat* is patchy, not covering all of his body. But spiritually, when that person is brought out of the camp, he cannot hide himself: he is to identify himself as unclean to the public. In this sense he progresses along the path towards purity.

A person who becomes clean after his body was completely covered by *ṣāraʿat* (v. 13) dwells inside the camp. Together with the leprous persons outside the camp, this case indicates that *ṣāraʿat* is not the person's ultimate problem, and that exclusion from the camp does not derive from hygienic concerns.

These circumstances bear some perennial spiritual significance. First, the whole prescription casts serious doubt on whether people living in the camp are existentially clean; i.e. in a state of uncovering themselves. In view of the potential presence of *ṣāraʿat* within the camp, which the Lord abhors, one cannot expect the Lord's presence inside the camp. It is, then, more favourable in the Lord's eyes that a person be declared unclean and dwell outside the camp even though he becomes a social outcast (cf. Num. 5:1–4 with 5:5–31). This is because humanity is essentially viewed as unclean before the Lord.

45. The leprous person must wear torn clothes, let the hair of his head hang loose, cover his lip and cry out, 'Unclean, unclean!'

'torn': *pĕrûmîm* The qal form *pāram* occurs three times in the OT, all in Leviticus (Lev. 10:6; 13:45; 21:10), and in all of these wearing torn clothes symbolizes sorrow in connection with funerary rites. Thus this gesture embodies the leprous person's sorrow at his affliction with *ṣāraʿat* and removal from the realm of life.

'hang loose': *pārûaʿ* The Hebr. term in this sense occurs often in conjunction with the above root *prm* (cf. Lev. 10:6; 21:10), and the gesture, as in wearing torn clothes, symbolizes sorrow. The mention of 'his head', echoing 'his head' in v. 44, also contributes to a smooth flow within the regulation.

'cover his upper lips': *ʿal śāpām yaʿṭeh* In this verse the verb *ʿāṭâ* does not mean 'cover' in the sense of shutting one's mouth. Rather it is an intransitive verb, as is also made clear from the preposition meaning 'on' (cf. Ezek. 24:17), and it means to 'shield his lips' with his hand. The sense of the rule is that the leprous person, without his lips seen by others, must cry, 'Unclean, unclean!' This gesture as a whole, then, conveys an ambivalent message: while he must indicate that he is unworthy to speak, he must also make it public that he is in the sphere of death.

46. The leprous person, as long as he is afflicted with *ṣāraʿat*, remains unclean, and must live alone outside the camp. This is expressed by the repetitive use of the root *yšb*, as follows:

> *Bādād* ***yēšēb*** Alone he shall dwell
> *Miḥûṣ lammaḥănēh* ***môšābô*** Outside the camp his dwelling

The assumption is that the camp must be clean, and thus all people pronounced unclean must live outside the camp. The command that he must live alone may reflect the legislator's intention to segregate him in such a way that his disease will not infect others. But in view of the symbolic meaning of *ṣāra'at* (see 'Explanation'), it is more likely that the prescription aims to indicate clearly to the public that he has been hiding himself. In this sense, these measures are punitive as well.

13:47–59

Lev. 13 adds to the various cases of *ṣāra'at* another case that occurs on clothes, or any articles made of skin. Most modern exegetes consider that the same term *ṣāra'at* is used, because for the ancients the appearance of human *ṣāra'at* looked similar to *ṣāra'at* of clothes and articles. Therefore they tend to call the *ṣāra'at* on clothes or articles 'fungus-like' or 'mildew-like', and some even identify it with fungus or mildew. But neither of these appears in the text: it is only a modern conjecture. It is questionable whether *ṣāra'at* on humans is different from *ṣāra'at* on clothes and articles. Does *ṣāra'at* on clothes and articles develop independently of *ṣāra'at* on humans? The next chapter discloses rules of purification from *ṣāra'at* on houses (14:33–53). Lev. 13 – 14 does not explain the connection between *ṣāra'at* in human beings and *ṣāra'at* on clothes and articles. But there are two things worth considering.

First, there is no evidence outside Leviticus that clothes or houses are afflicted by *ṣāra'at*: all the cases of *ṣāra'at* are those on humans, though this is not to say that the regulations in Lev. 13 – 14 are fictitious or purely imaginative. Second, and more immediately significant, is the positioning of the cases for *ṣāra'at* on clothes and articles immediately after the various cases of human *ṣāra'at*. Is it not reasonable to assume that *ṣāra'at* is an infectious disease, though the degree of its infectiousness is not as high as that associated with diseases people suffer in their reproductive organs (ch. 15)? Third, though the rules on *ṣāra'at* on clothes and articles appear independent of the foregoing rules, on closer inspection two literary connections are apparent. (1) 'Washing the clothes' has already appeared in vv. 6, 34. And if the symbolic meaning is to prevent further infection, then it is probable that the rule on *ṣāra'at* on clothes from v. 47 onwards is meant to be taken as addressing the result of the infection. (2) There is an association of ideas between 'his clothes' (*bĕgādāyw*) in v. 45 and 'the garment' (*habbeged*) in v. 47, so it is possible to conclude that the torn garment (v. 45) must be burnt if it is afflicted with *ṣāra'at* (see below). The position taken here is that by stipulating the manifestation for each type of *ṣāra'at*, the legislator confines humans to a fear of the disease, and that juxtaposing human *ṣāra'at* with that found on objects, as though they are separate, evinces the Lord's ironic viewpoint on the persistent nature of human self-hiding: that even if a person admits his clothes and articles are clearly affected by *ṣāra'at*, he treats the case as though it has nothing to do with him, although if he finds *ṣāra'at* in his clothes, it is highly unlikely he is free from *ṣāra'at*.

Now the treatment of infected garments and articles is harsher than that for *ṣāra'at* on human beings: if the garment or article is infected, it must be burned, whereas if the colour of the spot fades, then it is not called clean, but the diseased spot is to be torn out. Either way the garment or article must no longer be used. Moreover *ṣāra'at* is here called 'a persistent (*mam'eret*) *ṣāra'at*', and the fact that this case of *ṣāra'at* is more severe implies, in relation to human *ṣāra'at*, that the diseased spot of a person must be annihilated like it is in the case of *ṣāra'at* in clothes and articles; namely destruction of what is intended by *'ādām* (cf. 1:2).

Notice should be taken of the fact that the 'skin' (*'ôr*) is stressed in this prescription. While garments from various materials including skin can be infected, any articles made of skin can be as well: the latter may not necessarily be garments. But why does the prescription stress skin, presumably animal skin? The literary relationship to Gen. 3 provides an answer. Since the clothes made of animal skin were, in Gen. 3:21, a sign of the Lord's grace, it is surmised that here in Lev. 13, by expanding the areas of infection not just to garments but to articles made from animal skin, the destructive power of *ṣāra'at* over against grace is stressed (see 'Explanation'). At any rate, this final prescription is loaded with irony by the legislator's drawing attention to the fact that if a garment or article made of animal skin is infected, how much more the human who uses it is infected. Along with the people pronounced unclean who had to dwell alone outside the camp, this prescription on the *ṣāra'at* of garments and articles signals the potential presence of leprous people inside the camp using those garments and articles.

In terms of the human egocentric nature symbolized by *ṣāra'at*, this last prescription makes an incisive criticism of the incorrigibleness of human hypocrisy: even when a garment or article used by a man is desperately infected, he pretends he is not infected. Humans are very reluctant to admit that the cause of trouble, suffering or hardship lies within *them*. As is typical with humanity since the fall, we are like gods, knowing good and evil, and only rarely do we realize that we, or more specifically our egocentric nature, is the cause – even when our immediate environment is under heavy fire. Various catastrophes in the later history of Israel are incapable of changing the hearts of the Israelites. But the prescription clearly warns that the human egocentric nature must be destroyed (cf. the symbolic meaning of fat in the fellowship offering).

47. 'When there is a case of leprous disease in a garment': *wĕhabbeged kî*... The syntactic formulation is the same as before. See in Hebr. vv. 2, 9, 18, 24, 29, 38, 40.

48–49. The infected items include a woollen or linen garment, warp or woof of linen or wool, and anything made of skin. These are either worn or used by humans. If the spot is green or reddish, it is a *ṣāra'at*. The point in this case is that judgment can be made by the owner of those items before the latter are examined by the priest. It should be noted that while garments are the main focus of the prescription, articles made of skin include things other than garments (see vv. 49, 51–52 and 'Comment' above).

50–52. The priest looks at the spot and isolates it for seven days. Since it is known that it is a *ṣāra'at*, the quarantine period is not required to facilitate a decision as to whether it is *ṣāra'at*, but purely to determine if it spreads. As the following description shows, either case is unclean; they are different only in degree. Now, if it does spread within a week, then it is a persistent case of *ṣāra'at* and is unclean. The unclean item must be burnt with fire.

53–55. An alternative case and its handling is presented: if the disease has not spread, the priest commands that the infected item be washed and isolated for another seven days. On the seventh day the priest looks at the infected item after it is washed. If the spot remains the same and has not spread, then it is unclean and must be burnt, whether the rot is on the back or front of the article.

56–58. Another possible case, which the priest examines after seven days, is given: if the diseased area has faded after it has been washed, the person must tear it out of the item (v. 56). But if it reappears, it must be burnt (v. 57). However, any item that, after washing, retains no trace of the disease is considered clean after a second washing. As these cases indicate, *ṣāra'at* on clothes or other items has greater visibility and is worse than human cases.

59. This passage summarizes only the last section of this chapter: vv. 47–58. The summarizing statement of all the *ṣāra'at* cases comes at the end of ch. 14 (vv. 54–57). This raises the question as to why the *ṣāra'at* cases on humans are not summarized at this point. Milgrom (1991: 815) lists three possible reasons: (1) As Abrabanel commented (1979: 75), this subscript dealing with inanimate things sets the pericope off from the next chapter, where the person is at issue. (2) While the rules on garments and articles are complete within themselves, the rules on human *ṣāra'at* continue into the next chapter, which deals with purificatory rites (cited as the view of Wessely 1846). (3) Without the subscript it may give the impression that the purificatory rites also apply to garments and articles. In response to these reasons it may be first pointed out that the object of the purificatory rites in ch. 14 is specified, and there is no room for misunderstanding that they can apply to the case of *ṣāraʿat* on garments and articles. Only part of Abrabanel's view that the subscript sets the section on garments and articles apart from ch. 14 is acceptable. The major reason is that the rules on human *ṣāraʿat* are not exhausted by ch. 13: its purificatory rites are addressed in ch. 14. At least, the same literary phenomenon appears in 14:32 (see 'Comment' there). From the use of the formula *zōʾt tôrat* (or *tôrâ*), followed by the handled cases in 13:59 and 14:32, it appears that when the material in question appears to be capable of being taken by the readership as secondary, since these cases are not going to be referred to again, the legislator mentions the formula to emphasize that the instruction in question has the same importance as in the other cases (cf. 'Comment' on 6:9[2]).

Explanation

As the above comment on the symbolic meaning of *ṣāraʿat* indicates, this chapter is the first place in the OT that implies that the idea of outer cleanness/uncleanness has a deeper dimension. This is expressed by the traits of *ṣāraʿat* and its handling. Moreover by the destructive power of *ṣāraʿat*, the prescription clearly indicates that cleanness is a temporary state. Uncleanness is the state of a person before the Lord, but it also serves to lead men and women to inner cleanness via outer cleanness. In this respect, it is by the Lord's grace that he provides a way to cleanness. If a person uncovers all his heart, including his unconscious realm, then he becomes clean: though the text speaks in terms of outer purity, it points to inner purity.

The prescriptions of this chapter underscore several aspects of *ṣāraʿat*: it is persistent, nearly always hiding and indistinguishable from other skin diseases, and, most importantly, it is symbolic of existential self-hiding.

Even on the level of outer cleanness/uncleanness the rules are threatening when the Israelites have any kind of skin complication. For it can be easily surmised that the required self-examination introduced fear into the life of the Israelites, so people would not expose their case to a priest, for fear of learning they had a terminal illness or would experience public ignominy. In addition, a further threat is posed by the potential infection on clothes and articles by *ṣāraʿat*.

Now, when these features are seen in terms of their symbolism, they describe the condition of human nature before God. The whole thrust of the prescription in this chapter ironically insinuates that all humanity is incorrigibly unclean, and in a state of hiding before the Lord. The recognition of symbolism within this prescription is not a midrashic enterprise but the essence of the prescription. Since the chapter presents various cases or potential cases of *ṣāraʿat*, it is further proposed that the variety of cases represent a variety of manifestations of human self-hiding before the Lord.

Leviticus 13 in the light of Genesis 3

Self-hiding. In fact, the theme of human self-hiding from the Lord is the fundamental theme of Lev. 13, and this theme is traceable to the fall account in Gen. 3. Because of the importance of the narrative for understanding the symbolic meaning of uncleanness, we need to take a close look at the narrative's detail.

The fact that the man and woman before the fall were not ashamed of their nakedness (Gen. 2:25) suggests they were not self-conscious (like human beings after the fall are). Pre-fall they were assumedly unconscious even of their nakedness or non-nakedness (just like infants). In a word, they were unconscious of their fundamental existential condition. The human unconsciousness of their existential situation did not change after the fall, although the nature of their hearts changed fundamentally. Post-fall they became conscious of what they said and did (such as hiding behind trees, fear of God's voice), but were, at best, highly vague about their existential condition for the following reasons.

First, the fact that their eyes were opened (3:7) and they became ashamed of their nakedness reflects a radical transformation of heart, and this took place at the cost of their becoming blind to, or alienated from, God's presence. Henceforth this awareness of their nakedness became intrinsic to human nature.

Second, why did they not honestly admit their own offences? The reader may well label their conduct as self-justification and imputing the guilt to others (Gen. 3:12–13). However, this evaluation is from the reader's viewpoint. It is unlikely they were consciously justifying themselves or imputing their responsibility to others. Rather it is truer to say that they 'honestly' said what they thought. All this indicates that human beings from then on began to possess the propensity not to admit any violation they commit (cf. Luke 23:40–41). It is my view that the state of hiding from God manifests itself most clearly in their not admitting to the fact that they have violated his prohibition, since God's commandment cannot be separated from his presence (cf. Exod. 20:6).

Third, the unconscious nature that the violation of God's commandment involves exhibits itself in the very reason why they ate the fruit of the forbidden tree: because the fruit looked good and desirable (note the Hebr. root *ḥmd*) to their eyes, whereas all the other trees in the Garden are good (2:9), and once the fruit was seen this way, eating it no longer seemed evil (see 'Explanation' on chs. 4:1 – 5:13). This is the spiritual process by which the consciousness of the violation of God's commandment faded away in the presence of their own desires.

Fourth, the nature of the transformation of the first human hearts is best portrayed in 3:8, which runs, 'the man and his wife hid themselves from the presence of the LORD God among the trees of the garden' (ESV). Tangibleness and spirituality are one in this narrative, and it seems that this act approximates what I call by another Hebr. term *ḥāṭā'* (to hide oneself). Moreover the Hebr. root *ḥb'* appears in hith. form in v. 8 and ni. form in v. 10. Perhaps, though commonly their meanings are not differentiated, there is a difference between them. The former means 'he hid himself', connoting the presence of the man's will, whereas the latter just means 'he hid'. The former is an objective description of the narrator, whereas the latter reflects Adam's condition of heart, where he is unaware he hid *himself*.

These considerations show that their heart, namely a system as a whole, changed in the wake of their violation, the ultimate description of which is the egocentric making of themselves like God in 3:22: humans started to make their own standard of good and evil. Thus while they became self-conscious, their self-consciousness of what they thought and felt operated under the existential propensity to justify themselves, which they could not do anything about, nor did they intend to change. This state characterizes the 'egocentric nature'. Thus just as they were not conscious of their existential situation before the fall, they were so after the fall too.

Though the term *ḥāṭā'* does not appear in this narrative, the idea of hiding oneself unknowingly, which is inferred from an examination of all the occurrences of the term in the rest of the OT, suits this account in Gen. 3 as well (cf. Gen. 4:7 and Kiuchi 2003a: 67–68, 102–103). Further it is proposed that such an inner state of a human is what is termed 'unclean' in Lev. 11 – 15 in general and Lev. 13 in particular. Since this is a universal condition of all humanity since the fall, it is insufficient for people to remain content with what they are conscious of in their 'religious' life.

As uncleanness in a symbolic sense is primarily unconscious, an awareness of this state already places one on the road to cleanness. An unclean person is not aware of his uncleanness, whereas a clean person is (cf. 'Explanation' on ch. 11).

Flesh, skin and clothes. In Lev. 13 the human body (*bāśār*) is frequently mentioned as the place where diseases develop. In view of the hiding and persistent nature of *ṣāra'at*, it seems probable that the human body, though it was originally otherwise, now symbolizes the seedbed out of which the egocentric nature manifests itself. That is why a person relapses into an unclean state even after he or she is pronounced 'clean'. The continuation of a clean state cannot be expected unless the egocentric nature is completely removed.

Eleven times in this chapter the term 'body' (*bāśār*) is conjoined with 'skin' (*'ôr*), either in construct-genitive chains or by the suffix referring back to 'skin'. Why is it necessary to specify 'the skin of the flesh'? First, by referring to 'the skin of the flesh' the prescription emphasizes it is the most outer part of the body that is the focus of the rules. But this does not sufficiently explain the legislator's use of the phrase.

The root of the matter again lies in the account of the fall. After the man and woman hid themselves from God and received the sentence of judgment, they were clothed with 'garments of skins' (*kotnôt* '*ôr*) as Gen. 3:21 says, 'And the LORD God made for Adam and his wife garments of skins and clothed them' (ESV).

This note suggests a gracious act of God to cover their shame (cf. Gen. 3:7). After the fall human flesh symbolizes shame, and its skin is the most outward part that faces the outer world. Both in Gen. 3 and Lev. 13 the literal shame of being naked and covering oneself go hand in hand with spiritual shame and self-hiding from God. Lev. 13 assumes this human condition before God, and strongly encourages humans to return to their initial relationship with the Creator. But since human fallenness and its necessary consequence, death, cannot be altered, the only way to restore the broken relationship with God is through the uncovering of a person's spiritual condition. This is what is symbolized by *ṣāra'at* covering the *whole* body: the uncovering must be total, not partial.

In a word, Lev. 13 is a chapter that aims to bring humans into the Lord's presence, assuming our incorrigible propensity to self-hide.

Further developments in Leviticus 13

The prescription's symbolic meaning, that if a person's body is full of the leprous disease he or she is clean, and that all those pronounced unclean must live alone outside the camp, evinces the Lord's evaluation that it is far better for an individual to be outside the camp than to continue hiding himself inside the camp, because those who live outside the camp are on their way to inner purity. This is also corroborated by the presence of the *purificatory* ritual in the next chapter. Ch. 13 is the first chapter in Leviticus where the idea begins to surface that one is better off being excommunicated from the people (cf. 'Explanation' on ch. 11).

Over against the inherent human tendency to self-hide from the Lord, the Lord provides measures to overcome this: self-examination and examination by others. Symbolically this means that humans are often unconsciously bound by frameworks, doctrines or other human ways of thinking, above all by humanism. Differing viewpoints may open up what we have not noticed before. Hence the importance to listen to, and learn from, others. For humans to open their minds and hearts to conflicting viewpoints is painful and requires courage, but without this there is no hope of entering the way to inner purity. Obstinacy or stubbornness is the primary obstacle to this process.

As implied by leprous diseases on clothes and articles, the Lord also deals with the human heart in such a way that he sends various sufferings and catastrophes on human beings. But do humans realize their own state of self-hiding when they are deprived of all these things? OT spiritual history shows that even when the Lord withdraws his hand from people, they have a strong tendency to believe they are still experiencing his mercy and protection. But if we envisage the Lord's mercy even beyond this, is it not fitting that he puts outside the camp those who unconsciously pretend to be clean (cf. ch. 26)?

Seen in this way the prescription of Lev. 13 implies that its symbolic meaning applies to all humanity, not just to the Israelites. It is directly addressed to the Israelites as part of the Sinai covenant because Israel was a test case. Furthermore, though the prescription is to be observed by the Israelites in so far as the literal dimension is concerned, it is highly dubious whether they could follow the symbolic meaning of these prescriptions. Literal observation indeed produces social outcasts, but the message of the prescription is that there are far more 'leprous people' within the camp – indeed all humanity!

The only way this malignant disease (the egocentric nature) is overcome is by uncovering it before the Lord. But, as mentioned above, human pride and the desire to avoid the shame of being exposed make this purifying process almost impossible. No human can help, no god can assist in breaking this vicious circle. It is wishful thinking to consider that the Lord is the one who helps. He indeed helps those who, denying themselves, open their minds and hearts. But he allows those who do not do this to go their own way. Knowing oneself, particularly one's egocentric nature, is sound; to fight with oneself is respectable, but only victory brings peace with God.

New Testament implications

It was the scribes and Pharisees to whom Jesus' diatribe was directed. The human spiritual condition symbolized in Lev. 13 perfectly corresponds to those people who believe they worship the Lord 'properly'. While not all outcasts such as lepers were unbelieving people, and not all the scribes and Pharisees were criticized by Jesus, it was only natural that Jesus felt much more comfortable being with outcasts. He commonly associated with prostitutes, tax collectors and 'sinners' because their hearts and souls had become troubled to a greater degree by the results of their sinfulness. This corresponds to my explanation above that outcasts are more favourable in the Lord's eyes than people hiding themselves inside the camp (Matt. 21:31).

Although not previously recognized, given the symbolic meaning of *ṣāra'at*, there is the potential that St Paul used the term 'flesh' (*sarx*), assuming the symbolic meaning of *ṣāra'at* in Lev. 13 (cf. Thiselton 1975: 671–682). For him the 'flesh', which is opposed to the Spirit, is an existential entity where vices such as sexual immorality, licentiousness, idolatry, sorcery, enmity, strife, jealousy, anger, rivalries, dissensions and divisions occur. As long as people continue to do these things they will not inherit the kingdom of God (Gal. 5:19–21). Thus the NT also requires that the flesh be crucified in order for a person to grow strong in spirit. Compromise between flesh and spirit is neither assumed nor discussed. In this regard, the message of Lev. 13 is virtually the same as many Pauline passages. In most of his epistles he addresses himself to such 'believers' who still walk according to their flesh. To believe in Jesus Christ means that a person uncovers the selfishness that covers his or her heart and soul. If not destroying the egocentric nature, the law mandates self-uncovering. The kind of heart envisaged is that of little children (Gen. 2:25; Matt. 18:3; Luke 18:17).

LEVITICUS 14:1–57

Translation

[1]The LORD spoke to Moses, saying, [2]'This shall be the teaching of the leprous person for the day of his cleansing when he shall be brought to the priest. [3]The priest shall go out of the camp, and the priest shall look. If the case of leprous disease is healed in the leprous person, [4]the priest shall command them to take for him who is to be cleansed two live clean birds, cedar wood, scarlet yarn and hyssop. [5]The priest shall command them to kill one of the birds in an earthenware vessel over fresh water. [6]He shall take the live bird with the cedar wood, scarlet yarn and hyssop, and dip them and the live bird in the blood of the bird that was killed over the fresh water. [7]He shall sprinkle it seven times on him who is to be cleansed of the leprous disease. Then he shall pronounce him clean and shall let the live bird go into the open field. [8]He who is to be cleansed shall wash his clothes and shave off all his hair and bathe himself in water, and he shall be clean. And after that he may come into the camp, but live outside his tent seven days. [9]On the seventh day he shall shave off all his hair from his head, his beard and his eyebrows. He shall shave off all his hair, and then he shall wash his clothes and bathe his body in water, and he shall be clean.

[10]'On the eighth day he shall take two male lambs without blemish, and one ewe lamb a year old without blemish, and a loyalty offering of three-tenths of an ephah of fine flour mixed with oil, and one log of oil. [11]And the priest who cleanses shall set the man who is to be cleansed and these things before the LORD, at the entrance of the Tent of Meeting. [12]The priest shall take one of the male lambs and offer it for a reparation offering, along with the log of oil, and wave them for a wave offering before the LORD. [13]He shall slaughter the lamb in the place where they kill the sin offering and the burnt offering, in the Holy Place. For the reparation offering, like the sin offering, belongs to the priest: it is most holy. [14]The priest shall take some of the blood of the reparation offering, and the priest shall put it on

the lobe of the right ear of him who is to be cleansed and on the thumb of his right hand and on the big toe of his right foot. 15The priest shall take some of the log of oil and pour it into the palm of his own left hand 16and the priest shall dip his right finger in the oil that is in his left hand and sprinkle some oil with his finger seven times before the LORD. 17And some of the oil that remains in his hand the priest shall put on the lobe of the right ear of him who is to be cleansed and on the thumb of his right hand and on the big toe of his right foot, on top of the blood of the reparation offering. 18And the rest of the oil that is in the priest's hand he shall put on the head of him who is to be cleansed. Then the priest shall make propitiation for him before the LORD.

19'The priest shall offer the sin offering, to make propitiation for him who is to be cleansed from his uncleanness. And afterwards he shall slaughter the burnt offering, 20and the priest shall offer the burnt offering and the loyalty offering on the altar. The priest shall make propitiation for him, and he shall be clean.

21'If he is poor and cannot afford so much, then he shall take one male lamb for a reparation offering to be waved, to make propitiation for him, and a tenth of an ephah of fine flour mixed with oil for a loyalty offering, and a log of oil; 22also two turtle doves or two pigeons, whichever he can afford. The one shall be a sin offering and the other a burnt offering. 23On the eighth day he shall bring them for his cleansing to the priest, to the entrance of the Tent of Meeting, before the LORD. 24The priest shall take the lamb of the reparation offering and the log of oil, and the priest shall wave them for a wave offering before the LORD. 25When the lamb of the reparation offering is slaughtered, the priest shall take some of the blood of the reparation offering and put it on the lobe of the right ear of him who is to be cleansed, and on the thumb of his right hand and on the big toe of his right foot. 26The priest shall pour some of the oil into the palm of his own left hand, 27and shall sprinkle with his right finger some of the oil that is in his left hand seven times before the LORD. 28The priest shall put some of the oil that is in his hand on the lobe of the right ear of him who is to be cleansed and on the thumb of his right hand and on the big toe of his right foot, in the place where the blood of the reparation offering was put. 29The rest of the oil that is in the priest's hand he shall put on the head of him who is to be cleansed, to make propitiation for him before the LORD. 30And he shall offer one kind, of the turtle doves or pigeons, whichever he can afford, 31whichever he can afford – one for a sin offering and the other for a burnt offering, along with a loyalty offering. And the priest shall make propitiation before the LORD for him who is being cleansed. 32This is the teaching of him in whom is a case of leprous disease, who cannot afford the offerings for his cleansing.'

33The LORD spoke to Moses and Aaron, saying, 34'When you come into the land of Canaan, which I give you for a possession, and I put a case of leprous disease in a house in the land of your possession, 35then he who owns the house shall come and tell the priest, There seems to me to be some case of disease in my house. 36Then the priest shall command that they empty the house before the priest goes to examine the disease, lest all that is in the house become unclean. Afterwards the priest shall go in to see the house. 37He shall examine the disease. And if the disease is in the walls of the house with greenish or reddish spots, and if it appears to be deeper than the surface, [38]then the priest shall go out of the house to the door of the house and isolate the house seven days. [39]The priest shall come again on the seventh day, and look. If the disease has spread in the walls of the house, [40]then the priest shall command that they take out the stones which are affected with the disease and throw them into an unclean place outside the city. [41]He shall have the inside of the house scraped all around, and the clay that they scrape off they shall pour out in an unclean place outside the city. [42]Then they shall take other stones and put them in the place of those stones, and he shall take other clay and plaster the house. [43]If the disease breaks out again in the house, after he has taken out the stones and scraped the house and plastered it, [44]then the priest shall go and look. If the disease has spread in the house, it is a persistent leprous disease in the house; it is unclean. [45]The house shall be torn down – its stones and timber and all the clay of the house, and taken outside the city to an unclean place.

[46]‘Whoever enters the house while it is isolated shall be unclean until the evening, [47]and whoever sits in the house shall wash his clothes, and whoever eats in the house shall wash his clothes.

[48]‘But if the priest comes and looks, and if the disease has not spread in the house after the house was plastered, then the priest shall pronounce the house clean, for the disease is healed. [49]For making the house uncovered he shall take two small birds, with cedar wood, scarlet yarn and hyssop, [50]and shall kill one of the birds in an earthenware vessel over fresh water [51]and shall take the cedar wood, hyssop and the scarlet yarn, along with the live bird, and dip them in the blood of the bird that was killed and in the fresh water and sprinkle the house seven times. [52]Thus he shall make the house uncovered with the blood of the bird and with the fresh water and with the live bird and with the cedar wood, hyssop and scarlet yarn. [53]Then he shall let the live bird go out of the city into the open country. So he shall make propitiation for the house, and it shall be clean.’

[54]This is the teaching of any case of leprous disease: for an itch, [55]for leprous disease in a garment or in a house, [56]and for a swelling or an eruption or a spot, [57]to show when it is unclean and when it is clean. This is the teaching of leprous disease.

Notes on the text

2. How the clause *wĕhubbā’ ’el hakkôhēn* relates to the preceding *bĕyôm ṭohorātô* is variously understood. Most versions (RSV, NRSV, NASB, ESV) take 2b (*wĕhubbā’* ff.) as the new beginning of the prescription. But this majority view is inaccurate, since it produces the sense that the leper meets the priest somewhere he has not been. Since the next verse says it is the priest who goes to the recovered person, the NIV’s rendering ‘when he is brought to the priest’, which speaks *generally* of the following, is more accurate. See ‘Comment’ on 13:2.

4. ‘live’: *ḥayyôt* As Milgrom proposes, this may mean ‘wild’, on the ground that 'live birds' seems overly self-evident (1991: 832). However, as Milgrom admits, one should not overlook the fact that the common term *ḥāy* is attributed both to the birds and to water (vv. 4–5). The addition of this term, if not redundant, may aim to stress the idea that these birds and water give life to the healed leper.

7. 'pronounce him clean': *ṭiharô* LXX adds 'and he shall be clean', probably taking the verb as factitive, not declarative.

10. 'two male lambs without blemish' LXX and SamP add 'one year old', which appears logical but textually uncertain (cf. 9:3; 12:6).

'log' *HALOT* defines this as 'a small liquid measure'. This term occurs only in this chapter in the OT (vv. 10, 12, 15, 21, 24). The exact amount is uncertain, but one log is equivalent to 0.5 litres (Powell 1992: 904).

'ephah' The volume of an ephah is also uncertain, but according to Powell (1992: 903) is between ten and twenty litres.

17. 'on top of the blood of': *'al dam* Ancient versions (LXX, Syr and TgJon) read 'on the place of the blood of' etc., conforming it to v. 28.

22. *'eḥād ... hā'eḥād*: 'the one ... the other' LXX and other ancient versions read def. art. for both words, in conformity with v. 31. MT can be justified in view of 15:15.

31. 'whichever he can afford': *'et 'ăšer taśśîg yādô* Based on LXX, Syr and Vg, most modern exegetes delete this because of an apparent dittography with the same expression at the end of v. 30. However, note that *'ăšer taśśîg yādô* appears in v. 22, where it is unnecessary in terms of prescription (cf. v. 21). See 'Comment'.

34. 'When': *kî* This time designation refers to the general rather than the exact time. The same is true for *kî* in 19:23; 23:10; 25:2.

36. *Yiṭmā'* is variously rendered 'be declared unclean' (RSV, ESV), 'will be pronounced unclean' (NIV), 'need not become unclean' (NASB), 'may become unclean' (JPS), 'will become unclean' (NRSV), partly depending on how the clause *kol 'ăšer babbayit yiṭmā'* as a whole should be construed. However, *yiṭmā'* is not a pi. form, so the translations of RSV, ESV and NIV are unlikely. It simply means to 'become unclean'.

41. 'scrape': *yaqṣî'* This verb *qṣ'* hiph. occurs only here in the OT. Given that the subject is the priest, it must have a causative meaning, to 'make someone to scrape'.

'clay': *hē'āpār* This word occurs again in v. 42b, and ESV renders it 'plaster'. It actually means 'plaster dust'.

Hiqṣû (pour out) is a hapax legomenon and is generally emended to *hiqṣî'*, as in v. 41a (*HALOT*). Though it has some support in ancient versions (LXX, Syr, TgJon), another occurrence in v. 43 makes it unlikely that both occurrences resulted from scribal error. Since *qṣh* pi. means to 'break off, chop off', it may mean to 'scrape off' (cf. Youngblood 1997: 962). A play on the assonance between *yaqṣî'* and *hiqṣû* is more likely intended.

44. 'persistent': *mam'eret* Cf. 13:51–52.

49. 'making (the house) uncovered': *ḥiṭṭē'* See 'Comment' on 8:15.

Form and structure

The first half of this chapter deals with a case where a leprous person is healed (vv. 1–32). The second concerns a case of a *ṣāra'at*-afflicted house (vv. 33–53). The purification rites in the first half are new, though thematically they continue the previous chapter. On the other hand, the ritual procedure for the *ṣāra'at*-stricken house can be seen as a further development where *ṣāra'at* develops outside the human body: in a house. Not only does a case called 'persistent *ṣāra'at*' appear in both sections (13:51–52; 14:44), but the symptoms are common to those for clothes and articles in 13:47–58 in that they are 'greenish' or 'reddish' (13:49; 14:37). Moreover it is apparent that one of the two criteria, namely the diseased spot that appears deeper than the skin introduced in 13:3, is consistently applied to 13:47–58 and 14:33–53.

The material in chs. 13 – 14 is arranged as follows.

Ch. 13	A	*Ṣāra'at* on skin (1–46)
	B	*Ṣāra'at* on clothes and articles (47–58)
		Subscript (59)
Ch. 14	A′	Purification of the person who was healed from *ṣāra'at* (1–20)
		A concession to the poor (21–32)
	B′	*Ṣāra'at* on a house and its purification (33–53)
		Subscript (54–57)

The human *ṣāra'at* in A is followed by its purificatory ritual in A′, while the *ṣāra'at* on inanimate objects, such as clothes and articles in B, is followed by another instance of the *ṣāra'at* on an inanimate object: *ṣāra'at* on a house, in B′. Within ch. 14 the purificatory ritual prescribed for a healed leper in vv. 4–7 is applied to the purificatory ritual for the house cured of *ṣāra'at* (vv. 49–53). Thus the two chapters reflect a considered scheme of arrangement.

The later it appears in the literary corpus of chs. 13 – 14, the further removed is the *ṣāra'at* from the Israelites themselves. A healing from *ṣāra'at* in A′ would be rare (see 'Comment' on v. 3). In B′ the setting is the land of Canaan so that the prescription is not immediately relevant to the Israelites. A question naturally arises as to why the lawgiver saw it necessary to give such an unrealistic lengthy prescription (see 'Comment').

Comment

Although ch. 14 is a sequel to ch. 13 in that it contains the purificatory ritual for a healed person, it still conveys its own distinctive message. The prescriptions in ch. 14 consist of the rites necessary for reintegrating a once-leprous person into the covenant community (vv. 1–32) and the case of *ṣāra'at* in a house in the Promised Land and its purificatory ritual (vv. 33–53), both of which are presented as extremely rare cases. Still, the rarity of these cases is used as an occasion to stress the persistent and hiding nature of *ṣāra'at*; hence human stubbornness in hiding oneself. The ritual for the leprous person's reintegration into the camp is contrasted with the prescription in ch. 13, while the prescription for a *ṣāra'at*-afflicted house should be contrasted with all the preceding prescriptions in terms of human stubbornness. More incisively, the first half deals with a case where true purity is actualized, whereas the second half deals with a case of false purity, real uncleanness and most hypocritical situations.

14:1–13

As Wenham commented in the 1970s, the purpose of the ceremony in this chapter is not to cure but to purify the person before the Lord (1979: 207). At the same time it must be underscored that cleanness is different from physical cure: if a person is cured, he or she is not clean in the fullest sense of the word. The ritual for healed persons indicates that if they are physically healed, that is not enough to issue them into the Lord's presence. Also the provision of the ritual should not be taken as meaning that the disease was often healed. If healing ever occurred, it was miraculous (see 'Comment' on v. 3).

The purification of leprous people is performed in three stages: (1) before entering their house (vv. 2–9), (2) on the seventh day (v. 9), and (3) on the eighth day (vv. 10–20). Thus the requirement of these stages of purification indicates that a healthy body does not by itself provide grounds for entering the camp and house, not to mention the Lord's presence. Therefore a strong note of sarcasm is sounded against healthy people who live within the camp, yet potentially hide themselves.

The cleanness granted after each ritual is closely related to the person's location. Thus the ritual as a whole indicates that there are three degrees of cleanness. However, though the cleanness is outer, even from this viewpoint, the principle is that the closer proximity a person has to the Lord, the more demanding the rite becomes for that person. Symbolically the closer a person approaches the Lord, the more spiritually uncovered he or she must become.

1. 'to Moses' Rare is the case where the Lord addresses Moses alone without further commanding him to deliver his message to the Israelites. Such was the case in 5:14 and 6:1[5:20] (see Introduction 5.1.1). The prescription in the previous chapter was addressed to Moses and Aaron (13:1), but here the Lord does not even address Aaron, even though the rites of this chapter are conducted by priests. It is certainly assumed that the prescriptions in both ch. 13 and ch. 14 are to be communicated to the

Israelites, but both 13:1 and 14:1 show that the initial addressees were Moses and Aaron, and Moses alone respectively. Faced with such a situation, Milgrom (1991: 830) speculates that 'originally chaps 13 – 14 were an archival document of the priests, stored in the Temple, and only during the long course of redaction of the Pentateuch was it inserted in its present place'. As contemplated in 13:1, there seems to be an assumption that the prescription in ch. 13 is irrelevant to the Israelites, because, though that prescription is designed for all of the Israelites, the incidence of *ṣāra'at* is infrequent. In a similar vein, that 14:1 mentions neither Aaron nor the Israelites suggests that what is presented in this chapter is much rarer than the condition dealt with in ch. 13, making reference to Aaron and the Israelites unnecessary.

2. 'the leprous person' Though he is healed, he is so called presumably because he is regarded as a leprous person till he presents himself before the priest. However, he is still regarded as living within the realm of *ṣāra'at* until the purificatory rites are completed.

'for the day of his cleansing' As in Lev. 12 (see v. 7), the purification of the disease is distinct from physical recovery (see below).

'he shall be brought to the priest' This is not to say that the leprous person goes to meet the priest while the priest meets him on the way. It is a general statement to the effect that the person is to be brought before the priest for examination.

3. As prescribed in 13:45–46, the leprous person must dwell outside the camp. So the priest, upon hearing the report that the person has recovered, goes out of the camp, to see if the disease has really been healed. In the OT the disease was cured only by miracles (Exod. 4:6–7; 2 Kgs 5:1–14; implicitly in Num. 12:13–15 [note the Hebr. verb *'sp* ni., which means 'be brought in', but later the qal form came to have the sense of 'cure']. See 2 Kgs 5:3, 6–7). In other cases it appears that the disease was regarded as incurable, and was thus presumably a symbol of hopelessness (2 Kgs 7:3–4; 2 Chr. 26:21). It is also remarkable that the Lord punishes those people who trespassed the holy things by inflicting them with *ṣāra'at* (Num. 12:10 [Miriam]; 2 Kgs 5:27 [Gehazi]; 2 Chr. 26:19–20 [Uzziah]), though the cases in Lev. 13 are not presented as the result of rebelliousness.

4. The materials for cleansing (two live clean birds, cedar wood, scarlet yarn and hyssop) are unaffected by the presence of uncleanness: once appointed for the purpose, they symbolize life-giving material, common to animal blood and running water.

'cedar wood' Cedar wood was used abundantly in the construction of the Solomonic temple. In the later literature it symbolized majesty (Ezek. 31:2), beauty and stature (Ezek. 31:3, 8). It possibly symbolizes the same things in the context of Lev. 14, since these are conceivably what the leprous person desires.

'scarlet yarn': *šĕnê hattôla'at* The Hebr. phrase is the same as *tôla'at šānî*, both of which have been translated 'scarlet yarn' or 'crimson yarn'.

This is the material used for making the strips of cloth that cover the Tent of Meeting, the various screens of the sanctuary, including the *pārōket* veil, and the priestly garments (cf. Exod. 25:4; 26:1, 31; 27:16; 28:5 etc.). The choice of this material may be significant in view of the possible parallel between the leper's body and the Tent of Meeting (see below).

'hyssop' Hyssop first appears in the Passover rite (Exod. 12:22) and henceforth frequently appears in purificatory rites (Lev. 14:4, 6, 49, 51–52; Num. 19:6, 18; Ps. 51:7[9]). In contrast to cedar wood, hyssop is a small shrub (cf. 1 Kgs 4:33 [5:13]), the aroma of which may have functioned as a sort of deodorant (Taylor 1997: 334).

It is often considered that hyssop cleanses blood when thrown into it. But it is unlikely that the blood is viewed as unclean; both blood and hyssop combine in the symbolic cleansing of objects.

Thus the four objects of purification are taken from the worlds of fauna and flora. Their collective beauty symbolizes the realm of life and power, which the leprous person has been denied.

5–6. When the materials for purification are ready, the priest commands the offerer to slaughter one of the two birds in an earthenware vessel over fresh water. The running water, in combination with slaughtering, symbolizes the giving of life: the bird gives life by its substitutionary death. All of this enhances the picture of the slaughtered bird as a potent life-giving force. Then the priest takes another live bird, and the cedar wood, scarlet yarn and hyssop he has already prepared, and dips them in the blood of the bird slain over the running water.

7. The priest then sprinkles the diluted blood on the leprous person seven times, thereby purifying him, and lets the living bird go into an open field. By this the uncleanness of the person is symbolically removed.

'sprinkle': *hizzâ* See 'Comment' on 4:5–6. As when the Hebr. verb is conjoined with 'seven times', the phrase occurs only in the contexts of the purification of the Tent or the sancta therein; it is likely the lepers are treated just like the holy Tent (see below).

With regard to its ritual typology this ritual has been viewed as similar in type to the Azazel-goat ritual in ch. 16. It is unnecessary to conclude that differences in the details of the two rites suggest they are unrelated (*pace* Staubli 2002). Their two most significant elements are the same: (1) one living creature (a bird, a goat) is slain, whereas the other (a live bird, a live goat) is spared, and (2) after sprinkling the blood seven times on to defiled objects or a person, the live animal is sent away, thereby taking the uncleanness from the Tent or leprous person. That in both rites uncleanness is transferred from within the Tent or a person to the wilderness or an open field suggests that they aim to safeguard the Tent or the person in the presence of the Lord. In both, however, the 'life' envisaged for the ritual materials does not refer to physical life (the person is healed!) but spiritual life, a life that enables him or her to live before the Lord.

8. 'he who is to be cleansed' The appellation of the 'leprous person' gradually changes as follows: *mĕṣōra'* (v. 2), *haṣṣārûa'* (v. 3), 'he who is to be cleansed' (v. 4), 'he who is to be cleansed from *ṣāra'at*' (v. 7). Henceforth always 'he who is to be cleansed' (vv. 8, 11, 17–19). In keeping in step with the process of the ritual, the gradual change in appellation stresses that to be cleansed before the Lord is the ritual's purpose.

'wash his clothes', 'shaves off all his hair', 'bathe himself in water' The first two rites may well symbolize either that his clothes and hair are free from *ṣāra'at* or a wiping off of the uncleanness that possibly remains. Since this case of *ṣāra'at* is already healed, these rites have nothing to do with the cases of the previous chapter, which assumed the possible presence of *ṣāra'at*. As for 'bathing in water', it occurs only in this verse and the next in this chapter (it occurs frequently in ch. 15.). If the person is not suspected of having *ṣāra'at*, what is the purpose of these rites? A hygienic motive may underlie this regulation on this occasion (see Harrison 1980: 152; Hartley 1992: 195–196). Yet the heightened repetition in the next verse suggests that this collection of rites relates to more than a matter of hygiene. My proposal is that these rites symbolize the spiritual uncovering of a person. That is, because he has been hiding himself from the Lord, he now uncovers himself by the ceremonial washing of his clothes, the shaving of his hair, and his bathing in water. This interpretation is also in keeping with the symbolic meaning of 'clean' (*ṭāhēr*).

'his tent': *'ohŏlô* The choice of this term is deliberate. The 'tent' of ordinary people (as opposed to 'the *Tent* of Meeting') occurs only in Leviticus 14 (vv. 8, 11, 23). Note the concentration of its synonym, 'house' (*bayit*), in the chapter's latter half (vv. 34–55). Moreover it is explicitly stated that for seven days the person has to stay outside the camp. Thus his re-entry into his own 'tent' falls on the same day he presents his offerings to the Lord in the sanctuary: the eighth day. The legislator clearly attempts to highlight a correspondence between the leprous person's tent and the Tent of Meeting, where the Lord dwells (see 'Explanation').

9. On the seventh day the person repeats the same rites with greater thoroughness (cf. v. 8). The order of washing clothes and shaving hair in v. 8 are inverted in v. 9 with the addition of more details on shaving. 'Shaving *all his hair*' is further specified as 'his head', 'his beard' and 'his 'eyebrows', and then it is once again stressed at the end. Further, 'bathing in water' in v. 8 is replaced, using the same Hebr. verb *rāḥaṣ*, with 'washing his flesh in water'.

Undoubtedly these rites are not so much hygienic as symbolic. The rites function to remind the person of the disease he no longer has: his spiritual hiding of himself from the Lord.

10. Having completed the process of cleansing, the man can enter his own tent on the eighth day. On this day he prepares two male lambs, a one-year-old ewe lamb, a loyalty offering of three-tenths of an ephah of choice flour mixed with oil, and one log of oil. All of these are used by the priest to make propitiation (vv. 18–20) for him. These sacrifices would no doubt have been very expensive for a person unable to earn an income (see vv. 21–31). Thus it appears as though his recovery is viewed as far more valuable than the cost of his sacrifices.

'two male lambs, one ewe lamb a year old' One of the two lambs is used for the reparation offering (v. 12). Though it is not explicitly stated for which offering the other lamb is designated, it was presumably designated for the burnt offering because the animal for the burnt offering must be a male (see Lev. 1; Milgrom 1991: 844). Thus the year-old ewe lamb is designated for the sin offering. When a male lamb for the reparation offering is compared with the ram required for the reparation offering in 5:14 – 6:7[5:26], it is inexpensive, which indicates that though the person made a breach of faith in some way, the guilt was of a lesser kind than that envisaged in 5:14 – 6:7[5:26]. This is reasonable, since the person suffered from the disease involuntarily. The same applies to the lamb for the burnt offering. The year-old female lamb used for the sin offering is likewise less expensive than the case for the self-hiding of a lay individual in 4:32–35 or 5:6. But the qualification 'one year old' simultaneously marks the newness of the occasion: his recommencement of living in a relationship with the Lord.

'On the eighth day' See 'Comment' on 9:1.

'one log of oil' See 'Notes on the text'.

'three-tenths of an ephah of choice flour' The specification of the quantity of flour (roughly 4.5 litres) is relatively rare (cf. 5:11; 6:20[13] with 9:4).

For one person to prepare such an expensive offering for his reintegration into the covenant people is extraordinary. Probably the person is viewed as spiritually dead.

11. 'the priest who cleanses (*hakkôhēn hamĕṭahēr*) . . . the person who is to be cleansed (*hā'îš hammiṭṭahēr*)' For the first time in this ceremony the priest is called 'the priest who cleanses', which simultaneously corresponds to the 'person who is to be cleansed'.

12. The priest takes the oil and one lamb for the reparation offering, and waves them before the Lord. For the waving rite, see 'Comment' on 7:30. Both in this verse and the next the legislator is predominantly concerned with the priestly dues.

13. Then the priest slaughters the lamb in a holy place. Up to this point the ritual for the reparation offering follows the direction in 7:1–7.

The phrase *qōdeš qodāšîm* occurs with reference to the priestly prebends. Along with the waving of all the offerings (v. 12), v. 13b concludes by noting what accrues to the priest's work that follows. This way of summarizing the priest's dues at the beginning of the ceremony (vv. 11–13) serves to highlight the most important part of the ritual for the person who was leprous, which follows from v. 14 onwards.

14:14–18

The ritual for the person resembles that for the priestly ordination (8:22–24), when Moses applied the blood of a ram to the same body parts of Aaron and his sons. This is not to say the person becomes a priest. Rather the significance of the rite should be considered within the framework of the overall nature of the ceremony. In the ordination ceremony the animal is a ram, which is costlier than a lamb, and its purpose is to ordain the priestly candidates. In ch. 14 the rite serves to reintegrate the person into the covenant community.

But apart from the differences, the daubing of blood/water on the same specific parts of the body is a common element. It was proposed for ch. 8 that the rite indicates that Aaron and his sons are deemed, or are at least expected to be, equal to the altar: the condition of the priests is reflected in the condition of the altar. Although the person who is leprous is by no means expected to be a priest, it is likely he is expected to be spiritually one with the altar (see below). At any rate, the purification of the person is here achieved in the most potent way imaginable for a lay person.

The central sacrifice is the reparation offering. Given that the person has been hiding himself, symbolized by his *ṣāra'at*, it may appear strange that the central offering is not the sin offering. Two kinds of proposal have been offered thus far. One assumes that the reparation offering deals with an unknown sacrilegious 'sin' that the once-leprous person might have committed. The other assumes that, as the reparation offering deals with loss to God, it deals with compensation for the holy offerings the cured person cannot offer to God during his uncleanness, or for marring the image of God by the disease (see Snaith 1967: 102; Wenham 1979: 210; Hartley 1992: 197). Budd also sees the idea of compensation but conjectures that the offering is compensation for the damage that the priest has received by examining the disease (1996: 206). Since there is no assumption in the text that the once-leprous person has committed any particular offence, this element of the former view must be precluded. However, both views touch upon two important factors of the reparation offering, namely direct infringement against God, thus holiness, and compensation for the damage. Yet, unlike the three cases in 5:14 – 6:7[5:26], the offering here deals with *involuntary* infringement against holiness (cf. the Nazirite case in Num. 6:12), which matches the less expensive material of the offering. The damage to God may well lie in the fact that the once-leprous person dwelt outside the camp, presumably for a long period. Yet this requires explanation, since a person is not necessarily holy if he or she dwells within the camp. At this point it should be recalled that the Tent of Meeting symbolizes the human heart (see 'Explanation' on ch. 9). Thus the reparation offering as the central offering in this ritual evinces the assumption that the once-leprous person has lost his identity in God, which is tangibly expressed by his dwelling outside the camp. In view of my interpretation of ch. 13, that the rules have universal implications, this requirement of the reparation offering hints that all humanity has lost its identity before God.

14. The priest takes some of the blood of the reparation offering and puts it on the lobe of the right ear of the person who was leprous, on the thumb of his right hand, and on the big toe of his right foot. As proposed in ch. 8 (see 'Comment' on 8:23–24), these prominent parts of the body represent the spots where power, mental or physical, is expected to be present. Therefore the application of blood to these areas symbolizes the giving of life to the body, which corresponds to giving spiritual life to the person's spiritual death. Since, however, he has recovered from his disease, this 'life' cannot be physical life, but spiritual life before the Lord. In this regard he is likened to the altar: his re-entry into the people of God is welcomed with extraordinary treatment.

15–18. Oil in the ritual context symbolizes the Lord's presence. But what does sprinkling seven times towards the Tent symbolize? It is unlikely that the rite symbolizes the purification of the oil since it was already authenticated for ritual use when it was presented before the Lord in v. 11. Since the Tent is the symbol of the Lord's presence, the gesture seems to symbolize the priest's desire to receive the Lord's presence (cf. Num. 19:4). More ritually speaking, the oil, by some of it being related to the Tent, a symbol of the Lord's presence, becomes the means by which the same presence is conveyed to the person.

The rites prescribed in vv. 10–18 confirm that the idea of *kipper* lies in bringing the person into a relationship with the Lord by giving life and the Lord's presence to him. But simultaneously the very need for *kipper* assumes the presence of the Lord's wrath against the person who was leprous. Both positive and negative aspects of propitiation are commingled, but the negative is overcome by the positive, for the person becomes clean, and wrath is averted.

14:19–20

After the completion of the ritual for the reparation offering, the priest offers the sin offering, the burnt offering and lastly the loyalty offering. These three kinds of offerings are only briefly mentioned because their rituals are ordinary ones whose details may be presumed from chs. 1 – 7; if a ritual differs from what is conventional it is prescribed explicitly, as occurs for the reparation offering here. The mention of *kipper* (making propitiation) after each ritual indicates that while each offering has its own distinctive function it collectively contributes to the person's reconciliation with the Lord. It is notable that even the loyalty offering has a role in *kipper* (v. 20).

19. The ritual procedure for the sin offering is presumed (see 4:32ff.).

Explicit reference is again made to 'the person who is to be cleansed'. The mention of 'from his uncleanness' as the cause of propitiation indicates, however this phrase is interpreted, that uncleanness is still envisaged at this stage of the ritual. Thus the purification from uncleanness should not be conceived in a mathematical way: though the worshipper's uncleanness has been dealt with in the previous two stages, his uncleanness must be viewed anew before the Lord in the sanctuary. His uncleanness is now seen even more clearly, as though he stepped under a brighter light.

20. Lastly, the burnt offering and the loyalty offering are offered to make propitiation for him. The burnt offering symbolizes the annihilation of all his earthly desires and thus the Lord's acceptance of him, and the loyalty offering symbolizes his allegiance to the Lord alone. In offering these he is once again pronounced 'clean'. The three occurrences of *kipper* (vv. 18–20) as well as the thrice-mentioned 'he is clean' (vv. 8–9, 20) suggest that the person who is to be cleansed approaches the Lord stage by stage.

14:21–32

The lawgiver provides a concession for the case where the person requiring cleansing is poor. More specifically the concession relates to the sin and burnt offerings; they can be substituted by two turtle doves or by pigeons. The ritual of the reparation offering is practically the same as the ordinary one; only the formulation is slightly different (a few items in vv. 10–20 are omitted in this section): (1) No mention is made of the priestly due (see v. 13), probably because previous instructions are assumed to apply in this section as well. (2) The mention of *kipper* (make propitiation) is repeated three times in vv. 18–20, but the *kipper* for the sin offering and the burnt offering along with the loyalty offering is mentioned only once in v. 31. (3) The phrase 'he is clean' at the end of v. 20 is assumed and omitted in v. 31. On the other hand, as required by the particularity of the case, the phrase 'cannot afford' or 'afford' appears frequently, namely in vv. 21–22, 30–31, the latter three occurrences refer to the sin and burnt offerings. These slight differences imply this section is practical, showing the Lord's compassion towards the poor. As Hartley comments, it is most likely the relatives of the person who would have assisted in obtaining the required materials (1992: 198).

The very provision of the concession is not normative. In the rituals of the sin offering, the concession is found only in the cases where the guilt of the offender is conceived as lighter; i.e. in the cases of lay individuals (4:27–35; 5:6–13). Further, within the rituals of the sin offering it is observed that the more exposed the self-hiding is, the more options for the offering are provided. Such is the case with the new mother (12:8). Whereas, if within the cleanness and uncleanness regulations the degree of self-hiding is deemed as high as assumed in the cases of a man suffering from a discharge from his reproductive organ or a woman suffering from blood discharge, no concessionary measures are provided.

22. When concessions are made, as is the case here and in 5:6–13, it is the prescribed purpose of an offering that counts, not the material.

23–24. Cf. v. 12. But vv. 21–24 as a whole are related to vv. 10–12. Note the locations of 'on the eighth day'; namely in vv. 10 and 23.

25. Cf. vv. 13–14.

26. Cf. v. 15.

27. Cf. v. 16.

28. Cf. v. 17.

29. Cf. v. 18.

30–31. These verses address the priest's handling of the offerings other than the reparation offering: the sin, burnt and loyalty offerings. The twice-repeated 'whichever he can afford' may reflect the Lord's compassion for the offerer.

32. This is the summary statement of the concession case alone (vv. 21–31). See 'Comment' on 13:59.

14:33–53

This last section in the series of *ṣāra'at* cases deals with *ṣāra'at* associated with the houses the Israelites will occupy in the Promised Land. For the modern identification of *ṣāra'at* in houses, see 'Form and structure' on ch. 13. The placing of the section at this location, and not immediately after 13:59, is explained formally by the fact that as *ṣāra'at* on houses includes a cured case (v. 48ff.), the section must be placed after the prescription for the healed person in vv. 4–7 (see 'Form and structure'). However, there is another more essential reason that will be revealed by way of the following comments.

Section vv. 34–45 addresses itself only to the case of defilement and purification of a house afflicted with *ṣāra'at*; it does not address itself to a potential case where a house is not proven to be afflicted with *ṣāra'at*. This is due to the section starting from the revelation that the *ṣāra'at* was sent by the Lord. The reader is expected to see irony between this fact and the people's response. The case that the house is proven not to be seriously afflicted by *ṣāra'at* is dealt with in vv. 48–53, which are an alternative to vv. 43–45, the last stage of the first case.

The term *ṣāra'at* occurs only twice in vv. 34, 44. This is not because the term is replaced by a somewhat abbreviated *nega'* (some case of disease) but because the use of the latter reflects a fear or apprehension of the people living in the house that the spot or mark (*nega'*) may be *ṣāra'at*. In fact the mention of *ṣāra'at* in v. 34 is in the protasis, while the term appears only in v. 44 when the case is found to be a 'persistent *ṣāra'at*'. It is clear that the legislator deliberately hides the nature of the case until it is evidently found to be *ṣāra'at*, but where it is too late for the house.

The *reddish* or *greenish* symptom in the white wall signifies that it is a continuation of human *ṣāra'at* dealt with in ch. 13, and that it may well symbolize the presence of the egocentric nature (see below).

Also it is to be recalled (see above) that in the ritual for the purification of human *ṣāra'at* in vv. 2–20, it is tacitly assumed that the leprous person's tent and the Tent of Meeting are essentially one, and for the leprous person to dwell in the house again he must be made clean. In view of this assumption, it is entirely unlikely that while a house is already stricken with *ṣāra'at*, the people living in it are free from *ṣāra'at*. And yet this principle is deliberately not spelled out in the following prescription in order to highlight the human reality that even if the house were to be demolished, its inhabitants would still not admit that they had caused this. Moreover it is noteworthy that *ṣāra'at* is possibly viewed as infectious to some extent (vv. 46–47).

33. Unlike 14:1, where Moses alone is addressed, the Lord addresses Moses *and* Aaron, as he does in 13:1, and this signals the beginning of a new discourse. The assumption that the inclusion of Aaron in this formula suggests that the following instructions relate solely to the priesthood is inaccurate, since the prescription in 14:2–32, addressed solely to Moses, is also preoccupied with the actions of the priests. I have argued that the case of a healed person is extremely rare when there is no miraculous intervention by God. From the viewpoint of practical relevance, the prescription in this section is as relevant to the priesthood as the one in ch. 13. The Israelites are not addressed in either, which suggests that the prescription of this section is irrelevant to the people on a symbolic dimension, though apparently relevant in practice (see below).

34. The prescription will take effect when the Israelites settle in the land of Canaan, which the Lord gives them as a 'possession'. There are only three explicit references to 'Canaan' in Leviticus (14:34; 18:2; 25:38). When no time reference is made in Leviticus, it is assumed that the prescription in question is effective not just in the wilderness but also in Canaan. Thus the explicit specification of time suggests that the prescription in vv. 34ff. has no direct practical relevance to the Israelites at this point, though in so far as it is written down it has some relevance to them. The relevance is highlighted by a similar procedure to that applied to *ṣāra'at* on human beings, clothes and articles being prescribed for *ṣāra'at* in a house.

The latter half of this verse is highly significant: it says, 'I put a case of leprous disease in a house in the land of your possession'. 'Your (pl.)' refers to Moses and Aaron. This is the first time in chs. 13 – 14 that *ṣāra'at* is said to be sent by the Lord, though this is not to say that the one in ch. 13 is also assumed to be sent by the Lord. The idea that the Lord sends *ṣāra'at* into his own land may well be punitive, but it is also purificatory, since manifestations of *ṣāra'at* lead a person along the road to cleanness.

Now it must be observed that the ritual deals with the final stage of *ṣāra'at* when it appears on the wall of a house, which means that the *ṣāra'at* was hidden in the house long before its occupants found it. The explicit mention of its divine origin in v. 34 serves to stress the point, as background knowledge for the reader, that the following prescription deals with an unmistakable case of *ṣāra'at*.

'a possession': *'aḥuzzâ* In Leviticus the term occurs only here and in chs. 25 (thirteen times) and 27 (five times). The idea that the 'possession' is a gift from the Lord (Gen. 17:8; 48:4; Lev. 25:34; see Koopmans 1997: 359) contributes to creating the ironic situation where the Lord has marred his own gift.

'leprous disease' Significantly this term occurs only twice in vv. 33–53; i.e. vv. 34 and 44, where the possibility of the disease becomes a reality. Therefore until v. 44 the people dwelling in the house are uncertain whether the symptoms are those of *ṣāra'at* or if it was sent from the Lord.

How painful it would be for the Lord to send *ṣāra'at* on the very land he gave the Israelites as a gift! It is not known if there was some prior cause. At any rate, given that *ṣāra'at* symbolizes the human egocentric nature and its resultant self-hiding, it is because of the people's self-hiding that the Lord sent the disease.

35. This verse describes what occurs in the human realm as opposed to the divine providential realm mentioned in v. 34. In so far as the man reports the spot to the priest, he must suspect that it may be something ominous.

'tell': *higgîd* The Hebr. verb has a nuance stronger than 'say' or 'report'. See 5:1. The candidness of the report provides a striking contrast with the passiveness or unwillingness of the leprous person brought to the priest in ch. 13 (e.g. 13:2), perhaps because the house's owner assumes that the case has nothing to do with himself.

'some case of disease': *kĕnega'* In Hebr. the passage is constructed impersonally. Lit. 'It appears to me to be like a "spot" in the house'. Hebr. *nega'* refers to a 'spot' that may or may not be *ṣāra'at*. The term *nega'* is used in the following prescription until the case evidently becomes one of *ṣāra'at* in v. 44.

36. From this verse begins the apodosis of vv. 34–35. The occupants are commanded to remove the house's contents before the priest enters it to examine the spot, thereby ensuring that nothing in the house becomes defiled. Hartley's comment 'This step forcefully indicates that a growth did not make something unclean until a priest had officially pronounced it unclean' (1992: 198) is wrong. The existence of the *ṣāra'at* cannnot be separated from the state of being unclean (see 'Comment' on 13:3–5). The term 'become unclean' is ritualistic, not hygienic. Moreover there seems to be an assumption that if one item in the house is afflicted with the disease, the whole house becomes defiled.

37–38. When the priest looks at the spot, and the spot is greenish or reddish and it appears deeper than the surface of the wall, he orders the quarantining of the house for seven days. The two diagnostic criteria resemble those of other cases of *ṣāra'at* in ch. 13. But while whiteness is used as one of the criteria for diagnosing *ṣāra'at* in human beings, only greenness or redness is used in relation to house-related *ṣāra'at*. These latter colours would indicate that the wall was white (see v. 42). Obviously these two symptoms provide ample evidence for the priest to make a diagnosis, but to ascertain if the spot really is leprous, another criterion, namely its propensity to spread, is given. Though it would seem most likely that it is a case of *ṣāra'at*, the measure taken indicates that the Lord leaves the matter as it is. No possibility is envisaged that the case may not be that of *ṣāra'at*. The role of the priest is to make a judgment, as the matter grows worse and worse.

At the initial stage when the two criteria are met, it is probable that the case is *ṣāra'at*. But the prescription does not say this until the stones are replaced and the wall is plastered again with new plaster and seven days have passed. Also the grand-scale refurbishing of the house's interior may well alert the people who engage with the work that the case is one of *ṣāra'at*.

39–40. The priest once again examines the spot on the seventh day. If the spot has spread on the wall, the removal of the stones where the spot has spread is required. They should be thrown in an unclean place outside the city. 'An unclean place' (v. 40; see also vv. 41, 45 below) is grammatically in apposition to 'outside the city', but the whole area outside the city is not to be viewed as unclean: it is just that there is an unclean place outside the city. But this, in turn, implies that the city area is clean. At any rate, the priest orders the people to do so because he has concluded that the spot is *ṣāra'at*. Though his judgment is not mentioned in the text, it is implied.

The phrase 'unclean place' occurs only in ch. 13 in the whole OT (see vv. 41, 45, and cf. Jer. 19:13). It does not mean that it is a physically dirty place. 'Unclean' is a ritual term, and since it is never used without referring to a relationship with the Lord, it is a spiritual one. Further there is no place intrinsically 'unclean', though people may appoint a particular place as unclean.

It is clear that the house was stricken with *ṣāra'at*. The assumption that the place is unclean while the city is supposedly clean creates the incongruity that already inside the city there is an unclean place: the house afflicted with *ṣāra'at*. Most importantly, the threefold mention of 'outside the city, to an unclean place' (vv. 40–41, 45) creates a stark contrast with the putative cleanness the people removing the stones may have assumed in themselves. When it is considered that this case is undoubtedly one of *ṣāra'at*, even one sent by the Lord, these directions may reflect the occupant's attitude to the case that he has nothing to do with *ṣāra'at* himself. That the examined house has been defiled by *ṣāra'at* is, at any rate, indicated by vv. 46–47 below.

These considerations suggest that those people who took the stones out and threw them into the unclean place are unclean themselves (see 'Comment' on 4:12 and 6:4)! In other words, the expression 'unclean place' reflects both the house owner's consciousness that he is clean, and the Lord's evaluation that he is unclean.

41–42. The second reference to the unclean place makes it even comical that the more they throw the clay into the unclean place, the more they are confronted with the unwelcome fact that the house is seriously infected by *ṣāra'at*. It is strange that neither the priest nor the people, who engage in the demolition of the infected wall, explicitly indicate that the house was afflicted with *ṣāra'at*, a situation that possibly reflects their dull spiritual sense.

43–45. If after all this the spot manifests itself again and spreads in the house, the priest examines it and confirms that it is a malignant case of *ṣāra'at*, and commands the people to demolish the house, namely its stones, wood and clay, and to throw them into an unclean place outside the city. This case is similar to the *ṣāra'at*-stricken clothes or articles that must be burnt, in that both cases are called 'persistent (*mam'eret*) *ṣāra'at*' (cf. 13:51ff.). This implies that not just the people who carried the debris outside the city but also the house's occupants were stricken by *ṣāra'at*, though this is not stated. The third mention of 'an unclean place' (v. 45; see on v. 40) underscores this possibility.

14:46–53

This section presents additional regulations while the house is quarantined (vv. 46–47) and an alternative condition of the house where, after plastering, the spot does not spread. It finishes with the purificatory ritual required by such a case (vv. 48–53). The placing of this section after the rules on the case where the spot is undoubtedly one of *ṣāra'at*, rather than juxtaposing the two possibilities, as in ch. 13, derives at least from the fact that vv. 35–45 are a clear case (at least, for the readership) of *ṣāra'at*, as indicated by v. 34.

14:46–47

These verses deal with the contagion of uncleanness during the house's quarantine period. It is the first explicit reference in chs. 13 – 14 to the possibility that the *ṣāra'at* is infectious to some extent.

As 'while it is isolated' indicates, these verses refer back to the early stage of its examination by the priest in v. 38. During this period, anyone entering the house becomes unclean until evening. V. 47 stipulates that anyone who sits and eats in the house becomes unclean and must wash his clothes. It is unclear at first whether v. 47 constitutes a subcase of v. 46, or presents an alternative to v. 46. However, since it is unlikely that someone enters the house during its quarantine, v. 47 appears to present a separate rule, though v. 47 can include v. 46. The requirement for washing clothes indicates that it deals with a greater degree of defilement than in the case of a person waiting until evening. But more importantly, these additional rules imply that the people who used to occupy the house have already become even more defiled.

The mention of 'sits' (*haššōkēb*) first occurs here in Leviticus, and it adumbrates the regulation in ch. 15 (vv. 4, 20, 24, 26, 33).

The significance of washing clothes lies in the realm of purification, but it is also a gesture that pictorially represents the wiping off of any possible uncleanness from the person.

14:48–57

As v. 48 indicates, this section presents a possible parallel case to vv. 43–45. The placing of this section at the end of the prescription on the *ṣāra'at*-afflicted house is caused partly by the assumption that the case dealt with in this section is extremely rare, and partly and significantly by the structural and ideological scheme that attempts to contrast the ritual with the same ritual given in vv. 3–7.

First, with an awareness of the incorrigible stubbornness of the human heart that is related to the way the foregoing prescription is formulated, the 'healing' of the house would be even more unthinkable than the appearing of *ṣāra'at* on the house's walls. Again, as in vv. 2–7, the house's new-found *ṣāra'at*-free status does not mean it is clean before the Lord; hence the need for a purification ritual. Unlike the leprous person who had to stay outside the camp, the house could not move outside the city: the house, with all its uncleanness, remained in a supposedly clean area! Just as the leprous person needed propitiation (*kipper)* when he presented himself before the Lord, the house needs propitiation, since it has been defiling the city. This explains the mention of *kipper* in v. 53, which is lacking at the end of the bird rite in vv. 2–7.

Second and structurally, vv. 48–53 not only form an inclusio with the ritual in vv. 3–7; they leave the reader with the odd impression that while the bird rite purified the once-leprous *person*, the same rite does not deal with the purification of the *occupants* of the *ṣāra'at*-stricken house. Concentration on the purification of the house in this section and not of its occupants casts serious doubt on the 'clean' state of the occupants. Thus this prescription points ironically to the occupants' need for purification, and hence the incorrigible stubbornness of the occupants adumbrates the ritual of ch. 16 where both the Tent and the people are purified.

48. If the priest comes and examines the newly plastered house, and confirms that the previous spot has not spread, he pronounces the house clean because the spot is 'healed' (*nirpā*'; cf. 14:3). Since the case deals with the stage parallel to vv. 43–45, while the spot was already *ṣāra'at* in the previous cases, it would be extremely rare for the house to be 'healed' of its affliction.

49–52. The purpose of the ritual is twice specified as *ḥiṭṭē*' in vv. 49 and 52. As argued elsewhere (Kiuchi 2003a: 107–118), *ḥiṭṭē*' means to 'uncover' or 'make something or someone uncovered', and not 'decontaminate' or 'purge' as has been commonly assumed. In this ritual in particular, uncleanness materially conceived does not fit with the circumstance that the house was already free from *ṣāra'at*. In other words, the following ritual aims at uncovering the *ṣāra'at*-stricken house before the Lord.

Before the release, in v. 53, of the live bird into the open country the legislator mentions that the ritual succeeds in 'making the house uncovered'. This corresponds to the situation in v. 7, where the priest's purification is located between the sevenfold sprinkling and the dispatch of the live bird. Thus it may be inferred that *ḥiṭṭē*' and *ṭihar* (to cleanse) are synonymous in their reference to purification. However, *ḥiṭṭē*' describes the very process of uncovering, while *ṭihar* describes a change of status, from unclean to clean.

53. The ritual concludes with the release of the live bird, and the effect is described as making propitiation for the house (*kipper 'al habbayit*) 'The open country' does not mean some 'unclean' place.

With regard to the Hebr. term *kipper*, it is significant that it is stated after the release of the live bird and before the statement 'It shall be clean'. The whole ritual process from v. 49 to v. 53a aims at purification, the core of which is expressed by *ḥiṭṭē*', while the overall description is given by *kipper*, and the last status of the house by *ṭāhēr*. A similar ideological relation is found in ch. 16, where the Azazel goat also functions to make propitiation (see 16:10, 21).

In v. 7 there was no mention of *kipper* nor 'uncovering' (*ḥiṭṭē*'). However, a similar idea underlies v. 7 as well. It may be noted that in the purification of a *ṣāra'at*-afflicted person, *kipper* is most frequently used in the final stage of the ritual in the sanctuary (see vv. 18–20).

54–56. These verses are a summary statement regarding the various rules in chs. 13 – 14 headed by 'This is the teaching', which is repeated at the end of v. 57.

Explanation

The series of purificatory rites in vv. 2–32 reveal varying degrees of cleanness and make clear that the cleanness associated with mere physical recovery does not qualify a person to approach the Lord. Moreover, since cleanness symbolically refers to the state of being uncovered, the varying degrees correspond to different levels of uncovering. The closer a person approaches the Lord, the cleaner he must be. However, this idea is entirely different from the common or traditional understanding of purity where either amoral 'cultic' purity or some moral purity is assumed. Uncovering oneself means uncovering what one is: it does not mandate the rectification of particular moral conduct. Humans are imperfect and make mistakes, even hide from God, but cleanness symbolically refers to the condition of the heart, where people expose their whole condition before the Lord. Above all, in this purificatory process, people must uncover that they have been hiding themselves, not to mention any particular immoral conduct. Essentially, to hide is to be in a state of death before the Lord. The joyous occasion of the spiritual rebirth is unreservedly portrayed by the ritual prescription for putting blood on particular parts of the body (cf. Luke 15:11–24).

On a symbolic dimension this complicated purificatory ritual in vv. 2–32 casts an incisive irony over the previous regulations where people are pictured as trying to hide themselves *within the camp*. It is ironic in that this suggests the occupants of the camp must be clean, having undergone such a purificatory process. Yet the rules in ch. 13 strongly imply that such is not the case.

On the other hand, the prescription relating to *ṣāra'at* in a house and its associated purificatory ritual deals with the presence of uncleanness inside the city, a supposedly clean area. Thus the purification ritual in 14:2–31 forms a contrast with the prescription for *ṣāra'at* in a house in so far as the former deals with the entry of an unclean person into the 'clean' camp, whereas the latter deals with the presence of uncleanness within the 'clean' city. There is an assumed correlation between the house and its occupants. The occupants or other people who obey the priest's instructions are ironically, even comically, portrayed as those who do their best to pretend to be clean. In this respect, this final prescription is similar to the early part of ch. 13, where people try to hide themselves, while it is sharply contrastive with the early part of ch. 14.

Relatively speaking, which condition is healthier? The presence of uncleanness outside the camp requiring a series of purificatory rites for cleansing (vv. 1–32), or the presence of uncleanness within the camp (vv. 33–53)? Definitely the former (see 'Explanation' on 5:14 – 6:7[5:26]). Thus by juxtaposing two contrastive unrealistic cases, the healed person and the *ṣāra'at* in the house, the legislator stresses the potential appalling intractability of human self-hiding in the present and in the future. At the same time, the *ṣāra'at* in the house adumbrates ch. 16, where the uncleanness of the people living inside the camp is addressed in a double sense, in terms of the two-birds ritual and the presence of uncleanness inside the camp or a city.

The persistent propensity for self-hiding, of the Israelites in particular, is tacitly but strongly condemned in such a way that they do not easily admit their own guilt of self-hiding even when disasters or catastrophes befall them, such as are typically portrayed by the demolition of a house. It is even doubtful whether men see disasters or catastrophes themselves as being sent by God. While the latter are not necessarily the outcome of their own self-hiding, they are meant to serve as an occasion to reflect on their own ways. The time specification, effective from the beginning of life in Canaan, makes their stubbornness ever more hopeless. In fact the Israelites did not admit that various disasters and catastrophes were the result of their own self-hiding from the Lord. For instance, both in the Assyrian invasion of the northern kingdom and the Babylonian siege of Jerusalem the Israelites did not fully recognize their guilt (cf. Jer. 31:30; Ezek. 18:2; further see Kiuchi 2003a: 72–83).

Working from the symbolic meaning of *ṣāra'at*, then, all humanity, particularly the Israelites, are to live in their tents and meet the Lord only by undergoing a systematic spiritual uncovering of themselves. This, however, appears to be felt as inconceivable by the Lord, implied both by the fact that the Lord addresses the prescription only to Moses (v. 1), as well as by the likelihood that the disease is apparently conceived as incurable.

Thus hopelessness hovers over all humanity regarding the salvation of their hearts and souls, and casts a dark shadow on both the preceding and following chapters. The only way to salvation is to uncover oneself before the Lord (13:12–13).

Body-tent symbolism

The purificatory process for the healed person corresponds to that of the altar or chief priest, and also suggests that his body is the equivalent to his tent (see 'Comment' on v. 8). Some further evidence for this claim is provided below.

First of all, the tent (*'ōhēl*) of the unclean person (v. 8) is literarily associated with the Tent of Meeting (*'ōhēl mô'ēd*, v. 11). By implying that the day he enters his own tent is the same day he approaches the Tent of Meeting, the prescription suggests that his tent is substantially and spiritually the same as the Lord's Tent of Meeting.

Additional evidence for the relationship between a house and its occupant is found in the legislator's personification of the house. For example: (1) 'The disease is healed' (*nirpā' hannega'*, 14:48) is very similar to v. 3b. Though it is not said in 14:48 that the house is healed, the statement indicates that the *ṣāra'at* is the same as the *ṣāra'at* found on human beings. (2) Making propitiation (*kipper*) for the leprous person (vv. 18–20) parallels that undertaken for the house (v. 53b). Since the house appears inseparable from its occupants, its healing and purification from *ṣāra'at* implies that its occupants are likewise healed and purified. This correlation between house and occupants adumbrates the ritual in ch. 16. But here in 14:32–53 the whole purificatory ritual ironically highlights the persistent tendency of humans to hide themselves by concentrating on the purification of the house, the most immediate human environment apart from clothes (13:47–58).

The rite of applying the blood of the reparation offering to the prominent parts of the worshipper also reflects the same principle: the once-leprous person is now treated as though he is an altar or chief priest. The exposed condition of the person, which symbolically represents the uncovering of his heart, must also be the condition when he presents himself before the Lord. In other words, it is assumed that a person's dwelling place is a sanctuary: if a person is unclean in his house, he is likewise unclean in the Lord's dwelling place. Furthermore, since in the sanctuary the priest deals with the spiritual condition of the person (uncleanness), it can be inferred that the purificatory rites through outward gestures deal ultimately with his heart and soul. Thus not only is the house a sanctuary, but the person living in the house is a sanctuary, as are his heart and soul. This corroborates the fact regarding the sin offering that when one commits self-hiding, it defiles the sancta.

The body symbolism in vv. 2–20 gives additional ironic meaning to the case of *ṣāra'at* on houses in vv. 33–58. Indeed in the latter the prescription is formulated as though the house's occupant is distinct from the house, but this aims to highlight the unconscious hypocrisy of the occupant, as the case of *ṣāra'at* on clothes did in 13:47–58.

New Testament implications

The New Testament contains several accounts where Jesus heals lepers (Matt. 8:3; Mark 1:42; Luke 5:12–13). It is part of his messianic mission to heal the sick, among whom the lepers are counted (Matt. 10:8; 11:5; Luke 7:22). However, on the whole, the healed lepers are apparently unaware, or show no concern for, the symbolic meaning of their disease. Once they are healed, they nearly forget the Saviour (Luke 5:12–13; 17:11–19). The term 'clean' or 'cleanse' has become roughly synonymous with 'healing' (see Lev. 15:13, 28; 2 Kgs 5:10, 12–14). For the Pharisaic lifestyle, see 'Explanation' on ch. 13.

Indeed the Gospels appear to convey the message that it is more miraculous to be spiritually revived than to be healed from *ṣāra'at*. At the same time, Jesus' ministry to the sick is part of his overall mission to the poor and needy who live on the periphery of society, so on the whole his ministry casts irony on the 'people of God' inside the camp, who show disrespect towards, and discriminate against, *ṣāra'at*-afflicted persons. Those people inside the camp must, in the first place, be those who have gone through such a complicated purificatory process, but the reality is that they simply 'plaster' their outside rather than their inside (cf. Matt. 23:27; Acts 23:3).

It is in the Pauline epistles, particularly in Rom. 7:7–23, that the symbolic meaning of *ṣāraʿat* finds its concrete and definitive illustration. Paul knows God's law, but somehow does what he does not really want. This is the very condition referred to by the term 'unclean'. But he makes this confession consciously by recollecting his past or contemporary experience, hence his painful conscience. There is a world of difference between being conscious of one's own uncleanness and being unconscious of it: the former state is one of cleanness, while the latter is the very meaning of uncleanness. It is by his grace that Jesus saves Paul in the state the apostle is in. Paul is saved because he uncovers himself before the Lord.

This is not the place to discuss the NT idea of cleanness and holiness, but uncovering oneself is the way to cleanness and the prerequisite to holiness, unlike the popular idea that one becomes clean by improving one's own conduct. Indeed Paul's frequent mention of the believer's outward conduct has led many theologians to infer that cleanness results also from remedying outward conduct. But this inference may be simplistic, for it is more likely that Paul mentioned those statements as an encouragement to believers who consistently forget the foundation of Jesus' grace, and it is not his intention that they become legalistic. All his apparent references to the Law derive from the fact that the audience or readers of his epistles habitually tend to hide themselves, a matter that belongs to their hearts. However, Christ manifests himself when people uncover themselves, being powerless, or preferably remaining powerless.

LEVITICUS 15:1–33

Translation

1The LORD spoke to Moses and Aaron, saying, 2'Speak to the Israelites and say
to them, When any man has a discharge from his body, his discharge is unclean.
3This is the teaching of his uncleanness for a discharge: whether his body runs with
his discharge, or his body is blocked up by his discharge, it is his uncleanness.
4Every bed on which the one with the discharge lies shall be unclean, and everything
on which he sits shall be unclean. 5Anyone who touches his bed shall wash his
clothes and bathe himself in water and be unclean until the evening. 6Whoever sits
on anything on which the one with the discharge has sat shall wash his clothes and
bathe himself in water and be unclean until the evening. 7Whoever touches the body
of the one with the discharge shall wash his clothes and bathe himself in water and
be unclean until the evening. 8If the one with the discharge spits on someone who is
clean, then he shall wash his clothes and bathe himself in water and be unclean until
the evening. 9Any saddle on which the one with the discharge rides shall be unclean.
10Whatever touches anything that was under him shall be unclean until the evening.

And whoever carries such things shall wash his clothes and bathe himself in water and be unclean until the evening. [11]Anyone whom the one with the discharge touches without having rinsed his hands in water shall wash his clothes and bathe himself in water and be unclean until the evening. [12]An earthenware vessel that the one with the discharge touches shall be broken, and every vessel of wood shall be rinsed in water. [13]When the one with a discharge is cleansed of his discharge, then he shall count for himself seven days for his cleansing, and wash his clothes. And he shall bathe his body in fresh water and shall be clean. [14]On the eighth day he shall take two turtle doves or two pigeons and come before the LORD to the entrance of the Tent of Meeting and give them to the priest. [15]And the priest shall use them, one for a sin offering and the other for a burnt offering. And the priest shall make propitiation for him before the LORD for his discharge.

[16]'If a man has an emission of semen, he shall bathe his whole body in water and be unclean until the evening. [17]Every garment and every skin on which the semen comes shall be washed with water and be unclean until the evening.

[18]'If a man lies with a woman and has an emission of semen, both of them shall bathe themselves in water and be unclean until the evening.

[19]'When a woman has a discharge, and the discharge in her body is blood, she shall be in her menstrual impurity for seven days, and whoever touches her shall be unclean until the evening. [20]Everything on which she lies during her menstrual impurity shall be unclean. Everything also on which she sits shall be unclean. [21]Whoever touches her bed shall wash his clothes and bathe himself in water and be unclean until the evening. [22]Whoever touches anything on which she sits shall wash his clothes and bathe himself in water and be unclean until the evening. [23]Whether something is on the bed or on anything on which she sits, when he touches it he shall be unclean until the evening. [24]And if by any chance any man lies with her and her menstrual impurity comes upon him, he shall be unclean seven days, and every bed on which he lies shall be unclean.

[25]'If a woman has a discharge of blood for many days, not at the time of her menstrual impurity, or if she has a discharge beyond the time of her impurity, all the days of the discharge she shall continue in uncleanness. As in the days of her menstruation, she shall be unclean. [26]Every bed on which she lies, all the days of her discharge, shall be to her as in the bed of her menstrual impurity. Everything on which she sits shall be unclean, as in the uncleanness of her menstrual impurity. [27]Whoever touches these things shall be unclean, and shall wash his clothes and bathe himself in water and be unclean until the evening. [28]If she is cleansed of her discharge, she shall count for herself seven days, and after that she shall be clean. [29]On the eighth day she shall take two turtle doves or two pigeons and bring them to the priest, to the entrance of the Tent of Meeting. [30]And the priest shall use one for a sin offering and the other for a burnt offering. And the priest shall make propitiation for her before the LORD for the discharge of her uncleanness.

[31]'Thus you shall consecrate the Israelites away from their uncleanness, lest they die in their uncleanness by defiling my tabernacle that is in their midst.'

[32]This is the teaching for him who has a discharge and for him who has an emission of semen, becoming unclean thereby; [33]also for her who is unwell with her

menstrual impurity, that is, for anyone, male or female, who has a discharge, and for the man who lies with a woman who is unclean.

Notes on the text

2. 'say to them': *'amartem* Although LXX renders the verb in sg., Moses and Aaron are commanded to deliver the message to the Israelites. Further, the 2 m. pl. forms an inclusion with v. 31, where again Moses and Aaron are addressed.

'any man': *'îš 'îš* The idiom appears for the first time here in Leviticus and occurs increasingly frequent from here on, particularly in chs. 17ff. (cf. 17:3, 8, 10, 13 etc.). Contextually it clearly refers to males alone. So it means 'any man' rather than 'everyone'. More specifically the term refers to a man as opposed to a woman. When an interpersonal relationship between man and woman is not in view, *'ādām* is used (see 'Comment' on 1:2; 13:2).

'his body': *bĕśārô* It euphemistically refers to his penis. But note that later in this chapter *bāśār* is used to mean 'a body' (vv. 7, 13, 16).

3. 'is blocked up': *heḥtîm* The hiph. of *ḥtm* occurs as a hapax legomenon. Since it is followed by *min*, its meaning would be intransitive, 'be blocked up'.

'runs': *rār* This term is also a hapax legomenon. It means to 'secrete' (*HALOT*).

'blocked up by his discharge' SamP and LXX, while they differ from each other slightly, give an additional passage. LXX, for instance, reads after 'by his discharge' (*mizzōbô*), 'he is unclean during the entire period his body is discharging or his body is blocked by his discharge; it is his uncleanness'. Apparently this addition is supported by 11QPaleoLev. So it is possible to suppose that the section fell out of the MT by homoioteleuton. However, if so, the exact text cannot be ascertained due to small differences between SamP, LXX and 11PaleoLev. See Freedman and Matthews 1985: 32–33. Alternatively there is also the possibility that the addition was made in conformity with v. 25b (cf. 'Notes' below on vv. 14 and 27).

13. 'count': *sāpar* This term occurs here for the first time in Leviticus. Henceforth it occurs in 15:28; 23:15–16; 25:8.

'fresh water' Washing in fresh water is unique not only in Leviticus but in the whole OT.

'his body': *bĕśārô* Simultaneously it may mean his genitals; i.e. a double entendre.

14. 'and come': *ubā'* LXX, Syr and TgJon appear to harmonize the verb with *bw'* hiph. in v. 29. But as explained in 'Comment', it is stressed here that the man comes in person before the Lord.

19. 'in her body': *bibĕśārāh* As in v. 2 'body' refers euphemistically to her genitals.

23. ‘something is on the bed’: *‘al hammiškāb hû’* It appears ambiguous what *hû’* refers to at first sight. Most versions appear to take it as copulative, and understand that the verse deals with a case where a person touches either the bed or any article the woman uses. But in that case, the verse would say the same thing as vv. 21–22. Elberfelder is right in taking *hû’* as referring to ‘something’, probably the rule in v. 20. See ‘Comment’.

24. ‘by any chance’ For the use of this infinitive absolute, see ‘Notes on the text’ on 13:7.

27. ‘these’: *bām* Two Hebr. MSS and LXX read *bāh* (her). This may be an attempt to make the rule conform to v. 19b, which is unnecessary. See ‘Comment’.

31. ‘you shall consecrate’: *hizzartem* Opinions are divided over the identity of the root underlying this hiph. form. SamP and Syr suggest reading it as *hizhartem*, as does *BHS* margin. For the periphrastic *eulabeis poiēsete* in LXX, see Wevers 1997: 238. This assumes an elision of *hē*. Those who take the root of *hizzîr* as *zhr* divide over the meaning of the following preposition, *min*. Most modern Eng. translations correctly assume the root *nzr* and posit that it is the hiph. of *nzr* (the *nûn* assimilated), meaning to ‘separate’. See Num. 6:2–3, 5–6, 12. Based on the Numbers passages a meaning such as ‘consecrate’ is suitable here.

Form and structure

The rules in this chapter deal with the uncleanness that results from various discharges from male and female reproductive organs, and the purificatory rites associated with them. Though the topic may seem bizarre to the reader, it has a hidden meaning and aim. The interpretation that uncleanness represents human self-hiding before the Lord finds its clear expression in these rules, and as for the previous chapters, Gen. 3 also serves as the immediate background of this chapter (see ‘Comment’ and ‘Explanation’ on ch. 12).

As noted by recent commentators, the rules in this chapter are arranged in a chiastic order with sexual intercourse between man and woman forming its centre (v. 18):

A The Lord’s address to Moses (1–2a)
  B A man’s serious discharge (2b–15)
    C A man’s ordinary discharge (16–17)
      D Sexual intercourse (18)
    C' A woman’s ordinary discharge (19–24)
  B' A woman’s serious discharge (25–30)
A' The Lord’s concluding remark (31)

Subscript (32–33)

The opening clauses of the chapter divisions are similarly formulated: B (*'îš 'îš*), C (*wĕ'îš kî*), D (*wĕ'iššâ 'ăšer*), C' (*wĕ'iššâ kî*), B' (*wĕ'iššâ kî*). Both *'îš* and *'iššâ* carry interpersonal connotations. Thus though vv. 2b–30 are neatly grouped into male (vv. 2b–17) and female sections (vv. 19–30), and though each section is not mentioned without referring to the other, the whole chapter conveys its message as an organic whole.

Despite the symmetrical structuring of sections dealing with man and woman, and the serious and ordinary discharges, B is disproportionately longer than sections C and D, mainly owing to its additional rules concerning contagion. But as the comparison between C' and B' shows, the uncleanness contagion is not the sole determinant of the severity of case B': the criterion as to whether a case is normal or abnormal is also to be taken into account.

The clear chiastic pattern is unrelated to questions concerning the composition's originality (cf. Hartley 1992: 206). Rather it is possibly employed to express a particular message. One obvious point is that by stipulating the various rules on contagion this chapter aims to convey the differences between men and women (See 'Explanation').

It should be recognized that a large number of the rules in this chapter relate to primary and/or secondary uncleanness contagion. Since the rules are presented symmetrically, one may tend to assume that rules not mentioned in B must still remain applicable if they are found in B'. However, such a reading is problematical when it is remembered that the general rules are arranged chiastically and symmetrically, while the specific rules on the uncleanness contagion are not. More likely, the legislator aims at conveying some message through the disproportionate presentation of the contagion rules on the basis of the clear symmetrical pattern: the reader is expected to compare rules concerning men with the corresponding rules for women, and thereby see differences between men and women.

This chapter has literary and ideological links with chs. 11 – 14. Those links are mentioned in 'Comment' and 'Explanation', but the following linguistic, literary and ideological links should be noted here.

Links with chapter 11

At the end of ch. 11 (vv. 43–44) the aim or purpose of the observance of the laws is presented to the effect that the Israelites are led to holiness by their avoidance of detestable creatures (*šeqeṣ*). This passage adumbrates ch. 18 onwards, where the holiness of the Israelites becomes a major theme. However, the passage simultaneously states that coming into contact with detestable creatures brings about the defilement of one's soul (*nepeš*). By this statement the legislator assumes that various types of defilement in the following chapter also lead to the defilement of one's soul. Now, in 15:31 it is stated that a failure to observe the rules of this chapter leads to the defilement of the sanctuary. Moreover in chs. 11 – 15 *ṭimmē'*, in the sense of 'to defile' and not 'to pronounce unclean', appears only in these two places. Thus it is likely that the defilement of the human soul is viewed as paralleling the defilement of the sanctuary (see 'Comment').

In content ch. 11 is very similar to ch. 15. Both deal with defilement caused by contact with unclean entities: ch. 11 with detestable creatures, and ch. 15 with unclean persons. Incidentally, human defilement through contact with other unclean persons and things does not come to the fore in chs. 12 – 14. Also ch. 15 is possibly related to the principle that once seed (*zera'*) begins to have life, it becomes vulnerable to defilement (cf. 11:37–38). If so, ch. 15 stresses the prenatal uncleanness in childbirth in ch. 12, since the emission of semen is said to be defiling.

Links with chapter 12

The text itself (12:2) assumes the rules on menstrual uncleanness given in ch. 15. One may tend to consider that ch. 12 was somehow dislodged from ch. 15 or somewhere else. But as mentioned in ch. 12, its theme relates to childbirth, and in this sense it comes fittingly both before chs. 13 – 15, which relate to human life as a whole, and after ch. 11, which is preoccupied with the human environment (see below).

Links with chapter 13

There is a thematic relationship between chs. 13 and 15 in so far as the former deals with a serious disease called *ṣāra'at*, which symbolizes (as we have seen) human self-hiding, while ch. 15 deals with serious diseases of the male and female genitals, which are the most hidden parts of the human body (see 'Explanation'). Further it may be pointed out that *ṣāra'at* manifests itself on human skin, while discharges from the genitals are made public though the rules pertaining to contagion: the uncovering of human self-hiding is the aim of both passages.

Literarily the theme of *bāśār* (flesh, genital) links the two chapters.

Links with chapter 14

Ch. 14 contains body-sanctuary symbolism in vv. 2–20 (see 'Comment' there). This symbolism does not appear explicitly in ch. 15, but the causes for the need of propitiation in serious cases (vv. 14–15, 29–30) are stated explicitly as 'because of his discharge' (v. 15), and 'because of her discharge of uncleanness' (v. 30). These statements reflect the principle that the bodies of unclean persons parallel the condition of the sanctuary.

The section 14:46–47 refers to contagion for the first time in chs. 13 – 14, thereby adumbrating this topic in ch. 15.

As is clear from the above links between ch. 15 and the preceding chapters, this chapter is not an independent prescription on discharges associated with sexual organs, but is related to chs. 11 – 14 in various ways. To this may be added an observation alluded to above, namely that the arrangement of topics, each of which has the fall account in Gen. 3 as its immediate background, also attests to the unity of these chapters. Lev. 11 talks about the edible and inedible creatures, particularly the need for the Israelites to disassociate from detestable creatures. The prohibition on *eating* specific creatures, among which the serpent plays a central role without being mentioned, reminds the reader of the fall. In this sense, ch. 11 provides the human environment with a special reference to the prohibition against self-hiding (see 'Explanation' on ch. 11). Ch. 12, referring to God's sentence on the woman in Gen. 3:16, reminds the reader of the ongoing propensity of women to hide themselves and of the fact that a newborn baby is already defiled. In other words, the chapter is related to the beginning of life. Chs. 13 – 14 describe, through the prescriptions on *ṣāra'at*, a deep-seated human propensity to hide oneself, referring to the fact that the first man (and woman) hid himself immediately after violating God's commandment. This topic of *ṣāra'at* is related to the whole course of human life. And finally, ch. 15, keeping in mind that the first man and woman hid themselves with loincloths, addresses itself to male and female self-hiding through discharges from sexual organs. This topic is probably chosen because men and women use their genitals every day.

It is also observed that chs. 11 – 15 share a particular concern about the various dimensions of human beings. For example, in these chapters *nepeš* appears only in ch. 11 (see 11:43–44), *'ādām* appears only in ch. 13 (vv. 2, 9), while *'îš* first appears in the latter half of ch. 13 and then frequently in chapters 14 – 15. On the other hand, *'iššâ* appears as the mother of children in ch. 12, and in the latter half of ch. 13. It has been pointed out that the order of chs. 11 – 13 corresponds with the order of the divine verdict against the serpent and humans in Gen. 3:14–19. That *'îš* and *'iššâ* occur frequently from the latter half of ch. 13 onwards also suggests that in this section, the concept of self-hiding is examined from the interrelationship between men and women.

Comment

As for ch. 12, the rationale for the uncleanness associated with male and female genitals has posed a crux for exegetes (see 'Comment' on 12:1–2, 5). Although a variety of views on the rationale have been contributed (see Introduction 7.3.1), that offered by Wenham appears unique in that it offers a simple solution to the rationale for the defilement of both genders.

He proposes that semen, like blood, symbolizes life and that the loss of life is considered defiling because it leads to illness or death (Wenham 1983: 433–434). To interact with this view necessitates both the setting out once again of the position taken in this commentary as well as further clarification of the issue itself.

Several considerations militate against this inference.

(1) Life in the ritual context means life before the Lord, so poor health or physical death do not necessarily point to uncleanness. The case of *ṣāraʻat* in 13:12–13 is such a case. Indeed death is most defiling. But would it not be true that the ritual aims at teaching about spiritual life by employing an analogy with physical life and death?

(2) The assumption that semen symbolizes life can be accepted only by a common human experience and not by appealing to any biblical text.

(3) Further, menstrual blood defiles, but not human blood in general. And in regard to the cleanness/uncleanness regulations defiling blood is restricted to the blood from the female reproductive organ: blood flowing from lesions elsewhere on the body are not said to defile.

(4) That the first case of ch. 15 deals with the emission of pus indicates that it is not the emission of semen, but the disease within the *reproductive* organ that is the cause of uncleanness. Particularly, the last point suggests that as the discharge includes pus, not urine, it could be categorized as reproductive discharge, connoting sexuality. It seems that the rationale for the discharges should be sought from a broader perspective of these regulations.

My comments on chs. 11 – 14 have already made it clear that behind uncleanness lies the idea of hiding oneself. Moreover as for chs. 11 – 13, ch. 15 also exhibits a literary and ideological link with Gen. 3. In Gen. 3:1–7, Eve, in enticing her husband, proposed that he should eat the fruit from the forbidden tree. When they ate it, their eyes were opened just as the serpent had anticipated. Upon realization of their nakedness, they made loincloths from the leaves of a fig tree. They gained a sense of shame in relation to their genitals. Having made their loincloths, the couple hid themselves behind trees. Collectively, as already pointed out, these actions are a visible manifestation of the spiritual self-hiding in their hearts.

This idea reveals the intention of the whole prescription. The choice of male and female reproductive organs seems to be related to the fact that these are the parts of the body humans try to hide as much as possible. Thus the liquids or pus that come from these seem to be symbolically viewed as what comes from the innermost part of the human heart. They are evaluated as unclean, and thus the object of the Lord's wrath (see 'Links with chapter 11' in 'Form and structure').

With the fall account in view the legislator of Lev. 15 aims to urge the hiding man and woman to uncover themselves, by appealing to tangible and visible discharges from the most hidden parts of their bodies. This has an important implication: just as in ch. 11 the unclean creatures are ultimately not condemned, sexual intercourse and disease are not condemned either. Thus given that the legislator's aim is spiritual, though it is important to be meticulous about outer uncleanness and cleanness, to focus on this aspect of the legislation alone misses the legislator's ultimate goal.

Moreover there is a surprisingly tacit assumption in the text that the condition of male and female reproductive organs is reflected in the sanctuary. The term *bāśār* in this chapter refers both euphemistically to genitals and literally to human bodies, particularly that of a man (vv. 2–3, 7, 13, 16 for a man, v. 19 for a woman). Male genitals represent the man, while the man represents the Tent (v. 31). This accords with my interpretation of ch. 14 that the body of the healed person corresponds to his tent and the Tent of Meeting (14:2–20). Thus a number of directions for cleansing in the event of defilement, primary or secondary, function primarily to *uncover* the true condition of the person's most secret inner parts.

The nature of the self-hiding and the difference between man and woman in this regard are reflected in various literary devices used in formulating the prescription.

15:2b–15 (man with a serious discharge from his genitals)

The chapter begins with the case of a man who suffers from a reproductive discharge. This is a disease and is viewed as a case of serious uncleanness. The discharge could refer to pus in addition to semen. Since this is a disease, it is a source of major defiling. In addition to defiling the things he comes into contact with, these defiled things convey uncleanness to other objects and persons (vv. 4–12). When a person becomes defiled, he washes his clothes, bathes in water and waits until evening. If the defiled object is an earthenware vessel, it must be broken, and a wooden vessel must be rinsed. These prescriptions may well have a hygienic concern in mind. But this cannot explain why the defiled objects remain unclean until evening and why no direction is given to wash or rinse them (see vv. 4, 9–10).

Clearly his uncleanness would have defiled not only him but also those persons and objects he has physical contact with, so if he is aware of his disease, he must isolate himself from other people (cf. Num. 5:2–3).

The man suffers for an undetermined period of time. But the Law provides for the potential case where he is healed. After healing, he is required to undergo a two-stage purification process in the sanctuary. In the first stage he counts seven days, washes his clothes, bathes in fresh water and then becomes clean. In the second stage he goes in person before the Lord and presents his offerings to the priest: either two turtle doves or pigeons. The priest offers one as a sin offering, and the other as a burnt offering. Mention of 'he shall be clean' at the end of v. 13 suggests that the uncleanness he has had until then, as well as the cleanness he obtains after healing, is of a ritual rather than hygienic nature. Moreover the need for propitiation in the sanctuary indicates that his uncleanness was so severe that it defiled the sanctuary, the Lord's abode.

In this introductory case there is a significant literary device involving the term *bāśār*, which is suggestive of this section's purpose. *Bāśār* in vv. 2b, 3 refers euphemistically to the man's genitals, while the same term in vv. 7 and 13 apparently refers to his 'body' (see below on these verses). Except for these occurrences, the term occurs only in vv. 16 and 19 in this chapter. Thus the authorial intention may be conveyed through the subtle change of meaning resulting in his genitals becoming representative of his body. Thus when the man is healed, the direction to wash his body is expressed by the gesture of 'washing his body with fresh water', which is more potent than the ordinary 'washing his clothes' or 'bathing in water'; indeed the former is a combination of the two. So it is fitting that the prescription in v. 14 takes a formulation slightly different from that of v. 29: the man must present himself before the Lord, with a body that is both physically and symbolically clean. Further his very discharge becomes the object of propitiation that the priest makes for him (v. 15b). In other words, since his discharge is unclean (v. 2b), it is *uncovered* before the Lord as the object of purification and propitiation.

Compared with the case for a woman below, the provision of purificatory rites suggests that he is assumed as one taking responsibility for what he does. The offerings he presents to the Lord are the same as those brought in the concession case for a new mother in 12:8. Thus this man is apparently less defiling to the sanctuary than the woman, though the degree of his uncleanness' contagiousness is extremely high.

1–2a. The Lord's new address is introduced with what is the most typical introductory formula in Leviticus: he addresses Moses and Aaron, who are in turn to deliver it to the Israelites. The command to deliver the rules to the Israelites is understandable considering that they are highly relevant to their private life; such as 11:1 –2a and 12:1–2aa, but unlike 13:1 and 14:1. The Lord's command that *both* Moses and Aaron are to convey this message to the Israelites is relatively rare in Leviticus: it occurs here and 11:1 where not 'say' but 'speak' is used. A sense of urgency appears to be expressed by this form of the Lord's address.

2b–3. The first case refers to a situation where there is a discharge from a man's genitals. It is a serious disease where pus is discharged from the urethra, a condition that may even result in its blockage. The latter case is not an alternative to the former. The discharge itself is not only unclean but makes the whole person unclean.

4. The period for which things that come into contact with the unclean person remain defiled is not mentioned. But the handling of the defiled objects is stated later in vv. 11–12.

7. 'his body' is the same term employed euphemistically for the man's genitals in v. 2. But Milgrom (1991: 914) reasonably argues that here it refers to the *zāb*'s (the unclean person's in v. 7) body, for two reasons.

First, if the term refers to the genitals alone, the question naturally arises as to what happens if the rest of his body is touched. Second, and more logically, Milgrom adduces a rabbinic inferrence, and says, 'if touching any part of the menstruant's body is contaminating (v. 19b), all the more so touching any part of the *zāb*'s body, which is of a greater impurity'.

10–12. V. 10 summarizes the principle concerning the secondary contagion in its first half; i.e. whatever touches anything underneath the sufferer becomes unclean until evening. V. 11 is similar to v. 7 in that both deal with an occasion of direct contact with the sufferer. Anyone who is touched by the sufferer but does not rinse his hands becomes unclean. Some hygienic consideration seems to be at work here, though this is not the primary rationale underlying the concept of defilement.

13. In his purificatory process, the sufferer must 'count' seven days. Reference to 'counting' seems necessitated first of all by the sufferer's responsibility to determine when his condition is healed. He is to count seven days from this time. Second, counting (*sāpar*) occurs for the first time in Leviticus (see 'Notes on the text'), and it can be expressed otherwise. Thus counting the seven days is unlikely simply to refer to enumeration, and it seems possible to consider the symbolic meaning of 'counting time' in ritual texts. It may be that the person focuses his attention on his own spiritual condition before the Lord, a marked change from his former condition where he used to defile everything he contacted.

Thereafter, the man washes his body, including his genitals, with fresh water. Washing with fresh water is not found elsewhere in the OT. In this chapter, the defiled person is always to 'bathe in water' (*rāḥaṣ bammayim*, vv. 5–8, 10–11), so it is a heightened form of cleansing; i.e. this rite may convey the 'giving of life' (cf. 14:9).

14–15. The rites on the eighth day resemble those in ch. 12 (v. 6). Both kinds of offering are the same: one for the sin offering and the other for the burnt offering. Compared with the ritual in ch. 12, the one in 15:14 appears to stress, by placing 'before the Lord' at the front, the idea that the unclean man comes *in person* to the Lord. Note the sequence of the verbs: 'take', 'come' and 'give'.

The same ritual as 12:8 is prescribed. The need for making propitiation for the sufferer suggests that he has been defiling the sanctuary, or that he is seen before the Lord as one who has defiled the sanctuary. In other words, the person has been under the Lord's wrath, as the leprous person was in 14:18–20.

15:16–18 (man with an emission of semen and defilement through sexual intercourse)

These verses deal with defilement caused either by an emission of semen, or through a man's sexual intercourse with a woman. Vv. 16–17 belong to the section dealing with males (vv. 2a–17), while v. 18 bears a transitional nature, dealing with the common sexual experience of a man and woman. For an oft-raised question why sexual intercourse defiles, despite the fact that childbirth is God's blessing, see 'Comment' on 12:1–2. The emission of semen is defiling, not because it symbolizes the loss of 'life', but because it is symbolically viewed as what comes from the innermost part of the human heart.

All commentators appear to assume that the sexual intercourse in view is a legitimate one between husband and wife. But this assumption is one-sided: the text neither refers explicitly to it as occurring within a marital context (see below on v. 24), nor does it preclude that possibility.

The defiling power of semen is reflected in the purificatory measures taken against the defilement effected upon the man himself and those objects he comes into contact with. The man must wash *all* his body with water and wait until evening. In comparison with the persons who are defiled by coming into contact with a man suffering from a serious discharge (vv. 5–8), where washing clothes, bathing in water and waiting until evening are required, here he is simply required to wash his body and wait until evening. It is clear that the purificatory measures match the nature of the defilement, which comes from the man himself, while in vv. 5–8 it comes from outside. The defilement extends beyond his person to clothes and skin that come into contact with his semen. Those things must be cleansed, and remain unclean until evening. These purificatory rites strongly suggest that the uncleanness envisaged here is not of a hygienic nature: though the clothes and skin become dirty, it is improbable that 'unclean' means 'dirty'.

18. This verse addresses itself to sexual intercourse, and is located at the centre of the chapter's chiastic structure (see 'Form and structure'). Though in Hebr. the verse starts with 'a woman' (*'iššâ*), the case relates to men and women. When a woman has sexual intercourse with a man, both are defiled. So they both bathe in water and remain unclean until evening. If the emission of semen is defiling (v. 17), the woman who receives the semen is also defiled. But the difference in the cleansing rite ('washing all his body' and the purification of the defiled objects in v. 16 versus 'bathing in water' in v. 18) implies that sexual intercourse is less defiling than a man's emission of semen without having sexual intercourse.

15:19–24 (menstrual uncleanness)

The monthly discharge of blood from a woman's genitals is normal, but its contagiousness is particularly stressed in this section. Her uncleanness lasts seven days. The prescription stresses that its defiling force makes everything the woman comes into contact with unclean. As in the case of a man who suffers from a genital discharge, this woman defiles everything she comes into contact with, and brings secondary defilement to those who touch the objects she defiles. The degree of contagion, however, matches the length of defilement: seven days. Again, though it appears the blood defiles, it is the whole matter of the discharge of blood from her reproductive organ that defiles her and her environment.

In spite of the high degree of contagiousness associated with her period of menstruation, no direction for purification is given in vv. 19–24. This stands in sharp contrast with the man's case in 2b–15. The reason should be sought in the symbolic dimension of this rule, and not in the practical side (see 'Comment' on ch. 12). Practically, it seems to be assumed that with the passage of seven days purification is over.

The defiling power of the uncleanness in both this and the next case is contemplated only within the realm where a woman is likely to be active during her clean period: her bed, the contents of her house, and her husband – in a word, her home (cf. the man's case in vv. 2b–15). For the interpretation of v. 24, see below.

Thus menstrual uncleanness is characterized in such a way that while it looks less serious in so far as no direction is given for purificatory rites, it looks severe in that it is heavily contagious and requires purificatory rites for those subsequently defiled by it.

19. In Hebr. menstrual uncleanness is called *niddâ*. The tangible source is clearly the blood discharge from her reproductive organ. For the rationale, see above on vv. 16–17.

Some examples of its contagious power are given in vv. 20–24, and it is similar to that associated with the serious case involving a man in vv. 4–11, rather than that relating to a man's emission of semen in vv. 16–17. Hartley comments that this could be based on the difference in sex; 'the flow of the menstrual blood lasts longer than an emission of semen' (1992: 212). However, he seems to overlook that the woman's contagiousness is similar to the contagiousness of the serious case of a man in vv. 4–11. Why is the defiling force of a woman in her menstrual period similar to the first case of a man? Why does her flow of blood last longer than an emission of semen? There seem to be more than biological differences active between the sexes in this circumstance. As in ch. 12, any biological explanation is possible and may even be truthful, but in this case it does not fully explain the difference in the prescriptions between genders.

20–23. V. 20 concerns the defilement of objects the menstrual woman touches, while vv. 21–22 concern the secondary defilement incurred by persons who have touched her bed or belongings. The interpretation of v. 23 varies, as is reflected in the various translations. But besides the proposed interpretation in 'Notes on the text', it can be further pointed out that whenever human defilement caused by contagion is mentioned in this chapter, it is prescribed in such a way that a person must wash his or her clothes, bathe in water and wait until evening (vv. 5–8, 10b–11, 21–22).

By contrast, defiled things such as the bed or any articles the woman uses are described as remaining unclean only until evening. The case of v. 23 belongs to the latter. Therefore v. 23 talks about a secondary contagion from an inanimate object to a person. It is unlikely that any hygienic considerations lie behind this secondary contagion.

24. This verse addresses defilement that results from a man lying with a woman during the time of her menstrual period: he contracts uncleanness and becomes unclean for seven days. Some commentators view this prescription as in conflict with that found in 20:18 (cf. 18:19), where the offender is said to be cut off from his community (cf. Schwartz 1999: 26–27). Péter-Contesse (1993: 238), following Wenham (1979: 220), considers that the assumed intercourse is accidental, and that the case simply deals with a case between legitimate partners.

Thus two interpretive issues surround this verse. First, is such intercourse intentional or inadvertent? Second, is the 'man' (*'îš*) the husband, and the 'woman' (*'iššâ*) his wife, so this defilement takes place within legitimate bounds? The text provides no explicit answer to the first question and likewise says nothing about the second, as in v. 18. Yet the exegetical assumption that the ritual defilement in chs. 11 – 15 does not deal with 'moral' conduct, as is presumed to be the case in 20:18, which results in the *kāret* penalty, warrants challenging. A fundamental question to do with the relationship between ritual uncleanness and 'moral' uncleanness is involved. However, in so far as uncleanness is an existential matter, it can embrace moral conduct (see 'Explanation' on chs. 18, 20 and Introduction 7.4.3).

Now it is surprising that the seven-day defilement of a man is nowhere found except here. In addition to this, no purificatory measure is stipulated. This does not suggest that this case is less severe than the case of 18:10, as suggested by Hartley (1992: 212). 'Seven' is a number symbolizing 'complete' or 'perfect'. Thus it may be concluded that here the idea of 'completely hiding oneself' before the Lord is expressed by illicit sexual union, as well as by the absence of purification measures. For the verse's further relationship with 20:18, see 'Comment' there.

15:25–30 (woman who suffers from a serious discharge)

The last section of ch. 15 deals with the case of a woman who suffers from a serious blood discharge from her reproductive organs, which thematically parallels the first case involving a man (vv. 2b–15). Two alternative cases are envisaged: either she is experiencing an abnormally long period of discharge from her reproductive organ, or she has experienced an additional discharge outside her normal menstruation period. In either case she becomes unclean, and her uncleanness is presented just like that found in the case of menstruation. Some linguistic features of v. 25 (see below) suggest it is not just her blood discharge that is unclean but she has become unclean also.

Since this is a case of disease, it is understandable that no purificatory measures are required for the period leading up to her recovery. Instead when she recovers she is simply required to count seven days, which culminate in her becoming clean. Again this procedure contrasts with the case for a man in vv. 13ff., where he is ordered to wash his clothes and body in fresh water. On the other hand, the contagion of her uncleanness appears to be treated just like that associated with a menstruating woman: only persons defiled by contagion are commanded to bathe in water and wait until evening.

When she recovers from her disease, as in vv. 13–15 she enters into the purificatory process. Vv. 29–30 prescribe the gradual process by which she is to approach the Lord for reconciliation: 'take' – 'bring to the priest' – 'to the entrance of the Tent of Meeting' – 'the priest makes propitiation for her before the Lord' (see 'Comment' on v. 14; cf. 12:6–7). As in vv. 14–15, she first uncovers herself through the sin offering and dedicates herself by the burnt offering. It must be noted that the presence of this ritual does not mean that such a recovery frequently occurred in ancient Israel (cf. 14:2–20; see further Matt. 9:20–22; Mark 5:25–29; Luke 8:43–44).

25. 'as in the days of her menstruation' (*kîmê niddātāh*) refers to the degree of defilement, and not to the length of period (cf. 12:2).

The formulation of the law is not just a prescription, but is charged with a message. The subject of *tāzûb* in the alternative case (v. 25ab) is the 'woman' (*'iššâ*). Though *tāzûb* is commonly translated 'has a discharge', it may have a connotation that it is 'she' who emits or discharges, in the light of the use of *zwb* in its foregoing occurrences (cf. vv. 19, 25aa).

The phrase 'the discharge of her uncleanness' (*zôb ṭum'ātāh*) occurs only here and v. 30 in the whole OT. It appears to present her blood as the very source of uncleanness. But since this phrase occurs after the mention of *niddâ* (menstrual uncleanness), it literally expresses 'the discharge of her uncleanness'. The phrase certainly presumes that the discharge of her blood is unclean, but in this verse the law appears to express more than that: her very existence is unclean, symbolically equating the woman with her blood.

26. The phrases 'as in the bed of her menstrual impurity' (*kĕmiškab niddātāh*) and 'as in the uncleanness of her menstrual impurity' (*kĕṭum'at niddātāh*) abbreviate the description of the rules on contagion that are already mentioned in regard to a menstruating woman.

27. Cf. vv. 21–22

28. The woman suffering from an abnormal discharge is deemed to be clean after she has counted seven days from the time of her healing. No washing of her body or bathing in water (cf. v. 13) is prescribed. These rites are not necessarily assumed. For if the legislator has deliberately omitted this from the formulation, it may reflect his different attitude towards the woman, or that her defilement is of a lower degree than that of the man in vv. 2–15 (see 'Comment' on vv. 19–24 above and 'Explanation').

29–30. Cf. vv. 14–15. The sacrifices she brings are the same as those for the case of the new mother in 12:8.

For the phrase 'for the discharge of her uncleanness' (*mizzôb ṭum'ātāh*, v. 30), see 'Comment' on v. 25.

As for the first case relating to the man, the need for making propitiation likewise indicates that the woman is viewed as having been the object of the Lord's wrath, which was directed against the discharge's symbolic meaning.

15:31–33

31. See 'Notes on the text'. As 'you shall consecrate the Israelites away from their uncleanness' indicates, this passage is addressed to Moses and Aaron, and this corresponds to the Lord's address in v. 1. Self-evidently, then, this verse speaks about the role of Moses and Aaron. Does this mean that v. 31a speaks about the *observance* of the purificatory rites in vv. 2a–30? Certainly it does (Wenham 1979: 221; Kiuchi 1987: 61–62; Hartley 1992: 213). This view, however, rests on the assumption that the uncleanness in this chapter is mostly unavoidable (cf. Milgrom 1991: 945). Not only do they frequently defile themselves, particularly by sexual intercourse, but it may be that they remain *unaware* of their defilement resulting from contact with defiled things. But strictly speaking, the statement 'away from their uncleanness' presumes that uncleanness, as opposed to the observance of the purificatory measures, must be shunned by the Israelites.

The first part of this verse thus poses an apparently insoluble dilemma that while the Israelites must separate themselves from uncleanness, they cannot help but defile themselves.

However, does this mean that sexual intercourse, for instance, must be shunned or banned? This question is solved only by assuming that uncleanness means the state of hiding oneself, and that only because of its spiritual offence is the act said to be defiling: sexual intercourse is not itself condemned. Moreover, assuming this symbolic meaning of uncleanness, will the man and woman uncover themselves before the Lord? That seems very unlikely.

The latter half of the verse warns 'lest they die in their uncleanness by defiling my sanctuary that is in their midst'. Again, restricting this warning to the violation of purificatory rituals in this chapter cannot explain the fact that the serious cases of uncleanness, if not cured, constantly defile the sanctuary. Thus the conclusion is inevitable that any uncleanness, even that associated with sexual intercourse, defiles the sanctuary. The impossibility of not defiling the sanctuary explains why human beings die. In other words, the Lord speaks this concluding statement from the divine point of view, just as he did in 11:43–44, which is a divine necessity, even though it is diametrically opposed to the spiritual reality of humans.

'by defiling my sanctuary that is in their midst': *lĕṭamm'ām 'et miškānî 'ăšer bĕtôkām* 'My sanctuary' (*miškānî*) is co-referential with 'the Tent of Meeting' (*'ôhēl mô'ēd*) to the Lord's abode (e.g. Exod. 39:32; Lev. 17:4). In this chapter the latter appears in vv. 14 and 29. The idea prepares the way for the atonement ritual in the next chapter, where all the uncleanness of the Israelites is purified (16:16).

The term *ṭimmē'* in the sense of 'to defile', as opposed to 'to pronounce clean', occurs here for the second time; the first occurrence was in 11:44 where it is said, 'For I am the Lord your God. Consecrate yourselves [*hitqaddištem*] therefore and be holy, for I am holy. You shall not defile your souls [*wĕlō' tĕṭammĕ'û 'et napšôtêkem*] with any swarming thing that crawls on the ground.'

One may note the similar idea underlying this passage and 15:31, which is highly significant for the relationship between the sanctuary and the human soul (*nepeš*). First, 'consecrating oneself' is similar to 'separating from uncleanness' in 15:31a. Second, the clause 'not defiling your souls' is similar to 'not defiling my sanctuary' in 15:31b. Further, structurally 11:44 summarizes the intent of all the rules in ch. 11, just as 15:31 presents the intent of the rules in ch. 15 in summary form. One may argue that defiling the sanctuary is a different matter from defiling one's soul. But in view of the uncleanness or defilement envisaged in both passages it cannot be gainsaid that *the human nepeš is parallel to the sanctuary* (see 'Explanation' on chs. 9 – 11, 14). This parallel is further corroborated by the fact that uncleanness symbolizes hiding oneself in a spiritual sense. When a person hides himself, he hides his *nepeš* (see 4:2; 5:1). Since the presence of uncleanness among the Israelites parallels that found in the sanctuary, it is natural to infer that the uncovering of the hiding soul is what the ritual in the sanctuary achieves.

32–33. These verses summarize the content of this chapter. They are arranged in the following way:

A. *Zāb* and he who has an emission of semen (vv. 2–18)
B. A menstruating woman (vv. 19–23a)
C. *Zāb* (male and female) (vv. 2–15, 25–30)
D. A man who lies with an unclean woman (v. 24)

The ordering of the items calls for explanation, as the order is different from that of the rules in this chapter (cf. Milgrom 1991: 947). For C includes *zāb* in A, and overlaps with B, while D (v. 24) is located after B. A and B follow the order of the items in this chapter. The problem lies with C and D. C covers the serious diseases from male and female reproductive organs. Apparently the order of the list does not reflect the degrees of defilement (cf. A and B). However, the order of C and D appears to be based on the degrees of defilement. We cannot find any possible authorial intention behind the order if we look at just the formal aspect of the rules. Given the symbolic dimension of defilement, the resumptive nature of C and the ascending degrees of defilement in C and D imply that D is not just exceptional or additional, but that it is also resumptive, covering all the other cases: A, B and C. In other words, singling out a special case such as v. 24 as the last item of the list implies that man and woman are entirely unclean (see 'Comment' on v. 24, and 'Explanation' below), despite the Lord's words in v. 31.

Explanation

With the fall account as the immediate background, this chapter indicates particular aspects of uncleanness by way of its specific formulation of the rules relating to contagion.

First of all, in so far as uncleanness refers to a state of self-hiding, the contagiousness of uncleanness expresses the transference of self-hiding. Since the law strongly commands the Israelites to shun uncleanness, it is clear they are to disassociate from one another, a message similar to that found in ch. 11. This should not be misunderstood as meaning one should not make personal contact with others. However, if a person is affected by others so that he loses his concentration on, and dedication to, the Lord, he is viewed as defiled. In particular, the symbolic meaning of sexual intercourse between man and woman merits attention (v. 18). An emission of semen is defiling, so the partner becomes defiled. Although sexual intercourse is not wrong or discouraged by itself, the Lord shows his concern for the spiritual condition of man and woman after the fall. For by this act, man and woman tend to hide themselves from the Lord, for this act fosters a strong tendency to give priority to the sexual partner, unconsciously forgetting the Lord, if not defying him. Although the regulation does not restrict itself to marital relationships, the love between a husband and wife becomes meaningful only when each partner does not hide from the Lord (cf. Heb. 13:4). The marital relationship is the most difficult context in which to be clean before the Lord, and therefore it constitutes the touchstone for whether a person can uncover himself or herself before the Lord.

It may appear striking that the abnormal cases associated with men and women (vv. 2b–15, 25–30) occupy such a large part of this chapter. Are not these cases, being abnormal and relatively infrequent in society, irrelevant to the large majority of the Israelites? On a ritual level, these people are certainly to be separated from others who are 'clean', simply because the Lord so commands. But the emphasis on the abnormal cases in this chapter may well indicate that these people are part of Israelite society and are thus to be cared for. Furthermore on the same ritual level these people are not irrelevant to other 'clean' people, for the latter can be defiled by the former through contact. This potentially threatens those who are 'clean', because they may come into contact with an unclean person without knowing it. Moreover becoming conscious of the presence of abnormally unclean people would inevitably make 'clean' people check their own condition more punctiliously. This appears to be one of the major functions of the rules on abnormal discharges associated with men and women.

Moreover one may well wonder how often the two 'abnormal' cases of defilement, which are placed at the beginning and end of the chapter, were healed, despite the presence of purificatory rites at the sanctuary. Healing of such serious cases in ancient times was very unlikely (Mark 5:25–34). Thus even on the level of the outward ritual, not only do the serious cases of discharge defile the sanctuary for a long period; in all probability they may constantly defile the sanctuary; in which case 15:31 is not consonant with those serious cases.

However, as has been mentioned repeatedly, uncleanness symbolizes self-hiding, and it is on this level of the symbolism, which is the legislator's final intention, that the distinction between normal and abnormal virtually disappears. Indeed, just as in the cases of *ṣāraʿat*, the abnormal discharges of a man and a woman are utilized so as to highlight the strong human propensity to hide oneself. While uncovering is the aim of these prescriptions, the desire of those who suffer the most shameful of diseases to hide from the public represents the general nature of humans to hide themselves. The human propensity to hide is so deeply rooted in human nature after the fall that it powerfully contaminates all other humans and their immediate environment. It involves other humans in self-hiding from the Lord. In view of these considerations, these two special cases are not special or abnormal on a symbolic dimension; they just facilitate the description of what men and women are like: their propensity to self-hide from the Lord is incurable and hopeless.

Thus the abnormal and rare cases in ch. 15, like the cases of *ṣāraʿat* in chs. 13 – 14, which are *practically* relevant only to a very small number of people in Israelite society, ironically point to a universal significance. Therefore, despite the ritual differences between man and woman with regard to purificatory rites, both are essentially the same in terms of self-hiding. Moreover, as the things that issue from their most hidden body parts are a cause of defilement, the discharges symbolically mean that anything coming out of humans is defiled. When Jesus said, 'What comes out of a person is what defiles him. For from within, out of the heart of man, comes evil thoughts, sexual immorality, theft, murder, adultery, coveting, wickedness, deceit, sensuality, envy, slander, pride, foolishness. All these evil things come from within, and they defile a person' (Mark 7:20–23 ESV), he illustrates the prescription of Lev. 15. He is neither symbolizing the prescription, nor does he moralize the 'cultic' laws. The prescription in Lev. 15 already has a symbolic meaning, for the latter concerns the overall inner attitude of humans. Thus it is pretentious to conceive that some goodness can come out of human beings; the idea itself attests to the presence of self-hiding.

Thus the contagion of uncleanness and its purificatory rites should all be seen under the rubric of self-uncovering. Purity has been considered mainly as moral purity; i.e. in terms of how far one achieves perfection in morality, while not neglecting the purification of one's heart. But the ritual prescription essentially talks about inner purity, which refers to a state of being uncovered before the Lord.

Although the genitals of man and woman are the most hidden parts of their bodies, may it not be true that they look at them every day? The prescription thus exhorts man and woman to check regularly whether they are hiding themselves from the Lord. To uncover oneself means to expose oneself to shame, and sometimes to give up all kinds of earthly treasures, such as fame, wealth and humanistic concerns – in a word, all of one's selfishness. This chapter is thus not far from the exhortation of Jesus, who said, 'If anyone would come after me, let him deny himself and take up his cross daily and follow me' (Luke 9:23 ESV; Matt. 16:24; Mark 8:34).

At this point of Leviticus the man and woman who suffer from serious discharges are not commanded to remain outside the camp (cf. Num. 5:2–3). It is a glaring contradiction that those people stay inside the camp where the Lord resides (v. 31). It is even more contradictory if uncleanness takes on a symbolic dimension, for the prescription virtually says that all the Israelites hide themselves. In view of this interpretation, then, v. 31 bears ironic overtones: if the Israelites observe the prescription not just ritually but symbolically, the Lord's presence is guaranteed, but if not, they have to die. Thus though no explicit mention is made in Leviticus about the cause of human death, it is implied that their hiding themselves leads to physical death, which simultaneously symbolizes spiritual death.

Is the reader's natural response to this chapter not one of hopelessness with regard to his or her proximity to the Lord, as was also the case in chs. 12 – 14?

LEVITICUS 16:1–34

Translation

[1]The LORD spoke to Moses after the death of the two sons of Aaron, when they drew near before the LORD and died. [2]The LORD said to Moses, 'Tell Aaron your brother not to come at any time into the Holy Place inside the veil, before the propitiatory cover that is on the ark, so he may not die. For I will appear in the cloud over the propitiatory cover.

[3]‘But in this way Aaron shall come into the Holy Place: with a bull from the herd
for a sin offering and a ram for a burnt offering. [4]He shall put on the holy linen coat
and shall have the linen undergarment on his body, and he shall tie the linen sash
around his waist, and wear the linen turban; these are the holy garments. He shall
bathe his body in water and then put them on. [5]And he shall take from the
congregation of the Israelites two male goats for a sin offering, and one ram for a
burnt offering. [6]Aaron shall offer the bull as a sin offering for himself and shall
make propitiation on behalf of himself and his house. [7]He shall take the two goats
and set them before the LORD at the entrance of the Tent of Meeting. [8]And Aaron
shall cast lots over the two goats, one lot for the LORD and the other lot for Azazel.
[9]And Aaron shall present the goat on which the lot fell for the LORD and use it as a
sin offering, [10]but the goat on which the lot fell for Azazel shall be presented alive
before the LORD to sacrifice itself for him, being sent away into the wilderness
to Azazel.

[11]‘Aaron shall present the bull as a sin offering for himself, and shall make
propitiation on behalf of himself and his house. He shall slaughter the bull as a sin
offering for himself. [12]And he shall take a censer full of coals of fire from the altar
before the LORD, and two handfuls of sweet incense beaten small, and he shall bring
it inside the veil [13]and put the incense on the fire before the LORD, that the cloud of
the incense may cover the propitiatory cover that is over the testimony, so he does
not die. [14]And he shall take some of the blood of the bull and sprinkle it with his
finger on the front of the propitiatory cover on the east side, and in front of the
propitiatory cover he shall sprinkle some of the blood with his finger seven times.
[15]Then he shall slaughter the goat of the sin offering that is for the people and bring
its blood inside the veil and do with its blood as he did with the blood of the bull,
sprinkling it over the propitiatory cover and in front of the propitiatory cover.
[16]Thus he shall make propitiation for the Holy Place, because of the uncleanness of
the Israelites and because of their rebellions, all their self-hidings. And so shall he
do for the Tent of Meeting, which dwells with them in the midst of their
uncleanness. [17]No human may be in the Tent of Meeting from the time he enters
to make propitiation in the Holy Place until he comes out and has made
propitiation on behalf of himself, his house, and all the assembly of Israel. [18]Then
he shall go out to the altar that is before the LORD and make propitiation for it, and
shall take some of the blood of the bull and some of the blood of the goat, and put it
on the horns of the altar all around. [19]And he shall sprinkle some of the blood on
it with his finger seven times, and purify it and consecrate it from the uncleanness of
the Israelites.

[20]‘When he has completed making propitiation for the Holy Place and the Tent
of Meeting and the altar, he shall present the live goat. [21]And Aaron shall lay both
his hands on the head of the live goat, and confess over it all the guilt of the
Israelites, and all their rebellions, all their self-hidings. And he shall put them on
the head of the goat and send it away into the wilderness by the hand of a person
who is in readiness. [22]The goat shall bear all their guilt on itself to a remote area,
and he shall let the goat go free in the wilderness.

[23]‘Then Aaron shall come into the Tent of Meeting and shall take off the linen

garments that he put on when he went into the Holy Place and shall leave them
there. [24]And he shall bathe his body in water in a holy place and put on his
garments and come out and offer his burnt offering and the burnt offering of the
people and make propitiation on behalf of himself and the people. [25]And the fat of
the sin offering he shall burn on the altar. [26]He who lets the goat go to Azazel shall
wash his clothes and bathe his body in water, and afterwards he may come into the
camp. [27]And the bull for the sin offering and the goat for the sin offering, whose
blood was brought in to make propitiation in the Holy Place, shall be carried
outside the camp. Their skin and their flesh and their dung shall be burned up with
fire. [28]He who burns them shall wash his clothes and bathe his body in water, and
afterwards he may come into the camp.

[29]'It shall be a statute to you forever that in the seventh month, on the tenth day
of the month, you shall afflict your souls and shall do no work, either the native or
the stranger who sojourns among you. [30]For on this day shall propitiation be made
for you to purify you. You shall be clean before the LORD from all your self-hidings.
[31]It is a sabbath of solemn rest to you, and you shall afflict your souls; it is a statute
forever. [32]And the priest who is anointed and consecrated as priest in his father's
place shall make propitiation, wearing the holy linen garments. [33]He shall make
propitiation for the holy sanctuary, and he shall make propitiation for the Tent of
Meeting and for the altar, and he shall make propitiation for the priests and for all
the people of the assembly. [34]This shall be a statute forever for you, that
propitiation may be made for the Israelites once in the year because of all their
self-hidings.' And he did as the LORD commanded him.

Notes on the text

1. 'when they drew near': *bĕqorbātām* LXX, Syr, Tg, Vg read 'when they bring a strange fire', probably drawing on Lev. 10:1b or Num. 3:4.

2. 'the propitiatory cover': *hakkappōret* The Hebr. word has often been called 'the mercy seat' (e.g. RSV) or 'atonement cover' (e.g. NIV). It would seem that the *kappōret* here described functions as more than a 'cover' for the ark. Since the term probably derives from *kpr* pi., it is likely to be associated with the idea of *kipper*, which means to 'sacrifice oneself for propitiation'. In the light of LXX (*hilasterion*), it probably means 'propitiatory cover'.

8. 'for Azazel': *la'ăzā'zel* LXX reads *tō apopompaiō* (going away), as does Syr, which reflects the understanding that *'azā'zel* has a component of *'āzal*.

10. 'shall be presented': *yo'ŏmad* LXX reads 'shall present it', but this reading requires changing the consonant *yôd*. However, the rendering is not just *ad sensum*, as Péter-Contesse judges, but entails the interpretation that Aaron *kipper*s on/for the Azazel goat. See 'Comment'.

'to sacrifice itself for him': *lĕkapper 'ālāyw* Since some allege that propitiation is unlikely made by the Azazel, Elliger and Noth suspect a scribal error (Noth 1965: 121; Elliger 1966: 201). However, there is no need for this assumption (see 'Comment').

15. 'for the people': *lā'ām* LXX adds 'before the LORD'.

'bring its blood': *hēbî' 'et dāmô* LXX reading *apo tou haimatos autou* reflects *middāmô*.

17. LXX and Syr read 'the assembly of *the sons* of Israel'.

20. Only here and v. 33 does *kipper* take the accusative marker *'et* in the priestly literature (see also Ezek. 43:26; 45:20). The *'et* can be taken as an *'et* of dative accusative (cf. Kiuchi 2005: 57).

'and the altar' LXX adds 'and he shall make cleansing for the priests' (see also v. 24), but this is unnecessary.

21. 'in readiness': *'ittî* The Hebr. term is a hapax legomenon. It is an adjective deriving from *'ēt*, meaning 'occasion'. *HALOT* suggests it means 'timely', but this does not mean that whoever happened to be there at the time was suitable for the job. In view of another *'ēt* in v. 2a, some idea of definiteness is conveyed, something like 'a person who is appointed just for the occasion'.

22. 'a remote area': *'ereṣ gĕzērâ* *HALOT* suggests 'infertile land', since this phrase parallels 'to the wilderness', following Reymond 1958: 71. Other translations appear to take *gĕzērâ* as associated with Arab. *jazara*, 'to cut off'; hence 'an inaccessible region' (JPS) or 'a solitary place' (NIV), 'a solitary land' (RSV).

24. 'on behalf of himself ... and the people' LXX inserts 'and for his house', probably harmonizing it with v. 11.

'and the people' LXX adds 'as for the priests'. See above on v. 20.

26. 'Azazel' LXX, unlike in v. 8, here renders it by 'that has been set apart to be let go'.

29. *wĕhāyĕtâ* LXX reads *touto* (this), as in v. 34. The meaning remains the same without it.

'afflict your souls': *tĕ'annû napšôtêkem* Most translations take *napšôtêkem* as a reflexive pronoun, and translate 'afflict yourselves'. But see 'Comment'.

31. For *šabbātôn*, see *HALOT*.

hî' (it) The pronoun refers to *šabbāt*. Since there are cases where *šabbāt* is feminine (Exod. 31:14; Lev. 25:6), there is no need to contemplate the text's originality, as do Tg, TgJon and SamP.

34. 'he did': *wayya'aś* While Syr reads the verb in pl., LXX supplements 'it shall be done once in a year' for clarification, which is, however, unnecessary.

Form and structure

Lev. 16 is a chapter that prescribes the ritual for the annual purification of all the Israelites, the priests and the people alike. As it stands, the ritual is occasioned by the death of Aaron's sons, Nadab and Abihu, recounted in ch. 10.

Because of repetition and apparent internal discrepancies, Lev. 16 is often considered as a composite of two separate texts, behind which lie independent text histories. However, not only is this modern interpretation of these phenomena questionable, but it is possible to see the whole chapter as making perfectly good sense when its authorial intention is grasped (cf. Seidl 1999: 219–248).

Clearly the order of the description is inductive, starting from the historical reality of the death of Nadab and Abihu (vv. 1–2), rather than systematic. Also its form appears repetitive, often resuming what is already mentioned.

The chapter can be divided as follows:

Introduction (1–2)

A. Preparations: Aaron's garments (3–4)
B. Preparations and the ritual in general: offerings, sin offerings and burnt offerings (5–10)
C. Detailed description of the ritual: purification of sancta (11–20)
    The Azazel-goat ritual (21–22)
    Cleansing of the participants (23–28)
D. The duty of the people and the day as an institution (29–34a)
E. A report of Aaron's execution of the rites (34b)

The oft-alleged literary and ideological features in this chapter are explained by two factors: (1) various threads found until ch. 15 converge in the Day of Atonement ritual: it links to 4:1 – 5:13, chs. 8 – 10 and chs. 11 – 15. (2) The last section, vv. 29–34, both draws all of the preceding prescriptions to a conclusion, and adumbrates the content of ch. 17 onwards. As it stands, according to v. 2 ('Tell Aaron your brother'), all of the section vv. 2–34a is addressed to Moses, while v. 34b reports that Aaron carried it out (see 'Comment' there).

Based on the literary and theological meanings of the preceding chapters, the following notes may highlight the distinctive nature of this chapter.

In relation to chapter 4

The Day of Atonement ritual aims to overcome the insufficiencies latent in the rituals of 4:1 – 5:13, particularly in relation to those given for the anointed priest. Not only does Aaron enter the Holy of Holies only on this occasion, but the chapter prescribes the Azazel-goat ritual, which finally solves the question concerning who will ultimately bear the guilt that Aaron bears. Further, while the rituals in 4:1 – 5:13 consistently move from the outer court to the inner sanctuary, the opposite is true for the ritual of ch. 16: this ritual moves from the purification of the Holy Place to the Tent of Meeting and then further out to the altar of burnt offering. This direction is further stressed by the Azazel goat, which is sent away into the wilderness. Thus the whole ceremony flows from the innermost part of the sanctuary to the wilderness.

In relation to chapters 8 – 10

The purification of the outer altar in 16:18–19 is meant to achieve a rededication of the same altar that was consecrated in 8:15 (note 'round about' and see 'Comment' on 8:15). Aaron's garment in ch. 8 is far more extravagant than the one he wears in ch. 16 (see 'Comment' on v. 4).

The order of the rites in ch. 9, where Aaron brings both the priests and the people into the Lord's presence by making propitiation for himself and then the people, is the same as that given for the ritual in ch. 16. Note that the phrase *kipper bĕʿad* (to make propitiation on behalf of) occurs in 9:7 and 16:6, 11, 17, 24; it appears only in these chapters in Leviticus. Also the phrase *'ăšer lô* (for himself, 9:8) appears in 16:6, 11.

The early part of the ceremony responds to the need Aaron identified at the end of ch. 10, for propitiation to be made for the priestly house. Without it, any kind of atonement ritual loses its validity, since it is the priests who bear the guilt of the people. Yet on this occasion it is not Aaron and his house who ultimately bear the guilt of the people: the Azazel goat bears not only the people's guilt but also that of the priests. Thus without the Azazel goat, the bearing of all the guilt of the sons of Israel (which the term *kipper* has in view) cannot be accomplished. These circumstances, along with ritual proceeding from the innermost part of the Holy Place to the wilderness, clearly indicate that forgiveness and purification on other ordinary occasions are, though valid, temporary.

In relation to chapters 11 – 15

From the viewpoint of the body-sanctuary symbolism or house-Tent-of-Meeting symbolism, the Day of Atonement ritual, following the ironic overtones of the purification of the once *ṣāraʿat*-stricken house in 14:48–53, provides a concrete presentation of the fact that the sanctuary is defiled by the self-hidings of the Israelites, so the purification of the sancta leads to purification of the Israelites.

The core ritual of ch. 16 (the purification of sancta and removal of guilt by the Azazel goat) is typologically similar to the two bird rites in ch. 14 (vv. 5–7, 49–53). Both concern a dwelling place: the former, the Lord's, and the latter, the Israelites'. Moreover the overall structure of chs. 11 – 16 suggests that ch. 16 is a specific application of the rules in chs. 13 – 14. As chs. 13 – 14 convey, in general terms, the incorrigible hardness of heart in self-hiding and its almost putative purificatory rites, the message is expected that ch. 16 conveys the same message to the Israelites in particular. However, the ironic overtones in chs. 13 – 14 recede into the background, since the agent of defilement is specified in ch. 16 as 'the Israelites'. Yet the fact remains that even if the sanctuary is cleansed, it does not achieve its purpose if the Israelites fail to uncover themselves. The prescription does not address such a possibility, but only commands the Israelites to afflict their souls.

Two linguistic and thematic links with ch. 15 may be pointed out. One is that the whole content of ch. 16 clearly takes up the theme of defilement of the Lord's tabernacle that is mentioned in 15:31. The other is that a euphemistic use of the term *bāśār*, meaning 'a genital', occurs in 15:2 and 16:4 (see 'Comment').

The last part of ch. 16, vv. 29–34, continues the preceding prescription by drawing on the same terminology and ideas. This section adds that Aaron's entry into the Holy Place must take place once a year, on the tenth of the seventh month (cf. v. 3), and concludes that the purpose of his entry into the Holy Place is to make propitiation for himself, his house and all the Israelites. In terms of terminology, the previous use of 'people' (*'ām*, vv. 15, 24) and 'the assembly of Israel' (*qĕhal yiśrā'ēl*, v. 17) is replaced by 'the people of the assembly' (*'am haqqāhāl*) in v. 33.

At the same time, the section exhibits some new features: (1) The Lord's address (first, the 2nd person pl. in vv. 29–31; second, the 3rd person in vv. 32–33; third, the 2nd and 3rd person in v. 34); (2) a temporal concern (tenth of the seventh month); (3) the juxtaposition of the human soul (*nepeš*) and propitiation (*kipper*; see 'Comment'). Some other terms such as 'the native or the stranger' (v. 29), 'sabbath of solemn rest' (*šabbat šabbātôn*) and 'afflict a soul' (*'innâ nepeš*) are new in this section. All these anticipate what is dealt with in chs. 17 – 25.

Comment

16:1–2

The occasion for the prescription in ch. 16 is said to be the death of Aaron's sons Nadab and Abihu, recounted in ch. 10. Thus it is expected the following prescription relates to that incident in some way. Particularly in 10:16–19, Aaron bitterly expresses his concern to Moses regarding the propitiation of his own house (10:19). The content of what Moses is commanded to tell Aaron, his brother (16:2), is, at least in part, the Lord's response to Aaron's concern.

In v. 2a Moses commands Aaron not to enter the inner part of the Holy Place at any time. Though it was noted that 10:8, referring to the priests' entry into the 'Tent of Meeting' (*'ōhel mô'ēd*), implies that Nadab and Abihu entered the Tent of Meeting, it was not certain how far they went into the Tent. Here it is further implied that they even entered the inner part of the Tent, the Holy of Holies. Thus putting these pieces of information together, it appears that Nadab and Abihu entered the Holy of Holies, while drinking alcohol, and offered strange fire to the Lord. In view of the following instruction regarding smoke, they may have had a vague idea they needed to burn incense in order to approach the Lord, but did not use incense taken from the altar of incense. Above all, it was a grave violation to enter the inner sancta without authorization. That is why Aaron is warned not to enter 'at any time'. The verse does not specify that the occasion must be once a year (v. 34). The rules in this chapter develop gradually from matters relating to the occasion on which the innermost sanctuary may be entered, to this entry's purpose, and finally to the occasion and its purpose (see 'Form and structure').

'the propitiatory cover': *hakkappôret* The term *kappôret* appears here for the first time in Leviticus (frequently in Exod. 25 – 40). In later literature this part of the ark of the covenant is poetically expressed as the Lord's 'footstool' (Isa. 66:1; Pss. 99:5; 132:7; Lam. 2:1; 1 Chr. 28:2). It is made of pure gold, above which two cherubim cover it with their wings (Exod. 25:17–21). In Exod. 25:22 it is further said, 'There I will meet with you, and from above the mercy seat, from between the two cherubim that are on the ark of the testimony, I will speak with you about all that I will give you in commandment for the people of Israel' (ESV).

Here it is stated that the Lord appears above the *kappôret*. In Lev. 16:2 it is assumed that any human who sees God must die. Thus it was necessary to screen human sight with the smoke of the incense, which simultaneously functioned to appease the Lord's wrath. V. 2b provides the grounds for the injunction against entering the inner part of the Tent of Meeting: it is because the Lord manifests himself in the *kappôret* in smoke. It does not mean that the Lord is visible, but that the smoke is the visible sign of the Lord's presence in the Holy of Holies.

As *kappôret* is related to *kipper*, which means to 'sacrifice oneself (itself) for propitiation', it may well mean 'the propitiatory cover' (cf. Rom. 3:21). It is assumed the ark contains the two tablets on which are inscribed the Ten Commandments (cf. Deut. 10:2).

16:3–10

3. Preparations for Aaron's entrance into the Holy Place and instructions for what he is to do there are given in this section. First, he is to prepare a bull from the herd for a sin offering and a ram for a burnt offering. These offerings are to be sacrificed for himself and his house (v. 6; cf. 4:2–12; 8:2; 9:2). A comparison with the rituals in chs. 4, 8 and 9 indicates that this ritual on the Day of Atonement functions to return the sancta to their original pristine condition.

4. Aaron's wearing of the prescribed garment suggests he enters the Holy Place only by means of the Lord's holiness. Thus it is emphatically stressed that the propitiation achieved in the Holy Place is not of human origin (see v. 17).

Twice the term *bāśār* (body) appears in this verse. The first refers euphemistically to genitals (cf. Exod. 28:42), while the second literally means 'body' (Péter-Contesse 1993: 252). This literary phenomenon already appears in 15:2–3, 13, and here carries the same sense, so Aaron is presented as unclean and thus in a state of hiding himself. This is one of many examples where a person, who is holy by calling, is still regarded as unclean when he approaches the Lord (cf. chs. 8 – 9; Exod. 30:18–21). Washing his flesh in water symbolizes his uncovering, which is a part of his personal purificatory rites. Compared with the extravagant garments worn on the occasion of the ordination ceremony (8:7–9), these garments are strikingly plain. As Wenham succinctly points out (1979: 230), Aaron enters the 'other world', into the very presence of God as a sinner.

5. Then Aaron takes two male goats from the Israelites for the purification and propitiation of their self-hiding, and a ram for a burnt offering. The specification of 'goats for the whole of Israel' is similar to the one on the eighth-day service (9:3) but differs from the prescription in ch. 4; in ch. 4 a goat is specified for the propitiation of the tribal leader's self-hiding, whereas a bull is specified for the self-hiding of either an anointed priest or of the congregation. Rather than different traditions, these facts reflect different objects of expiation. In Lev. 9, the eighth-day service, the sin offering functioned to uncover the spiritual state of the Israelites as the first of a series of offerings, in anticipation of the Lord's visible manifestation. Thus the object of expiation is not rooted in the violation of one of the Lord's commandments, as in ch. 4. Here too the ceremony's occasion is not necessitated by any violation of the Lord's commandments by the Israelites, but, as in ch. 9, by the need for the Israelites to be completely purified. This is the reason why the purificatory offering for the people is less expensive than in ch. 4. Instead the burnt offering for the people is a bull, as in the sacrifice for Aaron and his family. A greater degree of self-dedication is expected of the people (cf. 9:3). This, in turn, implies that the priestly responsibility is underscored by the expensive offering Aaron offers: a bull (cf. 4:3).

6. Aaron's responsibility is first underscored by his making propitiation for himself and his house. Though resumed in v. 11, this verse completes the ritual for the priests in summary form. No mention is made of *kipper* in 4:2–12, which leads Péter-Contesse to suspect the presence of a different tradition. However, this is the very significance of the Day of Atonement: the ritual in ch. 4 is required on account of the anointed priest's self-hiding and, since he cannot bear his own guilt substitutionally, this ceremony on the Day of Atonement is given to overcome this insufficiency.

For *kipper bĕʿad* (to make propitiation on behalf of), see 'Comment' on 9:7 and 16:17 below. V. 6 is practically carried out from v. 11 onwards.

The chronological order of Aaron's propitiation for the priests and the casting of lots in relation to the two goats is not the main concern, though it is reasonably assumed that Aaron cast the lots after preparing the two goats and before making propitiation for himself and his house (cf. 'shall be presented alive' in v. 10). The repeated ordering of priestly matters *before* matters relating to the people pervades the whole chapter, and this suggests it is the responsibility of the priests over against the people that is stressed by this discourse.

7. It is not just v. 6 but vv. 7–10 that describe what should be done to the two goats for the people in summary form. The beginning of v. 7, 'He shall take', refers back to v. 5. Therefore it is not to say that the handling of the two goats in v. 7 took place just after propitiation was made for the priests in v. 6. A similar order is also found in vv. 18–19 below.

8. After taking and positioning the two goats before the Lord, Aaron casts lots, and determines which goat belongs to the Lord, and which belongs to Azazel. The etymology of *ʿăzāʾzēl* is uncertain. Three possibilities have been proposed: (1) the name of a demon, (2) a geographical designation meaning 'precipitous place' or 'rugged cliff', and (3) a combination of *ʿēz* (goat) and *ʾozēl* (to go away) (see Janowski 1998: 128–131). However, despite Janowski's scepticism, *laʿăzāʾzēl* is contrasted with *laYHWH*, and it is reasonable to infer that *ʿăzāʾzēl* is a spiritual being with personhood. It is certainly true that the Israelites committed their self-hidings by their own will, but the sending of their consequence to Azazel implies that Azazel was somehow deeply involved in the matter of their self-hidings.

9–10. Aaron is to bring the goat near the Lord and sacrifice it as a sin offering, but keep the goat for Azazel alive before the Lord. By saying *wĕʿāśāhû* (and use it), v. 9 summarizes what is later described in more detail in v. 15. Also v. 10b anticipates what is later prescribed in vv. 21–22.

The *ʿālāyw* in *lĕkapper ʿālāyw* (to sacrifice itself for him) in v. 10 is something of a *crux interpretum*. As the text stands, there are several translational possibilities, the major ones of which are as follows: (1) The agent of *kipper* is Aaron, and the pronominal suffix is the Azazel goat (Keil 1968: 398; Péter-Contesse 1993: 253–254). (2) The agent of *kipper* is Aaron and *ʿālāyw* means 'upon it [the goat]' (Milgrom 1991: 1023). (3) The agent of *kipper* is the Azazel goat and *ʿālāyw* means 'for him [Aaron]' (Kiuchi 1987: 151). First, it is entirely unintelligible why propitiation would be required for the Azazel goat: it is already holy. Option (2) is possible. But since the sancta are the extended personality of the Lord (cf. v. 16b), *kipper ʿal*, when followed by inanimate objects, should be translated as 'for'. (For other proposals, see Levine 1974: 65; Hartley 1992: 237; Péter-Contesse 1993: 253–254.) The third possibility, recently followed by Sklar (2001: 96–98), may appear surprising, but is most likely. Vv. 9–10 indicate a switch of agent from Aaron to the Azazel goat, analogous to the syntactical construction in 1:4 (*sāmak – nirṣâ*). Moreover my theory that *kipper* is synonymous with *nāśā' 'āwōn* (bearing guilt) supports this interpretation. This means that the Azazel goat's bearing of guilt for the Israelites in vv. 21b–22 is an act of *kipper* (see 10:17; Kiuchi 1987: 149–153; Sklar 2001: 96–98 [especially p. 97 n. 45] for his critique of Milgrom's view).

One rite analogous to the Azazel-goat rite is that performed for the purification of the *ṣāra'at*-afflicted house in 14:49–53. The live bird released into the open field outside the city parallels the Azazel goat. Yet in connection to the interpretation of 16:10 it is arguable that *kipper* in 14:53b encompasses what the live bird achieves. Therefore it is likely the Azazel goat *kipper*s in 16:10 as well.

Since the Azazel goat is not slaughtered, it is indeed unlike other ordinary sacrifices. Yet the assertion that it is not a sacrifice is problematical, for v. 5 explicitly states that the two goats are designated for the sin offering. The flow of the ritual procedure indicates that when a lot is cast, one of the goats ceased to be a sin offering in a normal sense. Whether it is a 'sacrifice' is another question, and the answer depends on the definition of 'sacrifice'. However, whatever the modern definition of the term, it is important to consider the question in biblical terms. In this regard, there is no reason why there cannot be a live sacrifice. As will be explained below, the difference of the two goats lies in the role each has in relation to the *kipper* act: whether or not the role is concerned with the Lord's dwelling place. In that the Azazel goat takes all the guilt of the Israelites away into the desert, it plays the concluding part in the *kipper* event for the whole of Israel.

16:11–15

Vv. 11–17 stipulate the ritual procedure for the propitiation made for Aaron and his house, and for the people. V. 11a resumes v. 6. Therefore vv. 11b–14 provide the details pertaining to v. 11a. On the other hand, vv. 15–16 are the details relating to v. 9. Thus the order of the rites in vv. 11–17 follows those of vv. 3–5 and 6–10, where Aaron's offerings are mentioned before those of the people. After slaughtering the bull, Aaron enters the Holy Place with a handful of incense. When he enters, he adds fire taken from the incense altar (cf. Exod. 30:34–38), so the smoke protects his life by preventing him from seeing the Lord's appearance above the *kappôret* (see v. 2). Then he sprinkles some of the bull's blood on the propitiatory cover seven times, and then does the same with the goat's blood.

The specification 'on the east side' (v. 14) may help Aaron do his job in darkness. However, this would appear somewhat superfluous, since the location was well known to Aaron. As for the designation in 1:16, it may suggest that the purification of the propitiatory cover is likened to the entrance of the Garden of Eden, which is likewise protected by cherubim (Gen. 3:24; see below). Sprinkling seven times towards the propitiatory cover would remind the reader of the similar ritual in 4:6, 17. There it was impossible for the anointed priest to enter the innermost sanctuary. So this is the occasion when the priestly self-hidings are expiated in a complete way. It is assumed the propitiatory cover is defiled by the self-hidings of the priests. Because of this the Lord is wrathful and requires appeasement.

On this occasion the same uncleanness and 'sins' that have defiled the propitiatory cover and the Holy Place are dealt with on a new dimension.

The defilement of the propitiatory cover shows that the Lord's commandments have been broken. Yet the violation is closely related to the idea of self-hiding. If the latter is purified by blood, the divine presence is again guaranteed. On the other hand, the presence of the cherubim has escaped the attention of exegetes. For just as they functioned to protect the way to the Tree of *Life* in Gen. 3:24, on this occasion too, their presence implies that even after purification of the propitiatory cover, the Israelites are not allowed to enter this *life* enjoyed by 'a living soul' (Gen. 2:7). This also points to the significant spiritual truth that the quality of life in the sanctuary, or even of the Holy Place, is likened to the quality of life outside the Garden of Eden (see 'Explanation' on ch. 11). With such limitations, however, the purification of the propitiatory cover and the Holy Place brings about the purification of the Israelites.

16:16

This verse summarizes the meaning and purpose of the ritual for the people, which are stressed further in v. 17b, in a more comprehensive way that refers to the propitiation made for Aaron and his house, in addition to the people.

V. 16b suggests a close linguistic and literary connection with 15:31, where it is said, 'so that they will not defile my sanctuary which is in their midst'. In this chapter, 'the Tent of Meeting' (*'ôhel mô'ēd*) and not 'sanctuary' (*miškān*) is used, whereas the use of the verb *šākan* refers back to 15:31. The significance of this is that despite the Lord's condescension to dwell among the people, the people who hide themselves constantly defile him.

The exegesis of v. 16a has seemingly reached an impasse mainly because of the loose definition of the Hebr. term *ḥaṭṭā't* (see below). Contextually v. 16 is the first place in Leviticus where the idea of uncleanness and *ḥaṭṭā't* are brought together in a single verse, so uncleanness (*ṭum'ōt*) should not be understood simply in a ritual sense but also as symbolically related to *ḥaṭṭā't* (see 'Comment' on ch. 4).

'because of the uncleanness of the Israelites and because of their rebellions, all their self-hiding': *miṭṭum'ōt běnê yiśrā'ēl umippiš'êhem lěkol ḥaṭṭō'tām* The phrase *běnê yiśrā'ēl* (the sons of Israel) must refer to the priests as well as the people, since v. 16 summarizes the foregoing rituals for both (see also 'Comment' on 4:2–3 and v. 19 below).

There are two important exegetical questions: (1) Syntactically does the last phrase *lěkol ḥaṭṭō'tām* refer not only to the preceding *piš'êhem* but also to *ṭum'ōt běnê yiśrā'ēl*? (2) What kind of uncleanness and 'sin' are envisaged here?

Peša' occurs only here and v. 21 in Leviticus, but often occurs in conjunction with *ḥaṭṭā't* or *ḥāṭā'* in other contexts as well (e.g. with *ḥaṭṭā't* Gen. 31:36; 50:17; with *ḥāṭā'* 1 Sam. 24:11[12]; 1 Kgs 8:50). It has been translated 'transgression' or 'rebellion'. But 'transgression' in the sense of breaking laws is inadequate. For, while *peša'* can be committed by some specific act, its meaning is much broader, referring to one's total attitude to God or a person, just as self-hiding can be committed by violating some specific commandment. Since the verbal form *pāša'* takes *bě* followed by persons, it must describe the breaking of a personal relationship. Thus 'to rebel' appears to be an appropriate rendering. Certainly rebellion or the breaking of a relationship can also be committed by violation of certain laws. The noun form *peša'* thus means 'rebellion' in the sense of breaking relationship with the Lord (cf. Isa. 48:8; Ezek. 2:3; 20:38).

In Lev. 16:16 further qualification of the term *peša'* is necessary, since it is followed by *lěkol ḥaṭṭō'tām*. With regard to the term *ḥaṭṭā't*, it means 'the state of hiding oneself' (Kiuchi 2003a: 41), and this rendering solves the somewhat ambiguous semantic relation between *peša'* and *ḥaṭṭā't* in this verse, for *lěkol* can be taken to mean 'in reference to' (for this use of *lěkol*, i.e. specification, in Leviticus, see 5:3–4; 11:42; 13:12, 51; 22:5). When the root *pš'* occurs in the forms *peša'* or *pāša'*, it is often accompanied by the root *ḥṭ'* in the forms of *ḥaṭṭā't* or *ḥāṭā'*. This strongly suggests that *peša'* and *ḥaṭṭā't* refer to two different descriptions of the same negative human relationship with the Lord. This does not mean these two terms are totally interchangeable: there are cases where each of them can describe certain situations better than the other. Lev. 16:16 is the only place in the OT where the two terms are not simply juxtaposed. This is probably because the Day of Atonement ritual concerns 'self-hiding': *lěkol ḥaṭṭō'tām* underscores the essential nature of the ritual.

Though *peša'* means 'rebellion', it does not follow that it is more 'heinous' or 'serious' than so-called 'sins'. Hence it is not right to say this ceremony deals only with serious 'sins' not dealt with by the ordinary rituals. Every transgression of the Lord's commandment constitutes rebellion, irrespective of how far individuals or a congregation are aware of their own act. Thus *peša'* is seen here as defiling the sanctuary, in so far as *peša'* is also self-hiding. For the notional relationship between uncleanness and rebellion, see Ezek. 14:11; 37:23.

The above considerations lead to the conclusion that on this occasion the same self-hidings dealt with by the sin offering are again in view, but from a different perspective: their role in defiling the innermost sanctuary.

With regard to the question of how *ṭum'ōt bĕnê yiśrā'ēl* relates to the following, there are two possibilities: (1) *Lĕkol ḥaṭṭō'tām* refers not just to the preceding *piš'êhem* but also to *ṭum'ōt bĕnê yiśrā'ēl.* (2) *Lĕkol ḥaṭṭō'tām* refers only to *piš'êhem*, and the latter comprises two separate matters: uncleanness and self-hiding. Point 1 implies that bodily uncleanness, such as touching unclean things or sexual intercourse, has not defiled the innermost sanctuary, as *ḥaṭṭō'tām* (their self-hidings) is the ultimate object of propitiation. On the other hand, point 2 may imply these incidents of uncleanness indeed defile the innermost sanctuary.

Some syntactical and notional observations are in order. First, the twice-repeated *min* may support possibility 2. However, since in legal parts of the Pentateuch *lĕkol* functions to sum up what precedes it (Lev. 22:5; Exod. 27:3; Lev. 5:4; 11:42; 13:12; see also Exod. 14:28; cf. Merwe et al 39.11), the presence of the twice-repeated *min* does not particularly support point 2. Second, *ḥaṭṭō'tām* is also uncleanness (see vv. 16b, 19b below), and in this regard, it may be possible to assume that by *lĕkol ḥaṭṭō'tām* 'uncleanness' (*ṭum'ōt*) is intended. The issue at question is the relationship between *ṭum'ōt* and *ḥaṭṭā't.* The solution lies in postulating that though *ṭum'ōt* means 'uncleanness', its symbolic meaning, the state of hiding oneself, is none other than the meaning of *ḥaṭṭā't.* These considerations appear to favour possibility 1.

However, the question still needs to be asked as to whether relatively minor defilements such as the touching of unclean things or having sexual intercourse defile the Holy Place. In chs. 11 – 15 these defilements do not appear to defile the sanctuary, since they are simply purified by a person's waiting until evening. However, while a 'minor' uncleanness does not defile the Tent in terms of *outer* cleanness/uncleanness, it does when its symbolic meaning is taken into account (see 'Comment' on 15:31). This means that the non-mention of sacrificial rituals in those cases of minor defilement does not indicate that the Tent went undefiled. This situation is similar to the one in 4:22 – 5:13, where the rituals only take place at the outer altar, even though it can be assumed the Holy of Holies was defiled. Thus this verse particularly unifies outer and inner cleanness.

Since the table of the Ten Commandments is ensconced in the ark, there is no reason to deny that the ritual on the Day of Atonement deals with self-hiding related to the violation of prohibitions such as the ones set out in chs. 18 onwards.

'for the Tent of Meeting' In this chapter 'the Tent of Meeting' refers to the outer part of the Tent where the priests officiate on ordinary occasions (see v. 20).

'which dwells with them in the midst of their uncleanness' (v. 16b). The 'Tent of Meeting' is personified, and this renders some support for the view that propitiation is made for sancta, as though the latter have a personality; indeed they represent the extended personhood of the Lord.

16:17–19

The instruction that no human (*'ādām*, see 'Comment' on 1:2) should be in the Tent of Meeting indicates that no priest, not to mention a lay individual, could involve himself with the purification of the Holy Place. Only Aaron performs the ritual, wearing his holy garment.

'to make propitiation on behalf of': *kipper bĕ'ad* The Hebr. phrase occurs in 9:7, and frequently in this chapter in vv. 6, 11, 17, 24. The preposition is used only for cases where the beneficiary of the *kipper* act is human.

Vv. 18–19 indicate how the altar of burnt offering is to be cleansed. Verse18a summarizes the purification of the altar, and vv. 18b–19 detail the procedure. Though some debate has focused on the identification of 'the altar' in v. 18 (i.e. whether it refers to the altar of incense or to the altar of burnt offering), v. 16b probably includes the purification of the incense altar, so 'the altar' in v. 18 is the outer altar (cf. Wenham 1979: 232–233). The language 'he put the blood on the horns of the altar *round about*' resonates with the language of 8:15, and implies that this rite is meant to rededicate the altar on this occasion. For the gesture's symbolic meaning, see 'Comment' on 4:7.

Nowhere else does Aaron *sprinkle* blood on to the altar of burnt offering. Compared with a similar ritual in 4:6–7, the one in 16:19 is unique in that it reverses the rite so that the sprinkling of blood now comes before the daubing of blood (cf. 4:6–7). These are probably meant to stress that the inefficiency of blood-handling on ordinary occasions is overcome by the potent blood that has purified the Holy Place (16:19b). Another analogue, which is more significant for the ritual in ch. 16, is the rite in 8:11. In this ordination ceremony, however, the oil is sprinkled on the altar of burnt offering. The order of the daubing and sprinkling of blood or oil in chs. 8 and 16 is as follows:

8:11, 15	*16:18–19*
Sprinkling of oil	Daubing of blood
Daubing of blood	Sprinkling of blood

This reversal of order is necessitated by the defilement of the altar of burnt offering. Its original sanctity, given by the sprinkling of oil, is now regained by the sprinkling of blood seven times.

Thus complete propitiation flows from the Holy Place; i.e. from the inner to the outer, and not the other way round. This is in accord with the prescription at the end of the chapter (vv. 29, 31) that the Israelites are to afflict their souls, their innermost parts (see below).

V. 19b describes the purpose of daubing and sprinkling blood on the altar; i.e. to 'purify it' (*ṭiharô*) and 'consecrate it' (*qiddĕšô*). This is the only place where the two terms *ṭihar* and *qiddēš* are juxtaposed. But the same idea is also assumed in v. 14, where Aaron sprinkles the blood on to the propitiatory cover. Further, though not mentioned explicitly, this can also be assumed in the same rites of 4:6, 17. Except for the rituals in chs. 8 and 16, the repetition of purificatory acts makes the unclean clean, but does not make it holy. That here the altar becomes holy by purification is grounded only upon the fact that the altar was consecrated previously by the oil and blood (ch. 8), suggesting that holiness is a God-given status or calling.

These two terms, 'purify' and 'consecrate', refer to the daubing of blood on to the horns of the altar as well as to the sprinkling of blood on it, and combine to express the content of *kipper* (v. 18a), which encapsulates the whole *process* from unclean to holy. When it is recalled that the ritual deals with the uncleanness of the Israelites, the ideas of purifying and consecrating are nothing more than a process of *uncovering*. This means the sancta have been hiding themselves, though this should not be seen as taking place independently of the Israelites. Since the state of sancta parallel the state of human soul (*nepeš*), uncovering the sancta symbolically uncovers the souls of the Israelites (see 'Explanation'). Aaron's purificatory rites, when they are complete, place an extreme demand upon the Israelites, for what took place in the sanctuary must take place in the souls of the Israelites (cf. vv. 29, 31).

The last phrase in v. 19, 'the sons of Israel' (*bĕnê yiśrā'ēl*), includes the priests, since the purifying blood is taken not just from the goat but also from the bull (v. 18b).

16:20–22

After completing the purificatory rites for the sancta, Aaron offers the live goat. He is to confess all the guilt and self-hidings of the Israelites over the goat, and to send it away into the wilderness. How is this rite related to the purification of the sancta? (For a variety of views on this question, see Kiuchi 1987: 145–148; Jenson 1992: 197–208.) The large majority of exegetes assume that the Azazel-goat ritual has its own independent history, and that it was incorporated into the ritual of the Day of Atonement. Others, who do not take such a view, leave the question of the relationship between the two rites unanswered.

Now, if the purification of sancta is not interconnected with the removal of guilt by the live goat, the question must be asked how the guilt Aaron bore in purifying the sancta is removed. Moreover what should Aaron do with his own guilt? The major reason why exegetes are unclear about these questions is partly because the meanings of key terms such as *kipper* and *ḥaṭṭā't* have not been elucidated sufficiently.

The term *kipper*, which, as we have seen, means to 'sacrifice oneself (itself) for propitiation', has two semantic elements, uncovering and bearing guilt. So when Aaron *kipper*s for the sancta, he uncovers the sancta and simultaneously bears the guilt associated with the self-hiding of the Israelites. Therefore the phrase *kipper 'al* in v. 10 does not present a difficulty. The Azazel goat sacrifices itself for Aaron, who has borne the guilt associated with the self-hidings of the Israelites.

As regards the ritual proper, Aaron acknowledges *all* the guilt and *all* the rebellion of the sons of Israel over the goat. This is the second occurrence of *hitwaddâ* in Leviticus (cf. 5:5; 26:40); it reveals what has been hidden, which befits the meaning of self-hiding. The *kipper* act finishes with the devolving of guilt on the Azazel goat when Aaron lays both hands on it, confessing all the self-hidings of the Israelites. While the laying on of both hands is associated with 'transference', in distinction to what occurs in the ordinary sacrificial context, it is not the distinction between one and two hands that determines its symbolic meaning, but the occasion on which the rite is performed (cf. Wright and Milgrom 1986: 884–885). Perhaps Aaron uses both hands, in keeping with the solemn nature of this occasion.

Compared with v. 16, sin terminology changes only with regard to 'guilt' (*'ăwōnōt*); uncleanness (*ṭum'ōt*) in v. 16 becomes 'guilt' (*'ăwōnōt*) in v. 21, which is the consequence of the former. In addition to this, the term *kol* is prefixed before all three terms. As in v. 16, it seems appropriate to take *lĕkol ḥaṭṭō'tām* as referring both to *kol piš'êhem* and *kol 'ăwōnōt bĕnê yiśrā'ēl* (cf. Exod. 14:28). Here in v. 21, however, *peša'* refers to the consequential aspect of 'rebellion'.

The phrase 'the sons of Israel' is used comprehensively, referring not just to the people but also to the priests (see v. 19). In this sense it should not be confused with the term 'people' (*'ām*) in vv. 15 and 24. In fact Aaron is not only confessing the guilt and rebellion of the people: he also confesses his own self-hiding alongside that of his house. Thus Aaron's role is not purely substitutionary.

The goat is sent away into the wilderness by a man in readiness (*bĕyad 'îš 'ittî*). The choice of the word *'îš* (a person) appears deliberate. It is used here in an interpersonal sense in that he is to be chosen from among the people. Cf. *'ādām* in v. 17.

Note the change of agent in vv. 21b–22: Aaron (21b) – the goat (22a) – impersonal or the person in office (22b). Thus v. 22b does not simply repeat v. 21b. V. 21b is stated from Aaron's point of view, while v. 22b is stated from the viewpoint of the role of the person in readiness; in the latter the person lets the goat go free *in* the wilderness. Although later Jewish tradition contemplated the further fate of the goat (Yoma 6:6; i.e. killed by falling off a cliff), this interpretation conflicts with the nature of the Azazel goat in that the rite symbolizes an *uncovering* of guilt and its removal from the sanctuary, and not that guilt's annihilation. Moreover, if Azazel is the name of a demon, the rite may aim at returning the guilt to the principal agent involved in the self-hidings of the Israelites. Thus the rite punishes Azazel. By watching the goat being sent away into the wilderness, the Israelites confirm, in a ritualistic sense, that all their self-hidings are uncovered, and removed from the sanctuary. Again, this ritual's purpose is defeated if the Israelites fail to uncover themselves. For the still imperfect nature of the rite, see 'Explanation'.

16:23–28

The foregoing is, however, not the end, but just the core part of the ceremony. These verses prescribe Aaron's changing of clothes, the offering of the burnt offering and the fat associated with the sin offering, and the burning of the remaining flesh of the sin offering, while simultaneously laying down the purificatory rites associated with each of these rites.

Aaron's leaving the holy garment in the Holy Place underscores again that propitiation for the Holy Place is not human work (v. 17a); even Aaron only performs his duty by wearing the holy garment. Changing his clothes from the holy linen garments to his ordinary ones after ablutions does not signify the removal of holiness (Hartley 1992: 242) but the purification of uncleanness. The rationale for this defilement is found in Aaron's movement from the highest degree of holiness to a lower degree of holiness. Since this is viewed as Aaron's hiding from the highest degree of holiness, he is regarded as hiding himself, i.e. becoming unclean, just as a Nazirite presents a sin offering when he successfully completes his vow (see v. 4; Num. 6:14; Kiuchi 2003a: 45–46). The phrase 'in a holy place' in v. 24 may contradict his state of uncleanness if holiness is simply conceived in a ritual sense. It demands he must bear inner holiness when washing.

Then he offers two burnt offerings for himself and the people (vv. 24b–25), which symbolize the total dedication of all the people, including Aaron. Only after the burnt offering, which symbolizes a total dedication that appeases the Lord's wrath, does the Lord accept Aaron and the people. However, all this is meaningless unless the people, including Aaron, really abandon all of their earthly desires.

The purificatory rite is for the man who handles the Azazel goat and becomes defiled (v. 26). This defilement presumably occurs because he comes into contact with the Azazel goat's holiness, and not with the sin and guilt of the Israelites that have been handled on a substitutionary dimension (see 'Comment' on 6:28 and Kiuchi 2006). He is allowed to enter the camp after he washes his clothes and bathes in water (cf. 14:8; 15:13; Num. 19:8). The juxtaposition of the same purificatory rites for the man who handles the Azazel goat and for the man who burns the flesh of the sin offering (v. 28) suggests that the latter rite, which takes place on ordinary occasions such as in ch. 4, also symbolizes a removal of guilt in the same way as the Azazel-goat ritual (see Kiuchi 1987: 134–135). In contrast with 4:12, where the person does not become defiled, when the perfect cleansing of the sanctuary is achieved on the Day of Atonement, the burning of the flesh brings about uncleanness, and the person who handles it becomes defiled. This observation suggests the rituals in ch. 4 are only temporal: though the ritual in ch. 4 is valid on its own, it is seen as insufficient and temporal in view of the more potent purification achieved by the Day of Atonement ritual.

16:29–34

The last section of the chapter, vv. 29–34, establishes the ceremony in vv. 3–28 as an annual institution: it must be observed once a year, the tenth of the seventh month. This section includes three major elements: (1) The Israelites must afflict their souls, doing no work on this day, since it is to be a day of solemn rest. (2) The qualification of the priest who makes propitiation is that he is anointed and the successor of his father. (3) On this day the priest makes propitiation for the sancta and for the priests and people, thus for all the sons of Israel, because of all their self-hidings. For the relationship with the following chapters, see 'Form and structure'.

Though this section may appear supplementary to vv. 3–28, it is an indispensable part of the institution for the Day of Atonement in that it includes a crucial prescription for 'afflicting one's soul', which applies to both Israelites and strangers – for without such affliction the ritual Aaron performs inside the Tent of Meeting becomes a mere formality.

Up to this point all the prescriptions are addressed to Moses (v. 2). It is not said that Moses delivered the message to Aaron. Though it appears the Lord addresses the rules from here on to the Israelites in general, including the priests, this would be a superficial reading. If this were so, the Lord would have addressed both Aaron and the Israelites through Moses in v. 2, or a new address may well have been expected to begin in v. 29. The fact that the Lord addresses only Moses in v. 2 suggests the section vv. 29–34a is also addressed to Moses (see on v. 29). This supports my exegetical conclusion that *wayya'aś* (and he did) should be sg., not pl., in v. 34 (see below on v. 34).

As regards the command to afflict one's soul, it is the soul that corresponds to the Holy Place in the sanctuary, and it is the object of purification. The Israelites' souls have been doomed by their hiding from the Lord. The body-sanctuary symbolism is already found in 14:10–20, while the defilement of souls in 11:44 corresponds to the Lord's abode; i.e. the Tent of Meeting in 15:31 (see 'Comment' there).

Just as the human body represents the outer part, and heart and soul the inner, the outer court, particularly the altar, represents the outer parts of the divine abode, and the Tent of Meeting, the centre of God's abode. Thus the release of the human soul from its self-hiding is tantamount to the complete purification of the Holy Place. Therefore whether or not the ritual on the Day of Atonement achieves such a goal depends on whether the Israelites observe the command to afflict their souls. Further, just as the purification of the sancta begins from the innermost part of the Holy Place and moves to the outer parts of the sanctuary, the purification of one's soul must come first, without which the accomplishment of purificatory rites has limited efficacy.

29. 'It shall be': *hāyĕtâ* Cf. v. 34. The subject, presumably 'this', refers to the content of the following verses till v. 33.

'a statute ... forever': *ḥuqqat 'ôlām* See 'Comment' on 3:17.

'for you [pl.]' Here, and in v. 34, 'you' refers to Moses and Aaron for two reasons: (1) No new addressee is specified here and the foregoing address was made to Moses. (2) That Aaron is included in 'you' is understandable, as all the content of the prescription in this chapter concerns Aaron (v. 2).

'afflict your souls': *tĕ'annû 'et napšōtêkem* The 'souls' of the Israelites, and not simply 'themselves', are at issue (note the pu. form of *'nh* in 23:29). The term *nepeš* is used in distinction from *'ādām* in v. 17 and *'îš* in v. 21. See also 'Comment' on 11:43–44. It is the human *nepeš* that hides itself from the Lord (4:2, 27; 5:1–2, 4, 15, 17, 21). Moreover, as explained in ch. 4, the hiding *nepeš* is usually unconscious of his own inner condition. Since the *ḥaṭṭā't* offering purifies such a condition of the human soul on this occasion, the Israelites must rigorously examine their own hearts and souls, to the extent that the unconscious realm of their hearts may be revealed. One practical outward means is prescribed: cessation from work. Although other outward means such as fasting were naturally added in the later interpretation of this passage, it must be admitted that nothing is mentioned other than the cessation from work, and that a piling up of outward actions more often than not leads human beings into replacing the affliction of their souls with outward actions; such actions tend to be viewed as meritorious until they become hypocritical (cf. Isa. 58:3–14). The Leviticus text does not command them to fast; rather it simply commands them not to work on the sabbath day.

The command to afflict one's soul presumes that one should have at least another self that supervises his own egocentric soul. However, as their whole existence is assumed to be hidden from themselves, it is extremely difficult to conceive of the existence of another self. This consideration suggests that the true observance of the Azazel-goat ritual, particularly Aaron's confession, is tantamount to something impracticable.

'the native and the stranger': *hā'ezraḥ wĕhaggēr* For the first time in Leviticus people are classified in this way. This classification certainly paves the way towards the following chapters. Even those who reside with the natives for a certain period of time defile the sanctuary.

30. This particle *kî* (for) introduces the ground for the statement in v. 29: the affliction of souls and cessation from work is required because propitiation is made so the Israelites can be cleansed from all of their self-hidings. What takes place inside the sanctuary (v. 30) must match the action of the people outside (v. 29). While the idea that the Israelites are atoned for (*kipper*) and purified (*ṭihar*) or 'forgiven' (*nislaḥ*, 4:20, 26, 31, 35; 5:10, 16, 18, 26; 19:22) is common in other contexts (see 12:7–8; 14:20 and implicitly in 15:15, 30), the expression that they are purified (*ṭāhēr*) from their self-hidings (*ḥaṭṭō't*) is new. This manifests the idea that uncleanness and self-hidings are related, which remained hidden in vv. 16 and 21. Because the self-hiding is ordinarily 'forgiven', it does not follow that on the Day of Atonement the same self-hiding is forgiven (cf. Hartley 1992: 243); rather on this day the clean state of the Israelites before the Lord is highlighted as the goal of the whole ceremony. Note that 'all your self-hidings' (*kol ḥaṭṭō'têkem*) in this verse is repeated in v. 34 as 'all their self-hidings' (*kol ḥaṭṭō'tām*).

It should be noted that the appearance of *kipper* and *nepeš* in this section, though not yet conjoined, adumbrates 17:11.

31. 'a sabbath of solemn rest': *šabbat šabbātôn* The noun *šabbat* as well as the phrase appears here for the first time in Leviticus. The phrase occurs further in 23:3, 32 and 25:4. In stipulating that the Israelites are to observe the day as a sabbath by afflicting their souls, the verse introduces a new aspect to the sabbath institution: true rest for the Israelites comes only when they afflict their souls.

32. This verse concerns the human agent of propitiation on the Day of Atonement. It is the anointed priest who succeeds his father, and who wears the holy linen garments. That the priest is what will be later called the high priest is indicated indirectly (see 'Comment' on 4:3–4).

'make propitiation': *kipper* The Hebr. term is used absolutely without a preposition. In vv. 29–34 *kipper* takes the prepositions *'et* or *'al*, or stands alone, and *bĕ'ad* is not used (see vv. 6, 11, 17, 24). In view of the interpretation that *bĕ'ad* appears in contexts where emphasis is laid on the beneficiary more than on the agent of *kipper 'al*, a more balanced relation between the agent and the beneficiary of the *kipper* act is conveyed by the use of *'al* (see above on v. 7).

33. The first term in Hebr. text, *kipper*, resumes the first term of the previous verse, *kipper*, and describes the objects and beneficiaries of propitiation. On the one hand, the priest makes propitiation for the Holy Place, the Tent of Meeting, and the altar; on the other, he makes it for the priests and all the assembly of the people.

'the holy sanctuary': *miqdaš haqqodeš Miqdaš* occurs in 12:4; 19:30; 20:3 etc. As opposed to *miškān*, it stresses the holy nature of the sanctuary. Cf. 12:4, where the woman is prohibited from coming into contact with a *holy* offering.

kol 'am haqqāhāl See 'Form and structure'.

34. 'This shall be': *hāyĕtâ zō't* These opening words form an inclusio with the beginning of v. 29 (Hartley 1992: 243). 'This' refers to the foregoing rules mentioned in vv. 29–33, and they are once again summarized by saying that propitiation may be made for the people of Israel once a year because of all their self-hidings. The construction *kipper* + *'al* + *min* is found in v. 16, but the word that comes after *'al* is different: in v. 16 it is the Holy Place, whereas in v. 34 it is the sons of Israel. Thus more emphasis on the personal aspect of propitiation is made in this last summary of the ceremony.

V. 34b reports that the prescription in this chapter was carried out just as the Lord commanded Moses. The subject of *wayya'aś* appears ambiguous, but since it is 3rd person sg., it is Aaron, not Moses (cf. Péter-Contesse 1993: 263 n. 58). This accords with the fact that vv. 29–34 and vv. 3–28 are addressed to Aaron through Moses (see 'Comment' on v. 29). This provides further resolution to the pending situation in 10:16–20 (see above on vv. 1–2).

In view of the symbolic meaning of the ritual presented above, one should not interpret this final remark as though Aaron fulfilled all the procedure including its symbolic meaning. The intent of this report is that he did what he could do according to the prescription.

Explanation

The Day of Atonement ritual provides for an occasion on which all the sins (self-hiding) of the Israelites and the priests are purified and removed by the Azazel goat. It is a perfect means of grace in that it purifies the defiled sancta with the most potent means of purification: the blood that purified the Holy Place. The comprehensiveness of the ritual in terms of its scope and power casts a shadow over the other ordinary purificatory rituals. The primary message of this chapter is that atonement comes only from the Lord, and that the process starts from the Holy of Holies, which symbolically corresponds to the innermost part of the human being.

Nevertheless the ritual still has some significant deficiencies and therefore awaits its complete substantiation in other ways. First of all, the interpretation that the offering for self-hiding (*ḥaṭṭā't*) functions to *uncover* the self-hiding of the people demands a radical reconsideration of the nature of this ritual. It is not specific violations of the Lord's commandments, but the existential and spiritual condition of the human *nepeš*, which hides itself, that is the object of propitiation. As mentioned in ch. 4 (see 'Comment' there), it is extremely difficult for people to realize their own self-hiding, since this primarily belongs to the unconscious realm. In v. 21 Aaron is to confess all the self-hidings upon the Azazel goat, but is this just a ritualistic formality? When due consideration is given to the nature of self-hiding, it is entirely unlikely that Aaron confesses *all* the self-hidings of the people, including his own. Moreover, if the offences in chs. 18 – 20, for instance, are related to self-hiding, which appears probable, the likelihood that propitiation is substantially made on this day seems remote. Last, does the Azazel goat understand Aaron's confession? This indicates that the goat cannot 'bear the guilt' of human beings in the true sense of the phrase. That the whole ritual culminates with such a situation points to an imperfection of the ritual on the Day of Atonement, let alone other expiatory rituals (cf. Ps. 40:6; Heb. 10:4–9).

Second, the purpose of the whole ritual lies in the purification of the Israelites through the purification of the sanctuary. Though the latter has dominated this chapter, this does not exhaust the ritual's purpose. In this regard, the command for the people to afflict their souls (i.e. vv. 29, 31) is of paramount importance. What happens if the whole sanctuary is purified from uncleanness but the people fail to afflict their souls? Since an uncovering of all their self-hidings is included in the ritual itself, the repetition of the ceremony without the essential part of the ritual being realized (i.e. the affliction of their souls) not only makes no sense, but it makes the accumulation of God's wrath inevitable, a situation that will ultimately culminate in his leaving the sanctuary.

The extreme danger and difficulty Aaron goes through in cleansing the propitiatory cover inside the Holy Place matches the difficulty the Israelites face in afflicting their own souls. Moreover, just as the Holy Place is barely cleansed substantially, so their souls are barely afflicted. In the latter, a fundamental purification, a reformation or creation of a new heart, is not achieved.

Before the New Testament, this perfect cleansing of the hearts and souls of God's people is predicted in the prophetic books, particularly in Ezekiel. 'The new heart and the new spirit', which though demanded of the Israelites was never achieved by them (Lev. 26; Ezek. 11:19; 18:31), are given in the last days from the Lord, so they can observe the Law (Ezek. 36:25–26; 36:33; 37:23).

New Testament implications

The ritual on the Day of Atonement is related to the central work of Jesus Christ: his death on the cross and its purifying power. He is without equal in his capacity as both High Priest and sin offering. The book of Hebrews elaborates on this in great detail. Jesus did not hide himself (traditionally expressed as his being 'sinless'), and became both High Priest and Sacrifice (Heb. 5:1–10). Therefore he did not need to make propitiation for himself, like Aaron had to, for he is holy, innocent and sinless (Heb. 7:26–29). It was by his blood, and not animal blood, that he made propitiation for the people, so his blood not only has the power to cleanse believers from all their self-hidings, but also their consciences (Heb. 9:9, 11–14). Christ's death is also presented in Rom. 3:25 as a *hilastērion*, which probably means 'propitiation', referring to the propitiatory cover. His death ransoms the sinful, but also propitiates the wrath of God.

The cessation of the old tabernacle worship is marked by the tearing in two of the curtain that separates the Holy Place and the Tent of Meeting when Jesus died on the cross (Matt. 27:51), which indicates that henceforth every believer can enter the Holy Place (Heb. 10:19–20).

However, just as in Leviticus, in the NT a spiritual gap is assumed between Christ's work on the cross and the people who approach him. It is one thing that Christ made atonement for the doomed souls of the people, but quite another to assume that the egocentric selves of the people are destroyed. In Romans Paul first urges Christians to *consider* that they are dead in their self-hiding (6:11) and gives testimony to his own inner struggle with self-hiding (*ḥaṭṭā't*). This demonstrates that real faith appears when one is totally dead to self-hiding, with the simultaneous destruction of the egocentric nature. Blurring the distinction between what Christ did on the cross and the real spiritual condition of humans, by assuming some coexistence of self-hiding with a verbal confession of faith, inevitably makes a person hypocritical. More dangerous is a consequent blurring of the truth that faith in Christ appears only when people are dead to themselves, for faith is the opposite of self-hiding (Rom. 14:23; cf. Kiuchi 2003a: 64–65), not just in the OT but in the NT too.

Rom. 12:1 exhorts the believers to present their bodies to God, as a sacrifice, living, holy and acceptable. The sacrificial idea is clearly used here to describe the Christian life. Now the OT sacrificial ideal is found in the burnt offering, where everything is reduced to ashes, and this may come closest to the idea of Christian self-sacrifice, in view in Rom. 12:1. However, a more plausible antecedent to the 'living sacrifice' in Rom. 12:1 may be found in the Azazel goal, which suffers for others, in that the goat is alive (note 'sacrifice', 'living'; see Kiuchi 2006). Since Christ has already made atonement for believers, there is no more need after Pentecost for believers to make further atonement (as a duty). Therefore Paul, by using the sacrificial metaphor, intends only to refer to the self-sacrificial attitude of the believer.

Thus the only hope for human beings in general and the Israelites in particular finds its expression in the cross of Jesus Christ, which allows for Ezekiel's vision to come true in reality. But as long as the egocentric selves of human beings remain, the spiritual condition is not beyond the level assumed in Leviticus. The following chapters give other approaches to this crucial issue.

LEVITICUS 17:1–16

Translation

[1]The LORD spoke to Moses, saying, [2]'Speak to Aaron and his sons and to all the Israelites and say to them, This is the thing that the LORD has commanded. [3]If any

one of the house of Israel slaughters an ox or a lamb or a goat in the camp, or kills it outside the camp, [4]and does not bring it to the entrance of the Tent of Meeting to present it as an offering to the LORD in front of the tabernacle of the LORD, bloodguilt shall be imputed to that man. He has shed blood, and that man shall be cut off from among his people. [5]This is in order that the Israelites may bring their sacrifices that they sacrifice in the open field – that they may bring them to the LORD, to the priest at the entrance of the Tent of Meeting, and sacrifice them as sacrifices of the fellowship offerings to the LORD. [6]And the priest shall dash the blood on the altar of the LORD at the entrance of the Tent of Meeting and burn the fat for a soothing aroma to the LORD. [7]so that they shall no more offer their sacrifices to goat demons, after whom they whore. This shall be a statute forever for them throughout their generations.

[8]'And say to them further, Any one of the house of Israel, or of the strangers who sojourn among them, who offers a burnt offering or sacrifice [9]and does not bring it to the entrance of the Tent of Meeting to offer it to the LORD, that man shall be cut off from his people.

[10]'If any one of the house of Israel or of the strangers who sojourn among them eats any blood, I will set my face against that soul who eats blood and will cut him off from among his people. [11]For the life of the flesh is in the blood, and I have given it for you on the altar to make propitiation for your souls, for it is the blood that makes propitiation by the life. [12]Therefore I have said to the Israelites, No soul among you shall eat blood, neither shall any stranger who sojourns among you eat blood.

[13]'Any one of the Israelites, or of any strangers who sojourn among them, who hunts any beast or bird that may be eaten shall pour out its blood and cover it with earth. [14]For the life of every flesh is its blood: its blood is its life. Therefore I have said to the Israelites, You shall not eat the blood of any flesh, for the life of every flesh is its blood. Whoever eats it shall be cut off. [15]And every soul who eats what dies of itself or what is torn by beasts, whether he is a native or a sojourner, shall wash his clothes and bathe himself in water and be unclean until the evening; then he shall be clean. [16]But if he does not wash them or bathe his flesh, he shall bear his iniquity.'

Notes on the text

3. 'the house': *bêt* LXX reads 'the sons' as in v. 10.

'of Israel': *yiśrā'ēl* LXX adds 'or of the strangers residing among you', conforming to the similar formulaic expression in vv. 8, 10, 13.

4. 'and does not bring it': *lō' hebî'ô* Instead of this, SamP and LXX present a lengthy statement: 'to make it a burnt offering or the fellowship offering to the LORD for your acceptance as a soothing aroma, and it is slaughtered outside and to the entrance of the Tent of Meeting he does not bring it'. In view of the overall tendency of this chapter to present the rules *gradually*, this addition along with others (see v. 3) is unlikely to represent the original.

'that man': *hā'îš hahû'* LXX reads 'that soul'; probably harmonizing it with the use of *nepeš* in this chapter, and not necessarily with 22:3, as *BHS* margin suggests.

6. 'the altar of the LORD': *mizbaḥ YHWH* LXX reads 'the altar round about before the LORD', a paraphrase according to the ordinary practice regarding the burnt and fellowship offerings (cf. 1:5; 3:2 etc.).

8. 'among them': *bĕtôkām* Two Hebr. MSS, LXX, Syr and Vg read 'among you (pl.)'. Note that LXX introduces the 2nd person address already in v. 3.

'offers': *ya'aleh* SamP and LXX reflect the Hebr. verb *'śh*, which is easier than *'lh* hiph. in view of its connection with *zebaḥ*. Yet the text highlights the offering of a burnt offering here.

10. Tg omits vv. 10–12; probably as a result of homoioarkton (see the beginning of v. 13).

11. 'in the blood': *baddām* LXX reads 'in its blood', like MT of v. 14.

13. 'the sons': *bĕnê* Some Hebr. MSS, SamP and TgJon read 'the house'. See above on v. 3.

'among them': *bĕtôkām* LXX, Syr, TgJon, Vg and some other ancient textual evidence read 'among you (pl.)', as in v. 8. See above on v. 8.

14. 'whoever eats it': *kol 'ōklāyw* Lit. 'all who eat it'. Though the subject does not match the object in number, and *BHS* margin proposes to read *'ōklô*, following Syr and Tg, *kol* appears to mean 'all', not 'every'. The subject is conceived as a unity.

Form and structure

This chapter deals with the handling of animal blood, a subject already mentioned sporadically throughout the preceding chapters. The words and phrases that appear for the first time in ch. 16 clearly gain more emphasis in this chapter. These include 'strangers' (*gēr*), goat demons and the goat for Azazel (v. 8; 16:10, 21), and most significantly the relationship between *nepeš* and *kipper* (v. 11; see 'Comment' on 16:30). As already mentioned (see 'Form and structure' on ch. 16), the last section of ch. 16 (vv. 29–34) exhibits a close literary and ideological relationship with this chapter. This suggests that the rules in this chapter partly explain the ritual of the Day of Atonement.

In terms of the broader literary structure of chs. 11 – 26, it should be remembered that just as ch. 11 introduces chs. 12 – 16, so does ch. 17 serve this purpose in relation to chs. 18 – 20. Moreover there is an ideological development between chs. 11 and 17. While ch. 11 deals with diet and cleanness/uncleanness, ch. 17 deals with offering a sacrifice and the theme of life/death, yet retains the issue of diet in the background (see 'Comment' on vv. 2b–7). Further the theme of 'defiling a soul' in 11:43–44 is dealt with on a deeper dimension in ch. 17, where the question of how a doomed soul can be atoned for is addressed. While ch. 11 symbolically prohibits contact with the egocentric selves of others, ch. 17 describes how a human soul can be saved (see also 'Comment' on vv. 15–16).

A cursory reading of the laws in this chapter makes it clear that they are not framed in a way moderns would expect legal material to be written. Though the chapter presents laws, their formulation is apparently repetitive, and a close reading suggests they have a literary character that facilitates the communication of a particular message. From this chapter onwards, the discourse's hortatory features become increasingly prominent: the reasons and rationales for rules, exhortation and threat. Another important stylistic feature is the divine 1st person discourse, which is relatively rare in the preceding chapters (cf. 6:17[10]; 7:34; 10:3: 14:34; 15:31).

The chapter as a whole is divisible into the following five sections (for the problem of the division of the chapter, see Schwartz 1999: 37–38):

I.	vv. 1–2	The Lord's address to Moses
II.	vv. 3–7	A prohibition against killing an animal outside the sanctuary, and a command to bring it to the Lord as a fellowship offering
III.	vv. 8–9	An expansion of the same rule, extended to strangers, and the burnt offering
IV.	vv. 10–12	The rationale for the injunction 'The blood is life'
V.	vv. 13–16	The handling of the blood of game, and purificatory measures in the case of defilement

Sections II, III, IV and V begin with 'Anyone' (*'îš 'îš*)' (vv. 3, 8, 10, 13). From v. 8 onwards 'the strangers who sojourn among them' is added (vv. 8, 10, 13), but the assumption that the rule in vv. 3–7 applies only to native Israelites is mistaken, because in content the rule of I is expanded or deepened in the following sections of III, IV and V. The legislator clearly aims at *gradually* expanding or deepening section I in terms of the kinds of sacrifices as well as in relation to the identity of those who must obey the rules. With regard to the kinds of sacrifice, it is 'an ox, a lamb and a goat' in I, a fellowship offering in II, 'the burnt offering and the sacrifice' in section III, and 'the blood' in section IV. Though a concern for the Israelites' diet permeates these rules, they more immediately relate to the matters of blood and its handling.

Already in I, the Lord's concern for blood is reflected in the statement in v. 4 'he has shed blood'. But it is striking that the term blood (*dām*) appears in various senses in this chapter. Animal blood first appears in v. 6, but then appears in v. 10 as part of the phrase 'eating blood', which, as we shall see, is more than a simple prohibition against eating blood. Last, in vv. 11–14 there is an alternation between the literal meaning of 'blood' and the symbolic meaning that underlies the term when it occurs in the phrase 'eating blood'. The rules increasingly focus on the issue of eating blood and the sanctity of blood in making propitiation for the souls of the Israelites. This parallels the shift from *'îš* to *nepeš* (v. 10). In vv. 10–12 there is a significant wordplay between the human *nepeš* and animal *nepeš*. Thus behind the injunction not to slaughter an animal outside the sanctuary lies a deeper rationale; namely that animal blood, which is life, functions to make propitiation for the souls of the Israelites.

Comment

17:1–2a

1–2a. The Lord addresses Moses, and Moses is to deliver his message to Aaron and his sons, and all the sons of Israel. At first sight it appears that this address by the Lord is no different from others found in the book of Leviticus. However, a closer examination reveals that this is the first time Moses is combined with Aaron, his sons and all the sons of Israel, as the primary and secondary addressees respectively. This suggests that the following directions concern both the priests and the common people, and that in some sense Moses takes responsibility for all the directions.

17:2b–7

Vv. 2–7 have challenged interpreters since the time of rabbinic exegesis on two accounts. First, does the prohibition against killing an animal apply to an offering or to food alone? Second, how should the permission granted for profane slaughter in Deut. 12 be reconciled with the prohibition against this in Lev. 17? In this regard, mention of 'This shall be a statute forever for them throughout their generations' (v. 7) is a difficult hurdle to overcome. However, as Schwartz argues, a superficial harmonization of this law with the Deuteronomic law is unnecessary (1999: 66–70). Some exegetical observations may clarify the intent of the law.

(1) 'slaughter' (*yišḥat*) in the camp or outside it (v. 3) does not by itself address the intention of killing. For example, it leaves room for the possibility that the killing was done for the purpose of obtaining food: the law prohibits such a killing if it is not related to the sanctuary.

(2) The law gradually reveals in four stages that the Lord is apprehensive of the intention to kill an animal outside: first, in v. 3, 'if any one kills an ox, or a lamb or a goat'; second, in v. 5, 'in order that the Israelites may bring their sacrifices that they sacrifice'; third, in v. 7a, 'So that they shall no more offer their sacrifices to goat demons'; and fourth, in vv. 8–9, 'who offers a burnt offering or sacrifice' (v. 8).

(3) If 'a statute forever for them throughout their generations' in v. 7b refers back to the content of vv. 3–7a, and not to v. 7a alone, it may contradict the Deuteronomic permission of profane slaughter (Deut. 12). However, some caution is advisable in relating the law of Lev. 17 to Deut. 12.

First, as is the case with other laws in Leviticus, the book basically presents the laws irrespective of the spiritual reality of the people (their stubbornness) revealed in Numbers and Deuteronomy. It is reasonable, then, to assume that in Deuteronomy the Lord was willing to compromise the practical side of the law in Lev. 17, once the hardness of their hearts had been experienced (cf. the levirate marriage in Deut. 25, and 'Comment' on 18:16). But he has not made a compromise in every detail: even though considerable freedom is given to the place of eating meat, the blood of the animal must not be consumed, in keeping with the command of Lev. 17. This freedom is in keeping with the general characteristic of Deuteronomy, which shows humanitarian concerns while still stressing the necessity of obedience to the Lord. On the other hand, Lev. 17 concerns itself with the inseparable bond between animal blood and the human soul. Moreover it uses the place of slaughtering as a reflection of people's motives in killing, to encourage an appropriate motive for offering their sacrifices to the Lord.

Second, all this does not mean the laws in Lev. 17 soon lost their significance. They retain their validity perpetually. Particularly the phrase 'a statute forever' does not mean the Israelites continued to live in the wilderness forever. The specification of the place of slaughtering as 'in the camp' or 'outside the camp' (v. 3) constitutes a practical direction relating to the 'statute forever', but not the statute itself; the 'statute' is that the Israelites must bring their sacrificial animals to the sanctuary and offer them to the Lord through the work of the priest, and not offer them to the goat demons. Other laws in Leviticus also assume the Israelites are about to enter the land of Canaan (cf. 14:52ff.; 18, etc.) and their lifestyle will change considerably. Not too much should be made of the reference to the 'goat demons'. For, although the demons were assumed to exist in the wilderness, the demons, who are spiritual beings, never ceased to exist: they still exist today.

From the viewpoint of harmony between Lev. 17 and Deut. 12, then, there is no contradiction between them once it is assumed the Lord made a particular compromise in Deuteronomy. So-called profane slaughter pertains to a practical side of the matter. It applies to the Deuteronomic law but not to the Levitical law, whose concern lies not exactly in the matter of 'eating meat'. In fact, there is no mention of 'eating meat' in this chapter. To the contrary, and interestingly, 'eating blood' predominates in this chapter.

(4) Schwartz is of the opinion that according to 'P' the Israelites punctiliously obeyed the Lord's commandments, as recorded in the erection of the

Tent of Meeting etc., and that reference to the idolatrous worship here is, if it reflects historical reality, incongruous with the overall picture of the reality of the people in the wilderness (Schwartz 1999: 73). However, the language of v. 7a, particularly the particle *'ôd* (any more), implies that such worship was a reality. Furthermore it must also be pointed out that the outward obedience of the Israelites to the Lord's commands through Moses does not necessarily reflect the real condition of their hearts. Furthermore so-called P reports surprisingly little in relation to the response of the people to Moses' speeches. Outside 'P' occurred the incident of the golden calf (Exod. 32), several reports of murmuring on the part of the Israelites, and some passages in the prophetic literature that attest to the fact that the Israelites used to offer their sacrifices to foreign gods (Amos 5:25–26; for the problem of this passage, cf. Weiss 1992: 182–187). Most significantly the structure of the sanctuary reflects the inner being of the people, and the laws in chs. 11 – 15 suggest they are far from a state of inner cleanness before the Lord. Thus it is not surprising they practised idolatrous worship while hearing the Lord's commandment as given through Moses.

(5) Thus the conclusion is that section vv. 3–7 commands the people to bring an ox, lamb or goat to the entrance of the Tent of Meeting to offer it as a fellowship offering rather than as an offering to the goat demons. Their potential behaviour is anticipated with ascending degrees of specification and focus: first slaughtering, then the offering of sacrifices, then the possibility of offering to the demons or to the Lord, and finally options of either destroying one's own soul by consuming the animal's blood or being saved by that same blood.

The Lord does not intend the people to slaughter an animal, drain its blood in the camp or outside the camp, and bring only the flesh to the sanctuary. Rather slaughtering and eating are considered the same, though the matter of eating meat does not constitute the Lord's primary concern here. Thus eating blood means not offering the animal to the Lord, but to the demons. In this sense, the laws in ch. 17 deal essentially with the matter of idolatry, which leads to the destruction of a human soul, and proper worship, which leads to salvation, a theme that becomes more detailed in the following chapters.

2b. 'This is the thing': *zeh haddābār* For the formula, see 'Comment' on 8:5.

3–4. The offender is guilty of shedding blood and is cut off from his people. Since the time of the flood it was legitimate to kill and eat an animal. Therefore this is the first time, since the establishment of the priesthood, that God commands slaughtering to be performed at the entrance to the Tent of Meeting; i.e. before him.

'anyone': *'îš 'îš* In ch. 17 this phrase marks the beginning of new discourses that have interpersonal connotations (vv. 3, 8, 10, 13), though in content the first and second sections constitute a unit.

'the house of Israel': *bêt yiśrā'ēl* 'Anyone' (*'îš 'îš*) is followed by 'the house of Israel' (*bêt yiśrā'ēl*). This combination appears also in vv. 7, 10, and 22:18. Apparently the 'house of Israel' is synonymous with the 'sons of Israel', but stresses the unity of the latter, as though it were one family (see 10:6).

'slaughters': *yišḥaṭ* Milgrom defines this verb as 'slit the throat' (Milgrom 2000a: 1453). The intention of a person who kills an animal outside the sanctuary is questionable. Vv. 5–7 reveal that an Israelite may have killed an animal to offer it to the goat demons (see below).

'blood-guilt shall be imputed to that man': *dām yēḥāšēb lā'îš hahû'* The word *dām* means 'blood-guilt'. In other words, if not authorized, killing an animal involves guilt. Thus the term *ḥāšab* underscores the identification between the blood and its offerer (cf. 7:18).

'He has shed blood': *dām šāpak* Not literally, but in view of the significance of the animal blood, i.e. life (see below on vv. 10–11), the act is tantamount to killing a human.

'shall be cut off': *nikrat* For the *kāret* penalty, see 'Comment' on 7:20.

5. The purpose of the commandment is stated; i.e. the Israelites may bring their sacrifices to the Tent of Meeting to the Lord and present them as fellowship offerings. Why is only the fellowship offering mentioned? Probably because it is the only sacrifice the offerer can consume. Yet a contrast between what the Lord desires and what the Israelite intends when killing outside the sanctuary is tacitly drawn here, for the main purpose of the fellowship offering is fellowship with the Lord; thus it implies the offerer's denial of this fellowship.

6. When a person brings his or her sacrifice to the entrance of the Tent of Meeting, the priest dashes its blood on the altar and burns the fat to make a soothing aroma to the Lord. As explained in ch. 3, the burning of fat symbolizes the destruction of one's egocentric nature (see 'Comment' on 3:3–4). Therefore these rites signify the offerer's total dedication to the Lord.

7. A further circumstance lying behind the commandment follows: that the Israelites no longer sacrifice their sacrifices to goat demons, after whom they whore. It is surprising to hear that this is the spiritual condition of God's people who have heard his commandments since ch. 1. At any rate, here it is made clear that the question of whether the Israelites bring their sacrifice to the sanctuary is simultaneously a question of whether they pay homage to the Lord or to goat demons.

'goat demons': *śĕ'îrîm* The Hebr. term simply means 'goats', but it is more likely that the word refers to some spirit antithetical to the Lord. Thus this contrast between the Lord and the goat demons resembles the contrast in the previous chapter, i.e. the Lord and the Azazel goat, and corroborates the assumption that 'Azazel' in ch. 16 is the name of a demon. Unfortunately, since the meaning of the term *'ăzā'zēl* is unclear, it is difficult to be precise about the nature of the association. However, since *'ăzā'zēl* is likely to be either a demon or Satan, or some kind of spiritual being at any rate, and since both it and the goats (*śĕ'îrîm*) in 17:7 are assumed as living in the wilderness, it is possible to assume some affinity between them. As 'goats' is pl., it may be that *'ăzā'zēl* is the head of the evil spirits.

'a statute forever ... throughout their generations': *ḥuqqat 'ôlām ... lĕdôrōtām* This should be taken literally except that the 'statute' refers to the principle, not the practical details of the rule that relate to a wilderness setting (cf. 'Comment' on 3:17).

17:8–9

The Lord continues to address Moses, emphasizing the same message while adding some further details. Whoever among the Israelites or foreigners offers a burnt offering or some other sacrifice, but does not bring it to the Tent of Meeting, will be cut off from his people. Here, the rule applies not just to 'the house of Israel' (vv. 2–7), but also to 'the sojourners'. Also, not just the killing of an animal is at issue, but the possibility that a person may offer the animal as an offering, even a burnt offering (note the order, a burnt offering and a sacrifice). Then the question remains as to whether the man or woman offers it to the Lord or to the goat demons. This possibility reflects the reality that he or she had not previously offered the burnt offering or other sacrifices to the Lord.

17:10–12

From v. 10 onwards the Lord focuses on the term *nepeš*. Correspondingly vv. 10–12 deal with the fundamental function of animal blood. The prohibition against eating blood already appears in 3:17 and 7:26–27. In these contexts the phrase appears to mean 'consume blood', but it is unclear how it is consumed, nor is the reason for its consumption provided. Thus this section provides a deeper rationale for the foregoing law, drawing attention to the role of the sacrificial blood in relation to the offerer. Although Milgrom has argued that the blood in this section, particularly in v. 11, refers exclusively to that of the fellowship offering (see Milgrom 2000a: 1474–1478), it is not the kind of offering but the general blood present in any kind of animal sacrifice that is at issue (for a recent critique, see Sklar 2001: 171–178). Also the twice-repeated *kî* in v. 11 deserves special note (see below).

10. The theme of vv. 3–7 relates to the slaughtering of an ox, a lamb or a goat, either in the camp or outside it. In that connection, the fellowship offering to the Lord is mentioned as an alternative to the custom of the people. In vv. 8–9 the emphasis shifts from animals, i.e. an ox, lamb or goat, to 'the burnt offering' or 'the sacrifice'. And in v. 10 the emphasis shifts to the subject of blood.

'eats any blood': *yō'kal kol dām* If taken literally, 'eating the blood' is a strange expression, for blood is presumably drunk as a liquid. And in fact the expression 'to drink blood' occurs in Num. 23:24; Ezek. 39:17–19; Ps. 50:13. There is, however, no evidence that the Israelites used to drink the blood itself. In other contexts the verb *'ākal* (eat) does not take the direct object *dām* (blood) but the prepositional phrase *'al* (or *'el*) *haddām* (with blood; see Lev. 19:26; 1 Sam. 14:32–34; Ezek. 33:25). Most significantly the idea itself already appears in Gen. 9:4, where it is said, 'But you shall not eat flesh with its life; i.e. its blood.' The appearance of the phrase 'eating the blood' is concentrated in those contexts primarily concerned with the relationship between blood and life. In Leviticus it has already appeared in 3:7 and 7:26–27, but it appears three times in this chapter (vv. 10, 12, 14), all of which appear in the context of the fellowship offering. The phrase probably has a general meaning of 'to consume' or 'to partake of', but it is a separate question as to why such an expression came about. One possibility is that in combination with 'to consume' the phrase means to 'consume the blood'; i.e. to destroy the very means of propitiation, life (see below). That something more than a physiological sense is intended is clear from the latter half of this verse. Therefore by not offering a sacrificial animal to the Lord, draining its blood and eating its flesh outside the sanctuary, one was in effect eating its blood; i.e. consuming the blood and destroying life.

'I will set my face against': *nātattî pānay bĕ* This expression 'set my face against' occurs four times in chs. 17 – 26 (17:10; 20:3, 6; 26:17), it is mostly followed by the *kāret* penalty. While the *kāret* penalty is expressed in a passive form (*nikrat*, 'to be cut off') in vv. 4, 9, here it is expressed in the 1st person, thereby pointing to its greater severity.

'against that soul who eats the blood': *bannepeš hā'ōkelet 'et haddām* This is the first appearance of the word *nepeš* in this chapter. *'îš* (a person, vv. 3, 8, 10) is deliberately replaced with *nepeš* (a soul). That a soul cannot eat the blood cannot be the reason for *nepeš* not meaning 'a soul', for the phrase 'eating the blood' symbolically means 'to forfeit the means of propitiation'. At any rate, the use of *nepeš* for the first time here in this chapter clearly derives from the legislator's need in the next verse to introduce the close relationship between the human soul and animal blood.

In relation to the human soul, it is stressed that if it is not revived by the life given by the animal blood, it must perish. On the whole, the human *nepeš* is viewed in Leviticus as doomed: unless given life, it is inevitably cut off from the covenantal community to which it belongs.

'from his people': *mē'ammāyw* See 'Comment' on 7:19–20.

11. This much-debated passage consists of three parts. For convenience' sake, I divide the verse as follows, setting aside the Masoretic punctuation:

11a *Kî nepeš habbāśār baddām hî'*
For the life of the flesh is in the blood,
11b *wa'ănî nĕtattîw lākem 'al hammizbēaḥ lĕkapper 'al napšôtêkem*
and I have given it for you on the altar to make propitiation for your souls,
11c *kî haddām hû' bannepeš yĕkapper*
for it is the blood that makes propitiation by the life.

First I shall address the general features of this passage, and then discuss the major problems in translating key terms such as *nepeš* and *kipper*.

V. 11a begins with *kî* and introduces the reason for the prohibition against eating blood in v. 10: it is because the *nepeš* of the flesh is in the blood and the blood was given by the Lord for the altar to make propitiation for the *nepeš* of the Israelites. While this is a reason in v. 10 for the prohibition against eating blood, it does not constitute the only reason. The second *kî* (11c) introduces the reason for the statement in 11b. The nature of the second *kî* seems to be different from the first, in that it gives the reason for the statement in 11a and 11b ('I am saying this because'), and not for the content of 11a and 11b (cf. Claassen 1983: 29–46): it provides the fundamental principle for what takes place on the altar, while simultaneously giving the background to 11a and 11b. Thus the use of *kî* in this verse suggests it talks about the significance of the animal blood, not just in the fellowship offering, but in all kinds of animal sacrifices (for the scope of the blood here, see Milgrom 2000a: 1474–1478; Sklar 2001: 171–178).

The animal blood mentioned here is not the full volume of blood circulating in the animal, but just the blood shed when it is slaughtered, so the life here is 'life yielded up in death' (Morris 1965: 116; see below). Now, the term *nepeš* appears once in each part, and the meaning should be considered seriatim. The one in 11a means 'the life of the (animal) flesh'. The second *nepeš*, in *napšôtêkem*, is more problematical and crucial. It refers to the Israelites; i.e. human beings. Modern English translations divide into three groups: (1) 'souls' (RSV, ESV), (2) 'lives' (JPS, NRSV), (3) 'yourselves' (NIV). In view of the obvious stress in v. 10 placed on the eating of blood by the *nepeš*, option (3) is most unlikely: it underplays the author's intention of relating the *nepeš* eating blood in v. 10 and *napšôtêkem* in v. 11b. Option (2) is possible. In this case, the general idea of what takes place on the altar is that animal life takes the place of human life. This leaves room for an understanding that animal life prevents the death of the offerer. But since 'life' in the sacrificial context means life before God (Kiuchi 2000: 44–46), the translation 'souls' is preferable. The third *nepeš* hinges on the interpretation of the meaning of *bĕ* in 11c. I maintain that it means 'by' or 'through' (cf. Kiuchi 1987: 104–106; Sklar 2001: 166–171), and that the *nepeš* in *banepeš* refers to the life of the animal. Thus it seems that the antecedent of *nepeš* in 11c is the life of the animal mentioned in 11a and that the animal blood symbolizes *spiritual life*.

It is vitally important to bear in mind that the human soul offering the animal's blood is assumed to be culpable in various senses, and that if this soul is left as it is, it will be cut off from the people. Thus the *kipper* act by the priest is undertaken to save the doomed soul. Concurrently the Lord is wrathful towards the offerer, as is conveyed by the idea of ransoming the *nepeš*.

As already argued, *kipper* means 'to sacrifice oneself (itself) for propitiation', which suggests the term presumes the idea of substitution (see 'Comment' on 1:4, and Kiuchi 2005: 52–58). How does substitution take place? The animal blood symbolizes life, but it is not that the animal blood replaces the doomed life: it gives life to the doomed *nepeš*. On the assumption that *kipper* relates to the idea of substitution, what is received by the blood in return for giving life to the doomed *nepeš*? It is most probably death. However, this death is not the physical death of the offerer, but the guilt he was to bear in the absence of sacrifice.

At this point, it is useful to remember that the offerer's soul is assumed as hiding itself before the Lord. Thus the above-stated guilt is the guilt of self-hiding before the Lord, which is existential and not directly related to a particular offence. So the doomed *nepeš* is a self-hiding *nepeš*, and the shed blood symbolizes life that uncovers the soul when the animal blood is substitutionally uncovered before the Lord. This postulate describes, in principle, what happens on the altar when an offerer presents a sacrificial animal and the priest handles its blood. As mentioned above, the details of what happens on the altar are not given in Leviticus until 17:11. The postulate shows that while it is not entirely wrong to say that the animal blood takes the place of the offerer, this does not explain the relationship between the blood and the altar. Moreover, as mentioned above, on its own this conclusion is misleading, for the animal blood takes the place of the doomed *nepeš* and not the physical death of the offerer. The postulate also implies that there is an invariable correspondence between the altar (sancta) and the people. And since the *nepeš* is the human being's innermost part, the revival of the doomed *nepeš* corresponds to that of the inner part of the Tent of Meeting, just as the purification of the Holy Place in the previous chapter corresponds to the affliction of the people's *nepeš*. Compare with the ritual of the burnt offering in ch. 1, where the animal, and not its blood, takes the place of the *'ādām* (man), a term that refers to the whole existence of the human being (see 1:4). In a word, the sacrificial blood prevents and saves the offerer from being cut off (*nikrat*) from his or her people and enables the person to remain within the covenant community.

12. 'Therefore': *'Al kēn* This phrase is unique in Leviticus. It introduces the fundamental consequence of the preceding, but in fact it has a repetitive nature. Cf. v. 11.

'I have said': *'āmartî* That the Lord says 'I said' is also unique in Leviticus. Moreover the exact wording of what follows has not appeared till here (cf. v. 14). Indeed the prohibition against eating blood is mentioned in 3:17; 7:26–27. Therefore 'I have said' does not mean the exact words the Lord said. In such cases it is reasonable to assume that what follows 'I have said' refers back to v. 10 and the relevant passages mentioned above. This, in turn, suggests that the verb *'āmar* does not necessarily refer to the exact statement. It is unnecessary, however, to assume it means to 'command'.

'(every) individual soul among you': *kol nepeš mikkem* This phraseology is also unique not just to Leviticus but to the whole OT. Cf. *'ādām … mikem* in Lev. 1:2.

17:13–14

Having finished his prescription relating to the animal whose blood is offered either to the demons or to the Lord, the Lord now turns to the blood of hunted animals and birds that are not taken to the altar, in contrast to sacrificial animals and birds.

13. 'any one': *'îš 'îš* Cf. the same phrase in vv. 3, 8, 10. The Israelites are addressed in the 3rd person, in contrast to vv. 11–12. It is assumed the Israelites are allowed to eat clean animals and birds not offered at the altar but that conform to the criteria outlined in ch. 11. In such a case they are to pour out the blood and cover it with earth. While 'shedding blood' outside the sanctuary is an illegitimate practice (v. 4), 'covering the blood with earth', used in a physical sense here, legitimates the practice by screening the blood from the Lord's sight, thereby cancelling the potential blood guilt (cf. Gen. 37:26; Isa. 26:21; Ezek. 24:7–8; Job 16:18). This 'covering the blood with earth' provides an interpretive key for the authorized ritual act of pouring the animal blood at the base of the altar; i.e. it is left uncovered.

14. This verse provides the rationale underlying v. 13, but has essentially the same content as vv. 10–12, 'for the life of every flesh, its blood is in its life' (*nepeš kol bāśār dāmô bĕnapšô*). Compared to v. 11 ('the life of the flesh is in the blood'), 'every' is added, which reflects the mention of game animals in v. 13. Further, the apparently awkward 'its blood is in its life' prepares the reader for the idea in v. 14b that the life is blood. Since life and blood are viewed as one and the same, and since both are instrumental in giving life to a doomed soul, the consumption of blood constitutes the loss of the very means of propitiation; thus the *kāret* penalty applies; i.e. the *kāret* penalty is not just a punishment, but a natural consequence of violating the Lord's ordinance. Here the interpretation of *nepeš* in *nepeš hā'ōkelet 'et haddām* as meaning 'a soul' and not 'a person' (v. 10) finds further support, for not only does *'ākal* mean to 'consume' rather than to 'eat' physically, but the expression underscores the idea that the consumption of blood results in the destruction of the means of propitiation.

17:15–16

Lastly, a law is laid down regarding those who eat the dead animal. Certainly the draining of blood is presumed, but if it were done, eating the flesh defiles a person, according to the rules of ch. 11, since he has come into contact with death.

15. If an individual soul, whether a native or stranger, eats the flesh of a dead animal, he must wash his clothes, bathe himself and wait until evening. Similar instructions are found in 11:39–40 (cf. 7:24).

The beginning of the Hebr. text, *kol nepeš*, is the same as in v. 12. It means 'an individual soul', and extends to the next verse. To eat the flesh of a dead animal is more defiling than simply touching it. However, since the subject of 'eating' is a soul (*nepeš*), the rule bears a symbolic meaning: it is not just the act of eating in a physical sense that matters, but, just like the other unclean animals, the dead animals symbolize human beings (see 'Explanation' on ch. 11). This is hinted at by this rule's immediate context. It comes after vv. 10–12, where the salvation of the human soul is addressed. Thus *eating* a carcass symbolizes having fellowship with spiritually dead people, and that endangers one's own soul. This assumes one's soul loses its life by having fellowship with the egocentric selves of other humans, and that as a consequence it needs cleansing.

16. The violation of v. 15 results in individuals bearing their own guilt. The 'bearing of guilt' is a consequence, and does not, by itself, address the question of whether the violation is expiable (whatever the sense is) or pardonable. Essentially the consequence is the same as 'being cut off' (v. 10; see also 'Explanation' on ch. 20). Thus the chapter, referring back to 11:40, 44–45, adds an additional dimension to the defilement of the soul: unless people become holy, they are to bear their guilt, which paves the way into the following chapters.

Explanation

Lev. 17 exhibits ideological links with both the preceding and following chapters on a deep dimension.

First, ch. 17 appears to make several references to the preceding chapters. Among other things, it provides the fundamental principle for the role of sacrificial blood (vv. 11–12). Until this chapter, no rationale for the sacrificial ritual is provided. For the first time in Leviticus it is explained that blood represents life (17:11), and that blood is instrumental in making propitiation for the souls of the Israelites. In sum, ch. 17 can be seen as conveying a deeper meaning to the idea of sacrifice.

Equally significant is the relationship between *kipper* and a human soul (*nepeš*). Though they appear loosely connected in the preceding chapter;

the *kipper* of the sancta must be accompanied by the Israelites' active affliction of their souls (16:29, 31). Thus the relationship between the purification of the sanctuary and the human soul in ch. 16 is elucidated in ch. 17 in a different context but in a more direct way.

As commented, however, v. 11 addresses itself to the role of animal blood in general. This means the burnt, fellowship, sin and reparation offerings deal with the human soul, a soul doomed because of its egocentric nature. That such a soul is constantly exposed to the danger of the *kāret* penalty is suggested by the need for the person to offer a sacrifice to the Lord whenever that person approaches him. Moreover within the context of ch. 17 the flow of the regulations indicates that killing a sacrificial animal at a place other than the altar is the equivalent to 'sacrificing to the goat demons after whom they [the Israelites] whore', an act of idolatry. In other words, this chapter tacitly informs the reader that in idolatry one sacrifices oneself to something else.

Now, alongside the literary and ideological relations ch. 17 has with the foregoing chapters, it also lays the foundational principle developed in the following chapters: it views the salvation of a human soul from a different perspective to that of chs. 1 – 16. That is, while in chs. 1 – 16 the human soul is dealt with by sacrifices and offerings, and individual human conduct remains in the background, the latter comes to the fore in chs. 18 – 26, though they still assume the regulations of chs. 1 – 16 (see 'Explanation' on ch. 18 onwards). Also, part of the reason why the fellowship offering is particularly stressed in this chapter is that this sacrifice deals symbolically with one's salvation (see 'Explanation' on ch. 3). However, in view of the hard fact that human beings remain in their uncleanness, namely in a state of hiding themselves before God and are not entitled to offer sacrifices unless they are in a clean state, how can they obtain life before him?

Last, in its broader context, ch. 17, with its theme of not eating blood, has literary and ideological links with ch. 11, and also reminds the reader of the injunction 'Do not eat from the tree of the knowledge of good and evil' in the Garden of Eden (Gen. 2 – 3). In Lev. 11 and 17, as well as Gen. 2 – 3, eating prohibited objects brings about death, particularly an exclusion from the Lord's presence.

In sum, Lev. 17 lays the ground for obtaining life for one's own doomed soul, which has been the major aim for the offering sacrifices in Lev. 1 – 16 and is developed from a different perspective in the following chapters.

New Testament implications

As a sequel to ch. 11 this chapter focuses on the question of whether one offers a sacrifice to the Lord or the demons, and strictly commands the people to offer their sacrifices to the Lord. However, one's merely offering a sacrifice to the Lord does not bring about the desired effect. If the blood's symbolic meaning is really achieved in the ritual, one's soul would surely be revived, but the text does not simply assume the soul becomes a 'living soul' (*nepeš ḥayyâ*). Sacrifices are holy, but a significant gap still exists between the inner state of the offerer and the sacrifice: if the offerer sacrifices himself just as the animal does, then he becomes a living soul. But as long as the offerer's egocentric nature remains alive, a gap between him and the sacrifice remains. Thus, though Lev. 17 prescribes how the Israelites are to approach the Lord, so as to gain a revived soul, it implies the presence of a limitation in the efficacy of a sacrificial animal to save the human soul in a definitive way.

The atoning power of animal blood is central to the background of the death of Jesus Christ on the cross. The blood of Jesus not only makes propitiation for the self-hiding of people but also purifies them, *on the condition* that people believe him. Problems surrounding the matter of 'believing' are mentioned in the comment sections of the preceding chapters. In this sense, the situation of 'standard' NT believers is not much different from OT believers as far as their souls are concerned: they are in danger of forfeiting their salvation.

In accordance with the once-for-all event of the cross and the resurrection and its accompanying power, it has an aspect of newness as well as of continuation of OT sacrificial ideas. Among other things, Jesus' words in John 6:53 are illuminating in this regard. Jesus said, 'Truly, truly, I say to you, unless you eat the flesh of the Son of Man and drink his blood, you have no life in you' (ESV). Here, it is not that the flesh of Jesus is likened to bread and his blood to drink, but it is explicitly said that the believer should eat his flesh and drink his blood, words that appear to contradict the law in Lev. 17; particularly the injunction against eating blood. This may be part of the reason why his disciples were offended by his words (John 6:60). However, the contradiction is only ostensible, due to the formal contradiction in the two expressions 'do not eat blood' and 'drink my blood'. The expression 'eating blood' in Lev. 17 does not mean the literal 'drinking of blood', but the consumption of life, referring to the forfeiture of the very means of atonement given for the doomed soul. On the other hand, Jesus' reference to his body as 'flesh and blood' is meant to be understood in a spiritual sense. Thus both Lev. 17 and John 6 talk about a person's benefiting from sacrifice and the body of Jesus in the spiritual sense respectively. Not only so, Jesus desired a spiritual depth of fellowship when he said 'Unless you drink my blood', an expression not used in sacrificial language. Thus the 'believers' are strongly encouraged to be united with him to the extent that the distinction between the symbol and the symbolized disappears; otherwise they will not be resurrected to eternal life. In other words, there is both a discontinuation with the OT world as well as a summation of it in Jesus' words.

LEVITICUS 18:1–30

Translation

[1]The LORD spoke to Moses, saying, [2]'Speak to the Israelites and say to them, I am
the LORD your God. [3]You shall not do as they do in the land of Egypt, where you
lived, and you shall not do as they do in the land of Canaan, to which I am bringing
you. You shall not walk in their statutes.

[4]'You shall follow my rules and keep my statutes and walk in them. I am the
LORD your God.

[5]'You shall therefore keep my statutes and my rules; if a man does them, he shall
live by them: I am the LORD.

[6]'None of you shall approach any one of his close relatives to uncover nakedness.
I am the LORD. [7]The nakedness of your father, i.e. the nakedness of your mother, you
shall not uncover; she is your mother, you shall not uncover her nakedness. [8]The
nakedness of your father's wife you shall not uncover; it is your father's nakedness.
[9]The nakedness of your sister, your father's daughter or your mother's daughter,
whether brought up among kindred or in another home – you shall not uncover her
nakedness. [10]The nakedness of your son's daughter or of your daughter's daughter –
you shall not uncover their nakedness, for their nakedness is your own nakedness.
[11]The nakedness of your father's wife's daughter, brought up in your father's
kindred, who is your sister – you shall not uncover her nakedness. [12]The nakedness
of your father's sister you shall not uncover; she is your father's relative. [13]The
nakedness of your mother's sister you shall not uncover, for she is your mother's
relative. [14]The nakedness of your father's brother you shall not uncover; i.e. you shall
not approach his wife; she is your aunt. [15]The nakedness of your daughter-in-law
you shall not uncover; she is your son's wife. You shall not uncover her nakedness.
[16]The nakedness of your brother's wife you shall not uncover; it is your brother's
nakedness. [17]The nakedness of a woman and of her daughter you shall not uncover,
and you shall not take her son's daughter or her daughter's daughter to uncover her
nakedness; they are relatives; it is depravity. [18]You shall not take a woman as a rival
wife to her sister, uncovering her nakedness while her sister is still alive. [19]You shall
not approach a woman to uncover her nakedness while she is in her menstrual
uncleanness. [20]You shall not lie sexually with your fellow's wife and so make
yourself unclean with her. [21]You shall not give any of your children to offer them to
Molech, and so profane the name of your God: I am the LORD. [22]You shall not lie
with a male as with a woman; it is an abomination. [23]You shall not lie with any
animal and so make yourself unclean with it, neither shall any woman give herself to
an animal to lie with it: it is perversion.

[24]'Do not make yourselves unclean by any of these things, for by all these the
nations I am driving out before you have become unclean, [25]and the land became
unclean, so I punished its iniquity, and the land vomited out its inhabitants. [26]But
you shall keep my statutes and my rules and do none of these abominations, either
the native or the stranger who sojourns among you [27](for the people of the land,
who were before you, did all of these abominations, so the land became unclean),

[28]lest the land vomit you out when you make it unclean, as it vomited out the nation that was before you. [29]For everyone who does any of these abominations, the souls that do them shall be cut off from among their people. [30]So keep my charge never to practise any of these abominable customs that were practised before you, and never to make yourselves unclean by them: I am the Lord your God.'

Notes on the text

5. 'a man': *hā'ādām* See 'Comment'.

9. 'her nakedness': *'erwātāh* Read with LXX, Syr, SamP and some Hebr. MSS instead of MT *'erwātān* (their nakedness).

11. LXX translates the verse freely but manages to capture the meaning correctly. The twice-repeated 'you shall not uncover her nakedness' and 'the same father' in LXX do not imply something about their *Vorlage* (see Wevers 1997: 277).

12. LXX, Syr and Vg and some Hebr. MSS insert 'for' before 'she', yet note there are cases where *kî* is not found, as in vv. 7–8, 14b, 15b, 16.

17. 'her nakedness': *'erwātâ* LXX and Syr read 'their [f.] nakedness'. However, it is possible to follow MT and interpret as suggested in 'Comment'.

'relatives': *šā'ărâ* The Hebr. word is a hapax legomenon, but the meaning would be the same as *šĕ'ēr*. LXX reads 'for they are your relatives'.

21. 'give ... to offer': *ha'ăbîr* SamP and possibly LXX suggest that the root is *'bd*. But this is unlikely, given the term *he'bîr* occurs in this idolatrous worship.

'Molech': *môlek* LXX, in giving *archonti* (ruler), did not recognize it as a pagan god, yet Wever reckons the translator's circumstance was in the third century BC in Egypt (see Wevers 1997: 282).

28. 'the nation': *gôy* LXX, Syriac and Tg reflect the pl. form *gôyîm* (nations), as in v. 24. But it is unnecessary in view of 20:23, where the sg. form is used.

29. 'souls that do them': *hannĕpāšôt hā'ōśōt* As in many other places in Leviticus, it is inappropriate to translate *nepeš* as 'a person'. In particular, when it occurs in combination with the verb *nikrat*, it is likely to mean 'a soul' (cf. 17:10). For the pairing of *nepeš* with *'āśâ*, see 23:30.

Form and structure

This chapter presents the Lord's statutes and warns the Israelites about the danger of defiling themselves and the land by giving concrete examples of Canaanite customs. The structure of the whole chapter is clear. Following the Lord's address to Moses in vv. 1–2a, it is divisible into three sections:

A. vv. 2b–5	The Lord's statutes versus the statutes of the Egyptians and Canaanites: warning with a promise (1st person pl.)
B. vv. 6–23	Prohibitions against the Canaanite customs, including Molech worship (2nd person sg.)
C. vv. 24–30	The Lord's statutes versus the statutes of the Canaanites: warning with grounds (3rd person pl.)

Since vv. 3–5 and vv. 24–30 are addressed in the 2nd person pl., while vv. 6–23 are 2nd person sg., the Israelites as a whole as well as each individual are the addressees of the Lord's commandments. Most of these prohibitions are mentioned again in ch. 20 in combination with their associated punishment. The relationship between chs. 18 and 20 is addressed in 'Form and structure' in ch. 20.

Some comments are in order for each section. Section A comprises prohibitions against behaving like Egyptians and Canaanites, and gives a command to walk in the way of the Lord. These are framed by the formula 'I am the LORD your God' (vv. 2ba and 30). This is accompanied by the promise that if one observes the Lord's statutes, he shall live (v. 5). Vv. 2a–5 are clearly an introduction to the following rules of this chapter, but as a similar reference is made to 'the statutes and rules' in 19:37 and 20:22, it also forms an introduction to all the laws of chs. 18 – 20 (see 'Comment' on 19:37).

In section B, and particularly in vv. 6–16, a number of so-called incestuous unions are prohibited, though vv. 7–16 do not cover all potential cases in a systematic way. The laws from v. 17 onwards exhibit a greater interest in extramarital unions, including worship. While it is generally agreed that vv. 6–23 have a twofold division, there is little agreement about the point of this division. It is, as Schwartz closely observes, appropriate to assume that the whole section moves *gradually* from so-called incestuous unions to other illicit unions, whereas even so the latter is written in a way that subtly echoes the former section (for a detailed discussion, see Schwartz 1999: 163–166).

V. 6 introduces and summarizes the following rules (see 'Comment' on v. 6). It is more questionable how vv. 6–16 are related to vv. 17–23, since the latter do not deal with cases of 'close relatives'. In fact, the various prohibitions of this section are stitched together by utilizing stylistic devices. First, v. 17 does not belong to the incestuous cases in a narrow sense, but the verse is cast in a form similar to vv. 7–16. That is, *'erwat* (the nakedness of) is followed by a noun, which is further followed by *lō' tĕgalleh* (you shall not uncover), and the term *šā'ărâ* (relatives) is employed, which is similar to *šĕ'ēr* (vv. 6, 12). All these elements, despite differences in their respective natures, are instrumental in associating this case with the preceding ones. The prohibition *lō' tiqqaḥ* (do not take) in

v. 17 reappears in v. 18 in a slightly different sense. V. 19 is formulated in a way similar to v. 6 in that both use *lōʾ tiqrĕbû/tiqrab* (you shall not approach). The beginning of v. 20 is similar to that of v. 19 ('To the woman of', *ʾel ʾiššâ*, *ʾel ʿešet*), while the mention of *zeraʿ* (semen) in v. 20 paves the way for prohibiting worship, which begins with the same term used in a different sense (offspring). The style of v. 22, which deals with homosexuality, is different from that of v. 21, but the introduction of the term *tôʿēbâ* (abomination), in a way similar to v. 17b, prepares for the summarizing statement in section C (vv. 26a, 27, 29–30). The last prohibition in v. 23 has a similar style to v. 20 (or v. 21) in that both use *lōʾ tittēn šĕkōbet . . . lĕṭomʿâ bāh* (see 'Comment' on vv. 17ff.).

The paraenetic style of the final section (C) strictly warns the Israelites of the danger associated with defiling themselves by engaging in any of the listed prohibited acts. The 2nd person pl. address refers to the first section vv. 2b–5(6). By using the terms *tôʿēbâ* (abomination) and *ṭāmēʾ* (become unclean), already used in vv. 20, 22–23, the list of things prohibited is revealed as representative of the Canaanite practices, and the Israelites are warned against doing the same by threatening them with expulsion from their land. The phraseologies found in vv. 4–5 (*ḥuqqôt, mišpāṭîm*) are found in v. 26. 'The Israelites' in A are detailed as 'the natives and strangers' in C (v. 26b).

On the whole, the flow of the discourse is natural and cast in a way that builds upon the foregoing.

Comment

Following ch. 17, which set out the fundamental requirements needed for the Israelites to live before the Lord, this chapter begins to relate the Lord's stipulations concerning their conduct. They consist of a set of prohibitions concerning sexual behaviour previously practised in Egypt and Canaan. While the immediate background for the prohibitions is the historical practice of the Canaanites, this chapter, as in other parts of Leviticus, reflects Gen. 2 – 3 on both theological and literary dimensions: (1) Observance of the statutes makes it possible for the man *to live* (v. 5), which echoes the primordial commandment in Gen. 2:17, where the consequence of the violation is expressed negatively as 'You shall surely die'. (2) The forbidden sexual unions find their suitable rationale in Gen. 2:24 (see 'Comment' on vv. 6–20), while since the fall the male and female genitals signified the shameful parts of the human body (see below). As in ch. 15, the human genitals are the focal point of the legislation in this chapter. (3) The laws in vv. 6–23 mandate the making of strict distinctions between man and woman, and between humans and beasts, thus highlighting the created order. (4) The driving out (*šillaḥ*) of the predecessors from the Promised Land may be in parallel to the driving out (*šillaḥ*) of the first man and woman from the Garden of Eden (Lev. 18:24; Gen. 3:22).

Thus vv. 6–23 singularly aim to restore the original created order upon the premise that humanity is fallen. They assume fallen humanity is liable to take the course of action represented by the abominations listed.

In particular, the characteristic idiom in Lev. 18 'to uncover nakedness' gains a double or triple significance when a link to fallen and pre-fallen humanity is considered. Though both man and woman were naked in their pre-fallen condition (Gen. 2:25), they desperately attempted to hide their genitals after the fall (Gen. 3:7). Therefore in terms of the fall, the act of uncovering nakedness is first of all a negation of the reality of human fallenness. Second, in view of the fact that *ḥāṭā'* means to 'hide oneself' and that 'uncovering oneself' in a *spiritual* sense is encouraged in chs. 11 – 17 (esp. 13 – 14), to 'uncover the nakedness of someone' in a *physical* sense in ch. 18 may be viewed as a total overturn of the creation and fall.

These prohibitions concern *secretive* behaviour, which means that apart from the violated person's testimony, there is no way of knowing the violation occurred. Thus when people uncover nakedness in a prohibited way, they do it while in a state of *self-hiding*. Thus the use of the phrase 'uncover the nakedness' bears ironic overtones.

As for the extent of the banned sexual unions, vv. 7–16 deal with forbidden unions within the first and second consanguinity. As has been noted, there are some glaring omissions in the list: e.g. unions with one's daughter. The solution of the question depends to a great extent upon what the exact meaning of *šĕ'ēr beśārô* (close relative) in v. 6 means, and its relation to the following cases. As mentioned in the comment below, I take the position that v. 6 summarizes the following rules, but that it also forms a principle, so the omitted cases are assumedly included in the statement of v. 6. Consequently the cases in vv. 7–16 mean what the phrase *šĕ'ēr beśārô* (close relative) refers to: the first and second consanguinity.

18:1–5

1–2. 'the Israelites': *bĕnê yiśrā'ēl.* While in ch. 17:5 the priests are addressed as distinct from the people, here there is no reason to assume the priests are excluded.

The first words Moses is to say to the Israelites is 'I am the LORD your God'. This is the second time the formula appears in Leviticus (cf. 11:44), and the first time in chs. 17 – 26. From now on the identification of the Lord in the 1st person appears frequently, and it appears in this chapter three times (vv. 2, 4, 30); the abbreviated form 'I am YHWH' appears in v. 21 (but note that the preceding words are 'your God'). From a structural point of view it is clear the last passage in ch. 11 shares a close literary and ideological relationship with this chapter (see 'Explanation'). As Wenham (1979: 250–251) elaborates on this formula, it functions to remind the Israelites of the Lord who delivered them from slavery in Egypt and became their Lord (cf. Exod. 20:2). Thus the people's allegiance to anything other than the Lord is deemed idolatrous.

3–4. The Israelites must behave according to the statutes of the Lord and not those of Egypt and Canaan. What these statutes are is explained from v. 6 onwards.

5. The content of v. 4 is repeated with a significant addition, to the effect that a man lives by observing the Lord's statutes and rules.

The word *hā'ādām* (a man) refers to the earthly manifestations of a human in distinction from *'îš* or *nepeš* (cf. vv. 6, 30). The propensity to hide oneself recedes into the background, at least theoretically. The Hebr. article before *'ādām* is meaningful and its meaning approaches 'humankind' (cf. 5:4; 6:3[5:22]; 27:29).

Since every human must die, the following 'and he shall live by them' has caused some conjecture with regard to what kind of life is in view. Early and medieval Judaism viewed this as a reference to 'eternal life'. Modern commentators generally reject this view. Christian exegetes (cf. Hartley 1992: 293) commonly consider it excessive, for only Jesus Christ guarantees eternal life. But this point appears to hold that the life assumed by 'and lives' will ultimately result in death, which is unlikely, as the consideration below suggests.

'he shall live': *wĕḥāy* Lit. 'and he lives'. In Leviticus the term *ḥāyâ* means to 'live' in the biological sense of moving freely (cf. 13:10, 14–16; 14:4–5; 16:10; Deut. 8:3; Ezek. 20:11, 13, 21). However, as this life is guaranteed by the observance of these rules, and not by food, the life envisaged here must mean more than just physical life, but primarily spiritual life, a life that embraces physical life (cf. Wenham 1979: 253).

After the fall, death is the inevitable outcome of human life, but it is questionable if this is taken for granted in Leviticus. It would seem a case of eisegesis to assume that a man lives by observing the statutes *and then dies*, despite the fact that all humans die. In Leviticus human death is always presented as caused by the violation of the Lord's commandments: it is never presented as a natural thing unrelated to the breaking of laws (see 'Comment' on 15:31). In view of this observation, it is possible to read this verse as saying that by 'and live' the Lord intends to say that a man lives for ever, on the assumption that the present life is part of eternal life (cf. Eccl. 3:11; Gen. 3:22). This may be an extraordinary interpretation for any modern who presumes a man must die. But Leviticus appears to assert that a man must die because he has violated the law; if he observes all of them, he lives. The postulate is just like that in Gen. 2 – 3: if the first man observes God's commandment, he lives; if not, he certainly dies. The hard fact that all humanity dies implies we fall short of the complete observance of the Lord's commandments that continue until at least ch. 20.

18:6–21

This section comprises prohibitions against incest within the second consanguinity (vv. 7–17), of taking another wife while the present one is still alive (v. 18), of intercourse with a woman in her menstrual uncleanness (v. 19), and of adultery. As Schwartz has shown, these rules are distinguishable from each other on the basis of content, but move gradually forward in style (Schwartz 1999: 166). Special attention should be paid to two aspects of the formulaic 'uncover the nakedness of someone', which includes 'your father' (v. 7), 'the wife of your father' (8) etc. Having sexual intercourse with these persons is regarded as disgracing the persons who are in close relation to the violator. Vv. 17–18, using the verb 'take' (*lāqaḥ*), which connotes marriage, prohibit sexual intercourse with a different relative. V. 19 deals with the offence of having intercourse with a menstruating woman. Lastly, v. 20 deals with an offence made in regard to another woman (adultery).

All of the cases in vv. 7–23 have something to do with the action of 'uncovering the nakedness' in v. 6. Schwartz considers that, in content, v. 6 anticipates all the rules until v. 16, while stylistically vv. 17–23 echo it (see 'Form and structure'). V. 6 is a fundamental principle that covers not only the following prohibitions but also what is not listed there, such as sexual union with one's daughter. Perhaps the latter cases are omitted simply because they are self-evident (cf. Wenham 1979: 254; Milgrom 2000a: 1527–1528). If so, the list (vv. 7–23) reflects the reality of the Canaanites *as examples*, and does not exhaust all possible cases.

One may well wonder why the Lord's statutes begin with prohibitions against incestuous unions. They no doubt strengthen family solidarity, and serve to protect the biological well-being of family members. But these rationales do not explain the cases given in vv. 19, 22–23. Schwartz concludes that the ultimate rationale is the Lord's will, while Milgrom says that 'the basic rationale is procreation within the ordered, patriarchal structure' (Milgrom 2000a: 1530). However, the central themes underlying these illicit sexual unions (their secretive nature, the distinction they make between man and woman and between human and beast) are best explained by the creation and fall in Gen. 2 – 3. Although more than a few exegetes refer to the creation and fall account for the purpose of illustration (e.g. Wenham 1979: 255; Noortzij 1982: 184; Rooker 2000: 243), the ideological relation these cases assume with Gen. 2 – 3 should not be viewed on the level of illustration: the rules clearly presume the Genesis account.

In terms of the creation, it is clear that as recounted in Gen. 2 the Lord created man and woman, and the woman as his helper. Gen. 2:24–25 states, 'Therefore a man shall leave his father and his mother and hold fast to his wife, and they shall become one flesh. And the man and his wife were both naked and were not ashamed' (ESV).

'One flesh' (*bāśār 'eḥād*) minimally means that they become part of each other, the symbolic picture of which is sexual intercourse. That they are not ashamed of their nakedness has something to do with both the absence of self-consciousness and the presence of God, for they became ashamed of it only after their violation of God's commandment. At any rate, herein lies the principle that explains the prohibitions in Lev. 18: since a man and a woman form one flesh, to uncover her is to uncover her husband (18:7). The reason why a man ought not to have sexual union with other females from his family is given as, 'a man shall leave his father and his mother and hold fast to his wife'. Separation from one's parents is given as the fundamental ground for a new couple. On the other hand, one's close relatives, including his parents, are part of his flesh in a broader sense, as the phrase *šĕ'ēr bĕśārô* indicates. Thus for a man to have sexual relations with a close relative brings shame not only upon the husband of the woman in question, but also on himself.

The Lord's intention to cover as wide a spectrum of illicit sexual unions as possible is seen particularly in the addition of the cases in vv. 17–23 where various literary devices are utilized (see 'Form and structure'). From v. 17 onwards the cases are not incestuous in a narrow sense. Almost all of them are illicit unions with women other than one's close relatives, but they are all common in 'uncovering the nakedness'. In other words, 'incest', 'adultery', 'polygamy', 'homosexuality' and 'worship' all refer to specific realms of illicit unions in modern terms.

It is artificial to make a distinction between marriage and sexual unions in reading the prohibitions. The gradual shift from 'uncover nakedness', 'to approach' (vv. 6, 14, 19) and then to 'take' (vv. 17–18) suggests no distinction is made between sexual union and marriage. Furthermore it is vital to comprehend that the overall nature of the list of abominations is designed to dissuade the Israelites from committing them, since they are the actual customs of the Canaanites. They do not aim to give the Israelites a comprehensive standard for marriage.

6. It is questionable whether 'his close relatives' is explained in the following verses or whether it also contains a rule. As Schwartz (1999: 163) observes, the verse exhibits six distinctive characteristics: (1) Only v. 6 refers to 'any one of his close relatives' (*šĕ'ēr bĕśārô*) and not to a certain woman. (2) Only v. 6 has 'anyone' (*'îš 'îš*), (3) Only here is the speech addressed in the 2nd person pl. (*tiqrĕbû*). (4) Only here is the verb 'to uncover' (*gillâ*) not followed by *someone's* nakedness. (5) The presence of the combination of *qārab* and *gillâ*. (6) The verse ends with 'I am the Lord'. However, v. 6 is not just a summary but the principle by which some missing cases in the following list are also included, as commented by Milgrom (Milgrom 2000a: 1533). Thus one can recognize both the independent nature of this verse and its nature as a summary.

The phrase *gillâ 'erwâ* (uncover nakedness) appears frequently in 18:6–19 and in 20:17–21. *'Erwâ* (nakedness) is euphemistic for the sexual organs of man and woman. Except for Leviticus, the phrase appears most frequently in Ezekiel (16:36–37; 22:10; 23:10, 18, 29).

Now alongside 'and he shall live' in v. 5, as well as the rationale for the injunctions (see above), this phrase 'uncover the nakedness' may derive from the fall. Since the fall, the uncovering of nakedness is shameful (cf. Gen. 2:25; see Gen. 9:22–23; Exod. 20:26).

7. The first of a series of illicit sexual relations relates to the nakedness of one's father. Since the addressee ('you') is a male, the partner is his mother. Having sexual intercourse with one's mother is 'uncovering the nakedness of your father'. Here 'nakedness' is figurative, but there is no distinction between literal and figurative, since his father's nakedness is seen as one with that of his mother (they are as 'one flesh'; cf. Gen. 2:24), hence the inviolability of the marital union.

The cases beginning from this verse reflect the actual customs among the Canaanites and Egyptians, but the rationale for the prohibitions lies in v. 6; it is not that potential untreated cases, such as polygamy, are approved.

8. 'The wife of your father' denotes a stepmother (Milgrom 2000a: 1538, 1541); hence the situation where a father had married another woman is presumed. The law does not address questions regarding whether the prohibition applies after the father's death, though it presumably does.

9. Next comes a prohibition against intercourse with one's sister who is further identified as 'your father's daughter' (a full sister) or 'your mother's daughter' (a half-sister). A further qualification is added to the effect that the rule applies to any sister whether she is born in the same household or not. Behind the rule lies the possibility that a woman remarries a man (the addressee's father) and has a daughter who grows up either with her half-brother (the addressee) or in her mother's new home. In this circumstance Wenham is right when he comments that 'whether brought up in the family or in another home' refers only to 'your mother's daughter' (Wenham 1979: 256).

10. Next comes a prohibition on intercourse with one's granddaughter, either a daughter of his son or daughter. Intercourse with one's granddaughter uncovers his own nakedness.

11. 'your father's wife's daughter' means a stepsister, on the understanding that the Hebr. term *môledet* (kindred) refers to a grouping wider than a core family but smaller than a tribe (Gen. 43:7; cf. Schwartz 1999: 179 n. 101). It is not necessarily the place where one is born. Cf. Abraham and Sarah (Gen. 20:12).

12–13. These verses prohibit one from having intercourse with an aunt (v. 12, his father's sister; and v. 13, his mother's sister), who is referred to as one of 'your relatives (*šĕ'ēr*).

14. The prohibition against intercourse with one's aunt: it is uncovering the nakedness of his father's brother. The words 'approach' and 'to uncover' in v. 6 are used here, though distributed to vv. 14a and 14b respectively. Cf. Amram and Jochebed (Exod. 6:20).

15. The prohibition against intercourse with one's daughter-in-law. Cf. Judah and Tamar (Gen. 38).

16. Intercourse with a brother's wife is prohibited, because that uncovers the nakedness of his brother. The relationship between this law and levirate marriage (Deut. 25:5–10) is often raised (for various views, see Milgrom 2000a: 1545). However, this verse and 20:21 cannot be harmonized with the Deuteronomic law on the same level, because the Levitical laws do not explicitly assume the death of 'your brother'. Furthermore an inability to have offspring is deemed in Leviticus as a punishment from God (20:21; cf. Kiuchi 2002). On the assumption that Deuteronomic law followed Levitical law, the law in this verse lost its practical validity for the Israelites in Deuteronomy.

17. Sexual union with both a woman and her daughter is prohibited. V. 17b appears to expand the case of 'her daughter' in v. 17a, assuming union with a woman. While up till v. 16 any union with one's relatives is prohibited, this law prohibits any attack on other relatives.

'take to uncover': *tiqqaḥ lĕgallôt* It is debatable whether 'take' signifies matrimony or simply means 'to take' in the sense of assault. The primary meaning is the latter, yet a marital connotation is not out of the question. It depends on how one defines 'marriage'. Since, however, the same verb 'take' (*lāqaḥ*) appears in the next verse, marital relationship appears to be in view.

18. This rule prohibits a man from having sexual relations with his wife's sister as a rival wife while his present wife remains alive. It is a ban on a special type of polygamy. Cf. Jacob in relation to Rachel and Leah (Gen. 29).

19. The rule bans intercourse with a woman while she is in a state of menstrual uncleanness. This case is often seen as incongruous with 15:24, which is thought to deal only with 'cultic' defilement. One proposal for harmonizing the two is to assume that the case in 15:24 deals with one's own wife, while the other deals with a woman who is not one's wife. But such an inference cannot be deduced from the text. As the occurrence of the phrase 'uncover nakedness' in this chapter ends at this verse, it is likely that one's wife is included, and that the phrase concerns marital relations. But as the next verse addresses a case of adultery with a neighbour's wife, there is a general arrangement of the rules, moving from marital intercourse to adultery. It is thus probable that v. 19, located between vv. 18 and 20, has in view both marital and extramarital intercourse. Therefore the man becomes unclean for seven days (15:24), namely completely unclean, which will be met by the *kāret* penalty (20:18).

It is noteworthy that the Hebr. root *ṭmʾ* ('unclean[ness]' or 'to become unclean') appears for the first time in this chapter and henceforth frequently (vv. 20, 23–25, 27–28, 30).

20. What is generally called 'adultery' is prohibited in this verse by using the characteristic phrase 'lie sexually' (*nātan šĕkōbet*; see v. 23 and 20:15;

Num. 5:20). In this chapter the phrase is used for cases concerning non-relatives (v. 23; 20:15).

Since the term 'fellow' (*'amît*, 6:2[5:21]; 18:20; 19:11, 15, 17; 24:19; 25:14–15, 17) clearly refers to a non-relative, this rule appears independent of what precedes. Yet it partially overlaps the potential case of v. 19 (see above).

The idea of defilement also links this verse to v. 19. Yet what is the nature of the term *ṭom'â* (becoming defiled)? Is it that *ṭum'â* in v. 19 is ritualistic, while *ṭom'â* is figuratively applied to moral conduct in this verse? This oft-made distinction is fallacious, because 'ritual' uncleanness already has a symbolic meaning: the state of hiding oneself. Rather it is more appropriate to assume that the idea of uncleanness is explicated in this chapter by illegal sexual *conduct* (see 'Explanation').

21. The regulations now move to a theme apparently different from the previous one: the prohibition against worship. In style it resembles v. 20: (1) The word *zera'* (seed), though different in meaning, echoes v. 19. (2) The Hebr. phrase *lō' tittēn* (lit. 'Do not give') appears in both verses.

In Leviticus the term *Môlek* occurs in 18:21 and 20:2–5, but it is reported in the books of Kings that worship was practised by the Ammonites and also by Israelite kings such as Solomon and others (1 Kgs 11:7; 2 Kgs 23:10; Jer. 32:35). Even where the term *Môlek* does not appear, such as in 2 Kgs 16:3, it appears to be assumed. According to Jer. 32:35, *Môlek* appears to be a god under the supremacy of Baal. And the ceremony is characterized by their transferring children through fire, expressed by the phrase *he'ebîr bā'ēš* (make someone pass through fire). The more exact nature of the worship as well as the identification of *Môlek* is a matter of scholarly debate (see Schwartz 1999: 187–196).

At any rate, to worship the *Môlek* god leads one to profane the name of his God on two major grounds: it is idolatrous and lacks reverence for life. 'Profaning' (*ḥillēl*) appears here for the first time in Leviticus, and henceforth frequently. That this worship is a direct affront against the Lord in a most extreme way is suggested by the mention of 'I am the Lord' at the end of the verse, which appears only in vv. 6 and 21.

Two factors, one, that this law is the only one in vv. 7–23 that deviates from the theme of sexual union, and two, that it is located between adultery (v. 20) and homosexuality (v. 22), have led exegetes since early times to assume that worship had something to do with sexual matters (see Schwartz 1999: 197 n. 46). But as Schwartz argues, worship is distinct from forbidden unions, though both are considered a major offence of Canaanite practice in the eyes of the Lord. Stylistically this law is suitably located after the mention of 'a seed' (v. 20) and through the formal similarity it shares with vv. 20–21, 23 in its use of *lō' tittēn* (lit. 'Do not give'; cf. Schwartz 1999: 199). However, v. 20 can be viewed as adultery, while v. 21 is adultery with a spiritual being. The latter is also prohibited because it blurs the distinction between humans and animals. Note that the following prohibitions in v. 22 (homosexuality) and v. 23 (bestiality) are related to the blurring of the distinction between man and woman, and between man and beasts. Vv. 21–23 give rules concerning an ignorance or rejection of the order God designed at the creation.

18:22–23

Two sexual aberrations are further prohibited: homosexuality and bestiality. The extravagant nature of the offences is expressed by somewhat milder expressions, such as 'lying' and 'standing', in contrast to the use of 'uncover the nakedness' in the earlier cases.

22. The addressee is a male, so homosexuality is at issue. One cannot, however, infer from the absence of a reference to lesbianism that lesbianism is permissible.

'Abominable thing' (*tô'ēbâ*) appears for the first time here in Leviticus and is concentrated in ch. 18 (vv. 22, 26–27, 29–30) and ch. 20 (v. 13).

23. Bestiality is prohibited through use of the similar form *lō;' tittēn* (lit. 'Do not give') as in vv. 20–21. It is prohibited for both men and women, and the rule is cast in parallelism. By lying with a beast, a man or a woman becomes defiled, which means he or she enters into the state of hiding. But he or she obviously hides even before the act (see 'Explanation').

18:24–30

This final section states the grounds for the above commandments in vv. 6–23, and commands the Israelites not to become defiled by any of those customs already prevalent in the land they are about to enter. Though the customs of 'Egypt' were mentioned in the introduction (v. 3), in this last section the Lord brings the attention of the addressees to the reality of Canaan. If the Israelites are not able to comply wholly with the Lord's direction, they will face the same fate the Canaanites are about to face; i.e. the Israelites will be expelled from the Promised Land too.

In this final section some Hebr. terms, the roots of which have already appeared in the preceding section (vv. 6–23), are frequently used to describe the nature of the consequences associated with the violation of these prohibitions: *ṭm'* and *tô'ēbâ*. The root *ṭm'* (to become unclean) appears in qal (vv. 25, 27), pi. (v. 28), ni. (v. 24) and hith. (vv. 24, 30). The subjects of the qal and ni. forms are 'the land', while the subjects of pi. and hith. forms are the Israelites in the 2nd person pl. Notice that the root *ṭm'* has already appeared in vv. 19–20, 23. Therefore it is nonsensical to say that only these cases are defiling, whereas the rest of the listed prohibitions are not defiling. Rather every case in vv. 7–23 is defiling; i.e. defiling to the offender. But what is new in this final section is that all the listed prohibitions are said to defile *the land* as well.

Similarly another repeated term, *tô'ēbâ* (an abomination), appears in v. 22, while it is repeated four times in thc final section (vv. 26–27, 29–30) in the pl. Thus all the listed prohibitions are *tô'ēbôt* (abominations). Clearly these stylistic features, not simply being literary, are instrumental in conveying the deliberate design of the Lord to bring all the prohibitions under the rubric of *tô'ēbôt*.

The land is personified: it *vomits out* its inhabitants (v. 25). Also it is implied that the land is the Lord's. By the use of the root *ṭm'* in the hith. (the people) and qal/ni. forms (the land) the idea is stressed that there is a concurrent defilement of both the land and its inhabitants. In 11:43–44, where the same grammatical conjugations appear, it was said contact with a swarming creature defiles one's soul. When one assumes defilement in ch. 11 has a symbolic meaning, rather than only a 'cultic' or 'ritual'meaning, it is gathered from 18:24 that defilement in ch. 11 can likewise result in the Lord's expulsion of the inhabitants from Canaan.

This means that the land, just like the sanctuary, is a reflection of the spiritual state of its inhabitants. However, while the sanctuary is purified by the ritual of the Day of Atonement, the land remains defiled until it vomits out the people living in it. The question arises, in what relation does the sanctuary stand to the land? In other words, does the ritual of the Day of Atonement purify the uncleanness caused by the violation of the prohibitions listed in this chapter? Prima facie, the latter defiles the sanctuary, and if all the self-hidings are confessed on the Day of Atonement, then both the sanctuary and the land are purified. However, the fact that the violations in this chapter are willfully committed, and their punishment is the *kāret* penalty, makes it unlikely the ritual in ch. 16 copes in practice with the defilement produced by the violation of the prohibitions in ch. 18. If the rules in this chapter are continually violated, there is no way the land, not to mention the sanctuary, can be purified, except by the land's vomiting out its inhabitants (see 'Explanation' on ch. 16).

Though this last section addresses all the Israelites, v. 29a, in particular, has the fate of an individual in view. Two significant facts are evident from this verse. First, the preposition *min* after '*āśâ* is partitive, so the violation of even one of these prohibitions is meant. The partitive sense of *min* is stressed in vv. 26a, 29a and 30. Though the idea of *one* violation is not stressed as it is in ch. 4 (see 'Comment' on 4:2), it appears to be assumed as self-evident. It is unnecessary to express the idea of 'one', for, as mentioned above, the very nature of the list of prohibitions in vv. 6–23 lies in that they are a unified whole, so one violation is closely related to others. Second, the term *nepeš* means 'a soul' and not the neutral translation 'person'. Thus the soul that offends any of the prohibitions will be cut off.

24. 'All these' should be taken literally: violation of one of them is prohibited. See vv. 26, 29–30.

26. V. 26aa is the same as v. 5aa and aims at responding to the further question as to why it is mandatory for the Israelites to observe the Lord's ordinances and judgments, which are this time contrasted with the 'abominations' (*tôʿēbôt*) of the land they are going to inherit. Note that all the customs listed in vv. 6–23 are called 'abominations', and not just the case in v. 22 (see also vv. 27, 29). Also notable is that the preposition *min* after *ʿāśâ* is partitive, so the Lord commands that *any of* the listed wrongs ought not to be done.

'the native or the stranger who sojourns among you' As in ch. 17, the law first mentions 'the Israelites', and afterwards details the components of it (cf. 17:2 versus v. 8).

27–28. The reason given for observance of the Lord's statutes (v. 26) is that the people of the land did commit these abominations and the land was defiled (v. 27). If the Israelites commit these abominations, the land will vomit them out too, just as the land will vomit out the Canaanites. Herein is presented a clear principle that the observance of the Lord's statutes must be universal, not just for the Israelites, but for foreigners too for as long as they dwell in the Promised Land.

29. Referring back to the injunction of v. 26ab, this verse lays further grounds for why the Israelites ought not to engage in any of the abominations: the souls of those who commit any of the listed abominations will be cut off from their people. For the meaning of the *kāret* penalty, see 'Comment' on 7:20 and 'Explanation' on ch. 20. It is noteworthy that the phrase 'the souls that do them' (v. 29b) indicates that the prohibited conduct emanates from the innermost part of people (see 'Explanation').

An intriguing contrast is formed in this chapter: that a man *lives* by observing the Lord's statutes (v. 5), while his soul may *be cut off* from the community if he does not observe them (v. 29). This leaves room for the situation that a person can live physically, yet be dead spiritually before the Lord; namely as a living corpse. Evidently there is no sacrificial ritual that can save such a soul.

30. The concluding exhortation is made in a comprehensive way.

'Keep my charge': *šĕmartem ʾet mišmartî* The phrase occurred in 8:35, and refers to a certain duty in a comprehensive way (cf. 22:9; Num. 1:53; 3:7 etc.).

The presence of 'the statutes (*ḥuqqôt*) of abominations (*tôʿēbôt*)' and 'make yourselves unclean' (*tiṭṭammāʾ*) in this last verse appears to have in view both vv. 4–5 and vv. 24. Furthermore the statement 'I am the Lord your God' at the end forms an inclusio with the same formula in v. 2.

Explanation

From this chapter onwards the moral nature of the Lord's commandments comes to the fore. However, as mentioned in Introduction 7.4.3, it is insufficient to assume that cultic 'uncleanness', expressed by the root *ṭm'*, is metaphorically applied in this chapter to moral conduct. In this chapter the root appears in vv. 19–20, 23–25, 27–28, 30, but as v. 24 indicates, all the violations are viewed as defiling, and the term is used as having a real spiritual force. Moreover the occurrence of the same root *ṭm'* both in this chapter and at the end of ch. 11 in qal, ni. and hiph. (see 'Comment' on vv. 20, 24–30) indicates that the idea of defilement in ch. 11 is explicated by moral conduct in ch. 18, rather than that the cultic/ritual shifts to the moral. Indeed the defilement in chs. 11 – 15 appears lenient compared to that in ch. 18, as the former, if serious, is expiable by animal sacrifice. But the principle is the same in both sections in that as far as one confesses his self-hiding, he is purified.

Furthermore to view the prohibitions in ch. 18 as consisting of cultic and moral elements is superficial. Since the behaviour mentioned is secretive, the violator is already hiding himself. This is probably the reason why *ḥāṭā'* or *ḥaṭṭā't* does not appear in this chapter; it is simply presumed. Thus the consequence of 'to become defiled', which is a ritual expression, functions both to refer the reader to the rules of chs. 11 – 15 and to make an ironic self-evident statement: because a person is unclean (in the state of hiding), he commits violations as presented in ch. 18 (for a further difference, see 'Explanation' on ch. 20).

But the approach to, and degree of, defilement in ch. 18 (and the following chapters), is different from those of chs. 11 – 15. In the former, the prohibitions begin hypothetically with secretive conduct, and only then mention the unclean state that ensues (similar to the address of Gen. 2:18). As regards the degree of defilement, the reader is reminded that sexual intercourse, even when legitimate, defiles a man and woman (15:18), while the rules in ch. 18, assuming this fact, present cases that result in higher degrees of defilement, since they are said to defile *the land*. And yet the consequence of these violations is said to be the same 'uncleanness'. Thus the relationship between chs. 15 and 18 is that ch. 15 presents the existential situation of a human by way of discharges from the reproductive organs, while ch. 18, assuming the presence of human self-hiding, presents possible defilement of a more serious nature that comes by way of conduct.

At first sight the injunctions against incestuous unions appear to be self-evident and axiomatic for the readers, but are naturally related, through stylistic devices, to other sexual offences in vv. 17–23; and the final section, vv. 24–30, brands all the violations as 'abominations' (*tô'ēbôt*). Thus the list of offences, through its literary devices, creates a homogenous balance of the sense of guilt on the part of the addressee, so the unspoken message of the list is that any violation of one of the prohibitions is no different, in essence, from others; for instance, any incestuous union is no different from Molech worship – both constitute rebellion against the divine created order. Therefore he cannot say he violates one prohibition but observes others.

Thus the immediate background, namely Gen. 2 – 3, of this chapter makes it likely that though the rules concentrate on outer conduct ('uncovering the nakedness'), they point to the root of the problem. These persons practise them because they hide themselves against the Lord.

This raises two further significant truths, which together form the essence of this chapter.

First, it is not just that the fate of one's soul is seriously affected by his conduct, but v. 29b explicitly states that the souls who do ('violate') (*hanněpāšôt hā'ōśōt*) them will be cut off. Herein lies the deepest cause of the abominations: the desire to violate a prohibition springs from the innermost part of the human, which is why the soul is said to be cut off. Despite the chapter's apparent emphasis on outward but hidden acts, an inner desire such as lust is assumed to be the source of the misconduct. Furthermore the phrase 'the souls that do' stresses the inseparable bond between one's inner motives and outward conduct (see 'Comment' on 5:4). And this opens up the possibility that all the acts prohibited in this chapter are merely manifestations of the human soul: the prohibitions assume no room to exist between what a person desires in the heart and how he or she behaves. It is only a small step towards Jesus' words in the Sermon on the Mount, 'But I say to you that everyone who looks at a woman with lust has already committed adultery with her in his heart' (Matt. 5:28 NRSV).

Second, while the prohibitions should be taken literally, they simultaneously convey spiritual principles that are developed in the following chapters: the ban on idolatry in the area of family and matrimonial matters (see the structure of chs. 17 – 22 in Introduction 4.1). Although the literal violations of the prohibitions are deemed heinous acts in almost all societies, people may find it difficult to separate spiritually from their parents and relatives, so they involve themselves with the egocentric nature of their relatives. Such a spiritual tendency can be seen as expressed in this chapter by incestuous relations.

New Testament implications

Sexual desire is not evil by itself, but since the fall such a desire has lost its proper control due to the fact that humans became like gods: they became the centre of their world and assumed the authority to do what they liked. The abominable customs of the Canaanites are just a manifestation of the fallen man and woman.

In principle, most of the abominations listed in this chapter are also condemned in the NT. Rom. 1 lists the same vices that result from humanity's willful alienation from the Creator (vv. 18–32). The chapter includes mercilessness, arrogance etc. (vv. 29–31) in addition to what is presented in Lev. 18, but St Paul's intention is that they are all the same. Any modern discussion about the degrees of heinousness of the abominations, which tends to treat abominations such as incest, adultery and homosexuality separately from each other, is at odds with the basic tenet of both Lev. 18 and Rom. 1, which regard them all as of equal gravity before the Lord. Therefore it is nonsensical to ask whether the violation of any of these abominations can be forgiven by the atoning work of Christ: they can indeed be forgiven, but only by the destruction of the human egocentric nature. If the latter is not achieved, the human situation before God remains the same as before. Also, the more moral a society looks, the higher its degree of self-hiding. The Lord dooms such a society to destruction.

LEVITICUS 19:1–37

Translation

[1]The LORD spoke to Moses, saying, [2]'Speak to all the community of the Israelites
and say to them, You shall be holy, for I the LORD your God am holy. [3]Everyone
shall revere his mother and his father, and you shall keep my sabbaths: I am the
LORD your God. [4]Do not turn to idols or make for yourselves any gods of cast
metal: I am the LORD your God.
[5]'When you offer a fellowship offering to the LORD, you shall offer it so that you
may be accepted. [6]It shall be eaten the same day you offer it or on the day after, and
anything left over until the third day shall be burned up with fire. [7]If it is eaten at all
on the third day, it is a desecrated offering; it will not be accepted, [8]and everyone
who eats it shall bear his guilt, because he has profaned what is holy to the LORD,
and that soul shall be cut off from his people.
[9]'When you reap the harvest of your land, you shall not reap your field right up to
its edge, neither shall you gather the gleanings after your harvest. [10]And you shall
not strip your vineyard bare, neither shall you gather the fallen grapes of your
vineyard. You shall leave them for the poor and for the sojourner: I am the LORD
your God.
[11]'You shall not steal; you shall not deal falsely; you shall not lie to one another.
[12]You shall not swear by my name falsely, and so profane the name of your God: I
am the LORD. [13]You shall not oppress your neighbour or rob him. The wages of a
hired servant shall not remain with you all night until the morning. [14]You shall not
curse the deaf or put a stumbling block before the blind, but you shall fear your
God: I am the LORD. [15]You shall do no injustice in court. You shall not be partial to
the poor or defer to the great, but in righteousness shall you judge your fellow.
[16]You shall not go around as a slanderer among your people, and you shall not
stand up against the life of your neighbour: I am the LORD. [17]You shall not hate
your brother in your heart; rather you shall reason frankly with your fellow, but
you should not bear punishment because of him. [18]You shall not take vengeance
or bear a grudge against the sons of your own people, but you shall love your
neighbour as yourself: I am the LORD.

[19]'You shall keep my statutes. You shall not let your cattle breed with a different kind. You shall not sow your field with two kinds of seed, nor shall you wear a garment of cloth made of two kinds of material. [20]If a man lies sexually with a woman who is a slave, assigned to another man and not yet ransomed or given her freedom, a distinction shall be made. They shall not be put to death, because she was not free; [21]but he shall bring his compensation to the LORD, to the entrance of the Tent of Meeting, a ram for a reparation offering. [22]And the priest shall make propitiation for him with the ram of the reparation offering before the LORD for his self-hiding that he has committed, and he shall be forgiven for the self-hiding that he has committed.

[23]'When you come into the land and plant any kind of tree for food, then you shall regard its fruit as forbidden. Three years it shall be forbidden to you; it must not be eaten. [24]And in the fourth year all its fruit shall be holy, an offering of praise to the LORD. [25]But in the fifth year you may eat of its fruit, to increase its yield for you: I am the LORD your God.

[26]'You shall not eat any flesh with the blood in it. You shall not interpret omens or tell fortunes. [27]You shall not round off the hair on your temples or mar the edges of your beard. [28]You shall not make any cuts on your body for the soul or tattoo yourselves: I am the LORD. [29]Do not degrade your daughter by making her commit fornication, lest the land fall into prostitution and the land become full of depravity.

[30]'You shall keep my sabbaths and revere my sanctuary: I am the LORD. [31]Do not turn to mediums or necromancers; do not seek them out, and so make yourselves unclean by them: I am the LORD your God. [32]You shall stand up before the elderly and honour the face of an old man, and you shall fear your God: I am the LORD.

[33]'When a stranger sojourns with you in your land, you shall not do him wrong. [34]You shall treat the stranger who sojourns with you as the native among you, and you shall love him as yourself, for you were strangers in the land of Egypt: I am the LORD your God. [35]You shall do no injustice in judgment, in measures of length or weight or quantity. [36]You shall have just balances, just weights, a just ephah, and a just hin: I am the LORD your God, who brought you out of the land of Egypt.

[37]'And you shall observe all my statutes and all my rules, and do them: I am the LORD.'

Notes on the text

1. 'all': *kol* LXX and possibly 11PaleoLev omit the word. However, MT is preferred in view of its uniqueness (Milgrom 2000a: 1602) and its counterpart in v. 37.

3. 'his mother and his father': *'immô wĕ'ābîw* LXX, Syr, Tg Neofiti and Vg invert the order, which is, however, deliberate (cf. 21:2 and see 'Comment').

7. *hē'ākōl yē'ākel* SamP reads *'ākōl ye'ākel*, which is unnecessary in view of 7:18.

11. 'against one another' This phrase appears to qualify the prohibitions against deception and lying.

12. 'I am the LORD': *'ănî YHWH* LXX adds 'your God'. However, this is unnecessary, since it is preceded by 'the name of your God'. LXX also adds 'your God' in vv. 14, 16, 28, 32 and 37.

13. *lō'* Some Hebr. MSS, LXX, SamP, TgJon read *wĕlō'*. However, when v. 13b is viewed as the second line of parallelism, this is unnecessary.

15. *ta'ăśû*: 'do' SamP reads it in sg. However, the use of pl. and sg. in the same law is common in this chapter. See vv. 12, 19, 27, 33–34.

16. 'among your people': *bĕ'ammêkā* SamP, Syr and some Hebr. MSS read *bĕ'ammĕkā* without *yôd*.

20. 'and not yet ransomed': *wĕhopdēh lō' nipdātâ BHS* margin proposes *hippādēh* (ni. inf. abs.) to correspond with *nipdātâ*. However, the juxtaposition of different conjugations in this construction is attested to elsewhere, such as in Exod. 19:13; 21:20, 22. For hoph. inf. abs., see Josh. 9:24; 2 Kgs 3:23.

'a distinction': *biqqôret* See 'Comment'.

23. 'regard ... as forbidden': *'araltem ... 'orlātô* Lit. 'regard as uncircumcised'. See 'Comment'.

26. 'with the blood': *'al haddām* LXX reads 'on the mountain', probably having read *'l hrm*, confusing *dālet* with *rēš*.

27. 'mar ... your [sg.] beard': *tašḥît ... zĕqānekā* SamP, LXX, TgJon read this part in pl. However, see on v. 15 above.

29. 'degrade': *tĕḥallel* Since the daughter is not holy, 'degrade' is better than 'profane', as Milgrom proposes (2000a: 1696).

'making her commit fornication': *hiznâ* See 'Comment'.

36. 'a just ephah': *'ēpat ṣedeq* LXX omits this; probably it is a case of homoioteleuton.

Form and structure

Lev. 19 contains laws relating to the divine–human relationship, inter-human relationships and various other relationships between the addressee, agricultural practices, sacrifices and offerings, clothes etc. They aim to encourage the Israelites to become holy. The variegated style of ch. 19 matches its variegated content. Not only does the chapter comprise positive and negative laws, but it addresses the reader with the 2nd person sg., 2nd person pl., 3rd person sg. and 3rd person pl. In content the chapter contains not just so-called moral laws but ritual laws as well (i.e. vv. 5–8, 20–22).

From a broader structural viewpoint, this chapter is the sequel of 11:44–45, which discusses holiness in terms of the symbolic meaning of creatures. By contrast, this chapter deals with human conduct in relation to holiness.

The latter half of ch. 19 (vv. 19–32) contains vague references to the language and themes of ch. 18, such as *hirbî‘* (let ... breed, v. 19; see 18:23), the phrase *ṭom'â bĕ* (make ... unclean by, v. 31; see 18: 20, 23), whoring after spiritual beings (soothsaying, witchcraft, contact with death), laws prohibiting various mixtures (v. 19) and a father causing his daughter to prostitute herself (v. 29), though the father–daughter relation is missing in ch. 18. Also, while reference to 'Egypt' is made in 18:3, it is not mentioned again until 19:34, 36. V. 37 is particularly significant: it is quite similar to what is found in 18:4–5, and this has implications for the structure of chs. 18 – 19. There is no mention of 'statutes and rules' between 18:5 and 19:37. It also makes sense that in 19:37 'all' (*kol*) is prefixed to 'statutes and rules' (cf. 18:4–5). These pieces of literary evidence indicate that 18:2b–5 is at least an introduction to all the laws from 18:6 to 19:36. A further recapitulation is found in 20:22–26.

Although various proposals are offered for the chapter's structure, this should be considered from the viewpoint of the content or theme (cf. Milgrom 2000a: 1596–1602). A consideration of the meaning of each cluster of laws shows that vv. 3–18 concern the addressee's relation to the Lord, parents and neighbours (i.e. extroversive), whereas vv. 19–29 concern the addressee's own inner condition (i.e. introversive). Vv. 3–4 are clearly related to vv. 30–32, while v. 19 (*'et ḥuqqôtay tišmĕrû*) is concluded by v. 37 (*ušĕmartem 'et ḥuqqôtay*). From this viewpoint the chapter appears to have the following palistrophic structure:

Panel 1 (focus on the relationship with the Lord and neighbours)

A 3–8 Reverence for parents, sabbaths:

B 5–8 Salvation of one's own soul

C 9–10 A prohibition against coveting (agriculture)

D 11–18 No damaging of 'your neighbour'; right judgment; love your neighbour as yourself

Panel 2 (focus on the addressee)

D' 19–22 No mixing the holy with the common: an example of right judgment

C' 23–25 Priority of the Lord to one's own (agriculture): prohibition against coveting

B' 26–29 Love of one's own soul and body

A' 30–32 Sabbath observance and reverence for the sanctuary and the elderly; ban on mediums

The evidence for this structure depends much on how each commandment is interpreted (see 'Comment' below). Panel 2 (D'C'B'A') complements Panel 1 (ABCD). The relationships between B–B' and D–D' require some explanation.

As mentioned above, Panel 2 focuses on the addressee's inner life after the need for true self-love is set out in D. On this assumption it appears that D^1 deals with a person who truly loves himself, a person able to make a strict and thorough differentiation between the holy and common, and vv. 20–22 can be seen as an example of just judgment (see 'Comment' there). As regards B–B^1, while B deals with the need to make a sharp distinction between the addressee's selfishness and the holy (it concerns his salvation), B^1 focuses on the addressee's soul and body. Note that 'eating with blood' in v. 26 symbolizes the forfeiture of the very means of making atonement.

Vv. 33–36 resume the same topics in D and expand on them. For the rest of the laws, see 'Comment'.

Comment

It is often, and rightfully, said that this chapter is preoccupied with holiness. Indeed the Lord introduces his speech with 'Be holy for I am holy' (v. 2). Although the following statutes and rules are evidently related to 'being holy' or 'holiness', how they are related is debatable. A discussion concerning this relationship is presented in 'Explanation'. Methodologically, it is safer to explore the significance they have for becoming holy by examining the meaning and nature of this chapter's laws within the wider context of Leviticus. Crucial for a correct reading of the laws are the following observations.

(1) Holiness is apparently related to observing *all* the laws, as stated in v. 37. Thus partial observance of the laws has essentially nothing to do with holiness, even though this is a commonly accepted idea (see 'Explanation').

(2) While it is right to say that the laws present *the road* to holiness, holiness lies not *in the road* but in the person who observes all the laws. Therefore one should consider what kind of person the holy person is.

(3) Although many of the rules are positive or negative commands relating to outward conduct, the key to their observance lies in the state or attitude of the human heart. In fact, some rules (vv. 5–8, 9–10, 19, 23–25) have, in all likelihood, symbolic meanings and refer to the condition of the human heart. Thus, though the Israelites are expected to observe the laws literally, it is more imperative to observe their symbolic meaning.

References to the Decalogue are evident throughout the laws. Indeed this chapter constitutes a further elucidation of the Decalogue with special reference to holiness.

19:1–2ab

As in the previous chapter (18:1), these laws are also addressed to the laity through Moses.

19:2b–4

2b. 'You shall be holy': *qĕdōšîm tihyû* The sons of Israel are commanded to be holy. Previously, the term *qādôš* is mostly ascribed to places in the 'holy place' in the sanctuary (6:16[9], 26[19], 27[20]; 7:6; 10:13; 16:24). It is only in 11:44–45 that the Israelites are commanded to be holy just as the Lord is holy. In view of the meaning of the commandment and the passage's significant location, it is arguable that what is outwardly indicated in 11:44–45, or ch. 11 as a whole, is detailed in a different way in this chapter. On the whole, while ch. 11 speaks about holiness gained by abstaining from detestable creatures that symbolize human beings, this chapter mainly speaks about the same holiness by addressing the particular conduct of the people, in terms of both the God–human relationship and interhuman relationships.

As mentioned in the Introduction (7.4.3), it is erroneous to assume that the holiness spoken of in chs. 1 – 16 is 'cultic' and essentially different from the so-called 'ethical' holiness in this chapter. In line with the relationship between chs. 1 – 16 and chs. 17 – 22, the concept of holiness in the former is the same as in the latter. Indeed, as holiness is graded in Leviticus, the Lord's holiness cannot simply be identifiable with that gained by the priests on the day of their ordination. At most, their holiness is outer. Also, noteworthy is that holiness in the Tent differs in degree from that assumed in the Holy of Holies. And yet the holiness of the Lord himself is even distinguishable from the Holy of Holies. But on the other hand, that the same term *qdš* is used in all these matters suggests they share a common element. The key to understanding the idea of holiness is found in the holiness of sacrifices and offerings that symbolize the existential condition of the offerer, and refers to the condition of the human heart.

The concept of *qōdeš* and *qādôš* is much debated. One major proposal for its basic meaning is 'separation'. Indeed several passages appear to point in that direction, such as 11:47 and 20:25–26. Schwartz (1999: 250–266) argues that what is common to God's holiness and human holiness is only the idea of 'separation'; in other respects God's holiness is different from human holiness, as God does not need to observe commandments such as those presented in both this and the preceding chapters. Schwartz correctly observes that the commandments as such do not represent holiness, and that the moral character of holiness is based only on a selection of laws pertaining to social justice in this chapter (Schwartz 1999: 264). However, that holiness ought to be separated from the common (10:10; Ezek. 22:26; 42:20) indicates that the idea of holiness is different from 'separation'. 'Separation' is an aspect of holiness and it, by no means, denotes the idea of *qdš* (see 'Explanation'). Thus that God does not need to observe the laws and that the same term *qādôš* is used for humans points to the possibility that it means something other than 'separation'. From this and the interpretation of the following commandments, I propose that it refers to the absence of an egocentric nature.

For the formulaic 'I am the LORD your God', see 'Comment' on 18:1–2.

3. The first concrete commandment is to 'fear' one's mother and father. This is a matter of the human heart. Note the order in 'his mother and his father', which differs from all other cases similar to this commandment. Indeed the order here is chiastic in relation to other cases (see the Fifth Commandment). Moreover the law is stressed in this instance by the verb 'fear' (*yārē'*); elsewhere the verb 'honour' (*kbd* pi.) is used. 'Fear' is normally used to describe one's attitude towards God. Clearly the law assumes the Decalogue, and it is the Lord's intention to push the Fifth Commandment to its extreme by commanding people even to fear their own mother, who is usually the object of affection, not fear. Yet who can observe this law?

The second part of the verse commands the observance of 'my sabbaths (*šabbĕtōtay*)'. *Šabbātōt* (pl.) includes not just the seventh day, but also the various festive days dealt with in ch. 23. On these occasions the Israelites are to rest completely, but here 'my' is important: those days belong to the Lord, not to the Israelites. The first part of this verse relates to the Fifth Commandment and the second to the Fourth Commandment. 'sabbath' means 'rest' both in the physical and spiritual sense. Negatively, it requires an abstinence from the work done over the previous six days. However, such a commandment is unlikely to be observed so long as a person entertains a covetous desire within his heart (cf. 16:31).

Vv. 3–8 clearly relate to the worship of the Lord. So the intention of mentioning the honouring of one's parents may derive from the premise that a person cannot fear or worship the Lord so long as they cannot fear their *visible* parents.

4. While v. 3 lists two positive commandments, this verse mentions a negative commandment; namely a prohibition against idolatry. This prohibition is necessitated by the propensity of people to turn away from the Lord. Note that the verb 'Do not turn to' (*'al tipnû*) refers to a person's inner motive.

Modern readers should not assume that, just because they no longer make graven images, this command is irrelevant. In modern society, where innumerable enterprises are pursued, idols, both visible and invisible, are innumerable. In the Decalogue, allegiance to the Lord is negatively expressed by the other side of the same coin: 'no coveting' (Exod. 20:2–5, 17). However, coveting refers to all kinds of expectations, aspirations and hopes in so far as they look pleasing to one's own eyes (cf. Gen. 3:6).

19:5–8

Why do the rules for the fellowship offering come within this context? This offering, by its symbolic depiction of its offerer's egocentric nature's destruction, concerns a person's spiritual salvation before the Lord. Note that the law concentrates on the issue of eating the remaining flesh. Since it symbolizes fellowship with the Lord *after* the removal of the worshipper's selfishness, the fellowship offering is singled out in order to highlight that one cannot have fellowship with the Lord while the egocentric nature still remains (see 'Comment' on chs. 3 and 7). The rule is reflective of human nature in so far as the destruction of one's selfishness is commonly temporary. Therefore it strictly prohibits eating the flesh of this offering on the third day. The severity of the punishment associated with this rule suggests that the Lord's holiness must not be infringed upon even when offering what was apparently the most common sacrifice. Reference to the *kāret* penalty (v. 8b) means, in view of 18:29, this violation is virtually as serious as that made against the Lord in the abominations listed in ch. 18. To observe this law, a deep sense of one's own egocentric nature is required. Paradoxically, then, the road to holiness begins with an awareness of one's selfishness.

The holiness (*qōdeš*) of the offering is essentially the same as the Lord's holiness, so it is artificial and erroneous to categorize the former holiness as cultic and the latter as moral.

Vv. 5–8 concern the fellowship aspect of the divine–human relationship, but if they reveal the difficulty of maintaining one's allegiance to the Lord, the commandments in vv. 3–4 seem even more difficult.

19:9–10

Following the rules relating to the divine–human relationship, this section stipulates several rules concerning interhuman relationships that function in the Lord's presence. The prohibitions against gleaning every corner of the field and against gathering what is left over after the harvest are arranged in a parallelistic form. As v. 10b indicates, these rules are meant to assist the poor and sojourner. In that it expresses an overall attitude to one's neighbour, by using a concrete situation as an example, it reflects the same attitude assumed in v. 18b. Obviously a person requires a heartfelt desire to care for others in order to implement this commandment. This is, at least, based on the condition that a person's heart is free from covetous desires. The literal observance of these rules is possible (Ruth 2), but they still aim to create an awareness of the covetous desires within one's heart. However, holiness assumes an absence of such desires. All this suggests holiness is found where there is a lack of interest in harvesting for oneself what remains for others, which seems nearly impossible for humans.

19:11–18

Along with vv. 3–4, vv. 11–17 are replete with allusions to the Decalogue. The laws in vv. 11–16 prohibit trespassing boundaries between neighbours (stealing, lying, oppressing, discriminating), and between the human and divine (swearing falsely). It is self-evident that all the prohibitions in vv. 11–13 aim to counter behaviour that derives from the human heart. Vv. 13–14 demand that no bias should exist in one's judgment of others. Put simply, they prohibit doing wrong to neighbours and the Lord. These laws become particularly concerned with inner matters in vv. 17–18a, where hatred is prohibited, and culminate in the golden rule 'Love your neighbour as yourself', where the addressee is commanded even to love those who *hate* him. That equity is of paramount importance (in this case equity in one's love for oneself and one's neighbour) even at this culminating point is worthy of note. For selfish human beings this requires the denial of oneself, or more exactly one's selfish nature. Thus the issue of selfishness, first addressed on a symbolic dimension in vv. 5–6, finds its culmination in v. 18b, where its denial is viewed as the essence of holiness. Or more exactly, the ability to observe the command to love presumes the existence of a heart free of selfishness. Holiness is found where there is unselfishness, which is also the essence of what a *holy* sacrificial animal symbolizes.

As Wenham observes (1979: 267), one's neighbour is called a 'fellow citizen' in vv. 11–12, 'neighbour' in v. 13–14, 'fellow citizen, people, neighbour' in vv. 15–16, and 'brother, fellow citizen, people, neighbour' in vv. 17–18, probably to highlight the great command to love his neighbour as himself in v. 18.

11. Prohibitions against stealing, deceiving and lying to one another. This verse and the following one are similar in content to the Seventh and Ninth Commandments.

'deal falsely': *kiḥēš* Cf. 'Comment' on 6:2[5:21].

'lie': *těšaqqer* The verb *šiqqer* occurs five times in the OT, and means to 'lie', the opposite of loyalty. It does not necessarily mean 'not telling the truth', as often assumed by modern exegetes. In this context the preposition *bě* in the adverbial clause *'îš ba'ămîtô* (to one another) means 'against', suggesting hostility (cf. Exod. 20:16).

12. Prohibition against swearing falsely by the name of the Lord. See 6:3, 5[5:22, 24]. It concerns the Third and Ninth Commandments (cf. Exod. 20:7a, 16).

13. Prohibitions against oppressing, or stealing from, others. See 6:2, 4[5:21, 23]. The second half of the verse provides an example of oppression (not paying the wage of a hired servant until morning). Though these prohibitions have a social dimension, the 2nd person sg. address suggests that, like the preceding commandments, their primary concern is the addressee.

14. Prohibitions against despising the deaf or blind. 'Curse' (*qillēl*) is both a verbal and non-verbal act of despising. One may do so by forgetting his creator. But in the biblical view it is the Lord himself who makes one person deaf and another blind, so to despise the handicapped is to despise their creator (cf. Exod. 4:11). A lack of fear of God engenders such an attitude. The placement of a stumbling block before a blind person is given as an example. Discriminations begin in the human heart and so an awareness of discrimination is expected to lead to an awareness of one's own egocentric nature.

15. A prohibition against injustice in court. Following the prohibition against the ill-treatment of the handicapped, this law prohibits partiality in matters of judgment motivated by the social status of the person being judged. 'Do not' recurs three times alongside one positive 'Do'. The first negative command ('do no injustice in court') is explained by the second ('You shall not be partial to the poor') and third ('you shall not defer to the great') commandments, and is formulated positively in 'You shall judge your fellow rightly'. However, can a human judge others justly? The very awareness of another's position should lead the addressee to an awareness of his own egocentric nature.

16. Prohibition against slandering. This verse consists of two parallel sayings that express the same idea. Note that, following vv. 14–15 and developed in vv. 17–18, this commandment also concerns a ban against partiality.

'go around as a slanderer': *tēlēk rākîl* The idiom *hālak rākîl* occurs five times in the OT (Lev. 19:16; Jer. 6:28; 9:5[3]; Prov. 11:13; 20:19). It refers to people who slander and reveal secrets. The second part of the verse reveals the act as the 'shedding of blood' (cf. Ezek. 22:9).

'stand up against the life of your neighbour': *ta'ămōd 'al dam rē'ekā* This is a unique expression in the OT. A comparable one is found in *'āmad 'al nepeš* in Esth. 8:11 and 9:16. In such cases the preposition *'al* means 'against' (cf. 1 Chr. 21:1) and the noun *dām* means 'life', so the whole expression virtually means 'to seek to destroy the life of your neighbour'. The significance of 'I am the Lord' at the end of the verse suggests that the neighbour's life is a life given by the Lord, and that to slander one's neighbour is to take offence with the Lord himself.

17. A prohibition against hating others. The cause of harmful conduct to others, such as slandering in v. 16, lies in its internal motive: hatred within one's heart. It seems that no human, if there are exceptions, can observe such a commandment. Vv. 17–18 show that *'āmît* (a fellow) is synonymous with *rēa'* (neighbour) and *'āḥ* (brother), and in this case it refers to non-relatives, only using the language of closest relatives to stress the close relationship between the addressee and the neighbour in question.

'your brother': *'āḥîkā* The term *'āḥ* does not primarily mean a blood brother but 'a brother' in a figurative sense, almost equivalent to *rēa'* in v. 16. Certainly 'your brother' includes one's blood brother. Yet the reason for the term's use here appears closely related to the use of the term 'to hate' (*śānē'*); as the prohibition concerns one's internal motive, one's neighbour is presented not just as a brother in a legal sense but as a brother who should be loved just like a blood brother.

The second part of the verse requires the addressee to reason frankly with the brother rather than hating him (cf. Prov. 27:5–6). It serves as the positive complement to the negative command of v. 17a ('Don't do this; rather do this'). However, its relationship with v. 17c is unclear. V. 17c is rendered 'lest you bear sin because of him' (RSV), 'or you will incur guilt yourself'. (NRSV), 'you shall not incur sin because of him' (ESV), 'but incur no guilt because of him' (JPS), 'so you will not share in his guilt' (NIV). Before considering the relationship that exists between 'Reprove your neighbour' and what follows, it is necessary to make clear what *nāśā' ḥēṭ* and *'ālāyw* mean. First, contra the majority of exegetes, it is important to distinguish between *ḥēṭ* and *ḥaṭṭā't*; the former means 'guilt', 'offence' or 'punishment'. Here 'bear punishment' seems intended. Second, in view of Lev. 22:9 and Num. 18:32, *'ālāyw* possibly means 'because of him'. Thus the whole passage means 'you shall not bear guilt/punishment because of him'. The question is, how does this sentence relate to the foregoing 'Reprove your neighbour'? Three possibilities exist:

1. Reproof of the neighbour would help you not to bear his guilt (RSV, NIV).
2. Reproof of the neighbour ought to be done in such a way that you should not bear guilt because of him (cf. JPS).
3. Reproof of the neighbour is mandatory; otherwise you will bear guilt because of him (cf. NRSV).

The presumption that the hated person has some guilt/punishment has no textual support and is therefore considered unlikely (*pace* option 1). Grammatically option 3 is possible, but it fails to explain the presence of *'ālāyw* (because of him). Thus option 2 is most likely. The text assumes that the reproof of another person in regard to some matter often brings guilt on the person who does the reproving. I hold that the relation between reproof and bearing guilt is disjunctive; hence the proposed translation.

The commandment in v. 17b is doubly difficult to observe. Given that it is extremely difficult to reprove a neighbour, how much more difficult it is to reprove a neighbour one hates in a way that he may not bear any guilt. For, since the person who reproves has his own problems, the reproof tends to result in an even deeper hatred (cf. 'Explanation' on ch. 4 [1.2]).

Both this commandment and the one in v. 16 prohibit one's involvement with another's egocentric nature.

18. A prohibition against taking vengeance and a command to love one's neighbour. The same theme of personal relationship evident in v. 18 is addressed, but now in relation to the addressee's anger. Taking vengeance means that one takes the initiative in repaying the wrong received from a neighbour. Such a responsibility is exclusively ascribed to the Lord (Deut. 32:35).

This prohibition is underscored by the Lord's prohibition against bearing a grudge. The addressee must not bear a grudge against a person who similarly shares membership in the same group of people who enjoy a covenantal relationship with the Lord. Taking vengeance and bearing grudges are aggravated human emotions fostered against a neighbour, and these two don'ts are followed by the most positive and comprehensive commandment, 'Love your neighbour as yourself.' The context in which v. 18b is placed is highly important in interpreting the commandment: it includes, as the forgoing verses indicate, potential situations where the addressee may hate his neighbour.

As this commandment is what is called the Golden Rule that summarizes all the Law in the Christian interpretation, some precision is required for its correct interpretation.

'love': *'āhab* This is an ordinary OT term for affection either between humans (e.g. Gen. 22:2; 25:28) or between humans and God (cf. Exod. 20:6; Deut. 6:5). But the context of hatred requires the addressee to envisage a situation where one ought to love one whom he does not love, which is impossible; if one cannot observe the commandment in v. 17, 'Do not hate your brother in your heart,' how much less is he able to observe this great commandment. The impossibility of its observance is further indicated by the following observations.

While the term is often taken as meaning something other than a human emotion, such as the will (e.g. Kleinig 2003: 412), the context of vv. 17–18 shows that it is an emotional term. Thus it is a command that says 'Love your neighbour whom you hate.'

'your neighbour': *rē'ăkā* The term *rēa'* has appeared in vv. 13 and 16, and it refers to all those people with whom the addressee has a relationship, including those whom the addressee hates.

'like yourself': *kāmôkā* An attempt has been made to connect this phrase to the immediately preceding *lĕrē'ăkā*, meaning that one ought to love one's neighbour, *who is like you* (e.g. Ehrlich 1908: 65; Muraoka 1978: 291–297). This reading may lessen the burden of the commandment. But, as Schwartz correctly observes (Schwartz 1999: 320–321), the phrase 'like yourself' is an adverbial one that qualifies the verb *'āhabtā* (cf. Lev. 19:34; 2 Sam. 9:8). While it appears possible to love one's neighbour, the text says that this love ought to be like the love one directs towards oneself. Such love is impossible (contra Schwartz 1999: 321) unless one's selfishness of all kinds and on all levels is destroyed. This consideration recalls the notion of sacrifice where the animal dies for the sake of saving a human soul. In other words, one can observe this commandment only when one becomes self-sacrificial in the true sense of the word. Since a sacrifice is holy, a person who possesses such an attitude is holy as is commanded in v. 2 (see further 'Explanation').

19:19

This verse begins with 'Keep my statutes'. Schwartz and Milgrom take 'my statutes' as referring only to the three laws of this verse (Schwartz 1999:

324; Milgrom 2000a: 1657); namely prohibitions on mating two different species, sowing two different kinds of seed, and wearing clothes made of two different kinds of textile. Yet there is not evidence for this interpretation: it more likely refers to the laws contained in all of the other chapters.

The prohibition against mating different kinds of animals is unique in the OT. In ch. 18 a number of illicit unions are presented, but they are either between human beings, or between humans and animals. The reason for the prohibition has been explained by suggesting that mixed breeding represents the introduction of disorder into God's creation. However, as Milgrom points out (2000a: 1659), it is more likely that the prohibition aims to inculcate the truth that mixtures belong to the holy realm.

One may rightfully argue that the literal observance of this law is mandatory. But this is not all there is to the law, for the observance of this law in v. 2 constitutes the idea of holiness, whereas it is suggested in the preceding verse that holiness lies in the state of the human heart. Therefore it is more likely that the Lord directs the addressee's attention to his own heart, to see whether or not his heart can make a distinction between what is common sense and what is not, *and* practise it (see also 'Explanation').

Second, sowing different kinds of seed is prohibited. Deut. 22:9 is significant: 'You shall not sow your vineyard with two kinds of seed, lest the whole yield be holy [*tiqdaš*], the crop that you have sown and the yield of the vineyard.'

Some versions translate *tiqdaš* 'be forfeited' (i.e. to the sanctuary). However, such a meaning is unusual in biblical Hebrew. Rather it seems the reason for the Deuteronomic prohibition lies in that to do so would make both the crop and the yield *holy*, with the result that they are forfeited and useless to the Israelites. This suggests the law in Leviticus 19:19 means that sowing two kinds of seed in the field is an act of making the whole crop holy. But what is wrong with making the whole crop holy in this context? Another passage, Isa. 28:23–25, suggests it was customary for a farmer to sow several kinds of seed in different but certain places in the field. Together these observations suggest that in Lev. 19:19 sowing *two* different kinds of seed is prohibited in order to symbolize the reality that the addressee does not belong in the holy realm. It is not a matter of whether or not sowing one, three or more kinds of seed is permitted. It is the symbolic meaning of the act in relation to the human heart that matters. The prohibition indicates a vast gap between what takes place in the holy realm and what takes place outside it: if the mixture is permitted in the holy realm, it is prohibited in the secular realm. The egocentric nature would blur the distinction. Paradoxically people are assumed to become holy though their realization that they are not part of the holy realm.

Third, wearing a garment made of two different textiles is prohibited. A parallel law is found in Deut. 22:11, where the meaning of the difficult term *šaʿaṭnēz* is explained by the additional phrase 'wool and linen'. It is notable that the priests, when officiating in the sanctuary, wore garments made only of linen, but the high priest wore both linen and yarn (wool) (cf. Ezek. 44:17; Exod. 28:5–6, 15; Haran 1985: 160). *Kil'ayim* is thus a mark of holiness (so Milgrom 2000a: 1661), and it follows that wearing clothes made of such a mixture of textiles is banned here. Thus the rationale for this prohibition is the same as the first and second cases: the addressee ought to recognize he is not in the holy realm, which, paradoxically, becomes the way to holiness.

Thus three instances from the practical life of Israel are used to encourage them to have a simple mind and pure heart that recognizes their true state before the Lord; i.e. they themselves are not in the holy realm. The goal of these laws is common to the more explicit commandments of vv. 3–8.

19:20–22

This law deals with the case of a man who has had sexual intercourse with a betrothed slave-girl. In that it deals with a case of an illegal sexual union, it is associated with the theme of v. 19: the nature of a union. It is formulated in the 3rd person, and no explicit addressee is mentioned, though ultimately the whole Israelite community is addressed. One may thus suppose that this law was taken from a different source, such as 'P' (e.g. Milgrom 2000a: 1665). But in view of the variegated style of this chapter, such a supposition is unlikely. The exegete's role is to determine this law's intention within the context of this chapter as a whole.

20. The beginning of this verse is quite similar to 15:18, but they are not exactly the same. At the very least, it reminds the reader of the theme of ch. 18 (cf. v. 20). But the following protasis is entirely different from other similar cases: it is the case where a man has had sexual intercourse with a woman who is not yet redeemed from her betrothal to another man.

'a distinction': *biqqōret* As mentioned by Schwartz, this term probably means 'a distinction' here and in 27:33, although the possibility that it has the meaning 'to inquire', as it does in passages such as Ezek. 34:11–12, cannot be excluded (Schwartz 1999: 332–335; cf. Milgrom 2000a: 1670–1671). Here the slave-girl's status is explicitly mentioned. Moreover the use of inf. abs. probably expresses certainty. The slave-girl's slave status makes the man's punishment lenient, so he is spared the death penalty. The slave-girl is regarded as the possession of another man who has betrothed her, so it is not exactly the same as adultery.

21–22. Since the offence involves the breaking of an oath between the slave-girl and her would-be husband, it is expiated by offering the reparation offering. Because this case is similar to adultery, it is not mentioned in chs. 4 – 5. However, the reason why the offence is called *ḥaṭṭā't* is evident from the literary position of the same psychological situation found in 5:1–4: the degree of offender's awareness lies between the *ḥaṭṭā't* offering in ch. 4 and the reparation offering in 5:14 – 6:7[5:26].

More importantly, what does this law intend to convey by its 3rd person address? From a structural point of view this law is a concrete example of the prohibition against impartial judgments in v. 15 (see 'Form and structure'). Thus it seems that *in the eyes of the addressee* such a judgment ought to take place, where clarifying the nature of the illicit union, particularly the status of the slave-girl, the nature of the offence (whether or not it is expiable) and in what degree the man hid himself against the Lord is self-evident.

19:23–25

This law assumes agricultural life in the Promised Land. It stipulates that all fruit from trees is forbidden as food for the first three years, that the fruit becomes a praise offering to the Lord in the fourth year, and that it can be eaten in the fifth year.

Who would be able to abstain from eating the fruit of trees for four years (cf. 25:20)? Presumably only those uninterested in the fruit or able to control their covetous desires. Such a person prioritizes his relationship with the Lord above his desire to benefit from his agricultural produce. Thus the law functions to confront the addressee with the presence of his coveting. Structurally this law parallels the one in vv. 9–10, where the law also points to the addressee's egocentric nature.

23. 'forbidden': *'orlâ* Lit. 'uncircumcised'. While the fruit of the trees is said to be 'uncircumcised', it is by no means 'unclean', for the fruit-bearing tree is a sign of God's blessing, which is consequential upon the observance of his commandments in the Promised Land (25:19; 26:4).

What is said to be 'uncircumcised' is unfit not just for eating but also for the sanctuary. It should be separated from holiness. But why is the root *'rl* ascribed to fruit of trees? Occurrences where this root is mentioned in relation to human beings include passages such as Exod. 6:12, 30 ('lips'); Jer. 6:10 ('ears'); Lev. 26:41; Jer. 9:25 ('heart'); Ezek. 44:7, 9 ('heart' and 'flesh'). Elsewhere there is no passage where the root refers to things other than human beings or any other parts of the human body. Thus the application of the root to fruit in Lev. 19:23 is unique in the OT. So what is the rationale for this law? Since in other passages the root *'rl* is related to human beings, the fruit probably symbolizes human beings. Moreover the use of *'rl* is interesting, for the fruit has 'skin' even in the fourth year. These observations suggest that the law has more in mind than simple literal observance.

What makes this law different from human circumcision is that while human circumcision marks the incorporation of people into the covenantal community, this law, concerning fruit, already assumes the Lord's blessing.

Thus if the latter symbolizes the state of the human heart, it is set in a context that follows a new spiritual birth.

24–25. In the fourth year the fruit becomes a holy thing of praise to the Lord (cf. 27:30). No explanation for such a transition is given except that three years have passed. The fruit automatically becomes a holy thing in the fourth year.

According to this reading, the people become holy in the fourth year after their spiritual rebirth. Though such a possibility is highly unrealistic, the law demands it. It means that if an individual, or people, begin life in the Lord's land in an undefiled state, three years must still elapse before they become consecrated (cf. St Paul's stay in Arabia for three years [Gal. 1:17–18]).

In the fifth year the fruit may be eaten (it becomes useful to humans), which is possible only after they are made holy. Similarly, though unrealistic, the Israelites can be useful to other people only after they are consecrated; i.e. after their egocentric nature is destroyed (cf. the degree of holiness contagion in 6:24–30[17–23] and 'Explanation' there).

19:26–29

Taking into account their symbolic meaning, this cluster of laws concern the maintenance of one's spiritual life before the Lord. It is closely related to the laws in vv. 5–8. In general, humans find it extremely difficult to refrain from modifying their souls and bodies (leaving them as they were created by God), but attempt to show others and themselves that they are something special. This is a further manifestation of the egocentric nature.

26. Examples begin with a law against eating flesh with its blood still in it, which intends that one ought not to forfeit the very means of making atonement for the soul, which negatively implies the committing of idolatry (cf. 17:10–12). The following prohibitions, against using interpretive omens and the telling of fortunes, concern having fellowship with spiritual beings (satanic forces) other than the Lord. Simultaneously, as those acts relate to the future, the laws indirectly prohibit human prediction of the future.

27. According to some Jeremianic passages, rounding off the hair on the temple or marring the edges of a beard were customs apparently practised by non-Israelites (Jer. 9:26[25]; 25:23; 49:32). It is true that these customs were performed when one was in grief or mourning in Israel. In this sense, the prohibitions exhibit a distincive feature of Israel's religion. However, while it may be a ban on having to do with death, to see the motif of death behind the prohibitions goes beyond the present context (cf. Milgrom 2000a: 1691). Letting the hair loose, or to grow it, signifies one's indifference to one's outward look; hence the need to be concerned with inner matters.

Since v. 26 addresses itself to spiritual matters, and this verse to outward matters, the addressee is commanded to be concerned with his or her inner state before the Lord but to be unconcerned with outward matters, such as hair and beard. The priests are also commanded to let their hair and beard grow (21:5), so there is no outward distinction between priests and lay people, a tacit command to possess *inner* holiness.

28. Making cuts on the body is mentioned here in relation to one's *nepeš*. *Nepeš* here and in 21:1, 11 has ordinarily been rendered 'dead'. However, this seems doubtful, considering that 'dead' is more likely conveyed by *mēt*. It seems that *nepeš* on this occasion means human 'soul', and it is used in this context because the human soul is assumed to be doomed (dead) in Leviticus. Also note that the *nepeš* is contrasted with the *bāśār* (body) here. A human, if he does not involve himself with the egocentric nature of others, would do violence to his own body, instead of afflicting his soul (cf. 16:29, 31). The violation of one's body for spiritual reasons is prohibited: one ought not to mar the divine creation. The psychology behind tattooing is complex, but it is possible that it aims to satisfy one's own egocentric soul. However, tattooing can sometimes be viewed as a desire to exhibit one's skin to others. This amounts to showing one's wounded soul to others, rather than showing one's soul to the Lord alone.

29. This verse prohibits the addressee from profaning his daughter by 'making her commit fornication' (*hiznâ*; cf. *HALOT*). Certainly 'a prostitute' is in view here, but the Hebr. verb appears to have a wider meaning, including various types of spiritual idolatry. The cause of the daughter's depravity is traced to her father. If this law is observed, then all the laws in 18:6–23 are observable. This topic is possibly placed within this context as a practical example of loving one's own soul (cf. *ḥillel* 'degrade' here and v. 8) and of showing reverence to the Lord in vv. 27–28; if one loves himself as created by God, he would not allow his daughter, who is under his care, to fornicate.

The omission from ch. 18 of the relationship between a father and his daughter would seem deliberate, considering it is dealt with here, albeit differently.

19:30–32

The laws in this section relate to the observance of sabbath days, reverence for the sanctuary, prohibitions against turning to mediums or necromancers, and the honouring of elders. These resemble the laws in vv. 3–4. In fact, vv. 30–32 augment vv. 3–4 and illuminate what is intended by the Lord in each section. It goes without saying that these commandments are essentially related to the human heart or attitude.

30. The sabbath days ought to be observed and the Lord's sanctuary revered. Though earlier the object of the verb 'revere' was the 'mother and father' (v. 3), here it is the Lord's sanctuary.

31. 'Turning' to mediums or necromancers is prohibited in a manner similar to v. 4 (note 'Do not turn [*tipnû*]' in both passages). It is presumed that deities who communicate through mediums or necromancers are not the Lord. In this sense those deities are examples of the 'gods' (*'ĕlîlîm*) mentioned in v. 4 (cf. Saul seeking a medium at En-Dor in 1 Sam. 28). What is prohibited is involvement with souls of the dead, which is also dealt with, albeit in a more general and mild way, in 21:11. This prohibition recurs two more times in Leviticus (20:6, 27).

'mediums': *'ôbōt* This term often appears in the OT with *yid'ônî*, as here (Lev. 20:6, 27; Deut. 18:11; 1 Sam. 28:3, 9; 2 Kgs 21:6; 23:24; Isa. 8:19; 19:3; 2 Chr. 33:6). Interpreters propose various translations for *'ôb*: a spirit, an ancestral spirit, a bag of skin, the pit from which spirits are called, a ghost, a demon (cf. Kuemmerlin-Mclean 1992: 468–471; Johnston 2002: 150–166). But the fact that *'ôb* is the grammatical object of *šā'al* (to ask), and that the purpose of asking is to 'inquire', suggests it has a personality. Since it is clearly associated with necromancy (cf. Deut. 18:11; 1 Sam. 28:3, 9; Isa. 8:19), it is surmised that an *'ôb*, possessed by an *'ôb* spirit, serves as 'a medium' between the living and the dead. However, what is the point of turning to mediums, given the assumption in Leviticus that the human soul is dead before God?

'necromancers': *yid'ônî* As for *'ôb* this term is also related to necromancy. The exact difference between it and an *'ôb* is hard to determine, since the term appears in conjunction with *'ôb*, but the root *yd'* suggests knowledge regarding the soul of the dead.

By the use of parallelism, the latter half of the verse adds that the essence of such conduct is tantamount to an attempt to make oneself unclean (for *ṭom'â bĕ* see 18:20, 23); namely hiding oneself before the Lord.

32. The commandment to revere the elderly is unique in the Bible. The added command 'and you shall fear your God' implies that revering the elderly leads one to fear the Lord. From a structural point of view this commandment is an extension of the command to revere parents in v. 3.

19:33–36

Structurally these verses stand outside the unified whole of vv. 3–32. They consist of commandments about the need to treat resident strangers with neighbourly love and to do justice in the practical matters of everyday Israelite life. These themes are also in vv. 9–18. To each of these the motive clause 'for you were strangers in the land of Egypt' (v. 34; cf. also v. 36) is added. The reference to Egypt (vv. 34, 36), which was outweighed by references to Canaan in ch. 18 (see v. 3), is here highlighted positively.

33–34. The neighbourly love mentioned in v. 18 is applied to the resident foreigner. Schwartz restricts the content of neighbourly love to not causing strangers distress within the Promised Land (1999: 359). However, the context of v. 18, namely hatred and resentment in one's heart, is probably assumed here so that the command 'to love the resident stranger as yourself' means more than helping and showing kindness to foreigners. In that this law expands the scope of v. 18b, its observance may well draw attention to a different kind of difficulty. For 'like yourself' requires the addressee to overlook the stranger's status and deal with him as though he is a compatriot (like the addressee himself). The motive clause introduced by *kî*, 'you were the strangers in the land of Egypt', emphasizes that strangers in the Promised Land ought to be given freedom, just as God liberated the Israelites while they were strangers in Egypt.

This law partly overlaps the law of vv. 9–10, and the latter is an example of the former.

35–36. The Lord then commands the process of fair justice in Israel's courts and commerce. Similar commandments are already given in v. 15, but, in essence, this law relates to all the laws contained in vv. 11–16. Thus since v. 33–34 are related to vv. 9–10 and v. 18, it appears that vv. 33–36 recapitulate the laws in vv. 9–18. The motive clause 'I am the Lord your God, *who brought you out of the land of Egypt*' appears to stress that justice and fairness characterize the Lord who righted the injustices done to the Israelites in Egypt, and freed them.

19:37

The last verse of this chapter commands the observance of *all* the statutes and rules. It may literarily correspond to '*all* the community' in v. 2. While exegetes fail to comment on the significance of this 'all', *can* one observe all the commandments? See 'Explanation'.

Explanation

The concept of holiness in ch. 19 is often said to contradict the concept of holiness in chs. 1 – 16 (see Introduction 7.4.3). However, the perceived differences simply reflect different approaches to the topic – the concepts are essentially the same. Among other things, the following points should be pointed out.

(1) That holiness is related to the observance of commandments is indicated by 4:2, where the human soul hides itself before the Lord by violating *one* commandment. Further on the Day of Atonement ritual, the ark is assumed as defiled by the self-hidings of the Israelites. These instances simultaneously show that the distinction commonly made between 'cultic' and 'ethical' in this regard is unwarranted.

(2) In chs. 1 – 16 the essence of holiness lies, at least, in the *self-sacrifice* expressed by the sacrificial animals. It is probable that the theme of human holiness (chs. 18 – 22) is deliberately placed after the long regulations on animal sacrifices (chs. 1 – 17) to underline that the essence of holiness is self-sacrifice rather than the outward observance of the laws.

(3) My interpretation of the human *nepeš*, that it is an egocentric nature, as well as the symbolism of *ṣāraʿat* in chs. 13 – 14 and the symbolic meaning of the veil in the Tent, indicates that holiness is closely associated with the state of the human heart. A holy person is someone who has had the egocentric nature destroyed.

Apparently, in this chapter and the next, holiness (19:2; 20:7–8) is closely related to the observance of laws (19:3–36; 20:2–6, 9–21). However, an exact formulation of the relationship between them is required.

First of all, only the observance of *all* the laws qualifies a person as holy (19:37; 20:22; cf. 4:2). Thus the violation of just one law makes a person unholy. The flipside of this is that any human endeavour, however respectable, does not result in holiness if the observance of the laws is less than perfect. Furthermore it is not human endeavour or a desire to observe the laws as much as possible, but the state of being able to observe the law that is equated with being holy (see 'Comment' on v. 18). Thus, for instance, if a person does not covet, he may well be able to observe all the laws. In this case the laws cease to have their function, since they have no object to prohibit.

Second, and consequently, the laws facilitate the addressee's experience of the gap between holiness and what he is able to do, thereby confronting him with the presence of his egocentric nature and the need for its destruction, by the inevitable feeling of hopelessness that accompanies a human's attempt to observe the laws. A person needs experiential, rather than notional, persuasion that he or she is unable to attain holiness. Paradoxically the person realizes he or she can become holy only after the death of the egocentric nature. This is taught not only by the laws in vv. 17–18 but also by other laws that demand an absence of selfishness and coveting. Otherwise the egocentric nature as 'a god' (cf. Gen. 3:22) would blur the distinction and merely pretend to do the right thing. Thus the laws presume the presence of an egocentric nature, and it is their role to expose it to the addressee.

Since the purpose of the law is to destroy the egocentric nature in order to lead a person to holiness, and not just to punish him, there is room for the possibility that a person who meets the *kāret* penalty becomes holy (see 'Explanation' on ch. 20).

In conclusion, the realization that the laws target the egocentric nature suggests that *qādôš* (holy) refers to the condition of the human heart, and that the holiness commanded in v. 2 concerns the state of a human heart that no longer has an egocentric nature.

The next question is, what state characterizes the holy human heart? The condition of the human heart that observes the laws in this chapter is one where the following features are found.

(1) The law in vv. 4–6 teaches that a person who observes the law is unselfish and does not covet. Practically the touchstone of one's belief in God is whether one is free from an egocentric nature, of which coveting of any sort forms one of the major aspects (vv. 7–9). Selfishness, along with a covetous desire, affects one's relationship with other humans, and it is v. 18b, 'Love your neighbour as yourself', that summarizes the essence of all the laws. This is practically impossible to carry out if one is not totally free of selfishness. And if selfishness remains, a person is regarded as committing idolatry, since he or she serves not only the Lord but themselves too.

(2) The laws of the latter half of the chapter, beginning with v. 19, concern one's attitude towards oneself. Holiness in this context includes, first of all, reverence for God's created order and the need to keep away from the holy realm (v. 19). The distinction between holy and common must translate into an experiential one. There is a paradox of holiness here: a holy person is characterized by an awareness that he is unholy, and therefore not part of the divine realm (cf. the offerer in Lev. 1; cf. also Isa. 57:15; 2 Kgs 4:13). Yet the laws assume that if one can distinguish clearly between holy and common, one's egocentric nature is destroyed. At any rate, holiness has the feature of separation, particularly from the divine and other human beings. To have such a heart enables a person to make judgments properly and without bias.

(3) Holiness is characterized by unselfishness, yet the latter does not mean an unbridled involvement with both the divine realm and other humans. A holy person clearly perceives the presence of the divine realm and makes himself separate from it (he has the ability to differentiate between holy and common), while refraining from unnecessary involvement with the egocentric nature of his neighbours. Further such a person is humble, untroubled by the future and uninterested in earthly matters. He loves justice without respect to human evaluation. His love for justice is untainted by a desire to seek the approval of others: such a person looks only at the Lord. It is vital to observe that such conditions are seen only by others and not by the person himself. The laws in this chapter assume that only those whose hearts are uninterested in their own gain, but with the gains of others, can observe all the laws.

The disappearance of the selfish nature practically means, like the burnt offering (cf. ch. 1), to experience the truth that one's humanistic tendency, namely to trust in human potentiality in all areas and in his own potentiality related to his earthly desires and aspirations, ultimately has no meaning. An experience of such hopelessness, the validity of which is tested by whether or not it continues, leads a man into the realm of holiness. This constitutes new birth of a man in a spiritual sense.

Holiness refers to the essential nature of the Lord. Though God's holiness is distinct from human holiness, each is characterized by selflessness. Practically this manifests itself in an independence of spirit and an unwillingness to damage either oneself or others – to live the command to love oneself and one's neighbour. Love and justice emanate from this condition of holiness. They are, so to speak, the fruit of the egocentric nature's destruction, analogous to the NT's 'fruit of the Spirit'.

Nevertheless the nature of this 'love' needs reconsideration, since the traditional exegesis of the laws in this chapter, as well as the common Christian attitude to neighbourly love, have become unwittingly infested with a humanitarian concept of love. For instance, love in vv. 17–18 is expressed by one's refraining from interacting with one's neighbour's egocentric nature. That is, these verses prohibit interaction with a neighbour's passions and emotions, including the conduct that arises from them. This is because the egocentric nature is polluted, and every emotion or passion arising from it is polluted. By avoiding interaction with a neighbour's egocentric nature, people indicate they understand their own limitations (cf. Rom. 12:3). By contrast, humanistic 'love' often goes beyond what a person should get involved with, and even tries to assist a neighbour's egocentric desire. This situation arises because people unconsciously assume they can change another's heart and soul, let alone their mind. This is the state of the human heart symbolized by the swarming creatures in ch. 11. But the whole OT, including Leviticus, asserts humans are unreliable, and in essence selfish, so to act with an unconscious selfish motive is not only contrary to the Lord's will, but bound to fail on the grounds that the egocentric nature is evil, and that the holy Lord accepts only that conduct which has nothing to do with the egocentric nature. Hence the beginning of neighbourly love lies in the destruction of a person's egocentric nature: all his expectations of what others ought to be must be destroyed. 'Love' in this elevated sense is the divine love, where a person looks objectively at himself as he is, and his neighbour as he is.

Once the egocentric nature is destroyed, the laws cease to function for a person, because their *raison d'être* is the human egocentric nature.

For those who struggle to live ethically, this may appear to relinquish and abolish the Law. Certainly it does. The Law functions to reveal one's egocentric nature, and as long as one sticks to the Law, that is an indication that his egocentric nature remains alive; perhaps he is either humanizing the Law or is unconsciously hypocritical, or both. Moreover, if the Law can be observed, it is only by a newborn heart. That is why the transformation of human hearts became the central concern in the prophetic literature (cf. Jer. 24:7; 31:33; Ezek. 11:19[18]; 18:31; 36:26). For this, however, a human heart and soul must go through a clinical operation: the destruction of the egocentric nature.

New Testament implications

Jesus' coming into this world was aimed at 'fulfilling' the Law (Matt. 5:17). The interpretation of the exact meaning of this varies (cf. Hagner 1993: 104–110), yet in view of the above interpretation of holiness, in that the Law aims to destroy the egocentric nature, the fulfilment of the Law can be paraphrased as the destruction of the egocentric nature. Indeed Jesus' teaching assumes that with an egocentric nature one cannot observe his teaching, let alone the Law.

Indeed his teaching is far more demanding than the Law. In contrast to 'Judge properly' in the Law, he says, 'Do not judge' (Matt. 7:1), 'Do not swear falsely,' 'Do not swear' (Matt. 5:33–37). For those who do not observe his command 'Do not hate your brother in heart' he declares eternal punishment (Matt. 5:22) etc.

In Jesus' teaching, the heavenly dweller is presented as one who, for example, is not self-gratifying, does not worry about the future, does not judge others, and does not even covet his own life (Matt. 5 – 7). In particular, such a person remains unconscious with regard to his own work (Matt. 6:3; 25:31–40). This person is a vessel of the Holy Spirit. In a word, Jesus gave the ultimate Law that presumes the death of the human egocentric nature, which culminates in 'Truly I say to you, unless you turn and become like children, you will never enter the kingdom of heaven' (Matt. 18:3 ESV; cf. Gen. 2:25; Luke 18:17).

St Paul also experienced the thorns of the Law when he said, 'For through the law I died to the law, so I might live to God' (Gal. 2:19 ESV; Rom. 7:5, 7–10). In talking about life lived by the Spirit and life lived by the flesh he suggests that holiness is not a matter of observance or non-observance of laws, but is found in the newly created heart (Gal. 5:16–24, especially v. 23). This is not antinomian, but the third way that finds its place outside and beyond the bounds of the Law. According to this understanding, it follows that living 'ethically', though venerated by human standards, is to live according to the desires of the flesh.

Although no mention is made in this chapter, or in Leviticus as a whole, of faith in God, faith underlies all the laws of this chapter. For only when one's egocentric nature is destroyed, can he become a true believer in God, which refers to his soul's salvation.

LEVITICUS 20:1–27

Translation

[1]The LORD spoke to Moses, saying, [2]'Say to the Israelites, Any one of the Israelites or of the strangers who sojourn in Israel who gives any of his children to Molech shall surely be put to death. The people of the land shall stone him

with stones. [3]I myself will set my face against that man and will cut him off from among his people, because he has given one of his children to Molech, thereby making my sanctuary unclean and profaning my holy name. [4]And if the people of the land close their eyes at all to that man when he gives one of his children to Molech, and do not put him to death, [5]then I will set my face against that man and against his clan and will cut them off from among their people, him and all who follow him in whoring after Molech. [6]If a soul turns to mediums and necromancers, whoring after them, I will set my face against that soul and will cut him off from among his people.

[7]'Consecrate yourselves, therefore and be holy, for I am the Lord your God.

[8]'Keep my statutes and do them; I am the Lord who sanctifies you.

[9]'Anyone who curses his father or his mother shall surely be put to death; he has cursed his father or his mother; his blood is upon him. [10]If a man commits adultery with the wife of a man, or with the wife of his neighbour, both the adulterer and the adulteress shall surely be put to death. [11]If a man lies with his father's wife, he has uncovered his father's nakedness; both of them shall surely be put to death; their blood is upon them. [12]If a man lies with his daughter-in-law, both of them shall surely be put to death; they have committed perversion; their blood is upon them. [13]If a man lies with a male as with a woman, both of them have committed an abomination; they shall surely be put to death; their blood is upon them. [14]If a man takes a woman and her mother also, it is depravity; he and they shall be burned with fire, that there may be no depravity among you. [15]If a man lies with an animal, he shall surely be put to death, and you shall kill the animal. [16]If a woman approaches any animal and lies with it, you shall kill the woman and the animal; they shall surely be put to death; their blood is upon them. [17]If a man takes his sister, a daughter of his father or a daughter of his mother, and sees her nakedness, and she sees his nakedness, it is a disgrace, and they shall be cut off in the sight of the children of their people. He has uncovered his sister's nakedness, and he shall bear his iniquity. [18]If a man lies with a woman during her menstrual period and uncovers her nakedness, he has made naked her fountain, and she has uncovered the fountain of her blood. Both of them shall be cut off from among their people. [19]You shall not uncover the nakedness of your mother's sister or of your father's sister, for that is to make naked one's relative; they shall bear their guilt. [20]If a man lies with his uncle's wife, he has uncovered his uncle's nakedness; they shall bear their punishment; they shall die childless. [21]If a man takes his brother's wife, it is impurity. He has uncovered his brother's nakedness; they shall be childless.

[22]'You shall therefore keep all my statutes and all my rules and do them, that the land where I am bringing you to live may not vomit you out. [23]And you shall not walk in the customs of the nation that I am driving out before you, for they did all these things, and therefore I detested them. [24]But I have said to you, You shall inherit their land, and I will give it to you to possess, a land flowing with milk and honey. I am the Lord your God, who have separated you from the peoples. [25]You shall therefore separate the clean beast from the unclean, and the unclean bird from the clean. You shall not make yourselves detestable by beast or by bird or by

anything with which the ground crawls, which I have set apart for you to hold unclean. [26]You shall be holy to me, for I the LORD am holy and have separated you from the peoples, that you should be mine.

[27]'A man or a woman who is a medium or a necromancer shall surely be put to death. They shall be stoned with stones; their blood shall be upon them.'

Notes on the text

2. 'of the Israelites': *mibbĕnê yiśrā'ēl* SamP has *mibbêt* (from the house of) as in 17:3, 8, 10. By itself, the reading is unnecessary, as 'the sons of Israel' is found in 17:12–14.

'to Molech' See 'Notes' on 18:21.

3. 'thereby making' etc.: *lĕma'an* For the consequential meaning of *lĕma'an*, see Brongers 1973: 89.

5. 'after Molech': *'ăḥărê hammôlek* LXX translates *eis tous arxontas*, probably reading *hammôlēk*, but this is unnecessary.

6. 'a soul': *hannepeš* The Hebr. article is used genetically. To translate *nepeš* as 'a person' downplays the significance of the term: the offence is one made by the human *soul*.

Some MSS add *qādôš* after *'ammô*, as followed by LXX. However, this is unlikely, considering that the basic assumption made by the laws in this chapter is that the people of Israel are commanded to become holy, which implies they are presently unholy (see 'Explanation').

'him ... his' SamP and LXX translate the pronouns as feminine, since *nepeš* is feminine. However, this is unnecessary, since the same phenomenon is found elsewhere (2:1; 17:15–16).

7. LXX and some Hebr. MSS insert 'holy' (*qādôš*) after 'for' (*kî*), probably in conformity with v. 26 and 11:44. However, the presence of *mĕqaddiškem* at the end of v. 8 makes the correctness of the addition doubtful.

10. 'of a man, or with the wife of': *'îš 'ăšer yin'ap 'et* LXX does not translate this part, and some modern versions (e.g. ESV) as well as *BHS* margin propose to delete it, probably because it appears redundant (see 'Comment'). A concurrent problem is the presence of the asyndetic *'ăšer*, so most ancient versions (LXX, SamP, TgJon, Vg) supply *wāw* and read *wa'ăšer*.

17. 'he shall bear his iniquity': *'ăwōnô yiśśā'* LXX and Syr read the verb in pl.

19. 'of your mother's sister or of your father's sister': *'ăḥôt 'immĕkā wa'ăḥôt 'ābîkā* SamP and LXX reverse the order, which, however, may be deliberate (see 'Comment').

21. 'shall be childless': *'ărîrîm yihyû* LXX translate 'he shall die childless'. In terms of the apparently decreasing degrees of punishment in vv. 17–21, this reading is unlikely.

23. 'the nation': *haggôy* One manuscript, SamP and some versions read it in pl. However, sg. and pl. forms appear in 18:24–30. So MT should be retained.

25. 'to hold unclean': *lěṭammē'* SamP, LXX and Syr read *lěṭum'â* (as uncleanness). In view of the declarative *ṭm'* pi. in 13:3, 8 etc., this is unwarranted.

Form and structure

Ch. 20 contains the same themes dealt with in ch. 18. Particularly the prohibition against Molech worship and certain sexual unions are common to both chapters. Yet the emphasis of ch. 20 is on the penalty associated with disobedience.

The location of ch. 20 is comparable to ch. 15, which forms a sequel to ch. 12 (see Introduction 4.1). Just as ch. 15 summarizes, in a sense, all the laws of chs. 12 – 15, so does ch. 20 summarize all the laws of chs. 18 – 20.

The chapter's internal structure is often considered to alternate between laws (2b–6, 9–21) and hortatory material (7–8, 22–26; cf. Wenham 1979: 276). Nevertheless it is debated as to whether vv. 7–8 is introductory to what follows it or concludes what precedes it (cf. Schwartz 1999: 138 n. 12). However, content similar to that in vv. 7–8 is found in 18:4–5, 19:2 and 19:37, making it likely the call to holiness in vv. 7–8 is meant to relate to material that both precedes and follows; i.e. it is a divine mandate that transcends its immediate context (cf. 'all the prohibitive commandments' in 4:2). Recognizing v. 27 as forming an inclusio with v. 6, the whole chapter has a loose thematic chiastic structure:

- A. vv. 2–5 A ban on Molech worship
  v. 6 A ban on soothsaying and fortune-telling
  - B. v. 7 A call to holiness
    - C. v. 8 Call to observance of the laws
      - D. v. 9 The cursing of one's parents
        vv. 10–21 Adultery and incest seen from the viewpoint of the husband of the woman involved
    - C' 22–24 A call to observe the laws with reference to the election and the land
  - B' 25–26 A call to holiness
- A' 27 A ban on soothsaying and fortune-telling

V. 27, often viewed as out of place (Budd 1996: 292), logically fits the above structure (cf. Milgrom 2000a: 1728). Complementing this structure is the inner structure of vv. 9–21. Milgrom (2000a: 1743) duly recognizes the rules are arranged according to their punishments as follows:

A. Prohibitions carrying the death penalty (vv. 9–16)
   1. Adultery (v. 10)
   2. Incest (vv. 11–12)
      a. Sex with a father's wife (v. 11)
      b. Sex with a daughter-in-law (v. 12)
   3. Male homosexuality (v. 13)
   4. Marriage to a woman and her mother (v. 14)
   5. Bestiality (vv. 15–16)
      a. By a male (v. 15)
      b. By a female (v. 16)
B. Prohibitions carrying the excision penalty (vv. 17–19)
   1. Marriage to a sister (v. 17)
   2. Sex during menses (v. 18)
   3. Sex with a paternal or maternal aunt (v. 19)
C. Prohibitions carrying the childlessness penalty (vv. 20–21)
   1. Sex with an uncle's wife (v. 20)
   2. Marriage to a sister-in-law (v. 21)

While one may tend to group vv. 2–6 with 18:21 and 19:31, it is more likely the legislator sets out the negative side of the rules in 19:3–4, 30–31 based on ch. 18. By beginning with Molech worship the legislator is asserting the Lord's sovereignty over the spiritual and interhuman realms, and then states the punishment for soothsaying, fortune-telling (v. 6) and cursing of one's parents (v. 9), all of which are already positively commanded in 19:3–4, 30–31. This explains the order of the rules in vv. 2–10.

Furthermore that adultery (v. 10) heads the following illicit sexual unions in this chapter suggests the list in vv. 11–21 is to be viewed under the rubric of adultery (cf. the location of the case for adultery in 18:20). Together with Molech worship, soothsaying and fortune-telling in vv. 2–6, vv. 12–21 deal with adultery in both a spiritual and a physical sense.

The literary relationship between this chapter and ch. 18 is discussed by Schwartz (1999: 135–144). After listing the similarities and differences between the chapters, he concludes that the differences support the assumption that these chapters are two independent creations. The following differences are cited as evidence for this conclusion.

(1) Although twelve cases are common to both chapters, five of the cases in ch. 18 have no counterpart in ch. 20. These include sexual intercourse with one's mother (18:7), niece (18:10), the daughter of a father's wife (18:11), a granddaughter of a woman (18:17) and the taking of two sisters as wives (18:18). On the other hand, two cases in ch. 20, mediums and necromancers (20:6, 27), and the one who curses his parents (20:9), are not cases of 'incestuous unions' and have no counterparts in ch. 18.

(2) With regard to punishment, ch. 18 mentions that the violations of the prohibitions are punished collectively (18:27–28); i.e. by expulsion from

the land, while the *kāret* penalty is pronounced on every perpetrator (18:29). In other words, though the penalty in ch. 18 is the *kāret* penalty, this is not so for all the offences in ch. 20.

First, as mentioned above, ch. 20 must be considered not just in relation to ch. 18 but also to ch. 19. The style of v. 2, namely the objective phrase coming before the verb *'āmar*, suggests a close link with ch. 19. Thematically the topics of 'mediums and necromancers' and 'fearing one's parents', the latter of which constitutes the opposite of 'cursing one's parents', do appear in 19:31 and 19:3 respectively. Moreover the call to holiness occurs for the first time in 19:2 in chs. 18 – 20, and recurs in 20:7, 26. The call to observe the Lord's statutes and rules in 18:4–5 is repeated with slight differences in formulation in 19:37 and 20:8, 22. This indicates that this theme pervades all three chapters. Other ideological links exist, though this depends on the interpretation of the rules in question. There are several examples. The ban on idolatry in 19:4 appears related to the ban against mediums and necromancers in 19:31 and 20:6. The ban in 19:19 against combining two species of seed is akin to the theme of illicit sexual intercourse in 18:6–23 and 20:10–21. If he prevents his daughter from committing adultery (19:29), then the types of illicit sexual intercourse in chs. 18 and 20 will be greatly reduced. Thus it is possible to view this chapter as a summary of chs. 18 and 19.

Further links to the previous chapters are evident. V. 25 recalls the rules of 11:44–45, which summarize ch. 11. Further the idea of 'defiling the sanctuary' in v. 3 may be related to the same idea in 15:31; between these passages no explicit mention is made of this idea, though the Day of Atonement ritual in ch. 16 deals with the defilement of the sanctuary (see below). Therefore ch. 20 serves to summarize various themes that have appeared thus far: the cleanness/uncleanness laws in chs. 11 – 16 and the holiness-oriented laws in chs. 18 – 19. In the concluding section, vv. 22–26, the Lord draws the addressees' attention to the Promised Land even more positively than he does in the concluding section of 18:24–30.

Second, it is unnecessary to see the five cases mentioned in ch. 18, but not in ch. 20, as evidence that the two chapters are independent compositions. (1) Ch. 18 presents its rules from the viewpoint of kinship, whereas ch. 20, though giving examples of illicit intercourse, stresses this activity's punishment. Moreover in ch. 20 the list is subordinated to the ban against adultery in general (20:10), a typical form of idolatry in the human realm. (2) There are unmistakable linguistic and stylistic similarities between chs. 18 and 20, some of which are also found in ch. 19: the phrase *nātan šĕkôbet* (give oneself to lie, 18:20, 23; 20:15), *rb'* (lie with, 18:23; 19:19; 20:16), estimative terms such as *zimmâ* (disgrace, 18:17; 19:29; 20:14), *tô'ēbâ* (abomination, 18:22, 26–27, 29–30; 20:13), *tebel* (perversion, 18:23; 20:12), *niddâ* (menstrual uncleanness, 18:19; 20:21). (3) The presence of various estimative terms such as *zimmâ* (18:17), *tô'ēbâ*

(18:22), *tebel* (18:23) and *niddâ* are an indication the legislator relied on the text of ch. 18. While *tô'ēbâ* and *zimmâ* are used for similar or identical cases (*tô'ēbâ*, 18:22; 20:13 [homosexuality]; *zimmâ*, 18:17; 20:14), *tebel* is used for bestiality in 18:23 and for an incestuous union in 20:12. A new estimative *ḥesed*, not found in ch. 18, is applied to a case in 20:17. The term *niddâ*, which is not an evaluation of the act in 18:19, comes as an estimative term in 20:21. Clearly the legislator in ch. 20 is well aware of the rules in ch. 18.

Third, the protases of the cases are cast in the 3rd person sg., except in v. 19. This contrast with ch. 18, where each case is expressed in the 2nd person sg. and begins with *'erwat*, is followed by the person attacked. It is unlikely that this is just stylistic, or a reflection of two different sources. The literary phenomenon that the first of a series of cases begins with *'îš 'îš* and the subsequent cases begin either with *'îš 'ăšer* (*kî*) or *'îššâ 'ăšer* appears also in ch. 15 (vv. 2, 5, 16, 18). Although these formulae are found in other places, such as 19:20, the similarity in style between chs. 20 and 15 is conspicuous. Together with the above-mentioned possible link with ch. 15 in terms of 'defiling the LORD's sanctuary/abode', it appears possible that ch. 20 aims to recall ch. 15, a chapter concerning defilement coming from sexual organs; just as ch. 15 describes defilement and its consequences, ch. 20 describes violations and their punishment.

It is a major characteristic of this chapter, in contrast with ch. 18, that it prescribes a punishment for the violation of each law. The death penalty in vv. 10–16 is formulated *môt yûmat* (he shall be put to death) or the like, *dĕmêhem bām* (their blood guilt is in them), and burning with fire. Punishment in vv. 17–21 is described by idioms such as *nāśā' 'āwōn/ḥēṭ* (bear guilt/punishment), *nikrat min* (be cut off from) and *'ărîrîm* (be childless). In view of the uniform punishment, namely the *kāret* penalty, in ch. 18, this variety of punishments in ch. 20 appears to confront the reader with the question of their meaning: are there degrees of punishment?

In sum, ch. 20 is a chapter that summarizes not only the preceding chs. 18 and 19, but also the cleanness/uncleanness regulations in chs. 11 – 16. On the one hand, it takes up the topics of chs. 18 – 19, stressing the gravity of the offences by stipulating either or both the *kāret* penalty and the death penalty. On the other hand, utilizing the motif of cleanness and uncleanness and the defilement of the sanctuary in chs. 11 – 15, ch. 20 integrates the theme of defilement with so-called moral conduct (see 'Explanation').

Comment

This chapter particularly stresses the punitive side of the offences, thus warning the Israelites against apostasy. At the same time, it positively stresses in two sections the need to become holy, vv. 7 and 26, which are inseparably connected with the observance of *all* the statutes of the Lord

(vv. 8 and 22a). The nature of the various punishments is considered in 'Explanation'.

20:1–2a

While v. 1 is the same in style as 18:1 and 19:1, the Hebr. of v. 2 is different from 18:2 and 19:2, in that the objective phrase comes first, before the verb 'to say' (*'āmar*). A similar style is also found in 17:8 (cf. 17:2; further 9:3 and 24:15 for *dibbēr*), and suggests that ch. 20 is a continuation of ch. 19. The Lord addresses himself to Moses, who must in turn deliver the message to the sons of Israel. As in chs. 18 and 19, this chapter concerns all the Israelites, excluding the priests.

20:2–6

The prohibition against Molech worship is already briefly mentioned in 18:21. Why then does this chapter begin with the same prohibition? The heinousness of this crime is highlighted by the fact that it not only involves worshipping a foreign god, but requires the sacrifice of one's own children. It appears that the placement of this heinous offence at the head of this chapter aims to convey the reality that the Lord has absolute claim and sovereignty over both spiritual and physical realms. By requiring the death penalty and the excision of the perpetrator and his family from the covenant community the legislator aimed to remove this practice from within Israel.

It is noteworthy that *'îš* is used in the Molech-worship section (vv. 2–5), while *nepeš* is used in referring to the necromancer (v. 6). This may derive from the distinct use of these terms: *'îš*, being a term used to refer to interpersonal relationships, is used for the Molech worship because the latter involves other people, whereas the use of *nepeš* (a soul) aims to stress the intimate relationship between the individual and the mediums/necromancers.

2b. The worshipper of Molech ought to be stoned to death. The formula *môt yûmat* suggests a humanly orchestrated death penalty sanctioned by a human court. Stoning to death is a common means of enacting the death penalty, occurring sixteen times in the OT (e.g. Lev. 20:27; 24:14, 16, 23; Num. 14:10; 15:35–36; Deut. 21:21). 'The people of the land' are ordered to execute the penalty. This phrase occurs three times in Leviticus (4:27; 20:2, 4) and connotes that the land is a good one, requiring their total obedience to the Lord (see v. 24).

3. The punishment for the violation of the law is further explained. The Lord will turn his face against the accused and cut his soul from his people. The act of the accused has defiled the Lord's sanctuary (*ṭimmē' 'et miqdāšî*) and profaned his holy name (*ḥillēl 'et šem qodšî*). The Lord's 1st person sg. address in vv. 3–6 is remarkable, given that the rest of the punishments in this chapter are mostly stated in the 3rd person sg. The difference probably reflects degrees of difference in the gravity of the respective offences, and thus of the Lord's wrath; namely this is the most heinous act, which consequently arouses the divine anger to the highest degree.

The convicted receives a double punishment: the death penalty and the *kāret* penalty. It is apparent that not just his physical life but his soul is lost forever; i.e. expelled from the Lord's presence. In the rest of this chapter there is no case other than this that requires both kinds of punishment. Methodologically, this appears to indicate that the punishment clause must be read literally; i.e. without blurring the distinction between the two kinds of punishment.

4. The nomenclature 'the people of the land' itself suggests an expectation that the people of the Promised Land are not to conceal such an act. Presumably the inevitable death of the offender would make the people hesitate in revealing it.

5. Then the Lord will set his face against the person and his family as well as all those who partake in the worship of Molech, and cut all of them off from their people. Those who protect the offender are regarded as guilty as the one who whored after Molech. This religious adultery is expressed by *zānâ* (here and v. 6), a term denoting human love and zeal for personalities other than the Lord (cf. 17:7).

The death and *kāret* penalties mentioned in vv. 2–3 are repeated in vv. 4–5, so the two are unmistakably distinct punishments stipulated for this law's violation.

6. Next come two forms of idolatry; namely the turning to mediums and necromancers (see 'Comment' on 19:31). Characteristically a person's soul (*nepeš*) is central to the offence. Most probably such an act involves contacting satanic beings. Again, as for Molech worship, the Lord himself directly punishes the offender by cutting him off from among his people. No mention is made of the death penalty here. But see v. 27.

20:7–8

These verses command the Israelites to become holy. V. 7 is similar to 19:2, while v. 8 reflects 18:5 and 19:37. Opinions divide as to whether vv. 7–8 belong to what precedes or follows. However, since the call to holiness is found in 11:44, 19:2, the hypercontextual nature of this commandment makes it likely that the verses belong to both the preceding and following material.

7. 'Consecrate yourselves': *hitqaddištem* In other contexts the hith. form of *qdš* means to 'consecrate' by washing one's clothes or body (e.g. 2 Sam. 11:4). But it is simplistic to make a distinction between a priestly and non-priestly sense for this term just by observing the ceremonial acts accompanying it, for in most of the cases where this term occurs the context is either that of a theophany or of people approaching the Lord (Exod. 19:22; Num. 11:18; Josh. 3:5; 7:13; 1 Sam. 16:5; Isa. 30:29; 1 Chr. 15:12, 14; 2 Chr. 29:5, 34; 30:15, 17, 24; 31:18; 35:6). The term is further distinguished from *ṭhr* hith. in Isa. 66:17 and 2 Chr. 29:15. In Leviticus the call to be holy is a commandment given to the Israelites wherever they are, not just when they approach the Lord in the sanctuary. Essentially, holiness refers to a human heart devoid of selfishness.

In relation to 11:44, the clauses 'for I am the Lord your God' and 'Sanctify yourselves and become holy' are inverted, an indication of the legislator's awareness of 11:44.

8. The call to become holy is coupled with the observance of the Lord's statutes. Though the observance of all the statutes (vv. 8, 22) appears to refer only to the statutes of this chapter, the repetitive nature of this call makes this unlikely. A similar command appears in 18:4–5, 26 and 19:37. Moreover in v. 22 the command comes as part of a section that summarizes all of the preceding laws from the beginning of ch. 18. This suggests the call to observe the Lord's statutes and rules in this verse and v. 7 refers not only to the statutes and rules in their immediate contexts, but also serves as a constant reminder for the addressees to keep all the commandments and rules of chs. 18 – 20.

'the one who sanctifies you': *mĕqaddišĕkem* This is the first indication in Leviticus that the Lord sanctifies the Israelites (cf. Exod. 31:13), and henceforth this idea occurs frequently.

Here it is not the laundering of clothes nor the washing of their body that sanctifies, but observing the Lord's statutes. Though commentators commonly notice this (e.g. Wenham 1979: 278; Hartley 1992: 338; Rooker 2000: 267), the means by which the Lord makes them holy remains unclear. It seems improbable that the Lord simply enables them to observe all his statutes. A deep chasm exists between one's capability for keeping all the laws and the Lord's consecration. Nevertheless, considering that holiness is an absence of selfishness (see ch. 19, 'Explanation'), it is possible to maintain a relationship with them. That is, as the Israelites strive to keep *all* his commandments, the Lord sanctifies them by reminding them they will be cut off from his presence if they continue in their egocentric ways. The tension between the Israelites and holiness is resolved only by assuming a transformation of the human heart. It is by this whole process that the Lord sanctifies a person (see further 'Explanation').

20:9–21

In this particular context, a law prohibiting adultery is highly significant, since it clearly designates adultery as a form of idolatry. The list beginning from v. 10 is formulated from the viewpoint of idolatry, the extreme case of which is Molech worship and divination (described as *zānâ*; vv. 5–6). Even the cases in vv. 13 (homosexuality), 14 (union with a woman and her mother), 15–16 (bestiality), 18 (union with a woman in menses), and 19 (union with the sister of one's mother) are seen from the viewpoint of sexual coveting. In comparison with ch. 18, there is an apparent tendency to stress adulterous rather than genealogical relations. In this regard, the use of *šākab 'et* (to lie with) is apt for expressing the illegality of this conduct. Thus as a whole, this chapter stresses idolatrous relations between humans and spiritual beings other than the Lord, although *nā'ap* or *zānâ* do not appear in vv. 11–21 (but see on v. 10).

As mentioned in 'Form and structure', the cases in vv. 9–21 are arranged according to their punishments. The violation of the laws in vv. 11–16 invokes the death penalty, whereas this penalty is not attached to the violation of those laws given in vv. 17–21; instead the accused is faced with the *kāret* penalty plus 'bearing guilt/punishment' (v. 17), the *kāret* penalty (v. 18), 'bearing guilt' (v. 19) or 'being (dying) childless' (vv. 20–21). It is questionable, however, whether the degree of an offence's heinousness determines the order in which it is treated; if this is the case, then it is still questionable in whose eyes it is viewed as detestable, the Lord's or a human's (see below and 'Explanation').

9. For cursing parents the offender is put to death. Why does this law follow a call to holiness? As mentioned in 'Form and structure', it is probably based on 19:3. Thus the flow of the laws can be seen in such a way that vv. 2b–6 deal with the divine–human relationship and vv. 9–21 deal with interhuman relationships, so the location of v. 9 is like that of the Fifth Commandment in the Decalogue. 'Cursing' can be non-verbal (see 'Comment' 19:14). The honouring of one's parents is fundamental to the patriarchal family. Most of the following violations should not occur when this is practised (see Milgrom 2000a: 1744–1745).

'his blood-guilt is in him': *dāmāyw bô* From this verse onwards, the formulaic *dam* in the sense of 'blood guilt' followed by *bĕ* and pronominal suffix appears frequently. When this formula occurs, it is always followed by the death penalty expressed by the formulaic *môt yûmat* (or *yûmĕtû*).

10. Those who commit adultery should be put to death.

The expression *'ešet 'îš* (a wife of a man) has been seen as a redundant reference to 'a wife of his neighbour'. This phrase occurs only twice in the OT, here and Prov. 6:26. Milgrom, having weighed various suggestions, adopts the view that the latter phrase functions to limit the jurisdiction of the law to the Israelite neighbour (Milgrom 2000a: 1747). However, the opposite is possibly true, since the phrase 'a wife of a man' may not exclusively refer to 'a wife who belongs to a fellow Israelite', but also to 'a woman of closest relative' listed in vv. 11–12, 20–21 (cf. Gen. 2:24 and 'Comment' on 15:18; 19:17). Thus the apparently additional 'a wife of his neighbour' seems to limit the scope of the partner of an adulterer to a woman who is not his closest relative. Yet, on the other hand, although this verse addresses an act of adultery with a neighbour's wife, the very connotation of 'a wife of a man' suggests that the cases in vv. 11–12, 20–21 also constitute the act of *nāʼap* (*pace* Greenberg 1985: 83–84).

'commit adultery': *nāʼap* The Hebr. root *nʼp* (including its pi. form) occurs thirty-one times in the OT, and it occurs first in the Decalogue (Exod. 20:14). The exact meaning of the term should be established, particularly in its relation to *zānâ*. These two terms are synonymous, but as Greenberg notes (1985: 83 n. 35), a distinction is suggested in passages such as Ezek. 23:2–3 and Hos. 4:14, where *zānâ* is ascribed to sexual union before marriage; *nāʼap* is limited to illicit sexual unions between the married, while this is not necessarily the case with *zānâ*. While this is so legally, *nāʼap* essentially begins with sexual coveting, and the object of the coveting is not always humans but things (cf. Prov. 6:25, 32; Job 24:15; Jer. 3:9). What is distinctive about *zānâ*, as opposed to *nāʼap*, is that it has spiritual and invisible beings as its objects.

11. A sexual union with the wife of one's father; as it is addressed in the 3rd person, as opposed to in ch. 18, this law relates both to 18:7 and 18:8. In the light of the fact that both perpetrators are to be punished, the phrase *šākab ʼet* (sleep with) connotes consensual sex.

12. Sexual union with one's daughter-in-law is punishable by death: both the offending man and woman shall be put to death (cf. 18:15). A case such as the incident between Judah and Tamar is at issue (Gen. 38).

The characterization of the offence as 'perversion' (*tebel*) is made in 18:23 in relation to the case of bestiality. Such a characterization may appear arbitrary, but since 'abomination' (*tôʻēbâ*; see v. 12 below) and 'depravity' (*zimmâ*; see v. 13 below) are used of the same cases in ch. 18, there is room to assume the legislator deliberately uses *tebel*. If this is the case, intercourse with one's daughter-in-law belongs to the same category of offence as bestiality.

13. Not listing the other cases of incestuous union, the legislator moves on to a different category of illicit union, homosexuality. This offence also carries the death penalty and is also called 'an abomination' (*tôʻēbâ*; cf. 18:22).

14. It is debated whether *lāqaḥ* means 'to take', 'to marry' (Milgrom 2000a: 1750) or 'to cohabit with' (Wenham 1979: 280). While such a union was probably practised publicly in Canaan, it was prohibited in Israel. In other words, the term is unlikely to refer to public marriage, though something more than sexual intercourse appears to be intended in view of 18:18. On the principle that a sexual union essentially means marriage, any of the suggested renderings listed above is acceptable, yet the ambiguous 'take' is preferred.

The evaluative term 'depravity' (*zimmâ*) is used here in relation to a case similar to that in 18:17. All people who commit such an offence ought to be burnt with fire. For *zimmâ*, see 19:29.

15–16. Bestiality is punishable by the death penalty: both the man and the animal must be killed. The idiomatic *nātan šĕkôbet bĕ* along with the verb *rāba'* is common to 18:23, which deals with the same case.

While *môt yûmat* is used for a male offender, *hārag* is used for killing a beast. Rather than summary execution (Milgrom 2000a: 1752), *hārag* may express a general method of execution.

Sexual intercourse between a woman and a beast (v. 16) is also punishable by death: both the woman and the beast must be executed. As in v. 15, this verse highlights both genders by mentioning 'a man' (*'îš*, v. 15) and 'a woman' (*'iššâ*), unlike in 18:23, which assumes the addressee is a man. A distinction is made between a man's case in v. 15 and the woman's case in terms of the means of execution, but the result is the same. The 2nd person imperatives (*tahărōgû, hāragtā*) indicate that the execution is not just a sentence but a commandment.

17. This verse deals with an illicit case of sexual intercourse between a man and his sister, either the daughter of his father or mother. Thus this case may be an abridged statement of the cases in 18:9, 11. Further the idea of 'uncovering nakedness' is conveyed here as 'seeing her nakedness and her seeing his nakedness'.

'a disgrace': *ḥesed* The Hebr. term normally means 'steadfast love', but obviously means something entirely different on this occasion, where it is possibly a euphemism (cf. Prov. 14:34; 25:9–10). The punishment of being cut off in public ('in the sight of the children of his people') is implemented for the first time here in the list of illicit sexual unions (vv. 10–21).

18. The case of having intercourse with a woman during her period of menstruation is mentioned in 15:24 and 18:19. The requirement that the *kāret* penalty be inflicted on both is given for the first time here. For *mĕqôrāh* (her fountain), see 12:7, and for the ideological relationship between the uncleanness regulations in chs. 12 and 15 on the one hand and the laws here, see 'Explanation'.

19. The case of intercourse between a man and his mother's or father's sister is related to the case in 18:12–13. Among the list of laws in vv. 10–21, which begins with 'If a man' (*'îš 'ăšer*), this law is the only one that begins with 'And the nakedness of' (*wĕ'erwat*), which reflects the style of 18:7–17. The significance for this is uncertain. Perhaps it is merely a stylistic variation. This law also presents a peculiarity in that the case is introduced in the 2nd person sg., whereas the clause beginning with *kî* is formulated in the 3rd person sg. and pl.

The order of 'the sister of your *mother*' and 'the sister of your *father*' suggests that, on the one hand, the law is the result of an abridgement of 18:12–13, but that, on the other, the formulation is affected by 19:3a.

The penalty for the violation is expressed by the idiom 'to bear guilt' (*nāśā' 'āwōn*). The concrete consequence of bearing guilt is not mentioned. It is noteworthy that 'bearing guilt' does not refer to the consequence of self-hiding (*ḥāṭā'*), but of the offence (see 'Explanation').

20. Intercourse with one's aunt is already prohibited in 18:14. The penalty formula is different from the previous ones; it consists of two parts: (1) to bear punishment (*ḥēṭ nāśā'*), and (2) to die childless (*'ărîrîm yāmûtû*).

(1) The phrase *nāśā' ḥēṭ* is synonymous with *nāśā' 'āwōn* (to bear guilt), and means to 'bear punishment/guilt'. See 'Comment' on 19:17. (2) The term *'ărîrîm* occurs four times in the OT, and except for this context occurs in Gen. 15:2 and Jer. 22:30. Childlessness was symbolic of hopelessness in OT times, not just in human society but before God. The apparently self-evident 'they shall die' (*yāmûtû*) deserves some attention, for undoubtedly this is not said to be a 'natural' death. In the rest of Leviticus *mwt* qal always means death by punishment (8:35; 10:2, 6–7, 9; 15:31; 16:1–2, 13). Indeed it is presumed that animals and creatures other than human beings die (11:31–32, 39), but as for human beings, death in Leviticus is not viewed as natural or inevitable. It is viewed as a consequence of violating some law or ordinance. Therefore in this verse both childlessness and death constitute the punishment for the offence.

In sum it is difficult to see any difference between the penalty in this verse and the previous ones where a person is cut off from his or her people.

21. The last in the series of illicit cases is sexual intercourse with a brother's wife. This prohibition is already given in 18:16. However, on this occasion the offence's punishment is prescribed; i.e. childlessness. Contra the previous case in v. 20 the death of the offender is not required. But the absence of any mention of the death penalty would not lessen the potential mental pain the offender may experience; if he keeps hiding his offence, he commits a self-hiding, and the penalty becomes eternal.

For *lāqaḥ*, see above on v. 14.

20:22–26

This section is a concluding exhortation for the Israelites to observe all the Lord's statutes and rules, and to become holy. It is delivered in the 2nd person. These positive exhortations are underscored by the warning against experiencing the fate of the previous occupants of the Promised Land and by the promise that the Israelites will inherit this land that flows with milk and honey. 'A call to holiness' (v. 7) and the 'observance of the Lord's statutes' (v. 8) are arranged chiastically in this section (vv. 22 and 26).

The language and themes used in this section closely resemble those of chs. 18 and 11. In this sense, this section is a concluding statement regarding not just chs. 18 – 20, but chs. 11 – 20.

22. With language similar to v. 8, the Lord exhorts the Israelites to observe all his statutes and rules. When compared with v. 8, 'all' is added before 'the statutes', while 'all the rules' is a new element. However, the combination of the terms 'statutes' (*ḥuqqôt*) and 'rules' (*mišpāṭîm*) appears in 18:3–5, 26 and 19:37, which makes it likely the Lord is here referring back to 18:3–5. Thus vv. 22–26 are meant to be a summary of chs. 18 – 20. The repetitive calls to holiness and observance of the Lord's statutes indicate that 20:22 refers not just to the statutes in this chapter, but to all the other statutes in chs. 18 and 19 as well.

V. 22b is the undesirable outcome of disobedience. Based on the idea of 'the land vomiting its inhabitants' in 18:25, 28, the Lord exhorts the people by stressing that the Promised Land is where he is leading them.

23. Based on the language of 18:3–4, where the phrase 'walk in the statutes of' is found, and on the language and idea of 'the Lord expelling the people before the Israelites' and 'the people having committed all these' in 18:24, 27, the Lord emotionally declares that 'I detest them' (v. 23b). This is the first direct mention of the Lord's personal abhorrence of all the Canaanite rules.

24. The Lord proceeds to mention further steps, to give the land of Canaan to his people. Up till now the term *'ereṣ* is used for the 'land', and not *'ădāmâ*. The latter term occurs only twice in Leviticus, in this verse and the next, and being synonymous with *'ereṣ* connotes an inhabited land. It is 'the land flowing milk and honey' (*'ereṣ zābat ḥālāb ûdĕbaš*). This description of the Promised Land is unique with Leviticus but first appears in Exod. 3:8 and then in Exod. 3:17; 13:5; 33:3. It is a good land the Lord will give the people *on the condition* they observe his statutes, as the following verses state. It represents the Lord's blessing to his people, which he promised to the Patriarchs.

It is the Lord's exclusive dealing with the people to single them out from among many other nations, with the expectation that the Israelites become holy like their God.

25. The theme of the Lord's 'separation' continues: because he has separated the Israelites from other peoples, the Israelites ought to separate the clean from the unclean, so they may not make their souls detestable in the Lord's sight. The language and theme closely resemble that of ch. 11, particularly 11:44–47. Some points crucial for the understanding of the relationship between the so-called cultic laws and moral laws need now to be addressed.

It is simplistic to identify the Israelites with the clean creatures. It is only an expectation of the Lord that they are clean; if not, he would not have commanded them to make a distinction between clean and unclean. Moreover it has been argued that the clean and unclean creatures in ch. 11 symbolize human beings, and that uncleanness is the state of hiding oneself (see 'Explanation' on ch. 11). Thus there is no intrinsic discontinuity between the so-called cultic laws and these moral laws in chs. 18 – 20. The present text is not the outcome of blending so-called cultic and moral materials: from the outset Israel made no such distinction.

To have contact with the swarming creatures defiles the souls of the Israelites, which, considering they have such souls, also requires they should detest themselves.

26. Beyond cleanness lies holiness. Cleanness refers to a person uncovered before the Lord, who may therefore approach his presence. Assuming this, the state of holiness is one of unselfishness. Both refer to the state of the human heart. Next to v. 7 this is the second call to become holy. Here, however, the ground for the people becoming holy is the Lord's holiness. The Lord's election and separation of the people from other peoples precede his call to holiness. If the people cannot live up to the Lord's expectation, their fate will be no different from these other people's.

20:27

This verse takes up the same theme mentioned in v. 6, punishment of people who turn to mediums or necromancers, and the penalty is being stoned to death.

The repetitiveness regarding this prohibition against turning to mediums or necromancers reflects, first, the chiastic literary structure of this chapter which is arranged from a thematic point of view (see 'Form and structure'), and second, the legislator's decision to adumbrate the rules in the next chapter (21:1–15), which concern the involvement of a human soul with other souls.

Explanation

Some explanation is required concerning the nature of the offences and their respective punishments, their relationship with chs. 11 – 15 and the meaning and significance of the call to holiness.

Nature of the offences

First, all the violations in this chapter are committed *in secret*. Because these violations have a furtive character, they tend to remain unknown to other people. However, the chapter presumes the Lord is aware the offences have been committed. Thus a stark contrast is drawn between the strong human impulse to hide a violation and divine omniscience (cf. 1 Sam. 16:7; Ps. 90:8). Severe penalties such as capital punishment or the *kāret* penalty most probably made the offences even more secretive. In my view of *ḥaṭṭā't*, this situation would make one hide to an extreme degree (cf. Rom. 7:13).

Second, while the prohibitions in ch. 18 are arranged with an emphasis on the divine created order, this chapter appears to stress the idolatrous aspects of the prohibited actions. Although, from a moral-ethical point of view, each of these cases tends to be dealt with in a fragmentary fashion, for instance, by posing a question as to whether or not homosexuality is allowed, this approach to their interpretation leaves much to be desired. All the prohibited cases in this chapter are prohibited.

kāret *penalty, death penalty and expiation of self-hiding*

Clearly these offences are committed by hiding oneself from the Lord. But how are these grave penalties related to the expiation of self-hiding? If one is sentenced to death, does one's self-hiding remain unforgiven forever? This raises a question concerning the relationship between the expiatory rituals in chs. 4 – 5 and the punishments listed in this chapter.

It is commonly assumed that the death and *kāret* penalties, being matters of the civil court or direct divine intervention, leave no room for expiation. However, this relies on the assumption that the violation of one of the Lord's commandments is identical with *ḥāṭā'* or *ḥaṭṭā't*, an assumption elsewhere argued as imprecise (Kiuchi 2003a; see 'Explanation', 'Consequence of self-hiding and recognition of guilt' on 4:1 – 5:13). In my interpretation of the terms *ḥāṭā'* and *ḥaṭṭā't*, the offering in 4:1 – 5:13 does not deal with the violation of a particular commandment as such. Rather it concerns the condition of the human heart. Along with my interpretation that the prohibitive commandments in 4:2 comprehend all kinds of laws, the *ḥaṭṭā't* offering is also related to those offences that warrant punishment by death or *kāret*. How? The offender is forgiven for his self-hiding when he realizes his guilt that derives from his self-hiding, although he still ought to be put to death for his offence (cf. the case of David and Bathsheba in 2 Sam. 12).

Degrees of gravity of the offences

The chapter begins with a prohibition against Molech worship and its punishment: the *kāret* penalty and death by stoning, both of the offender and his protectors. These two kinds of offence appear to be the gravest of all the offences in this chapter. Does the absence of the *kāret* penalty in relation to the sexual offences of vv. 10–16 imply they are less serious? Further does the absence of both the *kāret* penalty and the *môt–yûmat* formula in the cases of sexual violation in vv. 17–20 mean these offences are even less serious than these other sexual offences punished by death?

Is it possible a person can be sentenced to death even though he is not self-hiding? Or can a person be given life while he remains outside a covenantal relationship with the Lord? The answers to these questions are related to a further basic question regarding the difference between the *kāret* and death penalties.

The *kāret* penalty refers to the cutting off of a person from God's covenantal people. This cutting off may or may not involve the loss of the offender's physical life (cf. Hasel 1984: 363). On the other hand, the death penalty is a legal measure carried out by the court and the people. In this sense, it is a visible punishment: an offender is visibly cut off from both the people and the Lord. In such a case, the two penalties are not in conflict but overlap: in a sense the death penalty is part of the *kāret* penalty (cf. v. 6 with v. 27). Therefore the fact that 18:29 imposes the *kāret* penalty on all the cases in vv. 6–23 does not conflict with ch. 20, where the punishments vary according to the case in question; the death penalty for a series of sexual offences in vv. 10–16 can also be viewed as the *kāret* penalty.

The penalties in vv. 17–21 are formulated with a variety of expressions, none of which is accompanied by mention of the death penalty. However, those punishments appear even more sinister and dreadful considering that sooner or later the offender's own situation will betray he was punished by the Lord. If a person is said to be cut off from his people, that is no different from facing the death penalty.

Basically it can be observed that the penalties befit the nature of the crimes to some extent, and that there are degrees of the gravity of the offences, particularly as seen in the cases of Molech worship and soothsaying. However, the above consideration about the various formulations of the penalities exhibits an awareness of the common human assumption that the death penalty is the most dreadful punishment. Is this what the legislator ultimately assumes?

Thus there seem to be two factors here. First, by juxtaposing the *kāret* penalty with the death penalty, or various penalties without mentioning the death penalty, the Lord invites the Israelites to ponder the dreadfulness of the apparently less heinous punishments. Thus the meaning of one's receiving divine punishment while alive, or the meaning of living but bearing one's own guilt (vv. 19–21): there can be life without any meaning other than bearing one's own guilt or punishment. Thus the variety of formulations regarding punishment confronts one with a doomed life, which stands in contrast with the blessed life gained by observing all the statutes and rules (18:5).

Second, potentially as seen in prescriptions such as in chs. 7 (see 'Explanation' there), 14 (cf. 'Comment' on 14:39–40), 15 (cf. 'Comment' on 15:2b–15, 19–24) and 27 (see 'Explanation' there), here as well the various formulations of the penalties reflect a general *human* assessment of the penalties, such as the death penalty being the gravest: the Lord adjusts himself to that to a certain extent. In other words, the formulation of the penalties, while taking into account the human assessment, functions to convey the Lord's message that ultimately there is no substantial difference between the punishments before God.

Relationship with the uncleanness regulation in chapters 11 – 15

This chapter exhibits some linguistic and thematic relationships with the uncleanness regulations in chs. 11 – 15. There are two major points here.

First, in 20:25 the Lord integrates the uncleanness regulations in ch. 11 with the so-called moral-ethical laws in chs. 18 – 20. In accordance with this, scholars judge that the legislator sought to integrate cultic and moral motifs in this chapter. However, when it is assumed the violation of the symbolic meanings of these laws defiles one's soul (*napšôtêkem*), the supposed distinction between the cultic and moral becomes unwarranted. Thus an alternative view is more likely that the prohibited conduct in this chapter stems from the same root of the human unclean heart: the propensity to hide oneself.

Second, Molech worship is said in v. 3 to 'defile my sanctuary' (*ṭimmē' 'et miqdāšî*). A similar expression is found in 15:31, where it is said that uncleanness 'defiles my abode (*miškānî*)'. The Molech worshipper ought to *be put to death*, whereas in 15:31 uncleanness leads to the *death* of the Israelites (see 'Comment' there). On the traditional distinction between the 'cultic' and 'moral' realms, one may well infer that the defilement of the Lord's sanctuary in 20:3 is viewed as graver than the action in 15:31. However, if the regulations in ch. 15 are viewed simply as describing the human existential state and its consequence, Molech worship can be viewed as simply describing a violation of a concrete prohibition and its consequence (see 'Form and structure'). It is clear that the Molech worshipper hides himself from the outset. The same relationship is evident in 15:24 between the seven-day defilement that results from having sexual intercourse with a menstruating woman and the *kāret* penalty in 20:18.

Thus, however heinous the offence may look, it is just a manifestation of a human in an unclean state.

Call to be holy

The command clearly aims to summon the addressees to holiness. Holiness, particularly inner holiness, is never assumed in Leviticus, and the text presents holiness as the goal towards which the Israelites ought to strive. Whether they can achieve this is another matter. Moreover holiness is closely related to the observance of *all* the laws. By 'all the laws' the Lord means all the regulations in chs. 18 – 20. Yet as there is a reference in v. 25 to ch. 11, he implies that the laws also include those concerning cleanness and uncleanness.

The basic attitude underlying holy living is found, as set out in ch. 11, in maintaining a distinction between clean and unclean animals. These unclean creatures symbolize those human attitudes that tend to be insincere, double-tongued and selfish, all of which are manifestations of human self-hiding and the egocentric nature (see ch. 11). This is the condition of the implied reader. The egocentric nature manifests itself in various ways, yet this chapter stresses idolatry in relation to both the spiritual and the physical, the essence of which is coveting.

However, what does observance of the laws in vv. 2–21 (except for vv. 7–8) mean? They are not prohibitive commandments, but decrees the addressees ought to carry out so far as the human role is concerned. Yet the presence of direct divine punishment means that those laws as a whole are supposed to threaten the potential offenders, among whom are included the addressees themselves. Thus these laws function to pose a threat to the egocentric natures of both individual and community, out of which come various forms of idolatry. Thus, after ch. 19, where the nature of holiness is set out, 20:1–21 aims to destroy the human egocentric nature by inflicting severe punishments such as the *kāret* and death penalties, which humans fear the most, for holiness lies beyond the death of the egocentric nature. The offender is hard put before the choice of whether to take physical life without the Lord's presence, or forgiveness of self-hiding at the cost of his physical life. If the person resolves to choose the latter, he is to confess his self-hiding (his self-hiding before God), which makes him a forgiven sinner at the last moment. The punishments defeat their purpose when simply regarded as punishment for punishment's sake rather than as tools intended to keep the egocentric nature at bay.

Ironically the person who has not received either the sentence of *kāret* or death is in an even more precarious position than the person who has. This can be deduced from the fact that no person is able to observe all of the positive commandments of Lev. 19, which implies all people have an egocentric nature. Moreover it no doubt follows that all such people have committed some violation that requires either the death or *kāret* penalty. If so, the person who has not experienced the punishments of Lev. 20 may never have his or her egocentric nature destroyed. There are grave consequences for such persons, since if they continue hiding their violations till they die, this constitutes unpardonable self-hiding.

After all, that all humans die (cf. 18:5) is proof, according to Leviticus, that they have committed some violation that deserves the *kāret* or death penalty. Yet the book has already revealed that it is possible for a person who is cut off from his community to undergo a new spiritual birth. For example, in 13:1 – 14:32 the cut-off person is in a better position to pursue holiness via newfound cleanness. This is the only way for all humanity to become holy, even if physical life must be forfeited. And it is these kinds of people Jesus Christ came to save – not those who keep hiding in the temple.

New Testament implications

The coming of Jesus Christ assumes the spiritual reality that all humanity is cut off from God's presence. Now that the modus operandi of human salvation has changed: salvation is not by observance of laws but by belief in Jesus Christ. But the same responsibility to destroy the egocentric nature evident in OT times still applies to believers, and it does not take place easily.

However, there is a tendency to transform the original Law into a system of new and intricate rules (cf. Matt. 15:3–6). This is typical of any form of legalism, where the divine laws become essentially human laws. In legalism, humans are concerned about human rather than divine approval. The system is characterized by safety and convenience; it also provides a means by which humans can satisfy their desire to judge one another. In a word, the legalistic way of thinking matches the egocentric nature, or, more precisely, the latter generates the former.

However, 'ought to' characterizes both legalism and the Law. In this respect the hopelessness fostered by legalism may lead a person to the gospel. Until then the selfish nature remains alive.

The good news that Jesus brought was that God can pardon even the heinous acts listed in Rom. 1. Or, more precisely, what Jesus has pardoned on the cross is self-hiding rather than the acts themselves. The case of the forgiven criminal on the cross (Luke 23:40–43) eloquently testifies that pardon was given for his self-hiding rather than for the crimes he was being punished for on the cross. For as long as the human heart remains unchanged, an endless discussion of whether particular acts are right or wrong will continue. But if one opens one's heart to Jesus, abandoning all earthly desires and pride, the way is opened towards freedom from an egocentric nature that operates only legalistically. That heart is the heart of the 'children' (Matt. 18:3) the believer is to become like, which is holiness. This is the aim of the Levitical legislation.

It is thus the Law's purpose to make readers aware of their egocentric nature and produce a resultant state of hopelessness; thereby, if possible, leading to the death of the egocentric nature, and ultimately to holiness.

LEVITICUS 21:1–24

Translation

1The LORD said to Moses, 'Speak to the priests, the sons of Aaron, and say to them,
No-one shall make himself unclean for a soul among his people, 2except for
his closest relatives, his mother, his father, his son, his daughter, his brother, 3or his
virgin sister (who is near to him because she has had no husband; for her he may
make himself unclean). 4A husband shall not make himself unclean among his

people and so profane himself. 5They shall not make bald patches on their heads, nor shave off the edges of their beards, nor make any cuts on their body. 6They shall be holy to their God and not profane the name of their God. For they offer the LORD's offerings for annihilation, the food of their God which became holy things. 7They shall not marry a prostitute or a woman who has been defiled, neither shall they marry a woman divorced from her husband, for the priest is holy to his God. 8You shall sanctify him, for he offers the food of your God. He shall be holy to you, for I, the LORD, who sanctify you, am holy. 9And the daughter of any priest, if she profanes herself by whoring, profanes her father; she shall be burned with fire.

10'The priest who is chief among his brothers, on whose head the anointing oil is poured and who has been consecrated to wear the garments, shall not let the hair of his head hang loose nor tear his clothes. 11He shall not go in to any soul of the dead nor make himself unclean, even for his father or for his mother. 12He shall not go out of the sanctuary, lest he profane the sanctuary of his God, for the consecration of the anointing oil of his God is on him: I am the LORD. 13He shall take a wife in her virginity. 14A widow, or a divorced woman, or a woman who has been defiled, or a prostitute, these he shall not marry. But he shall take as his wife a virgin of his own people, 15that he may not profane his offspring among his people, for I am the LORD who sanctifies him.'

16The LORD spoke to Moses, saying, 17'Speak to Aaron, saying, None of your offspring throughout their generations who has a blemish may approach to offer the food of his God. 18For no-one who has a blemish shall draw near, a man blind or lame, or one who has a split nose or a limb too long, 19or a man who has an injured foot or an injured hand, 20or a hunchback or a dwarf or a man with a defect in his sight or festering sores or scabs or crushed testicles. 21No man of the offspring of Aaron the priest who has a blemish shall come near to offer the LORD's offerings for annihilation; since he has a blemish, he shall not come near to offer the food of his God. 22He may eat the bread of his God, both of the most holy and of the holy things, 23but he shall not go through the veil or approach the altar, because he has a blemish, that he may not profane my sanctuaries, for I am the LORD who sanctifies them.'

24So Moses spoke to Aaron and to his sons and to all the Israelites.

Notes on the text

1. 'Speak': *'āmar* Lit. 'say'. Thus *'āmar* appears three times in this verse. See 'Comment'.

'for': *lĕ* The root *ṭm'* in the hiph. form occurs elsewhere in Leviticus at 11:24 and 21:3. As on these occasions, here the preposition means 'because of' or 'for'.

'his kin': *'ammāyw* SamP, LXX, Syr, TgO, TgJon read *'ammô*.

The term *nepeš* is rendered a corpse in all modern English translations: 'any of his people who die' (NIV), 'any dead person' (JPS), 'the dead' (AV, RSV, ESV), 'a dead person' (NRSV). Also the commentators; e.g. Wenham

(1979: 290), Noortzij (1982: 215), Hartley (1992: 347), Budd (1996: 299), Rooker (2000: 273), Milgrom (2000a: 1797–1798); except for Ehrlich (1908: 73), who renders it as 'person'. LXX translates the term both here and v. 11 as *psyche*, and it gives an impression that the rendering is literal, so is hazardous to infer that LXX translators also understood it to mean 'a dead person' (cf. Wevers 1997: 331). For the possibility that *nepeš* means 'a soul', see 'Comment'.

'his people': *'ammāyw* As *BHS* margin notes, *'ammô* is expected. As has been commented on 7:20, however, the pl. form of *'ām* is a collective noun that conveys an awareness of distinct groups within a people (*IBHS* 7.4.1b).

lěnepeš lō' yiṭṭammā' Syntactically it seems correct to take *bě'ammāyw* as qualifying *nepeš*. In that case *bě* means 'among'. Such a construction is apparently required because of the long exceptional clause that follows in vv. 2–3. Certainly the term *nepeš* is fronted for emphasis.

2. 'closest': *haqqārōb* The def. art. expresses superlative (see *IBHS* 14:5c).

4. 'A husband': *ba'al* The anarthrous *ba'al* used absolutely is unique in the OT. LXX reads 'suddenly' (*exapina*), probably reading *bl'* (cf. *kěballa'* in Num. 4:20). Paran (1989: 216–217), followed by Milgrom (2000a: 1800), proposes to delete it, in order to see vv. 1b and 4 as forming an inclusio that surrounds seven instances of exceptions, each of which is headed by *lāmed*. However, is not the unique use of *ba'al* fitting for a rule that prohibits any involvement with other people, including a person's wife?

5. 'on their head' LXX adds 'for the dead'; probably influenced by Deut. 14:1.

6. 'which became holy things': *wěhāyû qōdeš* SamP, 11QPaleoLev and the versions read the pl. *qědōšîm*. Milgrom prefers MT, as it is a *lectio difficilior*. *wěhāyû qōdeš* is commonly rendered 'therefore they shall be holy'. However, given that the MT is original, the subject of *wěhāyû* still remains unclear. The lack of 'to the LORD' after *qōdeš* and the absence of any such case in the Pentateuch (cf. Ezra 8:28), where humans are called *qōdeš*, make it likely the priests are also subject. The possibility is more likely that *wěhāyû qōdeš* qualifies 'the LORD's offerings for annihilation' and 'the food of their God', meaning 'which became holy things'.

7. 'a prostitute': *'iššâ zônâ* The Hebr. phrase refers to a prostitute, not a woman who has the tendency to commit adultery. See Josh. 2:1; Judg. 11:1; 16:1; Jer. 3:3; Ezek. 16:30; Prov. 6:26.

'a woman who has been defiled': *ḥălālâ HALOT* interprets the term 'deflowered'.

8. 'you shall sanctify him': *qiddaštô* LXX reads 'he shall sanctify him'.

'who sanctify you [pl.]': *měqaddišěkem* SamP, LXX and 11QPaleoLev read 'who sanctify them'. See 'Comment'.

11. *napšōt* LXX and Syr. translate it with a sg. noun, perhaps influenced by Num. 6:6. However, there is no compelling reason for reading it as sg.

'any soul of the dead': *kol napšôt mēt* As for *nepeš* in v. 1 (see on v. 1 above), exegetes have unanimously taken the phrase as a whole to mean 'dead bodies'. But such a rendering is unwarranted, though *napšôt* may later have taken on such a meaning in the context of funerals. I propose it means 'souls'. See 'Comment'.

13. 'her virginity': *betûlêhā* LXX adds 'from his kin', as in v. 14b, which is unnecessary.

18. 'one who has a split nose': *ḥārûm HALOT* gives 'split nose'.

20. 'a hunchback': *gibbēn* The translation follows that of *HALOT*.

'dwarf': *daq* The normal word for 'thin', but here it must be a specific reference to some congenital disease. The translation follows Milgrom (2000: 1827).

'festering sores': *gārāb* Cf. 22:22 and Deut. 28:27.

'scabs': *yallepet* It occurs only here and 22:22. *Gārāb* and *yallepet*, though skin complications, are not mentioned in reference to *ṣāra'at* in ch. 13.

21. The following chiasm is discernible in this verse:

Lō' yiggaš lĕhaqrîb 'et'iššeh YHWH (He) shall not come near to offer the LORD's offerings for annihilation
mûm bô he has a blemish
'et leḥem 'ĕlōhāyw lō' yiggaš lĕhaqrîb the food of his God he shall not come near to offer

Lō' yiggaš lĕhaqrîb (shall not come near to offer) comes at the beginning and end, while *'iššeh YHWH* (the LORD's offerings for annihilation) parallels *leḥem 'ĕlōhāyw* (the food of his God). Thus the LXX reading 'the sacrifice to your God, for' for *'et 'iššeh YHWH* is unlikely the original.

23. 'my sanctuaries': *miqdāšay* LXX reads 'the Holy Place of his God'.

Form and structure

Chs. 21 and 22 deal with rules pertaining to priestly matters; ch. 21 deals with matters relating to the priesthood and ch. 22 deals with matters relating to the holy offerings. The rules in ch. 21 concern how Aaron and his sons should relate to other human beings. They encompass the nature of their marriage (21:1–15), the qualifications for approaching the altar with offerings (21:16–23) and a statement that Moses reported these laws to their intended recipients (21:24).

Ch. 22 deals with similar themes to those of ch. 21. It focuses on the holy offerings and their relationship with what is potentially unclean or unauthorized or unqualified (for the arrangement of the themes, see the next chapter). Thus these two chapters deal with what is institutionally called holy and its relationship with the unclean and unauthorized. As noted elsewhere (Wenham 1979: 289), the formula 'I am the LORD your (their) sanctifier' closes each section, both in this and the next chapter (21:8, 15, 23; 22:9, 16, 32). Thematically it is a special application of the rules in ch. 19, which are addressed to all the Israelites, just as ch. 16 is a special application of chs. 13 – 14.

The content of ch. 21 is as follows:

1a	The Lord's command to Moses to speak to the priests, the sons of Aaron
1b–9	Regarding Aaron's sons
1b–4	Prohibition against defilement by contact with the souls of relatives
5–6	Prohibition against making bald patches on one's head, shaving off the edges of one's head or making any cuts on one's body, accompanied by the prohibition's rationale
7–9	Prohibition against defilement by marriage, and rationale for prohibition
10–15	Regarding the chief priest
11–12	Prohibition against defilement by contact with the souls of the dead, and the prohibition's rationale
13–15	Restrictions on marriage partners
16–17a	The Lord's command for Moses to speak to Aaron
17b–23	Defects that disqualify priests from approaching the altar
24	The statement of Moses' execution of the Lord's command

The rules are generally stated in a negative form, *lō'* followed by *yiqṭol*, often further followed by the basis for the rule introduced by *kî* (cf. vv. 1b, 6–8, 10–11 etc.).

Despite the presence of many prohibitions, punishment in the event of violation is mentioned only at v. 9, a verse that appears to complement 19:29. But as the verb *ḥillel* (to profane) in vv. 6, 12, 15, 23 suggests, the penalty is supposed to be either the *kāret* or death penalty (cf. 19:8; 18:21/20:3). The reason for not mentioning the penalty is that it is obvious from the preceding chapters. Rather, as the three occurrences of *qdš* pi. (vv. 8, 15, 23) suggest, the whole chapter stresses the Lord's positive attitude to the sanctification of the priests.

Despite the appearance that this chapter addresses itself only to the priests, it provides further development of themes mentioned in previous chapters, such as defilement and marriage. First, for the first time it is stated that defilement is caused by one's coming into contact with a human soul (*nepeš*, vv. 1, 11; see 'Comment'). Up until this chapter, however, the closest statement to this is 11:43–44, where it is the 'swarming creatures' that defile. Second, there is already some development of the theme of illicit sexual relations in chs. 18 – 20. For example, though both chs. 18 and 20 are preoccupied with illicit sexual intercourse, ch. 20 introduces a matrimonial aspect, absent in ch. 18, by introducing the idea of adultery in 20:10. In line with this development, ch. 21 continues to deal with matrimonial matters, assuming the rules of chs. 18 and 20, but this time restrictions on the marriage partner, which are far more institutionally fundamental and restrictive, are dealt with. Thus though ch. 21 concerns the priests, it also provides some deeper meaning to the ideas of defilement and sexual union, mentioned in chs. 18 and 20. Rules on the basic qualifications for priests (physical blamelessness in vv. 17–23) are first introduced and are new in this chapter, and have their counterpart in 22:17–25.

Comment

As mentioned above, chs. 21 – 22 deal with priests: their qualifications in the matter of human relationships, particularly the defilement of their soul, and their marriage; various general warnings when handling offerings of the people, and rules on the common offerings, such as the fellowship offering. This flow of themes is, on the whole, similar to that found in chs. 6 – 7: from the purely priestly matters to matters relating to both priests and people. The basic message, a call to holiness, penetrates every rule in these chapters. From the viewpoint of the overall structure of Leviticus, ch. 21 and the following chapters can be seen as a special application of the message in ch. 19: the call to holiness to the people in general is applied to the priests who are holy by ordination. It is assumed the priests are demanded to live a higher degree of inner holiness because they are expected to have perfect outer holiness.

Inversely, though not stated explicitly, although the rules in chs. 21 – 22 concern mainly priests, they are indirectly directed to the laity, in so far as they describe the essence of the road to holiness (see 'Form and structure').

In each of the two sections vv. 1b–9 and 10–15 contact with death alternates with matrimony. As explained below, both themes concern one's involvement with another's egocentric nature. Stricter rules on marriage in the case of the priest or chief priest attest to the Lord's expectation that the priests should be holier than the laity. It is noteworthy that matrimony marks the very beginning of a priest's involvement with his lifelong partner. How the priest can maintain priority towards his God is of central concern to this chapter. Thus it is imperative for a priest to examine himself rigorously. The souls of other people, including his closest relatives, are indeed defiling, but his own soul is the key to this defilement.

The Hebr. term *qiddēš* (to sanctify) appears frequently from this chapter onwards. The idea of the Lord sanctifying the priests first appears in 21:8.

In this chapter it is further mentioned in vv. 15 and 23, and in the next chapter it appears in vv. 9, 16 and 32. In 21:8 Moses is commanded to sanctify the priest, while in vv. 15 and 23 it is the Lord himself who sanctifies the priest(s). One characteristic of the reference to divine sanctification is the final positioning of the term *qiddēš* at the end of each section, probably indicating that the term refers to the whole process, beginning from the observation of the rule in question (see on vv. 13–15). Practically the priests' road to inner holiness starts from their realization that they are full of idolatrous thoughts, deeply corrupt in their hearts, and thus in a state of hopelessness before the Lord. Paradoxically the fact that the priest has such a heart supervising his egocentric nature indicates he is on the road to inner holiness, though this ought not to become an axiom and a conscious basis on which to assert his own right.

21:1a

The Lord commands Moses to report to the priests, the sons of Aaron. The special way the Lord addresses Moses (by repeating *'āmar* three times) may express both intimacy and solemnity with regard to the content of the following rules. It should be noted that the following rules are not said to have been delivered to Aaron; so basically Moses remains the sole addressee until v. 23 (see on v. 8).

21:1b–9

Exegetes unanimously interpret this section as referring to defilement by contact with the dead, by rendering *nepeš* as 'corpse' (e.g. Milgrom 2000a: 1976). This interpretation is, in a sense, inevitable, as it stands on the assumption that uncleanness is related to *physical death*. However, the symbolic meaning of defilement proposed in this commentary, as well as the following observation, makes the above interpretation unwarranted, or, at least, one-sided (see also Michel 1994).

As is often mentioned (see on 2:1; 4:2 etc.), *nepeš* mostly means 'a soul' in Leviticus. In particular, translations such as 'a person' or 'life' are insufficient here. Yet what grounds are there for translating *nepeš* as 'corpse'? Is it because vv. 2–4 appear to refer to funerary rites? But there are no terms in these verses that suggest a funeral is in view, even if that is not precluded. Rather the combination of *nepeš* and *hiṭṭammā'* (to make oneself unclean) suggests a close ideological link with the rules of ch. 11 (cf. 11:24, 43–44; see also 20:25–26). Indeed interpreting the rule in question as a reference to a funeral appears to gain support from v. 10b, where the chief priest is commanded not to loosen his hair or his clothes, which are generally taken as gestures associated with a funeral. Indeed these express mourning (10:6), but are mentioned at v. 10, namely before v. 11, which is about 'all the *něpāšôt* of the dead', and this suggests the gestures are basically general in nature, symbolizing grief, particularly for human death, but are not restricted to a funeral context.

The phrase '*al kol napšôt mēt* appears in v. 11, a fact which may seem to strengthen the assumption that *nepeš* in vv. 1 and 11 means 'a corpse'. However, as noted elsewhere (Kiuchi 2003a: 127 n. 5), *napšôt mēt* means, first, 'the *napšôt* of the dead' and not 'dead *napšôt*'. At any rate, the translation 'corpse' makes the phrase redundant. Milgrom says that *nepeš* in v. 1 is an ellipsis of *nepeš mēt* in v. 11 (Milgrom 2000a: 1798). But would not the ordinary audience in Israel have understood that *nepeš* in v. 1 meant 'a corpse', if it did, without adding *mēt*? Then there would be no point in adding *mēt* in v. 11. Moreover such a meaning as 'a corpse' for *nepeš* has not appeared in this book (except for the debatable case in 19:28). For the meaning of *mēt*, see the comment on v. 11 below. Thus *nepeš* appears to mean 'a soul', but since this is defiling, it has an egocentric nature.

Thus this law in vv. 1 and 11 reveals a further stage of the same idea in ch. 11 that one defiles his soul by coming into contact with unclean creatures, which symbolize defilement by one's involvement with another's egocentric nature. That is, here in ch. 21 the defilement is explicitly said to be caused through contact with another's egocentric nature, regardless of whether the latter is physically alive or dead.

I take the prohibition in vv. 1b–3 as being against a priest's involvement with the egocentric natures of his closest relatives, including occasions on which such a relative has died. The prohibition has some exceptions for the case of ordinary priests: they are allowed to have contact with the souls of closest relatives. The very fact that this constitutes an exception indicates that even having contact with the corpse of one's dead relatives is not desirable in the Lord's eyes. Thus these exceptions constitute a compromise on the Lord's part. Particularly it should be pointed out that the permission granted for a priest to defile himself because of his father or mother is due to the common deep involvement with parents. But even this concession is not applicable to the chief priest (21:11; see below). This is because the souls of those relatives are implicitly assumed to be spiritually dead before God, for 'dead' should not be taken in a physical sense: a *dead* soul, as opposed to a living soul (*nepeš ḥayyâ*), means the soul is covered by the selfish nature.

2–3. An exception is prescribed. The priest is allowed to become defiled by coming into contact with the selfish natures of his closest relatives: his mother, father, son, daughter, brother and virgin sister. Notice should be made of the fact that the concept of 'closest relatives' on this occasion is narrower than in the prohibitions of incestuous unions in chs. 18 and 20. This is especially reflected in the case of 'his virgin sister'. The stress on virginity appears to suggest that once she marries she no longer belongs to the 'closest relatives' contemplated in this context, though she still remains a close relative in a wider sense (cf. 18:9; 20:17). This law rests on the principle that once a sister marries, she is regarded as belonging outside his 'close kin' (cf. Gen. 2:24).

It is not the death of a closest relative, but the selfish nature of such people that is assumed as defiling in these verses. It is extremely difficult not to have contact with the souls of the closest relatives, particularly those that live together; hence the Lord's compromise. Essentially a priest, being anointed, should not become defiled by his family, but the Lord saw that this was inevitable.

Exegetes have wondered why no mention is made of the wife of a husband as a source of defilement. Hartley (1992: 347) judges that the case of the wife is permissible, taking *šĕ'ēr* (kin) in a wider sense as in 18:6. But this is highly unlikely. A more probable solution is that the text takes for granted that a husband becomes defiled when he gets involved with the soul of his wife; i.e. in my interpretation, implied in v. 4 below and already suggested in ch. 15, where sexual intercourse makes both unclean (see 'Explanation' there). Indeed Leviticus sees the husband–wife relationship as one of the most defiling. Moreover such a spiritual tendency between spouses is indirectly and outwardly constrained by the regulations pertaining to marriage in vv. 7, 9, 13–14.

The rule assumes that marriage results in one becoming less than what is allowed in terms of spiritual purity. Such a situation did not exist before the fall, but became the inevitable spiritual relationship between a man and his wife (Gen. 3:12–13, 16b). Undoubtedly the defilement is that caused by spiritual idolatry under the circumstance that both the husband and wife hide themselves against the Lord: marriage tends to lead one to forget the Lord (cf. 1 Cor. 7:32–34). These considerations may help explain why in this chapter no explicit mention is made of a wife being a source of defilement.

4. The priest as the husband of a family should not defile himself by involving himself with any individual among his kin. Thus this verse states a principle concerning the head of the priestly family, resuming what is already said in v. 1bb. The use of *hēḥallô* (become desecrated) assumes that the priest is assumed as holy, at least in a God-given sense. The use of *bā'al* (a husband) implies that the priest should not defile himself with his wife (see on vv. 2–3, and 'Notes on the text').

5. As with ordinary people (see 19:27–28), the priests are prohibited from shaving their heads or the edges of their beards, or making cuts on their bodies. Though in other contexts, shaving the hair of one's head is a gesture of mourning and grief (Jer. 16:6; Ezek. 27:31; Mic. 1:16), it is not restricted to mourning. This commandment is not so much concerned with prohibiting a priest's participation in a funeral as with the condition of his heart: he must not sympathize with the death of people (see on 19:27–28).

6. The call to holiness in v. 6a refers both to the preceding and the following verses. It summarizes the intention of the preceding verses 1–5, to encourage holiness, and simultaneously paves the way towards the following rules about the priests' status as offerers of the divine food, and to appropriate marriage partners.

Vv. 6b–9 alternate between the themes of the divine food and marriage. The nature of these topics is related when we remember that marriage tends to make a person idolatrous. The priests must have fellowship only with the Lord.

Although the priests are holy in their capacities, they are only so in a formal sense. They must also be holy in their hearts. Here it is said, 'They shall be holy *to their God*,' stressing their responsibility concerning their role of handling sacrifices and offerings. Cf. with 19:2; 20:7, 26. What does 'the food of their God' refer to? It is undoubtedly not restricted to what the priests offer in the Tent of Meeting: it also includes sacrifices and offerings the people offer in general (cf. 3:11, 16). Thus on this occasion the meaning of *leḥem* is wider than food made from grain (cf. 7:13; 8:26, 31–32).

More importantly, the term *leḥem*, often paired elsewhere with *'iššeh* (3:11, 16; 21:21; 23:18; 24:7), appears five times in this chapter (vv. 6, 8, 17, 21–22). The bread or food of the Lord, being a soothing aroma, symbolizes the communion between the priest and the Lord. It is a symbol of the fellowship where the priest's selfishness ought to be destroyed, since that is the chief prerequisite of holiness. In this sense, the priests' fellowship with the Lord ought to be more intimate than that with any other human being, including their wives.

7. Although v. 7a is formulated in parallelism, it probably lists prohibited marriage partners in the order of descending degrees of disapproval: a prostitute, a non-virgin and a divorcee. Only virgins are potential marriage partners, which is explicitly mentioned in vv. 13–14. Clearly the rule is an outward standard, and not a stringent requirement. This suggests that this law aims beyond the initiation of marriage to encourage the priest to proceed in inner purity; i.e. committed to God. Thus marriage in the human realm is seen from the viewpoint of holiness: belonging to the Lord. To belong to the Lord is to marry the Lord in the true sense of the term. Therefore the law demands the priest to shun troubles originating from marriage in the human realm as much as possible.

8. This verse resumes the topic of v. 6b. The addressee shifts from the 3rd to 2nd person here. The assumption made by most exegetes that the addressee is 'the priests' or 'Israel' or both, is not possible. Since Moses is the addressee up till now, he is addressed here in the 2nd person (cf. Hoffmann 1906: 86). It is the Lord's command to Moses to sanctify the priest. Moses, as the installer of the priesthood, is responsible for the priests' holiness. However, it is the Lord who sanctifies both Moses and the priests. Thus the term 'responsibility' should not be pressed too far, because then the responsibility for the case of failure would rest on the Lord. The responsibility is ultimately that of the priests themselves, though Moses is expected to strive to make them self-sacrificial (see 'Explanation' on ch. 8, and 'Comment' on 10:16–20).

9. This verse addresses a theme similar to that in v. 7, but while in the latter it is about the priest's wife, here the focus is on his daughter. With the general background of 19:29, the law prescribes a severe punishment for prostituting a daughter: burning by fire. It is because her father is a *holy* priest and her conduct is a desecration of holiness. The Hebr. term *zānâ* is general, and does not necessarily refer to sexual intercourse alone, but also to spiritual idolatry, such as soothsaying, fortune-telling and the like (cf. 20:6).

21:10–15

This section addresses various restrictions pertaining to the so-called high priest. Moreover a comparison of the rules with those for the ordinary priests in vv. 1–9 reveals not just a distinction between the chief priest and the ordinary priests, but a higher degree of demand in the areas pertaining to human relationships and marriage.

10. *hakkôhēn haggādôl mē'eḥāyw* Lit. this means 'a priest who is the eldest among his brothers', and is not the name of the 'high priest' (*hakkôhēn haggādôl*) that appears later (Num. 35:25, 28; Josh. 20:6; 2 Kgs 12:10[11]; 22:4, 8; 23:4; Hag. 1:1; Zech. 3:1; Neh. 3:1; 2 Chr. 34:9). It is natural to infer that this is the original way of referring to the priest responsible for all the priestly work, and that only later it became abbreviated to *hakkôhēn haggādôl*. Although the following qualifying clause gives the impression that only the chief priest received the anointing with oil on his head, some texts indicate that all of Aaron's sons were anointed in this way (see on 4:3). Thus this qualification aims to lay more stress on the holy nature of the chief priest's mission than on that of the ordinary priests.

Dishevelling of the hair and tearing of clothes are gestures for mourning and grief, like the gestures in v. 5. Wenham (1979: 291) aptly comments, 'His hair had been anointed and his clothes specially designed for him. If he disturbed them, it could serve to nullify his consecration.'

11. By contrast with the permission granted to ordinary priests (see v. 1), the chief priest ought not to defile himself by involving himself with (*bā'* . . . *'al*; cf. Num. 6:6) the souls of the dead, even in the case of his father and mother. As mentioned in v. 1 above, *nepeš* here means 'a soul'. The text reads *napšôt mēt* (souls of the dead) and not *napšôt mētôt* or *nepeš mētâ*; *mēt* must be a collective noun, meaning 'the dead'. Then *napšôt* is unlikely to mean 'corpses', as taken by most exegetes. The phrase qualifies *nepeš* in v. 1 by adding 'the dead': the *nepeš* in v. 1 may or may not be that of the dead, but *nepeš mēt* in v. 11 is the souls of the dead. The prohibition evidently envisages the death of a person, but as the soul of the dead is at issue, it bears some invisible dimension.

Four considerations follow. First, 'the dead' appears here for the first time in Leviticus. Because 'death' is viewed as resulting from the violation of the Lord's commandments in Leviticus, 'all the souls' are those of egocentric people. Second, the phrase implies that one's soul does not die at his or her physical death, so the rule has a bearing on the prohibition against making enquiries of the spirits of the dead (19:31; 20:6, 27), though not to the extent of soothsaying – even grief over the death of a priest's parent is related to soothsaying. Third, and more essentially, since it is said 'all the souls of the dead', the Lord assumes that not just the physically dead but any human being is dead in his presence in so far as that person has an egocentric nature, which is seen as defiling even before physical death. Fourth, it is not so much the chief priest's attendance at his parents' funerals as his expression of grief over the death that is prohibited. The death of his parents is one of the most sorrowful events in his life. By prohibiting such an extreme occasion of grief, the law aims at inculcating the truth that this prohibition is even more applicable during the lifetime of the parents: if the chief priest can observe the rule when his father or mother dies, he can observe it even better while his parents are alive.

In Leviticus the question of whether the Israelites can observe the Lord's commandments is not explicitly addressed; at most, the rules reflect that it is not possible. Here the prohibition in v. 11 clearly assumes that all human souls violate his commandments. This means that all the Israelites remain outside the Lord's presence and are therefore spiritually dead even though they are physically alive. In the cleanness/uncleanness rules in chs. 11 – 15 the same truth was expressed, though they reveal the potentiality of a person's becoming clean. However, in this chapter not only is it said that the human soul is the source of defilement, but it is implied that this is a universal truth. If the chief priest frees himself from his own egocentric nature, he is the exception among all humanity. But is this possible (cf. 19:18)? His own selfish nature is the greatest obstacle to keeping himself clean before God. Holiness has nothing to do with death: eternal life results from the lack of an egocentric nature. How difficult it is for the chief priest to control his own heart, if his egocentric nature still remains!

For the relationship with 10:6, see 'Comment' there.

12. Here the chief priest is commanded not to leave the sanctuary, without any qualification being made, such as 'only when some of his kin dies'. Nor should the rigour of the command be weakened by the supposed later reality that the priests ordinarily live outside the sanctuary (cf. the discussion of Milgrom 2000a: 1816). Nevertheless the goal of the law lies in the allegiance of the chief priest to the Lord alone, not his physical distance from other people. Though the latter may guarantee the maintenance of his outer holiness (which by itself would be impossible to observe), and is stricter than that commanded for ordinary priests, it is just an outward restriction. Spiritually the same principle applies both to the chief priest and the other ordinary priests in that even the ordinary priests are prohibited from profaning the Lord's holy name outside the sanctuary.

13–15. As for the ordinary priests (cf. v. 7), the chief priest must marry only a virgin, and not a divorced woman, a prostitute, or one who has been defiled. A significant difference from the rules given for ordinary priests is that the chief priest should not marry a widow (*'almānâ*). But what is the point of adding 'a widow'? No possibility exists except that she is no more a virgin. The outward requirement certainly aims at something more than literal virginity. To have sexual intercourse involves idolatry, as far as a man or a woman has an egocentric nature. Thus the rule aims to remove any potential source of idolatry for the chief priest (see 'Explanation').

V. 15 prohibits the chief priest from profaning his offspring among his people (cf. 19:29). The reason for the statement is given in v. 15b: that it is the Lord who sanctifies his offspring (cf. 20:8; 21:8). As mentioned in 20:8, the Lord's sanctification lies not in carrying it out against the human will, but in accepting what the human being wills to become holy. Since Moses cannot make the heart of the chief priest unselfish, what he can do is, at best, to make him observe the rules concerning marriage. But as this is related to the inner attitude of the priests, Moses' success depends on the will of the priests, which, on all appearances, makes his attempts fruitless.

As with other rules in chs. 19 – 20, mere literal observance is entirely useless: their spiritual aim must be observed. Since it was impossible for a chief priest to have no egocentric nature, it is surmised that the subsequent history of Israel will inevitably become a history of desecrating the Lord's name. A high priest who has no selfishness is still awaited (cf. 2 Sam. 12:15–23).

21:16–23

This section addresses itself to the requirement that the priest ought to be normal in his physique. One may argue that it means nothing more than literal normality. Indeed just as the priest's body must be without blemish, so with the sacrificial animal (cf. 22:17–25). Hence the view has been advanced that physical normality is an important aspect of holiness.

However, despite the oft-labelled '*perfect* physique', the listed defects in vv. 18–20, though difficult to identify accurately, appear to be rather uncommon; if the priest's body is ordinary, this qualifies him to be a priest. Apparently the Lord desires to divert the attention of the priests and readers to inner holiness by listing these uncommon physical defects. This qualification is virtually the same as that of sacrifices and offerings in 22:17–25, and since the Hebr. term *tāmîm* (perfect) is the condition for the latter (22:19, 21), the same applies to the priest's heart (see 'Comment' on ch. 1). The fact that the priest ought to be 'perfect' means he believes in the Lord. A believing heart is wholehearted, sincere and has nothing to hide, just as with Noah (Gen. 6:9), Abraham (Gen. 17:1) and David (2 Sam. 22:24//Ps. 18:23[24]). Such a condition is, in fact, the essence of holiness. Thus the idea of a priest's meeting the outward qualifications without having the inner qualifications appears ridiculous.

Moreover as mentioned in 'Form and structure', the rules in this chapter are arranged in such a way that the priests' relationship with others is addressed first (vv. 1–15) and then the priests themselves are dealt with in terms of physical qualifications (vv. 16–23). With the spiritual dimension of the rules in view, the whole chapter tacitly conveys the message that the root of the priests' cleanness lies within themselves.

Indeed wholeheartedness is the goal of observing the rules, and it is tacitly assumed that the priests have not yet achieved inner holiness. The rules appear to be formulated to enhance the priests' dedication to the Lord in such a way that what they present to the Lord is the food of *his* God (see on v. 6 and 'Explanation' on ch. 3).

In this light it is ultimately inappropriate to see the physically handicapped as being short of holiness. Moreover those defects are presumably mostly congenital, and it is the Lord who is responsible for them (cf. Exod. 4:11). As an example of the opposite case in the OT, King Saul was just such man, with a 'handsome' appearance but an unstable heart, worrying about human evaluation, and undedicated to the Lord. He was a typical precursor to the Pharisees, against whom Jesus declared, 'Now you Pharisees cleanse the outside of the cup and of the dish, but inside you are full of greed and wickedness' (Luke 11:39 ESV). In view of the listed physical defects that are rather rare and prone to be socially discriminated against, one would have to examine one's own heart for spiritual defects that correspond to those physical defects, which is an indispensable step to inner holiness (cf. also Job's case).

22–23. Those who have defects in their bodies, however, are entitled to eat the remaining portions of the holy offerings. Again, the phrase 'the food of his God' (*leḥem 'ĕlōhāyw*) is highlighted as the continuation of the latter half of the previous verse. It is not that these people are cut off from the covenantal community; on the contrary, they have their God in their hearts. In so far as they belong to the priestly lineage, they are fed by the offerings. But because of the defects they bear they are prohibited from officiating in both the Tent of Meeting and at the altar of burnt offering, a major part of a priest's vocation.

In this chapter the pi. form of *qdš* (to sanctify) takes such objects as 'the priest' (v. 8) and 'the offspring of Aaron' (v. 15). The antecedent of the suffix of *mĕqaddĕšām* is commonly taken as either 'the priests' or 'the sanctuaries' (v. 23; Milgrom 2000a: 1832). However, the pronominal suffix is pl., while up to the motive clause in v. 23 the legislator has referred to the physically handicapped priest in the singular. The analogy in the sentence structure with v. 15 also supports that the suffix of *mĕqaddĕšām* is the 'sanctuaries' (the veil, altar and offerings).

21:24

This verse reports Moses' execution of the Lord's words. What section of the Lord's discourse does this verse refer to? The added 'to all the people of Israel' at the end of the verse makes it unlikely that it refers only to the content of this chapter, which is addressed to Aaron and his sons only (see v. 1). Notice should be made of the fact that the order of the addressees is Aaron, his sons and *all the Israelites*, and that the first two are arranged chiastically in reference to vv. 1–15 ('to the priests') and vv. 16–23 ('to Aaron'). Therefore it is more than likely that this verse refers to the preceding chapters as well. Yet, while the address formula of 19:1–2 ('all the community of Israel') or 18:1–2 ('the Israelites') may be the point of reference, exactly the same formula appears at 17:1–2. It is possible, then, that Moses spoke all the laws in chs. 17 – 21 to Aaron and his sons, and to all the people of Israel (see 'Comment' on 16:34). The reason why the statement comes at this point and not at the end of the next chapter, which forms a thematic whole with this chapter, is uncertain.

Explanation

Chs. 19 – 20 have shown that holiness is a condition of the human heart. Thus if it can be expressed by various visible objects such as offerings and sanctuaries, the latter ought to be seen as representations of the human heart: unselfishness, and not as something that bears specific characteristics independent of human beings. This assumption is vital in interpreting the various rules in this and the following chapters. Though ch. 21 addresses itself to the priests, the message indirectly applies to the laity as well, in so far as it addresses the essence of holiness. Conversely the observance of the laws pertaining to holiness in chs. 18 – 20, which were addressed to the laity, are demanded to a higher degree in this chapter by the outward institutions for the priests.

The areas that constitute the toughest hurdle for holiness lie within the family and marriage, where the human soul is most defiled, although this does not appear to be commonly perceived as such. This manifests itself typically when one of the family members dies. The prohibition against grief is a measure of whether the priest has involved himself with the egocentric nature of the dead. What is commanded of the chief priest is also commanded of the laity, as stated above. In order for people to observe the rule on grief they have to believe in the continuity of personhood even after death.

After receiving judgment through the prophet Nathan, David pleads for the sparing of his coming child. But once he knows this is impossible, he stops praying. His attitude evinces his total entrustment of everything to the Lord, and thus shows his attitude towards death, not just on this occasion but also at other times (2 Sam. 12:15–23).

As in chs. 10, 19 – 20, there is a tremendous gap between the rules themselves and the call to holiness, or holiness itself. For example, the prohibition against grieving the death of parents in this chapter appears inhuman for egocentric humans, even though the opposite is the case. To be holy means to love one's neighbour as oneself. But a common and serious misunderstanding is the view that one ought to involve oneself with a neighbour's inner life in order to love him. This is a serious misunderstanding derived from humanism. It is only through experiencing an inability to observe the Lord's commandments that one begins the road to inner holiness.

New Testament implications

In the NT Jesus said, 'Who is my mother, and who are my brothers?' (Matt. 12:48 ESV, NIV; Mark 3:33–34), and averred that his mother and brothers are those who hear the word of God and do it (Luke 8:21). On the other hand, Jesus' concern for his mother Mary should not be underestimated (John 19:25–27). St Paul and St Peter take pains to divert the attention of the married couple to the Lord first (1 Cor. 7; 1 Pet. 3:1–7); a husband's love for his wife should reflect what Christ showed to his church. That is, while self-sacrificing, Christ did not involve himself with the inner matters of various individuals (cf. John 2:24–25). When Lazarus died, it was probably the bystanders' *unbelief in the resurrection* that resulted in Jesus' weeping (John 11:33).

In the NT all believers are expected to be holy, just like the holy priests (1 Pet. 2:5). This presumes the breakdown of the selfish nature in a person's life, which is something like what occurred in Rom. 7:14–24 in the heart of St Paul. Thus sanctification begins with the uncovering of one's whole being, particularly one's egoistic and idolatrous heart and soul. It lies not so much in repenting from and rectifying certain acts, as in uncovering and exposing one's evil innermost part to the Lord. In Levitical terminology, cleanness can be achieved by such a process. But holiness is a condition of the heart as well, and it demands a total breakdown of selfishness, not just a temporary uncovering or confession of one's miserable inner situation. The ultimate key to sanctification is to maintain, as Job did (cf. 13:14), honesty and sincerity to the extent that one admits facts about oneself, even words of admonition hard to hear. The Holy Spirit works in and through such a condition of the human heart.

LEVITICUS 22:1–33

Translation

[1]And the LORD spoke to Moses, saying, [2]'Speak to Aaron and his sons so that they abstain from the holy things of the Israelites, which they dedicate to me, so they do not profane my holy name: I am the LORD. [3]Say to them, If any one of all your offspring throughout your generations approaches the holy things that the Israelites dedicate to the LORD, while he has uncleanness, that person shall be cut off from my presence: I am the LORD. [4]None of the offspring of Aaron who has a leprous disease or a discharge may eat of the holy things until he is clean. Whoever touches anyone who is unclean through contact with a soul or a man who has had an emission of semen, [5]and whoever touches a swarming thing by which he may be made unclean or a man from whom he may take uncleanness, whatever his uncleanness may be – [6]the soul who touches such a thing shall be unclean until the evening and shall not eat of the holy things unless he has bathed his body in water. [7]When the sun goes down he shall be clean, and afterwards he may eat of the holy things, because they are his food. [8]He shall not eat what dies of itself or is torn by beasts, and so make himself unclean by it: I am the LORD. [9]They shall therefore keep my charge, lest they bear their punishment on account of it and die, when they profane it: I am the LORD who sanctifies them.

[10]'A lay person shall not eat of a holy thing; no foreign guest of the priest or hired servant shall eat of a holy thing, [11]but if a priest buys a soul as his property for money, the slave may eat of it, and anyone born in his house may eat of his food. [12]If a priest's daughter marries a lay person, she shall not eat of the contribution of the holy things. [13]But if a priest's daughter is widowed or divorced and has no child and returns to her father's house, as in her youth, she may eat of her father's food; yet no lay person shall eat of it. [14]If anyone eats of a holy thing unintentionally, he shall add the fifth of its value to it and give the holy thing to the priest. [15]They shall not profane the holy things of the Israelites, which they contribute to the LORD, [16]and so cause them to bear punishment for the guilt, by eating their holy things: for I am the LORD who sanctifies them.'

[17]And the LORD spoke to Moses, saying, [18]'Speak to Aaron and his sons and all the Israelites and say to them, When any one of the house of Israel or of the sojourners in Israel presents a burnt offering as his offering, for any of their vows or freewill offerings that they offer to the LORD, [19]if it is to be accepted for you it shall be a male without blemish, of the bulls or the sheep or the goats. [20]You shall not offer anything that has a blemish, for it will not be acceptable for you. [21]And when anyone offers a sacrifice of fellowship offerings to the LORD to fulfil a vow or as a freewill offering from the herd or from the flock, to be accepted it must be perfect; there shall be no blemish in it. [22]Animals blind or disabled or mutilated or having a wart or a festering rash or scabs you shall not offer to the LORD or give them to the LORD as an offering for annihilation on the altar. [23]You may present a bull or a lamb that has a part too long or too short for a freewill offering, but for a vow offering it cannot be accepted. [24]Any animal that has its testicles bruised or crushed or torn or

cut you shall not offer to the LORD; you shall not do it within your land, [25]neither shall you offer as the food of your God any such animals gotten from a foreigner. Since there is mutilation, i.e. blemish in them, they will not be accepted for you.'
[26]And the LORD spoke to Moses, saying, [27]'When an ox or sheep or goat is born, it shall remain seven days with its mother, and from the eighth day on it shall be acceptable as an offering for annihilation to the LORD. [28]But you shall not slaughter an ox or a sheep and her young in one day. [29]And when you sacrifice a sacrifice of thanksgiving to the LORD, you shall sacrifice it so that you may be accepted. [30]It shall be eaten on the same day; you shall leave none of it until morning: I am the LORD. [31]So you shall keep my commandments and do them: I am the LORD. [32]And you shall not profane my holy name, that I may be sanctified among the Israelites. I am the LORD who sanctifies you, [33]who brought you out of the land of Egypt to be your God: I am the LORD.'

Notes on the text

3a. 'any one of all your offspring': *kol 'îš – zar'ăkem* The syntactic construction is the same as in 1:2a.

Modern translations have obscured the three terms *'îš*, *nepeš* and *'ādām* used here and in the following verses, vv. 4–6. But the text clearly differentiates them (see 'Comment').

4b. 'anyone who is unclean through contact with a soul': *ṭěmē' nepeš* The majority of Eng. translations take the phrase as referring to things. This view is also connected with the unanimous interpretation of *nepeš* to mean 'a corpse'. However, it has been argued it means 'a soul' (see 'Comment' on 21:1, 11). As Hag. 2:13 shows, it probably refers to humans. It refers to any person whether dead or alive, who has an egocentric nature. The idea is expressed frequently by the form *ṭāmē' lěnepeš* (Num. 5:2; 9:6–7; 9:10).

9. 'keep my charge': *šāměrû 'et mišmartî* For this phrase, see Lev. 8:35; 18:30.

'profane it': *yiḥallělûhû* It is questionable what 'it' refers to. It should refer to the same referent as the 3rd person sg. pronominal suffixes in the preceding *'ālāyw* and *bô*. The only possibility is that it refers to *laḥămô* (his bread) in v. 7.

'bear their punishment for it': *yiś'û 'ālāyw ḥēṭ'* For this phrase, see Lev. 19:17; 20:20; 24:15; Num. 9:13; 18:22, 32; Isa. 53:12. The meaning of *'al* is 'on account of', as in 19:17. Cf. Gen. 20:3.

sanctifies them: *měqadděšām* Milgrom takes 'them' as referring to 'priests' and not 'holy offerings' on the ground that 'the referent is the plural subjects of all the verbs in this verse' (Milgrom 2000a: 1860). I prefer to take it as referring to the 'holy offerings', because the major theme in vv. 2–9 is the offerings, and 'I am the Lord who sanctifies' is spoken on a level different from that of v. 9a.

10. From this verse, the term *tôšāb* (a guest) occurs frequently, often in conjunction with *śākîr* (a hired servant). See 25:6, 23, 35, 40, 45, 47.

11. 'a soul': *nepeš* Some Eng. translations render it 'a person' (JPS), 'a slave' (ESV, NIV), 'anyone' (NRSV). However, the idea of buying a *nepeš* is unique in the OT, and something more than 'a person' or 'a slave' seems intended.

12. 'a lay person': *zār* This term first appears in Exod. 29:33, and as is the case there, this term means 'an outsider', practically 'a lay person'.

16. *'ăwôn 'ašmâ* The latter term *'ašmâ* occurs elsewhere in Lev. at 4:3, 6:5, 7[5:24, 26], and is synonymous with *'āwôn* (cf. Ezra 9:6–7, 13). Clearly the punitive side of guilt is at issue, so 'punishment for the guilt' is proposed as the translation. See 'Comment'.

22. 'disabled': *šābûr* If a living creature is said to be 'broken', this means the animal is nearly or actually dead (cf. 1 Kgs 13:26, 28).

'mutilated': *ḥārûṣ* This term is a hapax legomenon, and may derive from *ḥrṣ* (to make an incision). See *HALOT* s.v.

'a wart': *yabbelet* The derivation is uncertain. *HALOT* lists Akk. *ublu* (wart), as taken by LXX.

'a festering rash': *gārāb* Elsewhere this term appears in Lev. 21:20 and Deut. 28:27. *HALOT* renders it 'a festering rash'.

'scabs': *yallepet* This term occurs here and 21:20.

25. Most English versions supplement verbs like 'gotten' (ESV) or 'accept' (JPS, NIV) for 'from the hand of a foreigner'.

Form and structure

Lev. 22 provides rules intended to preserve the holiness of the Israelite offerings to the Lord. Warnings directed at the priests begin the chapter because it is they who directly handle the offerings and can potentially desecrate the holy name (vv. 1–16). After this, rules governing the very quality of the offerings are addressed not only to the priests but also to the Israelites, since the latter will select what animals are presented before the Lord. It is stressed that the animals must be without blemish (vv. 17–30). In the last section the Lord restricts his address to Moses, the one who installed the priesthood. He gives him some additional qualifications for sacrificial animals (vv. 26–33) and apparently rounds out a major part of the divine–human relationship, referring to his initial purpose in installing the priesthood and sanctuary worship. In addition to this, he concludes with a warning against desecrating the holy God who brought the people out of the land of Egypt (vv. 31–33).

For the structure of chs. 21 – 22, see 'Form and structure' on ch. 21.

The chapter as a whole is divisible into three parts, each of which is addressed to different addressees: A. vv. 1–16 (Aaron and his sons), B. vv.

17–25 (Aaron and his sons, and the Israelites) and C. vv. 26–33 (Moses). The chapter can be outlined as follows.

A. 1–16	Warnings against desecrating priestly food
B. 17–25	Rules pertaining to the sacrificial use of animals (votive and freewill offerings)
C. 26–33	Further basic rules on the sacrificial use of animals (thanksgiving sacrifice, 27–30), and a final warning and exhortation to observe the laws (31–33)

Section A deals with how priests ought to handle the offerings, B presents defects that disqualify an animal from sacrificial use and describes how acceptable animals ought to be offered to the Lord, and C deals with what must characterize a sacrificial animal from the time of its birth to its being offered on the altar.

The way in which the rules are presented is inconsistent across the three sections. In A the principle is stated in two stages (vv. 2ab and 3). It is followed by a section beginning with *'îš 'îš*. Though *'îš 'ăšer* (v. 5) and *'îš kî* (v. 14) appear, they merely serve to delineate the new subsections. In section B *'îš 'îš* in v. 18 and *'îš kî* in v. 21 correspond to the burnt and fellowship offerings respectively. The rules in C are interconnected, at least formally, by an association of words and ideas, such as *šôr* (vv. 27–28), *rṣḥ* (vv. 27, 29) and 'in one day' versus 'on that day' (vv. 28, 30).

Despite the lack of any formal demarcation within each section, the chapter unmistakably indicates a consistent warning on desecrating the holy offerings and, as a consequence, the Lord's name (vv. 2ab, 9, 15–16, 32–33).

Comment

22:1–9

The Lord's concern regarding the possible desecration of the holy offerings is outlined in several stages, from general to particular.

First, the priests should exercise the utmost caution in handling the offerings the Israelites offer to the Lord, so they may not profane the holy name (v. 2). The priest has the potential to destroy not only the offerer's self-dedication but also the Lord's holy name. In Leviticus *nzr* hiph. appears in 15:31, where the Lord commands Moses and Aaron (15:1) to make the Israelites abstain from their uncleanness lest they die by defiling the Lord's abode. Here it is the priests who are to abstain (*nzr* ni.) from the holy offerings the people offer the Lord. If the people abstain from uncleanness and present their offerings, the mediating priest can undermine the very act of offering sacrifices by profaning them.

Second, the cause of potential desecration lies in the potential uncleanness of the priest (v. 3). The punishment for such desecration is the cutting off of the soul of the defiled priest from the Lord's presence. Up till now, the penalty is stated in such a way that a person will be cut off *from his people*. This suggests that 'to be cut off *from his people*' has not been a stereotyped phrase, and that 'to be cut off *from the Lord's presence*' is used here because of the priest's higher standing and responsibility before the Lord. As already argued, uncleanness symbolizes the state of hiding oneself, so if the priest becomes defiled, this indicates that he has hidden himself from the Lord. Thus the *kāret* penalty is a natural consequence of his defilement.

Third, what the uncleanness is, and how it ought to be handled, is the theme of vv. 4–9, which continues up to v. 14. V. 4 begins with *'îš 'îš* (any one), and introduces a new subsection spanning from v. 4 to v. 8, which explains what the uncleanness in v. 3 refers to. In distinction to v. 3, where only the priest who officiates with holy offerings is at issue, this subsection has a wider group of people in view: all the priests, even those who do not officiate, as indicated by the phrase 'the offspring of Aaron' (cf. 21:17, 21).

Sacrificial animals constitute an important food source for the priests but since the former are holy, there are naturally restrictions relating to how these animals are to be eaten, and the violation of such restrictions is punishable by death (see below). The principle governing the rules in vv. 4–7 is that any offspring of Aaron cannot eat sacrificial meat unless he or she is clean. The sources of defilement include leprosy, various discharges, contact with unclean people, and contact with swarming creatures. When Aaron's offspring become defiled in any of these ways, they cannot eat a holy sacrifice until after they have washed their body with water and waited until evening. Although the observance of these rules may appear easy, the opposite would seem to be true considering that it would seem impossible to know if a particular person had had an emission of semen, or some other kind of discharge. Likewise could the priests always be sure they had not unwittingly come into contact with an unclean creature? Whether a priest's uncleanness is inadvertent or not, the rules say he cannot eat any holy offerings until he becomes clean.

The symbolic dimension of uncleanness, not taken into account previously, makes it harder for the priest to observe these rules. The occurrence of *nepeš* at v. 4 (*ṭĕmē' nepeš*) and v. 6 (*nepeš kî*) suggests that the Lord is preoccupied with the inner cleanness of the priest. As 21:1–15 has shown, the defilement is that of the human soul, not 'cultic' defilement. Uncleanness symbolically refers to the state of hiding oneself (See 'Explanation', 'Nature of the regulation', on ch. 11). Given these postulates, it is imperative the priest examines whether he is hiding himself from the Lord. Without such rigorous introspection or self-examination the priest will be punished by either the death or *kāret* penalties. Practically if the priest is aware of his own defilement, namely self-hiding, he must follow the prescription in ch. 4; if he is unaware of it, he will be cut off from the Lord's presence. For the idea of sanctification, see 'Comment' on 20:8.

The prohibition against eating either what is killed by another animal or dies of natural causes was previously mentioned in 11:40 and 17:15. Purificatory rites, namely the washing of clothes, bathing in water and waiting until evening, are not mentioned as they were in 17:15b. The priests must receive their sustenance from the sacrificial animals as far as meat is concerned. The violation of the rules in vv. 4–8 constitutes an offence of desecration and is punishable by death (v. 9). In v. 3, however, the *kāret* penalty is prescribed for desecration. Since v. 3 is a general principle for the following details, it follows that the offender receives both penalties. Although this punishment appears greater in its severity than that prescribed in cases for the laity, there is no substantial difference. As for the priests here, when the laity become unclean, they wash their clothes or bodies, and wait until evening. Moreover the imposition of the death penalty upon the priest who violates the Lord's command in Leviticus 22 complements the stipulation of the same punishment for the laity in 15:31. Thus the difference between the priests and the laity simply reflects that the priests have more opportunities to eat holy offerings and, consequently, more chances of desecrating the holy name.

What consequences are associated with the failure of a priest to undergo self-examination? Later, OT prophets condemned the priests of each generation for the offences they committed before the Lord. For example, the avarice and greed of the priestly family are narrated in 1 Sam. 2:12–13. In particular the core problem of Eli's house appears to be that Eli the chief priest could not reprove his two sons, Hophni and Phinehas, who had rampantly ignored the ritual procedure and thus the Lord himself (1 Sam. 2:29), which led to the destruction of the temple at Shiloh (1 Sam. 2:30; 3:11–13). The prophetic critique of the priests' selfishness and greed suggests that the self-hiding of the latter also played a part in bringing about the Babylonian exile (Jer. 5:31; 6:13; 23:11; Ezek. 22:26; 44:10–13).

22:10–16

This section applies various restrictions for eating the holy offerings to those who are not priests: a guest of a priest, a hired servant, a slave of a priest, one who was born in a priest's house, and the daughter of a priest. With the exception of a purchased slave and a person born in the priest's house, all of these people are called 'the unauthorized' (*zār*). Vv. 14–16 warn the laity and the priests, particularly the latter, against desecrating the holy offerings; thereby causing the guilt to fall upon the offerers.

Vv. 10–14 stipulate rules for eating holy meat: on principle unauthorized people cannot eat it (v. 10a). After this follow cases concerning people who have personal contact with a priest in ascending degrees of intimacy: a guest or a hired man of the priest (v. 10b), a person purchased by the priest or born into the priest's house (v. 11), and the daughter of a priest (vv. 12–13). Of these only those who are regarded as belonging to the priest can partake in the eating of the holy meat. The case of a priest purchasing a *nepeš* (a soul) does not necessarily mean the purchased one becomes a slave, as is commonly interpreted, though such a possibility is not precluded. Rather the act of purchasing a soul implies affection on the part of the priest (cf. Exod. 12:44). Also those born in a priest's house can eat the meat the priest eats even if they no longer live in the same house. Such an expansion of the scope of those authorized to sit at the priestly table reflects the Lord's initial desire that the people of Israel may become the 'kingdom of priests' and 'holy nation' described in Exod. 19:6.

However, when the daughter of a priest marries a lay person, which appears permissible, she is no longer regarded as belonging to her father's house and can no longer eat the holy meat (v. 12). A compassionate provision is made for the daughter in v. 13: if she is left alone without offspring for whatever reason, and has no means of living, then she should return to her father's house and may eat the holy meat until her death. Nevertheless, despite the provision's compassionate nature, it probably does not allow her to remarry. This is inferred from the fact that a divorced woman cannot marry a priest (21:7), and that childlessness is a sign of the divine curse (cf. 20:20–21). Thus this measure is a maximal compromise of the Lord that apparently aims at keeping the extent of defilement to a minimum (cf. 19:29; 21:9). V. 13b forms an inclusio with v. 10a, both of which state the principle that no outsider can eat the holy meat.

V. 14 adds the potential case where someone who is not a priest has inadvertently eaten holy meat. On such an occasion compensation is made by adding one-fifth of the offering's value and giving the total of six-fifths as a substitute to the priest. If a person commits this offence, breaking faith with the Lord, then he must present a reparation offering (5:14–16). On the surface this case resembles the case of 5:15–16, but the chief difference lies in that here the inadvertent eating (*'ākal bišěgāgâ*) of a sacrifice is at issue, whereas the case in 5:15–16 addressed itself to a person's inner attitude to the holy offerings as a whole (*ma'al, ḥāṭā' bišěgāgâ*; see 'Comment' there).

Vv. 15–16 warn the priests against desecrating the holy offerings offered by the Israelites; thereby imputing the very punishment of the guilt the offering bears to the offerers who eat them. These verses underscore the principle in v. 2. *'Ăwōn 'ăšmâ* means 'the punishment of realizing guilt': 'punishment of guilt' (cf. 4:2). Though the offering is meant to bear the punishment, the punishment is returned to the offerer when the offering is desecrated.

The failure of the priests in this regard results not only in the offering of sacrificial animals being done in vain, but also in the offerer bearing his own guilt. In the last statement 'I am the one who sanctifies them' it is questionable who 'them' refers to. Against Hoffmann, who takes it as a reference to 'the sacred donations', Milgrom suggests it refers to 'the priests', as he does for v. 9 (2000a: 1870; see 'Notes on the text' on v. 9). However, as in v. 9 the Lord directs his warning against the priests, so it is unlikely the Lord here intends to protect them against profaning the offerings the Israelites offer. If 'them' refers to the holy offerings, it is also likely the object of the Lord's sanctification includes the offerers as well, as an offering symbolizes its offerer. Thus the passage says it is the Lord who sanctifies the offerings offered by the Israelites, and therefore the priest should not impede this process.

Therefore whether an offering is properly offered to the Lord depends ultimately on a priest's perfect preparation of his own heart. In view of these restrictions on the priest's condition, both external and internal, one may wonder if it is possible for a priest to handle the offerings of the laity properly.

22:17–25

In this section the Lord addresses himself not just to Aaron and his sons but also to the Israelites, and stipulates rules on holy offerings, specifically focusing on the burnt (17–20) and fellowship (21–30) offerings. Regulations are provided for these offerings because they are the most common for the Israelites, and the holiness of the offerings ought to be guaranteed at the first stage of offering, even before the offerer comes to the sanctuary. The Lord addresses the priests because it is they who supervise everything relating to sacrifices. The principle governing all these cases is that any sacrifice, except for the free-will offering, should be unblemished.

18. That the burnt offering ought to be without blemish is already stated in 1:3. This is the first time the reader is informed of two motivations for offering the burnt offering: votive or free will. Ch. 1 confirmed that the sacrifice represents its offerer, so the sacrifice without a blemish represents the condition of the offerer's heart.

19–20. This is the apodosis of v. 18b and its main point. A burnt offering should be offered in such a way that the offerer may be accepted (*lirṣōnĕkem*); the animal ought to be without blemish, must be a male taken from the cattle, sheep or goats (cf. 1:3, 10), and must take the place of the offerer (1:4). Thus when an offering is not accepted, neither is the offerer. The same applies to the fellowship offering (v. 21). The nature of the blemish is explained in v. 22 below.

21–25. Basically there should be no blemish in the animal for the fellowship offering, though a minor blemish is permitted in the case of a free-will offering (v. 23). The list of blemishes is detailed in vv. 22 and 24. These outline what blemishes disqualify an animal for the fellowship and burnt offerings (vv. 18b–20). It is something like 'blind', 'mutilated', 'having a wart or a festering rash' or scabs. Significantly two of these symptoms, *gārāb* (a festering rash) and *yallepet* (scabs), appear among the defects that disqualify priests from offering the people's offerings (21:20). Moreover, taking the root *šbr* into account, the disabled animal may be likened to a person with an injured leg or hand (21:19).

Since a sacrificial animal represents the offerer, or, more precisely, his heart, the outer defects tacitly point to the spiritual side of the offering: the offerer's heart. His heart ought to be without blemish, completely honest and sincere.

The mention of two inner motives for bringing the offering reflects the following circumstance (cf. 'Comment' on 7:15–16).

In the votive offering and thanksgiving sacrifice (see v. 29 below) the offerer has already received a blessing/salvation; the former, one-sidedly, and the latter, as a response to a worshipper's prayer. In other words, the *holy* Lord has unilaterally involved himself with the worshipper in the case of the thanksgiving sacrifice, while he responded to the worshipper's prayer in the case of the votive offering. In both cases, in response to the Lord's holy will the offerer has to present himself in a holy way by offering a sacrifice without blemish; otherwise he may profane the Lord's holiness. On the other hand, in the free-will offering, the initiative comes from the offerer himself. By stipulating that the sacrifice in this case can afford to be defective to some extent, the Lord shows his general estimation that the human will towards God is defective at best.

A rather prolonged legislation on defects that disqualify animals from sacrificial use (vv. 22–25) reflects that the Israelites were entirely capable of contemplating using such animals as their offerings. This reflects the offerer's potentially mean spirit. Note that the phrase 'the food of your God', frequent in ch. 21, occurs only here in this chapter. It is incredible that a defective animal is bought or accepted from a foreigner and offered to the Lord as his food, when the latter is envisaged as the host (cf. Mal. 1:8–14). If such should not happen even among human beings, what would be the consequence if it were done to the Lord?

These rules on disqualifying physical defects presume the condition of animals offered to the Lord reflects the condition of the offerer's heart. Later in the prophetic literature, the Lord uses various prophets to indict the Israelites for the hypocritical attitudes they held towards him, often pointing out their heartless offering of sacrifices (e.g. Isa. 1:11–12; Jer. 6:20; 7:21–22). However, it is important to observe that the Israelites for their part did not recognize in themselves what the prophets criticized them for. Ultimately both the physical quality of the sacrifices and the proper execution of their sacrificial procedures mirrored the inner attitude of the offerer.

22:26–33

This section is addressed to Moses alone, though it comprises rules that relate to the Israelites. This reflects that the rules are concerned with the very foundation of the holy things for which Moses is responsible (cf. 5:14; 6:1[5:20]). This leads to the restatement of the rule concerning the consumption of the remaining flesh of the thanksgiving sacrifice (vv. 29–30), which is omitted in the preceding rules of vv. 18–25. Vv. 31–33 summarize the command of chs. 21 – 22. They look back to the initial purpose of the priesthood.

While the meanings and sequence of the rules in vv. 27–28 and vv. 29–30 are somewhat difficult to understand, this task is made easier when the symbolic meaning of the offering is kept in mind.

27. A kid is to remain with its mother for seven days after its birth, only becoming fit for an offering for annihilation to the Lord from the eighth day onwards (see 'Notes on the text' on 1:9). Although the number 8 marks a new start on various occasions (9:1; 12:3; 14:10 etc.), contextually it is preferable to assume that the world of the sacrificial animal is likened to the human world; thus to the circumcision of a human baby (12:2–3). More importantly, as circumcision symbolizes the uncovering of oneself in a spiritual sense, the lawgiver apparently conveys the message that the offerer ought to have uncovered himself before expressing the annihilation of his egocentric nature.

28. Slaughtering is the first major thing done to a sacrificial animal. Slaughtering both an animal and her offspring on the same day is prohibited. The kid may be either male or female. Referring to similar prohibitions against boiling a kid in its mother's milk (Exod. 23:19; 34:26; Deut. 14:21) or taking a bird and its egg (Deut. 22:6–7), exegetes have proposed that the prohibition seeks to preserve life; i.e. 'avoiding wanton destruction of God's given creation' (Wenham 1979: 296). However, this view appears to be slightly out of context.

Exegetically it is noteworthy that the slaughtering (v. 28) and offering of an animal to the Lord (v. 28) are already included in v. 27. Thus the theme of a kid and its mother in v. 27 partly overlaps with a parent and his or her male kid in v. 28.

Since I have already demonstrated that a parallel is drawn between the sacrifice and the offerer, the prohibition against slaughtering the kid *on the same* day should be compared with the human world here too. It probably expresses a cruel form of annihilation (on divine punishment, see 1 Sam. 2:34; Isa. 9:14[13]; 10:17; 47:9; Zech. 3:9. On the human realm, see Gen. 27:45; Esth. 3:13). Sacrificial animals have their own parental–filial relationship, and are destined to be sacrificed for the human egocentric nature. A tender and considerate attitude towards the animals would be a natural and necessary attitude on the part of the offerer (see 'Comment' on 1:5).

29–30. The Lord then introduces the topic of the thanksgiving sacrifice. By way of an association of ideas, two contrasts may be drawn between v. 28 and this verse. First, 'one day' in v. 28 is contrasted with 'do not leave until morning' in this verse. Second, rather than annihilating the animals on the same day, the offerer's egocentric nature ought to be annihilated on the same day an animal is slaughtered. As commented on 7:15–16, the prohibition against leaving the flesh until morning is founded on the rationale that the offerer's selfishness ought not to desecrate the holy offering.

Therefore the introduction of the matter of the thanksgiving sacrifice at this point is appropriate, since the other kinds of fellowship offering, namely the votive offering and free-will offering, whose permitted period of eating is longer, are already mentioned in vv. 21–25.

31. The exhortation to observe the Lord's commandments (*miṣwôt*) has in view at least all the rules in chs. 21 – 22. But even more than these rules may be intended. Though this verse resembles the exhortations of 19:37 and 20:8, 22, the combination of *šāmar* (keep) and *miṣwôt* occurs only twice in Leviticus, both here and in 26:3. Since *miṣwôt* encompasses both *ḥuqqîm* and *mišpāṭîm* (cf. 'Comment' on 4:2), it is entirely possible that v. 31 has in view all the commandments given in Leviticus up until this point.

32. The Lord's fundamental concern regarding holiness is again underscored by a warning and the exhortation he delivers to Moses, the priests and the laity. It is expressed, first, by the prohibition against desecrating the Lord's name, which resumes v. 2ab, followed by a statement of the result of not desecrating it; namely the Lord's sanctification among the Israelites.

'that I may be sanctified': *wĕniqdaštî* Here the Lord alludes to his initial statement of the purpose concerning sanctuary worship in Exod. 29:45–46, the major protagonists of which are the priests. The *qdš* ni. appears just three times in Exodus–Leviticus (Exod. 29:43; Lev. 10:3; 22:32). The purpose of the Lord's self-identification and sanctification in Exod. 29:43 is mentioned; i.e. the priests are to become like the God of the Israelites (vv. 45–46). Moreover the idea of the purpose clause in Lev. 22:33 'to be your God' is very similar to the same idea in Exod. 29:45. Undoubtedly Lev. 22:32 refers to that passage.

In vv. 31b–32 the Lord presents himself as the one who sanctifies the Israelites and who has brought them out of Egypt to become their God. For the meaning of *qiddēš*, see 'Comment' on 20:8 and 'Explanation'. The idea of 'bringing up the Israelites from Egypt' has appeared in 11:45 and 19:36, so from a structural point of view the addition of 'to be your God' in 22:33 indicates those passages adumbrate this last section of ch. 22. In a word, this last section of ch. 22 rounds out the details of sanctuary worship in Leviticus up to this point.

However, the Israelites ought to observe the Lord's commandments to become holy and to have him within their midst. In so far as the Shekinah is contingent upon their obedience to the Lord's commandments, the Israelites' holiness, both inner and outer, must be seen as yet unattained.

Explanation

While there are similarities between the priests and the holy offerings in that both are related to holiness, a significant difference exists between them. Priests are made holy by anointment and they are called to engage in the Lord's work (8:12, 30). But priests are never called 'holy' (*qādôš*), except in 21:7. Rather they sometimes hide themselves against the Lord (4:3–12). In fact, in ch. 21 they are exhorted to become holy (vv. 8, 15, 23). This is in conformity with my assumption that the holiness they acquired in the ordination ceremony is outer holiness. Therefore the priests are expected to behave in a way that befits their outer holiness. The content of becoming holy is elucidated from ch. 11 up to ch. 21 in various ways. By contrast, offerings are always conceived as holy. The two major obstacles to offering a sacrifice so that it will be acceptable are the priests and the offerer. An offering's holy status is dependent on the condition of the officiating priest and on those who eat its remaining portions. Further a serious problem, whether or not the offerer becomes substantially wholehearted, may separate the offerer from his sacrifice. Yet this chapter, setting aside this potential problem, first addresses the priestly responsibility for handling the offerings that the lay people have offered. They are required to bear inner holiness in handling the offerings.

In view of the stringent rules this chapter attaches to holy offerings, particularly the symbolic meaning of uncleanness, one wonders who can really offer a holy offering. And if it is possible, how can a holy offering be accepted by the Lord without its holiness becoming defiled and desecrated by the priests? Thus these chapters challenge both the priests and the laity extremely by warning them that if the offering is not accepted, both priest and offerer will bear their guilt, each in his own way. This challenge becomes more acute when account is taken of the spiritual aspect of the offerings: the offerer's heart ought to be without blemish, namely completely honest and sincere, and in offering a burnt offering or a fellowship offering, the offerer ought to yield himself to the Lord, completely destroying his selfishness.

Though the Law never states so much explicitly, the very presence of the egocentric nature within the priests and the offerer implies that no offering can be offered to the Lord in a holy condition, and no priest can truly mediate between the offerer and the Lord.

Thus the human heart that is tacitly assumed by the rules in this chapter appears to be in a hopeless situation before God. It is just at this point that the essence of the Lord's sanctification (*qiddēš*) lies. When people are confronted with their own egocentric nature, becoming dumfounded by a complete inability to observe the Lord's commandments, they have, paradoxically, begun on their way towards inner holiness.

New Testament implications

In the NT Christ became the unique and perfect offering to God by dying on the cross. It is demanded of those who believe in him (and confess they follow him) to die in a similar way; this is a death of the egocentric nature that allows the believer to become a holy offering to the Lord (Rom. 12:1). The holiness of Christ and his church is essentially not moral or ethical as is commonly suggested. When St Paul says in Eph. 5:27, 'so that he might present the church to himself in splendour, without spot or wrinkle or any such thing, that she might be holy and without blemish' (ESV), he refers to the wholeheartedness of the believers, rather than moral perfection, by alluding to the spotlessness of a sacrifice discussed in Lev. 22. That believers are holy means their 'flesh' is destroyed by the Holy Spirit. However, since this outcome is rarely realized among egocentric humans, who have a strong tendency to criticize others or themselves on an ethical dimension, St Paul often has to talk in terms that appear to have ethical or moral connotations (see 1 Tim. 3:1–13). In fact, his words oscillate between outer and inner holiness, depending on what the context is. But one should not equate outer holiness (the observance of commandments) with the essence of holiness, since the former aims to bring believers to realize their hopelessness. It is only by the Holy Spirit that human selfishness is destroyed, though he may use other humans or suffering to achieve this.

LEVITICUS 23:1–44

Translation

[1]The LORD spoke to Moses, saying, [2]'Speak to the people of Israel and say to them, These are the appointed meetings of the LORD that you shall proclaim as proclamations of holiness; these are my appointed meetings.

[3]'Six days shall work be done, but the seventh day is a sabbath of solemn rest, a proclamation of holiness. You shall do no work. It is a sabbath to the LORD in all your dwelling places.

[4]'These are the appointed meetings of the LORD, the proclamations of holiness, which you shall proclaim at the time appointed for them. [5]In the first month, on the fourteenth day of the month at twilight, is the LORD's Passover. [6]And on the fifteenth day of the same month is the Feast of Unleavened bread to the LORD; for seven days you shall eat unleavened bread. [7]On the first day you shall have a proclamation of holiness; you shall not do any ordinary work. [8]But you shall present an offering for annihilation to the LORD for seven days. On the seventh day is a proclamation of holiness; you shall not do any ordinary work.'

[9]The LORD spoke to Moses, saying, [10]'Speak to the people of Israel and say to them, When you come into the land that I give you and reap its harvest, you shall bring the first sheaf of your harvest to the priest, [11]and he shall wave the sheaf before

the LORD, so you may be accepted. On the day after the sabbath the priest shall wave it. [12]And on the day when you wave the sheaf, you shall offer a male lamb a year old without blemish as a burnt offering to the LORD. [13]And the loyalty offering with it shall be two-tenths of an ephah of fine flour mixed with oil, an offering for annihilation to the LORD with a soothing aroma, and the drink offering with it shall be of wine, a quarter of a hin. [14]And you shall eat neither bread nor grain parched or fresh until this same day, until you have brought the offering of your God: it is a statute forever throughout your generations in all your dwellings.

[15]'You shall count seven full weeks from the day after the sabbath, from the day that you brought the sheaf of the wave offering. [16]You shall count fifty days to the day after the seventh sabbath. Then you shall present a loyalty offering of new grain to the LORD. [17]You shall bring from your dwelling places two loaves of bread to be waved, made of two-tenths of an ephah. They shall be of fine flour, and they shall be baked with leaven, as first fruits to the LORD. [18]And you shall present with the bread seven lambs a year old without blemish, and one bull from the herd and two rams. They shall be a burnt offering to the LORD, with their loyalty offering and their drink offerings, an offering for annihilation with a soothing aroma to the LORD. [19]And you shall offer one male goat for a sin offering, and two male lambs a year old as a sacrifice of fellowship offerings. [20]And the priest shall wave them with the bread of the first fruits as a wave offering before the LORD, with the two lambs. They shall be holy to the LORD for the priest. [21]And you shall make proclamation on the same day. You shall hold a proclamation of holiness. You shall not do any ordinary work. It is a statute forever in all your dwelling places throughout your generations. [22]And when you reap the harvest of your land, you shall not reap your field right up to its edge, nor shall you gather the gleanings after your harvest. You shall leave them for the poor and for the sojourner: I am the LORD your God.'

[23]The LORD spoke to Moses, saying, [24]'Speak to the people of Israel, saying, In the seventh month, on the first day of the month, you shall observe a day of solemn rest, a memorial by a loud cry; it is a proclamation of holiness. [25]You shall not do any ordinary work, and you shall present an offering for annihilation to the LORD.'

[26]The LORD spoke to Moses, saying, [27]'Above all, on the tenth day of this seventh month is the Day of Atonement. It shall be for you a proclamation of holiness, and you shall afflict your souls and present an offering for annihilation to the LORD. [28]And you shall not do any work on that very day, for it is a Day of Atonement, to make propitiation for you before the LORD your God. [29]For any soul that is not afflicted on that very day shall be cut off from his people. [30]And any soul that does any work on that very day, that soul I will destroy from among his people. [31]You shall not do any work. It is a statute forever throughout your generations in all your dwelling places. [32]It shall be to you a sabbath of solemn rest, and you shall afflict your souls. On the ninth day of the month beginning at evening, from evening to evening shall you keep your sabbath.'

[33]The LORD spoke to Moses, saying, [34]'Speak to the people of Israel, saying, On the fifteenth day of this seventh month there shall be the Feast of Booths to the LORD to last seven days. [35]On the first day shall be a proclamation of holiness; you shall not do any ordinary work. [36]For seven days you shall present offerings for

annihilation to the LORD. On the eighth day you shall hold a proclamation of holiness and present an offering for annihilation to the LORD. It is a solemn assembly; you shall not do any ordinary work.

[37]'These are the appointed meetings of the LORD, which you shall proclaim as proclamations of holiness, for presenting to the LORD offerings for annihilation, burnt offerings and loyalty offerings, sacrifices and drink offerings, each on its proper day, [38]besides the LORD's sabbaths and besides your gifts and besides all your vow offerings and besides all your freewill offerings, which you give to the LORD.

[39]'Surely, on the fifteenth day of the seventh month, when you have gathered in the produce of the land, you shall celebrate the feast of the LORD seven days. On the first day shall be a solemn rest, and on the eighth day shall be a solemn rest. [40]And you shall take on the first day the fruit of splendid trees, branches of palm trees and boughs of leafy trees and willows of the brook, and you shall rejoice before the LORD your God seven days. [41]You shall celebrate it as a feast to the LORD for seven days in the year. It is a statute forever throughout your generations; you shall celebrate it in the seventh month. [42]You shall dwell in booths for seven days. All native Israelites shall dwell in booths, [43]that your generations may know that I made the people of Israel dwell in booths when I brought them out of the land of Egypt: I am the LORD your God.'

[44]Thus Moses declared to the people of Israel the appointed meetings of the LORD.

Notes on the text

2. 'the appointed meetings of the LORD': *môʿădê YHWH* The term *môʿēd* occurs forty-nine times in Leviticus and thus far it has appeared exclusively in the form of *'ōhel môʿēd* (the Tent of Meeting). This is the first time the term appears in conjunction with another term such as 'YHWH' in this book. Eng. translations render the phrase 'the fixed times of the LORD' (JPS), 'the appointed feasts of the LORD' (NIV, ESV), 'the appointed festivals of the LORD' (NRSV). However, 'time' seems to lose the nuance of 'an event', whereas 'feasts' or 'festivals' goes too far, though the occasions are ones of festivity or feasting. Moreover the latter idea may well be expressed by *ḥāg* (cf. 23:6, 34, 39, 41). Thus it appears more accurate and desirable to render the phrase 'the appointed meetings of the LORD'. See 'Comment'.

'proclamations of holiness': *miqrā'ê qōdeš* Commonly *miqrā'îm* is rendered 'convocations' (RSV, NRSV), 'assemblies' (NIV, ESV), 'occasions' (JPS), *Versammulungen* (Luther, Elberfelder), 'conventions' (Wenham 1979: 297, 301). Probably also LXX's *klētas* (cf. Wevers 1997: 365). *HALOT* also supplies 'assembly' as the basic meaning of the term. However, the term itself does not seem to have the nuance of 'gathering people' (see 'Comment'). Tg reads *miqrā'ê* in sg. both here and in v. 4.

3. 'be done': *teʿāśeh* LXX reads it as an active verb that corresponds to *ta'ăśeh*. Yet, considering the parallelistic balance it has with *ta'ăśû* in the same verse (LXX read it in sg.), MT is preferable.

'a sabbath of solemn rest': *šabbat šabbātôn* See 'Comment' on 16:31.

5. 'at twilight': *bēn hā'arbayim HALOT* gives the explanation 'lit. between the two evenings, i.e. the time between sunset and nightfall, the evening twilight'.

7. 'an ordinary work': *mĕle'ket 'ăbôdâ* In regard to the sabbath it is simply stated, 'Six days shall work be done' (v. 3). *Mĕlā'kâ* occurs alone in vv. 3, 28, 30–31, while *mĕlā'kâ* appears as part of a construct genitive chain with *'ăbôdâ* in vv. 7–8, 21, 25, 35–36. These two expressions are clearly differentiated. While the difference would appear to be minor, the facts that the mention of *mĕlā'kâ* alone concerns the rules pertaining to the sabbath and Day of Atonement, and that the *kāret* penalty is laid down for the violation of these rules, show that these occasions are viewed as more demanding in terms of the quality of work. Thus it appears that *mĕle'ket 'ăbôdâ* refers to a kind of work that is heavier than *mĕlā'kâ* alone.

8. 'an offering for annihilation': *'iššeh* LXX reads 'a burnt offering' instead, while Geniza MSS add 'a burnt offering'. Both, however, seem influenced by Num. 28:19.

10. 'sheaf': *'ōmer* SamP and TgJon add an article, thus making the term appositional to the following. LXX translates it 'handful' (*dragma*).

13. 'an offering for annihilation': *'iššeh* LXX adds 'to the LORD', which is, however, unnecessary, since *'iššeh* is preceded by 'to the LORD'.

19. 'a sacrifice of fellowship offerings': *zabaḥ šĕlāmîm* LXX adds 'with the bread of first fruits'. As the latter is mentioned in v. 20, this is unnecessary.

20. LXX adds 'it will be for him who offers them'. Cf. 7:8–9.

24. 'a memorial by a loud cry': *zikrôn tĕrû'â* The phrase is unique in the OT. *Tĕrû'â* means loud blasts. While the day was meant to be marked by the trumpet sound, it does not follow that *tĕrû'â* itself means 'loud blasts with a trumpet' as LXX (*salpingōn*) and all the modern translations render it. It simply means a loud cry (Josh. 6:5, 20; 1 Sam. 4:5–6), while, if the sound is that of a trumpet, either the term for a trumpet or the verb *tāqa'* (blow) occurs (cf. 25:9; Num. 10:5). Cf. 2 Sam. 6:15; Jer. 20:16; Ps. 27:6. Practically, however, it may well have included a blast of trumpets (cf. Ps. 81:1–3[2–4]). Basically the loud cry is one given by the Israelites. The semantic relationship between *zikrôn* (a memorial) and *tĕrû'â* (a loud cry) could be expressed as 'a memorial by a loud cry'.

25. Syr adds 'Speak to the sons of Israel, saying' after *lē'mōr*. But there is no need for this addition. See 'Comment'.

27. 'Above all': *'ak* The particle cannot be restrictive in sense. It emphasizes the following content. Basically so does *'ak* in v. 39.

36. 'a solemn rest': *'ăṣeret* This term is synonymous with *miqrā' qōdeš* (proclamation of holiness), but, as the root meaning ('restrain', 'withhold') suggests, it conveys a complete rest with the connotation of self-dedication to either the Lord or some other deity (cf. Deut. 16:8; 2 Kgs 10:20; Joel 1:14; Amos 5:21).

37. 'burnt offerings . . . and drink offerings': '*ôlâ uminḥâ zebaḥ unĕsākîm* LXX reads 'the burnt offerings and their sacrifices and their drink offerings' and leaves out *minḥâ*. The referents of the pronominal suffixes in LXX, which are not present in MT, are also unclear.

41. LXX does not translate 'You shall celebrate it as a feast to the LORD for seven days', probably due to the same 'for seven days' at the end of vv. 40 and 41. It is 'a case of parablepsis due to homoioteleuton' (Wevers 1997: 385).

Form and structure

From ch. 23 onwards holy *time*, as opposed to holy offerings and priests, becomes the major theme. The theme of holy time will be developed more fully in ch. 25 (see Introduction 4.1).

This chapter lists seven appointed meetings of the Lord, giving their dates and basic requirements. As Wenham observes (1979: 300), the formula 'I am the LORD your God' appears in vv. 22 and 43, and functions to divide the feasts as spring feasts (5–22) and autumn feasts (23–43). In grasping the structure of the chapter, two kinds of divine statements must be taken into account: the Lord's address to Moses in vv. 1–2, 9–10, 23–24, 33–34, and the statement 'These are the LORD's appointed meetings' in vv. 2, 4, 37. It is worth inquiring into the functions of these introductory words, for they do not always appear before every appointed meeting of the Lord. The structure of the chapter presented in terms of the two kinds of the introductory address is as follows:

A.	1–2	The Lord's address to Moses
	2	The Lord's appointed meetings etc.
		the weekly sabbath
	4	The Lord's appointed meetings etc.
		the Passover
B.	9–10	The Lord's address to Moses
		the Sheaf
		the Weeks
C.	23–24	The Lord's address to Moses
	25	the first day of the seventh month
D.	26	The Lord's address to Moses
	27–32	the Day of Atonement
E.	33–34	The Lord's address to Moses
	35–36	the Booths
	37–38	The Lord's appointed meetings etc.
	39–43	the Booths

The lengths of explanations given for each appointed meeting varies. The shorter abbreviated sections concern the weekly sabbath and the first day of the seventh month. The longer detailed sections concern the Sheaf, the Weeks, the Day of Atonement, and the Booths. Part of the reason for the presence of the longer detailed sections is that they provide prescriptions for the kinds of offerings and rituals undertaken on the occasions specified (see vv. 10–14, 15–22, 39–40). With the exception of the weekly sabbaths, every feast contains two common elements: first, the absence of ordinary work, and second, the command to make offerings for annihilation (*'iššeh*, 7–8, 25, 27–28, 35–36).

As regards the introductory address, 'The Lord's appointed meetings' etc., it appears three times in vv. 2, 4, 37. The one in vv. 2 and 37 is understandable, since the former heads a list of various appointed meetings and the latter summarizes all the preceding appointed meetings. However, the concluding one in v. 37, since it appears to refer to all of the feasts except for the weekly sabbath, practically sums up all six feasts (see 'Comment'). The one in v. 4 marks it off from the weekly sabbath and makes the Passover an independent occasion within A.

Closely related to the function of 'the Lord's appointed meetings' etc. is the function of 'the Lord's address to Moses'. The latter appears five times and functions as an overarching framework of 'the Lord's appointed meetings'. Thus in E, though its content is interrupted by the concluding statement in vv. 37–38, the two divided sections share a single theme. Similarly, in B, the two distinct but related occasions are subsumed under the same address. In this case the close relation in content of the two occasions requires only one address. In A, however, both the weekly sabbath and the Passover fall under the same address. The two occasions are closely related by the theological rationale that the weekly sabbath symbolizes salvation from bondage at the exodus.

Thus, according to 'the Lord's address to Moses', the entire chapter is divisible into five sections. However, according to 'the Lord's appointed meetings', it is divisible into seven sections. And if seen from the viewpoint of occasions, it can also be divided into seven occasions. Thus the two formulaic introductions together function to make the Lord's feasts seven, as well as showing the interrelatedness between the weekly sabbath and the Passover (A), between the Sheaf and the Weeks, and between abstinence and joy in E (see 'Comment').

Seen this way, these considerations indicate the two kinds of introductory address are used not arbitrarily, but deliberately with distinct functions.

While a detailed prescription of the kinds of offerings is given in B and E, it is remarkable that no mention is made of the offerings in A, C, D and E, with the exception of the apparently stereotyped *wĕhiqrabtem 'iššeh* (you shall offer the offering for annihilation to the Lord, vv. 8, 25, 27, 36). In this regard, scholars like Knohl and Milgrom assume that Lev. 23 depends on Num. 28 – 29, where detailed prescriptions on the offerings are given (e.g. Knohl 1995: 8–45; Milgrom 2001: 1979). But first of all, the very linking of Lev. 23 with Num. 28 – 29 in this way is problematical. An exhaustive analysis of these chapters goes beyond the scope of this commentary. Yet Num. 28 – 29 may have been composed in a situation different from that of Lev. 23 with a different purpose. Second, the position taken by Milgrom and Knohl assumes that the provision of the details concerning the *material* of the offerings was necessary in Lev. 23. A close examination of the phrase *hiqrîb 'iššeh* shows that it is used in a general sense of self-dedication (see 'Comment') and that therefore the materials of *'iššeh* are of secondary importance, at least in sections A, C, D and E. Indeed section B is unique among the seven sections in its provision of detailed rituals (including the material for the offerings) for the two occasions of the Sheaf and the Weeks. The reason for this is not that this feast comes for the first time in Exodus–Leviticus (cf. the feast of a loud cry in vv. 23–25), but in the nature of the feast, particularly the theological emphasis placed on the Lord's blessing and the people's responsibility in receiving it (see 'Comment'). That the section includes a ritual involving the priest as well as time suggests that the listing of various kinds of offerings is not by itself the major purpose of this section. Note that Num. 28 – 29 does not mention any ritual, let alone that for this feast.

All in all, the purpose of this chapter lies in presenting the Lord's appointed meetings throughout the year, their respective dates and basic requirement; namely self-dedication in the annihilation of one's egocentric nature.

Apart from the first section on the weekly sabbath, the other six sections relating to the Lord's appointed meetings is comparable with the six days of creation in Gen. 1 from literary and theological points of view. In Gen. 1, what is created on the third day (trees and grass) is, in content, brought to bear on the sixth day (as food for the living creatures). Similarly the third feast, namely the feast of Weeks, is related to the sixth feast, the feast of Booths, in that both feasts are characterized by joy (see 'Comment'). Another structural significance of the feasts is provided in 'Explanation'.

Comment

The stipulation concerning the weekly sabbath is followed by six feasts that begin with the Passover and end with the feast of Booths (for a general idea of festivals and feasts, see Amerding 2003: 300–313).

23:1–2

1–2. The Lord addresses himself to Moses and directs him to speak to the Israelites. The same or a similar address occurs in vv. 9–10a, 23–24,

33–34, while in v. 26 the Lord addresses Moses and does not command him to deliver the ensuing message. The reason for this is discussed below. Although five occurrences of the Lord's address appear too numerous to reflect a homogeneous theme, they are, together with another phrase 'the appointed meeting of the Lord', possibly intended to create seven occasions; thus alluding to God's creation in Gen. 1.

The phrase *mô'ădê YHWH* (the appointed meetings of the LORD) is significant, for the Lord expresses his willingness to *meet* with the Israelites on the specific occasions prescribed in what follows.

'proclamation of holiness': *miqrā'ê qōdeš* Though the term *miqrā'* occurs in the phrase *miqrā' qōdeš*, the latter is almost always followed by the injunction to rest from work (Exod. 12:16; Lev. 23:3, 7–8, 21, 24b–25, 35–36; Num. 28:18, 25–26; 29:1, 7, 12). These occurrences suggest it is unnecessary to infer that the term has something to do with 'a convocation' or any kind of 'gathering'. Num. 10:2 attests to either an infinitival use of *qārā'* (to call, proclaim) or its verbal noun, though in this case *miqrā'* is better rendered 'summon'. On the other hand, the presence of 'proclaim' in such phrases as *qārā' dĕrôr* (proclaim freedom, Lev. 25:10; Isa. 61:1; Jer. 34:8 etc.) suggests that *miqrā'* simply means 'a proclamation', and that *miqrā'ê qōdeš* means 'proclamations of holiness'. A negative implication of this proposal is that the Lord does not command a gathering of people, and that a visible gathering of people does not prove the people are holy.

V. 2aa first introduces a prolonged treatment of a topic taken up by *'elleh*, and the whole is so composed that the location of *mô'ēd* is arranged chiastically with *qr'*, thus:

Mô'ădê YHWH 'ăšer tiqrĕ'û miqrā'ê qōdeš
The appointed meetings of the Lord
that you shall proclaim as
proclamations of holiness
'Elleh hēm mô'ădāy
These are my appointed meetings.

The same literary feature is found in v. 4 below. It is remarkable that the appointed meetings of the Lord in the 3rd person are rephrased as '*my* appointed meetings'. Since the appointed meetings are *meetings*, 'my appointed meetings' naturally calls for the presence of those who are met by the Lord and who fulfil his requirement: holiness.

23:3 (sabbath)

The first appointed meeting mentioned is the weekly sabbath. The people should work for six days, but not on the seventh. It is assumed the institution is grounded in the Lord's creation of the universe (Gen. 2:1–3; Exod. 20:9–11). In Leviticus the term *šabbat* has appeared in 16:31 and 19:3, 30, and appears frequently from here onwards.

This commandment is important in that it provides the basis of the following festivals. The idea of *šabbat* is common to all.

First, the cessation from (ordinary) work is the most fundamental requirement of the weekly sabbath, and constitutes one of the two fundamental demands made for the other six holy feasts. While the general pattern in God's creation of six days' work followed by a seventh day of rest ought to be imitated, the work (*mĕlā'kâ*) of God is different from human work (*mĕlā'kâ*), particularly after the fall. In the wake of the first violation of God's commandment, the earth was cursed and human work became toilsome and laborious (Gen. 3:17–19). On the surface, the command to rest on the sabbath may appear easy to observe, yet human covetousness and greed make this very difficult. In particular, how can one be holy on the sabbath but not on the other six days? It is achieved by not doing any work at all. Moreover the sabbath is said to be 'to the Lord', which means the rest is not commanded in order to revitalize a person before the next week of work, let alone for the last six days. People's work must be forgotten: they must separate themselves from the work they have done in the previous six days and what they will do in the following six days. Can anyone achieve such rest?

By doing nothing, one can approach himself as he is. This is made difficult when one's mind is preoccupied with matters of work. In a word, 'doing no ordinary work' symbolizes the rejection and negation of one's selfishness and any concern about worldly affairs.

The phrase 'appointed meetings of the LORD' clearly indicates the Lord is willing to meet each individual of Israel on the condition that he or she ceases from doing work and makes a self-dedication. Since the Lord is holy, the people also must be holy when they meet him. This suggests holiness is found where there is an absence of preoccupation with one's own business.

As the phrase 'in all your dwelling places' (*bĕkol môšĕbōtêkem*; cf. 3:17; 7:26) indicates, the sabbath is thus the day on which the Lord is willing to meet the people, not by their going to the sanctuary, but in their own settlements.

However, despite the simplicity of the requirements it is easily surmised that it is impossible for the Israelites to cease from work to dedicate themselves as they are to the Lord only on the appointed occasions; if they cannot dedicate themselves in the days other than those appointed as festivals, then they are very unlikely to meet the requirements on the appointed days (see below) – for the condition of the human heart is unlikely to change just on those fixed days.

23:4–8 (Passover)

The first of what are commonly called 'festivals' is the Passover. It was presumably celebrated in early spring, between the end of May and the early part of April (see Exod. 23:15; 34:18). Three requirements are set out: (1) eating unleavened bread for a week, (2) a cessation from ordinary work, and (3) an offering for annihilation to the Lord. Points 1 and 2 are already mentioned in Exod. 12:15–16. These are intended for the people to remember their own salvation from slavery in Egypt. Element 3 is new. While it can be assumed that the people offer certain kinds of offering for annihilation to the Lord, it is questionable how their self-dedication is expressed. Is it expressed by doing something other than work, or is it the opposite of work cessation? The very rationale for the cessation of work suggests that self-dedication is a further stage of one's cessation from work, the essence of which is found not in doing something, but in self-examination and self-dedication (see below on the Day of Atonement).

The introductory 'These are the appointed times of the Lord' etc. sets this section on the Passover apart from the weekly sabbath in v. 3. Yet, on the other hand, since it is subsumed under the Lord's address to Moses in vv. 1–2, the meaning of the Passover must be closely related to the idea of the sabbath (see 'Form and structure').

4–5. The beginning of this verse resumes the last part of v. 2, perhaps to distinguish it from the weekly sabbath and to solemnize the occasion.

The Passover should be celebrated on the fourteenth day of the first month, from evening to evening. From the following day, the Israelites are to eat unleavened bread for seven days: the first day is a proclamation of holiness, and as for the sabbath, no work should be done. In this chapter the Passover is incorporated into the sabbatical system (cf. Exod. 12:16–19).

6–8. The Feast of Unleavened Bread to the Lord begins on the following day, the fifteenth day of the month: unleavened bread is eaten for seven days (Exod. 12:15–20; 13:6–7; 23:15; 34:18). The Passover is foundational to the nation's history. The event and the ritual symbolize that Israel as a nation owes everything to the Lord, even their existence. The rapid consumption of the unleavened bread symbolizes the event of the exodus, but the symbolic meaning of the unleavened bread is of equal importance: that the Israelites are to show pure dedication to the Lord, free from any corruption that may be caused by humanism (see 'Comment' on 2:4–5). Compared to the previous prescription for this feast, only this prescription commands the offering of an offering for annihilation to the Lord to be offered for seven consecutive days. While offerings such as the burnt, fellowship and loyalty offerings may be assumed, the symbolic meaning of 'offering the offering for annihilation to the Lord' is stressed here; it culminates in a soothing aroma (*rēaḥ nîḥôaḥ*) to the Lord, symbolizing the annihilation of one's egocentric nature. Though the feast celebrates the nation's birth, it goes without saying that each member of Israel is expected to remember that his or her existence depends entirely on the Lord. All this begins with the cessation from ordinary work on the first and seventh days of this proclamation of holiness.

'but you shall present an offering for annihilation to the Lord' (v. 8): *wĕhiqrabtem 'iššeh laYHWH* The details of the offering for annihilation are not mentioned here, and it is commonly and reasonably assumed it is mentioned in Num. 28:16–25. The same question arises also for vv. 25, 27 and 36b. However, as already mentioned (see 'Form and structure'), Lev. 23 should be interpreted within its own context. There are other major cases of seemingly glaring omissions in Leviticus, the details of which are given in the book of Numbers. For instance, while no explicit rule is prescribed for the case when *a lay person* comes into contact with the *nepeš* of a dead human, this is provided in Num. 19 (cf. Lev. 21). So the reader must remain contented with the absence of various details and determine the intended meaning from the present context, rather than systematically trying to see these texts as reflecting some historical process regarding the 'priestly cultic calendar'. Since *'iššeh* means 'an offering for annihilation', *hiqrîb 'iššeh* symbolizes self-dedication through the annihilation of one's own egocentric nature, by the outward offering of sacrifices. That not all the cases of *'iššeh* are detailed suggests that the occasions where it occurs stress the self-dedication of the Israelites to the Lord, and that the details at this point are unnecessary.

23:9–14 (sheaf of barley)

This section deals with the offering of a sheaf of first fruits when the Israelites are settled in the land and reap their harvests (for a similar introduction, see 14:34; 19:23; 25:2). The statement of the Lord's address in vv. 9–10aa is exactly the same as 1–2aa, and the next address of the Lord does not appear till v. 23. This may imply that this section on the first fruits should be viewed as forming a single unit with the next topic, the Feast of Weeks (vv. 15–22). People are commanded to bring the first sheaf to the priest with accompaniments of various loyalty offerings. As noted by Wenham (1979: 303), the rules on the first sheaf are more specific than those provided in Exod. 23:15 and 34:18–20.

The priest waves the offering, so the offerer may be accepted. For the symbolic meaning of *tĕnûpâ*, see 'Comment' on 7:30. The latter half of v. 11 adds that the ritual ought to be done 'on the day after the sabbath'. Considerable debate surrounds when 'the sabbath' took place. The traditional formulation of the question is whether it refers to the first sabbath after the beginning of the festival of unleavened bread, or to the first day of the unleavened bread (for the arguments, see Wenham 1979: 304). However, the common assumption of these two views that the rules in vv. 9–15 deal with the continuation of the rules on the unleavened bread in vv. 5–8 is questionable. The two sets of rules, vv. 5–8 and 9–15, are separated by the statement of the Lord's address in vv. 9–10aa, and have their own independent introductory statements (vv. 4, 10aa). Thus it is unlikely that *haššabbat* (the sabbath) in v. 11b refers to the Feast of Unleavened Bread. The article in *haššabbat* does not refer to the previous mention of *šabbat* but functions to make a genetic reference to the sabbath (*IBHS* 13:5.1f): it refers to the Saturday immediately after the people are ready to bring the sheaf to the priest, and the rule says that the priest waves it on the Sunday. Additionally it may be assumed, in view of v. 15 below, that the day of waving is the same day on which the people bring the sheaf.

The eighth day symbolizes a new beginning. So in conformity with the nature of the first fruits, the priest's waving of the sheaf before the Lord on the first day of the week symbolizes a total dedication of that year's produce to the Lord.

On the same day the priest waves the sheaf, the people are to offer a year-old male lamb without blemish for a burnt offering, two-tenths of an ephah of fine flour mixed with oil as a loyalty offering, and a quarter of a hin of wine as a drink offering (vv. 12–14). The specification 'a year old' for the lamb symbolizes a new beginning, as it does in 9:3, 12:6 and 14:10. The ritual progresses from the offering of the sheaf, to the burnt offering and then the loyalty offering. Though this order may appear unusual, this is the intended order (see on vv. 17–20 below).

The use of wine as a drink offering appears for the first time in Leviticus, and only in this chapter (vv. 13, 18, 37). Undoubtedly the addition of wine alone suggests that this is a joyful occasion, at least, from a human standpoint, not to mention that it is part of the produce. But it needs to be borne in mind that this joy must first be shared by the Lord, for all these offerings are given to the Lord, and then to the priests. Until the people have offered the sheaf, the burnt offering, the loyalty offering and the wine to their God, they must abstain from bread and parched or fresh grain.

On the other hand, as in chs. 1 – 2, the mention of 'acceptance' (v. 11) as well as the soothing aroma (*rēaḥ nîḥôaḥ*) of the burnt and loyalty offerings suggest the presence of the Lord's wrath and its propitiation, though not to the degree it is present in the offerings for sin (self-hiding) and reparation. These offerings symbolize that the people ought to dedicate not only all of their earthly desires but also commit their full allegiance to the Lord. This reflects that they neither dedicate nor commit themselves to the Lord in reality; at least not until that occasion.

23:15–22 (Weeks)

The Feast of First Sheaf is followed by the Feast of Weeks, fifty days after the day on which the sheaf was waved. It is also called 'the Feast of the

Harvest' (Exod. 23:16) or 'the Day of the First fruits' (Num. 28:26) or 'the Feast of the Weeks' (Deut. 16:10). On this day the people are to bring a new loyalty offering, further accompanied by the burnt offering, a sin offering and the fellowship offering. This day is to be observed in the same way as the weekly sabbath, so a cessation from work takes place. A commandment that the people should show generosity towards the poor and strangers is added at the end of the section (v. 22).

15–16. The Israelites are to count fifty days from the day after the sabbath, when they brought the sheaf to the priest. In Hebr. 'the day after the sabbath' is equated with 'the day of your bringing the sheaf of the wave offering' (cf. v. 11 above). The seven weeks from the day of the sheaf would make the people aware of the time in between. Therefore, though the Feast of the Weeks is just one day, the people are made aware of the seven consecutive weeks within a year. On the fiftieth day the people must offer a new loyalty offering to the Lord (v. 16). The seven full weeks and 'fiftieth' recalls the Jubilee year. Therefore the day is like a small Jubilee within a year, and it is consequently no wonder that the day should be observed with the spirit of generosity.

17–20. On that day people ought to bring three kinds of offerings. One characteristic of the ritual of the sheaf, that the grain is accompanied by ordinary sacrifices and offerings, receives even more emphasis here: (1) Two loaves of bread for waving are made from two-tenths of an ephah of flour and are baked with leaven as first fruits to the Lord (v. 17). This is one of the rare occasions in the year when leavened bread is offered (cf. 2:11; 7:13). (2) Accompanying the bread are seven yearling lambs without blemish, one bull of the herd and two rams, along with their loyalty offerings and drink offerings (v. 18). It is remarkable that these accompaniments are clearly richer and costlier than the bread for waving. (3) Finally, one male goat for a sin offering and two yearling lambs for a fellowship offering ought to be sacrificed; the latter offering is waved by the priest upon the bread of first fruits to the Lord (vv. 19–20). That the priest uses the first fruits in the last waving gesture indicates that vv. 17–20 should be taken as prescribing the procedure sequentially, and that the bread of first fruits is the main element of this ritual.

While the new loyalty offering is of central importance, the addition of other animal sacrifices reverses the ordinary sacrificial sequence. Ordinarily, expiatory offerings are offered first and less expiatory ones later. In other words, on this occasion more emphasis is laid on the spiritual fact that the Lord approaches the people, rather than that the people approach the Lord, though the latter is expressed by offerings and sacrifices. Thus it is commanded that just as the Lord is gracious to the Israelites, so must the Israelites act graciously towards the poor and strangers when reaping their harvests (v. 22; cf. 19:9–10).

It is probably because of this idea that the bread can be baked with leaven, which symbolizes not only richness but also corruption; since it is the Lord who blesses the people by the latter's offerings, there is no danger of corruption.

Nevertheless that not only the burnt offering but also the sin offering are required reflects that the spiritual state of the people is less than what is required for acceptance by the Lord.

23:23–25 (feast of the first day of the seventh month)

The first day of the seventh month is a special day that warrants the Israelites' remembrance of the seventh month. It is announced by a loud cry. The term *tĕrû'â* (a loud cry) should be seen in connection with *qārā'* (call), which has appeared several times thus far (vv. 2, 4, 21); *tĕrû'â* is louder and more powerful than *qārā'*. As is well known, the importance of the number seven begins in the creation account. Just as the Lord rested on the seventh day, so the people must rest on the seventh day, and here in the seventh month. The two subsequent important feasts (the Day of Atonement and Booths) in this month make it the people's month of rest. This particular day makes them prepare for these coming feasts by way of abstinence and self-dedication.

23:26–32 (Day of Atonement)

The tenth day of the seventh month is the Day of Atonement. This ritual is prescribed in ch. 16. Though afflicting one's soul is prescribed in 16:29–31, here the emphasis is laid on the people's attitude to the day, and on warning them against non-observance of the law. The proclamation of holiness consists of three elements: (1) afflicting one's soul, (2) offering an offering for annihilation to the Lord, and (3) cessation from work.

Though the Lord speaks to Moses, he does not command him to deliver the message to the Israelites (v. 26), unlike the other addresses of this chapter (vv. 1–2, 9–10, 23–24, 33–34). That this is neither coincidental nor an abridged formulation is evident from vv. 33–34, where the Lord's address reverts to normal. As commented at 22:26, this is probably because Moses is responsible for the proper observance of the Day of Atonement, it being one of the most fundamental institutions. Nevertheless all of these rules are eventually related to the Israelites (see 'Comment' on 16:34).

The special emphasis on the day's importance is expressed by 'Above all' (*'ak*) at the beginning of v. 27. The logic given in v. 28, that no work ought to be done on that day because it is the Day of Atonement, is already found in 16:29–30. Atonement concerns the salvation of the human soul. It is noteworthy that *nepeš* (a soul) occurs five times in vv. 27, 29–30, 32. Therefore the Israelites ought to lay bare their egocentric selves as much as possible, which practically begins with a cessation from ordinary work. The examination of one's own self is what is commanded.

29–31. Thus the *kāret* penalty is imposed on those souls that are not afflicted and work on that day. The law assumes that their souls are less than *living* souls (i.e. full of selfishness and arrogance), all of which results in self-hiding from the Lord. Therefore any person who violates the law is punished by the extermination of his soul from his people. In so far as the human soul is not cleansed or set free from a selfish ego, the following Feast of Booths as well as all the preceding feasts, the sabbath, Sheaf of First Fruits, and the first day of the seventh month, are observed in vain and are hypocritical (see further below). Special attention should be paid to the truth that afflicting one's soul constitutes a stage that follows the cessation of work, and that therefore the former provides the direction of the latter; even when only a cessation from work is commanded, it is more desirable that the people afflict their souls. V. 29 is formulated in the passive, while v. 30 is in the active sense. Such a strict punishment is, however, in line with what takes place inside the Tent of Meeting on that day: what takes place there must parallel what the Israelites do in their settlements.

32. This verse repeats the warning and prohibition in a unique and emphatic way. Stylistically, it begins with *šabbat šabbātôn* (it is a complete rest) and ends with *tišbětû šabbatěkem* (you shall keep your sabbath), thus stressing the idea of 'rest' or 'doing no work'. In content the verse is a fine example of parallelism: the command of the first half of the verse to afflict one's soul in the evening of the ninth of that month is supplemented by 'from evening to evening shall you keep the sabbath'. According to these rules, afflicting one's soul means to take a rest, which is none other than the rest of a human soul.

23:33–36 (Booths)

The form of the Lord's address reverts to those given in vv. 1–2, 9–10, 23–24, and introduces the Feast of Booths.

The last of the series of annual feasts is the Feast of Booths on the fifteenth of the seventh month. While this section appears to be interrupted by vv. 37–38, this is due to the differing function of the two introductory expressions: the Lord's address and the enumeration of the Lord's appointed meetings (see 'Comment' on vv. 1–2 above, and 'Form and structure'). The lengthy addition of vv. 39–43 concerning the details of the feast stresses that it ought to be celebrated with joy, as the section is replete with terms like *ḥāgag* (to celebrate), *ḥag* (feast) and *śāmēaḥ* (to rejoice).

This feast is, in a sense, a summary of the other feasts in that it refers to all of them (cf. the similar formula of introduction in vv. 2ab–b, 4); it is observed at the time of harvest (v. 39), which is the culmination of the

Feast of the Weeks. Also it refers back to the Passover (v. 43) as well as to the Day of Atonement. In contrast to the rigorous mood of the Day of Atonement, the Feast of Booths is a feast of joy and relaxation. The two divided sections, vv. 33–36 and 39–43, have their own functions. As for most of the other feasts, people are first commanded, in vv. 33–36, to cease from their work and offer their offerings to the Lord; i.e. dedicate themselves. But in vv. 39–43 they are commanded to rejoice before the Lord. Rather than looking at these two sections as giving different laws regarding the Feast of Booths, it is more appropriate to see the ideological connection between the two: the cessation from work and self-dedication to the Lord lead to joy before the Lord in response to his salvation of them from bondage in Egypt and his guidance thereafter. This joy is a heavenly joy that springs out of the affliction of one's own soul, which was previously full of selfishness, arrogance and self-indulgence, and should be distinguished from any kind of joy that satisfies human selfishness.

23:37–38

These verses summarize the preceding seven appointed meetings in a general way. V. 38 ('besides the Lord's sabbaths') indicates that v. 37 refers to the preceding six festivals, except for the weekly sabbath in v. 3. The purpose of the six occasions is to make the people dedicate themselves by offering sacrifices. Reference to the burnt, loyalty and fellowship offerings, and the drink offerings in v. 37b, does not refer only to the two rituals of the sheaves and the weeks (vv. 10–20), but to all the feasts. It is not that these verses assume Num. 28 – 29. They simply imply that the practical content of 'the offering for annihilation to the LORD' consists in such offerings. The concern for detail is secondary in this chapter (see 'Form and structure').

23:39–44

The additional section in vv. 39–42 begins with *'ak*, which probably means 'surely'. As for *'ak* in v. 27, this particle can begin a new discourse. The Feast of Booths is characterized by the time of the produce's ingathering. The first and eighth days are days of complete rest. The way to celebrate the feast is to take, on the first day, the fruit of splendid trees, branches of palm trees and boughs of leafy trees, willows of the brook, to make a booth and dwell in it for seven days. It is a visible way of invoking the memory of the exodus and particularly the wilderness period. The feast has the purpose of reminding the Israelites of all generations that the Lord made them dwell in booths when he brought them out of the land of Egypt. Thus the design of the festival serves to remind them of the Lord's guidance after the exodus. In this way the Feast of Booths rounds out the initial theme of the Passover in vv. 4–8.

Though this feast is practically observed in the Promised Land, there are ironic overtones in that the law is addressed to the Israelites who, though they have just experienced the exodus, have often complained about it (e.g. Exod. 16:1–3). On the other hand, while it may appear easier to observe the law in the Promised Land, one passage (Neh. 8:17) reveals that the Feast of Booths was not celebrated from the time of Joshua to the reformation headed by Nehemiah. Moreover when it was recommenced at the time of Nehemiah, the great joy of the people was evoked out of their response to the word of God (Neh. 8:8–9). It seems in the light of the self-indulgence that characterizes general human nature that the people soon forgot their God who had saved them in the Promised Land. Thus contrary to what would seem easy to observe, the Israelites proved themselves to be powerless in observing the law. In view of these considerations, the section vv. 39–43 is an appendix, not in the source-analytical sense but in the true sense of the word: it reflects the Lord's sentiment that if the people really afflict their souls, they will get joy, but this was unlikely to happen.

V. 44 records Moses' execution of the Lord's command in v. 2.

Explanation

From this chapter onwards the Lord's speech focuses on holiness in relation to time, the sabbath and various annual festivals the Israelites are to observe from this time on. In that the main theme is *time*, the nature of the rules differs from the themes addressed up to ch. 22. Nevertheless the theme of time and holiness is dealt with on various occasions and in various rules before this chapter. The ordination ceremony in ch. 8 and various purificatory rituals comprise a time element. The first required a seven-day stay at the sanctuary, the second commanded an unclean person to wait until evening, or pronounced people unclean for seven days. These references to time signify that human beings lack the Lord's presence until they become clean. Indeed it is argued in connection with the law on the leprous person (ch. 13) that the status of cleanness is only temporary. To become holy, then, one's egocentric nature ought to be destroyed, since holiness is a condition of the human heart. The duration of time in the case of purificatory rituals indicates both the state of self-hiding and the purificatory process. From this perspective, the duration of time can be seen as redemptive or salvific, though an unclean person does not experience the presence of the Lord during that fixed period. That time has a redemptive nature is relevant for understanding the various feasts of this chapter.

Šabbat is viewed as holy (Exod. 16:23; 31:14–15; 35:2). But why is the sabbath holy? It is because God rested on that day from his creative work.

Thus the holy nature of time is inseparable from what God did or who he is. When the principle is applied to human beings, it is assumed that they are not holy. While the appointed meetings can be taken as a gracious gift to the Israelites, they clearly demand more than formal or outward observance. Those holy times are grounded upon the divine–human relationship. To be more specific, the Lord is holy and the fact that he is going to meet the people demands holiness on the part of the people, which is characterized by the lack of an egocentric nature. In other words, since holiness resides in personality, the holy Lord is to meet with holy people on those occasions.

Seven kinds of appointed meetings are listed, with significant theological messages, and the sequence of the occasions are, on the whole, divided into spring and autumn feasts. They are arranged as follows.

1. The weekly sabbath – creation
2. (Spring) the Passover – salvation
3. The Sheaf of First Fruits – birth and growth
4. The Weeks – the beginning of the harvest
5. (Autumn) the first day of the seventh month – towards inner salvation
6. The Day of Atonement – inner salvation
7. The Booths – joyful remembrance of the Lord's guidance

Clearly the sabbath principle in point 1 permeates the rest of the appointed meetings. That is, the cessation from ordinary work is basic to these appointed occasions, and this is an important element of observing them as holy. It is also clear that while some of these feasts, particularly the feasts of First Fruits and Booths, are characterized by the agricultural life of the people, it is the divine–human relationship that is to be expressed through these feasts.

Except for the weekly sabbath, then, the other six feasts all concern the salvation of the Israelites (the Passover and the Day of Atonement), and their fellowship with the Lord (the Weeks and the Booths). This means that both in spring and autumn the Israelites are expected to meet the Lord from two different viewpoints, salvation and fellowship.

The two basic requirements for feasts are the cessation from ordinary work and the dedication of oneself to the Lord by way of offerings. These two elements by themselves suggest that the observance of rules is a matter of the human heart (see below).

The spiritual significance of the various feasts is as follows: the Passover provided the people with an opportunity to express their complete allegiance to the Lord; the Feast of Weeks reminded them of the Lord's blessings; on the Day of Atonement the people demonstrated their complete allegiance to the Lord by afflicting their souls, and this was followed by their sharing joy in God's presence.

In addition to the sabbath principle, all seven feasts concern human salvation. It is not too much to say that God expresses his creativity in bringing salvation to humans. Not only is the sabbath directly related to the creation, but this principle brings the notion of creation into the other six feasts God gave. That is, it suggests that God's salvation creates a new humanity, starting from the Passover to the Day of Atonement. Since these feasts are called holy and are closely related to human salvation, it can be posited that holiness is, in its essence, salvific. This does not contradict my observation that the essence of holiness is found in self-sacrifice (see 'Explanation' on ch. 19). Though practically the salvation rejoiced over is salvation from slavery in Egypt, more essentially it constitutes salvation from one's own egocentric nature.

As Wenham comments, holy days 'constituted major interruptions to daily living and introduced an element of variety into the rhythm of life' (Wenham 1979: 301). More essentially Greenberg crystallizes the difference between holy time and secular time by suggesting that the former is circular or repetitive and the latter, linear. He points out that holy occasions remind the celebrating people of God's redemptive event, which was holy and eternal, thus actualizing the eternal (for further points, see Greenberg 1982: 1–4). While these considerations are appropriate, they fail to take human sinfulness into account. Thus they need balancing by what I have proposed in regard to the concept of holiness: the absence of an egocentric nature. Clearly both the call to holiness (11:44–45; 19:2; 20:7, 26 etc.) and the plethora of feasts, not to mention the weekly sabbath, indicate that the Lord intends to make all days holy. Since this is not possible for humans, who live under the general curse of God, the Lord graciously permitted the feasts listed in this chapter. On such days he is prepared to meet the people, not necessarily in the sanctuary but in all their dwelling places, so long as they are holy. Thus, by instituting the numerous feasts throughout the year, the Lord makes the people not only aware of the appointed days, but also of all the other days, in order to encourage the Israelites to lift their thoughts to the heavenly world characterized by a cessation of work, relaxation and joy. But that ordinary life is interrupted by such special days points to the fact that the Israelites remain otherwise preoccupied with themselves and what they can gain from their own work. This suggests that their selfish natures still remain alive. Balentine also aptly points out that human beings tend to organize their time around their ordinary work (2002: 181–183). But a holy occasion is neither just a matter of time nor living 'ethically'. Rather the observance of holy feasts is achieved only when people present themselves before God by killing their egocentric natures.

The eternal heavenly world is meant to be found within the human heart (see 'Explanation' on ch. 19). In this sense, the holy feasts are days on which the Israelites are invited to enter eternal life even in this world. However, in view of the hardness of the human heart it may be surmised that the people are unlikely to observe the laws in this chapter. More is discussed on holiness in relation to time in ch. 25 (the Sabbatical and Jubilee year). Thus, as for the other commandments, this legislation concerning holy feasts is also designed to confront the people with the presence of their egocentric natures; this time, from the viewpoint of time.

The postulate that the essence of holy time lies in the human heart may indicate that the goal of instituting the holy feasts lies not so much in the observance of the 'holy days' but in the people's caring for their own souls on those occasions; holiness does not lie in the linear experience of time but is meant to be found in the human heart, and the institution of the holy feasts is one of the Lord's means to this end. This is the major reason why an increasing emphasis is placed on the eternal 'today' in terms of salvation in the later literature (Pss. 2:7; 95:7) even though it is acknowledged human beings have a limited physical lifespan on this earth. Ps. 90 is suggestive in this regard. While it begins by reflecting on God's eternal nature (vv. 1–2), the psalmist moves on to the 'thousand years' of God, then to the seventy or eighty years of human age (v. 10) and ends with 'every morning' (v. 14).

New Testament implications

Some of the feasts listed in this chapter have parallels in the NT world. Jesus healed the sick and expelled demons on the sabbath: he demonstrated the principle that the sabbath is made for the good of humans, rather than for burdening them. Despite much discussion, it is difficult to prove a relationship between the OT and NT sabbath, except for their theological relationship (cf. Shead 2000: 749–750). The cross, the ultimate event of God's series of saving works, coincides both in timing and significance with the Passover (John 19:36; 1 Cor. 5:7; see Alexander 1995: 79–81). Over and above the literal and physical deliverance from slavery in Egypt, the cross achieved atonement for the self-hidings of many. Comparable with the Feast of Weeks is the passing of the fifty days following Christ's resurrection (Pentecost), after which the Holy Spirit came upon the believers (Acts 2:1). Indeed the Christian life is, in some contexts, described by using the language of OT festivals (1 Cor. 5:8).

Despite the correspondence between OT festivals and some of the Christian festivals, there are some fundamental differences. Christ fulfilled the Law, thereby putting an end to it (Rom. 10:4). This means that Christian believers no longer need to observe the feasts literally (Col. 2:16–17), just as they do not need to offer the various sacrifices and offerings literally. This is because Christ bore our curse and cancelled it on the cross. As its background, this was the experience of the people of Israel who could not observe the Law, nor believe in God. The NT asserts that whoever believes in Jesus Christ will be saved and resurrected on the last day.

Christ is our rest, and has worked for our salvation since the world began (John 5:17). This salvation is ultimately that of a human soul considered dead as a result of the desires of the flesh. Jesus' healing of the sick, leprous persons, on the sabbath is merely an outward salvation given because of their response to Jesus and his power. It is, however, not the same as the salvation of the human soul. Indeed the Gospels indicate human nature is such that the physically healed soon forgot not only their healer but even the source of their previous suffering and how intensely they sought healing (Luke 17:11–19). Those who believe in Jesus have their selfish nature destroyed and enter God's eternal kingdom even while they remain on this earth. For eternity resides in the human heart (Eccl. 3:11). In fact, the real work, salvation, is done through the cessation of 'work'. Such people are called holy, and if their heart gains such a condition, they meet continually with the Lord. This is virtually the same as what the author of Hebrews calls 'the Lord's rest' (Heb. 4:3–11). Therefore in principle the Law's demand for holiness in the Israelites is the same as the NT demand of believers. However, in NT times the outpouring of the Holy Spirit is guaranteed, but is possible only for those who are wholehearted.

The condition of the human heart that celebrates the feasts in the true sense of the word is what characterizes those who dwell in the heavenly kingdom. Such a person does not worry about tomorrow (Matt. 6:24–34; Jas 4:13–15) and is content with what is given to him, even a simply built booth (1 Tim. 6:6–7), for believers are aliens on this earth (cf. Lev. 25:23).

LEVITICUS 24:1–23

Translation

1The LORD spoke to Moses, saying, 2'Command the Israelites to bring you pure oil
from beaten olives for the lamp, that a light may be kept burning regularly.
3Outside the veil of the testimony, in the Tent of Meeting, Aaron shall arrange it
from evening to morning before the LORD regularly. It shall be a statute forever
throughout your generations. 4He shall arrange the lamps on the lampstand of
pure gold before the LORD regularly. 5You shall take fine flour and bake twelve
loaves from it; two-tenths of an ephah shall be in each loaf. 6You shall set them in
two piles, six in a pile, on the table of pure gold before the LORD. 7You shall put
pure frankincense on each pile, that it may go with the bread as a token portion as
an offering for annihilation to the LORD. 8Every sabbath day Aaron shall arrange
it before the LORD regularly; it is from the Israelites as a covenant forever.
9And it shall be for Aaron and his sons, and they shall eat it in a holy place, since
it is for him a most holy portion from the offerings for annihilation to the LORD, a
perpetual due.'

10Now an Israelite woman's son, whose father was an Egyptian, went out among
the Israelites. And the Israelite woman's son and a man of Israel fought in the camp,

[11]and the Israelite woman's son blasphemed the Name, and cursed. Then they
brought him to Moses. His mother's name was Shelomith, the daughter of Dibri, of
the tribe of Dan. [12]And they put him in custody, till the will of the LORD should be
made clear to them.
[13]Then the LORD spoke to Moses, saying, [14]'Bring out of the camp the one who
cursed, and let all who heard him lay their hands on his head, and let all the
congregation stone him. [15]And speak to the Israelites, saying, Whoever curses his
God shall bear his punishment. [16]Whoever blasphemes the name of the LORD shall
surely be put to death. All the congregation shall stone him. The sojourner as well
as the native when he blasphemes the Name shall be put to death. [17]Whoever takes
a human life shall surely be put to death. [18]Whoever takes an animal's life shall
make it good, life for life. [19]If anyone injures his fellow, as he has done it shall be
done to him, [20]fracture for fracture, eye for eye, tooth for tooth; whatever injury he
has given a man shall be given to him. [21]Whoever kills an animal shall make it
good, and whoever kills a man shall be put to death. [22]You shall have the same rule
for the sojourner and for the native, for I am the LORD your God.'
[23]So Moses spoke to the Israelites, and they brought out of the camp the one
who had cursed and stoned him with stones. Thus the Israelites did as the LORD
commanded Moses.

Notes on the text

2. 'you': *'ēlêkā* LXX reads 'to me'. As Milgrom (2001: 2086) judges, the consistent reference to the Lord in the 3rd person throughout this pericope favours the MT.

3. 'Aaron' LXX, SamP and Hebr. MSS add 'and his sons'. This should be dismissed, as it may well be a harmonization with Exod. 27:21.

4. 'arrange': *ya'ărōk* LXX reads it in 2nd person pl., here and in vv. 5 ('you shall take'), 6 ('you shall set') and 7 ('you shall put'), in conformity with its reading in v. 3 that not only Aaron but his sons too arrange the light.

'of pure gold': literally 'pure lampstand'. Yet in the light of Exod. 25:31, 31:8 and 39:37 it is probable 'pure' refers to the material of the lampstand.

'regularly': *tāmîd* LXX and SamP read 'until morning' instead, which is unlikely, since *'ārak* (arrange) is not a verb that expresses continuous action.

7. 'frankincense' LXX adds 'salt'; probably based on 2:13.

12. 'be made clear': *liprōš* For the root *prš*, see also Num. 15:34.

15. 'his God': *'ĕlōhāyw* LXX simply reads 'God'.

16. 'the Name': *šēm* LXX adds 'of the LORD'; perhaps conforming it with the beginning of this verse.

17. LXX adds 'and he dies' after 'human life'. The same goes for vv. 18 (after 'an animal's life') and 21 (after 'a man').

18. 'take life': *makkeh nepeš* Some Hebr. MSS, LXX and Vg omit *nepeš* (life).

21. LXX omits 'Whoever kills an animal shall make it good'.
23. Syr adds 'so that he dies' after 'with stones'.

Form and structure

Lev. 24 deals with two apparently separate matters. The first (vv. 1–9) provides instructions for two ritual activities: the preparation of the oil for the candelabrum, and the bread called *tāmîd*. The second (vv. 10–23) reports an incident of blasphemy that occurs in the camp, and is followed by some basic principles by which this incident and some other potential civil cases should be handled. There are a couple of fundamental questions pertaining to this chapter; the first relates to how the juxtaposition of vv. 1–9 and 10–23 can be explained. The second asks what rationale there is for locating this chapter where it is. Relevant to both of these questions might be an answer for why a 'legal' prescription is followed by a narrative account.

First, it has been observed that the first part (vv. 1–9) is unrelated in content to the second part (vv. 10–23). Hartley even concludes, 'Thus this material seems to be arbitrarily dropped in between chaps. 23 and 25' (Hartley 1992: 396). Critics, engaging with literary analysis, identify two literary layers underlying vv. 10–23; vv. 10–14 (P) and vv. 15–22 (H) (e.g. Grünwaldt 1999: 90). However, apart from their different literary genres, is the conclusion that they are unrelated really warranted? Some exegetes point out that the incident in vv. 10–23 took place immediately after the Lord gave the instructions of vv. 1–9 (Keil 1968: 453; Harrison 1980: 220). Wenham and Rooker both suggest the legal material is actually set within a narrative context, not just in this chapter but in the whole book of Leviticus (Wenham 1979: 308–309; Rooker 2000: 295). I agree with this view, but even so, such an explanation does not resolve the seemingly anomalous juxtaposition of the two parts.

As is the case elsewhere in Leviticus, the interpretation of this chapter is hindered by the modern distinction between law and narrative. This chapter appears to consist of laws (vv. 1–9) and narrative/laws (vv. 10–23). This is not a rare phenomenon in Leviticus. Ch. 10 is introduced with a report of the Nadab and Abihu incident, moves on to instructions from the Lord, and finally returns to the introductory narrative. Moreover the artificialness of making a clear distinction between narrative and law is exemplified by the nature of chs. 8 – 9, which report Moses' implementation of the Exod. 28 – 29 instructions. Thus, though these chapters appear legal, they are not laws in the modern sense of the word.

The placement of the account of an incident regarding blasphemy after the prescription for the lampstand and shewbread appears puzzling. A proposal for their relationship is given in 'Explanation', but a close reading of vv. 10–23 as well as a consideration of the symbolic meaning of the ritual acts performed in the Holy Place give the impression that the two parts are not merely arranged to convey chronological sequence but a certain theological message as a whole.

Second, regarding the question of why the instructions pertaining to the light of the lampstand and the *tāmîd* offerings (vv. 1–9) come at this point, ancient rabbis suggest it is because of the association of ideas, both in ch. 23 and this chapter, about agricultural produce. Gispen (1950: 337) speculates that the concept of time forms the nexus between the festivals and this law. At least, the connection seems to lie in the continuous theme of time: the fixed times of ch. 23 and the concept of continuity (*tāmîd*) in ch. 24.

I propose that the rationale for the location of 24:1–9 is explained by paying attention to the overall flow of chs. 18 – 26. Just as chs. 18 – 22 were divisible into chs. 18 – 20 and 21 – 22, chs. 23 – 26 are divisible into chs. 23, 24, 25 and 26. A similar structure characterizes both in so far as chs. 19 and 24 are enveloped by chs. 18 and 20, and chs. 23 and 25 respectively. And just as the content of ch. 19 is characteristically positive and general in its teaching on holiness and is subsequently applied more specifically to the priests and offerings in chs. 21 – 22, so too does the content of the central ch. 24 present positive and general teaching on the theme of holy *time* (see Introduction 7.4.2.d), which is subsequently applied specifically to the Israelites in ch. 26. In ch. 24 time relates to 'perpetuity', while in chs. 23 and 25 fixed time is in view (the former deals with annual cycles and the latter with the seventh or fiftieth years). Thus it may be inferred that ch. 24:1–9 stresses the perennial aspect of time, particularly, in reference to the relationship between the Lord and the people, which is mediated by the priests.

Comment

24:1–9

These verses set out what the priests should regularly do in the Holy Place, other than their work at the altar of burnt offering in the outer court. They should keep the light burning throughout the night and offer shewbread every sabbath. The rationale for mentioning these rules at this location, i.e. after ch. 23, is connected with the symbolic meaning of these ritual acts. As the various elements of these acts are essentially related to the loyalty offering in the court, their symbolic meanings may shed light on the relationship between them, and the significance of placing the laws in this location.

24:1–4

1–2. The section vv. 1–9 is a fundamental regulation to be carried out by Moses for the people and Aaron. As with other institutions, Moses is the one responsible for this institution. But because of the commandment's nature, it is first addressed to the Israelites, i.e. to bring materials such as pure oil, and then Aaron is informed as to what should be done with these materials. The oil for the lampstand is already prescribed in Exod. 27:20–21 in an almost identical form. Nevertheless a more detailed prescription is made, placing more emphasis in these verses on the idea of *tāmîd* (regularly). *Tāmîd* cannot mean literal continuation, since the priests are commanded to burn the oil 'from evening to morning' in the next verse (cf. Haran 1985: 207). 'Oil from beaten olives' means the best oil.

3. The lampstand is located on a table top 90 cm by 45 cm in size located outside the Holy of Holies, near the incense altar. Aaron is to arrange it in this position regularly from evening to morning. Since the lamp is lit from evening to morning, it follows that there should never be a time when the room is dark; though this is not to fulfil any practical purpose. The act naturally has its symbolic meaning. Compared with the perpetual fire in 6:9ff.[6:2ff.], where it probably symbolizes a consuming power, it is the light emitted from this fire that is emphasized and it solely symbolizes the Lord's presence (spiritual light). And if so, it is definitely related to the condition of the human heart (see on v. 4 and 'Explanation').

4. Compared with the instructions in Exod. 27:20–21, it is clear that the idea of *tāmîd* is stressed here; the term appears in vv. 2–4. Yet this regulation intends not so much to prescribe the *maintenance* of light, which is given in Exod. 27:20–21, as to emphasize the light's *perpetuity*. This observation fits well with the idea that the prescription in vv. 1–9 is meant to remind the Israelites that they ought to show continual allegiance to the Lord. Furthermore this ought to be considered alongside the light's symbolic meaning. While the light must symbolize the divine presence (see on v. 3), such a symbolic meaning is too general: the same presence of the Lord may be expressed by other symbols, such as clouds (e.g. Exod. 13:21). It would seem the light symbolizes the light of the Spirit of the Lord (cf. Gen. 1:3).

At any rate, since the visible light illuminates the outer part of the Tent, the Israelites, including Aaron, ought to be illuminated by the Spirit's invisible light.

That this regulation concerns the human heart is particularly suggested by the fact that, though not explicitly mentioned, the light is to be lit on a candelabrum, which probably symbolizes the Tree of Life in the Garden of Eden. However, that the cherubim are located within the Holy of Holies, and not in the Holy Place, implies that the divine presence is not present to the same extent that it is in the Holy of Holies, let alone the pre-fall Garden of Eden. Thus the symbolic meaning of the candelabrum and its location reflect the hearts of the Israelites: if the symbolic meaning is actualized, their hearts are far from the condition of the first man and woman in Eden.

The Israelites are also commanded to bring the purest possible oil, the best oil. The requirement for them to prepare the best possible oil is not merely practical in meaning but, since the oil symbolizes the Lord's presence, it indicates that their efforts must reflect a zeal for maintaining this presence.

Aaron, or any succeeding chief priest, must also realize that in arranging the fire each day he ought to be holy before the Lord, not just uncovering himself, but also destroying his egocentric nature.

24:5–9

5–7. From v. 5 to v. 7 Aaron is addressed in the 2nd person. As has been noticed, the relatively small size of the table implies that the two loaves of twelve pieces of bread were apparently piled up rather than positioned in a row. Although it is Moses who is commanded to take and bake the flour, he is viewed as the one responsible for this institution; it is presumably the people who bake it. The twelve pieces of bread undoubtedly symbolize the twelve tribes of Israel. Thus Aaron, the representative of all Israel, offers the food to the Lord on behalf of the people. It is also noteworthy that this bread is leavened, unlike the large majority of cases for the loyalty offering in the outer court.

The use of frankincense as a token portion suggests that it, together with the oil and the twelve pieces of bread, functions as a *minḥâ*, the loyalty offering. This frankincense differs in quality from that mentioned in ch. 2 in that a finer grade of frankincense is required here (Exod. 30:34). Yet the nature of this offering appears to be more mundane and anthropomorphic compared with the one of the outer court (see 'Explanation'). There is a reason for this. In the court, where the rituals are witnessed by various people, and the destruction of human selfishness is of central concern, the phrase 'soothing aroma' is used; for selfish humans cannot easily imagine that the true bread comes from the Lord. The ritual inside the Tent assumes such a level of transformation in the human heart. For the priests who are theoretically assumed to have gone through an inner transformation, the bread can be ordinary, because they are assumed as not owning or coveting it.

Thus, by offering the twelve pieces of bread, the Israelites pay symbolic tribute to the Lord in a more pure form than what is achieved by the loyalty offerings made in the outer court.

8. Aaron is to arrange the bread every sabbath, and this constitutes an eternal covenant. Elsewhere the phrase *bĕrît 'ôlām* (a covenant forever) occurs on several occasions in the Pentateuch; namely the Lord's covenant with Noah (Gen. 9:16), with Abraham (Gen. 17:7, 13, 19) and in relation to sabbath observance (Exod. 31:16). However, more immediately, sabbath observance is stipulated in 23:3. Thus it follows that perfect loyalty to the Lord is added to the cessation of work as constituting the holy nature of the sabbath. The people ought not only to cease from their work, which symbolizes the destruction of their selfishness, but must also show perfect allegiance to the Lord based on the former. Yet this would seem impossible to implement, not just for the Israelites but for all humanity.

9. The weekly bread is given to Aaron and his sons. They are to consume it in a holy place, which means they ought to be holy in eating it. If holiness is outward, the observance of this law is possible, but if inward, then it would appear extremely difficult to consume it without profaning its holiness.

24:10–23

It is the Lord's will to be present with the people so long as the latter maintain constant allegiance to him. The following incident of blasphemy illustrates the very opposite of the Lord's will.

10. Following the regulation for the holy loyalty offering in the Tent, this section reporting the case of blasphemy comes unexpectedly. It should be noted that in Hebr. the verse begins literally 'and he went out' (*wayyēṣē'*). It is not specified from where, but as Ibn Ezra comments, it is reasonable to infer that he went out 'from his tent' (see below on v. 14). This verse presents the setting for the quarrel, identifying the lineage of the two men in question. One is a person who had an Israelite mother and an Egyptian father, while the other is an Israelite. They quarrelled within the camp. The exact cause of the quarrel is not stated, but some indications concerning the nature of the quarrel are given: (1) The mention of 'a son of an Israelite woman' precedes 'a son of Egyptian man'. (2) The blasphemer is stressed as 'the son of the Israelite woman' in v. 10b. (3) The blasphemy was committed against the God of Israel. These literary features along with the blasphemy's content suggest the offender was influenced by his mother into thinking the God of Israel was to be blamed, and this led him to his act of blasphemy. Thus, though the exact reason for the blasphemy remains unclear, it would appear the quarrel concerned a debate regarding which god is superior.

11. Two terms appear in this incident in relation to the idea of blasphemy, *nqb* qal (vv. 11, 16) and *qll* pi. (vv. 11, 14–15, 23). While *qillēl* means to 'curse' or 'look down upon', whether it is verbal or not, the exact nuance of *nāqab* needs clarification. Though the term can be rendered 'to slander', its nuance lies in the pronouncing of a name, since the verb is conjoined with names in vv. 11, 16 (see also Num. 1:17; Isa. 62:2; Ezra 8:20; 1 Chr. 12:31[32]). Thus the blasphemer may well have pronounced the Tetragrammaton in cursing the God of Israel. Nevertheless the Lord's name is not specified in the text: it is just expressed by *haššēm* (the Name). The term *qillēl*, which follows *nāqab* in v. 11, describes the overall nature of the culprit. Though the blasphemer pronounced God's name, the biblical writer does not explicitly mention the name of the blasphemer, but only of his mother, Shelomith, the daughter of Dibri, of the tribe of Dan. The reason why the culprit's name is not mentioned is unclear. But perhaps the logic is that while the divine name was not to be pronounced, the culprit's name ought to be erased; thus it is not worth mentioning it.

12. Even uttering the divine name in vain deserves divine punishment (Exod. 20:7); here is a case of blasphemy. Elsewhere in Leviticus, even looking down on handicapped people is prohibited, and the cursing of one's parents deserves capital punishment (19:14; 20:9). Thus a punishment of greater severity is naturally expected. Therefore the people arrest the culprit and wait expectantly for the Lord's reply through Moses.

13–14. The Lord answers that the culprit has to be brought outside the camp, and the people must lay their hands on his *head* before stoning him to death. The Lord's first word, *hôṣî'* (bring out), seems to be literarily associated with *wayyēṣē'* (and he went out) at the beginning of v. 10, suggesting that since the person went out from his tent by his own will and had a quarrel in the camp, it is the Lord's will to 'bring him out of the camp' (see Wright and Milgrom 1986: 884–888).

For 'stoning to death', see 'Comment' on 20:2. There is some ambiguity around the meaning of the people's laying their hands on the head of the culprit. One explanation is that since the blasphemer, along with those who overheard the blasphemy, becomes defiled, it is the duty of the latter to put the culprit to death, so the death will make atonement for the guilt of both parties (Wenham 1979: 311; Rooker 2000: 297). However, this seems to read too much into the rite. Rather than seeing the ideas of transference of guilt or identification behind the rite, it is preferable to see that the idea is one of testifying under divine authority: by laying their hands on the offender, the people testify before the Lord that they are witnesses of his blasphemy. Such a meaning of the hand-leaning rite is also found when Moses lays his hands on the head of Joshua (Num. 27:18, 23).

15–16. A principle regarding blasphemy is given to the Israelites: whoever curses God should be put to death by stoning. The practical details associated with the general principle given in v. 15 are provided in v. 16: the mode and agent of execution, and the persons subject to the law. By 'his God' (v. 15) the lawgiver does not contemplate a foreign god, but uses the pronominal suffix to indicate that it is the person's personal God (see 'Comment' on 2:13). The idiomatic expression *nāśā' ḥēṭ* means to 'bear the offence', and refers either to the death penalty (cf. 22:9) or the *kāret* penalty (Num. 9:13; 18:22, 32; see also Lev. 19:17). First, the cursing (*qillēl*) in v. 15 is specified as slandering (*nāqab*) the name of the Lord. The blasphemer has to be stoned (*rāgam*) to death by the hands of the congregation, the representative body of the people, and the law applies not just to the resident Israelites but also to resident foreigners. As human hands carry out the execution, it is expressed by the formulaic *môt yûmat*, which should be distinguished from the divine execution expressed by other forms. Such a punishment is comparable to the death penalty required for a person who kills another person.

17–18. The verdict that the person who curses God has to be stoned to death becomes an occasion for the Lord to give further instructions regarding interhuman civil cases: the principle of a life for a life (commonly expressed by the *lex talionis* or *talion*) is applied to such cases. However, there is no element in this that connotes a sense of vengeance or retaliation, just the principle of 'measure for measure' – that the one who injures must receive the same injury.

Second, whoever takes the life of an animal, which presumably belongs to another person, must make compensation for it. The principle that life should be compensated by life is added at the end of v. 18. This principle is mentioned in Exod. 21:23, and with a slightly different form in Deut. 19:21. Compared with Exod. 21:23–25, the Leviticus section exhibits two major differences: (1) Leviticus is more comprehensive in that it includes the case for murder. (2) Also the penalties for divine–human and interhuman cases are presented as a corollary of the principle of 'a life for a life'. Indeed the principle is also emphasized by a chiasm (see below on vv. 21–23). Furthermore the placing of the interhuman cases just after the case of blasphemy serves to persuade the Israelites of the Lord's reasonableness in sentencing the blasphemer to death.

19–20. These verses deal with cases of physical injuries resulting from interhuman relationships. Here again it is observable that *'îš* is used when interpersonal relations are at issue, while *'ādām* is used when reference is being made to a person's body.

21. This verse reiterates and summarizes what is said in vv. 17–18, so the entire section of vv. 17–21 forms a thematic chiasmus, as follows:

A v. 17 Killing of a human
  B v. 18 Killing of a neighbour's animal
    C vv. 19–20 Injuries between humans
  B' v. 21a Killing of an animal
A' v. 21b Killing of a human

22–23. The same principle applies to Israelites and resident foreigners. This is because both groups live in the same land. Following the Lord's words, Moses spoke to the people, and they brought the culprit outside the camp, and stoned him to death, just as the Lord has commanded. The order of Moses' relating of the Lord's words to the people and the people's taking the culprit outside the camp are also chiastically arranged when compared with vv. 14 and 15.

Though she experiences the loss of her son, it may seem unfair that the culprit's mother escapes the punishment meted out to her son. But the principle enunciated here suggests that what the mother did will be repaid to her in some other way (see 'Explanation' below).

Explanation

The location of the chapter's first section and the rationale for the juxtaposition of the two apparently unrelated materials requires some explanation.

Significance of the ritual in verses 1–9

The nature of the priestly activities in the Holy Place takes such a form that Aaron lights the candelabrum every evening and presents the shewbread every sabbath. That the materials for both are taken from the Israelites indicates that Aaron mediates between the people and the Lord, a role that cannot be carried out by the people in the outer court. Thus his activities represent the closest access the people have to the Lord. The rites are relatively more anthropomorphic than the loyalty offering made in the outer court, and this suggests that the former assume the symbolic meaning of the latter. Oil is used here for gaining light, while bread is not consumed by the fire but by the priests. These features assume the destruction of the Israelites' egocentric natures in the court. Once complete allegiance is shown through the loyalty offering made in the court, an ordinary meal is possible without any concern for disloyalty. This reflects the parallel between what takes place in the hearts of the people and what takes place inside the Tent through Aaron's mediation. Since the priests are given the privilege of participating in the communion, it follows that the ritual symbolically requires them to maintain constant intimate fellowship with the Lord.

However, the imperfect nature of the priestly activities inside the Tent is indicated by the symbolism of the candelabrum and the veil that separates the Holy Place from the Holy of Holies. First, the candelabrum probably symbolizes the Tree of Life in the Garden of Eden. Second, the pattern of cherubim is woven into the veil, and cherubim sit on the ark in the Holy of Holies. Taking into account that in Gen. 3 the cherubim are said to have been placed as the guardians of Eden, it would seem the candelabrum points to a spiritual reality beyond the cherubim on the ark. This implies the following: (1) All the ritual activities, not just in the Tent but also in the outer court, are intended to bring both priests and people to experience the quality of life the first man and woman enjoyed in Eden. (2) However, the divine presence envisaged in the outer part of the Tent is still far removed from what was experienced in Eden. (3) Since the Tree of Life gave eternal life, it is fitting that the idea of perpetuity is stressed in this prescription. (4) Though, after the fall, the ritual activities of the priests inside the Tent are meant to guarantee the presence of the Lord, this cannot yet be fulfilled in an institutional sense. The reason becomes evident when the cause of banishment from Eden is considered: it lay in the self-hiding of the first man and woman. It has been argued that a human's self-hiding before the Lord goes hand in hand with stubbornness, a major characteristic of the egocentric nature. Since the spiritual condition of humanity corresponds to the sanctuary and the Tent, the division of the latter into two parts as well as the prescribed rituals in the Holy Place imply that humans are far removed from the Tree of Life, and that this is due to their stubbornness. Thus, as will be mentioned below, it is reasonable to assume that the ritual in this chapter reflects the condition of the Israelites' hearts.

Despite the above limitations of the ritual and what they symbolize, the Israelites are sternly commanded to bring the best oil and bread for the ritual acts in the Holy Place. And if they obey this command, then the Lord's presence among his people is guaranteed, since this is a covenant between the Lord and the people.

In relation to verses 10–23

How the account in vv. 10–23 relates *in content* to the prescription in vv. 1–9 is rarely answered by commentators. Yet an answer may be forthcoming if the structural relationship between the Tent (or the sanctuary) and the camp is kept in mind, as well as the significance of slandering the Lord's name. The ritual in the Holy Place represents the hearts of the people if they dwell in the camp. This means that, even in the camp, people have the Holy of Holies in their hearts. On this assumption, the designations of location in both sections stand out: in vv. 1–10 the ritual is to be performed *outside the veil* (v. 3), while in vv. 10–23 the blasphemy took place inside the camp (v. 10), even though the blasphemer was stoned to death *outside the camp* (vv. 13, 23). The area of the camp is assumed to be where the Lord is, as long as the people embody the symbolic meaning of the ritual. That the blasphemer is stoned to death outside the camp is a necessary corollary to his blaspheming the Lord, who appears in the Holy of Holies. Just as he rejected the Lord who appears in the Holy of Holies, so the Lord rejects him by having him executed outside the camp.

The rest of the chapter (vv. 17–22) can also be viewed in such a way that the mirroring between the Lord and the people is further applied to relationships between human beings in terms of civil matters.

Moreover, though the second part (vv. 10–23) appears to deal with blatant crimes, it also addresses itself to the inner part of the human heart. For the mother of the culprit, who supposedly incited her son's anger against the Lord, is not punished. The text does not mention the responsibility of his parents, but it does hint that a person may curse God in his or her heart, even though this may not result in verbal blasphemy. Is the presence of the Lord guaranteed in such cases? It seems entirely unlikely. Thus the absence of any cases other than visible/tangible offences allows the Israelites as well as the readers to ponder the presence of offences that may be committed in the human heart, in relation to the ritual performed by Aaron in the Holy Place. Indeed the oil and bread the people offer to Moses and Aaron symbolize the former's wholehearted dedication to the Lord. And if some of the people deny, neglect or ignore the Lord in their hearts (even if they do not express this verbally), it is tantamount to denying the Lord. Such an offence is even more serious than a case of outright blasphemy, because it involves hiding from the Lord (*ḥāṭā'*) while still expressing allegiance to him. If mirroring is applied to the human spiritual condition, is it not likely that all the people in the camp, who worship in the sanctuary, are doomed to eternal condemnation?

The inability of the people to show perfect allegiance to the Lord matches the priests being allowed to officiate only in a place *outside* the Holy of Holies, which symbolically represents the innermost part of the human heart. As in ch. 13, where the symbolic meaning of *ṣāra'at* (leprous disease) implies that all humanity ought to dwell outside the camp, so here all of the Israelites have the potential to be brought outside the camp and to be stoned to death. This becomes all the more likely when the talionic principle is applied to the inner state of the people.

Therefore, on the whole, the first part of this chapter presents the positive and spiritual side of the divine–human relationship through the symbolism of the ritual in the Holy Place, while the second part relates its negative side by reporting a blatant act of blasphemy. The central message of the chapter is that the Lord deals with humans just as humans deal with him. Moreover this is not just the case in affairs relating to civil lawsuits but in all realms (cf. Hoffmon 1992). Examples are numerous, but see 'Comment' on ch. 26 and cf. Ps. 18:25[26]–26[27]. The Lord's handling of humans in this way suggests that the human reality, however unsatisfactory or evil, is ultimately God's will in the sense that it reflects his verdict.

New Testament implications

By the death of Christ on the cross the curtain separating the Holy Place and the Holy of Holies was abandoned, as 'he entered once for all into the Holy Places, not by means of the blood of goats and calves but by means of his own blood, thus securing an eternal redemption' (Heb. 9:12 ESV).

However, if Jesus Christ has removed the curtain and the way to eternal life is opened, so-called believers are unable to enter the Holy of Holies (not to mention gaining access to the Tree of Life beyond the cherubim) *if they still possess even the slightest residue of selfishness in their hearts.* That is why NT writers give numerous warnings about the dangerous state of believers and exhort us strongly to take up the cross and endure the

Lord's tests, because by going through this process our human egocentric nature is destroyed (Jas 1:12; Matt. 10:38; 16:24; Mark 8:34; Luke 9:23).

The theme of blasphemy is related to the spiritual transformation of believers. Jesus averred, 'Truly, I say to you, all sins will be forgiven the children of man, and whatever blasphemies they utter, but whoever blasphemes against the Holy Spirit never has forgiveness, but is guilty of an eternal sin' (Mark 3:28–29 ESV). Needless to say, forgiveness is given only to those who realize their self-hiding. Yet according to this standard, the blasphemy in Lev. 24 can be forgiven. This suggests capital punishment is not the final destiny for the offender and that the believer should realize that an even more terrifying fate awaits those who blaspheme the Holy Spirit. Though the latter is commonly interpreted as the sin of saying that Jesus, as head of the demons, expels demons, it has a much wider reference. Since the Holy Spirit leads one to realize one's self-hiding, the egocentric nature hinders him from accomplishing this.

Jesus' teaching shows a higher standard to his followers in that they must show selfless love to their persecutors (Matt. 5:38–39), which is far from a way of life characterized by 'measure for measure'. Those who meet such a standard have the kind of heart characteristic of people who dwell in the kingdom of heaven, totally and experientially persuaded they deserve the death penalty. On a higher dimension, then, mirroring takes place; reaping what one sows is to be applied to the question of whether one has lived on the basis of Jesus' teaching. As Wenham comments, 'it is on this basis that God will judge mankind' (Wenham 1979: 313; see Rom. 2:6–16).

Since the light in the Holy Place symbolizes the light of God, it points forwards to the light of the Holy Spirit in the NT. Essentially such light is that given after the complete burning of the egocentric nature in the forecourt. Yet because of the remaining human egocentric nature, the light is dim. The labour on the part of the people to bring the purest possible oil and offer it to the Lord recalls the endeavour of the wise women in Matt. 25:1–13, where this motif of tending to an oil supply is said to divide humankind into those who have two entirely different fates. Where the Lord is, there ought to be nothing to hide from him. The NT is replete with admonitions not to quench the Spirit who is given to believers (e.g. 1 Thess. 5:19), which means to keep uncovering oneself and killing one's egocentric nature, since these represent respectively the processes of purification and sanctification.

LEVITICUS 25:1–55

Translation

[1]The LORD spoke to Moses on Mount Sinai, saying, [2]'Speak to the Israelites and say to them, When you come into the land that I give you, the land shall keep a

sabbath to the Lord. [3]For six years you shall sow your field, and for six years you shall prune your vineyard and gather in its fruits, [4]but in the seventh year there shall be a sabbath of solemn rest for the land, a sabbath to the Lord. You shall not sow your field or prune your vineyard. [5]You shall not reap what grows of itself in your harvest, or gather the grapes of your undressed vine. It shall be a year of solemn rest for the land. [6]The sabbath of the land shall provide food for you, for yourself and for your male and female slaves and for your hired servant and the sojourner who lives with you, [7]and for your cattle and for the wild animals that are in your land: all its yield shall be for food.

[8]'You shall count seven weeks of years, seven times seven years, so the time of the seven weeks of years shall give you forty-nine years. [9]Then you shall sound the loud trumpet on the tenth day of the seventh month. On the Day of Atonement you shall sound the trumpet throughout all your land. [10]And you shall consecrate the fiftieth year, and proclaim liberty throughout the land to all its inhabitants. It shall be a Jubilee for you, when each of you shall return to his property and each of you shall return to his clan. [11]That fiftieth year shall be a Jubilee for you; in it you shall neither sow nor reap what grows of itself nor gather the grapes from the undressed vines. [12]For it is a Jubilee. It shall be holy to you. You may eat the produce of the field.

[13]'In this year of Jubilee each of you shall return to his property. [14]And if you make a sale to your fellow or buy from your fellow, you shall not wrong one another. [15]You shall pay your fellow according to the number of years after the Jubilee, and he shall sell to you according to the number of years for crops. [16]If the years are many, you shall increase the price, and if the years are few, you shall reduce the price, for it is the number of the crops that he is selling to you. [17]You shall not wrong one another, but you shall fear your God, for I am the Lord your God. [18]Therefore you shall carry out my statutes and keep my rules and perform them, and then you will dwell in the land securely. [19]The land will yield its fruit, and you will eat your fill and dwell in it securely.

[20]'And if you say, What shall we eat in the seventh year, if we may not sow or gather in our crop? [21]I will command my blessing on you in the sixth year, so it will produce a crop sufficient for three years. [22]When you sow in the eighth year, you will be eating some of the old crop; you shall eat the old until the ninth year, when its crop arrives.

[23]'The land shall not be sold conclusively, for the land is mine. For you are strangers and sojourners with me. [24]And in all the country you possess, you shall allow a redemption of the land.

[25]'If your brother becomes poor and sells part of his property, then his nearest redeemer shall come and redeem what his brother has sold. [26]If a man has no-one to redeem it and then himself becomes prosperous and finds sufficient means to redeem it, [27]let him calculate the years since he sold it and pay back the balance to the man to whom he sold it, and then return to his property. [28]But if he has not sufficient means to recover it, then what he sold shall remain in the hand of the buyer until the year of Jubilee. In the Jubilee it shall be released, and he shall return to his property. [29]If a man sells a dwelling house in a walled city, he may redeem it

within a year of its sale. For a full year he shall have the right of redemption. [30]If it
is not redeemed within a full year, then the house in the walled city shall belong
conclusively to the buyer, throughout his generations; it shall not be released in
the Jubilee. [31]But the houses of the villages that have no wall around them shall
be considered as the fields of the land. They may be redeemed, and they shall be
released in the Jubilee. [32]As for the cities of the Levites, the Levites may redeem at
any time the houses in the cities they possess. [33]And the houses that one redeems
from the Levites, their sold house and his possessed city shall be released in the
Jubilee. For the houses in the cities of the Levites are their possession among
the Israelites. [34]But the fields of pastureland belonging to their cities may not be
sold, for that is their possession forever.

[35]'If your brother becomes poor and cannot maintain himself beside you, you
shall support him as though he were a stranger and a sojourner, and he shall live
with you. [36]Take no interest from him or profit, but fear your God, that your
brother may live beside you. [37]You shall not lend him your money at interest, nor
give him your food for profit. [38]I am the LORD your God, who brought you out of
the land of Egypt to give you the land of Canaan, and to be your God.

[39]'If your brother becomes poor beside you and sells himself to you, you shall
not make him serve as a slave: [40]he shall be with you as a hired servant and as
a sojourner. He shall serve with you until the year of the Jubilee. [41]Then he shall
go out from you, he and his children with him, and go back to his own clan
and return to the possession of his fathers. [42]For they are my servants, whom I
brought out of the land of Egypt; they shall not be sold as slaves. [43]You shall
not rule over him ruthlessly but shall fear your God. [44]As for your male and
female slaves whom you may have: you may buy male and female slaves from
among the nations that are around you. [45]You may also buy from among the
strangers who sojourn with you and their clans that are with you, who have been
born in your land, and they may be your property. [46]You may bequeath them to
your sons after you to inherit as a possession forever. You may make them
work, but over your brothers the Israelites you shall not rule, one over another
ruthlessly.

[47]'If a stranger or sojourner with you becomes rich, and your brother beside him
becomes poor and sells himself to the stranger or sojourner with you or to an
offshoot of a stranger's clan, [48]then after he is sold he may be redeemed. One of his
brothers may redeem him, [49]or his uncle or his cousin may redeem him, or a close
relative from his clan may redeem him. Or if he grows rich he may redeem himself.
[50]He shall calculate with his buyer from the year when he sold himself to him until
the year of Jubilee, and the price of his sale shall vary with the number of years. The
time he was with his owner shall be rated as the time of a hired servant. [51]If there
are still many years left, he shall pay proportionately for his redemption some of his
sale price. [52]If there remain but a few years until the year of Jubilee, he shall
calculate and pay for his redemption in proportion to his years of service. [53]He
shall treat him as a servant hired year by year. He shall not rule ruthlessly over him
in your sight. [54]And if he is not redeemed by these means, then he and his children
with him shall be released in the year of Jubilee.

[55]'For it is to me that the Israelites are servants. They are my servants whom I brought out of the land of Egypt: I am the LORD your God.'

Notes on the text

5. 'what grows of itself': *śĕpîaḥ* SamP and Tg read it in pl. construct, as in v. 11.

14. 'you [pl.] make a sale': *timkĕrû* SamP, LXX, Vg and versions read it in sg. in accordance with the sg. suffixes in this verse. Such a concordance in number is needed in translation, but by no means reflects the original, as there are many such cases where there is no concordance in number.

18. 'my statutes ... my rules': *ḥuqqōtay ... mišpātay* LXX affixes 'all' before the words.

20. 'our crop (sg.)': *tĕbû'ātênû* Hebr. MSS, SamP, LXX, Syr and Vg read it in pl.

21. 'it will produce': *wĕ'āśāt* The expected form is *wĕ'aśtâ* (so SamP). The MT may have an older form (cf. *GKC* 75m).

23. 'conclusively': *liṣĕmîtût* The term occurs only here and in v. 30 in the whole OT. From within this chapter it is possible to say it is synonymous with *lĕ'ôlām*. *HALOT* (s.v.) explains the term as meaning 'with irrevocable validity', which seems correct.

25. 'your brother': *'āḥîkā* LXX adds 'with you', as in v. 39. However, in view of the deliberate variations concerning the four protases in vv. 25, 35, 39, 47 (see 'Form and structure'), MT should be retained.

30. *'ăšer lō'* This *lō'* should be read *lô* (to it) as is done by SamP and the versions.

33. *wă'ăšer* This verse is not independent but is a continuation of v. 32. The antecedent of the phrase is *bātê 'ārê 'ăḥuzzātām* (the houses of the cities of their possession) in v. 32. The phrase *'îr 'ăḥuzzātô* has been considered difficult to translate (*BHS* suggests reading *bêt 'îr* instead of *bayit wĕ'îr*). However, its use aims to indicate that the city, where the purchased house is located, will be returned to the Levites anyway, though one would not purchase a whole Levitical city.

35. 'cannot maintain himself': *māṭâ yādô* Lit. 'his hand becomes in trouble' The verb comes from the root *mwṭ* and the phrase is unique in the OT.

'beside you': *'immāk* JPS translates it 'under your authority'. Lit. 'with you', but either the JPS translation or the proposed one is clearer. See also v. 39.

'as though' Though the corresponding Hebr. term is missing, it is translated this way. So does LXX (like).

'live': *wāḥāy* A few Hebr. MSS, SamP and LXX add 'your brother', perhaps influenced by v. 36b.

39. 'you shall not make him serve': *lō' ta'ăbod bô* LXX reads 'Do not let him serve you'.

46. 'You may make them work' LXX does not translate this part. However, it is necessary in view of *'bd* in v. 39 and *rdh* in v. 43; both are used again in v. 46.

'forever': *lĕ'ôlām* The Masoretic accentuation understands this phrase as qualifying the following and not the preceding *'ăḥuzzâ* (property). But it is preferable to take it as qualifying *'ăḥuzzâ*, as do the large majority of Eng. translations.

47. 'the stranger or sojourner': *gēr tôšāb* There is no *wāw* before the latter, which was apparently corrected in some Hebr. MSS, SamP, LXX and Syr.

'or to an offshoot': *'ô lĕ'eqer* LXX omits this.

49. 'Or if': *'ô* 'Ô has the meaning of 'or if'; see also 26:41b.

Form and structure

Lev. 25 deals with the sabbatical year and the year of Jubilee. In that ch. 23 deals with holy festive days this chapter is considered to be its continuation. Both deal with *holy time*, but the sabbatical year and the year of Jubilee relate to much longer periods of time than the annual festivals. As in ch. 23, this chapter challenges the human egocentric nature by commanding the consecration of the sabbatical and Jubilee years (for more details, see 'Explanation').

In assessing form and structure it is important to keep in mind the lawgiver's intention. Indeed this chapter is applicable to all of Israelite society in terms of the land and property as well as the Israelites themselves. However, although no sufficient attention is previously paid elsewhere to the significance of v. 18 (see 'Comment' there), this institution makes sense only when the people observe the commandments of the Lord. In fact, not only are some fundamental principles explicitly mentioned, such as 'You shall fear your God' (v. 17), 'You shall carry out my statutes and keep my rules and perform them' (v. 18), but in order to observe the rules on the Jubilee and sabbatical years, one ought to be unselfish, as is clear from the rules pertaining to impoverished fellow Israelites. The spirit of neighbourly love commanded in ch. 19 pervades the regulations throughout. Cf. *'ămît/'aḥ* (cf. vv. 14–15 with 19:17), *hônā'* (cf. v. 17 with 19:33), *yārē'tā mē'ĕlōhêkā* (cf. v. 17 with 19:14, 32). Thus, as is summarized in v. 18, the complete observance of the Lord's commandments is assumed, which demands or assumes an existential transformation of the Israelites if they are to observe the rules: they must truly become the Lord's slaves to the extent that they accept they possess nothing in this world (see 'Explanation'). Conformably the idea of 'consecrating' the fiftieth year requires a heart with such a condition. Thus contrary to the chapter's appearance it addresses the presumed holiness of the Israelites and how the Lord will respond with blessing. The general outline of the chapter is as follows:

	1–2aa	The Lord's address to Moses to speak to the Israelites
A	2ab–7	The sabbatical year
B	8–19	General stipulations for the year of Jubilee
	8–12	The fundamental aspects of the institution
	13–19	Specifics of the celebration of the year Return to one's inherited land Selling and buying the land and including method
A′	20–22	The Lord's blessing on the seventh year
	23–24	The theological reason for the inalienability of the land
B′	25–54	Four cases where a fellow Israelite becomes impoverished, and their measures
	25–34	Rules on selling/leasing land or houses
	35–38	Rules on loans to a poor Israelite
	39–46	Rules on slaves, both in the case of an Israelite and the foreigner
	47–54	Rules on the Israelite who is held by a resident alien or a stranger
	55	The theological reason for the above rules on the slave

In v. 1 the Lord is said to speak 'on Mount Sinai'. This geographical note reappears in 26:46 and 27:34. Partly because of this, some exegetes take chs. 25 – 26 as a single literary unit (e.g. Hartley 1992: 414). It is true that in style and content ch. 25 exhibits a close relationship with ch. 26 (see 'Form and structure' in ch. 26). At least, some stress is laid on the fact that these three chapters are revealed on Mount Sinai (see 'Comment' on v. 1). However, the significance of the geographical note lies on a different level to the content of this chapter (see 'Form and structure' in ch. 27 for more detail).

As a whole, A–B sets out a general principle that receives a more detailed treatment in A′B′. Yet the whole is knit together by an association of ideas and words, so to assume a clear division may not reflect the text's true nature. For the question of whether vv. 23–24 belong to what precedes or follows, see 'Comment'. These verses can be taken as relating to both. Nevertheless the theological rationale given in vv. 23–24 relates to vv. 25–34 but not the whole of B′. Therefore these verses may better be classified as belonging to A′.

Now A begins with rules on the sabbatical year and ends with the people's apprehension about what they will eat in the seventh year (vv. 20–22), A'. Though this query refers directly to the sabbatical year, it also applies to the year of Jubilee. B addresses itself to various cases of selling and purchasing land and property up until the year of Jubilee. Therefore it is, in a sense, a sequel to the rules on the year of Jubilee in vv. 8–19, so the entire chapter is constructed something like A (2–7) – B (8–19) – A' (20–24) – B' (25–55), which is a frequent structure in Leviticus (see Introduction 4.1).

B' is divisible into four sections, the first three of which begin with (*wĕ*) *kî yāmûk 'āḥîkā* ('when your brother becomes poor', vv. 25, 35, 39), and the fourth with *wĕkî* (v. 47). It deals with four cases where an Israelite becomes impoverished for various reasons. The addressee is called 'you' in the 2nd person sg. throughout.

The fellow Israelite who becomes poor is consistently called 'your brother' (*'āḥîkā*), probably to stress that the Israelites are 'brothers' who share the same status before the Lord (v. 55). It is notable that the first and fourth cases involve the addressee indirectly, whereas the second and third involve him directly.

The four cases are arranged according to increasing degrees of predicament fellow Israelites find themselves in (cf. Chirichigno 1993: 324–343). The first case deals with a case where an Israelite is forced to sell part of his land, but the land is redeemable at any time. The second deals with a man's poverty, the third with the case where a man sells himself to an Israelite with the warning that the purchaser should not treat him like a slave, and the fourth with a case where a man sells himself to a stranger. The rule on the slave (vv. 44–46) makes the fourth case the most serious in terms of the status of the impoverished Israelite.

Two further observations should be made: (1) While the method of redemption (*gĕ'ullâ*) is mentioned in the first and fourth cases, the fourth supplements what is not mentioned in the first; i.e. the identity of the redeemer (*gô'ēl*; cf. v. 25 with vv. 48–49). (2) In terms of what relationship the addressee has with the impoverished Israelite, this is expressed in a subtle way by the use of the preposition *'im* (*'immekâ*). In the first and fourth cases the addressee does not involve himself with the man in need, whereas he does involve himself with this person in the second and third cases.

That AB and A'B' form a literary unit is further suggested by use of particular terms, such as *'āmît/'āḥ*, *yāṣā'*, *g'l*. First, *'ămît* and *'āḥ* are terms in ch. 19 used to discuss neighbourly love (e.g. v. 17). The two terms appear in this chapter in a significant way. *'Āmît* is found only in A–B (vv. 14–15, 17), whereas the occurrence of *'āḥ*, though it appears just once in v. 14, is concentrated in B' (vv. 25, 35–36, 39, 46–48). The spreading of this pair over the two halves points to the unity of this chapter. Second, within B' *yāṣā'* and the root *g'l* play special roles. *Yāṣā'* may well be a specific legal term that connotes the cancellation of a contract (vv. 28, 30–31, 33, 54), whereas the same root *yṣ'* is used to describe an impoverished Israelite's 'going out' from his fellow Israelites or a stranger (vv. 41, 54) and the Lord's bringing out (*hôṣî'*) the Israelites from Egypt (vv. 38, 42, 55). Clearly this literary feature is instrumental in inculcating the idea in the minds and hearts of the Israelites that, spiritually, the year of Jubilee corresponds to the Lord's deliverance of them from Egypt. The same purpose is achieved by expressing the redemptive measure by *gā'al* or *gĕ'ullâ* (nineteen times in B^{I}). It is a measure, before the year of Jubilee, to return the status of land, a house or an impoverished Israelite back to the status they had when the Israelites were delivered from the Egyptians. Just as the Lord redeemed them, so should the Israelites display such acts of salvation towards their fellow Israelites. As a whole, the four cases exhibit an artful structure.

As evidence for different literary layers, some exegetes point out the alteration that occurs between the 2nd person sg. and 2nd person pl. addresses in this chapter (Hartley 1992: 426). But this hardly constitutes such evidence, since the same literary phenomenon is found in other chapters (e.g. 2:11–15; 18:2b–6, 6–23, 24–30; 19:12, 15, 19).

More questionable is the mention of the Levitical cities and their land in vv. 32–34. This is the first time 'the cities of Levites' is mentioned, not just in Leviticus but in the whole Pentateuch. 'The cities of Levites' is later detailed in Num. 35:1–8 and Josh. 21. To assume that this passage betrays the hand of a writer who assumes the Numbers passage is tenuous. First, the legislation is a necessary extension of the rulings given for the possessed land (*'ăḥuzzâ*, vv. 10, 13, 24–25, 27–28), and in vv. 32–34 it is mentioned in the context of the 'city' (*'îr*, v. 29). Second, some laws in Leviticus that are descriptive or symbolic do not have their practical aspects expounded until Numbers. Examples include 'The priest who is chief among his brothers, on whose head the anointing oil is poured' (21:10; see 'Comment' there), 'an offering for annihilation' in 23:8 etc. (see 'Comment' on 23:6–8). It seems safer to see this tendency as simply characteristic of Leviticus. With regard to the Levitical cities, it is no more or less implied in 25:32 than that the Levites have their own cities, and that this phenomenon will be treated later. Rather than the practical details, the law appears to stress the spiritual message it conveys (see 'Comment' there).

Relationship with other related laws

Exod. 21:2–11, 23:10–11 and Deut. 15:1–8 contain laws on the manumission of slaves in the seventh year and the fallow land. However, there is no mention of the Jubilee year in these laws. Thus it is clear that the legislation in Lev. 25 is entirely different from the other two sets of laws: in Lev. 25 the sabbatical year contains no laws on the manumission of slaves in the seventh year; rather that subject is incorporated into the laws for the year of Jubilee. In other words, the Hebrew slaves are potentially redeemable at any time.

Although it is not my intention to comment on the literary and ideological relationship between the three laws dealing with similar topics, Exod. 21, 23, Lev. 25 and Deut. 15 (cf. Japhet 1986: 63–89; Chirichigno 1993), one factor seems to be of paramount importance in dealing with this question: the practicability/impracticability of the sabbatical or Jubilee years. The very way the laws are presented in Lev. 25 as well as the institution itself appears to make its implementation extremely difficult. For instance, the people's apprehension in vv. 20–22 concerns the sabbatical year and not the year of Jubilee. If they find it difficult to comprehend observing the sabbatical year, how much more difficult will it be for them to do so for the Jubilee year? Moreover, apart from the potential difficulties associated with observing the laws of vv. 25–55, it must be stressed that the institution of the year of Jubilee assumes complete observance of the Lord's commandments (v. 18), though this aspect is, at least on the surface, not dominant in this chapter. Among other factors surrounding the year of Jubilee, as the rules in vv. 25ff. show, the observance of the year of Jubilee is not limited to that year alone, but to all time as far as the status of land, houses and Israelites are concerned. In view of the impracticability or impossibility of observing this institution, it is no wonder that no clear historical evidence exists on the observance of the year of Jubilee, and that the Deuteronomic law reverted to the law, something similar to the one in Exod. 21 and 23, if the relative chronological order of Exod. 21 and 23, Lev. 25 and Deut. 15 is assumed (cf. Japhet 1986; Milgrom 2001: 2254–2257).

As for the prevalent tendency to date the composition of this chapter after the exile, Chirichigno has argued for an early date of the Jubilee legislation on the ground of its literary analysis and its parallel to the *mîšarum* (justice) edicts in Babylon (Chirichigno 1993: 357). He also argues for the possiblity that the Deuteronomic law existed contemporaneously with the Levitical law. Bergsma also lists various considerations that make such a date unlikely (Bergsma 2003: 225–246). However, as the following 'Comment' and 'Explanation' show, it is also unlikely that there ever was a period in the history of Israel where such legislation needed to be produced by a human hand.

Comment

25:1–7

1. The Lord commands Moses on Mount Sinai to relate the following rules concerning the sabbatical year and Jubilee to the Israelites. The phrase 'on Mount Sinai' has not appeared since 7:38, the concluding passage of

6:8[1] – 7:36 and 1:1 – 7:36. In Leviticus the phrase again appears in 26:46 and 27:34. Should such a geographical reference be taken only as a literary embellishment or as indicating the literal location? Possibly both. At least, the content of the last three chapters of Leviticus was delivered to the people through Moses on Mount Sinai. However, as 27:34 appears to say that all the rules and statutes in Leviticus were given on Mount Sinai, it would be more advisable to read the geographical designation as emphasizing that the following rules were given on the very mountain where Moses received the Ten Commandments. Thus it seems that while the designation does not rule out that the other rules in Leviticus were given on Mount Sinai, it certainly emphasizes that the following laws are given from the lofty point of the mountain that corresponds to the Holy of Holies in the Tent (cf. the three divisions in the Sinai event in Exod. 19).

2. 'When you come to the land': *kî tābō'û 'el hā'āreṣ* Similar introductions appear in 14:34, 19:23 and 23:10. In all of these the land is assumed to be a gift from the Lord. All the stipulations of this chapter assume an agricultural setting in the Promised Land. Every seventh year is to be a sabbatical year, where the land rests (an absence of agricultural activity): Israel's seven-year calendar should reflect the creational pattern of six days' work and a sabbath.

'the land shall keep a sabbath to the Lord': *šabtâ hā'āreṣ šabbāt laYHWH* In the Pentateuch, instances where *šbt* qal appears with an impersonal object are found in Gen. 8:22 and Lev. 23:32. More importantly, this is the first instance in the Pentateuch where the idea of the land taking a rest appears. While the land's taking a rest is conditional on the Israelites' observance of the regulation in this chapter, the starting point of the sabbatical year is with the deliberate resting of the land, and not with the people who are subordinated to the need of the land. It is as if to say, 'Because the land needs a rest, you must not work on it.' This is stressed by the following details.

3–5. The six-plus-one cycle of the weekly sabbath is here extrapolated to years. For six years the people sow, prune the vineyards and harvest crops, but in the seventh year there is a complete rest for the land: they are not to sow or prune their vineyards. V. 5 underscores this principle by referring to the specific aspect of the people's work: *sāpîaḥ* (what grows of itself), *'innĕbê nĕzîrĕkā* (the grapes of your undressed vine) as well as the new verb *bāṣar* (gather) appear to stress the need for a complete rest from work on the part of the people. While some scholars posit that the lying fallow of this sabbatical year is not simultaneously universal, but particular and rotating (e.g. North 1954: 119–120), Chirichigno stresses that it is universal and simultaneous but that it applies to some part of the field and not all the land, while other parts are still cultivated (Chirichigno 1993: 308–310). However, the text does not appear to make such distinctions. The fallow must be universal and simultaneous, extending to all the fields in every seventh year.

In 19:9–10 the people in the Promised Land are required not to harvest their field to its corners, a rule meant to curb the selfishness of the people. But here in ch. 25 they are to cease from all work in their fields. Could a person who is unable to observe the law in 19:9–10 observe this law in 25:3–5?

The sabbatical year is not said to be 'holy', but so much is undoubtedly assumed, since the year is not only referred to as a sabbath, but even as a complete sabbath (*šabbat šabbātôn*, 'a sabbath of solemn rest') (v. 4). It appears that the legislator intends to incorporate the holy nature of the sabbatical year into that of the Jubilee year (see vv. 10, 12). Similarly the land is said to be holy not just in this chapter but throughout Leviticus, which is related to the overall view of the land–people–sanctuary. The sanctuary is consistently viewed as a holy realm, but the land, being distinct from the people, belongs to the Lord. Nevertheless the conduct or spiritual state of the Israelites is reflected in the land and the sanctuary: what happens to the sanctuary happens to the land.

6–7. The merit of observing the sabbatical year is mentioned in vv. 6–7: the Israelites, their slaves, maidservants, cattle and all the living creatures can rest and live off the land's produce. It is not stated how this comes about. That resting the land results in food for the cattle and creatures therein is more understandable, since they may eat the unharvested produce. This also encourages the reader to take the sabbatical year in conjunction with the Jubilee year. The answer is, in fact, given in vv. 20ff. The pending nature of these verses is meant to stress the absolute nature of the rest of the land: if the latter is secured all will go well for the living creatures in the land, including humans.

25:8–12

This section, building on the sabbatical year, sets out the year of Jubilee, which is celebrated the year following forty-nine years (seven multiplied by seven). As is implied by the first Hebr. word, 'You shall count' (v. 8), the seven intervening sabbatical years are designed to prepare the people for the Jubilee (see 'Comment' on 15:13 and 23:15). Thus the year of Jubilee should not be taken just as a year that comes around once in fifty years: it is the culminating year of the preceding sabbatical years, beginning with the observance of a weekly sabbath.

The basic principle underlying this year is described in this section, while the subsequent sections starting from v. 13 detail and expand the principle. The principle is as follows: (1) The fiftieth year is the Jubilee year, and this year is holy (*qōdeš*, v. 12). (2) On the tenth of the seventh month a ram's horn blast must be heard to announce the beginning of the Jubilee. The trumpet sound signifies, in both Testaments, God's direct manifestation or involvement in the human realm (Exod. 19:16, 19; 20:18; Josh. 6:4–6;

Judg. 6:34; 1 Kgs 1:34 etc.). That the sound is to be blasted on the Day of Atonement should not be overlooked. The significance of the Jubilee's commencement on the Day of Atonement is that on this day all the self-hidings of the people are atoned for, so the Israelites are cleansed from inner defilement. Though in Exod. 19 the people feared God's dwelling near them on Mount Sinai, no such fear is envisaged on this occasion, for this is a year of freedom and joy. (3) During this year the release of all debt is carried out throughout the country; of greatest significance is that every Israelite returns to his inherited land and family. (4) No work can be done during this year.

As in the observance of a weekly sabbath (Exod. 20:8), the consecration of the Jubilee year is actualized when the people become holy. Thus, while the year of Jubilee itself is holy (12), failure to consecrate the year constitutes the profanation of its holiness. In the Pentateuch the construction *qiddēš* followed by a reference to time has appeared only several times thus far in connection with the sabbath day (Gen. 2:3; Exod. 20:8, 11; Deut. 5:12). However, this is the first appearance of *qōdeš* as an independent form. This is significant, particularly because *qdš* pi. does not appear in ch. 23 where the holy occasions are set out, even though all of the festive days were to be consecrated. In view of the literary and ideological relationship between chs. 23 and 25, the absence of 'consecrate' (*qiddēš*) in ch. 23 may deliberately anticipate the law on the Jubilee in ch. 25. Neither is the sabbatical year said to be holy in this chapter, though this is assumed. Perhaps a desire to emphasize the year of Jubilee is responsible for this omission.

In principle the consecration of the Jubilee year is commensurate with that of the weekly sabbath, yet the Jubilee institution reveals rich manifestations of the holy nature of time in view of the following regulation.

As for the weekly sabbath (Exod. 20:8), the consecration of the Jubilee year is deeply related to human beings. It is stated in this commentary that holiness is a matter of the human heart, which is primarily characterized by an absence of the egocentric nature. This is to be expressed outwardly and institutionally by the people doing no agricultural labour throughout the year, the observance of which depends on whether the egocentric nature is destroyed. Thus as v. 10 commands the people to consecrate (*qiddēš*) the whole year, it is assumed that the people do not commit self-hiding, nor contract uncleanness, for they are assumed to be unselfish. However, this is entirely unlikely to happen. Moreover how can a person become holy only in the year of Jubilee when he has not been so in the preceding years? But the rules in this chapter are set out with the assumption that the people become holy irrespective of the human predicament. Some comments are required concerning the following words and phrases.

'the fiftieth year': *šĕnat haḥămîššîm šānâ* In view of v. 8, this 'fiftieth year' simply refers to the year following the forty-nine years, so there are two successive fallow years. Some scholars reject this reading because the rule would seem too hard to implement. Instead they suggest that the forty-ninth year overlaps with the Jubilee year (inclusive reckoning), or, alternatively, they suggest reading v. 8b as 'the forty-nine days of the seven cycles of sabbatical years shall be for you a year, intercalated in the seventh month of the forty-ninth year' (for details, cf. Chirichigno 1993: 317–321). However, the adoption of such interpretations is unnecessary. The law's apparent infeasibility in this regard is meant to demand faith in God's provision. This is more explicitly suggested in vv. 20–22.

'liberty': *dĕrôr* The biblical Jubilee has been discussed in relation to the Babylonian *andurārum*, which likewise stipulates the release of slaves and debt, but no connection has as yet been proven (cf. Olivier 1997).

'a Jubilee': *yôbēl* The OT attests to various meanings for this term, and even its basic meaning is uncertain (cf. Hartley 1992: 428; Milgrom 2001: 2169). Though it can refer to a 'ram' or some specific type of the ram's horn (see Exod. 19:13; Josh. 6:4–5 etc.), in this chapter and ch. 27 (vv. 27–28 etc.) it bears an abstract meaning such as 'remission', 'release' or 'liberty'. The first meaning may well underlie the latter ones, considering a blast from a ram's horn accompanied such occasions. However, it is possible that it derives from the ordinary sense of *yābal*, meaning 'to be carried' or 'to be led', though the qal form is not found in the OT. If so, the noun form would mean something like 'what carries' or 'what leads'; in particular, where the term appears to suggest that the person carried or led either by persons or the Lord is innocent (Isa. 53:7; 55:12; Jer. 11:19; Ps. 45:14[15], 15[16]; Job 10:19 etc.).

Vv. 11–12 comprise two sets of parallelisms. Within each the first half mentions the Jubilee's general character, and the second half refers to concrete aspects that relate directly to the people, first negatively (11, no harvesting) and second positively (12, eating). Note the linguistic variations between vv. 11b and 5a, and between vv. 12b and 6–7. The additional element in the Jubilee year compared with the sabbatical year is that the people return to their inherited land and family.

25:13–19

13–14. First, the fundamental rule that all should return to their inherited land in the Jubilee year is set out (v. 10b). This is a unique feature of the Jubilee, absent in the sabbatical year. The term *mimkār* ordinarily connotes the selling and purchasing of immovable estate. So this word and the last word in v. 13, 'his inherited land', combine to suggest that the Lord intends to introduce the topic of selling or purchasing the property.

From v. 14 onwards the lawgiver begins to address one's attitude to his neighbour in business years other than the Jubilee year: he is not to exploit his neighbour.

15–16. The price of the property or estate is calculated with reference to how many years have elapsed since the Jubilee year. In this regard, the price is fixed according to the number of non-fallow years remaining. This implies that the amount of annual produce is fixed, for to worry that there might be poor crops or famine would be at odds with the spirit of the Jubilee.

17. Referring back to v. 14, this verse stresses that a person must not oppress his neigbour by exploiting him. *'al tônû* (v. 14) is paralleled by *lō' tônû* (v. 17). Moreover *'ămît* and *'îš*, which are found in both parts of v. 14, are combined in this instance in the form *'îš 'et 'ămîtô*. The motive for not oppressing one's neighbour is twofold: on the one hand God must be feared; on the other, the Lord is the God of both him and his neighbour. In dealing with others he must keep in mind that there is a God who judges him, and that before God he is no different from his neighbour.

18–19. As is indicated by the repetitive 'observing the Lord's statutes and rules' (18:4–5, 26; 19:37; 20:22), the Lord is referring to all the statutes and rules of Leviticus in addition to those of this chapter: the latter are included in the former. It is questionable how this command to observe the Lord's rules and statutes relates either to the preceding verse or the one following. While v. 18 can be taken as an elaboration of the fear of God in v. 17, v. 18 can be taken as the necessary condition for abundant production and a secure dwelling in v. 19. Thus it seems reasonable to take v. 18 as related to both vv. 17 and 19.

Security within the land along with abundant production is contingent upon the people's observance of *all* the Lord's rules and statutes (cf. 26:3–5). Is this condition unrelated to the content of 'consecrating' or 'hallowing' the Jubilee year mentioned in v. 10? Indeed the Jubilee year comes automatically, but the people's consecration of the year is not automatically guaranteed.

The mention of 'the land' in v. 18b and at the beginning of v. 19 reveals that the land will be responsive to their observance of all the Lord's commandments, yielding rich produce so that the people will eat to their satisfaction and live securely.

25:20–22

This section deals with the possible apprehension the people may feel at the prospect of not sowing or harvesting in the seventh year (vv. 3–7). What will they eat? The Lord declares that he will greatly increase the production of the sixth year, so much so that the resultant abundance of produce will last until the end of the ninth year. Since the people will commence agricultural activity again in the eighth year, they will continue eating the old produce into the ninth year. Thus within the context of instructions on the sabbatical year, this section simultaneously aims to answer the inevitable question of how Israel will survive during the two consecutive fallow years that will occur at the time of the Jubilee year. Essentially even more faith will be required of the people at this time. The implicit logic is, if the Lord's blessing on the seventh year is such, how much more on the year of Jubilee!

That the law envisages the people as worrying about their food rather than their ability to observe the Lord's commandments is ironic (v. 18), for the promised blessing of the seventh year is contingent upon complete observance of the laws, the essence of which is unselfishness.

At the same time, the belated mentioning of this potential query implies that such a worry is of no importance in the Lord's opinion compared with the standard that the Lord expects from the faith of his people. If they cannot observe the sabbatical year, they cannot observe the Jubilee either, and to observe both, faith in the Lord's promise is required. Two elements surrounding the sabbatical year and Jubilee merge at this point: 'Consecrating the year of Jubilee' (v. 10) must go hand in hand with the observance of all the Lord's commandments (v. 18). Faith is not explicitly discussed in Leviticus, but it should be stressed that the biblical understanding of faith requires that a person who believes in the Lord is holy and observes all the commandments. But to have such a faith requires that a person not only understand or realize, but be completely persuaded that nothing in this world belongs to him.

25:23–24

Opinions are divided as to whether these verses conclude what precedes or introduce what follows (cf. Hubbard 1991: 8). Yet it is not always necessary to make such a distinction, particularly within a hortatory context. As they stand, these verses both serve to give the principle for selling the land and introduce the rules that follow regarding an impoverished brother. In other words, they are transitional.

The central and profound rationale for the sabbatical and Jubilee institutions is set out here: the land shall not be sold in perpetuity, for the land belongs to the Lord. The inalienability of the land is basic to the Jubilee institution. The Israelites will simply dwell there as 'strangers' or 'sojourners', though such appellations are used on a different level to their literal meanings. By declaring that the ownership of the land does not fall to the Israelites, the Lord underscores that no land belongs to them. They are tenants who are permitted to use it providing certain conditions are met.

The sale of inherited land (*'ăḥuzzâ*) occurs with the commencement of a Jubilee year. This prohibits the purchasing of property on a deeper dimension, reflecting the fact that the land ultimately belongs to the Lord. As such, the Israelites are viewed as tenants permitted to make commercial transactions according to prescribed conditions. That is, though the land is a gift from the Lord, it is not to be used as the Israelites would like, but only within the parameters set by certain conditions that reflect the Lord's ownership. Hence provisions are made in v. 24 for the possible repurchase (*gĕ'ullâ*) of land, which by association is linked to the following regulations on what should take place during the years leading up to the year of Jubilee. A corollary of the Lord's ownership of land is that all the produce belongs to him.

Reference to the Israelites as 'strangers and sojourners' in the Promised Land has great theological significance: just as they were in Egypt, so shall they be even within the Promised Land. The difference between Egypt and the Promised Land is one of Lordship. It is only a small step to the idea that, apart from the Lord, the believer possesses nothing in this world (Ps. 39:12[13]; Heb. 11:13; 1 Pet. 2:11).

25:25–34

25. The first concrete economical case is that of a person who becomes so poor that he has to sell (practically, 'lease'; cf. vv. 15, 23 and Japhet 1986: 86) some of his inherited land. The context in which the person became poor is not provided, yet the sale of his land implies bankruptcy. The positioning of these cases after the description of the blessed year of Jubilee ironically implies that this situation resulted from human selfishness and violation of the Lord's commandments (cf. vv. 18–19). In such a case, the person's closest relatives are expected to repurchase the sold land to help provide an income for him.

'a redeemer, repurchaser': *gô'ēl* This term refers to a 'kinsman-redeemer' in the context of family affairs. When trouble occurs, one of the family members assumes the duty of *gĕ'ullâ* (redemption). Practical instances include avenging the blood of a relative as a redeemer of blood (Num. 35:19 etc.), receiving reparation (Num. 5:8), but presumably the responsibility would have covered all areas of family life. Already in the Pentateuch such a redeeming act has been ascribed to the Lord with reference to the exodus event (Exod. 6:6; 15:13).

26–27. When an impoverished person has no such relative to save him from his predicament, he calculates the years between his selling of the land and the approaching Jubilee year, and pays the new owner the appropriate sum of money; then he may return to his inherited land.

28. If that is not feasible, i.e. he cannot afford to pay the price, then the land remains in the hand of the buyer until the Jubilee year, at which time the sold estate reverts to the original owner.

'in the Jubilee it shall be released': *yāṣā' bayyôbēl* The verb *yāṣā'*, which appears in vv. 30–31, 33, 54 and 27:21, has a specific connotation in legal contexts. It has an Akkadian counterpart *waṣia*, and both this and the Hebr. *yāṣā'* probably refer to the condition in which the legal validity of a certain decree loses its force (Tsumura 2000: 73–79).

29–31. If a house to be sold is in a walled city, the right of repurchase is valid only until the end of the year in which it was sold. If it is not repurchased within that year, it belongs to the buyer thereafter (note the term *ṣĕmîtût* in vv. 30 and 23); it is not released in the Jubilee (vv. 29–30). The reason for this has been explained by comparing it with the case in v. 31; i.e. it is claimed that a contrast is drawn between a house in a city and a house in a village (Hartley 1992: 439; cf. Wenham 1979: 321). Rooker adduces Oehler's explanation that 'houses within walled cities fell outside the jurisdiction of family property inheritance and were not critical for the economic survival of the family' (Rooker 2000: 308). However, the differences between city and village houses, and the different value of each, would not seem compelling enough to make such a conclusion.

A comparison with the houses in v. 31 shows that the difference between the two cases lies in whether or not walls surround them. While walls in the OT signify 'protection' and 'security', they remain a human convention, a convention that seems to be regarded as at odds with the spirit of the Jubilee, which was meant to make human attempts at self-protection unnecessary. On the other hand, houses in unwalled villages are regarded as the fields of the land. In line with this, they are sold and purchased with the Jubilee year in view, since at that time they will be returned to their original owners. This truth is applicable to various dimensions of human life. First and foremost, houses without walls are regarded as vulnerable to the enemy's attack and are counted as less valuable than houses with walls. But this typical human view runs contrary to the Lord's: he who protects himself loses his life. In addition to this, these rules may be a veiled criticism of a city life used to increase one's prosperity (cf. Ps. 55:10[11]).

32–34. The houses of the Levites are an exception to the previous law. They can redeem houses sold in cities at any time. The phrase 'at any time' is a translation of *'ôlām*, and guarantees that the right of repurchase always remains. This means that the legal status of the Levite houses is equivalent to that of the land. V. 33a deals with a case where a person other than a Levite purchases a Levite house: such a purchase must revert to the Levites in the Jubilee year (see JPS and NRSV). The reason is significant: the houses of the Levitical cities are their inherited land amid the sons of Israel. Note that it does not say 'amid the land of Israel'. In other words, the Levite houses belong to the sons of Israel, representing the latter. While the Levite houses are saleable, the fields belonging to the houses are not, on the grounds that they remain the perpetual possession of the Levites (v. 34). The phrase *'ăḥuzzat 'ôlām* (possession forever) was used for the Promised Land in general in Gen. 17:8 and 48:4. Here, however, the term is used in a more restricted sense.

Theologically the Levites demonstrated allegiance to the Lord during the Golden Calf incident (Exod. 32:26). Here it is implied they have their own cities and a special status among the Israelites. In v. 23 it is said that the land belongs to the Lord and here the pasture land of the Levites is never to be sold. This seems to imply that their fields continually have the condition that ordinary land has only at the time of the Jubilee. In view of the status of the Levites and the special nature of their property, it is no wonder that the right of repurchase is less restrictive for the Levites than it is for the other Israelites. Such exceptional protection for the Levites and their cities and houses strongly suggests that a Levitical lifestyle is far closer to the spirit of the Jubilee than is the life of ordinary people.

25:35–38

The second case of a fellow Israelite coming into financial difficulty envisages a situation where the person is, or lives with, the addressee (*'immāk*). In this case the addressee is commanded to support him as a stranger and sojourner, so he may live. In particular the addressee should not charge interest for money lent (cf. Exod. 22:25[24]). If the destitute man is dealt with as a stranger, he is dealt with in the spirit of neighbourly love commanded in 19:33. Following the command is the most fundamental rationale for Israel's existence: that they were brought out of slavery in Egypt and led into Canaan by the Lord; as such they possess nothing of their own. Moreover that the person in need ought to be treated just like a stranger or sojourner (*gēr wĕtôšāb*) should remind the addressee and reader alike that the Israelites share the same status before the Lord (see v. 23). Selfish desires are prohibited when dealing with a fellow Israelite. Observance of this rule is, however, impossible unless the addressee has become convinced he owns nothing, and has given up all desire to acquire anything.

25:39–46

39–41. The third case of a poverty-stricken Israelite envisages a situation where he, living with the addressee, sells himself to the addressee. By definition this Israelite becomes a slave, but the Lord sternly rules that such a person should not be treated as an ordinary slave. In v. 39b the root *'bd* appears three times. By associating the term 'a slave' (*'ebed*) with 'work' (*'ăbōdâ*) the Lord commands the addressee not to treat his brother harshly, as the Egyptians treated the Israelites (note the same construction, *'bd* followed by *bĕ* in Exod. 1:14). Rather the impoverished person should work like an Israelite hired man with the addressee until the Jubilee, after which time he can return to his home along with his family. It is notable that the prepositional phrase *'immāk* (lit. 'with you') appears four times in this section (vv. 39a, 40a, 40b, 41a), apparently with the nuance of 'together with'. In other words, just as the Lord treats the Israelites as sojourners or strangers (see v. 23), so should the addressee treat his fellow Israelite.

42–43. The exceedingly generous treatment of impoverished Israelites is grounded upon their identity as the Lord's 'slaves' (*'ăbādîm*), having been saved by him. As his slaves they should not be sold like ordinary slaves, since they can belong to no-one else. While the same term *'ebed* is used in relation to both the Lord and humans in v. 42, differentiating their translation by rendering one 'a slave' and the other 'a servant' possibly weakens the thrust of the message that the exodus worked a change of master for the Israelites.

In v. 43 the prohibition against forced labour is expressed in a way reminiscent of their days of slavery in Egypt, namely a labour in harshness (*bĕpārek*; cf. Exod. 1:13, 14; Ezek. 34:40), followed by the commandment 'you shall fear your God'. As in vv. 17 and 36, this latter prohibition appears when a shift is made to the topic of pressurizing one's neighbour.

44–46. This passage identifies three sources from where the Israelites may purchase their slaves and maidservants: (1) from neigbouring countries, (2) from strangers living among them, and (3) from members of clans of strangers, who were born in the Promised Land. All those who become slaves or maidservants become an inheritance for the Israelites, and are treated as such. But these people should not be treated harshly like slaves. As commented by some exegetes (Wenham 1979: 322; North 2000: 59–61), slaves in Israelite society would have enjoyed far more freedom than, say, the slaves of a galley-ship. True, they were bought, but they were not ordinarily subjected to torture or harsh treatment, though to an extent this would depend entirely on their individual masters.

That slaves from surrounding countries or strangers become the 'property' (*'ăḥuzzâ*) of the Israelites indicates that such slaves have a status similar to that of the inherited land, so, if bought from someone else, they return to their homes in the year of Jubilee. In other words, while purchased slaves are legally distinct from the Israelites, they indirectly inherit the Promised Land. From the viewpoint of the purchased slaves, their engrafting into an Israelite family would hold out the prospect of a promising future, in that they could expect to receive 'crumbs' fallen from their masters' table (Matt. 15:27//Mark 7:28), which means their being recipients of forgiveness and patience, since it is assumed (at least in this chapter) the Israelites will observe all the Lord's commandments. The Lord's blessing on the Israelites belongs to these purchased slaves also.

25:47–55

47–49. V. 47 introduces a case where, after a sojourner or stranger becomes wealthy, the very Israelite he lives with becomes impoverished and sells himself to the sojourner or a member of the stranger's clan. After the Israelite is sold, he has the right to be repurchased by a person from among the nearest of kin in his clan, a matter not mentioned in the comparable situation described in v. 26. If one attaches importance to the order of these options, it is noticeable that his parents are not included among the people who may repurchase him. This is probably due to the assumption that he has already separated from his parents (Gen. 2:24). Further it is imaginable that the law assumes a redeemer who is close in age to the one redeemed in order to convey the idea that a brother redeems a brother. The priority of a brother as a redeemer is significant, considering the emphasis this chapter places on the brotherhood of Israelites: the Israelites are expected to show the same brotherly love evidenced between relatives. However, if the person in question accumulates enough resources, he may redeem himself.

The relationship the addressee has to each person, the stranger and the fellow Israelite, is uppermost in the lawgiver's consciousness: both are related to the addressee. And it is strongly anticipated that the addressee will be vigilant in his rigorous keeping of all the rules (see v. 53b). However, what circumstance would force a fellow Israelite to sell himself to a sojourner or stranger rather than to the addressee assumed in v. 39? Undoubtedly it was because the impoverished Israelite found it more congenial to work with these other people and to be repurchased by one of his relatives than working with the addressee until the year of Jubilee. Presumably some unspecified circumstances might lie behind the impoverished Israelite's decision; but, in view of the fact that no economic factors come into play, the assumption seems to be that the impoverished Israelite loves the sojourner or stranger more than the addressee. This would pose a challenge to the addressee, for he is supposed to observe the commandment of neighbourly love in 19:18b. The addressee is, instead, to supervise the whole process, and particularly to monitor the treatment of the fellow Israelite; this is, by itself, the Lord's discipline.

50–54. The method of pricing the repurchase is similar to that used for evaluating the land (see vv. 15ff.). The only difference is that while the criterion used in the case of the land is the quantity of the annual produce, the hired man's wage is used in the case of impoverished Israelites. The redeemer ought to pay the sojourner or stranger the equivalent of the man's wage from the time he is purchased to the year of Jubilee, regardless of how many years remain. If he is not redeemed by any of the means permitted, he will be released in the year of Jubilee along with his sons. Of great importance is that in this case the right of redemption is applied to the Israelites in contrast with the first case, where it is applied to the land (v. 25). This implies that the Israelites have the same status as that of the land: just as sold land needs to be repurchased as soon as possible, so do the Israelites (see Japhet 1986: 85–86).

Thus these methods of redeeming an Israelite from impoverishment function to rescue him from becoming a slave to a stranger, the condition experienced by the Israelites in Egypt.

55. This last verse of ch. 25 sets out the grand principle that underlies the second (vv. 35–38), third (vv. 39–46) and fourth sections (vv. 47–54) above. That is, the Israelites belong to the Lord who brought them out of Egypt, and should not become the slaves of any other person or people. Thus in the second part of this chapter (vv. 25–54) the establishment of the Jubilee year is the most definitive means of preserving the Israelites as the Lord's slaves, even during the period leading up to the Jubilee, simultaneously rescuing them from the kind of experience they had in Egypt.

It must be borne in mind that the reference to the Israelites as the Lord's slaves is a theological statement. Nevertheless unless this statement becomes actualized in the hearts of the Israelites, they cannot observe all the preceding laws. In particular, this statement is, in content, closely related to the statement given in v. 23 that the Israelites are sojourners with the Lord, and that therefore they possess nothing in the Promised Land. When the Israelites cease claiming things as their own property, they will become the Lord's slaves.

Explanation

In so far as Lev. 25 provides stipulations concerning the sabbatical year and the Jubilee, the chapter is a continuation of ch. 23, which addresses holy *time*. Compared with the annual festival days of ch. 23, ch. 25 deals not only with a longer period of holy time (one year), but also with a longer intervening period (six years, forty-nine years).

Though a surface reading of the chapter may suggest that it simply deals with Israel's so-called infrastructure (the land, trade, social status of Israelite slaves), it should not be overlooked that its underlying principle is the same as that mentioned in ch. 23: time is consecrated, becoming holy when the people's hearts are holy, without which the observance of these institutions is impossible.

In conformity with this, the institution of the Jubilee year is designed to inculcate in the mind of the Israelites the realization that they possess nothing in this world and that the land and its produce are only a gift from the Lord. In a true sense, this truth means that in the year of Jubilee the Israelites are to return to the state they had when they were redeemed from the land of Egypt.

Holiness of the year of Jubilee – eternity

Since the year of Jubilee is holy (v. 10), it follows that its holiness ought to be enacted by the Israelites even before that time, and that consecration does not exist independently of the Israelites. As mentioned in 'Comment' on vv. 18–19, the consecration or hallowing of the year of Jubilee assumes the observance of the Lord's commandments (v. 18), where neighbourly love for both the fellow Israelites and strangers is included (see 19:18b, 33–34). By itself, the latter assumes the absence of an egocentric nature. The practice of such neighbourly love is assumed in the rules regarding the redemption of the land, and their support of the impoverished fellow Israelite.

The addressee, every Israelite, is assumed to be the agent of this neighbourly love, as well as the redeemer (*gô'ēl*). They are expected to be selfless and show no interest in worldly affairs. In dealing with the various situations of their fellow Israelites they are expected to implement the Lord's will even before the year of Jubilee. However, it is entirely impossible to consecrate only the fiftieth year when the Israelites remain unholy in the foregoing years. This makes the reason for which the various cases of an impoverished Israelite are presented just after the ideal nature of the year of Jubilee understandable.

Thus holiness has a twofold aspect: on the one hand, it is related to the experience of human beings, but on the other hand, it belongs to the divine realm. More significantly, the year of Jubilee can be viewed as a year *representing* all the time experienced by human beings (Kiuchi 1995), as all the rules that ought to be enforced before that year indicate. Such a situation derives from the deeper truth that all 'time' belongs to the Lord and ought to be holy.

As briefly mentioned (see 'Explanation' on ch. 23), holy times are related to eternity, which should exist within the human heart. The year of the Jubilee, held every fifty years, is the culmination of the sabbath principle, starting from the weekly sabbath, annual feasts and sabbatical years. Above these occasions lies the idea of 'eternity', expressed in this chapter by *li(a)ṣĕmîtût* (conclusively, vv. 23, 30) and *'ôlām* (vv. 32, 34, 46). In this chapter, these two expressions do not appear to depict a concept of time unrelated to the Jubilee years; rather they are depicted as an extension of the sabbatical and Jubilee years. They relate to the rules of the land and purchased foreign slaves unaffected by the Jubilee legislation. In a sense these regulations concern a deeper dimension than the holiness of the Jubilee, for they represent the essence of holiness, just like the burnt offering, which is never said to be holy, although other offerings are (see 'Explanation' on ch. 1).

As is well known, the idea of *'ôlām* in Hebr. is not identical with the philosophically conceived idea of eternity. While *'ôlām* means perpetuity in an empirical sense, it, after all, involves timelessness, for it refers to a limitlessness of duration. Thus timelessness and unchangeableness of the land and foreign slaves are the essence of holiness in this chapter. The chapter focuses on the legislation of the Jubilee year, but the latter is a bridge, or pointer, to the essence of holiness.

Since the 'consecration' of the Jubilee year is inseparable from the observation of the laws, the essence of which is summed up by the destruction of the egocentric nature, and the same spirit pervades all the laws in this chapter, it must be concluded that holiness in this chapter is also viewed as a condition of the human heart, and that a holy eternity lies if it does, in the human heart.

Reality reflected in chapter 25 and the history of Israel

The ideal or utopian nature of the year of Jubilee is evident in a few fundamental premises. The institution assumes the complete observance of the Lord's commandments (v. 18). Moreover, unless one's selfish ego is not removed, one cannot hallow the sabbatical year, not to mention the Jubilee year (cf. Greenberg 1990: 55). Thus it appears that people would find it easier to observe the seventh year, which involves only a cessation from work, than the year of Jubilee with all its accompanying rules. As though sharing the people's sentiment, at the end of the presentation of the institution's fundamental part (vv. 20–22) the Lord anticipates and responds to the potential anxiety the people may have about this year. But this by itself implies that it is hard for the people to observe even the sabbatical year. All in all, the Jubilee years, while they are theoretically a time of liberation, challenge the condition of human hearts corrupted by an egocentric nature.

References to the year of Jubilee are scarce in the rest of the OT, and there is no evidence that the institution was ever practised (cf. Jer. 34:8–17). A plethora of opinions have been advanced to explain this fact (for a variety of views, see Hartley 1992: 427–430; North 2000: 101–114; Milgrom 2001: 2257–2270). But none of these explanations takes the above fundamental premises into serious account. According to those premises, it is natural to infer that it is impossible to observe the institution. If this is true, then the subsequent Israelite history would naturally be a history of profaning holiness (cf. ch. 26 and 2 Chr. 36:21). On the other hand, it is unnecessary to doubt that the Lord spoke these words on Mount Sinai. Thus it must be concluded that the Lord presented these words to the Israelites as the standard, from *his* viewpoint, by which they should live in the Promised Land, without thought for whether the people were capable of observing them. Yet that the Lord knows the true condition of the people's hearts is betrayed by the year of Jubilee's aim to address human selfishness.

Thus it is imagined that this institution was never carried out in practice in Israel's later history. In my view, this is why the rules on the Hebrew slave and the sabbatical year in Exodus (21:2–11; 23:10–11) come up again in Deuteronomy (15:1–18; cf. Barker 2003: 704).

Implications for Isaiah and the New Testament

The prophetic literature envisages a time in the future when the Lord will become the redeemer of his people, particularly in Isaiah, where *gô'ēl* is consistently used to refer to the Lord (Isa. 41:14; 43:14; 44:22; but see also Exod. 6:6; 15:13). While the redeemer Lord in Isaiah is presented as strong and reliable, the original legal connotation of *gô'ēl* should not be forgotten: the person is, above all, a brother, an aunt or the son of an aunt, which means the redeemer is one who offers a brother's helping hand. What the *gô'ēl* actually does culminates in the work of the Lord's 'servant' (*'ebed*, Isa. 52:3, 9). Within Isaiah the theme of the Jubilee is combined with that of the Messiah's work (61:1–2). This imagery possibly persists into the NT, where Christ is said to be our Redeemer.

Christ has come into this world as the one who fulfils the Jubilee (Luke 4:17–19). He is also the Lord of the sabbath (Matt. 12:8; Mark 2:28; Luke 6:5). Thus it can be said that Christ is holy and represents all the various kinds of holy time based on the sabbatical principle. He came to bring rest to all humanity, but such rest is not to be purely thought of in terms of physical healing or protection from various calamities. Rather it refers ultimately to that rest in the human heart that endures even amid outward sufferings and calamities. It is a heavenly rest granted by the Holy Spirit. On the other hand, as the laws in Lev. 25:35–54 show, holiness lies in the selfless helping of fellow humans. The depiction of the Israelites as the Lord's slaves tacitly demands that they serve each other like slaves. In this regard, Jesus surpasses all the rulings in Lev. 25, since he came into this world as the true servant of all (Matt. 20:28; John 13:1–11; 1 Pet. 2:17–18). So Jesus' followers are expected to show a lifestyle of higher calling than the one presented in Lev. 25. It could be easily surmised that if the year of Jubilee is difficult for all humanity, to follow Jesus is even more difficult. Yet the redeeming love shown on the cross encourages the hearts of believers to follow him.

Relief, rest and peace characterize the holiness the Lord grants believers. And as the year of Jubilee reveals through its legal stipulations, it sheds light on the significance of human labour. How the Israelites could rest for a whole year and yet continue to eat the land's produce is beyond human imagination. Likewise Jesus says on one occasion that he along with his Father in heaven have been working on the sabbath (John 5:17). For a believer, then, faith that the Lord will take care of everything is the secret of fruitful labour (Ps. 127:1–2).

While such is the case for true believers, the NT presumes the large majority of 'believers' have not attained this level of faith. This is because they still retain their egocentric nature. The practical wisdom of the year of Jubilee, thus includes the following:

1. The New Testament is replete with warnings against amassing wealth; hence the need to become contented with what is given.
2. It encourages cheerful giving to others.
3. Being sojourners and strangers with the Lord in this world.

4. As humans, particularly believers, are brothers, they should assist and serve each other as much as possible.
5. Believers are saved by grace, and therefore possess nothing in this world.

All these items concern the presence within the human heart of coveting. In terms of the spiritual condition of the so-called people of God, the NT believers are the same as the Israelites, despite Christ's death and resurrection. In principle this situation does not change when Christ fulfils the Law, and the Holy Spirit focuses on the transformation of the human heart. For the ultimate obstacle to complete observance of the laws in the OT as well as to obedience to Christ in faith is the presence of the egocentric nature, the chief elements of which are a desire to earn more, greatness and arrogance.

LEVITICUS 26:1–46

Translation

[1]'You shall not make idols for yourselves or erect an image or pillar, and you shall not set up a figured stone in your land to bow down to it, for I am the LORD your God. [2]You shall keep my sabbaths and revere my sanctuary: I am the LORD.

[3]'If you walk in my statutes and observe my commandments and do them, [4]then I will give rains to you in their season, and the land will yield its increase, and the trees of the field will yield their fruit. [5]Your threshing will last to the time of the grape harvest, and the grape harvest will last to the time for sowing. And you will eat your food to the full and dwell in your land securely. [6]I will give peace in the land, and you will lie down, and none shall make you afraid. And I will remove harmful beasts from the land, and the sword shall not go through your land. [7]You shall chase your enemies, and they shall fall before you by the sword. [8]Five of you shall chase a hundred, and a hundred of you shall chase ten thousand, and your enemies shall fall before you by the sword. [9]I will turn to you and make you fruitful and multiply you and will confirm my covenant with you. [10]You shall eat old store long kept, and you shall clear out the old to make way for the new. [11]I will make my dwelling among you, and my soul shall not abhor you. [12]And I will walk among you and will be your God, and you shall be my people. [13]I am the LORD your God, who brought you out of the land of Egypt, that you should not be their slaves. And I have broken the bars of your yoke and made you walk erect.

[14]'But if you will not listen to me and will not keep all these commandments, [15]if you spurn my statutes, and if your soul abhors my rules, so you will not keep all my commandments, so that you shall break my covenant, [16]then I will do this to you: I will visit you with panic, with wasting disease and fever that consume the eyes and what makes the heart ache. And you shall sow your seed in vain, for your enemies shall eat it. [17]I will set my face against you, and you shall be struck down

before your enemies. Those who hate you shall rule over you, and you shall flee
when none pursues you.
[18]'And if in spite of this you will not listen to me, then I will add to your discipline
sevenfold for your self-hidings, [19]and I will break the pride of your power, and I will
make your heavens like iron and your earth like bronze. [20]And your strength shall be
spent in vain, for your land shall not yield its increase, and the trees of the land shall
not yield their fruit.
[21]'Then if you walk in defiance with me and will not listen to me, I will continue
striking you, sevenfold for your self-hidings. [22]And I will let loose the wild beasts
against you, which shall bereave you of your children and destroy your livestock
and make you few in number, so your roads shall be deserted.
[23]'And if by this discipline you are not turned to me but walk in defiance with me,
[24]then I also will walk in defiance with you, and I myself will strike you sevenfold for
your self-hidings. [25]And I will bring a sword upon you, which shall execute
vengeance for the covenant. And if you gather within your cities, I will send
pestilence among you, and you shall be delivered into the hand of the enemy. [26]When
I break your supply of bread, ten women shall bake your bread in a single oven and
shall dole out your bread again by weight, and you shall eat and not be satisfied.
[27]'But if in spite of this you will not listen to me, but walk in defiance with me,
[28]then I will walk in defiance with you in fury, and I myself will discipline you
sevenfold for your self-hidings. [29]You shall eat the flesh of your sons, and you shall
eat the flesh of your daughters. [30]And I will destroy your high places and cut down
your incense altars and cast your dead bodies upon the dead bodies of your idols,
and my soul will abhor you. [31]And I will lay your cities waste and will make your
sanctuaries desolate, and I will not smell your soothing aromas. [32]And I myself will
devastate the land, so your enemies who settle in it shall be appalled at it. [33]And I
will scatter you among the nations, and I will unsheathe the sword after you, and
your land shall be a desolation, and your cities shall be a waste. [34]Then the land shall
enjoy its sabbaths as long as it lies desolate, while you are in your enemies' land;
then the land shall rest, and enjoy its sabbaths. [35]As long as it lies desolate it shall
have rest, the rest that it did not have on your sabbaths when you were dwelling in it.
[36]And as for those of you who are left, I will send faintness into their hearts in the
lands of their enemies. The sound of a driven leaf shall put them to flight, and they
shall flee as one flees from the sword, and they shall fall when none pursues. [37]They
shall stumble over one another, as if to escape a sword, though none pursues. And
you shall have no power to stand before your enemies. [38]And you shall perish
among the nations, and the land of your enemies shall eat you up. [39]And those of
you who are left shall rot away in your enemies' lands because of their guilt, and also
because of the guilt of their fathers they shall rot away. [40]And they confess their guilt
and the guilt of their fathers in their treachery that they committed against me,
and also in walking in defiance with me. [41]I will walk in defiance with them and
bring them into the land of their enemies – or if then their uncircumcised heart is
humbled and they make amends for their guilt, [42]then I will remember my covenant
with Jacob, and I will remember my covenant with Isaac and my covenant with
Abraham, and I will remember the land. [43]But the land shall be abandoned by them

and enjoy its sabbaths while it lies desolate without them, and they shall make amends for their guilt, because they spurned my rules and their soul abhorred my statutes. 44Yet for all that, when they are in the land of their enemies, I will not spurn them, neither will I abhor them so as to destroy them utterly and break my covenant with them, for I am the LORD their God. 45But I will for their sake remember the covenant with their forefathers, whom I brought out of the land of Egypt in the sight of the nations, that I might be their God: I am the LORD.'

46These are the statutes, namely the rules and teachings, that the LORD established between him and the people of Israel through Moses on Mount Sinai.

Notes on the text

1. 'for': *kî* LXX and Syr omit this word.

6. 'and the sword shall not go through your land': *wĕḥereb lō' ta'ăbōr bĕ'arṣĕkem* In LXX this part comes at the end of v. 5.

11. 'my dwelling': *miškānî* LXX reads 'my covenant'.

'my soul': *napšî* Modern translations tend not to use 'soul' for *nepeš* in Leviticus (except for ESV and Elberfelder), but it seems required, particularly in the phrase *gā'al nepeš* (see 'Comment').

13. 'that you should not be their slaves': *mihyōt lāhem 'ăbādîm* LXX reads 'where you were slaves' instead.

'erect': *qômĕmîyût* A hapax legomenon. It appears that this word adverbially qualifies *hôlîk* (lit. 'guide').

14. LXX does not read *kol* (all).

17. 'shall rule over you': *rādû* LXX reads 'and will persecute', reflecting the Hebr. *wĕrādĕpû*. Perhaps this reading was influenced by vv. 7–8.

18. 'sevenfold': *šeba'* See 'Comment'.

20. '(the trees of) the land': ('*ēṣ*) *hā'āreṣ* MT is supported by 11QPaleoLev, but some Hebr. MSS, SamP, TgJon and LXX read 'the field'; probably in conformity with v. 4.

25. *ḥereb nōqemet nĕqam bĕrît*: lit. 'revenging sword, the vengeance of the covenant' The collocation of *nāqām* with *bĕrît* appears only here in the OT. For the meaning of *nāqām*, see 'Comment'.

31. 'your sanctuaries': *miqdĕšêkem* Many Hebr. MSS, SamP and Syr read it in sg.

34. 'it lies desolate': *hŏššammâ* It is hoph. inf. of *šmm* (*HALOT*; see also 2 Chr. 36:21). SamP reads *šmh* here and in v. 35.

'enjoy': *hirṣāt* The ordinary form is *hirṣĕtâ* as SamP reads, yet it can be taken as its archaic form (*GKC* 75m).

39. 'because of their guilt': *ba'ăwōnām* LXX reads 'because of your [pl.] sins'; thereby apparently harmonizing the number with the 2nd person address in vv. 38–38. However, this is unnecessary, since the second half of v. 39 is in the 3rd person (see also v. 36a).

'because of the guilt of their fathers' LXX translates 'through your sins'.

However, this may not reflect their *Vorlage*, as LXX uses 'sin' for *'āwōn* in 5:1, 17, 7:18 and 10:17.

40–41. Translations vary, depending upon how the beginning of v. 40 is to be understood in relation to its context. NIV, NRSV and ESV take the whole section of vv. 40–41 as the protasis of a conditional sentence by translating v. 40 'But if they (shall) confess' etc., followed by the apodosis in v. 42. On the other hand, JPS takes v. 40 (the people's confession) as a sequel to the desolation of the land and the people's rotting away in their guilt, which are mentioned in v. 39. The former translations seem artificial, since there is, in the text, no particle expressing condition at the beginning of v. 40. Indeed the latter understanding may create logical redundancy in v. 41a, since the people are in v. 40 to confess their guilt in the foreign land, whereas the Lord talks in v. 41b about the possibility of their recognizing their guilt. I, however, take v. 41 as resumptive of the preceding words, representing a different level of discourse (see 'Comment').

41. 'and bring': *wĕhēbē'tî* LXX reads 'and I will destroy', which is probably a paraphrased translation.

'or if then': *'ô 'āz* LXX simply translates it 'then' [*tote*]. RSV, NRSV and ESV similarly take the *'ô 'āz* as meaning 'if then', while JPS renders it 'then at last'. The former entails the understanding that the people's submission is one option, whereas JPS assumes it is a necessary outcome. On this occasion *'ô* cannot mean 'or', since the second half of the verse does not naturally follow the first. However, *'ô* has the meaning of 'or if' (cf. 25:49b; Exod. 21:36). It is proposed here that *'ô 'āz* means 'or if then'.

42. 'my covenant, with Jacob': *bĕrîtî ya'ăqōb* The syntax has posed some difficulties for exegetes (see Hartley 1992: 455). LXX omits the suffix, thus making the phrase an ordinary genitive-construct chain, while Syr supplies 'with'. However, the text may well represent the very process of the Lord's remembering: 'my covenant, yea Jacob'.

46. 'teachings': *tôrôt* LXX reads it in sg.

Form and structure

Lev. 26 begins with a basic principle of conduct (vv. 1–2, see below) and sets out the blessings that follow obedience (vv. 3–13) and curses that follow disobedience (vv. 14–45). Although this chapter concerns the 'blessings and curses' pertaining to the Sinai covenant, the concluding section makes reference to the Abrahamic covenant. All these covenants have in common their aim for the people to have only the Lord as their God (see 'Comment' on vv. 42, 44–45).

The chapter exhibits close literary and ideological connections with the preceding chs. 24 and 25. First, as in other sections of Leviticus, ch. 26 can be viewed as a special application of the permanent principle given in ch. 24 to the future of the Israelites. Ch. 24 has dealt with the Lord's *perennial* handling of the people in a positive (vv. 1–9) and negative way (vv. 10–23); i.e. his actions towards them mirrors their attitude towards him, in blessing and curse. As the following 'Comment' shows, this mirroring is emphatically set out in this chapter as well.

Second, this chapter utilizes the language and ideas of Lev. 25. In the blessing section the ideas of 'dwelling safely in the land' and 'eating the old food' are common to both chapters (cf. v. 5 with 25:18, and v. 10 with 25:21–22). In the curse section, the theme of sabbath in ch. 25 is utilized in a rather gloomy way. In ch. 25 it is not even questioned whether or not the people will observe the statutes and rules (cf. 25:18); rather the institution of the Jubilee year is grounded upon the people's observance of the Lord's commandments. But in ch. 26 it is said that even when the statutes and rules are not observed and the dwellers are deported to a foreign land, the land of Israel will enjoy its rest (sabbath). This gloomy use of the sabbath theme reminds the reader of the repeated injunction not to follow the Canaanite customs listed in chs. 18 and 20, thus rounding out the larger literary unit of chs. 18 – 26.

The structure of the whole chapter is as follows:

1–2 Basic commandments: allegiance to the Lord and prohibition against idol worship

3–13 Blessings brought about by obedience
- Condition (3)
- Blessings (4–12)
  1. fertility (4–5)
  2. peace (6–8)
  3. multiplication of offspring (9–10)
  4. the presence of God (11–12)

14–46 Curses brought about by disobedience
- A series of calamities
  - 1st stage: plague and defeat in war (14–17)
  - 2nd stage: famine (18–20)
  - 3rd stage: wild animals (21–22)
  - 4th stage: sword, plague, famine (23–26)
  - 5th stage: Cannibalism, destruction of the sanctuary, exile (27–38)
  - Possibility of restoration
    - People: realizing their own guilt (39–40)
    - God: remembering the covenants (41–45)

While the overall structure is simple, some specific exegetical questions need to be answered in relation to each of the three sections vv. 1–2, 3–13 and 14–46.

Vv. 1–2. Some exegetes take these verses as the conclusion of ch. 25 (e.g. Cassuto 1954: 886; Noth 1965: 193; Levine 1989: 181–182), while others take them as the introduction to what follows (Wenham 1979: 327; Hartley 1992: 449 with a slightly nuanced view). A couple of considerations exist for the location and role of these verses: (1) The introductory formula for the Lord's address is in 25:1, which may suggest that ch. 25 forms a unit with ch. 26. (2) 26:2 is exactly the same as 19:30. Moreover both the language and content of 26:2 (a ban on making idols) closely resemble that of 19:4.

It must be observed that the first consideration is not necessarily true. While most literary units are demarcated by the Lord's introductory statements in Leviticus, some cases have the formulae repeated for the same kind of theme: 5:14; 6:1[5:20], 8[6:1] and 23:1–2, 9–10, 23–24, 26, 33–34. The absence of the Lord's address at the beginning of ch. 26 may be supplemented by 26:46, which summarizes all the laws in Leviticus (see 'Comment' there). Thus I assume that the matter of the Lord's address belongs to a different dimension to the content of these two chapters; its absence in ch. 26 may reflect an urgency felt by the Lord towards his people. The linguistic and ideological link to ch. 19 is significant, for this implies that 26:1–2 resumes and summarizes what has been set out before the Israelites. And as these verses encapsulate all the rest of the commandments, in that their observance attests to that of the others (see 'Comment' there), they form a summary of the Lord's commandments. On the other hand, though the theme of the Jubilee is clearly part of the Lord's commandments, the fact that the institution is maintained only when the Israelites are free from self-centredness and trust in the Lord shows a marked difference between it and the theme in 26:3–45, where a strong emphasis is laid on the opposite possibility. Thus it would seem preferable to view 26:1–2 as the heading of what follows, rather than as a summary of the preceding chapter.

Vv. 3–13. The section on blessings in the event of the people's obedience is introduced by *'im* (if) followed by various blessings. It enumerates four kinds of blessing in the case of obedience: fertility (4–5, 10), peace (6–8), posterity (9), the Lord's presence and protection (vv. 11–13). Exegetes are divided as to the number of blessings (see Milgrom 2001: 2287–2288). While the number can be four as presented above, two points deserve attention: (1) Blessings such as fertility, peace and posterity are blessings of a different kind to the presence of God. (2) There is a noticeable cause and effect between fertility and peace, and between these and posterity, so it is somewhat artificial to enumerate the blessings. God's presence guarantees all the rest of the blessings. Moreover not only do these blessings and their language pave the way for the delineation of the calamities in the event of disobedience that follow, but it is also notable that the phrase *gā'al nepeš* (a soul abhors), in particular, appears frequently henceforth, as one of the key terms of this chapter.

Vv. 14–49. This long section on curses in the event of disobedience also begins with *'im* (if), but the repeated disobedience of the people is envisaged, and every potential case begins with *'im* or *wĕ'im* (14, 18, 21, 23, 27). Thus it is reasonable to see the whole section as comprising five stages. In addition to the themes of blessing, fertility, peace, posterity and the Lord's presence, this section on curses exhibits the following remarkable features.

(1) At every stage the protasis is introduced by characteristic expressions such as 'If you do not listen to me' or 'If you walk in defiance against me [*hālak 'immî qĕrî*]' or 'If you are not chastised by them' or a combination of such expressions. On four occasions, following the second stage, the Lord declares that he will punish the people 'exactly according to your self-hidings' (for the meaning of 'sevenfold', see 'Comment' on v. 18).

(2) The vocabulary that appears in the fifth stage also appears in the first stage: the people's detesting (*mā'as*) and abhorring (*gā'al*) the Lord's commandments (vv. 15, 44). The idea of breaking the covenant (*hēpēr bĕrît*) appears in vv. 15 and 44.

The fifth stage is the longest of all, and one may tend to divide it into subsections. There are two major interpretive questions surrounding the division of the last section, vv. 27–45. The first is whether it is possible to divide the section at v. 39, with v. 40 beginning a new subsection. Such a position is taken by Steymans (1999: 279–280) and others, and is reflected in some modern translations. He takes the beginning of v. 40 as conditional, and forming a new beginning (see 'Notes on the text'). However, though this interpretation is possible, the double occurrence of the same phrase *ba'ăwōnām* (because of their guilt) and *ba'ăwōnōt 'ăbōtām* (because of the guilt of their fathers) in vv. 39 and 40 make it artificial to see *wĕhitwaddû* (they confess) in v. 40 as conditional (for other difficulties admitted by Steymans himself, see Steymans 1999: 280). Another major problem from a structural point of view is the transition from v. 40 to v. 41. However, it is clear that v. 41, while repeating the language of v. 40b, recapitulates what has been happening between the Lord and the people. Thus v. 41 marks a renewed viewpoint on the part of the Lord, but it cannot be separated from the content of v. 40. Thus it may seem that any inner division of vv. 27–45 from the viewpoint of its content is artificial. This last section describes the future of Israel in the event of their disobedience, starting with cannibalism and ending with the deportation of the people. While vv. 40ff. can be taken as describing the possibility of their spiritual transformation, it cannot be separated from vv. 28–39, in that it is set in the context of the catastrophe of the exile. In sum, the Lord's discourse in this section is resumptive, yet it gradually moves forward the final possibility for the Israelites; the flow of the discourse in the section is seamless, in its language and content.

Comment

26:1–2

As discussed in 'Form and structure', these verses belong to what follows rather than to the preceding chapter. The reference to the ban on idols and observance of the Lord's sabbaths in 19:4 is chiastically reversed here. Equally important is the fact that v. 2 was stated in 19:30 in exactly the same way. These literary and ideological connections to ch. 19 are indeed in the Lord's mind, which indicates that these prohibitions form the basic principles the Israelites should live by. Thus just as in 19:3–4, here too the two commandments represent a summary of all the Lord's commandments and function to introduce the blessing and curse sections that follow. Vv. 1–2 reflect the First, Second and Fourth Commandments (Exod. 20:3–6, 8–11), while the mention of *hištaḥăwâ* (to bow down) in v. 1 suggests an additional literary link to the Second Commandment (Exod. 20:5; see further Exod. 23:24; 34:14).

1. The strictness of the prohibition against making idols for oneself is achieved by using a unique word pair, *pesel/maṣṣēbâ* (image/pillar), with the addition of *'eben maśkît* (a figured stone). The purpose of the three acts *'āśâ* (to make), *hēqîm* (to erect) and *nātan* (to set up) lies in *hištaḥăwâ* (to bow down), which appears only here in Leviticus.

2. While v. 1 is formulated in a negative form, v. 2 is positive. The relationship between the two verses from the viewpoint of their content needs to be clarified, which depends on the meaning of 'keeping the sabbaths' and 'revere the sanctuary'.

First, exactly the same passage is found in 19:30. The term *šabtōtay* (my sabbaths) refers to holy occasions such as weekly sabbaths, the Lord's appointed times, the sabbatical year and the year of Jubilee. 'My sanctuary' refers not just to the sanctuary as a holy place as such but to all the rituals conducted there, including sacrifices and offerings. Second, taken this way v. 2 is the other side of the same coin: v. 1 states allegiance to the Lord in a negative way, while v. 2 states the same in a positive way. Thus the relationship between these two verses is not just antithetical in form; more essentially they complement each other: they are two different ways of encouraging allegiance to the Lord. In other words, if a person can observe the First Commandment, he can observe all the rest of the Lord's commandments, since that presumes the death of his selfish nature (see 'Comment' on 19:4).

26:3–13

3. The condition for blessing is that one walks according to the Lord's statutes (*ḥuqqôt*) and observes his commandments (*miṣwôt*), a combination that appears only here (cf. v. 15). Ordinarily *ḥuqqâ* appears with *mišpāṭîm*, and as v. 15 indicates (see below), *miṣwôt* is a comprehensive term that encompasses both of them in terms of reference (see Introduction 4.5, figure). This condition is similar to what is assumed in 25:18. Thus, although no explicit mention is made here of the blessing brought about by observance of the statutes and the keeping of the rules, it is assumed.

Notice should be taken that while in v. 15 *kol* (all) is added before *miṣwôt* (commandments), it is not here. This certainly does not mean that people need not observe all the commandments in order to receive blessing. That 'statutes' is first mentioned without 'all' and later mentioned with 'all' or 'all' implied is found also in ch. 18 (cf. v. 5 with v. 30) and ch. 19 (cf. v. 19 with v. 37).

4–8. The first item of blessing is a bountiful and constant supply of food for the people. It begins with regular rainfall that will increase the harvest by supporting greater crop yields. This is a reversal of the original divine curse on the ground (Gen. 3:17–18). The second blessing (vv. 6–8) comprises a life of peace and protection from enemies and harmful animals. Even when the land is attacked by enemies, the Israelites will always be victorious.

9. The third blessing relates to their posterity. The pairing of the two verbs 'make fruitful' (*hiprâ*) and 'to multiply' (*hirbâ*) first appears in the blessing given by the Lord God when he created the heavens and earth (Gen. 1:22, 28). After this it occurs in the Noachic covenant (Gen. 9:1, 7), and in his covenant with Abraham (Gen. 17:2). Thus, though the Lord refers to the Sinaitic covenant when he mentions 'my covenant', he is always ready to provide blessings for obedience. And in this regard there is a continuation between the one he made with Abraham and the one he made with the exodus generation.

'to turn to': *pānâ 'el* This phrase refers to the positive attitude shown towards the person and matter following *'el*. As in 19:4, 31, it refers to the agent's existential situation (cf. further Lev. 20:6; Num. 16:15; Deut. 31:18, 20; Judg. 6:14; 1 Kgs 8:28; 2 Kgs 13:23; Isa. 45:22; Ezek. 36:9; Pss. 40:4[5]; 69:16[17] etc.), and it is expected that such a turning will result in concrete blessing.

'my covenant': *bĕrîtî* What covenant is referred to (see further vv. 15, 25 below)? Considering that the covenants with Abraham, Jacob and Isaac are mentioned in v. 42, the 'covenant' mentioned in vv. 9, 15, 25 probably refers to the Sinaitic covenant as a whole: the Decalogue and its related rules in Exodus in addition to what is found in Leviticus.

10. By mentioning an abundance of food, this verse reverts to the theme of v. 5 and gives further description of the Lord's blessing; thus forming an inclusio. The idea is the same as in 25:21–22.

11. The phrase *nātan miškān* (to make a dwelling) is found in the OT only here and Ezek. 25:4. It virtually refers to the divine presence. Yet in content it is the same as 'I will dwell among you' in Exod. 29:45a. The phrase *lōʾ tigʿal napšî ʾetĕkem* (my soul shall not abhor you) is another and emphatic way of expressing God's intimate presence promised in the first half. It paves the way towards the description of the curse that follows (see vv. 15, 30, 43 and 44 [without *nepeš*]).

'my soul abhors': *gāʿal napšî* In this chapter this phrase occurs in vv. 11, 15, 30, 43 and in Jer. 14:19 and Ezek. 16:5. In Jer. 14:19 it is synonymous with *māʾas* (to detest), as it is in this chapter (vv. 15, 43). As is often the case with expressions of emotion and will, *lōʾ tigʿal* (not abhorring) in this verse is not a logical negation but serves to stress the opposite of abhorrence, namely 'to love' or 'to delight in' (cf. Pss. 51:17[19]; 84:11[12]), though not so in v. 44, where the phrase has a less positive sense.

The striking aspect of the phrase's use in this verse is that on this occasion the *nepeš* refers to that of the Lord, and not of a human being. This is also the case in v. 30 below. While it is not wrong to translate 'I, even myself', there is an unmistakable correspondence drawn between the Lord's *nepeš* and the *nepeš* (sg.) of the Israelites in this chapter (cf. vv. 11, 30 with 15, 43). First, there seems no reason to suppose that the agent of *gāʿal* should be stressed. On the other hand, the verb does not necessarily require *nepeš* as its subject (cf. v. 44 and Ezek. 16:5). Such a linguistic usage is also found in Jeremiah and Ezekiel, and the one case in Ezek. 16:5 (*bĕgōʿal napšēk*), where the genitive-construct chain indicates that *nepeš* means 'a soul' whenever it is conjoined with *gāʿal*. Moreover it has been pointed out that *nepeš* in Leviticus is not simply a substitute for an emphatic pronoun ('myself', 'yourselves'), nor does it mean 'a person' (see 'Comment' on 4:2; 17:10–11; 11:43).

These observations suggest that *nepeš* ought to be translated as 'a soul' when conjoined with *gāʿal*; probably because the latter refers to the innermost feelings of the human heart. The term is characteristically conjoined with emotive terms such as 'hate' (Isa. 1:14), 'be satisfied' (Isa. 42:1), 'beloved' (Jer. 12:7) etc., which provides additional support for the translation proposed above of *gāʿal nepeš*.

Although humanly speaking God's *nepeš* is indescribable, it would seem certain that he has a *nepeš*, since he made humans in his own likeness (Gen. 1:27; for God's *nepeš*, see Isa. 1:14; 42:1; Jer. 32:41; Amos 6:8 etc.). Moreover, in contrast to the human *nepeš*, that of God is unselfish. His soul is characterized as 'merciful, gracious, slow to anger, abounding in steadfast love and faithfulness' and 'forgiving iniquity and transgression, not clearing the guilty, visiting the iniquity of the fathers on the children, to the third and the fourth generation' (Exod. 34:6–7; Num. 14:8). These characteristics are also found in this chapter (see 'Explanation').

12. 'I will walk among you': *wĕhithallaktî bĕtôkĕkem* Although *hithallēk* can take various subjects, the nature of the blessings mentioned in vv. 4–5 (food) and v. 9 (offspring) together with his divine presence suggests that 'I will walk among you' is the blessing the Lord bestowed upon the first humans in Eden (see Gen. 3:8). As a whole the verse is also similar to Exod.

29:45, and this, combined with the similarities of the verse that follows with Exod. 29:46, suggests it clearly echoes the passage in Exod. 29. In other words, the Lord guarantees the blessing granted previously in Eden, the consecration of the sanctuary, and the installation of the priesthood that took place after the exodus.

Thus vv. 11–12 display a close literary and ideological relationship with Exod. 29:45 and the Garden of Eden.

13. The divine self-introduction is qualified by a reference to the exodus event. A further allusion to Exod. 29:45–46 is discernible here.

Notice should be taken of the fact that the roots *qwm* and *hlk* occur frequently in this blessing section: *hālak* (v. 3), *hēqîm* (v. 9), *hithallēk* (v. 12), *hôlîk*, *qômĕmîyût* (v. 13), all of which give the impression of the firmness and stability that ensue from the Lord's blessing upon a people who walk in obedience.

26:14–17 (Stage 1)

14. The first stage of the curse in the event of disobedience. Vv. 14–15 present the fundamental condition, while vv. 16–17 set out the consequences of the disobedience: calamities such as disease, a poor harvest and defeat in war. This stage is indeed the first of a series of curses, but the listed calamities appear in the subsequent stages, albeit with some variations.

The condition is formulated generally in v. 14 and specifically in the next verse. The phrase *šāma' lĕ* (listen to), meaning obedience, appears only in the curse section (vv. 14, 18, 21, 27). Moreover, compared with v. 3, v. 14b adds *kol* (all) to 'these commandments' (*hammiṣwôt hā'ēlleh*), suggesting that obedience to the Lord ought to be expressed by observing *all* of his commandments. Thus retrospectively it is learnt that the observance of *all* the commandments is intended at v. 3 as well, though *kol* is not mentioned there.

15. A more detailed formulation of the condition is set out here, by the use of terms that refer to the more specific aspects of the commandments (*miṣwôt*), such as *ḥuqqôt* (statutes) and *mišpāṭîm* (rules). The latter two have appeared since ch. 18 as synonymous terms (18:4–5, 26; 19:37; 20:22; 25:18; 26:15, 43). The four terms *ḥuqqôt*, *mišpāṭîm*, *miṣwôt* and *bĕrît* clearly exhibit, in terms of reference, an ascending degree of generalization. More importantly the accompanying verbs, especially 'detest' and 'abhor', show that a breach of the covenant begins with the condition of the people's hearts.

'you spurn my statutes': *bĕḥuqqōtay tim'āsû* The verb *mā'as* occurs here for the first time in the OT. It often takes *bĕ*, since it describes the human emotion.

'(if) your soul abhors my rules': *'et mišpātay tig'al napšĕkem* This is the second appearance of *nepeš* plus *gā'al* in this chapter. While the object of 'abhorring' is the Lord's rules, the chapter as a whole makes no distinction between abhorring the rules and abhorring the Lord (see vv. 30, 44). As is discussed below and more fully in 'Explanation', it is highly likely that the people are assumed as unaware of the condition of their own hearts.

'so you will not keep all my commandments': *biltî 'ăśôt 'et kol miṣwôtay* Following the previous verse, the idea of 'doing all the commandments' is once again emphasized. Since *miṣwôt* refers to both positive and negative commandments, this condition of the covenant includes the cases dealt with in ch. 4, where the violation of one of the Lord's prohibitive commandments is in view. It is obvious that the people will fail in observing all the commandments, because, not to mention the prohibitive commandments, such a positive commandment as 19:18b assumes that the selfish souls of the Israelites must be destroyed in order to observe the golden rule.

'so that you shall break my covenant': *lĕhaprĕkem 'et bĕrîtî* For the referent of 'my covenant', see v. 9 above. A breach of the Sinaitic covenant will result in the people being cut off from the Lord. While the Sinaitic covenant as a whole is meant, it ought to be borne in mind that the violation of *one* divine commandment leads to dire consequences.

16. Both this and the verses that follow set out the consequences of disobedience. This verse mentions panic caused by a wasting disease, fever and famine. Attention should be drawn to the fact that while tangible disasters will befall the people, their hearts are primarily targeted by the Lord: *behālâ* (panic) and *mĕdîbōt nāpeš* (what makes the soul ache).

17. Defeat in war and foreign rule by an enemy also culminate in needless fear on the part of the people when they flee non-existent pursuers.

26:18–20 (Stage 2)

18. The second stage of the curse is brief compared to the initial one. As for the previous stage, calamities such as drought and poor harvest are not only outward hardship but aim at weakening their stubborn hearts. If the people do not turn their hearts to the Lord, he will discipline and punish them to the full extent.

'sevenfold': *šeba'* Although modern English translations render it 'seven times' or 'sevenfold' or the like, it is unlikely that 'seven' is meant literally, since the Lord has already set out the principle of the *lex talionis* in 24:15–21. For 'sevenfold' or 'fourfold' there are such expressions as *šib'ātayim* (Gen. 4:15; Ps. 12:6[7]; Prov. 6:31) and *'arba'tayim* (2 Sam. 12:6). The word *kiplayim* in Isa. 42:2 may be helpful in solving the matter. Just as it probably means 'fully' (cf. Oswald 1998: 43 n. 5; see Kiuchi: 2003: 18), so here does *šeba'* mean 'fully', though the translation should be 'sevenfold'. Moreover *šeba'* should be construed as adverbially qualifying the verb *yisser* (discipline).

'for your self-hidings': *'al ḥaṭṭō'têkem Ḥaṭṭā't* means the state of hiding oneself through violating certain commandments of the Lord. It assumes the people remain unaware of the condition of their own hearts.

Some exegetes take the repetitive use of the phrase *šeba' 'al ḥaṭṭō'têkem* (vv. 18, 21, 24, 28) as indicating increasing degrees of punishment. However, while this interpretation is often coupled with the assumption that *šeba'* means 'seven times' or 'sevenfold' (see above), the latter means 'fully' or 'exactly' and does not, by itself, carry the more particular meaning of intensifying the degree of punishment. Yet the people's suffering intensifies, because they increasingly harden their hearts, while the reality of the previous calamities presumably remains.

19–20. The additional punishments of drought and poor harvests are given, yet their main purpose is to break the pride of the people (*gĕ'ôn 'uzzĕkem*).

26:21–22 (Stage 3)

21. The third stage is introduced by the new phrase 'walk in defiance with me', followed by clauses that differ slightly from the beginning of v. 18. The phrase 'walk in defiance against' appears again in the fourth (vv. 23–24) and fifth stages (v. 27). As in v. 18b, the phrase *šeba'* means 'fully', and *šeba' kĕḥaṭṭō'têkem*, 'fully as much as your self-hiding'.

22. The concrete calamity is described as an incursion of wild animals that will kill some of the people and derange the course of their lives. But the latter comes at the end of v. 22, unlike the second stage, where the punishment's major purpose comes at the beginning (v. 19a). From this verse onwards the root *šmm*, whose basic idea is to be desolate, appears frequently: *šmm* hiph. (v. 32), *šmm* qal (v. 32), *šĕmāmâ* (v. 33), *hŏšammâ* (vv. 34–35, 43).

26:23–26 (Stage 4)

23. The fourth stage is longer than the second and third, and its formulation and the calamities described reflect the wrath of the Lord to a higher degree, which manifests itself in the wielding of his sword throughout the land, plagues and famine.

The conditional clause in v. 23 is formulated by using the first and third elements in v. 21 in a chiastic manner: discipline and walking in defiance against the Lord.

24. This is the first time the Lord is said to walk in defiance against the people. The very mention of his overall attitude to the people at the beginning of this verse stresses his increasing anger with them. This is also expressed by his direct attack against the people's lives ('I will strike you' [*hikkêtî 'etĕkem*]), in contrast with the milder and more concrete forms of sending calamities in v. 18b ('I will add to discipline you') and v. 21b ('I will continue striking you').

25. The calamities, which are exactly opposite to the blessings in vv. 6bb–7, are part of the Lord's vengeance. This divine vengeance is an extrajudicial act, and should be distinguished from human vengeance (cf. 19:18, Greenberg 1983: 13). Out of fear the people will gather in the city but the Lord will send pestilence into their midst. Being weakened, they will necessarily be delivered into the hand of their enemy.

26. In addition to the divine sword, the people will face an extreme lack of food. The situation is described by ten women baking in one oven, sparingly doling out bread to people whose hunger is never satisfied. This is the exact opposite to the abundant supply of food promised in vv. 5 and 10. Note that until this verse in the curse section no mention has been made of 'bread', just sowing (v. 16) and harvesting (v. 20).

26:27–45 (Stage 5)

27–31. This last stage is the longest, and describes what befalls the people if they continue to disobey the Lord. As with the foregoing stages, the most important point to make about the nature of the calamities is that they aim to damage the arrogant *nepeš* (soul) of the people. The calamities that will befall the people are described with harsh language. As set out in 'Form and structure', the whole section cannot be further divided, since it by and large describes the sequential calamities that will befall the people and how they will respond.

In vv. 27–28, while the components of the conditional clause are taken from those of the previous stages, the Lord's harsher response is reflected in '(walk) in defiance with you *in fury*'. The first calamity (v. 29) results from famine: the people will eat the flesh of their own children. This is more than plain 'cannibalism'! At this stage the people are envisaged as so self-centred that they lose any natural feelings they previously had for blood relatives, which is also the consequence of their accumulated self-hiding.

The second calamity (v. 30) is the destruction of their high places and incense altars, and the death of their bodies beside their idols. Both *bāmâ* (a high place) and *ḥammān* (incense altars) occur here for the first time in the OT. The 'high places' (*bāmōt*) can be legitimate (cf. 1 Sam. 9:12–14, 19; 1 Kgs 3:2), but since the latter term *ḥammān* connotes idolatry (Isa. 17:8; 27:9; Ezek. 6:4, 6; 2 Chr. 14:5[4] etc.), it seems likely the text assumes the people are offering their offerings and incense on altars designated for foreign gods.

While the Lord is said to destroy their religious centre, this destruction is practically implemented by the hand of their enemies, which is fitting, considering the people intend to turn to their deities; just as the people turn from the Lord, the Lord turns from them. The Lord's slaying of them next to their idolatrous altars (cf. Ezek. 6:5) underscores that the people belonged to foreign deities rather than to him.

All these calamities express the Lord's abhorrence of the people. In Hebr. this is expressed by the phrase *gā'al* and *nepeš* (subject), which appears in vv. 11, 15. The destruction of the sanctuary and the ensuing exile both express divine anger, and in this regard they invert the blessed situation mentioned in v. 11.

The religious activities essentially function to achieve the people's acceptance by the Lord, an outcome expressed by the Lord's smelling of the soothing aroma. Yet he will refuse to accept this aroma if the people become apostate (v. 31). While the soothing aroma (*rēaḥ nîḥôaḥ*) symbolizes the people's self-dedication to the Lord, it appears that by this stage their hearts have become so far removed from the observance of his commandments, that their burning of offerings is now a mere formality. Thus it is surmised that the people at this stage no longer distinguish between the Lord and foreign gods. Though they are aware they present offerings to the Lord, within their subconsciousness all these religious activities have become directed towards foreign gods. Yet they feel no incongruity in their hearts. This is the condition of the human heart that hides itself from the Lord, which is expressed by *ḥaṭṭā't* (see Kiuchi 2003a). Though it obviously has a spiritual dimension, the Lord's smelling of the soothing aroma is a strongly anthropomorphic expression. Therefore this passage and the mention of a 'soothing aroma' in chs. 1 – 3 assume the Lord actually smells the aroma (cf. Gen. 8:21); it is insufficient just to say 'anthropomorphic'. That the Lord would not smell the aroma indicates he has cast the people out of his presence.

32–38. The Lord's devastating (*hăšimmōtî*) to the land appalls (*šāmĕmû*) those enemies living in the land, probably because of the sight of the desolation (v. 32). Yet the people still have to fear the sword (v. 33). Assumedly it is the human agent that unsheathes the sword, though we are meant to interpret this as the work of God himself. The complete destruction of the land is stressed at the end of the verse (cf. vv. 31a and 32a) by the association of the assonant *ḥereb* (a sword) and *ḥorbâ* (a waste).

While the people are in exile, the land is said to enjoy the rest previously withheld by its inhabitants (vv. 34–35). This piercing irony is conveyed by using wordplays with assonance such as *tirṣeh hā'āreṣ* (the land shall enjoy), *hā'āreṣ wĕhirṣāt* (the land and enjoy), *lō' šabĕtâ bĕšabbĕtōtêkem bĕšibtĕkem 'ālêhā* (that it did not have on your sabbaths when you were dwelling in it). In v. 34 the assonance of ' and *r*, and in v. 35 of *š* and *b*, can be observed, each word having a different meaning. Clearly these verses assume reference to the sabbatical and Jubilee years in ch. 25. Retrospectively it can be confirmed from these words that those institutions are based on the people's wholehearted obedience to the Lord's commandments (see 25:18ff.). All this suggests that the destinies of the sanctuary and the land are inseparable.

Even the survivors will suffer in the land they are deported to, fleeing from the sword of their enemy and fearing even the sound of wind-rustled leaves, even though no-one pursues (36–38). This is because the Lord will send 'faintness' (*môrek*; lit. 'what weakens') into their hearts. Confusion will ensue as they stumble over each other as they attempt to escape the sword of a phantom, a situation that stands in complete contrast to that described in v. 8. It is noticeable that for the first time in the curse section the Lord directly sends spiritual power (*môrek*) into their hearts; until now he has aimed at transforming their hearts by sending calamities. V. 38 conveys that the nation will come to a complete end in such a humiliating way that the people will have to perish among a foreign people, and be devoured in a foreign land. This is, however, said in regard to the nation as a whole and not to every individual, since the following passage assumes the existence of survivors.

39–45. V. 39 summarizes the fate of the survivors in a foreign land: they perish because of their own guilt (*'ăwōnām*) and the guilt of their forefathers (*'ăwōnōt 'ăbōtām*). By now the cause of suffering lies in their guilt and not in something else, such as drought, wild beasts, pestilence or international political turmoil.

When the survivors suffer to the extreme, they confess their guilt and the guilt of their fathers, admitting they have broken faith with the Lord and have walked in defiance against him (40).

'confess their guilt': *hitwaddû 'et 'ăwōnām* Since the 'guilt' is that of self-hiding, the confession is existential in character, not just confessing violations of various commandments. Also 'the confession' betrays that the survivors have until this time remained unaware of the condition of their own hearts. In fact the foregoing description of the people (vv. 36–37) shows that they cannot afford to realize their own situation. Their guilt is seen as consisting of 'breaking faith with [*mā'al*] the LORD' and 'walking in defiance against the LORD'. For the conceptual relationship between *ḥāṭā'* and *mā'al*, see Lev. 5:15, 6:2[5:21], Ezek. 14:13 and my analysis in Kiuchi 2003a: 18–23.

Though the content of v. 41a resumes what is said previously, this is treated on a different level from the foregoing discourse. The latter half of the verse begins with *'ô 'āz*, which probably means 'or if then' (see 'Notes on the text'). The people's repentance is presented as a possibility. This seems to conflict slightly with what is said between vv. 39 and 40, where the connection appears natural. Yet the apparent discrepancy dissolves when it is seen that vv. 29–40, particularly v. 40, describe the general course of an event from a divine point of view, while v. 41b addresses the details of a confessing heart with an emphasis on human responsibility: repentance is a necessary result, but even that hinges on the will of the survivors. At the same time, one's interpretation of the tension depends much on how the nature of the Lord's whole discourse in this curse section should be viewed. If one assumes the Lord says these things in order to bring the people to confess their guilt and salvation, the conditional nature of v. 41b strikes a jarring note. However, if the Lord speaks these words in anger, the apparent limitation on the ability of the survivors to humble themselves in v. 41 is possibly just a natural expression of the Lord's anger, for he has repeatedly experienced the deception and rebellion of this people. This latter view seems more fitting, considering the nature of the Lord's discourse.

'their uncircumcised hearts': *lĕbābām he'ārēl* This phrase appears only here in the whole OT, though it is substantially the same as the one found in Jer. 9:25 and Ezek. 44:7, 9 (*'arlê lēb*). Indeed it is the transformation of the human heart that is the focus of the new covenant (Ezek. 11:19; 18:31; 36:26; cf. Jer. 31:33–34). Within the particular context of Lev. 26 it is important to observe that such a human heart is one that detests and abhors the Lord's commandments (v. 15) and that the people had hearts like this from the beginning, before their exile from the land (v. 15). As the second half of the verse intimates, such a heart is characterized by arrogance (cf. 2 Kgs 22:19).

'make amends for their guilt': *yirṣû 'et 'ăwōnām* This phrase appears again in the verse that follows (v. 43). The phrase indeed conveys the idea that guilt is paid for by suffering. But as the context indicates, the suffering should be one that leads humans to the destruction of their egocentric nature. The idea that human guilt is compensated by suffering and the confession of guilt is new within the context of Leviticus, but this observation need not imply a particular historical reality within the history of Israel (*pace* Milgrom 2001: 2330). Notice should be taken of the fact that v. 41 is part of a discourse where the Lord addresses the *possibility* of a recalcitrant people humbling themselves after the destruction of the sanctuary.

The submission of their arrogant hearts marks the last phase of compensation for their guilt, and this is expressed by the force of the second *'āz* in v. 41b. Moreover the Lord's words are not a law but a compromise, considering the standard the rest of the laws in Leviticus set.

The Lord's response to the people's repentance is his remembering the covenant he made with Jacob, Isaac and Abraham (v. 42). The chronologically reversed sequence of patriarchal names may reflect the process of the Lord's remembering (see 'Notes on the text'). The covenant includes the multiplication of offspring, the possession of the land, and the intimate relationship between the Lord and the people. The very mention of the Lord's *remembering* indicates he will implement these promises in reality. It also mentions he remembers the land that has been laid waste. In v. 43 the fate of the land is contrasted with the fate of the people: the land, though forsaken, will enjoy (*rāṣâ*) its sabbath rest during the time in which its occupants are expelled, whereas these occupants will have their guilt satisfied (*rāṣâ*). The cause for this course of events is emphasized by the words *ya'an* and *bĕya'an* (because): it is solely because the people detested the Lord's rules and abhorred his statutes (cf. v. 15). Note that the order of *mā'as* and *gā'al* in v. 15 is reversed here.

Despite the fact that the people detested and abhorred the Lord's commandments, the Lord avers that he will not detest and abhor them so much as destroy them completely; thereby breaking his covenant with them (v. 44). A strong literary and ideological connection with v. 15 appears to be made by *mā'as*, *gā'al* and 'breaking my covenant'. 'My covenant with them' that the Lord mentions refers here to that made with the Patriarchs. Yet except for what is mentioned in the following verse, the Lord makes no mention of his positive attitude to the fulfilment of the other items of his promise: multiplication of offspring and possession of the land. His mercy must be acknowledged here and could be an expression of his 'love', but the latter is of a nature far different from humanly conceived 'love'.

It is the covenant at Sinai, a more recent covenant than the covenant with the Patriarchs, that the Lord will fulfil at this critical stage of his people: he will be their God in the sight of the nations (v. 45). Thus, though the Lord's covenant with the Patriarchs will be remembered (v. 42), he will fulfil the principal goal of the covenant that is common to the Sinai covenant: to become their God. The mention of 'their forefathers' is ironic in that it refers to the present audience of the Lord's speech.

26:46

This verse summarizes not just the content of the chapter but the content of all the statutes given on Mount Sinai through Moses. Another similar statement appears at the end of the next chapter (see 'Comment' there). Thus all the commandments in Leviticus are summarized in two stages, here and in 27:34. The comprehensive nature of its reference is indicated by the three terms *ḥuqqîm*, *mišpāṭîm* and *tôrôt* (see Introduction 4.5).

'statutes': *ḥuqqîm* As mentioned at 10:11, the pl. form of *ḥōq* appears only twice in Leviticus, 10:11 and here, and is synonymous with *miṣwôt* (commandments), thus covering all the statutes given through Moses.

'rules': *mišpāṭîm* This appears in Leviticus in conjunction with *ḥuqqôt*, in chs. 18 – 26 (see 'Comment' on v. 15 above).

'laws': *tôrōt* In Leviticus this refers to various ritual prescriptions (6:9[2], 14[7], 25[18]; 7:1, 7, 11, 37; 11:46; 12:7; 13:59; 14:57; 15:32) and does not overlap with what *mišpāṭîm* refers to; the latter appears in 18:4 for the first time in Leviticus.

The overall sense relation of these three terms shows that while *mišpāṭîm* and *tôrôt* mostly do not overlap, *ḥuqqîm* is comprehensive. Therefore *wāw* before *hammišpāṭîm* would be explicative.

Explanation

In general the laws in Leviticus reflect the heart of the people, and this chapter is no exception. On the contrary, Lev. 26 is a rare chapter in Leviticus, not just in that it is devoid of rituals and legal instructions, but also because it portrays the real condition of the people's hearts in a hypothetical manner.

Both the curse and blessing sections are always set forth as hypothetical situations; i.e. 'if you obey' or 'if you do not obey'. Therefore the consequence of obedience or disobedience is consistently hypothetical. A corollary of this observation is that despite the much longer nature of the curses section, the Lord never reveals to what extent the Israelites will suffer the calamities mentioned therein. But the strong emphasis laid on the disproportionately longer section of curses indicates the Lord considers that the people's disobedience is most likely to become a reality. If one assumes God's omniscience, then it can be surmised the method in which the blessing and curse sections are presented derives from his conviction that the people will certainly disobey. In fact the blessing section can be seen as a mere preparation for the curse section in terms of its language and content. Until ch. 25 the laws are addressed to the Israelites on a level that does not imply the Israelites are as stiff-necked as what is described in this chapter. Although it is generally true that their spiritual reality is increasingly revealed through the regulations as the book progresses.

The Lord's goal to become the only God of the people is actualized only with the transformation of their hearts. In particular the curse section addresses itself to the mechanism between the people's *souls*, on the one hand, and the Lord and his commandments, on the other, thus answering the question of why the people disobey the commandments, and thus the Lord himself. It is clear the listed calamities are also aimed to facilitate the Lord's targeting of the people's hearts. They are, as mentioned above, designed to puncture pride and arrogance. Since pride and arrogance derive from human power, the calamities sent by the Lord are intended to destroy the Israelites' reliance upon such power. Thus, more than just setting out blessings and curses, this chapter demonstrates that the condition of the people's hearts is all that matters.

This chapter is more explicit than any other part of Leviticus in drawing a parallel between human stubbornness (uncircumcised hearts) and the state of self-hiding before the Lord. It would be no problem if the Israelites could observe the Lord's commandments, but the Lord's discourse, albeit hypothetical, presumes from the outset this is impossible for them. For they remain in a state of self-hiding. Thus freedom from the state of self-hiding requires the destruction of the uncircumcised heart, and these commandments are a means to this end.

Although there is no term for 'faith' in Leviticus, it is the condition of a human heart devoid of an egocentric nature (cf. the meaning of *mā'al* being 'to break faith with'): such a heart is 'holy' according to my definition of that term. Thus, since faith comes only after the destruction of the egocentric nature, the historical process by which the Lord destroys the people's hearts can be viewed as the process of sanctification. Generally, however, if faith is set against the observance of the laws, one inevitably tends to become legalistic, forgetting the essence of faith. This results in 'faith in the Lord' camouflaging legalism, which is characterized by humanism that camouflages an insufficient view of God's required standard. The condition of the human heart in such a situation is called the state of self-hiding, which is characterized by unconscious hypocrisy, where one is almost unaware of what is in his or her subconscious. When one begins to be troubled by, or suffer from an inner struggle, that person approaches the state of St Paul's heart in Rom. 7:7–25. The fact that the Israelites come to their senses when everything is stripped from them amply attests to this truth.

Now the people's failure or inability to observe the Lord's commandments finds its root in their 'uncircumcised hearts' (v. 41), which they have had from the beginning. 'Uncircumcised' is another expression for not observing any of the Lord's commandments, detesting the Lord, and hardness of the heart. By itself, what comes out of the uncircumcised heart is no different from blasphemy if it is contained inside, and in this regard Lev. 26 elaborates further on the blasphemy theme of ch. 24. This is most significant for understanding the meaning of the confession of guilt in v. 40. The object of the confession is the guilt (*'āwōn*) for the people's self-hiding, not to mention for their violation of particular commandments. It can be said that here for the first time in the long history of Israel the people come to have faith in the Lord. In other words, 'faith in the Lord' essentially refers to an acknowledgment of one's true condition: his subconscious is laid bare. This situation eventuates, the text says, after the Israelites are stripped of all their power, and even expelled from the land. How difficult it is to remove the human egocentric nature, and how fearful it is to deviate from the Lord's standard!

The Leviticus text does not indicate how the Lord will establish the ancient promise he made with the Patriarchs and the first generation redeemed from exodus. This is understandable, since the book has the nature of setting forth God's standard to the Israelites, how humans can come into close proximity with God, not how to handle people who repeatedly break the commandments and harden their hearts. It was the prophets who later appeared and endeavoured to turn the hearts of the people to the Lord, by drawing attention to and accusing them of their violation of the Law. But all their efforts failed in human eyes, and the covenants appeared broken. Yet from the midst of Babylonian exile the Lord began to stress that the only way to keep his promises to their forefathers was to transform their hearts. In Jer. 31:31–34 a 'new covenant' is announced, where the law is put in the hearts of the people, so they will no longer need to teach one another about the Lord. The prophet Ezekiel also speaks about the Lord's transformation of the human heart. In Ezekiel the Lord says he will create a 'new heart', which is not a heart of hard stone but of soft flesh. It is obvious that this takes place by the power of the Holy Spirit. Yet for all this, the principle that the people's hearts must be transformed is already present in Lev. 26.

Lastly, special attention should be paid to the fact that the Lord is said to establish his covenant with his people when the latter's heart is humbled, even if the sanctuary is non-existent. This raises the question as to why a sanctuary and all the holy things, such as offerings, priesthood, holy times, was ever needed. In so far as the historical and spiritual process mentioned in this chapter reflects a compromise on the Lord's part, his establishment of the covenant is gracious. However, this process, particularly its last phase, shows that even if the sanctuary is destroyed and the people are expelled from their land, it is the hearts of the people that the Lord is most concerned about. Indeed as prophets in later history announced, the observance of the Law is impossible without a transformation of the heart. Thus Lev. 26 indicates that the Lord deems the condition of the human heart as more important than the visible sancta.

It is already suggested that holiness is a matter of the human heart, and that things called holy only symbolize the condition of a person's heart. The punishment that follows the violation of holy things and time is severe because the violation has been made in the spiritual realm. In formulating rules that specific and tangible things such as offerings are holy, the Lord intended to teach the Israelites about the invisible spiritual realm, which is a matter of the heart. As mentioned in connection with the burnt offering (see 'Explanation' on ch. 1), the essence of holiness lies in the disappearance of all the offerer's earthly desires. In ch. 1, however, the burnt offering expresses its essence in a positive way, within the framework of the sanctuary and offerings. Yet in ch. 26 the essence of holiness is demonstrated negatively through the Lord's promised discipline. The same relationship is also present in the next chapter.

Thus it may be concluded that the Lord is satisfied with the people so long as their hearts are holy even when there is no sanctuary, priests or offerings, for holiness is intrinsically a matter of the human heart. In view of this the Lord's sanctification must inevitably take the form presented in this chapter in order to inculcate holiness within the hearts of the people.

New Testament implications

Chronologically the gospel of Jesus Christ, which finds its final expression in his cross and resurrection, came after the following truths became evident: that humans cannot and will not observe the Lord's commandments, that they cannot improve their own selfish nature and are constantly inclined to hide themselves, and thus only hopelessness remains for humanity. These are theological truths that a large part of OT narrative, laws and prophecies aim to inculcate within the reader. Although in Lev. 26 the Lord addresses the Israelites, his message concerning the condition of their hearts is universally applicable.

The New Testament also attests to the above truths. As humans cannot satisfy the Lord's standard, it is inevitable that the whole NT focuses on the transformation of the human heart. The Sermon on the Mount sets out a standard for the sons of the heavenly kingdom, but it is clear that all of Jesus' words cannot be observed unless a person's egocentric nature is destroyed and transformed into the heart of a child (Matt. 18:3). The sermon is not just a Christian *ideal* but must be *experienced* in order for a person to enter the heavenly kingdom. St Paul, in addressing salvation before God, stresses that the circumcision required is not physical but is circumcision of heart (Rom. 2:25–29). The process by which an uncircumcised heart is transformed into a circumcised one is elucidated by way of Paul's personal experience in Rom. 7:7–25, where he suffers from his inner conflict between what the Law says and his flesh desires. Thus both Paul's experience and the supposed history of the Israelites are essentially the same – both have a long spiritual history, where they hid themselves unconsciously, only later realizing their guilt.

The Holy Spirit brings the elect to an awareness of their own inner inconsistency and hypocrisy when he sends suffering, financial predicaments, conflicts, the fracturing of personal relationships, and various incidents including what are sometimes called catastrophes. These are occasions where people should turn their attention to and ponder their past lifestyles and the condition of their hearts. It is extremely difficult for individuals to realize on their own that they have hidden themselves from the Lord. Nor is it easy for this to be pointed out by others, unless a person is honest and humble in the way assumed by Lev. 4. At any rate, the Holy Spirit works within 'believers' so that they become aware of their guilt and become true disciples of Jesus.

Thus one would have to realize that the selfish nature requires destruction before one can be saved. It is insufficient just to believe a set of doctrines. A person whose heart still leaves room for hardness and stubbornness cannot be called a believer. Just as in Lev. 26 people reconcile themselves with the Lord after confessing they have detested both him and his commandments, people today ought also to confess their self-hiding and the way they have detested the Lord even while hypocritically observing religious practices. This means they admit to the presence of their own flesh, which is hostile to the good Law.

Thus faith in the proper biblical sense is not so much a belief in a set of doctrines as in the condition of the human heart. This is the condition of the saved heart, and the Lord dwells with such a person (cf. Isa. 57:15).

Under the category of 'sanctification', believers tend to assume, consciously or unconsciously, that they ought to live an increasingly ethical life, as this is pleasing to God. However, this brings a believer to his former condition of heart, and offers an occasion for his flesh to revive under the guise of ‘holy living’. Though not perceived, this merely betrays that the ‘believer’ has not completely undergone the operation of the Holy Spirit. As long as the selfish nature lives within the human heart, the Law challenges and puts one in a sinful state (cf. Selman 2003: 514).

The road to the salvation of the human heart is hard and harsh (Matt. 7:14), but made easier if one is humble, innocent and honest.

LEVITICUS 27:1–34

Translation

1The LORD spoke to Moses, saying, 2‘Speak to the people of Israel and say to them, If anyone makes a special vow to the LORD at the evaluation of lives, 3then the valuation of a male from twenty years old up to sixty years old shall be fifty shekels of silver, according to the shekel of the sanctuary. 4If it is a female, the valuation shall be thirty shekels. 5If the age is from five years old up to twenty years old, the valuation shall be for a male twenty shekels, and for a female ten shekels. 6If the age is from a month old up to five years old, the valuation shall be for a male five shekels of silver, and for a female the valuation shall be three shekels of silver. 7If the age is sixty years old or over, then the valuation for a male shall be fifteen shekels, and for a female ten shekels. 8If one cannot afford to pay the valuation, then he shall be made to stand before the priest, and the priest shall value him; the priest shall value him according to what the vower can afford.

9‘If the vow is an animal that may be offered as an offering to the LORD, all of it that he gives to the LORD is holy. 10He shall not exchange it or make a substitute for it, good for bad, or bad for good; and if he does in fact substitute one animal for another, then both it and the substitute shall be holy. 11If it is any unclean animal that may not be offered as an offering to the LORD, then he shall stand the animal before the priest, 12and the priest shall value it as either good or bad; as the priest values it, so it shall be. 13But if he wishes to redeem it, he shall add a fifth to the valuation.

14‘When a person dedicates his house as a holy gift to the LORD, the priest shall value it as either good or bad; as the priest values it, so it shall stand. 15And if the donor wishes to redeem his house, he shall add a fifth to the valuation price, and it shall be his. 16If a man dedicates to the LORD part of the land that is his possession, then the valuation shall be in proportion to its seed. A homer of barley seed shall be valued at fifty shekels of silver. 17If he dedicates his field from the year of Jubilee, the valuation shall stand, 18but if he dedicates his field after the Jubilee, then the priest shall calculate the price according to the years that remain until the year of Jubilee, and a deduction shall be made from the valuation. 19And if he who dedicates the field wishes to redeem it, then he shall add a fifth to its valuation price, and it shall remain his; 20but if he does not wish to redeem the field, or if he had sold

the field to another man, it shall not be redeemed anymore. [21]But the field, when it
is released in the Jubilee, shall be a holy gift to the LORD, like a field that has been
devoted. The priest shall be in possession of it. [22]If he dedicates to the LORD a field
that he has bought, which is not a part of his possession, [23]then the priest shall
calculate the amount of the valuation for it up to the year of Jubilee, and the man
shall give the valuation on that day as a holy gift to the LORD. [24]In the year of
Jubilee the field shall return to him from whom it was bought, to whom the land
belongs as a possession. [25]Every valuation shall be according to the shekel of the
sanctuary: twenty gerahs shall make a shekel.

[26]'But a firstborn of animals, which is treated as a firstborn to the LORD, no man
may dedicate; whether ox or sheep, it is the LORD's. [27]And if it is an unclean animal,
then he shall buy it back at the valuation, and add a fifth to it; or, if it is not redeemed,
it shall be sold at the valuation. [28]But no devoted thing that a man devotes to the
LORD, of anything that he has, whether man or beast, or of his inherited field, shall be
sold or redeemed; every devoted thing is most holy to the LORD. [29]No-one devoted,
who is to be devoted for destruction from mankind, shall be ransomed; he shall
surely be put to death. [30]Every tithe of the land, whether of the seed of the land or of
the fruit of the trees, is the LORD's; it is holy to the LORD. [31]If a man wishes to redeem
some of his tithe, he shall add a fifth to it. [32]And every tithe of herds and flocks, every
tenth animal of all that pass under the herdsman's staff, shall be holy to the LORD.
[33]One shall not differentiate between good or bad, neither shall he make a substitute
for it; and if he does substitute for it, then both it and the substitute shall be holy; it
shall not be redeemed.'

[34]These are the commandments that the LORD commanded Moses for the people
of Israel on Mount Sinai.

Notes on the text

2. 'makes a special vow': *yaplî'* *BHS* proposes its pi. form *yĕpalle'*, as in 22:21. However, this is unnecessary, considering the use of *yaplî'* in relation to a Nazirite's vow (Num. 6:2).

'at the evaluation of lives': *bĕ'erkĕkā nĕpāšōt* This phrase is variously rendered in English translations. The key term is *nĕpāšōt*, pl. of *nepeš*. It has been understood as meaning 'persons' or 'human beings'. However, *nepeš* is unlikely to mean 'a person', which is better expressed *'îš*, a term that, in this regulation, occurs only in v. 1aa (*'îš kî*). On this occasion *nepeš* probably means either 'life' or 'soul'. Since the salvation of a soul is not at issue here, 'life' may be preferable. LXX translates it as sg.: *tēs psychēs autou* (his life). Perhaps the pl. form refers to the different kinds of *nepeš* that follow in vv. 3–7.

5. 'the age' Though there is no corresponding Hebr. word for this term, it is supplemented as in JPS. So in vv. 6 and 7.

8. 'be made to stand': *he'ĕmîdô* The agent of the Hebr. verb is impersonal, and the person who is to stand is the one who makes the vow.

9. 'may be offered': *yaqrîbû* A few Hebr. MSS, Tg and Vg take it in sg. both here and v. 11.

20. 'or if': *wĕ'im* If a single apodosis is contemplated, this 'if' would not normally be necessary; hence the understanding that two alternative cases are set out here.

'had sold': *mākar* Since the rule assumes that a person has already dedicated the land to the Lord, the pluperfect tense fits this context better.

23. 'the amount of': *miksat* This term appears elsewhere only in Exod. 12:4.

26. 'treated as a firstborn': *yĕbukkar* As another instance of *bkr* pu. in Deut. 21:16 shows, the sense of this verb can cover such a case that an animal or person that is not actually firstborn is treated as such (cf. Gen. 27 and McConville 2002: 330).

27. 'buy back': *pādâ* In Leviticus the qal form appears for the first time here and in the next verse. The hoph. form has already appeared in 19:20. The idea of the root is to 'buy something back to give it freedom' and should be distinguished from *gā'al*. Nevertheless in this chapter these terms are not distinguished but are used as synonyms, as evidenced by this verse.

'add a fifth to it' LXX adds 'and it will be his' both here and v. 31.

30. 'of the fruits of the trees': *mippĕrî hā'ēṣ* Many Hebr. MSS, SamP, LXX, Syr and Vg read '*and* from the fruits of the trees'.

31. *mimma'aśĕrô* LXX and Vg read *ma'aśĕrô*; i.e. as a direct object, and without the preposition *min*.

33. 'differentiate': *biqqēr* For this meaning, see 'Comment' on 19:20.

'differentiate ... bad' LXX translates this part 'exchange good by bad', something closer to v. 10.

Form and structure

The final chapter of Leviticus provides rules relating to human vows made to the Lord. Various restrictions are given concerning the offerings and dedications that may be used. Essentially these rules are concerned with the will of the person who makes a vow.

The content is as follows:

A. Introduction (1–2)
B. Vows concerning
  1. a. persons (2–8)
     b. animals (9–13)
C. Vows concerning dedications
  1. of a house (14–15)
  2. of a field (16–24)
     the statement of the value of a shekel (25)

D. Restrictions on other objects that may be vowed (26–33)
   1. firstborn (26–27)
   2. things devoted (28–29)
   3. tithes (30–33)
E. Summary

Sections B and C begin with *wĕ'îš kî* (and if a person, vv. 2, 14), while their subsections are introduced by *wĕ'im* (and if, vv. 4, 9, 16, 22 etc.). Thus the chapter divides into two parts, B on the one hand, and C, D, on the other. On the whole, though every vow is limited by certain conditions, the rules move from what is redeemable to things that are not.

The placement of this chapter after ch. 26 may appear puzzling to modern readers, and it is generally labelled as an appendix. However, the appropriateness of the location in terms of its content has been advocated by recent commentators such as Wenham (1979: 336) and Hartley (1992: 479). Following Wenham's understanding that this chapter dealing with human vows naturally follows ch. 26, a chapter comprising a kind of divine vow (curses and blessings), Hartley observes that until ch. 27 there is no appropriate place to position the content contained in ch. 27. More specifically, there is an unmistakable contrast drawn between God's unyielding faithfulness to his own promises (ch. 26) and the untrustworthy resolutions of humans (ch. 27). Both present the same view of human spirituality: in ch. 26, its ever-growing stubbornness, while in ch. 27, an outwardly pietistic but inwardly covetous reality (see 'Explanation' and 26:31).

The links with ch. 25 are not purely lexical, such as references to the year of Jubilee (27:17–18, 21, 23–24), but theological, as suggested by the use of the term *gā'al* (redeem). The benevolent character of the year of Jubilee in ch. 25 is replaced by a restrictive one in Lev. 27, and becomes an even more severe institution for those who make vows and those who desire to 'redeem' what they have already dedicated. Conformably, monetary units never mentioned in ch. 25 are referred to in this chapter (vv. 16, 25).

In the light of the above it even seems possible to recognize the presence of the wordplay between *gā'al* (abhor) in ch. 26 and *gā'al* (redeem) in this chapter.

Another structural issue is the mention of 'on Mount Sinai' that occurs in 25:1, 26:36 and 27:34, which, at least, suggests there are some literary connections between the three chapters. The fact that the comprehensive term *miṣwôt* (commandments) appears in 26:15 but not at the end of ch. 26 (v. 46), while it appears at the end of ch. 27, suggests ch. 27 was intended as the concluding chapter from the outset.

In view of these observations, along with ch. 26, ch. 27 forms the concluding chapter, and clarifies the human self-dedication to the Lord dealt with in ch. 24 (see 'Form and structure' of ch. 26).

For the relationship between chs. 27 and 1, see 'Explanation'.

Comment

This chapter deals with vows involving a person, dedications of an animal, a house, a land, and bans and tithes. The common element is the transference of things or persons to the divinity by invoking God's name. While until this chapter the Lord makes promises to the Israelite, this chapter focuses on human beings making their promises to God.

The OT contains a number of instances where men and women make vows on various occasions of predicaments or in the face of death. Thus Jacob vowed to his God, saying if God were present and would protect him in every way, he would make a tithe to God (Gen. 28:20). The people of Israel made a vow of destroying the Canaanite cities if God delivered their enemies to them (Num. 21:1–3). Hannah vowed a vow by saying, if the Lord gave her a child, she would dedicate him to the Lord as a permanent Nazirite (1 Sam. 1:11). Especially, many references to vows in the psalms indicate that making a vow was regarded as an ordinary and legitimate act for believers (e.g. Pss. 50:14; 65:1[2]; 132:2; cf. 'Comment' on 7:15–17 and 22:21–25).

However, since the human resolution often betrays its foolishness in making a vow, and any failure to fulfil it constitutes an offence against God, this chapter apparently warns the Israelites not to make hasty resolutions, by stipulating that what is dedicated to the Lord belongs to him and by imposing heavy penalties on its repurchase (cf. 5:4 and 'Comment' there, and also Num. 6:2, 5, 21). Some legislations in the Pentateuch, beginning with this chapter, envisage this potentiality, give warnings (Deut. 23:22–24) and present cases where apparent violation can be forgiven (Num. 30). More than human weakness or foolishness, however, Lev. 27 tacitly implies the presence of human covetousness or the egocentric nature as the cause of making vows in general.

27:1–8

2. The situation envisaged here is that of a person making a special vow involving human life (see below). However, the text's silence about the specific circumstances of the vows appears to presume them. Instead the legislation draws attention to the cost of the vows, rather than the supposed varying motives of the vowers. Thus when people vow by saying they will be God's servant, or that, as Hannah did, they will dedicate one of their offspring to be the Lord's servant for the rest of his or her life, the cost will be more than the sum total of the estimation listed below, although it varies depending on how long the vowed person lives. If one shekel corresponds to the average monthly wage of a worker, as Wenham comments (1979: 338), the potential for violation of the vow inevitably becomes high. However, the absence in the OT of the explict application of the rule in v. 2 may reflect the fact that a person scarcely realizes the true cost of his or her vow.

'lives': *nĕpāšōt* This term refers to human life (see 'Notes on the text'). An additional exegetical question is whether this term also includes the life of the person who makes the vow. The fact that the following valuations do not specifically answer this question suggests that the term refers to both. Moreover v. 8 implies that the person who makes the vow is included.

3–7. The estimation of the person involved in a vow is set out according to gender and age, as follows:

male	twenty to sixty years	fifty shekels
female		thirty shekels
male	five to twenty years	twenty shekels
female		ten shekels
male	one month to five years	five shekels
female		three shekels
male	sixty years and more	fifteen shekels
female		ten shekels

What these valuations were based on is not immediately apparent. Wenham has proposed that they were based on the slave market (1979: 338). However, Hartley points out that 'the price of the slaves varies in different times and locations' (Hartley 1992: 481, citing Mendelsohn's view), and judges that it has nothing to do with a person's intrinsic value as a human being but is based on the relative strength of men and women. Meyers, drawing on Graham, says, 'This structure indicates exactly the way in which the vowed persons contributed to the shrine; i.e. in terms of labour' (1988: 171, followed by Wegner 1992: 47). However, though this latter view appears reasonable, any explanation resorting to human strength or labour cannot fully explain why infants are included. The best solution would be to assume that these valuations reflect an investment one receives from others, particularly one's parents, an average cost of living for each of these age groups. The valuations above the age of sixty decrease because those elderly people are assumed to have received the fruits from the investment made in themselves.

The differences in valuation according to gender still requires some explanation. It would be slightly inaccurate to explain this as reflecting a patriarchal society, since the prices are sanctuary prices made by God and unchangeable in relation to time and situation. As in other parts of Leviticus, it seems that, as far as human life on earth is concerned, more is expected of a man, as the head of a family, than of a woman, though the human souls are priceless regardless of gender.

Thus this rule stipulates the values for human beings according to gender and age, thereby revealing the cost of making a vow.

8. A provision is made for the case where a person who has made a vow becomes impoverished and unable to pay the specified amount. In such a case the priest revalues him according to his income. This verse addresses itself to the re-evaluation of the very person who made a vow rather than another person who was vowed (cf. Hartley 1992: 481). As mentioned above, this implies that the *nĕpāšōt* in v. 2b includes the person who made the vow, so the valuation system in vv. 3–7 also concerns this person. This measure implies that the vow ought to be fulfilled by any means. However, it also indicates the foolishness of making a vow involving human life, because it does not take into account the possibility of becoming poor.

27:9–13

9–10. The above main case (vv. 2ab–8) is followed by this subcase, which is further followed by its own subcases in vv. 11–12 and 13, all of which are introduced by *'im* (if). When a person makes a vow, he may do it by offering an animal in the form of a fellowship offering or burnt offering (cf. 22:21) rather than a monetary payment. Unlike monetary payments, animals have different qualities. 'Good for bad, or bad for good' does not mean that badness disqualifies an animal. Even within the bounds of a qualified animal there can be different qualities (cf. 22:18–25).

These verses stipulate that once an animal is given to the Lord it remains his, so the person who dedicated it cannot exchange it for an animal of either greater of lesser quality. If he does, both animals become the Lord's property. The point is that the Lord is not concerned about the offerer's decision rather than the quality of the animal; once it is offered to the Lord, it must not be tampered with by the human will. The rule demands purity or sincerity of heart on the part of the person who makes the vow. However, who would dare exchange the one with another, knowing how costly such an act would be?

11–13. If a vow involves offering an unclean animal, which is prohibited in the case of an offering to the Lord, it ought to be converted into monetary value by the priest. But if he does wish to 'redeem' (*gā'al*) it, then he must pay six-fifths of the animal's value. It is obvious that this payment has the nature of a penalty for profaning a vow to the Lord (cf. 5:16; 6:5[5:24]), though more specifically for changing his initial decision.

One wonders what urges the offerers to use an unclean animal if it must be converted into money. Why do they have to make a vow in this way? Undoubtedly the rule, as for the one in vv. 9–10, aims to curb the desire of the one who makes the vow to hold on to what has already been offered, or has been vowed to offer, to the Lord.

'repurchase': *gā'al* This term appears frequently in ch. 25 and appears for the first time here in this chapter. But its connotation is quite unlike the ordinary one. In ch. 25, for instance, the redeemer (*gō'ēl*) is one who, because of the relative in question, repurchases land so that the relative may return there. In other words, the redeemer extends a benevolent helping hand to a person because he is a relative; it is not the relative's fault that the land was sold. Equally important is the fact that one repurchases or redeems something (land, house) that originally belonged to him. By contrast, the use of *gā'al* beginning from 27:13 to the end of the chapter exhibits an unusual character, for what is to be 'redeemed' belongs to the Lord. Moreover it is not someone else but the person who vows or dedicates himself who repurchases or redeems (*gā'al*). Such usage of the term is found nowhere else, whether in 'secular' or 'religious' contexts. Indeed one may define the meaning of the term simply as 'to repurchase', but the meaning is also conveyed by *mākar*. The conclusion is inevitable that *gā'al* is used in this chapter in an ironic or sarcastic sense, and that it is used in this way because the Lord assumes that the one who vows takes for granted that the things offered, dedicated or even devoted are his own, or, at least because the person takes his vow lightly; hence the heavy penalty (see 'Explanation').

27:14–25

This section addresses the dedication of a house (14–15) or land (16–25) to the Lord. The latter is further divided into the dedication of an inherited land (16–21) and a purchased land (22–25). The issue of repurchasing property is based on the principle of the Jubilee year set out in ch. 25.

14–15. The principle of dedicating a house is stated: when it is dedicated to the Lord, it becomes a holy gift and its valuation is made by the priest. Lev. 25:29–31 stipulated how a house is to be sold. Here, however, it is the Lord who receives the dedication. Though not stated, repurchasing what is already holy profanes it so that the payment of a penalty is required. Again, the decision to repurchase it from the Lord presumes a change of mind on the part of the person who dedicated it, the roots of which are traceable to his initial decision. Yet considering the presumably very high value of a house, he would, in all likelihood, relinquish his desire to take it back. Thus these rules appear to function to discourage any human attempt to tamper with a holy thing, thereby stressing that once a house is dedicated to the Lord it is his. As in the previous rules, this rule also points to the need for having a pure heart. Thus when it is said in v. 15, 'If the dedicator redeems his house', it ironically portrays the dedicator as one who has not truly dedicated his offering.

Here the human resolution to repurchase (*gā'al*) is legal, though offensive to the Lord. As in v. 13, 'redeem' (*gā'al*) in v. 15 sarcastically refers to the impure motive of the dedicator. It appears that the Lord uses *gā'al* in this instance to draw the reader's attention to the fact that far from serving the Lord, the house remains the donor's main concern. That is, the once-dedicated house has become his idol (cf. Ezek. 20:39).

16. This verse, along with vv. 17–18, sets out the principle of dedicating part of one's inherited land to the Lord. Ch. 25 has stipulated the rule concerning the selling or buying of land between the Israelites. Here the dedication is assumed to be to the Lord. This sounds slightly strange, for the land is the Lord's (25:23). However, the Lord legally permits the Israelites to dedicate part of his own land to himself, so they can express their dedication to him, on the assumption that the people consider the land is not the Lord's but theirs.

As in 25:16 the valuation of a house should be based on the amount of barley produce, which is here specified; a homer of barley corresponds to fifty shekels of silver. However, that this specific standard is given here and not in ch. 25 suggests that this chapter assumes a calculating people. Inevitably legalistic people would apply this specific rate to 25:16, where the exact amount is not specified. However, if the people's attitude is assumed to be such, would they attempt to observe the year of Jubilee?

17–18. If a piece of the inherited land is dedicated, the value of the land depends on its annual agricultural yield. This amount is multiplied by the number of years: if the dedication is made on the year of Jubilee, the annual production is multiplied by forty-nine. This multiple is reduced by one for each year the land is dedicated after the Jubilee year.

19. Again, as in vv. 13 and 15, the possibility is envisaged that the donor desires to repurchase the house he already dedicated to the Lord. As for the previous case, he is to make a payment of six-fifths of the original value. This presumably exorbitant expense would curb his desire to redeem the land. Yet the land is the Lord's from the beginning!

20–21. Two further principles are introduced to underline the irrevocable nature of the inherited land. First, if the donor does not redeem the land he has already dedicated, the land remains unredeemable. Second, if he sells the land to another man, the land remains unredeemable. The first rule does not preclude the possibility that the donor redeems the land, but strongly suggests that once the land is dedicated to the Lord, he forfeits forever his right to redeem it. The second rule envisages some irresponsible or even criminal conduct, for it assumes the donor, while dedicating the land to the Lord, sold it to someone else. In such a case, the land becomes unredeemable. Such land, which is either unredeemable or neglected, belongs to the Lord until the year of Jubilee, and on that year it becomes holy as a *ḥērem*-land and belongs to the property of the priests. It should be noted that the *ḥērem*-land does not revert to the original owner on the year of Jubilee, as in the case of the interhuman dealings of ch. 25.

The term *ḥērem* refers to things or persons that are irrevocably devoted to the Lord. It occurs here for the first time in Leviticus, and only in this chapter (see further vv. 28–29). As the mention of the term is incidental, the concept may have been well known to the original readership. A fuller definition of this term is given in vv. 28–29. In this verse, however, it is observable that *ḥērem*-land belongs to the Lord; hence its holy character.

Nevertheless more significantly, *ḥērem*-land has a history of circumstances or situations that led to the profanation of its once-holy status, the root of which lies in the human will. So, though such a field eventually ends up having a holy status, it is not the same as other holy objects in that it has gone through the process of profanation.

Thus the idea of *ḥērem* presumes the process of profanation, and this incidental reference to *ḥērem* along with the first reference to 'It shall not be redeemed' (*lō' yiggā'ēl*) in v. 20 paves the way for a comprehensive reference to *ḥērem* in vv. 28–29.

On the whole, these regulations give the impression that despite being an honourable act, the dedication of part of one's inherited land tends to incur serious consequences, unless the initial intention of the dedication is pure and simple.

22–25. In the case where the land a person dedicates to the Lord is not part of his inherited land but is saleable land, the priest calculates the value of the land until the year of Jubilee, and the devotee pays that amount on the day of dedication, a detail not mentioned in the case for selling part of inherited land (16–18). The currency rate is that of the sanctuary: one shekel is twenty gerahs, another additional detail of the rule in v. 16b. According to Exod. 30:13 half a shekel ransoms the life of an Israelite.

As stated in ch. 25, the land reverts to the original owner on the year of Jubilee. While the land becomes holy by dedication (v. 23b) it seems reasonable to assume that the devotee himself cultivates the land, since the land is not the property of the priests. The possibility that the land can be redeemed is precluded and therefore not mentioned, because redemption (*gā'al*) of land is inherently related to its original owner. In view of the following rules regarding the firstborn, *ḥērem* and tithes, one should observe the gradual shift in legal emphasis from redeemable to unredeemable.

27:26–33

This last section is a continuation of the preceding in that both deal with the theme of dedication, but as stated above, the theme in this section shifts to one of cases where the very possibility of dedication is ruled out: for the firstborn, *ḥērem* and tithes. The last of these has essentially nothing to do with dedication or redemption. Though not explicitly mentioned, the Lord tacitly suggests, by this flow of rules, that everything belongs to the Lord, so 'dedication' or 'redemption' has something to do with the human sinful drive (see 'Explanation').

26. The case of the first-born is introduced by *'ak* (but). It is contrasted with all the preceding cases where one can redeem a house (v. 14) and land (vv. 16, 22). One cannot redeem a firstborn animal, whether it is a sheep or an ox, for it is inherently the Lord's. Every firstborn, whether it is a human or an animal, has to be consecrated to the Lord (Exod. 13:2).

27. In the case of an unclean animal, such as a donkey (Exod. 34:20), one must ransom it by paying 120% of its value. But if it is not redeemed (*gā'al*), it must be sold at its normal value. Behind this rule is the idea that an unclean firstborn must be separated from the owner's hand. Thus, far from 'dedicating' a firstborn, the owner of the unclean firstborn animal is compelled either to redeem or sell it.

28–29. Both this and the following verse deal with *ḥērem* relating to animals, humans and land. The opening Hebr. *'ak* contrasts the rules in these verses with 'it shall be sold at the value' at the end of v. 27. So the relationship with the previous rules is partly associative.

Following the earlier mention of *ḥērem* in v. 21, this verse stipulates that any *ḥērem* (human, animal or inherited land) cannot be sold or redeemed: it is most holy and belongs to the Lord.

'most holy': *qōdeš qodāšîm* As has been mentioned, this phrase is not necessarily related to the degree of holiness. The superlative form rather conveys the message that extra caution should be paid to the handling of what has a *ḥērem* character. This conforms to the nature of *ḥērem*, which is both non-saleable and irredeemable: any human involvement with it is banned. Ironically this situation arose from the circumstance that a once-holy thing was profaned prior to becoming a *ḥērem* object (see above on v. 21).

V. 29 stipulates that whoever is devoted ought to be put to death. The formula *môt yûmat* suggests that the act of execution is carried out by the court.

The hiph. and hoph. forms of *ḥāram* appear in these verses, and both assume the people can devote inanimate things and humans as *ḥērem* to the Lord. In other words, while there are cases such as the one in vv. 20–21, where land eventually becomes *ḥērem* (in the course of the circumstances), there are cases, as here, where people offer humans, animals or land as *ḥērem* by their own will. What exact situation these rules envisage has been discussed (see Stern 1991: 131–132). The case of a human *ḥērem* poses a special problem. But as Stern observes, it refers to slaves, since the text explicitly states 'from what he possesses'. However, Stern, in attempting to refute the possibility of seeing idolatry behind the rules, further qualifies the slave as a foreigner, since Hebrew slaves are provided with good care. Also, referring to Deuteronomy, he maintains that 'the execution of an individual is a communal matter; it was not the job of the individual to eliminate his compatriots when he suspected them of worshipping alien gods' (Stern 1991: 132). A couple of comments are necessary.

First, there is a problem with the common definition of 'idolatry': the worshipping of other gods. The essence of idolatry lies not just in making visible idols or uttering the names of foreign gods but in covetousness (see on v. 21 and 'Comment' on 19:4). This inevitably calls Stern's assumption that foreign slaves are more 'idolatrous' than the Israelites into question. Further, why, if not the case of a human, is the once-dedicated land in

vv. 20–21 called *ḥērem*-land? It is because its initial holiness has been profaned, and it is more than likely that this was caused by its original owner's covetousness when he dedicated it. Thus legally the Israelites are indeed allowed to make a special vow, but the very act of devoting a human, if the person is his own slave, indicates that the offerer deems himself to be an absolute judge free from any covetousness. In other words, the offerer is tacitly viewed as highly dangerous spiritually, unknowingly equating himself with a god. For fairness' sake, if idolatry lies in coveting or the egocentric nature, then the dedicator ought to dedicate his life to a death sentence.

Second, while it is indeed extremely difficult for a slave owner to devote his slave to the Lord even superficially, it would be appropriate, in view of the nature of other Leviticus laws, to assume the law simply sets out the rules by taking into account the human propensity to make oneself a god. This reading seems to conform to other rules in this chapter, where the superficiality of human involvement with the holy is viewed as ironic (see 'Explanation'). Thus, while the Lord commands Israelites to devote persons such as the Canaanites (e.g. Deut. 7:1–2, 26; 20:17; cf. McConville 2002: 87–90 *et passim*), the matter is different when a human being is the devotee. More important than the legal side of these rules is the observation that the Lord, accommodating himself to the mind of human beings, provides a means to 'devote' one of their slaves; thereby challenging the potentially deep and incorrigible hypocrisy within human beings.

Seen this way, the rules in vv. 28–29 challenge the readers with regard to the devoted animals and land as well. For, the fact that a person devotes an animal or a piece of land to the Lord presumes he himself is free from any covetousness. A concrete example of these rules may be envisaged in a person's devotion of an animal or a piece of land because it has become an idol, a god to him; he then devotes it to the Lord relinquishing every desire towards it forever. Such an act may be religiously honourable, but the very stipulation of irredeemability regarding *ḥērem* suggests that there is something unnatural in the dedication.

30–33. After the section on irredeemable things comes the theme of tithes made from agricultural produce and animals: one-tenth of produce and animals belong to the Lord – they are holy. This theme probably comes last in a series of dedications, partly because the tithes are inherently holy, so there is no need to dedicate them as is done for firstborn animals (v. 26; notice that in this connection these verses form a literary unit with vv. 26–33), and partly because the Lord here indicates that humans, far from dedicating something to him, have a deeply calculating mind, as shown by the rule in vv. 31–33.

The redemption of tithes is permitted. But in such a case a person ought to pay six-fifths of the original value. Undoubtedly, as for other similar cases in this chapter (see vv. 13, 15), this 'redemption' has a character of profanation and penalty. But what prompts a person to repurchase a holy tithe to make it his own? Whatever circumstance or excuse one might suggest, it is undoubtedly traceable to the covetousness of the 'redeemer'. This is clear in the rule of vv. 32–33. While the tenth animal that comes under a rod becomes the Lord's, the prohibition against differentiating the animal reflects the human calculating mind. The penalty in the case of substituting one for another (both becoming holy and irredeemable) aims at curbing the inner drive of the 'dedicator'.

Compared with v. 10, v. 33 adds 'it shall not be redeemed'. The 'irredeemability' of the profaned tithes give them a status similar to that of the *ḥērem*, particularly because the whole process involves itself with the covetousness of a person who has exchanged one animal for another.

27:34

This concluding statement refers at least to the rules in this chapter. It is similar to 26:46, and as regards the mention of 'on Mount Sinai' is also related to 25:1. The possibility exists that this verse also refers to all the preceding rules, judging from the semantic range of *miṣṣwôt* (commandments). As has been argued (see Introduction 4.5, 'Comment' on 4:2 and 26:15), this term is most comprehensive, encompassing the rules (*ḥuqqôt*) and statutes (*mišpāṭîm*). For the further structural implications of this, see 'Form and structure' and 'Explanation'.

Explanation

Why does a human dedicate something or someone to the Lord? Does he or she know the costliness of his or her decision? The priceless value in vv. 3–7 of the person's life dedicated and in vv. 15, 19 the redemption of the devoted house or land by paying six-fifths of its original value are undoubtedly intended to underline the foolishness of making vows to the Lord indiscreetly. Why would they make a vow risking such a large amount of money? The reason is that the devotee deems that the person devoted is worth that risk, or that he temporarily has the will or emotion to dedicate a thing or person, without considering the gravity of his decision. However, the huge penalty associated with making vows raises the question of why one would consider making a vow to the Lord in the first place. These considerations suggest that though the making of vows is permissible and looks like a pious act in human eyes, it often betrays the unbelief of the devotee. Such a human spiritual condition is apparently presumed not just in this chapter but also in the rule pertaining to the Nazirite (Num. 6:1–21).

Thus these penalties, though they can simply be taken as rules, aim at curbing the desire of the people to make dedications to the Lord lightheartedly. The dedication of a house or land is respectable, but only so far as the dedicator remains steadfast in a decision to relinquish these things to the Lord. In fact the chapter assumes a person who forgets an initial desire to dedicate something.

Thus this chapter, while dealing with the legal dimensions of 'redemption' and 'repurchase' of what has been consecrated to the Lord, addresses itself to the wastefulness of the human will that prompts people to make vows, dedicate things and devote things and persons to the Lord. Envisaged in, or underlying, these rules is the presumption of human covetousness and greed that make one's whole decision to dedicate things foolish and hypocritical, even though such an act looks pious. In other words, they function to inculcate in the minds and hearts of the Israelites the absolute truth that whatever belongs to the Lord remains his, and should thus not be tampered with. The introduction of two items towards the end of the chapter, namely firstborns and tithes, both of which belong to the Lord from the beginning, underscores this message, though human beings still tend to presume they own what belongs to the Lord.

Thus the rules in this chapter reflect the Lord's accommodating gracious stance towards the calculating mind of human beings. However, what is holy is holy, and the rules show that the Lord does not make a compromise with anything that threatens his holiness. The reader should be reminded that holiness is a state of the human heart (cf. 'Explanation' on ch. 19). Though holy things are naturally the Lord's, they are called holy just because they represent the will of those who vowed or dedicated them.

The book of Leviticus began with a chapter on the burnt offering, which symbolizes total self-dedication to the Lord. Yet it ends with a chapter that clearly betrays the human egocentric nature. It is noteworthy that the most absolute self-dedication, namely the proscription, is deeply related to the human egocentric nature. In this sense, ch. 27 stands in sharp contrast to ch. 1, even though both deal with self-dedication. If the Lord cannot accept a person unless he offers himself totally, thus effectively destroying his egocentric nature, how daunting it is for a human to be accepted by the Lord, considering that the rules in this chapter reflect the real condition of the people!

Later literature increasingly attests to the negative aspects of making vows (Prov. 20:25; Eccl. 5:4–5; Ps. 15:4), even though they were permissible throughout the biblical period. More important than the outward act of making a vow is the condition of the human heart. Jesus prohibited swearing, and commanded the believers to have a heart that says 'Yes' to 'Yes' and 'No' to 'No' (Matt. 5:33–37; cf. Jas 4:13–16), a heart characterized by wholeheartedness.

BIBLIOGRAPHY

COMMENTARIES ON LEVITICUS

Abrabanel, D. I. (1979), *A Commentary on the Pentateuch* [Hebrew], Jerusalem: Bnei Arbel.

Balentine, S. E. (2002), *Leviticus*, Interpretation, Louisville: John Knox.

Budd, P. J. (1996), *Leviticus*, NCB Commentary, London: Marshall Pickering.

Dillmann, A. (1880), *Exodus und Leviticus*, Kurzgefasstes exegetisches Handbuch zum Alten Testament, Leipzig: Hirtzel.

Elliger, K. (1966), *Leviticus*, Tübingen: Mohr.

Gerstenberger, E. S. (1993), *Das 3. Buch Mose Leviticus*, ATD 6, Göttingen: Vandenhoeck & Ruprecht.

Gispen, W. H. (1950), *Het Boek Leviticus*, Commentar op het OT, Kampen: Kok.

Harrison, R. K. (1980), *Leviticus: An Introduction and Commentary*, TOTC, Leicester: IVP.

Hartley, J. E. (1992), *Leviticus*, WBC, Dallas, TX: Word.

Hoffmann, D. (1905–6), *Das Buch Leviticus I–II*, Berlin: Poppenlauer.

Ibn Ezra, A. (1977), *A Commentary on the Pentateuch* [Hebrew], Tel-Aviv: Mossad Harav Kook.

Keil, C. F. (1968 rep.), *The Pentateuch II–III*, Biblical Commentary on the OT, Grand Rapids: Eerdmans.

Kellogg, S. H. (1988 rep.), *Studies in Leviticus*, Grand Rapids: Kregel.

Kleinig, J. W. (2003), *Leviticus*, Concordia Commentary, St. Louis: Concordia.

Levine, B. (1989), *Leviticus*, JPSTC, Philadelphia, PA, and Jerusalem: JPS.

Luzzatto, S. D. (1965, 1st ed. 1871), *S. D. Luzzatto's Commentary on the Pentateuch* [Hebrew], Tel Aviv: Dvir.

Milgrom, J. (1991), *Leviticus 1–16*, AB, New York: Doubleday.

——— (2000a), *Leviticus 17–22*, AB, New York: Doubleday.

——— (2001), *Leviticus 23–27*, AB, New York: Doubleday.

Noortzij, A. (1982), *Leviticus*, BSC, trans. R. Togtman, Grand Rapids: Zondervan.

Noth, M. (1965), *Leviticus*, London: SCM.

Péter-Contesse, R. (1993), *Lévitique 1–16*, Geneva: Labor et Fides.

Porter, J. R. (1976), *Leviticus*, CBC, Cambridge: SPCK.

Rendtorff, R. (1985), *Leviticus*, BKAT 3.1, Neukirchen-Vluyn: Neukirchener.

——— (1990), *Leviticus*, BKAT 3.2, Neukirchen-Vluyn: Neukirchener.

——— (1992), *Leviticus*, BKAT 3.3, Neukirchen-Vluyn: Neukirchener.

Rooker, M. F. (2000), *Leviticus*, NAC, Nashville: Broadman & Holman.

Ross, A. P. (2002), *Holiness to the Lord: A Guide to the Exposition of the Book of Leviticus*, Grand Rapids: Baker Academic.
Snaith, N. (1967), *Leviticus and Numbers*, NCB, London: Oliphants.
Wenham, G. J. (1979), *The Book of Leviticus*, NICOT, Grand Rapids: Eerdmans.

OTHER WORKS

Ahitub, Y. (1982), 'tôr', *EM* 8:468–469.
Alexander, T. D. (1995), *From Paradise to the Promised Land*, Carlisle: Paternoster.
Amerding, C. E. (2003), 'Festivals and Feasts', *DOTP*, 300–313.
Anderson, G. A., and S. M. Olyan (eds.) (1991), *Priesthood and Cult in Ancient Israel*, JSOTSup 125, Sheffield: JSOT.
Ashley, T. R. (1993), *The Book of Numbers*, NICOT, Grand Rapids: Eerdmans.
Auld, G. (2003), 'Leviticus: After Exodus and Before Numbers', in R. Rendtorff and R. A. Kugler (eds.), *The Book of Leviticus: Composition and Reception*, VTSup 93, 41–54, Leiden: Brill.
Averbeck, R. E. (1997), 'kpr', *NIDOTTE* 2:689–710.
Barker, P. A. (2003), 'Sabbath, Sabbatical Year, Jubilee', *DOTP*, 695–706.
Beckwith, R. T. (1995), 'The Death of Christ as a Sacrifice in the Teaching of Paul and Hebrews', in Beckwith and Selman 1995: 130–135.
Beckwith, R. T., and M. J. Selman (eds.) (1995), *Sacrifice in the Bible*, Carlisle: Paternoster.
Bergsma, J. S. (2003), 'The Jubilee: A Post-Exilic Priestly Attempt to Reclaim Lands?', *Bib* 84:225–246.
Brongers, H. A. (1973), 'Die Partikel *lĕma'an* in der Biblisch-Hebräischen Sprache', in *Syntax and Meaning: Studies in Hebrew Syntax and Biblical Exegesis*, *OtSt* 18, 84–96, Leiden: Brill.
——— (1977), 'Fasting in Israel in Biblical and Post-Biblical Times', in H. A. Brongers, F. F. Bruce et al. (eds.), *Instruction and Interpretation: Studies in Hebrew Language, Palestinian Archaeology and Biblical Exegesis*, *OtSt* 20, 1–21, Leiden: Brill.
Carpenter, E. E. (1997), "ēdâ', *NIDOTTE* 3:326–328.
Carson, D. A. (1984), *Matthew*, EBC 8.
Cassuto, M. D. (1954), 'wayyiqrā'', *EM* 2:878–887.
Chirichigno, G. C. (1993), *Debt-Slavery in Israel and the Ancient Near East*, JSOTSup 141, Sheffield: JSOT.
Claassen, W. T. (1983), 'The Speaker-Oriented Function of *kî* in Biblical Hebrew', *JNWSL* 9:29–46.
Cranfield, C. E. B. (1975), *A Critical and Exegetical Commentary on the Epistle to the Romans I–II*, ICC, Edinburgh: T. & T. Clarke.
Dennis, J. (2002), 'The Function of the "hattat" Sacrifice in the Priestly Literature: An Evaluation of the View of Jacob Milgrom', *ETL* 78:108–129.

Douglas, M. (1966), *Purity and Danger: An Analysis of the Concept of Pollution and Taboo*, London: Routledge & Kegan Paul.
——— (1993), 'The Forbidden Animals in Leviticus', *JSOT* 59:3–23.
——— (1999), *Leviticus as Literature*, Oxford: Oxford University Press.
Drinkard, Jr., J. F. (1992), 'East', *ABD* 2:248.
Eberhart, C. (2002), 'Beobachtungen zum Verbrennungsritus bei Schlachtopfer und Gemeinschafts-Schlachtopfer', *Bib* 83:88–96.
Ehrlich, A. (1908), *Randglossen zur hebräischen Bibel*, vol. 2, Leipzig: Hinrichs.
Fabry, H.-J., and H.-W. Jüngling (eds.) (1999), *Levitikus als Buch*, BBB 119, Berlin: Philo.
Firmage, E. (1990), 'The Biblical Dietary Laws and the Concept of Holiness', in J. A. Emerton (ed.), *Studies in the Pentateuch*, VTSup 41, 177–208, Leiden: Brill.
Fleming, D. (1998), 'The Biblical Tradition of Anointing Priests', *JBL* 117:401–414.
Freedman, D. N., and K. A. Matthews (1985), *The Paleo-Hebrew Leviticus Scroll (11QPaleoLev)*, Winona Lake: Eisenbrauns.
Greenberg, M. (1976), 'On the Refinement of the Conception of Prayer in Hebrew Scripture', *AJSR* 1:57–92.
——— (1982), 'heḥāg bĕmiqrā' uzĕman mĕquddaš', *Proceedings of the 1981 Convention of the Rabbinical Assembly* 43:1–4.
——— (1983), *Biblical Prose Prayer: As a Window to the Popular Religion of Ancient Israel*, Berkeley: University of California Press.
——— (1985), 'The Decalogue Tradition Critically Examined' [Hebrew], in B.-Z. Segal (ed.), *The Ten Commandments: As Reflected in Tradition and Literature Throughout the Ages*, 67–94, Jerusalem: Magnes.
——— (1990), 'Biblical Attitude toward Power: Ideal and Reality in Law and Prophets', in E. B. Firmage, B. G. Weiss and J. W. Welch (eds.), *Religion and Law: Biblical-Judaic and Islamic Perspectives*, 101–112, Winona Lake: Eisenbrauns, 1990.
Grisanti, M. A. (1997), 'šqṣ', *NIDOTTE* 4:243–246.
Grünwaldt, K. (1999), *Das Heiligkeitsgesetz Leviticus 17–26*, BZAW, Berlin: de Gruyter.
Hagner, D. A. (1993), *Matthew 1–13*, WBC, Dallas, TX: Word.
Hall, R. G. (1992), 'Circumcision', in *ABD* 1:1025–1031.
Haran, M. (1985), *Temples and Temple-Service in Ancient Israel*, Winona Lake: Eisenbrauns.
Harrison, R. K. (1997), 'ṣr'', *NIDOTTE* 3:846–847.
Hasel, G. F. (1984), 'kāret', *ThWAT* 4:355–367.
Hawk, L. D. (2003), 'Altars', *DOTP*, 33–37.
Head, P. M. (1995), 'The Self-Offering and Death of Christ as a Sacrifice in the Gospels and the Acts of the Apostles', in Beckwith and Selman 1995: 111–129.
Heller, J. (1970), 'Die Symbolik des Fettes im AT', *VT* 20:106–108.
Hoffmon, H. B. (1992), 'lex talionis', *ABD* 4:321–322.

Houston, W. J. (1993), *Purity and Monotheism: Clean and Unclean Animals in Biblical Law*, JSOTSup 140, Sheffield: Sheffield Academic Press.
——— (2003), 'Towards an Integrated Reading of the Dietary Laws of Leviticus', in Rendtorff and Kugler 2003: 142–161.
Hubbard, Jr., R. L. (1991), 'The Go'el in Ancient Israel: Theological Reflection on an Israelite Institution', *BBR* 1:3–19.
Hübner, H. (1992), 'Unclean and Clean', in *ABD* 6:741–745.
Hugenberger, G. (1994), *Marriage as a Covenant: Biblical Law and Ethics as Developed from Malachi*, Leiden: Brill.
Hurvitz, A. (1982), *A Linguistic Study of the Relationship between the Priestly Source and the Book of Ezekiel: A New Approach to an Old Problem*, Cahiers de la *RB*, Paris: Gabalda.
Janowski, B. (1998), 'Azazel', in K. van der Toorn, B. Becking and P. W. van der Horst (eds.), *Dictionary of Deities and Demons*, 128–131, Leiden: Brill; Grand Rapids: Eerdmans.
Japhet, S. (1986), 'The Relationship between the Legal Corpora in the Pentateuch in Light of Manumission', in S. Japhet (ed.), *Studies in the Bible*, 63–89, Jerusalem: Magnes.
Jenson, P. (1992), *Graded Holiness*, JSOTSup 106, Sheffield: JSOT Press.
——— (1997), ''ēpōd', *NIDOTTE* 1:476–477.
Johnston, P. S. (2002), *Shades of Sheol: Death and Afterlife in the Old Testament*, Leicester: Apollos.
Joosten, J. (1996), *People and Land in the Holiness Code*, VTSup 67, Leiden: Brill.
Kaufmann, Y. (1937–56), *The History of Israelite Religion* [Hebrew], 4 vols., Tel-Aviv: Dvir.
Kedar-Kopstein, B. (1993), 'qeren', *ThWAT* 7:181–189.
Kiuchi, N. (1987), *The Purification Offering in the Priestly Literature*, JSOTSup 53, Sheffield: Sheffield Academic Press.
——— (1994), 'Elijah's Self-Offering', *Bib* 75: 74–79.
——— (1995), 'The Jubilee and *qdš*' [Japanese], *Exeg* 6:31–48.
——— (1997), 'zānāb', *NIDOTTE* 1:1122.
——— (1999a), 'On the Existence of the so-called Holiness Code' [Japanese], *Exeg* 10:33–64.
——— (1999b), 'Spirituality in Offering a Peace Offering', *TynB* 50:23–31.
——— (2000), 'A Living Sacrifice (Rom 12:1)' [Japanese], *Exeg* 11:21–51.
——— (2001a), 'A Paradox of the Skin Disease', *ZAW* 113:505–514.
——— (2001b), 'The Faith of Cain and Abel' [Japanese], *Exeg* 12:1–30.
——— (2002), 'From Law to Salvation – By way of the Levirate Marriage' [Japanese], *Exeg* 13:21–45.
——— (2003a), *A Study of Ḥāṭā' and Ḥaṭṭā't in Leviticus 4–5*, FAT 2.2, Tübingen: Mohr.
——— (2003b), 'The Road to the Salvation of the Heart: Lev 26' [Japanese], *Exeg* 13:1–30.
——— (2003c), 'Leviticus, Book of', *DOTP*, 522–532.

——— (2005), 'Propitiation in the Sacrificial Ritual', *Christ and the World* 15:35–60, Inzai, Chiba: Tokyo Christian University.
——— (2006), 'Living Like the Azazel-Goat in Romans 12:1b', *TynB* 57:251–261.
Klawans, J. (2000), *Impurity and Sin in Ancient Judaism*, Oxford: Oxford University Press.
Klingbeil, G. A. (2004), 'Altars, Ritual and Theology – Preliminary Thoughts on the Importance of Cult and Ritual for a Theology of the Hebrew Scripture', *VT* 54:495–515.
Klostermann, A. (1983), *Der Pentateuch: Beiträge zu seinem Verständnis und seiner Entstehungsgeschichte*, Leipzig: Bohme.
Knierim, R. P. (1992), *Text and Concept in Leviticus 1:1–9*, FAT 2, Tübingen: Mohr.
Knohl, I. (1995), *The Sanctuary of Silence*, Minneapolis: Fortress.
Koopmans, W. T. (1997), ''ăḥuzzâ', *NIDOTTE* 1:358–360.
Kuemmerlin-Mclean, J. K. (1992), 'Magic: Old Testament', *ABD* 4:468–471.
Kurtz, J. H. (1980), *Sacrificial Worship of the Old Testament*, Grand Rapids: Eerdmans (original German ed. 1863).
Latham, J. E. (1982), *The Religious Symbolism of Salt*, ThH 64, Paris: Edition Beauchesne.
Leeuwen, J. H. van (1988), 'The Meaning of tupîn in Lev. 6, 14', *ZAW* 100:268–269.
Levine, B. (1974), *In the Presence of the Lord*, SJLA 5, Leiden: Brill.
——— (1992), 'Leviticus, Book of', *ABD* 4:311–321.
Maass, F. (1973), ''ādām', *ThWAT* 1:91–94.
Magonet, J. (1996), 'But if it a Girl She Is Unclean for Twice Seven Days: The Riddle of Leviticus 12.5', in Sawyer 1996: 144–152.
McConville, J. G. (2002), *Deuteronomy*, AOTC 5, Leicester: Apollos.
Meyers, C. L. (1976), *The Tabernacle Menorah: A Synthetic Study of a Symbol from the Biblical Cult*, D. N. Freedman (ed.), ASOR Dissertation Series 2, Missoula: Scholars Press.
——— (1988), *Discovering Eve: Ancient Israelite Women in Context*, New York: Oxford University Press.
Michel, D. (1994), 'nœfœš als Leichnam', *ZAH*, 81–84.
Milgrom, J. (1970), *Studies in Levitical Terminology*, vol. 1: *The Encroacher and the Levite, the Term 'Aboda*, Berkeley: University of California Press.
——— (1972), 'The Alleged Wave-Offering in Israel and the Ancient Near East', *IEJ* 22:33–38.
——— (1976), 'The Concept of Ma'al in the Bible and the Ancient Near East', *JAOS* 96:236–247.
——— (1996), 'The Changing Concept of Holiness in the Pentateuchal Codes with Emphasis on Leviticus 19', in *Reading Leviticus*, 65–75, Sheffield: Sheffield Academic Press.
——— (2000b), 'The Dynamics of Purity in the Priestly System', in Poorthuis and Schwartz 2000: 29–32.

Morris, L. (1965), *The Apostolic Preaching of the Cross*, Grand Rapids: Eerdmans.
Muraoka, T. (1978), 'A Syntactic Problem in Lev XIX. 18b', *JSS* 23:291–297.
Nielsen, K. (1986), *Incense in Ancient Israel*, VTSup 38, Leiden: Brill.
North, R. (1954), *Sociology of the Biblical Jubilee,* Rome: Biblical Institute Press.
——— (2000), *The Biblical Jubilee ... after Fifty Years*, AnBib 145, Rome: Biblical Institute Press.
Olivier, J. P. J. (1997), 'dĕrôr', *NIDOTTE* 1:986–989.
Oswald, J. N. (1998), *The Book of Isaiah Chapters 40–66*, NICOT, Grand Rapids: Eerdmans.
Paran, M. (1989), *Forms of the Priestly Style in the Pentateuch* [Hebrew], Jerusalem: Magnes.
Parry, D. W. (1994), 'Garden of Eden: Prototype of Sanctuary', in D. W. Parry and S. D. Ricks, *Temples of the Ancient World*, 126–152, Salt Lake City: Deseret.
Paschen, W. (1970), *Rein und Unrein: Untersuchung zur biblischen Wortgeschichte*, SANT 24, Munich: Kösel-Verlag.
Poorthuis, M. J. H. M., and J. Schwartz (eds.) (2000), *Purity and Holiness: The Heritage of Leviticus*, Jewish and Christian Perspectives Series 2, Leiden: Brill.
Powell, M. A. (1992), 'Weights and Measures', *ABD* 6:897–908.
Ratschow, C. H. (1978), 'Altar I', *Theologische Realenzyklopädie* 2:305–308, Berlin: de Gruyter.
Rendsburg, G. A. (1993), 'The Inclusio in Leviticus XI', *VT* 43:418–421.
Rendtorff, R. (1996), 'Is it Possible to Read Leviticus as a Separate Book?', Sawyer 1996: 22–35.
Rendtorff, R., and R. A. Kugler (eds.) (2003), *The Book of Leviticus: Composition and Reception*, VTSup 93, Leiden: Brill.
Reymond, P. (1958), *L'eau, sa vie, et sa signification dans l'Ancien Testament*, VTSup 6, Leiden: Brill.
Ringgren, H. (1986), 'nwp', *ThWAT* 5:318–322.
Rodriguez, A. M. (1979), *Substitution in the Hebrew Cultus*, Berrien Springs: Andrews University Press.
Rooy, H. F. van (1997), 'rō'š', *NIDOTTE* 3:1015–1020.
Sailhamer, J. H. (1992), *The Pentateuch as Narrative: A Biblical-Theological Commentary*, Grand Rapids: Zondervan.
Sarna, N. M. (1986), *Exploring Exodus: The Heritage of Biblical Israel*, New York: Schocken.
——— (1989), *Genesis*, JPSTC, New York: JPS.
Sawyer, J. F. A. (ed.) (1996), *Reading Leviticus: A Conversation with Mary Douglas*, JSOTSup 227, Sheffield: Sheffield Academic Press.
Scharbert, J. (1968), *Prolegomena eines Alttestamentlers zur Erbsündenlehre*, QD 37, Freiburg: Herder.
Schearing, L. S. (2003), 'Double Time ... Double Trouble?', in Rendtorff and Kugler 2003: 429–450.

Schenker, A. (1992), *Studien zu Opfer und Kult im Alten Testament, mit einer Bibliographie 1967–1991 zum Opfer in der Bibel*, FAT 3, Tübingen: Mohr.

Schwartz, B. J. (1991), 'The Prohibition Concerning the "eating" of Blood in Leviticus 17', in Anderson and Olyan 1991: 34–66.

——— (1999), *The Holiness Legislation: Studies in the Priestly Code* [Hebrew], Jerusalem: Magnes.

——— (2000), 'Israel's Holiness: The Torah Tradition', in Poorthuis and Schwartz 2000: 47–59.

Seebass, H. (1986), 'nepeš', *ThWAT* 5:531–555.

Seidl, T. (1999), 'Levitikus 16 – "Schlußstein des priesterlichen System der Sündenvergebung" ', in Fabry-Jüngling 1999: 219–248.

Selman, M. J. (2003), 'Law', *DOTP*, 497–515.

Seybold, K. (1986), 'māšaḥ', *ThWAT* 5:46–59.

Shead, A. G. (2000), 'Sabbath', *NDBT*, 745–750.

Sklar, J. A. (2001), 'Sin, Impurity, Sacrifice, and Atonement', PhD dissertation, Cheltenham and Gloucester College of Higher Education.

Speiser, E. A. (1960), 'Leviticus and Critics', in M. Haran (ed.), *Y. Kaufmann Jubilee Volume*, 29–45, Jerusalem: Magnes.

Staubli, T. (2002), 'Die Symbolik des Vogelrituals bei der Reinigung von Aussätzigen (Lev 14,4–7)', *Bib* 83:230–237.

Stern, P. D. (1991), *The Biblical Ḥerem: A Window on Israel's Religious Experience*, BJS 211, Atlanta: Scholars Press.

Steymans, H.-U. (1999), 'Verheißung und Drohung: Lev 26', in Fabry-Jüngling 1999: 263–307.

Taylor, R. A. (1997) ''ēzôb', *NIDOTTE* 1:334–335.

Thiselton, A. C. (1975), 'Flesh', *NIDNTT* 1:671–682, Grand Rapids: Zondervan.

Tomes, R. (1988), 'A Perpetual Statute throughout your Generations', in B. Lindars (ed.), *Law and Religion: Essays on the Place of the Law in Israel and Early Christianity*, 20–33, Cambridge: James Clarke.

Tsumura, D. T. (2000), 'Fulfilment and Abolishment of the Law – a Meaning of Hebrew yāṣā' [Japanese], *Exeg* 11:73–79.

Van Dam, C. (1997), ''ûrîm', *NIDOTTE* 1:329–331.

Warning, W. (1999), *Literary Artistry in Leviticus*, Biblical Interpretation Series 3, Leiden: Brill.

Wegner, J. R. (1992), 'Leviticus', in C. A. Newsom and S. H. Ringe (eds.), *Women's Bible Commentary*, Louisville: Westminster John Knox.

Weinfeld, M. (1972), *Deuteronomy and Deuteronomic School*, Oxford: Clarendon.

Weiss, M. (1987), *The Bible and Modern Literary Theory* [Hebrew], Jerusalem: Bialik Institute.

——— (1992), *The Book of Amos* [Hebrew], Jerusalem: Magnes.

Wenham, G. J. (1979), *The Book of Leviticus*, NICOT, Grand Rapids: Eerdmans.

——— (1982), 'Christ's Healing Mininstry and his Attitude to the Law', in H. H. Rowdon (ed.), *Christ the Lord*, FS D. Guthrie, 115–126, Leicester: IVP.

——— (1983), 'Why Does Sexual Intercourse Defile (Lev 15.18)?', *ZAW* 95:432–434.
——— (1986), 'Sanctuary Symbolism in the Garden of Eden Story', in *Proceedings of the Ninth World Congress of Jewish Studies, Division A: The Period of the Bible*, 19–25, Jerusalem: World Union of Jewish Studies.
——— (1996), 'Pentateuchal Studies Today', *Them* 22:3–13.
——— (1999), 'The Priority of P', *VT* 49:240–258.
Wessely, N. H. (1846), *Netivot Ha-shalom*, ed. M. Mendelssohn, Vienna: Schmid & Busch.
Wevers, J. W. (1997), *Notes on the Greek Text of Leviticus*, Atlanta: Scholars Press.
Wright, D. P. (1987), *The Disposal of Impurity*, SBL Dissertation Series 101, Atlanta: Scholars Press.
——— (1992), 'Unclean and Clean', *ABD* 6:729–741.
Wright, D. P., and R. N. Jones (1992), 'Discharge', *ABD* 2:204–207.
Wright, D. P., and J. Milgrom (1986), 'sāmak', *ThWAT* 5:880–888.
Youngblood, R. (1997), 'qṣ'', *NIDOTTE* 3:962.

INDEX OF SCRIPTURE REFERENCES

INDEX OF AUTHORS

INDEX OF SUBJECTS